Adobe® Creative Suite® 6 Web Tools: Dreamweaver®, Photoshop®, and Flash®

ILLUSTRATED

Bishop • Botello • Waxer

COURSE TECHNOLOGY
CENGAGE Learning

Australia • Brazil • Japan • Korea • Mexico • Singapore • Spain • United Kingdom • United States

COURSE TECHNOLOGY
CENGAGE Learning·

Adobe® Creative Suite® 6 Web Tools:
Dreamweaver®, Photoshop®, and
Flash®—Illustrated
Bishop, Botello, Waxer

Editor-in-Chief: Marie Lee

Executive Editor: Marjorie Hunt

Associate Acquisitions Editor: Amanda Lyons

Senior Product Manager: Christina Kling Garrett

Product Manager: Kim Klasner

Editorial Assistant: Brandelynn Perry

Director of Marketing: Cheryl Costantini

Developmental Editors: Marjorie Hopper, Ann Fisher,
 Mary-Terese Cozzola

Senior Content Project Manager: Cathie DiMassa

Print Buyer: Fola Orekoya

Art Director: GEX Publishing Services

Proofreaders: Harold Johnson, Kim Kosmatka

Indexer: BIM Indexing

QA Manuscript Reviewers: John Freitas, Jeff Schwartz,
 Danielle Shaw, Ashlee Welz Smith

Cover Designer: GEX Publishing Services

Cover Artist: Mark Hunt

Compositor: GEX Publishing Services

For product information and technology assistance, contact us at
Cengage Learning Customer & Sales Support, 1-800-354-9706

For permission to use material from this text or product, submit all requests online at **www.cengage.com/permissions**
Further permissions questions can be emailed to
permissionrequest@cengage.com

Library of Congress Control Number: 2012948806

ISBN-13: 978-1-133-62974-0

ISBN-10: 1-133-62974-1

Course Technology
20 Channel Center Street
Boston, MA 02210
USA

Cengage Learning is a leading provider of customized learning solutions with office locations around the globe, including Singapore, the United Kingdom, Australia, Mexico, Brazil, and Japan. Locate your local office at
www.cengage.com/global

Cengage Learning products are represented in Canada by Nelson Education, Ltd.

To learn more about Course Technology, visit **www.cengage.com/coursetechnology**

To learn more about Cengage Learning, visit **www.cengage.com**

Purchase any of our products at your local college store or at our preferred online store
www.cengagebrain.com

Adobe product screen shot(s) reprinted with permission from Adobe Systems.

Adobe®, Dreamweaver®, Fireworks®, Flash®, InDesign®, Illustrator®, and Photoshop® are either registered trademarks or trademarks of Adobe Systems Incorporated in the United States and/or other countries. THIS PRODUCT IS NOT ENDORSED OR SPONSORED BY ADOBE SYSTEMS INCORPORATED, PUBLISHER OF ADOBE® DREAMWEAVER®, FLASH®, FIREWORKS®, INDESIGN®, ILLUSTRATOR®, AND PHOTOSHOP®.

Printed in the United States of America
Print Number: 04   Print Year: 2018

Brief Contents

Contents

Photoshop CS6

Preface

Welcome to *Adobe® Creative Suite® 6 Web Tools: Dreamweaver, Photoshop, and Flash—Illustrated*. The unique page design of this book makes it a great learning tool for both new and experienced users. Each skill is presented on two facing pages so that you don't have to turn the page to find a screen shot or finish a paragraph. See the illustration on the right to learn more about the pedagogical and design elements of a typical lesson.

This book is an ideal learning tool for a wide range of learners—the "rookies" will find the clean design easy to follow and focused with only essential information presented, and the "hotshots" will appreciate being able to move quickly through the lessons to find the information they need without reading a lot of text. The design also makes this book a great reference after the course is over!

Coverage

21 units offer thorough coverage of essential skills for working with Adobe Dreamweaver, Photoshop, and Flash CS6, including coverage of Web 2.0 tools in Dreamweaver, creating eye-popping effects in Photoshop, incorporating video and sound and exporting Flash content to the web and mobile devices; introducing Bridge and integrating Flash with other Adobe CS6 programs.

Written by Sherry Bishop, a digital media instructor at North Arkansas College; Chris Botello, a professional designer who works on movie posters and theatrical campaigns for the entertainment industry; and Barbara Waxer, a professional writer, media instructor, and copyright educator, this text offers a real-world perspective with exercises designed to develop the practical skills and techniques necessary to work effectively in a professional environment.

Each two-page spread focuses on a single skill.

Introduction briefly explains why the lesson skill is important.

A case scenario motivates the steps and puts learning in context.

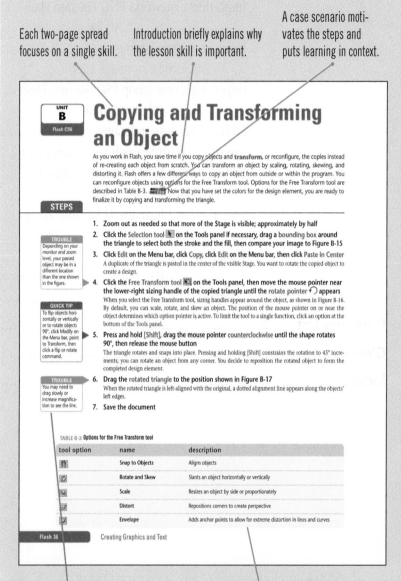

Tips and troubleshooting advice, right where you need it—next to the step itself.

Tables provide helpful summaries of key terms, buttons, or keyboard shortcuts.

Large screen shots keep
students on track as
they complete steps.

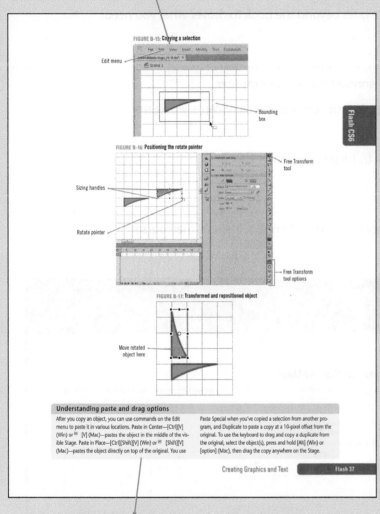

Sidebars provide useful
information related to the
lesson skill.

Assignments

The lessons follow a real world case study. The assignments on the light yellow pages at the end of each unit increase in difficulty. Additional case studies provide a variety of interesting and relevant exercises for students to practice skills.

Assignments include:

- **Concepts Reviews** consist of multiple choice, matching, and screen identification questions.

- **Skills Reviews** provide additional hands-on, step-by-step reinforcement.

- **Independent Challenges** are case projects requiring critical thinking and application of the unit skills. The Independent Challenges increase in difficulty, with the first one in each unit being the easiest. Independent Challenges 2 and 3 become increasingly open-ended, requiring more independent problem solving.

- **Real Life Independent Challenges** are practical exercises to help students with their everyday lives by developing their own projects. Students work on this project throughout the text, using the skills they learn in each unit.

- **Advanced Challenge Exercises** set within the Independent Challenges provide optional steps for more advanced students.

- **Visual Workshops** direct students to the Internet to visit websites and view projects for critical review and inspiration.

CourseMate

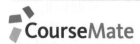

ENGAGING. TRACKABLE. AFFORDABLE.

Cengage Learning's CourseMate brings course concepts to life with interactive learning, study, and exam preparation tools that support the printed textbook. Watch student comprehension soar as your class works with the printed textbook and the textbook-specific website. CourseMate goes beyond the book to deliver what you need!

FOR STUDENTS:

Interactive eBook that you can read, highlight, or annotate on your computer.

Total Training videos with audio-visual, step-by-step instructions reinforce concepts you learn.

Glossary and Flashcards to help you master key terms.

Interactive exercises give you immediate feedback to help you learn.

FOR INSTRUCTORS:

Engagement Tracker, a first-of-its-kind tool that monitors student engagement in the course.

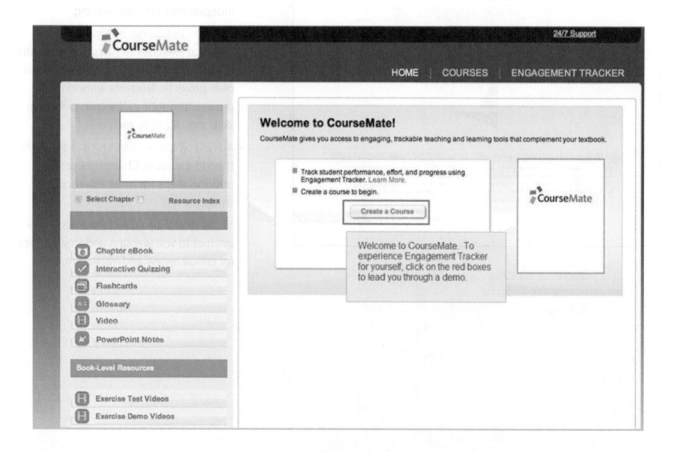

Instructor Resources

The Instructor Resources CD is Course Technology's way of putting the resources and information needed to teach and learn effectively into your hands. With an integrated array of teaching and learning tools that offer you and your students a broad range of technology-based instructional options, we believe this CD represents the highest quality and most cutting edge resources available to instructors today. Many of these resources are available at www.cengage.com/coursetechnology. The resources available with this book are:

- **Instructor's Manual**—Available as an electronic file, the Instructor's Manual includes detailed lecture topics with teaching tips for each unit.

- **Sample Syllabus**—Prepare and customize your course easily using this sample course outline.

- **PowerPoint Presentations**—Each unit has a corresponding PowerPoint presentation that you can use in lecture, distribute to your students, or customize to suit your course.

- **Figure Files**—The figures in the text are provided on the Instructor Resources CD to help you illustrate key topics or concepts. You can create traditional overhead transparencies by printing the figure files. Or you can create electronic slide shows by using the figures in a presentation program such as PowerPoint.

- **Solutions to Exercises**—Solutions to Exercises contains every file students are asked to create or modify in the lessons and end-of-unit material. Also provided in this section, there is a document

outlining the solutions for the end-of-unit Concepts Review, Skills Review, and Independent Challenges.

- **Data Files for Students**—To complete most of the units in this book, your students will need Data Files. You can post the Data Files on a file server for students to copy. The Data Files are available on the Instructor Resources CD-ROM, the Review Pack, and can also be downloaded from cengagebrain.com. For more information on how to download the Data Files, see the inside front cover of this book.

- **ExamView**—ExamView is a powerful testing software package that allows you to create and administer printed, computer (LAN-based), and Internet exams. ExamView includes hundreds of questions that correspond to the topics covered in this text, enabling students to generate detailed study guides that include page references for further review. The computer-based and Internet testing components allow students to take exams at their computers, and also saves you time by grading each exam automatically.

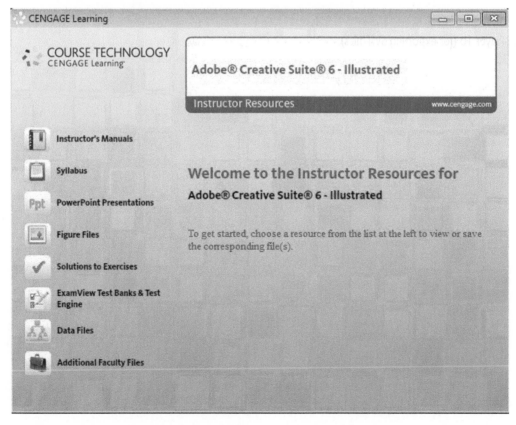

Read This Before You Begin

This book assumes the following:

1. The software has been registered properly. If the product is not registered, students must respond to registration and dialog boxes each time they start the software.
2. Default tools in the Tools panel might differ, but tool options and other settings do not carry over to the End-of-Unit exercises or between units.
3. Students know how to create a folder using a file management utility.
4. After introduction and reinforcement in initial units, the student will be able to respond to the dialog boxes that open when saving a file. Later units do not provide step-by-step guidance.
5. Panels, windows, and dialog boxes have default settings when opened. Exceptions may occur when students open these elements repeatedly in a lesson or in the unit.
6. Students will be instructed in the early units on how to update missing links. Later units do not provide step-by-step guidance.
7. The few exercises that do contain live type were created using commonly available fonts. Nevertheless, it is possible, that students may run into a missing font issue when opening a data file. In that case, students should use an available font that is similar to the size and weight of the type shown in the lesson.

Frequently Asked Questions

What are the Minimum System Requirements (Windows)?

- Intel® Pentium® 4 or AMD Athlon® 64 or faster processor with 1GB RAM (2GB recommended)

- Microsoft® Windows Vista or Windows 7

- 1.6GB of available hard disk space (2GB recommended)

- Color monitor with 16-bit color video card

- DVD-ROM

- Adobe Flash Player 10 (for exporting SWF files)

What are Data Files?

A Data File is a partially completed animation, graphic, or video file that you use to complete the steps in the units and exercises to create the final document that you submit to your instructor. The Data Files that you need for each unit are listed in the back of this book.

Where are the Data Files?

Your instructor will provide the Data Files to you or direct you to a location on a network drive from which you can download them. As you download the files, select where to store them, such as a hard drive, a network server, or a USB drive. The instructions in the lessons refer to "the drive and folder where your Data Files are stored" when referring to the Data Files for the book.

What software was used to write and test this book?

This book was written and tested on a computer with a typical installation of Microsoft Windows 7. The browsers used for any steps that require a browser are Mozilla Firefox 13, Google Chrome 19, and Internet Explorer 9.

This book is written and tested on both the Windows version and the Macintosh version of Adobe Flash Professional CS6. The two versions of the software are virtually the same, but there are a few platform differences. When there are differences between the two versions of the software, steps written specifically for the Windows version end with the notation (Win) and steps for the Macintosh version end with the notation (Mac). In instances when the lessons are split between the two operating systems, a line divides the page and is accompanied by Mac and Win icons.

Also, in this book, Macintosh commands instruct users to press the [return] key to enter information. On some newer Macintosh keyboards, this key may be named [enter] or the keyboard may include both [return] and [enter].

Do I need to be connected to the Internet to complete the steps and exercises in this book?

Some of the exercises in this book assume that your computer is connected to the Internet. If you are not connected to the Internet, see your instructor for information on how to complete the exercises.

What do I do if my screen is different from the figures shown in this book?

This book was written and tested on computers with monitors set at a resolution of 1280 × 1024. If your screen shows more or less information than the figures in the book, your monitor is probably set at a higher or lower resolution. If you don't see something on your screen, you might have to scroll down or up to see the object identified in the figures. In some cases, the figures will not match your screen because the Flash windows have been resized or moved in an effort to make the figures as easy to read as possible. Note that the appearance of commands on menus and in dialog boxes will vary.

What do I do if I see an Adobe Flash Player security warning?

In the Integration unit, you may encounter the Adobe Flash Player Security warning dialog box when you click a button in a SWF or HTML file that links to a URL. This is a Flash security feature that requires you to allow access to the URL in the Global Security Settings Panel. Although you access the Panel through Flash Player Help online, the security settings affect your local computer. To allow access to a URL, click Settings in the Adobe Flash Player Security dialog box. On the Flash Player Help, Global security settings for content creators page, click Edit locations. Next, click Add location, click Browse for Files, navigate to where you store the SWF, select it, click Open, then reopen the SWF file in your browser. Instructors should confirm with their IT departments that institutional policy will allow access. To adjust security settings, navigate to http://www.macromedia.com/support/documentation/en/flashplayer/help/settings_manager04a.html, then click the Global Security Settings Panel link at the left.

How do I use Dreamweaver on multiple computers?

If you are using Dreamweaver on multiple computers, such as one in the classroom and one at home or in a lab, you must set up each Website on each computer before you can access your Website files on each computer. You only have to do this once for each Website, but the site root folder must be accessible from both machines. For instance, if you are storing your Websites on a USB storage device and using it on a computer in a lab and your computer at home, you must set up the Website on each machine. Once you tell Dreamweaver where to find the files (the USB drive), it will find them automatically from that point forward.

What if I can't find some of the information in the exercises on the Internet?

This book uses the Internet to provide real-life examples in the lessons and end-of-unit exercises. Because the Internet is constantly changing to display current information, some of the links used and described in the book may be deleted or modified before the book is even published. If this happens, searching the referenced Websites will usually locate similar information in a slightly modified form. In some cases, entire Websites may move. Technical problems with Web servers may also prevent access to Websites or Web pages temporarily. Patience, critical thinking, and creativity are necessary whenever the Internet is being used in the classroom.

What if my icons look different?

Symbols for icons, buttons, and pointers are shown in the steps each time they are used. Icons may look different in the Files panel depending on the file association settings on your computer.

What if my screen fonts look different?

Your screen fonts may be larger or smaller than they appear in figures. The figures were captured using the default Windows display setting of Smaller - 100% (default). Use the Control Panel to compare your settings in the Appearance and Personalization, Display window.

What if I can't see my file extensions?

The learning process will be easier if you can see the file extensions for the files you will use in the lessons. To do this in Windows, open Windows Explorer, click Organize, click Folder and Search Options, click the View tab, then uncheck the box Hide Extensions for Known File Types. To do this on a Macintosh, go to the Finder, click the Finder menu, then click Preferences. Click the Advanced tab, then select the Show all file extensions check box.

What if I can't see Flash content in my browser?

To view objects such as Flash movies, you must set a preference in your browser to allow active content to run. Otherwise, you will not be able to view objects such as Flash buttons. To set this preference in Internet Explorer, click Tools, click Internet Options, click the Advanced tab, then check the box Allow active content to run in files on My computer (under Security). Your browser settings may be slightly different, but look for similar wording. When using Windows Internet Explorer 7, you can also click the information bar when prompted to allow blocked content.

What do I do if I see a Server Busy dialog box?

You may see a message that says "This action cannot be completed because the other program is busy. Choose 'Switch To' to activate the busy program and correct the problem." when you are attempting to import Word content. This is probably a memory problem. If it happens, click Word when the Start menu opens. Repeat again if necessary, then switch back to Dreamweaver. You should see the imported text.

How do I use Flash with other Adobe CS6 programs?

The lessons in the Integration unit assume students have access to Adobe Fireworks, Adobe Photoshop, Adobe Dreamweaver, and Adobe Illustrator. To take full advantage of these lessons, set your file association for PNG files to Fireworks.

How do I create Websites that have not been built through previous consecutive units? (Windows)

If you begin an assignment that requires a Website that you did not create or maintain earlier in the text, you must perform the following steps:

1. Copy the Solution Files folder from the preceding unit for the Website you wish to create onto the hard drive or USB storage device. For example, if you are working on Unit E, you need the Solution Files folder from Unit D. Your instructor will furnish this folder to you.
2. Start Dreamweaver.
3. Click **Site** on the Application bar, then click **Manage Sites**.
4. Click **New**.
5. Type the name you want to use for your Website in the Site Name text box. Spaces and uppercase letters are allowed in the Site name.
6. Click the **Browse for folder icon** next to the Local Site Folder text box.
7. Navigate to the location of the drive and folder of your newly copied folder to set the local site root folder. The local site root folder contains the name of the Website you are working on. For example, the local site root folder for The Striped Umbrella Website is called striped_umbrella.
8. Double-click the local site root folder, then click **Select**.
9. Click **Advanced Settings** in the category list in the Site Setup dialog box, click the **Browse for folder icon** next to the Default Images folder text box. A message appears stating that the site cache is being updated. This scans the files in your site and starts tracking links as you change them.
10. Double-click the assets folder in your site root folder, then click **Select**.
11. Verify that the **Links relative to: Document option** is checked.
12. Click **Save** to close the Site Setup dialog box.
13. Click **Done** to close the Manage Sites dialog box.

How do I create Websites that have not been built through previous consecutive units? (Macintosh)

If you begin an assignment that requires a Website that you did not create or maintain before this unit, you must perform the following steps:

1. Copy the Solution Files folder from the preceding unit for the Website you wish to create onto the hard drive, or USB storage device. For example, if you are working on Unit E, you need the Solution Files folder from Unit D. Your instructor will furnish this folder to you.
2. Start Dreamweaver, click **Site** on the Menu bar, then click **New Site**.
3. Click **Site** in the category list in the Site Setup dialog box (if necessary).
4. Type the name you want to use for your Website in the Site name text box.
5. Click the **Browse for folder icon** next to the Local Site Folder text box, and then navigate to the location of the drive and folder of your newly copied folder to set the local site root folder.
6. Click the local site root folder, then click **Choose**.
7. Click **Advanced Settings** in the category list in the Site Setup dialog box, then click **Local Info** if necessary.
8. Click the **Browse for folder icon** next to the Default Images folder text box. If necessary, click the drive and folder of your newly copied folder to locate the assets folder.
9. Click the assets folder, click **Choose**, then click **Save** to close the Site Setup dialog box.
10. Click **Done** to close the Manage Sites dialog box.

Acknowledgements

Author Acknowledgements

This book is one of my favorites—I was so excited by the challenge of teaching Photoshop in the Illustrated book format, and even more excited that we made it work. This is the book I use to teach my Photoshop 1 class at Tabor Academy.

Thank you to my development editor Ann Fisher for guiding the book through to completion (and for all the extra work she does and never mentions). Special thanks to the technical editors, John Freitas, Ashlee Welz-Smith, Danielle Shaw, and Susan Whalen, who took great care to be sure that the exercises all worked. Thank you guys for having my back.

I would also like to thank Marie Lee, Editor-in-Chief at Course Technology, Marjorie Hunt, Executive Editor, and Amanda Lyons, Associate Acquisitions Editor. I would also like to thank our Content Project Manager, Jennifer Feltri-George, and Christina Kling-Garrett, our Senior Product Manager.

Finally, thank you to the production and editorial teams for their hard work in putting it all together.

– Chris Botello

It is so difficult to fully express my appreciation to the many dedicated members of the Illustrated team. Christina Kling-Garrett, the Senior Product Manager, was at the helm and did a wonderful job guiding the process. It was amazing to be a part of such a wonderful team with so many talented professionals.

This was my first time working with Marj Hopper, our Developmental Editor. Her sharp eye, keen perspective, and sense of humor were so appreciated by all of us. Thank you, Marj! Cathie DiMassa, the Senior Content Project Manager, and Louise Capulli, the Project Manager, moved the units along smoothly, ensuring that this book would be ready for each of you. We thank them for keeping up with the many details and deadlines. I am always so appreciative of the work so many do to ensure that the book is technically accurate: Kim Kosmatka, our Proofreader; and Jeff Schwartz, Danielle Shaw, Susan Whalen, and Ashlee Welz Smith, QA Manuscript Reviewers.

Thank you, Adobe, for giving us this outstanding web development tool. It is an exciting program that is easy to use whether you are a professional web developer or a beginning design student. I hope each of you enjoy exploring its many exciting features.

Thanks to the Beach Club in Gulf Shores, Alabama, for being such a delightful place to visit. Several photographs of their beautiful property appear in The Striped Umbrella website.

Thanks, also, to my encourager and sounding board, my husband Don. Our travels with our children and grandchildren provide happy memories for us and content for each website.

– Sherry Bishop

I am fortunate to be surrounded by a cadre of talented and dedicated colleagues who share best practices and suffer my humor, mostly of their own volition. My thanks to Marie Lee, Editor-in-Chief at Course Technology, Marjorie Hunt, Executive Editor, and Associate Acquisitions Editor Amanda Lyons for keeping Flash in the Illustrated repertoire. Product Manager Kim Klasner, Senior Content Project Manager Cathie DiMassa, and GEX Project Manager Louise Capulli kept us spot-on organized and informed through every phase. Many thanks to our ace quality assurance testers John Freitas, Jeff Schwartz, and to Ashlee Welz Smith who also shot the Macintosh figures. Big thanks also to Senior Product Manager Christina Kling Garrett and her sons Jack and Keith, on whom itzyBotz is modeled.

This book benefits from the many talents of MT Cozzola, my developmental editor and friend. Her guidance and humor are superb. Evidence of her sound advice and editorial impact is embedded throughout.

Kudos to Anita Quintana, my friend and colleague in the Media Arts and Film Department at Santa Fe Community College, for translating my babblings and scribbles into such amazing art for the Data Files.

Finally, the warmest of acknowledgement always to my partner, Lindy, who waved gamely as I disappeared into my office and marveled at my alleged ability to write with cats ensconced around my keyboard and person.

– Barbara Waxer

Advisory Board Acknowledgements

We would like to thank our Advisory Board for their honest feedback and suggestions that helped guide our development decisions for this edition. They are as follows:

Rich Barnett, Wadsworth High School

Lisa Cogley, James A. Rhodes State College

Trudy Lund, Smoke Valley School District

Diane Miller, James A. Rhodes State College

Charles Schneider, Red Clay Consolidated School District

Other Adobe® CS6 Titles

Adobe® Dreamweaver® CS6—Illustrated
Sherry Bishop (9781133526025)

Eleven units provide essential training on using Adobe Dreamweaver CS6 to create websites. Coverage includes creating a website, developing web pages, formatting text, using and managing images, creating links and navigation bars using CSS to layout pages, and collecting data with forms.

Adobe® Flash® Professional CS6—Illustrated
Barbara M. Waxer (9781133526001)

Eight units provide essential training on using Adobe Flash Professional CS6, including creating graphics, text, and symbols, using the Timeline, creating animation, creating buttons and using media, adding interactivity, and integrating Flash projects with other CS6 programs.

Adobe® Illustrator® CS6—Illustrated
Chris Botello (9781133526407)

Eight units cover essential skills for working with Adobe Illustrator CS6 including drawing basic and complex shapes, using the Pen tool, working with blends, compound paths and clipping masks, creating pattern fills and gradient fills for objects, and designing stunning 3D effects.

Adobe® InDesign® CS6—Illustrated
Ann Fisher (9781133187585)

Eight units provide essential training on using Adobe InDesign CS6 for designing simple layouts, combining text, graphics, and color, as well as multi-page documents, layered documents, tables, and InDesign libraries.

Adobe® Photoshop® CS6—Illustrated
Chris Botello (9781133190394)

Eight units offer thorough coverage of essential skills for working with Adobe Photoshop CS6 from both the design and production perspective, including creating and managing layer masks, creating color effects and improving images with adjustment layers, working with text and combining text and imagery, and using filters and layer styles to create eye-popping special effects.

Adobe® Creative Suite 6 Web Tools: Dreamweaver, Photoshop, and Flash Illustrated
(9781133629740)

Covers essential skills for working with Adobe Dreamweaver CS6, Adobe Photoshop CS6, and Adobe Flash CS6 with ten Dreamweaver units, four Photoshop units, one Bridge unit, five Flash units and one unit on integration.

Adobe® Creative Suite 6 Design Tools: Photoshop, Illustrator, InDesign Illustrated
(9781133562580)

Covers essential skills for working with Adobe Photoshop CS6, Adobe Illustrator CS6, and Adobe InDesign CS6 with seven Photoshop units, seven Illustrator units, six InDesign units, and one unit on integration.

For more information on the Illustrated Series, please visit:
www.cengage.com/ct/illustrated

Using Adobe Bridge to Manage Assets

Adobe Bridge is a media content manager integrated with many Adobe products for quick access to project files. Bridge is very easy to use as a "bridge" between your library of assets and the project files you are developing in programs such as Dreamweaver, Photoshop, Fireworks, Flash, Illustrator, and InDesign. In Bridge, you can open and preview any file format that Adobe recognizes such as JPGs, SWFs, PNGs, PDFs, MP3s, and MP4s. Although the most common use of Bridge is to organize and view media, it has many powerful features that you will find useful, such as adding metadata and keywords to files. **Metadata** is file information you add to a file with tags (words) that are used to identify and describe the file. **Keywords** are words you add to a file to identify, group, and sort files.  You work for a marketing firm that designs and maintains websites for several business clients. They include a beach resort, a nursery, a travel agency, a canoe outfitter, and a catering business. You will use Bridge to manage all of the media files that will be used to create the sites, so you begin by looking at the organizational functions Bridge has to offer.

OBJECTIVES

Start Adobe Bridge CS6

Explore the Bridge workspace

Use metadata

Starting Adobe Bridge CS6

Adobe Bridge is packaged with the Adobe Creative Suite. There are several ways to access the program: by opening it directly from your Applications or Program Files folder on your computer's hard drive, or within Adobe Illustrator, Photoshop, or InDesign either with the Bridge button on the Menu bar (in Windows, it's next to Help), or by choosing File on the Menu bar, then Browse in Bridge within the program. In Flash, the Bridge button is on the Document toolbar. A streamlined version of Bridge called **Mini Bridge** is also available in Photoshop and InDesign; it appears as a panel that opens directly within the Photoshop and InDesign programs. You use Bridge as your primary tool for viewing, copying, and moving media files similar to the way you use Windows Explorer or Macintosh Finder. You can also configure Bridge to start automatically each time you log in or start your computer or device by choosing Start Bridge At Login on the Advanced tab in the Adobe Bridge Preferences dialog box. To access the Preferences dialog box, click Edit on the Menu bar, then choose Preferences. You begin your work by starting Bridge and locating your media files.

STEPS

Win

1. Click the Start button 🔵 on the taskbar
2. Point to All Programs (if necessary), click Adobe Bridge CS6, then proceed to Step 3

Mac

1. Click Finder in the Dock, then click Applications

2. Click the Adobe Bridge CS6 folder, double-click the Adobe Bridge CS6 application, then proceed to Step 3

From an Adobe Creative Suite 6 component that is integrated with Bridge

1. Click File, click Browse in Bridge, then proceed to Step 3

Or

1. Click the Adobe Bridge button 🔳 on the Standard toolbar (Dreamweaver), then proceed to Step 3

Or

1. Press [Ctrl][Alt][O], then proceed to Step 3

All users

3. Verify that you are in the Essentials workspace (the default workspace), as shown in Figure BR-1

   Your panels probably show a darker background than the panels in Figure BR-1. To increase the readability, the Bridge interface was lightened for the figures. See Editing Bridge Preferences on page 3.

4. Use the breadcrumb trail across the top of the Bridge window on the Path bar or use the Folders panel to navigate to and select the Bridge_data folder from the drive and folder where you store your Bridge data files, as shown in Figure BR-1

   Thumbnails of each file in the Bridge Data Files folder appear in the Content panel. These are the same media data files you will use to complete each of the lessons in Dreamweaver.

FIGURE BR-1: Starting Bridge

Path bar

Folders panel

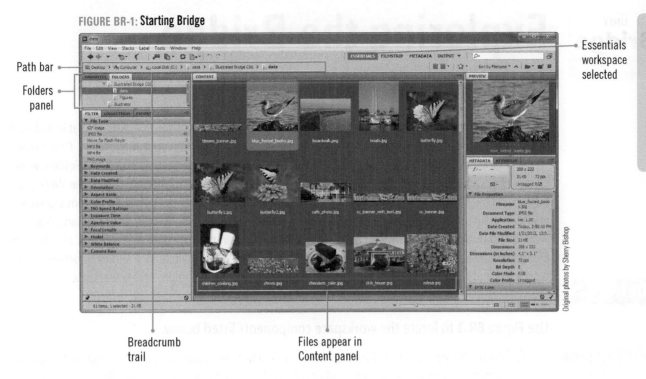

Essentials workspace selected

Original photos by Sherry Bishop

Breadcrumb trail

Files appear in Content panel

Editing Bridge Preferences

The panels in the Bridge CS6 interface have dark gray backgrounds that help you focus better on the images displayed in the Content panel. You can lighten the Bridge interface if you prefer by choosing a different color theme. To do this, click Edit on the Menu bar (Win) or click Bridge CS6 on the Menu bar (Mac), choose Preferences, then view the General tab in the Preferences dialog box. Four color boxes ranging from a dark gray to a light gray appear next to Color Theme. Click one of these boxes to select a different color theme or use the User Interface Brightness slider to create your own color theme. You can also enable (or disable) a script that enables other applications to communicate with Bridge when you start Bridge by checking the Adobe Bridge CS6 check box on the Startup Scripts tab in the Preferences dialog box.

Exploring the Bridge Workspace

When you start Bridge, you see the Bridge **Essentials workspace**, the default workspace that includes all of the menus, panels, buttons, bars, and panes that you use to organize your media files. Other workspace choices are the Filmstrip, Metadata, Output, Keywords, Preview, Light Table, and Folders workspaces. You can change workspaces by using the Window menu or by clicking one of the Workspace buttons on the Application bar. You can also arrange the panes and panels to create a custom workspace and then assign it a unique name using the Window > Workspace > New Workspace command. You can work in **Compact mode**, which is a mode with a smaller, simplified workspace window, as shown in Figure BR-2. Press [Ctrl][Enter] (Win) or [command][return] (Mac) to switch back and forth between your workspace and Compact mode. You spend some time exploring the Bridge workspace.

DETAILS

Use Figure BR-3 to locate the workspace components listed below.

- The Essentials workspace is divided into three panes, which are arranged in columns and further divided into panels. Each panel can be expanded or collapsed by double-clicking the panel title bar. You can also hide panels using the Windows > (panel name).

- The left pane includes the Favorites, Folders, Filter, Collections, and Export panels. You can use the **Favorites panel** to quickly access folders that you designate as folders you use frequently. The **Folders panel** is used to navigate through your folders to select a folder to view the folder contents. The **Filter panel** is used for filtering files to view in the Content panel. The **Collections panel** is used to group assets into collections. The **Export panel** is used to optimize images by saving them as JPEGs for use on the web.

- The center pane is the **Content panel**, where thumbnails of the files from the selected drive and folder in the Folders panel appear. You can change the size of the thumbnails by using the **Thumbnail slider** at the bottom of the workspace.

- The right pane includes the Preview, Metadata, and Keywords panels. The **Preview panel** is where a preview of a selected file appears. The **Metadata panel** lists the metadata for a selected file. You use the Metadata panel to assign new metadata to a file. The **Keywords panel** lists the keywords assigned to a file. You use the Keywords panel to add new keywords to a file.

- The **Menu bar** with the program commands is at the top of the Bridge workspace. Below the Menu bar is the **Application bar** that contains navigation buttons, the Workspace buttons, and the Search text box. Under the Application bar is the **Path bar**, where you see the path for the selected folder in the Folders panel that you are currently viewing. The Path bar makes it easy to navigate quickly from folder to folder.

FIGURE BR-2: Bridge in compact mode

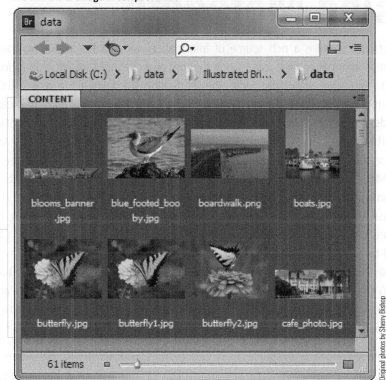

Content panel
is the only
panel displayed

Original photos by Sherry Bishop

FIGURE BR-3: The Bridge Essentials workspace

Menu bar
Application bar
Path bar
Favorites
and Folders
panels
Filter,
Collections,
and Export
panels

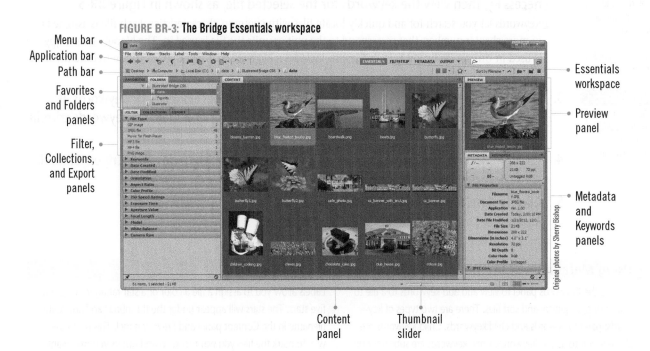

Essentials
workspace

Preview
panel

Metadata
and
Keywords
panels

Content
panel

Thumbnail
slider

Original photos by Sherry Bishop

Using Metadata

The Metadata panel is a rich source of information about a file, including the camera settings used (descriptive information that you cannot change) and copyright information (additive data that you can change). You can view and edit the copyright information in the IPTC (International Press Telecommunications Council) Core section of the Metadata panel. Image resolution, author name, and keywords are also examples of metadata you can view in the Metadata panel. Metadata is saved using the **Extensible Metadata Platform (XMP) standard.** XMP metadata is used by Adobe products, such as Illustrator, InDesign, Flash, and Photoshop, and is usually stored with the file name. If a file contains metadata, XMP allows the metadata to stay with the file when the file is converted to a different file type or placed in a project. You can add metadata using the File > File Info command.

You use the Keywords panel to view and add keywords to a file to help group, organize, and sort files. There are two types of keywords: **parent keywords** and **child keywords**. Child keywords are also referred to as **sub keywords**. Child keywords are subcategories of parent keywords. For instance, you could have a parent keyword "food" and a child keyword "desserts." After you have added keywords to files, you can use the Filter panel to sort files by their keywords.  You have added keywords to each of the media files you will use in your websites. You view each group separately to quickly verify that you added the correct keywords to each file.

STEPS

> **QUICK TIP**
> You cannot add metadata to .gif files.

> **QUICK TIP**
> Your other keywords will vary as keywords are deleted or added as you use Bridge or as files are selected with additional keywords associated with them.

> **QUICK TIP**
> If the files are not listed in alphabetical order, click View > Sort > By Filename.

1. **Click the** Metadata panel tab **to open the Metadata panel, click the first file listed in the Content panel,** blooms_banner.jpg, **then click** File Properties **(if necessary) to expand the panel to view the file size, dimensions, and resolution of the selected file, as shown in Figure BR-4**

2. **Click the** Keywords panel tab, **double-click the parent keyword** Unit **to expand it if necessary, then view the keywords for the selected file, as shown in Figure BR-5**

   Keywords let you search for and quickly locate files with common characteristics. Each file is assigned one or more chapter numbers that correspond to the unit or units the file is used in. The blooms_banner.jpg file is used in Units A, B, E, and F. Each file also includes a keyword that corresponds to the website the file is associated with.

3. **Double-click the** Filter panel tab **to expand the panel if necessary, click** Keywords, **if necessary to expand it, then click to select** striped_umbrella **under the Keywords criteria**

   Fourteen files appear in the Content panel, as shown in Figure BR-6.

4. **Click to select** blooms **under the Keywords criteria, then click to deselect** striped_umbrella

   The Content panel now shows seventeen files listed for the Blooms & Bulbs website.

5. **Click to deselect** blooms **under the Keywords criteria**

   All sixty-one files appear in the Content panel.

Using Metadata to label and rate files

You use the Keywords panel to view and add keywords to a file to help group, organize, and sort files. There are two types of keywords: parent keywords and child keywords. Child keywords are also referred to as sub keywords. Child keywords are subcategories of parent keywords. For instance, you could have a parent keyword "animal" and a child keyword "dog." After you have added keywords to files, you can use the Filter panel to sort files by their keywords. You can also identify groups of files by using labels.

Labels allow you to assign a file a color or a star rating from zero to five stars. The stars will appear under the thumbnail and above the filename in the Content panel and Preview panel. This is an easy way to mark the files you want to keep and others you may want to delete. You can also add labels such as "Approved" to indicate art that has been approved for a project. After you have entered labels for files, you can filter them with their labels in the Filter panel. To remove a label, use the Label > No Label command.

FIGURE BR-4: Viewing the metadata for the blooms_banner.jpg file

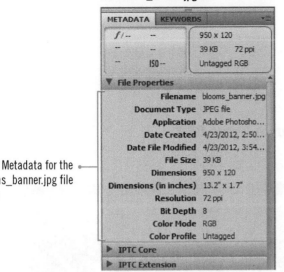

Metadata for the
blooms_banner.jpg file

FIGURE BR-5: Viewing the keywords for the blooms_banner.jpg file

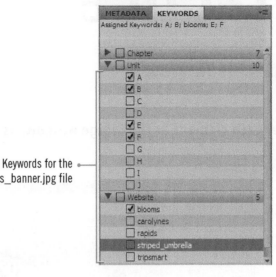

Keywords for the
blooms_banner.jpg file

FIGURE BR-6: Viewing files with the striped_umbrella keyword

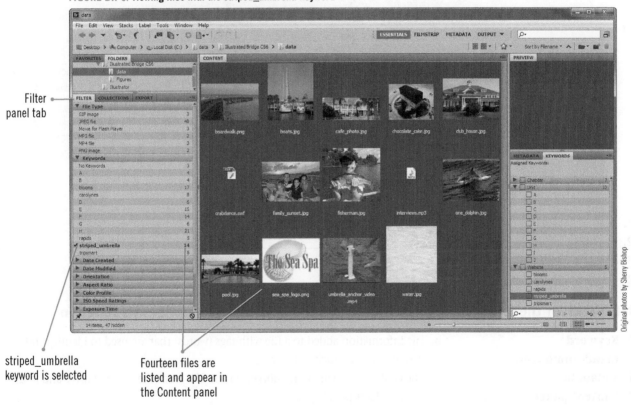

Filter
panel tab

striped_umbrella
keyword is selected

Fourteen files are
listed and appear in
the Content panel

Adding and applying keywords

To add a keyword to the Keywords panel, click the **New Keyword button** ➕ in the Keywords panel, then enter the keyword. To add a new sub keyword, click the **New Sub Keyword button** ➕ in the Keywords panel, then enter the sub keyword. To apply a keyword or a sub keyword to a file, select the file, then click the check box by the keyword or sub keyword you want to apply.

Practice

Concepts Review

Label each element in the Bridge window, as shown in Figure BR-7.

FIGURE BR-7

Original photos by Sherry Bishop

1. _____
2. _____
3. _____
4. _____

5. _____
6. _____
7. _____
8. _____

Match each of the following terms with the statement that best describes its function.

9. **Keyword**
10. **Breadcrumb trail**
11. **Metadata**
12. **Content panel**
13. **Folders panel**
14. **Menu bar**
15. **Application bar**
16. **Metadata panel**

a. File information added to a file with tags (words) that are used to identify and describe the file, such as keywords

b. The center pane, where thumbnails of the files from the selected drive and folder in the Folders panel appear

c. The bar that contains navigation buttons, the Workspace buttons, and the Search text box

d. The bar at the top of the Bridge workspace where program commands are listed

e. The path used to access a selected file; listed on the Path bar

f. Used to assign new metadata to a file

g. The panel used to navigate and select a folder to view the folder contents

h. Words you add to a file to identify, group, and sort files

Getting Started with Adobe Dreamweaver CS6

Files You Will Need:

To view a list of files needed for this unit, see the Data Files Grid in the back of the book.

Adobe Dreamweaver CS6 is a web design program used to create media-rich web pages and websites. Its easy-to-use tools let you incorporate sophisticated features, such as animations and interactive forms. In this unit, you learn to start Dreamweaver and examine the workspace. Next, you open a web page and learn how to use the Help feature. Finally, you close the web page and exit the program. You have recently been hired as a manager at The Striped Umbrella, a beach resort in Florida. One of your main responsibilities is to develop the resort's website using Dreamweaver. You begin by familiarizing yourself with the Dreamweaver program.

OBJECTIVES

Define web design software

Start Adobe Dreamweaver CS6

View the Dreamweaver workspace

Work with views and panels

Open a web page

View web page elements

Get help

View a web page in a browser

Close a web page and exit Dreamweaver

Defining Web Design Software

Adobe Dreamweaver CS6 is a powerful **web design program** that lets you create interactive web pages with text, images, animation, sounds, and video. You can create web page objects in Dreamweaver as well as import objects created using other programs. Although you can create several different types of files with Dreamweaver, you will be saving files with the .html file extension throughout this book. **HTML** is the acronym for **Hypertext Markup Language**, the language web developers use to create web pages. ▚▚▚▚ You need to learn some basic Dreamweaver features for your new position.

Using Dreamweaver you can:

- **Create web pages or websites**

  You can use Dreamweaver to create individual web pages or entire websites, depending on your project needs. **Web pages** are pages of text in HTML format combined with images in various image formats. **Websites** are collections of related web pages. Websites are stored on **servers**, which are computers connected to the Internet. Users can view websites using a **web browser**, which is software used to display pages in a website; some of the most popular browsers are Internet Explorer, Mozilla Firefox, Google Chrome, Opera, and Safari. You can also import web pages created in other programs, edit them in Dreamweaver, and then incorporate them into an existing website. Dreamweaver provides predefined page layouts called **templates** that you can apply to existing pages or use as a basis for designing new ones.

- **Add text, images, tables, and media files**

  You can add text, images, tables, and media files to a web page by using the Insert panel. The **Insert panel** (also referred to as the **Insert bar**) contains buttons for creating or inserting objects, such as tables, images, forms, and videos. Using the Insert panel, you can also insert objects made with other Adobe software programs, including Fireworks, Flash, and Photoshop. Table A-1 describes the Insert panel categories.

- **Display web pages as they will appear to users**

  Dreamweaver is a **WYSIWYG** ("What You See Is What You Get") program. As you design a web page in Dreamweaver, you see the page exactly as it will appear in a browser window.

- **Use the Property inspector to view and edit page elements**

  The **Property inspector** (also referred to as the **Properties panel**) is a panel that displays the characteristics of a page's currently selected object. Figure A-1 shows a web page open in Dreamweaver. Note that the properties of the selected text appear in the Property inspector. The Property inspector changes depending upon the type of page object selected. For example, when an image is selected, the Property inspector displays image properties. When text is selected, the Property inspector displays text properties with either the HTML Property inspector or the CSS Property inspector.

- **Manage websites**

  Dreamweaver lets you manage website pages to ensure that all the **links**, or connections among the pages, work properly. The importance of proper site management increases as new pages are added to a website. Part of managing a website involves identifying problems or challenges as content is added and the site becomes more complex. There are several types of reports that you can run to check for problems across the website. Dreamweaver also has special tools that help you manage a site when you are working as part of a team on a project.

FIGURE A-1: Web page open in Dreamweaver

Tab displays filename of open file (Macintosh users will not see tabs unless multiple pages are open.)

Web page

Property inspector showing properties for selected text

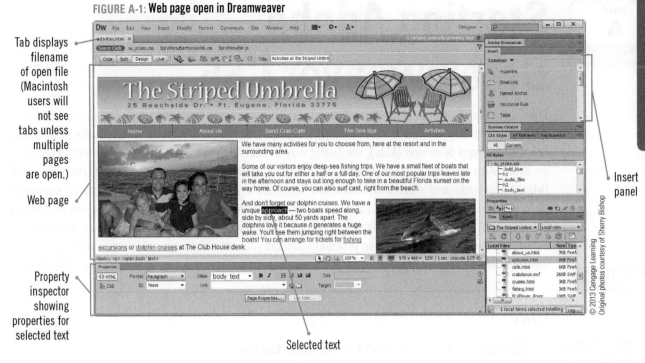

Insert panel

Selected text

TABLE A-1: Insert panel categories and corresponding buttons

category	buttons
Common	Commonly used buttons, such as images, media, and hyperlinks
Layout	Buttons for inserting divs, tables, Spry objects, and frames
Forms	Buttons for inserting form objects, such as check boxes and radio buttons
Data	Buttons for inserting Tabular Data, Dynamic Data, and Recordsets
Spry	Buttons for inserting Spry data sets, Spry validations, and Spry panels
jQuery Mobile	Buttons for inserting widgets in jQuery Mobile Pages
InContext Editing	Buttons for creating editable regions to allow others to add content
Text	Buttons for formatting text; for example, strong, headings, and lists
Favorites	Buttons you can customize; Dreamweaver will add those you use most frequently

Getting Started with Adobe Dreamweaver CS6

Starting Adobe Dreamweaver CS6

There are several ways to start Dreamweaver, depending on the type of computer you are using and the type of installation you have. Although the steps below start the program using the Start menu (Win) or the hard drive icon (Mac), the fastest way to start Dreamweaver is to place a shortcut (Win) or an alias (Mac) for Adobe Dreamweaver CS6 on your desktop or add it to the taskbar (Win) or Dock (Mac). **Shortcuts** and **aliases** are icons that represent a software program stored on your computer system. When you double-click a shortcut (Win) or an alias (Mac), you do not need to use the Start menu (Win) or open submenus (Mac) to find your program. When you initially open Dreamweaver, the Welcome Screen appears. The Welcome Screen provides shortcuts you can click to open files or to create new files or websites.  You are given your first web-related assignment and begin by starting Dreamweaver.

STEPS

WIN

1. **Click the** Start button 🌐 **on the Windows taskbar**

   The Start menu opens, which lists the names of the software programs installed on your computer.

2. **Point to** All Programs, **click** Adobe Web Premium CS6 **or** Adobe Design Premium CS6 **(if you have one of these suites of Adobe products), then click** Adobe Dreamweaver CS6

   Dreamweaver opens and the Welcome Screen appears, as shown in Figure A-2.

3. **Click** HTML **in the Create New column on the Dreamweaver Welcome Screen**

   A new blank HTML document named Untitled-1 opens.

MAC

1. **Click** Finder **in the Dock, then click** Applications

2. **Click the** Adobe Dreamweaver CS6 **folder, then double-click the** Adobe Dreamweaver CS6 program

   Dreamweaver opens, and the Welcome Screen appears, as shown in Figure A-2.

3. **Click** HTML **in the Create New column on the Dreamweaver Welcome Screen**

   A blank document named Untitled-1 opens.

Using Dreamweaver layouts

Dreamweaver has several preset workspace layouts that you can choose between. In the **Designer layout**, the panels are docked on the right side of the screen, and Design view is the default view. In the **Coder layout**, the panels are docked on the left side of the screen, and Code view is the default view. The **Dual Screen layout** is used with two monitors: one for the Document window and Property inspector and one for the panels. Other layouts include App Developer, App Developer Plus, Business Catalyst, Classic, Coder Plus, Designer Compact, Fluid Layout, and Mobile Applications. You can change the workspace layout by using a feature called the **Workspace switcher**. The Workspace switcher allows you to quickly change between different preset workspace layouts. You can also create and name your own custom layout with the New Workspace command on the Workspace switcher menu. You can reset your workspace back to the preset Designer layout after you have moved, opened, or closed panels with the 'Reset Designer' command.

FIGURE A-2: The Dreamweaver Welcome Screen (Win)

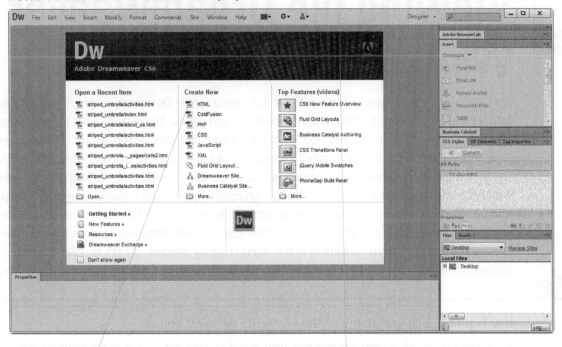

Create New HTML

Depending on the size of your screen,
the Menu bar may appear as two
different bars, one above the other

FIGURE A-2: The Dreamweaver Welcome Screen (Mac)

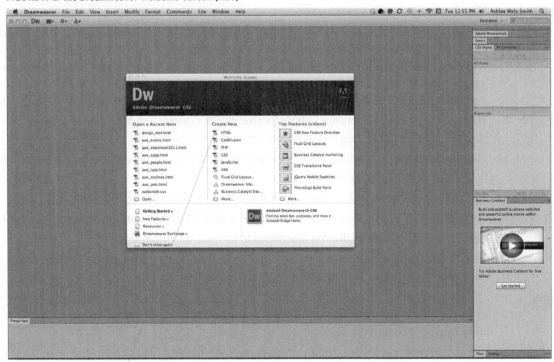

Create New HTML

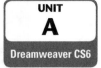
Viewing the Dreamweaver Workspace

The Dreamweaver **workspace**, shown in Figure A-3, consists of the Document window, the Application bar (Win) or Menu bar (Mac), toolbars, Property inspector, and panels. The default layout in Dreamweaver is called the Designer layout. Other layouts include the Coder and Dual Screen layouts. The Designer and Coder layouts are built with an integrated workspace using the **Multiple Document Interface (MDI)**. This means that all Document windows and panels are positioned within one large application window. **Panel Groups** are sets of related panels that are grouped together. The Property inspector, or Properties panel, is a panel that changes to display the properties of the currently selected web page object. It contains text boxes, shortcut menus, and buttons that allow you to make formatting changes without having to open menus. Its contents vary according to the object currently selected. ▓▓▓ In order to continue with your website project, you want to spend some time familiarizing yourself with the Dreamweaver workspace.

DETAILS

Use Figure A-3 to find many of the elements detailed below.

- When a document is open, the filename, path, and document type appear in the **Browser Navigation toolbar**. This toolbar, located directly above the Document window contains navigation buttons you use when following links on your pages in Live view. **Live view** displays an open document with its interactive elements active and functioning, as if you were viewing the document in an actual browser window.

- The **Application bar** (Win) or **Menu bar** (Mac), located at the top of the Dreamweaver workspace, includes menu names, a Workspace switcher, and other program commands. The Application bar (Win) or Menu bar (Mac) appears as one bar or two bars, depending on your screen size and resolution. You use commands by using shortcut keys or by clicking corresponding buttons on the various panels. We will simply refer to this as the Menu bar from this point forward.

TROUBLE

If you don't see the Insert panel, click Window on the Menu bar, then click Insert.

- The Insert panel contains buttons that allow you to insert objects, such as images, tables, and horizontal rules. The buttons on the Insert panel change depending on the category you select using a drop-down menu. Each category contains buttons relating to a specific task. When you insert an object using one of the buttons, a dialog box opens, letting you choose the object's characteristics. The last button selected becomes the default button for that category. The Insert panel's drop-down menu also has an option to show the program icons in color.

TROUBLE

To see hidden toolbars, click View on the Menu bar, point to Toolbars, then click the toolbar name. The Standard and Style Rendering toolbars do not appear by default.

- The **Document toolbar** contains buttons for changing the current web page view, previewing and debugging web pages, and managing files. The Document toolbar buttons are listed in Table A-2.

- The **Standard toolbar** contains buttons for some frequently used commands on the File and Edit menus, such as the Copy and Paste commands.

- The **Style Rendering toolbar** contains buttons that can be used to display different media types.

- The **Coding toolbar** is useful when you are working with HTML code; it can only be accessed in Code view.

- The **Related Files toolbar** displays files related to an open and active file.

- The **Document window** is the large area under the Document toolbar that encompasses most of the Dreamweaver workspace. Web pages that you open in Dreamweaver appear in this area.

- The **Status bar** appears under the Document window. The left side displays the **tag selector**, which shows the HTML tags being used at the insertion point location. The right side displays window size data and page download time estimates.

QUICK TIP

To make an open panel active and display its contents, click the panel tab. To expand or collapse a panel, double-click the panel tab.

- **Panels** are small windows containing program controls. Related panels appear together in panel groups, such as the CSS Styles panel and the Files panel. You display a panel by choosing its name from the Window menu. You can dock panel groups to the right side of the screen, or undock them by dragging the panel tab. When two or more panels are docked together, you can access the panel you want by clicking its tab name to display its contents.

FIGURE A-3: The Dreamweaver CS6 workspace

Menu bar (Application bar)
File tab with file name
Related Files toolbar
Document toolbar
Style Rendering toolbar
Standard toolbar
Document window
Status bar
Property inspector

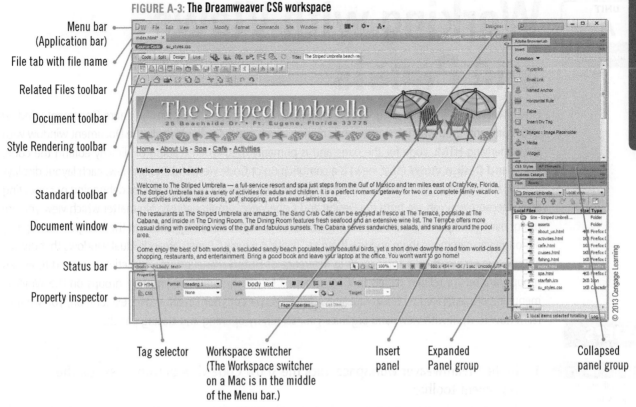

Tag selector

Workspace switcher
(The Workspace switcher
on a Mac is in the middle
of the Menu bar.)

Insert panel

Expanded Panel group

Collapsed panel group

© 2013 Cengage Learning

TABLE A-2: Document toolbar buttons

button	name	function
Code	Show Code view	Displays only the Code view in the Document window
Split	Show Code and Design views	Displays both the Code and Design views in the Document window
Design	Show Design view	Displays only the Design view in the Document window
Live	Switch Design View to Live View	Displays the page with interactive elements active and functioning
	File management	Displays file management options
	Preview/Debug in browser	Activates the browser for viewing the page
	Multiscreen	Displays the page in three devices in one integrated window; list arrow lets you select options
	W3C Validation	Submits the page to the W3C service for validation
	Check browser compatibility	Checks the page for problems when viewed in browsers
	Visual Aids	Displays options for visual display of information
	Refresh Design View	Reloads the page to reflect any changes made in Code view

Working with Views and Panels

Dreamweaver has three working views. **Design view** shows a page within the entire Document window and is primarily used when designing and creating a web page. **Code view** fills the Document window with the underlying HTML code for the page and is primarily used when reading or directly editing the code. **Code and Design views** (Split view) is a combination of Code view and Design view; each layout displays in a separate window within the Document window. This view is a good choice for debugging or correcting errors because you can see both the Design and Code views simultaneously. No matter which view you are using, panels and panel groups appear on the right side of the screen by default in the Designer workspace, although you can move them and use them as "floating panels." Panels are individual windows that display information on a particular topic, such as Reference or History. Panel groups, sometimes referred to as Tab groups, are sets of related panels that are grouped together. Panels are listed by groups on the Window menu and are separated by horizontal lines. ▨▨▨ As part of your Dreamweaver exploration, you want to learn how to work with views and organize your screen by opening and closing panels.

STEPS

QUICK TIP

The icons shown in the figures are in color, although the icons by default are not in color. To change to color icons, click the Insert panel drop-down menu, then click Color Icons.

1. **In the Dreamweaver workspace, click the** Show Code view button `Code` **on the Document toolbar**

   The HTML code for the untitled, blank document appears, as shown in Figure A-4. The code for a blank, untitled page is very limited since the page has no content. As content is added, the number of lines of code will increase as well. Notice in the first line of code that this is an XHTML document type, although the file extension is .html.

2. **Click the** Show Code and Design views button `Split` **on the Document toolbar**

   A split screen appears. The left side displays the HTML code, while the right side displays the open page. The open page is blank because the current document, Unitled-1, doesn't have any content.

3. **Click the** Show Design view button `Design` **on the Document toolbar**

   A blank page appears again because there is no page content to view.

TROUBLE

If you don't see the CSS Styles panel, click Window on the Menu bar, then click CSS Styles.

4. **Click the** CSS Styles panel tab, **if necessary, to expand the panel group.**

   The CSS panel group expands so you can see the contents of the active panel. The CSS Styles panel is the active panel in the default Designer workspace when the program is opened initially. An **active panel** is displayed as the front panel in an expanded panel group with the panel options displayed. Panels open in the position they held when the program was last closed. The CSS Styles panel contains two buttons, All and Current, which are used to view specific information in the panel. When two or more panels are docked together, you can access the panel you want by clicking its tab to display its contents.

5. **Click the** AP Elements panel tab **on the CSS Styles panel group**

   AP Elements becomes the active panel with the panel contents displayed. As you click each panel tab, the panel tab changes color and the panel contents are displayed. See Figure A-5.

QUICK TIP

If you want to restore your workspace to the original settings, click Window on the Menu bar, point to Workspace Layout, click Reset 'Designer'; click View on the Menu bar, scroll down, if necessary, then click Color Icons if you want to view your icons in color.

6. **Click the** CSS Styles panel tab **to display it, then double-click the** CSS Styles panel tab

   The panel group collapses. When a panel is collapsed, you click the panel tab to expand it. If a panel group is expanded, you simply click the panel tab to make the panel active.

7. **Click** File **on the Menu bar, click** Close **to close the untitled document, then click** No **if necessary if you are asked about saving the untitled page**

FIGURE A-4: Code view for a blank document

Show Design view button
Show Code view button
Show Code and Design views button
Code for blank document
Document type code
Workspace switcher
Your Property inspector might be collapsed; double-click to collapse or expand the panel.
All button
CSS Styles panel tab
Current button
AP Elements panel tab

FIGURE A-5: Viewing a panel in an expanded panel group

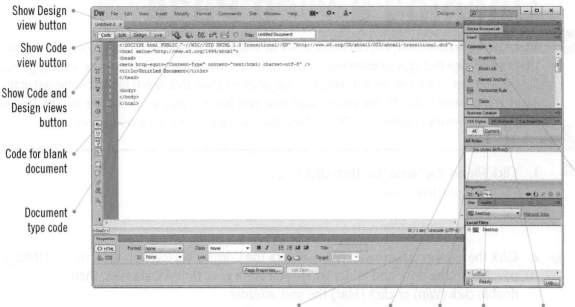

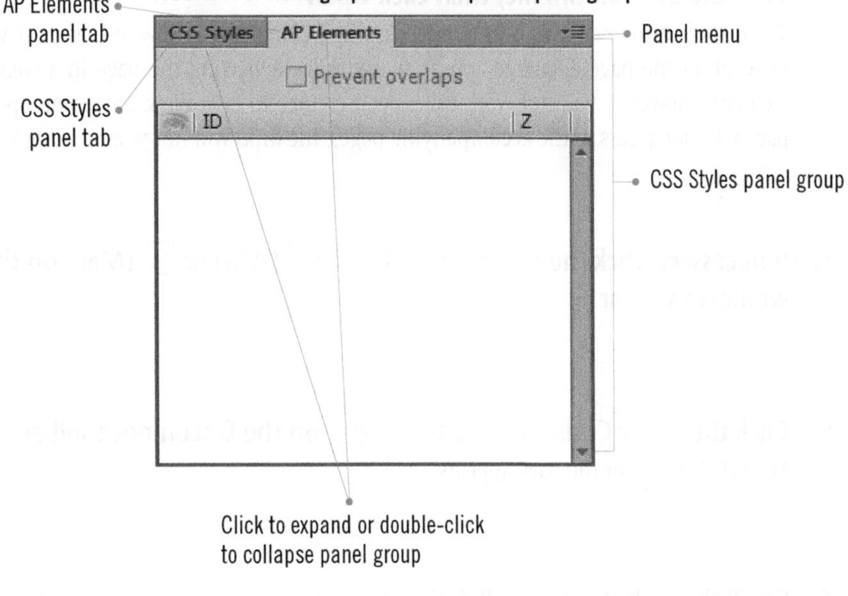

AP Elements panel tab
CSS Styles panel tab
CSS Styles
AP Elements
Prevent overlaps
ID
Z
Panel menu
CSS Styles panel group
Click to expand or double-click to collapse panel group

Using panel groups

By default, the Adobe BrowserLab panel, Insert panel, CSS Styles panel group, Business Catalyst panel, and Files panel group open when you first start Dreamweaver in Windows. The panels will retain their arrangement from one session to the next. For instance, if you open the Files panel and do not close it before exiting Dreamweaver, it will be open the next time you start Dreamweaver. To close a panel group, right-click (Win) or [control]-click (Mac) its title bar, then click Close Tab Group. The **panel group title bar** is the dark gray bar at the top of each panel group. The Panel menu lets you choose commands related to the currently displayed panel. You can also rearrange the workspace using your own choices for panel placement and save the workspace with a unique name using the "New Workspace" and "Manage Workspaces" commands on the Workspace switcher. The Workspace switcher is shown in Figure A-4.

Opening a Web Page

After opening Dreamweaver, you can create a new website or page, or open an existing website or page. The first web page that appears when you access a website is called the **home page**. The home page sets the look and tone of the website and contains a navigation structure that directs the user to the rest of the pages in the website. The resort's marketing firm has designed a new banner for The Striped Umbrella. You begin by opening The Striped Umbrella home page to view the new banner.

STEPS

TROUBLE
If you do not have your preferences set to show file extensions, you will not see the file extensions for each file. To show file extensions, open Windows Explorer, click Organize, click Folder and search options, click the View tab, then uncheck Hide extensions for known file types.

1. **Click File on the Menu bar, then click Open**
   The Open dialog box opens.

2. **Click the Look in list arrow ⏷ (Win) or click the Current file location list arrow ⬍ (Mac), navigate to the drive and folder where you store your Unit A Data Files, then double-click (Win) or click (Mac) the unit_a folder**
   The list of the data files in the unit_a folder, along with an assets folder where the image files for this unit are stored, appear in the Name column. See Figure A-6.

QUICK TIP
You can also double-click a file in the Open dialog box to open it. Or click File on the Menu bar, then click one of the recently opened files listed in the Open Recent submenu.

3. **Click the dwa_1.html file, then click Open**
   The document named dwa_1.html opens in the Document window in Design view. Since you are in Design view, all of the page elements appear as if you were viewing the page in a web browser. The interactive elements, however, will not work unless you change to Live View. Since you opened this page as a single page without access to the accompanying pages, the links will not work in Live View or in a browser.

4. **If necessary, click the Maximize button 🔲 (Win) or ⊕ (Mac) on the Document window title bar**

5. **Click the Show Code view button [Code] on the Document toolbar**
   The HTML code for the page appears.

6. **Scroll through the code, click the Show Design view button [Design] on the Document toolbar to return to Design view, then, if necessary, scroll to display the top of the page**

Design Matters

Opening or creating different document types with Dreamweaver

You can use either the Welcome Screen or the New command on the File menu to open or create several types of files. For example, you can create HTML documents, XML documents, style sheets, and text files. You can create new documents from scratch, or base them on existing pages. The predesigned CSS page layouts make it easy to design web pages based on Cascading Style Sheets without an advanced level of expertise in writing HTML code. Predesigned templates save you time and promote consistency across a website. As you learn more about Dreamweaver, you will find it worthwhile to explore each category to understand what is available to you as a designer.

dwa_1.html
data file

Look in list arrow

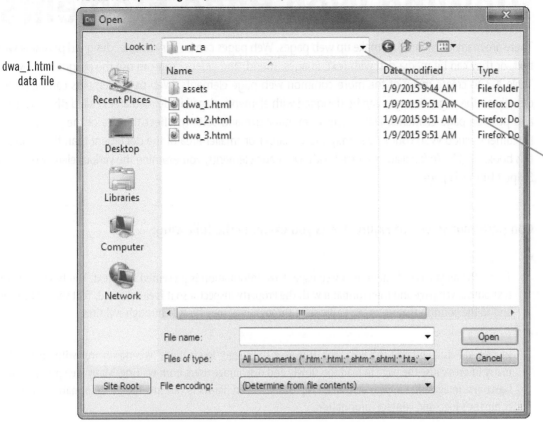

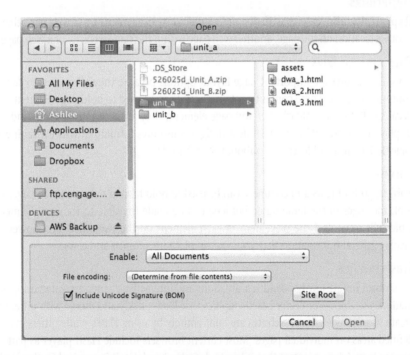

Displaying and docking panel groups

You can move panel groups to a different area on the screen by dragging the panel group title bar. To dock a panel group, drag the panel group to the right side of the screen. A heavy blue bar indicates the position it will take when you release the mouse button. This position is called the **drop zone**. You can also minimize all panels to icons by clicking the Collapse to Icons button in the top-right corner of the top panel. You can hide and show all panels by pressing the F4 key (Win).

Viewing Web Page Elements

There are many elements that make up web pages. Web pages can be very simple, designed primarily with text, or they can be media-rich with text, images, sound, and videos. You can use the programs shown in Table A-3 to create many of the more common web page elements. Web page elements can be placed directly on the page, or pages can be designed with elements placed in defined areas called **divs** to format and position page elements. Differences in monitor size and settings affect the size of the program and Document windows so your screen may show a larger or smaller area of the document than the figures in this book.  To familiarize yourself with web page elements, you examine the various elements on the Striped Umbrella page.

DETAILS

Compare your screen to Figure A-7 as you examine the following:

- **Text**

  Text is the most basic element on a web page. Most information is presented with text. You type or import text onto a web page and then format it with the Property inspector so it is easy to read. Text should be short and to the point so that users can easily skim through it as they browse through websites.

- **Images**

  Images add visual interest to a web page. However, the adage "less is more" is certainly true with images. Too many images cause the page to load too slowly and discourage users from waiting. Many web pages contain **banners**, images that appear across the top of the screen. Banners can incorporate information, such as a company's logo and contact information.

- **Hyperlinks**

  Hyperlinks, also known as **links**, are graphic or text elements on a web page that users click to display another location on the page, another web page within the same website, or a web page in a different website.

- **Divs and AP Divs**

  Divs and AP divs are important page layout options because they allow you to "draw" or insert blocks of content on a page. These content containers can then be used to hold page elements, such as text or images. Because AP divs can "float" over any page element, they are easy to reposition and can be programmed to display according to set criteria. Most designers use divs formatted with Cascading Style Sheets (CSS) for page design. You will learn more about CSS in Unit D.

- **Tables**

  Tables, grids of rows and columns, can be used to hold tabular data on a web page. When used as a design tool, the edges of the table (table borders) can be made invisible to the user. Elements are then placed in table cells to control the placement of each element on the page. Div tags, however, are the best way to display general information that you want to place in columns and rows.

- **Flash movies**

  Flash movies are low-bandwidth animations and interactive elements created using Adobe Flash. These animations use a series of vector-based graphics that load quickly and merge with other graphics and sounds to create short movies. Some websites are built entirely by using Flash, while others may have Flash content in defined areas on individual pages. Most current browsers include Flash player as part of the software. **Flash player** is an Adobe program that is free to download and use. It is required to play Flash animations.

- **Flash video**

  Flash videos are videos that have been converted from a digital video file format to an .flv file using Adobe Flash. The big advantage to Flash videos is that they can be **streamed**, which means that they begin playing before the entire file has been downloaded.

FIGURE A-7: **Viewing web page elements**

Banner •

Links to • other pages in the website

Text •

Image •

Page layout based on divs

© 2013 Cengage Learning
Original photo courtesy of Sherry Bishop

TABLE A-3: **Programs used to create web page elements**

source program	elements created
Adobe Edge	Used to create animation and interactive content
Adobe Fireworks	Used to create and optimize images for the web
Adobe Flash	Used to create animation and vector graphics
Adobe Illustrator	Used to create and edit vector graphics
Adobe Photoshop	Used to edit and enhance bitmap images

Getting Help

Dreamweaver has an excellent Help feature that is comprehensive and easy to use. When questions or problems arise, you can use the Adobe Community Help window. This window contains two tools that you can use to search for answers in different ways: the link to the PDF and a Search box. Clicking the link to the PDF opens the Dreamweaver Help PDF file that is saved locally on your computer and that contains a list of topics and subtopics by category. The Search box at the top-left corner of the window enables you to enter a keyword to search for a specific topic. You can see context-specific help by clicking the Help button in the Property inspector (Win). The Help feature in Dreamweaver CS6 is based on Adobe Air technology. **Adobe AIR** is an Adobe product used for developing content that can be delivered with a browser or as a desktop application. Context-specific help can be accessed by clicking the Help button on the Property inspector (Win). ▓▓▓ You decide to access the Help feature to learn more about Dreamweaver.

STEPS

1. **Click Help on the Menu bar**

   The Help menu appears, displaying the Help categories. See Figure A-8.

2. **Click Dreamweaver Help**

   The Dreamweaver Help/Help and tutorials window opens. Since the help feature is online content, you must have Internet access to use it. This also means that since it is Web content, the pages are live pages subject to change. Your screens will probably not match the figures exactly.

3. **Type "workspace switcher" in the search box on the left side of the window under the words Adobe Community Help, click the drop-down menu next to the search text box, click Dreamweaver if necessary, then press [Enter]**

   A list of topics related to the workspace switcher appears.

4. **Click the option button next to "Only Adobe content" as shown in Figure A-9 then read the information in the Content pane**

   The list repopulates to show only content from the Adobe website. Community content includes content that has been posted from other approved sources outside of Adobe.

5. **Click one of the links listed**

6. **Scroll through and read some of the information, as shown in Figure A-10, then close the Dreamweaver Help window**

Using Adobe Help

When you access the Help feature in Dreamweaver, you have the choice of downloading a PDF for offline help (which is similar to searching in a Dreamweaver manual) or using online help. The online help feature is called Adobe Community Help.

Adobe Community Help is a collection of materials such as tutorials, published articles, or blogs, in addition to the regular help content. All content is monitored and approved by the Adobe Community Expert program.

FIGURE A-8: **Help menu**

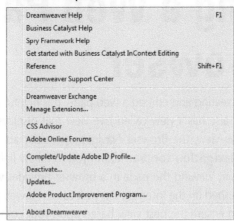

Dreamweaver Help   F1
Business Catalyst Help
Spry Framework Help
Get started with Business Catalyst InContext Editing
Reference   Shift+F1
Dreamweaver Support Center

Dreamweaver Exchange
Manage Extensions...

CSS Advisor
Adobe Online Forums

Complete/Update Adobe ID Profile...
Deactivate...
Updates...
Adobe Product Improvement Program...

Macintosh users will see this on • — About Dreamweaver
the Dreamweaver menu

FIGURE A-9: **Displaying the Help topics**

Search text box •

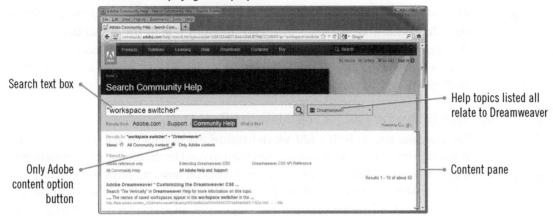

Only Adobe
content option
button

Help topics listed all
relate to Dreamweaver

Content pane

FIGURE A-10: **Displaying Help content**

Viewing a Web Page in a Browser

During the process of creating and editing a web page, it is helpful to frequently view the page in a web browser. Dreamweaver also has a view called Live view that displays the page as if it were being viewed using a browser. In Live view, the Browser Navigation toolbar above the Document window becomes active. The **Browser Navigation toolbar** allows you to follow links in Live view as if you were viewing the pages in the browser. Viewing the page in a browser provides visual feedback of what the page will look like when it is published on the Internet. It is best to view a web page using different browsers, screen sizes, and resolutions to ensure the best view based upon your computer's capabilities. It is important to remember that you cannot print a web page in Dreamweaver except in Code view. You use the Print command on your browser toolbar or menu to print the page. You decide to view The Striped Umbrella home page in your default browser.

STEPS

TROUBLE

If the status bar is out of view, then resize and reposition the Document window as necessary for it to be visible. Drag a corner to resize the window and drag the title bar to reposition it.

1. **In Design view, click the Maximize button** ▫ **(Win) or** ⊕ **(Mac) on the Menu bar, then click the Window Size pop-up menu on the right side of the status bar**

   The Window Size pop-up menu appears, as shown in Figure A-11. The Window Size pop-up menu lists several options for simulating commonly used screen sizes. You may need to double-click the right side of the Property inspector to collapse it in order to see the Window Size pop-up menu.

2. **Click 1000 × 620 (1024 × 768, Maximized)**

   The screen size is set to 1000 × 620, which translates to a monitor set at a 1024 × 768 screen resolution. When you choose your screen size, it is important to consider the equipment your users may have when they view your page in their browser. You need to consider how your pages will look, not only with different size desktop monitors, but also on tablets and other mobile devices. The Status bar also has Mobile size ▣ , Tablet size ▣ , and Desktop size ▣ buttons you can use to view pages with these device sizes. See Table A-4 for window size options.

QUICK TIP

You can change the browser list by using the Edit > Preferences > Preview in Browser command, then using the Add or Remove Browser buttons to add or remove browsers from the list.

3. **Click the Preview/Debug in browser button** ◉ **on the Document toolbar, then click Preview in [browser name]**

   The browser opens, and the Striped Umbrella web page previews in the browser, as shown in Figure A-12.

TROUBLE

If you don't see a menu bar, press [Ctrl] [P] to print.

4. **Click File on the browser Menu bar, then click Print**

   The Print dialog box opens.

5. **Click Print**

   A copy of the web page prints. The black background that appears on the web page will not print unless you have selected the Print background colors and images option in your printer settings.

FIGURE A-11: **Window size pop-up menu**

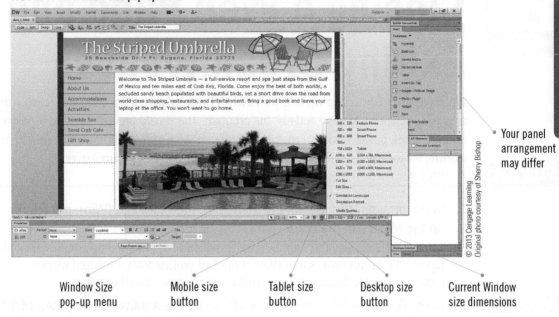

© 2013 Cengage Learning
Original photo courtesy of Sherry Bishop

Your panel
arrangement
may differ

Window Size
pop-up menu

Mobile size
button

Tablet size
button

Desktop size
button

Current Window
size dimensions

FIGURE A-12: **Web page previewed in a browser window**

Your path
will differ

© 2013 Cengage Learning

TABLE A-4: **Window size options**

window size (inside dimensions of browser window without borders)	corresponding resolution
240 × 320	Feature Phone
320 × 480	Smart Phone
480 × 800	Smart Phone
592w	
768 × 1024	Tablet
1000 × 620	(1024 × 768, Maximized)
1260 × 875	(1280 × 1024, Maximized)
1420 × 750	(1440 × 900, Maximized)
1580 × 1050	(1600 × 1200, Maximized)

Getting Started with Adobe Dreamweaver CS6

Closing a Web Page and Exiting Dreamweaver

When you are ready to stop working with a file in Dreamweaver, it is a good idea to close the current page or pages you are working on and exit the program. This should prevent data loss if power is interrupted; in some cases, power outages can corrupt an open file and make it unusable.  You are finished working for the day so you want to close the web page and exit Dreamweaver.

1. **In the browser, click File on the Menu bar, then click Exit (Win), or click [Browser name] on the Menu bar, then click Quit [Browser name] (Mac)**

   The browser closes, and The Striped Umbrella Web page reappears in the Dreamweaver window, as shown in Figure A-13. In this book, screen shots of finished projects feature enlarged windows to display as much content as possible. You may have to scroll to see the same amount of content.

   QUICK TIP
   You may need to click the Dreamweaver CS6 title bar to activate the program.

2. **In the Dreamweaver workspace, click File on the Application bar, then click Exit (Win) or click Dreamweaver on the Menu bar, then click Quit Dreamweaver (Mac)**

   Dreamweaver closes.

Saving and closing Dreamweaver files

It is wise to save a file as soon as you begin creating it and to save frequently as you work. A quick glance at the title bar shows whether you have saved your file. If you haven't saved the file initially, the filename shows "Untitled" rather than a filename. This does not refer to the page title, but the actual filename. After you save the file and make a change to it, an asterisk appears at the end of the filename until you save it again. It is always wise to save and close a page on which you are not actively working. Keeping multiple files open can cause confusion, especially when you are working with multiple websites which have similarly named pages. Each open page has a tab at the top of the page with the filename listed. You use these tabs to switch between each open page to make it the active page. You can also press [Ctrl] [Tab] (Win) or [command][tab] (Mac) to move between open documents.

Design Matters

Designing for multiple window sizes

It is not enough today to simply design for several different screen resolutions and sizes for prospective users using desktop monitors. Although desktop sizes are probably your main focus, you should have a design plan in place for tablet sizes and mobile phone sizes in both portrait and landscape modes. Your first thought may be that your users can just enlarge their screens using gestures. **Gestures** are interactions with a touchscreen, usually with a combination of fingers and a thumb. Gestures can be used to enlarge or reduce a screen. When users pinch their thumb and finger together, the screen zooms out. When users move their thumb and finger apart (a reverse pinch), the screen zooms in. Although most people are familiar with how to use gestures, you should not make them use them in order to read your content. Dreamweaver can help you develop a design plan for multiple window sizes with the new Fluid Grid Layout, a system for designing an adaptive website based on a single fluid grid. Another option is to use Media Queries, a tool that uses CSS3 and HTML5 to identify the device a page is being displayed in and apply the appropriate styles for optimum viewing. We will learn more about Media Queries in Unit J.

Practice

Concepts Review

Label each element in the Dreamweaver window as shown in Figure A-14.

FIGURE A-14

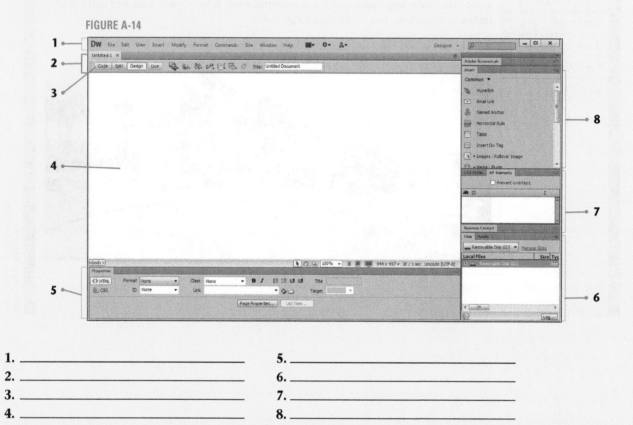

1. _____   5. _____
2. _____   6. _____
3. _____   7. _____
4. _____   8. _____

Match each of the following terms with the statement that best describes its function.

9. Standard toolbar
10. Document toolbar
11. Code view
12. Tag selector
13. Workspace
14. Design view
15. Insert panel
16. Menu bar

a. The Document window, the menu bar, toolbars, inspectors, and panels
b. Allows you to choose program commands
c. Shows the page layout
d. Contains buttons that allow you to insert objects, such as images
e. Contains buttons for some of the more commonly used options under the File and Edit menus
f. Shows the HTML code
g. Contains buttons for changing the current Dreamweaver view
h. Shows the HTML tags being used at the current insertion point

Select the best answer from the list of choices.

17. You display panels using the _____ menu.
   a. Window
   b. Edit
   c. Panel
   d. View

18. The tool that allows you to show the properties of a selected page element is called the:
   a. Tool inspector.
   b. Element inspector.
   c. Insert panel.
   d. Property inspector or Properties panel.

19. Most information on a web page is presented in the form of:
   a. text.
   b. images.
   c. links.
   d. video.

20. The view that is best for designing and creating a web page is:
   a. Code view.
   b. Design view.
   c. a combination of both Code and Design views.
   d. any of the above.

21. Which of the following is one of the Dreamweaver default panel groups?
   a. History
   b. Design
   c. Application
   d. Files

Skills Review

1. Define web design software.
   a. Write a short paragraph describing at least three features of Dreamweaver.
   b. Add another paragraph describing three views that are available in Dreamweaver, then describe when you would use each view.

2. Start Adobe Dreamweaver CS6.
   a. Start Dreamweaver and create a new HTML page.
   b. Write a list of the panels that currently appear on the screen.

3. View the Dreamweaver workspace.
   a. Locate the document title bar.
   b. Locate the Menu bar.
   c. Locate the Document toolbar.
   d. Locate the Insert panel.
   e. Locate the Property inspector.

4. Work with views and panels.
   a. Switch to Code view.
   b. Switch to Code and Design views.
   c. Switch to Design view.
   d. Expand the CSS Styles panel group.
   e. Collapse the CSS Styles panel group.

5. Open a web page.
   a. Open dwa_2.html from the drive and folder where you store your Unit A Data Files. Maximize the window, if necessary. (*Hint*: The file will open in the window size last selected. You can change it by using the Window Size menu.)
   b. Display the page in Code view.
   c. Display the page in Design view.
   d. Display the page in Live view, as shown in Figure A-15.
   e. Return to Design view.

6. View web page elements.
   a. Locate a banner.
   b. Locate text.
   c. Locate an image.

FIGURE A-15

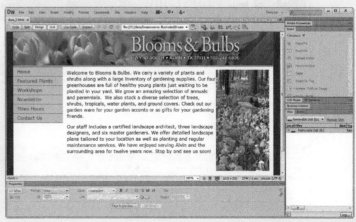

© 2013 Cengage Learning
Original photos courtesy of Sherry Bishop

Skills Review (continued)

7. Get Help.

a. Use Dreamweaver Help to search for topics relating to the Assets panel.

b. Display Help information on one of the topics.

c. Print the topic information.

d. Close the Help window.

8. View a web page in a browser window.

a. Note the window size that is currently selected in Dreamweaver.

b. Change the window size to a different setting.

c. Preview the page in your web browser.

d. Print the page.

e. Close the browser.

9. Close a web page and exit Dreamweaver.

a. Close the web page.

b. Exit Dreamweaver.

Independent Challenge 1

You have recently purchased Adobe Dreamweaver CS6 and are eager to learn to use it. You open a web page and view it using Dreamweaver.

a. Start Dreamweaver.

b. Open the file dwa_3.html from the drive and folder where you store your Unit A Data Files. Your screen should resemble Figure A-16. (*Hint*: The file will open in the window size last selected. You can change it by using the Window Size menu.)

c. Change to Code view.

d. Change back to Design view.

e. Collapse the Files panel group if necessary.

f. Expand the Files panel group.

g. Change the window size, then preview the page in your browser.

h. Close the browser, close the file, then exit Dreamweaver.

FIGURE A-16

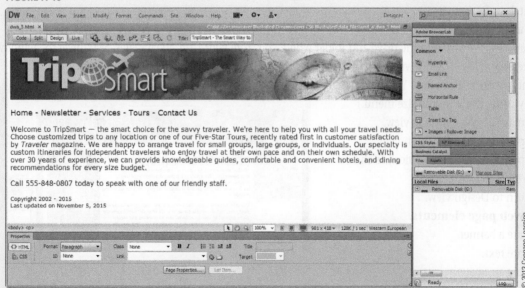

© 2013 Cengage Learning

Independent Challenge 2

When you work in Dreamweaver, it is important to organize your panels so that you have the information you need where you can access it quickly.

a. Start Dreamweaver.

b. Use Dreamweaver Help to locate information on how to collapse or expand panel groups.

c. Read and print the information.

d. Close the Help window, then exit Dreamweaver.

 ## Independent Challenge 3

The Adobe website has a feature called Customer Showcase, which includes links to websites that were created using Adobe software such as Dreamweaver, Flash, and Fireworks. The Customer Showcase feature includes the Site of the Day and Customer Showcase Features. The Customer Showcase Features links provide information about spotlighted companies, the challenges that were presented to the design team, the solution, and the resulting benefits to the companies. You visit the Adobe website to look at some of the featured websites to get a feel for what constitutes good page design.

a. Connect to the Internet, then go to the Adobe website at adobe.com.

b. Click the Company link at the top of the screen, then click Customer Showcase. Scroll down and click one of the examples.

c. Read the success story, then print the page from the browser.

d. Close your browser.

e. Using a word processing program or paper, write a short summary (two paragraphs) of the success story, then list three things that you learned about the Adobe software that was used. For example: "I learned that the Adobe Digital Publishing Suite can be used to develop tablet applications."

 ## Real Life Independent Challenge

You are about to begin work on an original website. This site can be about anything you are interested in developing. It can be about you and your family, a hobby, a business, or a fictitious website. There will be no data files supplied. This site will build from unit to unit, so you must do each Real Life Independent Challenge to complete your website.

a. Decide what type of website you would like to build.

b. Find sites on the Internet that are similar to the one you would like to design to gather some ideas.

c. Evaluate what works on these sites and what doesn't work.

d. Write down at least three ideas for your new site.

e. Write down the screen resolutions you will use for designing your pages.

Visual Workshop

Open Dreamweaver, create a new HTML file using the Welcome screen, then use the Window menu to open the panels and document, as shown in Figure A-17. If necessary, collapse or expand the panels into the position on the screen shown in Figure A-17. Exit (Win) or Quit (Mac) Dreamweaver.

FIGURE A-17

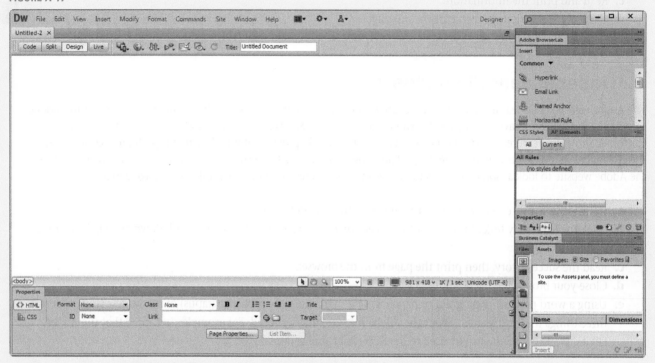

Creating a Website

Files You Will Need:

To view a list of files needed for this unit, see the Data Files Grid in the back of the book.

Creating a website requires lots of thought and careful planning. Dreamweaver CS6 has many tools to help you plan, create, and manage your sites. In this unit, you use these tools to plan and design a new website.  The owners of The Striped Umbrella meet with you to discuss their ideas for a new and improved website. You assure them that you can create a great site for them with Dreamweaver.

OBJECTIVES

Plan a website

Create a folder for website management

Set up a website

Add a folder to a website

Save a web page

Copy a new image to a website

Add new pages to a website

Planning a Website

Developing a website is a process that begins with careful planning and research. You should plan all development phases before you begin. Figure B-1 illustrates the steps involved in website planning. Your plan should include how you will organize and implement your site. It should also encompass testing your pages on different types of computers and modifying the pages to handle challenges such as page elements appearing inconsistently in different devices or browsers. Careful planning of your website may prevent mistakes that would be costly and time-consuming to correct. After consulting with the lead member of the web development team, you review the steps described below to help you create a plan for The Striped Umbrella site.

DETAILS

QUICK TIP

You can easily create a simple, or low-fidelity, wireframe using a program such as Microsoft PowerPoint, Adobe Illustrator, or Adobe Fireworks. To create a more detailed wireframe that simulates site navigation and user interaction, use a high-fidelity wireframe program such as OverSite, ProtoShare, or Microsoft Visio.

- **Research site goals and needs**

  When you research your website, you determine the site's purpose and requirements. Create a checklist of questions and answer them before you begin work. For example: "What are the company's or client's goals for the website? What tools will I need to construct the site? Will the site require media files? If so, who will create them?" The more questions that you can answer about the site, the more prepared you will be to begin development. Once you have gone through your checklist, create a timeline and a budget for the site.

- **Create a wireframe**

  A **wireframe** can range from a small sketch that represents the relationship between every page of a website to a complex prototype of each page's content on a website, including filenames, navigation, images, text, and link information. Like a flowchart or storyboard, a wireframe shows the relationship of each page to the other pages on the site. Wireframes are used throughout the development process. Consult your wireframe before beginning work on a new page to use as your "blueprint" and compare each completed page to its prototype to make sure you met the specifications. The wireframe example shown in Figure B-2 is helpful during the planning process as it allows you to visualize how each page on the site is linked to the others.

- **Create folders**

  Before you create your website, you can plan for your file storage needs by creating a system of folders for all of the elements you will use in the site. Decide where on your computer you will store your site. Start by creating a folder for the website with a descriptive name, such as the name of the company. Then create a subfolder to store all of the files that are not web pages—for example, images, audio files, and video clips. An organized folder system makes it easier to find files quickly as you develop and edit your website. Figure B-3 shows the folder structure of the Striped Umbrella site.

- **Collect the page content and create the web pages**

  This is the fun part! After studying your wireframe, gather the files you need to create the pages—for example, text, images, buttons, videos, and animations. Some of these elements will be imported from other software programs, and some will be created in Dreamweaver. For instance, you can create text either directly in Dreamweaver or in a word processing program and then import it into Dreamweaver.

- **Test and modify the pages**

  It is important to test your web pages using a variety of web browsers. The four most common browsers are Microsoft Internet Explorer, Apple Safari, Google Chrome, and Mozilla Firefox. You should also test your website using different versions of each browser, a variety of screen resolutions (as discussed in Unit A), and various connection speeds (dial-up modems are considerably slower than cable or DSLs (Digital Subscriber Lines). Your web pages will need to be updated on a regular basis as new information is released and older information becomes outdated. Each time you modify a website element, it is wise to test the site again.

- **Publish the site**

  To publish a website means to make it available for viewing on the Internet or on an **intranet**, an internal website without public access. Many companies have intranets to enable them to share information within their organizations. You publish a website to a **web server**, a computer that is connected to the Internet with an **IP (Internet Protocol) address** and has software that enables it to make files accessible to anyone on the internet or an intranet. Until a website is published, you can only view the site if you have the files stored on a hard drive, USB disk, or other storage device connected to your computer.

FIGURE B-1: Steps in website planning

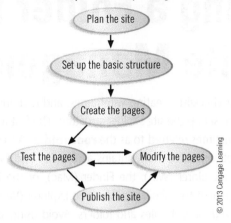

© 2013 Cengage Learning

FIGURE B-2: The Striped Umbrella website wireframe

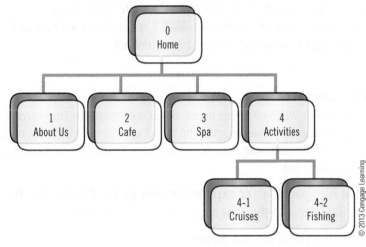

© 2013 Cengage Learning

FIGURE B-3: Folder and file structure for The Striped Umbrella website

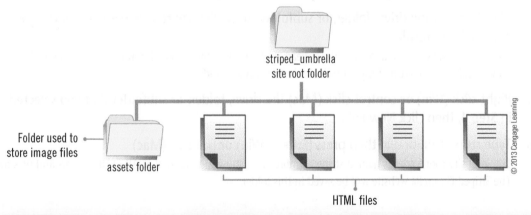

© 2013 Cengage Learning

Design Matters

IP addresses and domain names

To make a website accessible over the Internet, you must publish it to a web server with a permanent IP (Internet Protocol) address. An **IP address** is an assigned series of four numbers, each between 0 and 255 and separated by periods, that indicates the address of a specific computer or other piece of hardware on the Internet or an internal computer network. To access a web page, you enter either an IP address or a domain name in the address box of your browser window. A **domain name** is expressed in letters instead of numbers, and usually reflects the name of the business, individual, or other organization represented by the website. For example the domain name for the Adobe website is adobe.com, but the IP address (at the time of this writing) is 192.150.18.200. Because domain names use descriptive text instead of numbers, they are much easier to remember.

Creating a Folder for Website Management

After composing your checklist, creating wireframes, and gathering the files and resources you need for your website, you then set up the site's folder structure. The first folder you create for the website is called a local site folder, sometimes referred to as the **root folder**. A **local site folder** is a folder on your hard drive, USB disk, or network drive that contains all the files and folders for a website. You can create this folder using Windows Explorer (Win), the Finder (Mac), or the Files panel in Dreamweaver. The **Files panel** is a file management tool similar to Windows Explorer (Win) or Finder (Mac), where Dreamweaver stores and manages your website files and folders. Avoid using spaces, special characters, or uppercase characters when naming files or folders to prevent problems when you publish your website. When you publish the website, you transfer a copy of the local site folder contents to a remote computer, usually hosted by an Internet Service Provider (ISP). ▓▓▓▓ You want to create the local site folder (root folder) for The Striped Umbrella website and name it striped_umbrella.

1. **Start Dreamweaver**

   The Dreamweaver Welcome Screen opens. If you don't want the Dreamweaver Welcome Screen to open each time you start Dreamweaver, click the "Don't show again" check box on the Welcome Screen. If you change your mind later, select the Show Welcome Screen check box in the General category of the Preferences dialog box.

2. **Click the** Files panel tab **or expand the Files panel, if necessary, to view its contents**

   The Files panel displays a list of the drives and folders on your computer.

3. **Click the** Files panel Site list arrow

   The drop-down menu displays the list of drives on your computer. See Figure B-4.

4. **Click to select the drive, folder, or subfolder in the list where you want your local site root folder to reside**

   The name of the selected drive or folder appears in the Files panel list box. Dreamweaver will store all of the folders and files you create for your websites in this drive or folder.

5. **Right-click (Win) or control-click (Mac) the drive, folder, or subfolder that you selected in Step 4, then click** New Folder

6. **Type** striped_umbrella, **then press [Enter] (Win) or [return] (Mac)**

   The local site root folder is named striped_umbrella, as shown in Figure B-5. All of the folders and files for The Striped Umbrella website will be saved in this folder.

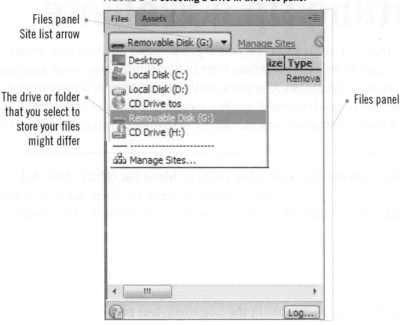

FIGURE B-4: Selecting a drive in the Files panel

Files panel
Site list arrow

The drive or folder
that you select to
store your files
might differ

Files panel

FIGURE B-5: Creating a local site root folder using the Files panel

striped_umbrella root
folder; the file folder is
yellow because you have
not created a website
yet (the folder will be
blue on a Mac)

Design Matters

Managing files

It is imperative that you understand the basics of good file management before you can master Dreamweaver. You should be able to create new folders and new files in a specified location. You should also learn the basic file naming conventions for web content. To ensure that your files are available to all users regardless of their operating system, do not use uppercase letters or spaces in filenames. Although files with uppercase letters or spaces in their names may look fine on your screen, they might not when they are published on a web server and might appear as broken links. If you do not have a basic understanding of file management, a quick review on how to use your operating system will pay big dividends and shorten your Dreamweaver learning curve.

Setting Up a Website

After you create a local site folder, the next step is to define, or set up your website. When you set up a website, you specify the site's local site root folder location to help Dreamweaver keep track of the links among your web pages and related files. After you set up the site, the program displays the local site root folder in the Files panel. The Files panel commands also help you publish your website to a remote computer. See Unit J for more information on publishing your site. ░░░░░ You are ready to define The Striped Umbrella site.

QUICK TIP

If you have created another new site since you have opened Dreamweaver, your Unnamed Site number might be different.

1. **Click Site on the Application bar (Win) or Menu bar (Mac), then click New Site**

   The Site Setup dialog box opens, as shown in Figure B-6. (From this point forward, we will refer to "Application bar (Win) or Menu bar (Mac)" as "Menu bar" to simplify the instructions.)

QUICK TIP

You can also create a new site by clicking Dreamweaver Site under Create New on the Welcome Screen.

2. **Type The Striped Umbrella in the Site Name text box**

   The site is renamed The Striped Umbrella.

QUICK TIP

It is acceptable to use uppercase letters in the site name because it is not the name of a file or folder.

3. **Click the Browse for folder button 📁 to the right of the Local Site Folder text box, click the Select list arrow ▾ (Win) or the Current file location list arrow ⬍ (Mac) in the Choose Root Folder dialog box, navigate to the drive and folder where you created your Local Site Folder, double-click (Win) or click (Mac) the striped_umbrella folder, then click Select (Win) or Choose (Mac)**

   The Choose Root Folder dialog box closes and the Site Setup dialog box reappears with "The Striped Umbrella" as the new name, confirming that you have defined The Striped Umbrella website with the name "The Striped Umbrella". The local site folder, striped_umbrella, is designated as the location for the website files and folders. See Figure B-7.

4. **Click Save in the Site Setup dialog box**

   The Site Setup dialog box closes. Your Files panel should resemble Figure B-8. You can use the Site Setup dialog box at any time to edit your settings. Notice that the striped_umbrella folder is green. In Dreamweaver, this indicates that it is a website folder. Other types of folders are displayed in yellow.

Design Matters

Using the web as your classroom

Throughout this book, you are asked to evaluate real websites. You learn basic design principles parallel to the new skills you learn using Dreamweaver. Learning a new skill, such as inserting an image, will not be very useful if you do not understand how to use images efficiently and effectively on a page.

The best way to learn is to examine how live websites use page elements such as images to convey information. Therefore, you are encouraged to complete the Design Quest Independent Challenges to gain a practical understanding of the skills you learn.

FIGURE B-6: Site Setup dialog box

Your default
Site number
might differ

Default
name for a
new site that
has not yet
been named

FIGURE B-7: Site Setup for The Striped Umbrella dialog box

Site Name

The Striped
Umbrella local
site folder
(your path
might differ)

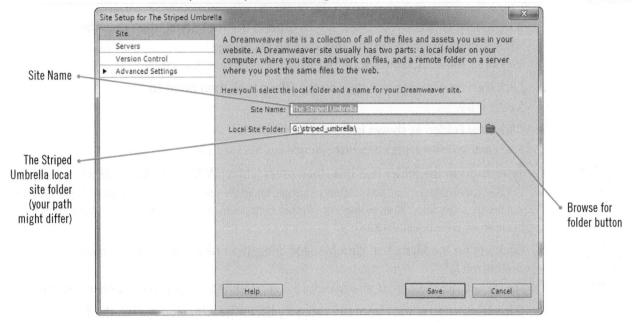

Browse for
folder button

FIGURE B-8: Files panel

The Striped Umbrella local
root folder—your path might
differ—the file folder is now
green, rather than yellow,
indicating that a website has
been created

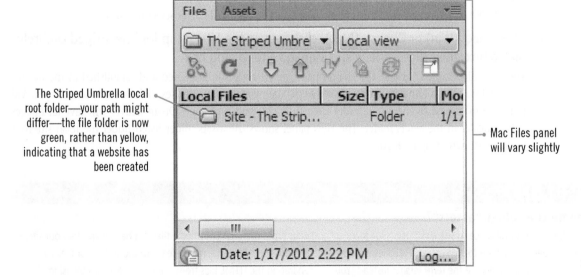

Mac Files panel
will vary slightly

Adding a Folder to a Website

After defining your website, you need to create folders to contain the non-HTML files that will add content to the site. Creating a folder called "assets" or "images" is a good beginning. Complex websites with many types of media or text files may have organizing subfolders within this folder—for example, separate folders for text files, image files, sound files, and video clips. It is better to create these folders in Dreamweaver rather than in Windows Explorer or Macintosh Finder; once you have defined a site, it is much easier to avoid errors if you let Dreamweaver perform all of the file management tasks. ▓▓▓▓ You want to create a folder called assets for The Striped Umbrella website and set this as the default folder for the images you save in the website.

STEPS

1. **If necessary, click the** Files panel tab **to expand the Files panel, then click the** striped_umbrella folder **in the Files panel if necessary**
   The striped_umbrella folder is highlighted, indicating that the site is selected.

2. **Click the** Panel menu button 📑 **on the Files panel, then point to** File
   See Figure B-9.

3. **Click** New Folder, **as shown in Figure B-9**
   A new untitled folder appears beneath the striped_umbrella folder in the Files panel.

   TROUBLE
   If you are using a Mac, you may not see the new folder if the striped_umbrella folder is collapsed. To expand it, click the triangle to the left of the striped_ umbrella folder.

4. **Type** assets **in the folder text box, then press [Enter] (Win) or [return] (Mac)**
   The Files panel displays the assets subfolder indented under the site root folder, as shown in Figure B-10. You will use the assets folder to store images and other elements used in the website. But first the assets folder has to be set as the default folder.

5. **Click** Site **on the Menu bar, click** Manage Sites, **then click the** Edit the currently selected site button 🖉
   The Site Setup for The Striped Umbrella dialog box opens with The Striped Umbrella website selected.

6. **Click** Advanced Settings **from the category list in the left column, click the** Browse for folder button 📁 **next to the Default Images folder text box, then click the** Select list arrow ▾ **(Win) or the** Current file location list arrow ⬍ **(Mac) if necessary to display the** striped_umbrella folder **in the Select text box**

7. **Click the** assets folder
   The Choose Image Folder dialog box shows the assets folder listed in the Select text box.

8. **Click** Select **(Win) or** Choose **(Mac), click** Save **in the Site Setup for The Striped Umbrella dialog box, then click** Done **in the Manage Sites dialog box**
   The new folder called "assets" for The Striped Umbrella website is created and established as the default location for saving all images. This will save steps when you copy image files to the website because you will not have to browse to the assets folder each time you save an image. Dreamweaver will save all images automatically in the assets folder. The Files panel shows the assets folder listed under the local site root folder, as shown in Figure B-10.

Design Matters

Why name the folder "assets"?
There is no particular significance to the word *assets* for the name of the folder you will use to store non-HTML files in your websites. Many web designers use the term *images* instead. You can name the folder anything you want, but the term *assets* is a good descriptive word for a folder that can be used to store other types of graphic or media files besides images for your site, such as sound files. The main idea is to organize your files by separating the HTML files from the non-HTML files by using a folder structure with appropriately named folders to reflect the content that they store.

FIGURE B-9: Creating a new folder in the Files panel

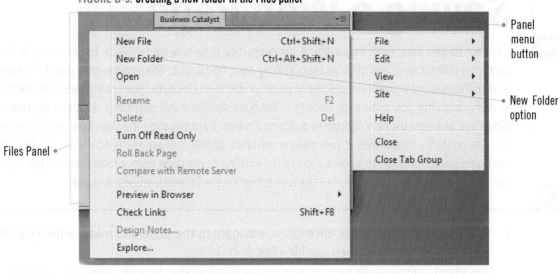

Files Panel •

Panel menu button

• New Folder option

FIGURE B-10: Files panel with the assets folder added

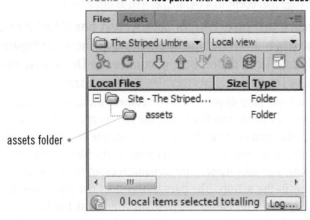

assets folder •

Using the Files panel for file management

You can use the Files panel to add, delete, move, or rename files and folders in a website. *It is very important that you perform these file maintenance tasks in the Files panel rather than in Windows Explorer (Win) or the Finder (Mac). If you make changes to the folder* *structure outside the Files panel, you may experience problems.* If you move or copy the site root folder to a new location, you must define the website again in Dreamweaver, as you did in the lesson on defining a website.

Saving a Web Page

It is wise to save your work frequently. A good practice is to save every five or ten minutes, before you attempt a difficult step, and after you successfully complete a step. This ensures that you do not lose any work in the event of a power outage or computer problem. In this book, you are instructed to use the Save As command after you open each Data File. The Save As command duplicates the open document and allows you to assign the new document a different name. By duplicating the Data Files, you can repeat an exercise or start a lesson over if you make a mistake. ▨▨▨▨ You are ready to create the first draft of the home page. You want to open a copy of the existing home page from a folder outside the new website, rename it, and then save it in the site root folder for the Striped Umbrella website.

STEPS

1. **Click File on the Menu bar, click Open, navigate to the drive and folder where you store your Unit B Data Files, then double-click dwb_1.html**

   The Striped Umbrella home page opens in the Document window in Design View. This is the home page that users will see when they first visit The Striped Umbrella website.

QUICK TIP
The file extension php stands for PHP: Hypertext Preprocessor. It is a server-side scripting language.

2. **Click File on the Menu bar, click Save As, click the Save in list arrow ⊡ (Win) or the Current file location list arrow ⬍ (Mac) to navigate to the striped_umbrella local site root folder, then double-click (Win) or click (Mac) the striped_umbrella folder**

   The home page will be saved in the Striped Umbrella website root folder, striped_umbrella. Because it will be the home page for your site, you save the file using the name "index.html", the conventional name for a site's home page. Web servers are programmed to search for files named "index.html" or "default.html" to display as the initial page that opens in a website, as well as other file types such as index.php.

QUICK TIP
You can just type the filename "index"; the program automatically adds the .html file extension to the filename after you click Save.

3. **Click in the File name text box (Win) or Save As text box (Mac) if necessary, select the existing file name (dwb_1.html), type index.html, as shown in Figure B-11, click Save, click No in the Update Links dialog box, maximize the Document window if necessary, then click the Show Design view button ⌜Design⌟ if necessary**

   The Striped Umbrella home page displays in the Document window, as shown in Figure B-12. If you are not viewing the page in a separate window (Win), the path to the site root folder and the filename is displayed to the right of the document tab. If you are viewing the page in a separate window, this information appears on the document title bar. Mac users point to the file tab to see this information. The drive designator, folder name, subfolder names, and filename is called the **path**, or location of the open file in relation to any folders in the website. The page banner does not appear and is replaced by a gray box, indicating the link is broken. This means the program cannot link to the image, which currently resides in the Data Files folder. In the next lesson you will repair the link so that the image appears.

TROUBLE
If you don't see the index.html file listed in the Files panel, click the Refresh button ↻.

4. **Click the Close button ☒ on the dwb_1.html file tab, click the Insert panel drop-down menu, then click Color Icons if necessary to show the icons in color**

   The dwb_1.html page closes. You leave the index.html page open to correct the link to the banner image.

Design Matters

Choosing filenames

When you name a file, you should use a descriptive name that reflects the file's contents. For example, if the page is about a company's products, you could name it "products." You must also follow some general rules for naming web pages. For example, the home page should be named "index.html" or "default.html". You can also use the file extension "htm" instead of "html." Do not use spaces, special characters, regular or back slashes, or punctuation in web page filenames or in the names of any images that will be inserted in your website. Another rule is not to use a number for the first character of a filename. To ensure that everything loads properly on all platforms, including UNIX, assume that filenames are case sensitive and use lowercase characters. A good practice is to limit filenames to eight characters.

FIGURE B-11: **The Save As dialog box (Windows and Mac)**

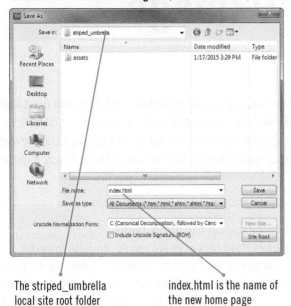

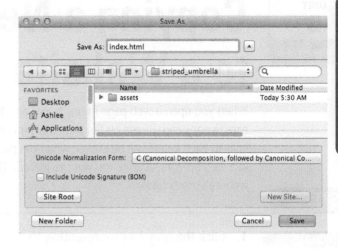

The striped_umbrella
local site root folder

index.html is the name of
the new home page

FIGURE B-12: **The Striped Umbrella home page**

Close button

Banner link
is broken
because the
image file
has not been
copied into
the website
assets folder

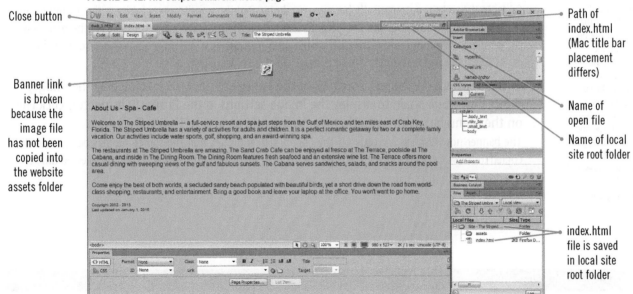

Path of
index.html
(Mac title bar
placement
differs)

Name of
open file

Name of local
site root folder

index.html
file is saved
in local site
root folder

Copying a New Image to a Website

When you open a web page in one folder and then save a copy of it in a different folder, you must take care to copy each image on the page from the original folder into the new folder. If you don't do this, the links to each image will be broken when the page is published to a web server and subsequently viewed in a web browser. ▰▰▰▰ You want to identify The Striped Umbrella banner source file and copy it to the website's assets folder.

STEPS

TROUBLE
If your index.html page does not appear in the Files panel, click the Refresh button ⟳ on the Files panel toolbar.

1. **Click the gray box representing the broken image on the index page**

   Selection handles appear on the lower and right edges of the broken image and the Property inspector displays the banner's properties. The Src (Source) text box in the Property inspector displays the location: assets/su-banner.gif, but it is referencing the assets folder in the unit_b Data Files folder, not the assets folder in the website folder. The Striped Umbrella banner, which is the source file, currently resides in the unit_b assets folder. You navigate to the Data Files and select the source file. The concept of broken links will become clearer upon completing Unit F which explores the relationship between absolute and relative links.

TROUBLE
If the path for an image or a link begins with the word *file*, you will have linking problems. Delete all extraneous path information in the Src text box or the browser will not be able to find the image when the website is published. A good practice is to go to Code view and search for the word *file*. If you find *file* in your code, you must evaluate each occurrence to see if you need to remove unnecessary code.

2. **If necessary, double-click the right side of the Property inspector to expand it, click the Browse for File button ▢ next to the Src text box, click the Look in list arrow ▾ (Win) or the Current file location list arrow ⬍ (Mac) if necessary to navigate to the drive and folder where you store your Data Files, double-click the unit_b folder, double-click the assets folder, then double-click the su_banner.gif file**

   The correct source file is selected from the Data Files folder. Dreamweaver copies the file to the assets folder in the website automatically because you designated the website assets folder as the default location for images when you set up the site. The Src text box in the Property inspector displays the path "assets/su_ banner.gif" without any extra path designation in front of it. If you see a path in front of the word *assets*, Dreamweaver is trying to link the image file to the Data Files folder.

3. **Click anywhere on the page outside of the banner, if necessary, to display the image, select the image again to display the image settings in the Property inspector, click File on the Menu bar, click Save, then compare your screen to Figure B-13**

   The banner now displays correctly on the page which indicates that the source file has been successfully copied to the website assets folder. The Property inspector displays the properties of the selected image.

Design Matters

Making a good first impression

Since the home page is the first page users see as they enter a website, it is important to make a good first impression. When you enter a store, you immediately notice the way the merchandise is displayed, whether the staff is accessible and friendly, and the general overall appearance and comfort of the interior. The same is true of a website. If you see pleasing colors and images, friendly and easy-to-understand text, and a simple navigation system, you are favorably impressed and want to explore the site. If you see poorly organized content, misspelled words, and confusing navigation, you will probably leave the site. It is much faster and easier to leave a website than to leave a store, so you have less time to correct a bad first impression. Have others evaluate your home page before you finalize it so you understand how others see your page.

FIGURE B-13: Property inspector showing properties of The Striped Umbrella banner

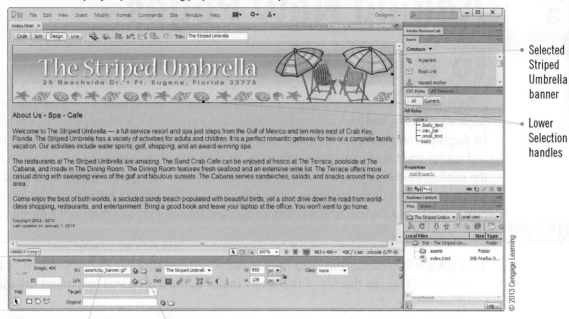

Selected Striped Umbrella banner

Lower Selection handles

Property inspector provides details about the selected image

Source is pointing to assets folder

Browse for File button

© 2013 Cengage Learning

Planning the page layout

When you begin developing the content for your website, you must decide what to include and how to arrange each element on each page. You must also design the content with the audience in mind. Who is your target audience? What is your audience's age group, sex, race, and residence? What reading and computer literacy level is appropriate? Should pages be simple, containing mostly text, or rich with images and media files? To ensure that users do not get "lost" in your website, make sure all the pages have a consistent look and feel. This can be accomplished easily through the use of templates. **Templates** are web pages that contain the basic layout for each page of a site. You can create original templates with the File menu in Dreamweaver or download them from the Internet. See the Appendix for more information on templates.

Adding New Pages to a Website

Websites may be as small as one page or contain hundreds of pages. In Dreamweaver, you can add new pages to a website, and then add content such as text and images. The blank pages serve as placeholders for pages that you anticipate designing. That way you can set up the navigation structure of the website and test the links between the pages. When you are satisfied with the overall structure, you can then create the content for the pages. You add new pages by using the Files panel. ▰▰▰▰ After consulting your wireframe, you decide to create new web pages to add to The Striped Umbrella website. You create new pages called about_us, spa, cafe, activities, cruises, and fishing, and place them in the site root folder.

STEPS

1. **Click the Refresh button ⟳ on the Files Panel, then click the plus sign (Win) or the triangle (Mac) to the left of the assets folder in the Files panel to expand the folder if necessary**

   The assets folder expands to display its contents, as shown in Figure B-14. The su_banner.gif file is located in the assets folder.

   > **TROUBLE**
   > Be careful not to delete the .html file extension when you name the file.

2. **Click the site folder under the Local Files column to select it, right-click the site folder, click New File, click in the filename text box to select untitled if necessary, type about_us, then press [Enter] (Win) or [return] (Mac)**

   The about us page is added to the website. You can also click the Files panel menu button ▰, point to File, then click New File to create a new file.

3. **Repeat Step 2 to add five more blank pages to The Striped Umbrella website, and name the new files spa.html, cafe.html, activities.html, cruises.html, and fishing.html**

   The new pages appear in the striped_umbrella root folder.

   > **TROUBLE**
   > If you accidentally create your new files in the assets folder rather than the site root folder, select and drag each one to the site root folder.

4. **Click the Refresh button ⟳ on the Files panel toolbar**

   The file listing is refreshed and the files are now sorted in alphabetical order, as shown in Figure B-15.

5. **Click File on the Menu bar, click Close, click File on the Application bar, click Exit (Win) or click Dreamweaver on the Menu bar, then click Quit Dreamweaver (Mac)**

Managing a project with a team

When working with a team, it is essential that you define clear goals for the project and a list of objectives to accomplish those goals. Your plan should be finalized after conferring with both the client and team to make sure that the purpose, scope, and objectives are clear to everyone. Establish the **deliverables**, or products that will be provided to the client upon project completion, such as creation of new pages or graphic elements, and a timeline for their delivery. You should present the web pages to both your team and client for feedback and evaluation at strategic points in the development process. Analyze all feedback objectively, incorporating both the positive and the negative comments to help you make improvements to the site and meet everyone's expectations and goals. A common pitfall in team management is scope creep. **Scope creep** occurs when impromptu changes or additions are made to a project without accounting for corresponding increases in the schedule or budget. Proper project control, resource allocation, and communication between team members and clients can minimize scope creep and achieve the successful and timely completion of a project.

FIGURE B-14: **Files panel showing su_banner.gif in the assets folder**

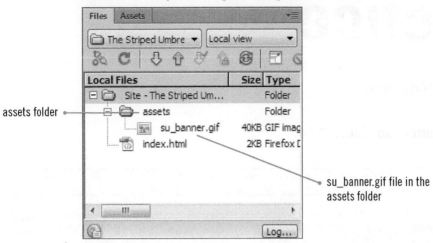

assets folder

su_banner.gif file in the
assets folder

FIGURE B-15: **New pages added to The Striped Umbrella website and sorted**

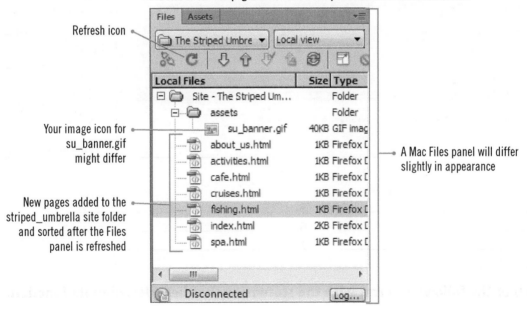

Refresh icon

Your image icon for
su_banner.gif
might differ

New pages added to the
striped_umbrella site folder
and sorted after the Files
panel is refreshed

A Mac Files panel will differ
slightly in appearance

Practice

Concepts Review

Label each element in Figure B-16.

FIGURE B-16

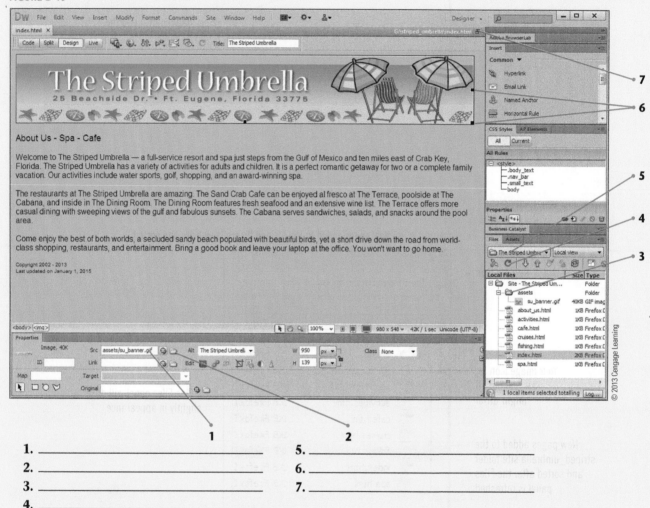

1. _____
2. _____
3. _____
4. _____

5. _____
6. _____
7. _____

Match each of the following terms with the statement that best describes its function.

8. **Domain name**
9. **Wireframe**
10. **Assets**
11. **IP address**
12. **web server**
13. **Local site folder**
14. **Intranet**
15. **Home page**
16. **Publish a website**

a. An address on the web expressed in numbers
b. Computer connected to the Internet with an IP address and software that enables it to make files accessible for viewing on the Internet
c. An internal website without public access
d. To make a website available for viewing on the Internet
e. A folder that holds all the files and folders for a website
f. Usually the first page users see when they visit a website
g. A folder that contains non-HTML files
h. A diagram of a website's folder structure showing links and placement of main page elements
i. An address on the web expressed in letters

Select the best answer from the following list of choices.

17. An internal website without public access is called a(n):
    a. Internet
    b. Intranet
    c. Domain
    d. Extension

18. The first step in designing a website should be:
    a. Setting up web server access
    b. Testing the pages
    c. Planning the site
    d. Creating the pages and developing the content

19. Which icon or button do you click to refresh the Files panel after you have changed files listed there?
    a.
    b.
    c. Code
    d.

20. Web pages that contain the basic layout for each page in a website are called:
    a. Templates
    b. Examples
    c. Shells
    d. Forms

Skills Review

1. **Plan a website.**
   a. Create a wireframe with five pages for a company called Blooms & Bulbs.
   b. Name the pages **index**, **plants**, **workshops**, **newsletter**, and **tips**. (The plants, workshops, newsletter, and tips pages will be linked to the index page.)

2. **Create a folder for website management.**
   a. Start Dreamweaver, then open or expand the Files panel if necessary.
   b. Select the drive or folder in the Site list box where you will store your website files.
   c. Create a new folder with the name **blooms** to store your website files.

3. **Define the website.**
   a. Create a new site using the Site > New Site command. Name the site **Blooms & Bulbs**.
   b. In the Site Setup dialog box, browse to select the root folder you created for the website.
   c. Save the site definition and exit the site setup.

4. **Add a folder to the website.**
   a. Use the Files panel to create an assets folder for the website.
   b. Use the Site Setup dialog box to set the assets folder as the default images folder for storing your image files.

5. **Copy a new image to a website.**
   a. Open dwb_2.html from the drive and folder where your unit_b Data Files are stored.
   b. Save the file as **index.html** in the blooms folder in the Blooms & Bulbs website, and do not update the links.
   c. Close the dwb_2.html file.
   d. Select the gray box representing the broken link to the banner image on the page.
   e. Using the Browse for File button next to the Src text box on the Property inspector, navigate to the assets folder inside the unit_b folder where you store your Data Files, then select blooms_banner.jpg.
   f. Refresh the Files panel, click on the page to deselect the banner, then verify that the banner was copied to the assets folder in your Blooms & Bulbs site, then save the index.html file.

Skills Review (continued)

6. Add new pages to a website.

a. Using the Files panel, create a new page called **plants.html**.

b. Create three more pages, called **workshops.html**, **tips.html**, and **newsletter.html**.

c. Use the Refresh button to sort the files in alphabetical order, then compare your screen to Figure B-17.

d. Close the index page, then exit Dreamweaver.

FIGURE B-17

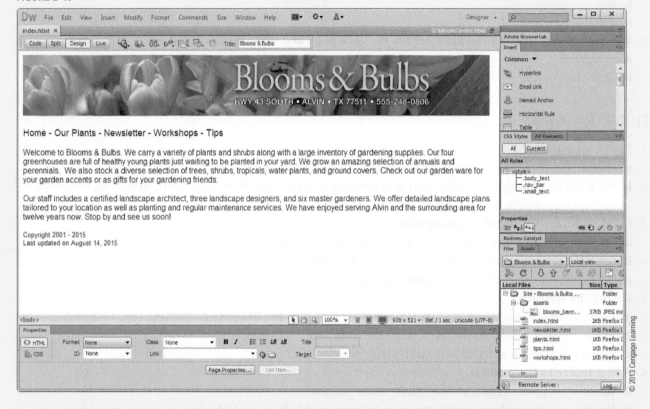

Independent Challenge 1

You have been hired to create a website for a river expedition company named Rapids Transit, located on the Buffalo River in Arkansas. In addition to renting canoes, kayaks, and rafts, they have several types of cabin rentals for overnight stays. River guides are available, if requested, to accompany clients on float trips. The clients range from experienced floaters to beginners. Refer to Figure B-18 as you work through the following steps:

a. Create a website plan and wireframe for this site.

b. Create a folder named **rapids** in the drive and folder where you save your website files.

c. Define the site with the name **Rapids Transit**, setting the rapids folder as the site root folder for the website.

d. Create an **assets** folder, then set it as the default images folder.

e. Open dwb_3.html from the drive and folder where your Unit B Data Files are stored, then save it in the site folder as **index.html**. Do not update the links.

f. Close dwb_3.html.

g. Save the rt_banner.jpg image in the assets folder for your site and save the index.html file. (*Hint*: Use the Browse for File button next to the Src text box to navigate to the unit_b assets folder to locate the image.) Refresh the Files panel and verify that the rt_banner.jpg image was copied to the site assets folder.

h. Create four additional files for the pages in your site plan, and give them the following names: **guides.html**, **rates.html**, **lodging.html**, and **before.html**. Refresh the Files panel to display the files in alphabetical order.

i. Close the index page, then exit Dreamweaver.

FIGURE B-18

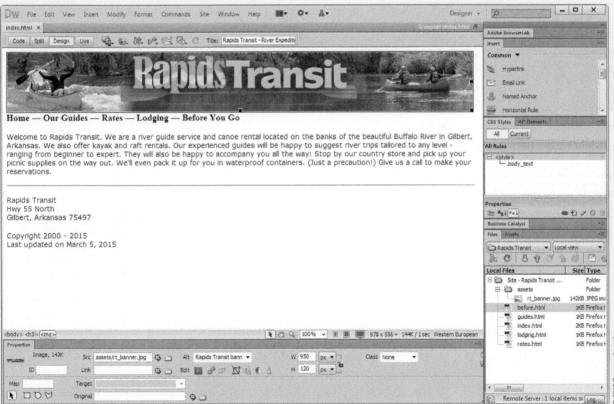

Independent Challenge 2

Your company is designing a new website for a travel outfitter named TripSmart. TripSmart specializes in travel products and services. In addition to selling travel products such as luggage and accessories, they organize trips and offer travel advice. Their clients range from college students to families to vacationing professionals. The owner, Thomas Howard, has requested a dynamic website that conveys the excitement of traveling. Refer to Figure B-19 as you work through the following steps:

a. Create a website plan and wireframe for this site to present to Thomas.

b. Create a folder named **tripsmart** in the drive and folder where you save your website files.

c. Define the site with the name **TripSmart**, then set the tripsmart folder as the site root folder.

d. Create an assets folder, then set it as the default images folder.

e. Open the file dwb_4.html from the drive and folder where you store your Unit B Data Files, then save it in the site root folder as **index.html**. Do not update the links.

f. Close dwb_4.html.

g. Save the tripsmart_banner.jpg image in the assets folder for the site, save the index.html file, then refresh the Files panel to display the image file in the assets folder.

h. Create four additional files for the pages in your plan, and give them the following names: **catalog.html**, **newsletter.html**, **services.html**, and **tours.html**. Refresh the Files panel to display the files in alphabetical order, then compare your screen to Figure B-19.

i. Close the index page, then exit Dreamweaver.

FIGURE B-19

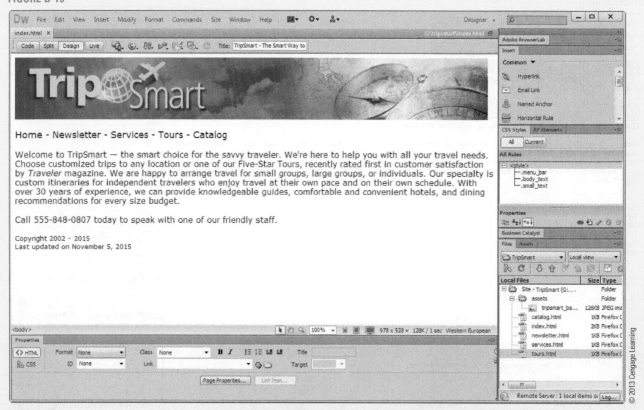

Independent Challenge 3

Patsy Broers is interested in a national program that encourages high school students to memorize and recite poetry. This program is sponsored by the National Endowment for the Arts (NEA), so she goes to the NEA website, shown in Figure B-20, to look for information on the program. (As this is a live site, your figure may differ due to content changes.) Record your answers to the questions below.

FIGURE B-20

National Endowment for the Arts website (nea.gov)

a. Connect to the Internet and go to the NEA website at nea.gov.

b. Click the Site Map link at the bottom of the page. What do you think is the purpose of the site map?

c. How has the NEA organized its information to help you navigate its website?

d. Can you find the information that Patsy needs?

e. Did you feel that the site map helped you navigate the website?

f. Do you feel that the site map link is beneficial for users?

g. Close your browser.

Real Life Independent Challenge

In this assignment, you create a personal website entirely on your own. There will be no Data Files supplied. These Independent Challenges will build from unit to unit, so you must do each unit's Real Life Independent Challenge assignment to complete your website.

a. Decide what type of website you would like to build. It can be a personal website about you and your family, a business website if you have a business you would like to promote, or a fictitious website. Your instructor may direct your choices for this assignment.

b. Create a wireframe for your website and include at least four pages.

c. Create a site root folder where you store your website files and name it appropriately.

d. Define the site with an appropriate name, using the site root folder that you created.

e. Create an assets folder and set it as the default location for images.

f. Begin planning the content you would like to use for the home page and plan how you would like to organize it on the page.

g. Use the Files panel to create the pages you listed in your wireframe.

h. Collect information to use in your website, such as images or text. Store these in a folder (either electronic or paper) that you can bring with you to class as you develop your site.

i. Exit Dreamweaver.

Visual Workshop

Your company has been selected to design a website for a catering business called Carolyne's Creations. In addition to catering, Carolyne's services include cooking classes and daily specials available as take-out meals. She also has a retail shop that stocks gourmet treats and kitchen items. Create the website pictured in Figure B-21, using **Carolyne's Creations** for the site name and **cc** for the site root folder name. Use the files dwb_5.html for the index (home) page and cc_banner.jpg for the banner. These files are located in the drive and folder where you store your Data Files. Next, add the files **catering.html**, **classes.html**, **recipes.html**, and **shop.html** to the local site root folder.

FIGURE B-21

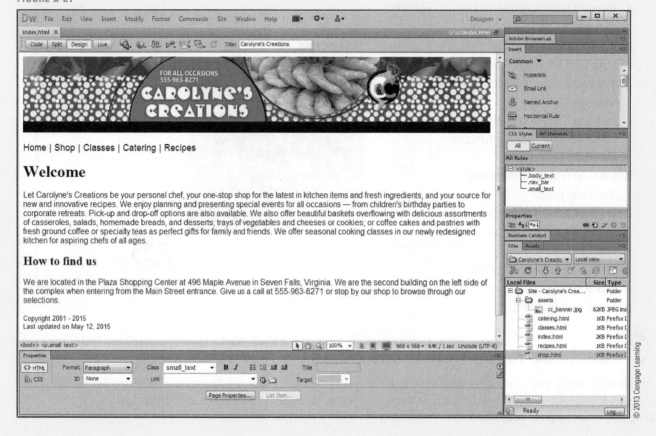

Developing a Web Page

When you begin developing web pages, you should choose the page content with the purpose of the website and the target audience in mind. A website designed for a large professional corporation should be designed quite differently than an educational website for children. You can use colors, fonts, and images to set a formal or casual tone. In this unit, you learn about planning a website, modifying a web page, and linking it to other pages. Finally, you'll use Code view to modify some of the page code, and test the links to make sure they work. 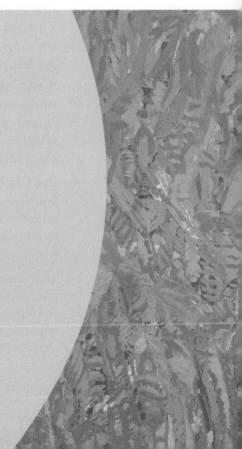 The Striped Umbrella website should appeal to families, singles, and maturing baby boomers with leisure time and money to spend. You improve the design and content of the home page to attract this broad target audience.

OBJECTIVES

Plan the page layout

Create the head content

Set web page properties

Create and format text

Add links to web pages

Use the History panel

View HTML code

Test and modify web pages

Planning the Page Layout

When people visit your website, you want them to feel at home, as if they know their way around the pages in your site. You also want to ensure that users will not get lost on the site due to layout inconsistencies. To help maintain a common look for all pages, you can use templates. Templates are web pages that contain basic layouts you can apply to your website pages, standardizing elements, such as the location of a company logo or a menu of buttons. As you will learn in Units D and G, the use of **Cascading Style Sheets (CSS)** provides a way to easily position and format objects or entire pages by providing common formatting characteristics that can be applied to multiple objects. And, as you will learn in Unit G, many designers use tables, simple grids of cells in rows and columns, as a page layout tool to position lists of tabular data on the page easily.  Before you begin working on The Striped Umbrella home page, you want to identify key concepts that govern good page layout.

When planning the layout of your web pages, remember the following guidelines:

- **Keep it simple**

  Often the simplest websites are the most appealing. Websites that are simple in layout and design are the easiest to create and maintain. A simple website that works is far superior to a complex one with errors.

- **Use white space effectively**

  Too many text blocks, links, and images can confuse users, and actually make them feel agitated. Consider leaving some white space on each page. **White space** is the area on a web page that is not filled with text or graphics. (Note that white space is not necessarily white in color.) Using white space effectively creates a harmonious balance on the page. Figure C-1 shows how white space can help emphasize strong visual page elements, yet still achieve a simple, clean look for the page.

- **Limit media objects**

  Too many media objects—such as graphics, video clips, or sounds—may result in a page that takes too long to load. Users may tire of waiting for these objects to appear and leave your site before the entire page finishes loading. Placing unnecessary media objects on your page makes your website seem unprofessional.

- **Use an intuitive navigation structure**

  A website's navigational structure should be easy to use. It can be based on text links or a combination of text and graphic links. Users should always know where they are in the website, and be able to find their way back to the home page easily. If users get lost on your website, they may leave the site rather than struggle to find their way around.

- **Apply a consistent theme using templates**

  A theme can be almost anything, from the same background color on each page to common graphics, such as buttons or icons that reflect a collective theme. Common design elements such as borders can also be considered a theme. Templates are a great way to easily incorporate consistent themes in websites.

- **Use CSS for page layout**

  When you use CSS as the basis for page layout, you can control both how the entire page appears in browser windows and how the various page elements are positioned on the page in relation to each other. This allows a page to look the same, regardless of the size of a user's screen.

- **Be conscious of accessibility issues**

  There are several techniques you can use to ensure that your website is accessible to individuals with disabilities. These techniques include using alternate text with images, avoiding certain colors on web pages, and supplying text as an alternate source for information that is presented in audio files. Dreamweaver can display Accessibility dialog boxes to prompt you to insert accessibility information for the page objects, as shown in Figure C-2.

FIGURE C-1: An example of an effective web page layout

First Federal Bank website used with permission from First Federal Bank (ffbh.com)

FIGURE C-2: Accessibility attributes for inserting objects on a page

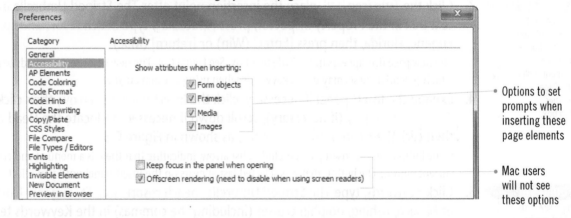

• Options to set prompts when inserting these page elements

• Mac users will not see these options

Designing for accessibility

It is extremely important to design your website so that individuals with disabilities can successfully navigate and read its web pages. In fact, government websites must be made accessible pursuant to Section 508 of the Workforce Investment Act of 1998, based on the Americans with Disabilities Act (ADA). On May 5, 1999, the first Web Content Accessibility Guidelines (WCAG) were published by the World Wide Web Consortium (W3C). The levels of accessibility are grouped into three priority level checkpoints. Although all websites should comply with the Priority 1 checkpoints, government websites *must* comply with them, such as providing a text equivalent for every non-text element. For more

information about priority level checkpoints, go to w3.org. Adobe's Accessibility Resource Center (adobe.com/accessibility); this site provides specific information about website compliance with Section 508 guidelines, such as suggestions for creating accessible websites, an explanation of Section 508, and information on how people with disabilities use assistive devices to navigate the Internet. These guidelines are based on four principles called the POUR principles: websites should be Perceivable, Operable, Understandable, and Robust. For more information about the POUR principles (Putting People at the Center of the Process) for website accessibility, go to webaim.org.

Creating the Head Content

A web page consists of two sections: the head section and the body. The **body** contains all the page content users see in their browser window, such as text, graphics, and links. The **head section** contains the **head content**, including the page title that is displayed in the browser title bar (not to be confused with the filename which is used to save the page), as well as some very important page elements that are not visible in the browser. These items are called meta tags. **Meta tags** are HTML codes that include information about the page such as keywords and descriptions. **Keywords** are words that are representative to the content of a website. Search engines find web pages by matching the title, description, and keywords in the head content of web pages with keywords users enter in search text boxes. A **description** is a short summary of website content. Before you work on page content for the home page, you modify the page title and add a description and keywords that will draw users to The Striped Umbrella website.

TROUBLE
If you don't see the index.html file listed, click the plus sign (Win) or triangle (Mac) next to the striped_umbrella folder to expand the folder contents.

1. **Start Dreamweaver, click the Site list arrow ▾ (Win) or ▼ (Mac) on the Files panel, then click The Striped Umbrella if it isn't already selected**
   The Striped Umbrella website opens in the Files panel.

2. **Double-click index.html in the Files panel, make sure the Document window is maximized and you are in either Design view or Split view, click View on the Menu bar, then if necessary click Head Content to select it**
   The head content section appears at the top of The Striped Umbrella home page, as shown in Figure C-3. The head content section includes the Meta tag icon 🔲, the Title tag icon 🔲, and the CSS icon 🔲.

QUICK TIP
You can also change the page title using either the Title text box on the Document toolbar or the Page Properties dialog box.

3. **Click the Title icon 🔲, place the insertion point after The Striped Umbrella in the Title text box in the Property inspector, press [spacebar], type beach resort and spa, Ft. Eugene, Florida, then press [Enter] (Win) or [return] (Mac)**
   The new page title appears in the Title text box. See Figure C-4. The new title uses the words *beach* and *resort*, which potential guests may use as keywords when using a search engine.

4. **Expand the Insert panel if necessary, click the Insert panel list arrow, then click the Common category (if necessary), scroll down if necessary to locate the Head object, then click the Head button list arrow, as shown in Figure C-3**
   Some buttons on the Insert panel include a list arrow, indicating that there is a menu of choices beneath the current button. The button that was selected last appears on the Insert panel until you select another.

QUICK TIP
Multiple keywords should always be separated by commas.

5. **Click Keywords, type The Striped Umbrella, beach resort, spa, Ft. Eugene, Florida, Gulf of Mexico, fishing, dolphin cruises (including the commas) in the Keywords text box, as shown in Figure C-5, then click OK**
   The Keywords icon 🔑 appears selected in the head section, indicating that keywords have been created for the page.

6. **Click the Head button list arrow on the Insert panel, click Description, type The Striped Umbrella is a full-service resort and spa just steps from the Gulf of Mexico in Ft. Eugene, Florida. in the Description dialog box, as shown in Figure C-6, then click OK**
   The Description icon 🔲 appears selected in the head section, indicating that a description has been entered.

TROUBLE
You may see embedded style tags above the title, keywords, and description. Scroll down to see the rest of the head content code.

7. **Click the Show Code view button [Code] on the Document toolbar, click anywhere in the code, then view the head section code, as shown in Figure C-7**
   The title, keywords, and description appear in the head section of the HTML code. The title is surrounded by title tags, and the keywords and description are both surrounded by meta tags.

8. **Click the Show Design view button [Design] on the Document toolbar, click View on the Menu bar, then click Head Content**
   The Striped Umbrella home page redisplays without the head content section visible above the Document window.

FIGURE C-3: Viewing the head content section

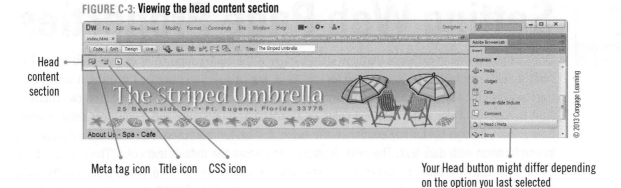

Head content section

Meta tag icon   Title icon   CSS icon

Your Head button might differ depending on the option you last selected

© 2013 Cengage Learning

FIGURE C-4: Property inspector displaying new page title

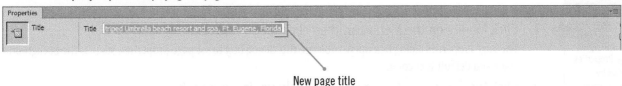

New page title

FIGURE C-5: Keywords dialog box

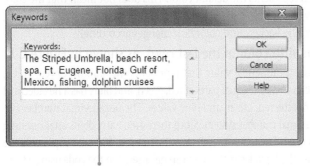

Keywords separated by commas

FIGURE C-6: Description dialog box

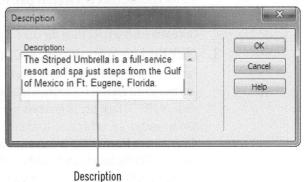

Description

FIGURE C-7: Code view displaying the code for the head content

Your lines of code may appear in a slightly different order

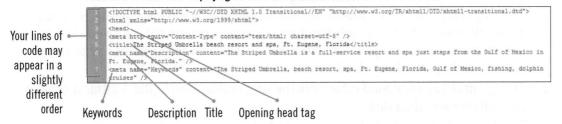

Keywords   Description   Title   Opening head tag

Design Matters

Entering titles, keywords, and descriptions

Search engines use titles, keywords, and descriptions to find pages after the user enters search terms. It is therefore important to anticipate what your potential customers will use for search terms, and to try to include those in the keywords, description, or title. Many search engines print the page titles and descriptions when they list pages in their search results. Some search engines limit the number of keywords that they will index, so again keep your keywords and description to a minimum. It is usually sufficient to enter keywords and a description only for the home page or any other page you want users to find, rather than for every page on the website. To choose effective keywords, many designers use focus groups to learn which words potential customers or clients might use. A **focus group** is a marketing tool that asks a group of people for feedback about a product, such as the impact of a television ad or the effectiveness of a website design.

UNIT
C
Dreamweaver CS6

Setting Web Page Properties

One of the first design decisions that you should make is the background color of your web page. This color should complement the colors used for text, links, and images you place on the page. A strong contrast between the text and background colors makes it easier for users to read the text. You can choose a light background color and a dark text color, or a dark background color and a light text color. A white background, though not terribly exciting, is the easiest to read for most users, and provides good contrast in combination with dark text. The next decision is to choose the default text color. The **default text color** is the color the browser uses to display text when a color is not specified. Settings such as the page background color and the default text color are specified using CSS. ▚▚▚▚ You want to set the background color and choose a default text color for The Striped Umbrella home page.

STEPS

QUICK TIP

You can also open the Page Properties dialog box by clicking the Page Properties button on the Property inspector.

1. **Click Modify on the Menu bar, then click Page Properties**

   The Page Properties dialog box opens. You use this dialog box to set page properties, such as the background color and default text color.

2. **Click the Background color box [icon], as shown in Figure C-8**

   The color picker opens, and the pointer changes to an eyedropper [icon]. When Dreamweaver is first installed, the Background color box appears gray, which represents the default color. This does not mean that the color gray will be applied *unless* gray has previously been selected as the default color for the selected page element. Once you select a color from the color picker, the Background color box changes accordingly.

3. **Click the blue color swatch, #9CF (the fifth color in the last row), as shown in Figure C-8**

   Each color is assigned a **hexadecimal value**, a numerical value that represents the amount of red, green, and blue in the color. For example, white, which is made of equal parts of red, green, and blue, has a hexadecimal value of FFFFFF. Each pair of numbers represents the red, green, and blue values. The hexadecimal number system is based on 16, rather than 10 as in the decimal number system. Since there aren't any digits after reaching the number 9, letters of the alphabet are then used. The letter A represents the number 10, and F represents the number 15 in the hexadecimal number system. The hexadecimal values can be entered in the code using a form of shorthand that shortens the six characters to three characters. For instance: 99CCFF becomes 9CF and FFFFFF becomes FFF. The number value for a color is preceded by a pound sign (#) in HTML code.

4. **Click Apply in the Page Properties dialog box**

   The background color of the web page changes to a different shade of blue while the text color remains the default color, which is black. The Apply button allows you to see changes that you have made to the page without having to close the Page Properties dialog box. The blue background does not provide the best contrast between the page background and the text.

QUICK TIP

The Background color box appears blue (the last color selected) until you click the white color swatch.

5. **Click [icon] next to Background color, click the white color swatch (the rightmost color in the bottom row), then click Apply**

   The white page background provides a better contrast.

6. **Click the Text color box [icon], shown in Figure C-9, use the eyedropper [icon] to select a light shade of blue, then click Apply**

   The light blue text color on the home page is not quite as easy to read as the black text.

7. **Click [icon] next to Text color, then click the Default Color icon [icon] at the top of the color picker**

   The Page Properties dialog box shows the text color setting restored to the default color. See Figure C-9. The Default Color button restores the default color setting after either the Apply button is clicked or the dialog box is closed.

8. **Click OK**

   The Page Properties dialog box closes and The Striped Umbrella web page redisplays with the default black text color and new white background color.

Developing a Web Page

FIGURE C-8: Page Properties dialog box

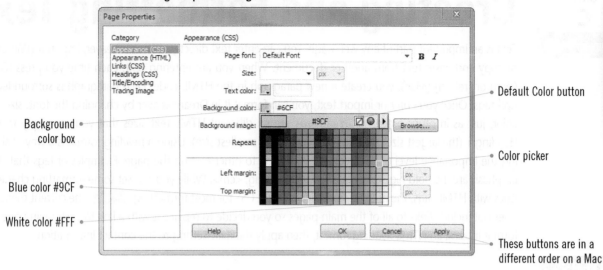

Background color box

Blue color #9CF

White color #FFF

Default Color button

Color picker

These buttons are in a different order on a Mac

FIGURE C-9: Page Properties dialog box

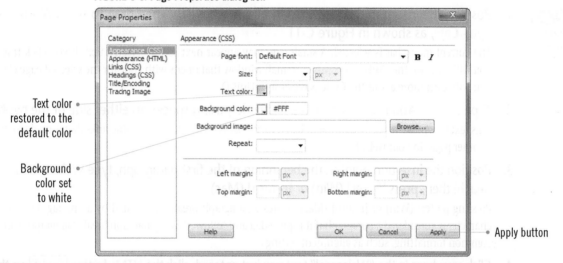

Text color restored to the default color

Background color set to white

Apply button

Design Matters

Choosing Colors to Convey Information

Prior to 1994, colors appeared differently on different types of computers. In 1994, Netscape developed the first **web-safe color palette**, a set of colors that appears consistently in all browsers and on Macintosh, Windows, and UNIX platforms. The evolution of video cards has made this less relevant today, although understanding web-safe colors may still be a factor when you are designing for some devices, such as cell phones and PDAs. The use of appropriate colors is an important factor in creating accessible pages. Be sure to only use colors that provide good contrast on your pages. Dreamweaver has two web-safe color palettes: Color Cubes and Continuous Tone. Each palette contains the 216 web-safe colors. Color Cubes is the default color palette; however, you can choose another one by clicking Modify on the Menu bar, clicking Page Properties, clicking the Appearance (CSS) or (HTML) category, clicking the color box next to the Background or Text color boxes, clicking the color palette list arrow, then clicking the desired color

palette. Figure C-10 shows the list of color palette choices. Another WCAG guideline states that color should never be the only visual means of conveying information. For instance, don't say "Refer to the brown box"; rather, say something like "Refer to the box immediately below this paragraph."

FIGURE C-10: Color palettes

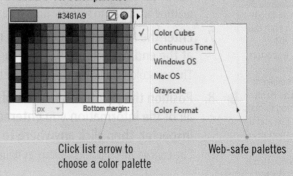

Click list arrow to choose a color palette

Web-safe palettes

Creating and Formatting Text

Text is an important part of any web page. You can enter text directly in Dreamweaver, import it (Win only), or copy and paste text from another document. When you are entering text, each time you press [Enter] (Win) or [return] (Mac), you create a new paragraph in the HTML code. Each paragraph is surrounded by <p> tags. Once you enter or import text, you can format it in Dreamweaver by changing the font, size, and color, just as in other programs. **Headings** are six different HTML text sizes that you can apply to text: Heading 1 (the largest size) through Heading 6 (the smallest size). Using a heading format is a way of showing the importance level of selected text in relation to other text on the page. Examples of tags that show emphasis are the bold tag, <strong>, and the italic tag, <em>. While you can set some formatting characteristics with HTML tags, the preferred practice is to use CSS for most formatting. 🖿🖿🖿 The current menu bar does not include links to all of the main pages so you decide to replace it with a link to each main page and format it using an HTML heading format, then apply the italic setting to the contact information.

STEPS

QUICK TIP

Make sure the text is selected properly—the next keystroke will replace the selected items. If you have difficulty selecting text, try [Backspace] or [Delete].

1. **Position the insertion point to the left of A in About Us, then drag to select** About Us - Spa - Cafe, **as shown in Figure C-11**

   The current menu bar is selected. A small icon may appear next to the selected text. If you click this icon, you will bring up the **Code Navigator**, a small window that opens with code for the selected page element. You will learn more about the Code Navigator in Unit D.

2. **Type** Home - About Us - Spa - Cafe - Activities, **using spaces on either side of the hyphens**

   This text becomes the page's new menu bar. A menu bar is a set of text or graphic links that is used to navigate to other pages in your website.

3. **Position the insertion point at the beginning of the first paragraph, type** Welcome to our beach! **then, press** [Enter] **(Win) or** [return] **(Mac)**

   Pressing [Enter] (Win) or [return] (Mac) creates a paragraph break represented by a <p> tag. Even a single character is considered a paragraph if it is preceded and followed by a paragraph break. Paragraphs can share common formatting, such as alignment settings.

4. **Click anywhere in the "Welcome!" text you just entered, click the HTML button** `<> HTML` **on the Property inspector to open the HTML Property inspector if necessary, click the** Format list arrow **in the HTML Property inspector, then click** Heading 1

   The Heading 1 format is applied to the text "Welcome to our beach!" as shown in Figure C-12.

QUICK TIP

Line breaks are useful when you want to apply the same formatting to text but place it on separate lines. The HTML code for a line break is <br />.

5. **Position the insertion point after the period following "...want to go home", as shown in Figure C-12, press** [Enter] **(Win) or** [return] **(Mac), then type** The Striped Umbrella

6. **Press and hold** [Shift], **press** [Enter] **(Win) or** [return] **(Mac) to create a line break**

   You can create separate lines within a paragraph by entering a line break after each line. A **line break** places text on separate lines without creating a new paragraph, which enables you to apply common formatting attributes to separate lines of text.

QUICK TIP

The Italic button is located in both the CSS and HTML Property inspectors, but each one produces different results. The HTML Italic button formats selected text and the CSS Italic button will ask you to create a new CSS rule to use to format the text.

7. **Enter the following information, repeating the instructions in Step 6 to place a line break at the end of each line:** 25 Beachside Drive; Ft. Eugene, Florida 33775; (555) 594-9458

   The semicolons indicate where the line breaks go.

8. **Position the pointer to the left of The Striped Umbrella, click and drag to select it and all of the information you entered in Step 7, click the** Italic button `I` **in the Property inspector, then click anywhere to deselect the text**

   The contact information appears as italicized text. See Figure C-13.

FIGURE C-11: **Replacing the current menu bar**

Selected text

FIGURE C-12: **Formatting the new heading**

New heading with Heading 1 format applied

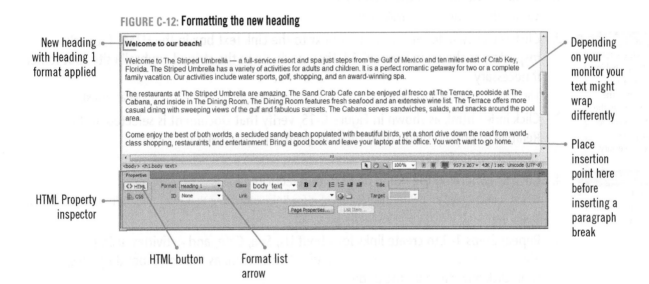

Depending on your monitor your text might wrap differently

Place insertion point here before inserting a paragraph break

HTML Property inspector

HTML button

Format list arrow

FIGURE C-13: **Adding and formatting the contact information**

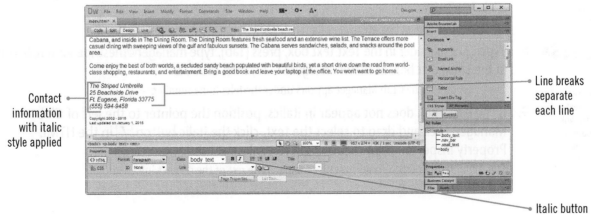

Contact information with italic style applied

Line breaks separate each line

Italic button

Adding Links to Web Pages

Links, or hyperlinks, are specially formatted text or images that users click to navigate through and between websites. Users are more likely to return to sites that have a user-friendly navigation system and interesting links to other web pages or sites. After a link has been clicked in a browser window, it is called a **visited link**, and it changes by default to a purple color in the browser window. The default color for links that have not yet been clicked is blue. When creating web pages, it is important to avoid **broken links**, which are links that are unable to access the intended destination file. In addition to the links that you create to enable users to move from page to page, a helpful link to include is a **point of contact**, a place on a web page that gives users a means of contacting the website if they have questions or problems. A **mailto: link**, an email address for users to contact the website's headquarters, is a common point of contact.  You create links for each of the menu items to their respective web pages in The Striped Umbrella website. You also create an email link to the club manager at The Striped Umbrella.

STEPS

1. **Double-click Home in the menu bar**
   You use this selected text to make a link.

2. **Click the Browse for File button next to the Link text box in the HTML Property inspector, as shown in Figure C-14, then navigate to the striped_umbrella site root folder if necessary**
   The Select File dialog box opens. The contents of the striped_umbrella site root folder are listed.

3. **Click index.html, as shown in Figure C-15, verify that Document is selected in the Relative to pop-up menu then click OK (Win) or Open (Mac)**
   The Select File dialog box closes.

4. **Click anywhere on the home page to deselect Home**
   Home is underlined and blue, the default color for links, indicating that it is a link. When users click the Home link in a browser, the index.html page opens.

5. **Repeat Steps 1–4 to create links for About Us, Spa, Cafe, and Activities, using about_us.html, spa.html, cafe.html, and activities.html as the corresponding files, then click anywhere on the page**
   All five links are now created for The Striped Umbrella home page. See Figure C-16.

6. **Position the insertion point immediately after the last digit in the telephone number, press and hold [Shift], then press [Enter] (Win) or [return] (Mac)**
   A line break is created.

7. **Click the Insert panel list arrow on the Insert panel, click Common if necessary, then click Email Link**
   The Email Link dialog box opens.

8. **Type Club Manager in the Text text box, press [Tab], type manager@thestripedumbrella.com in the Email text box, as shown in Figure C-17, then click OK**
   The email link to the Club Manager appears under the telephone number.

9. **If the email link does not appear in italics, position the pointer to the left of Club Manager, click and drag to select the text, click the Italic button *I* in the HTML Property inspector, then click anywhere to deselect the text**
   The Club Manager link appears in italics to match the rest of the contact information.

FIGURE C-14: Creating a link using the Property inspector

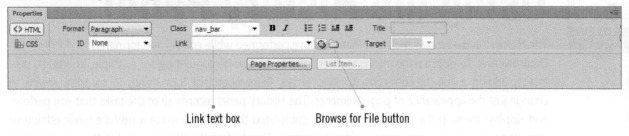

Link text box

Browse for File button

FIGURE C-15: Select File dialog box

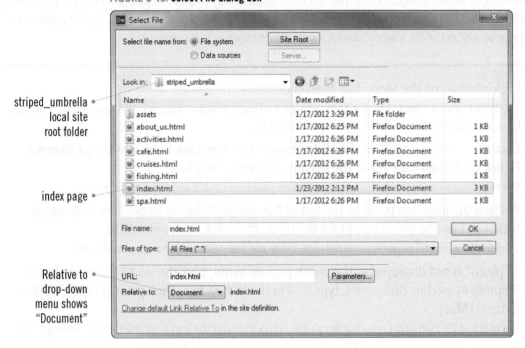

striped_umbrella local site root folder

index page

Relative to drop-down menu shows "Document"

FIGURE C-16: Links added to menu bar items

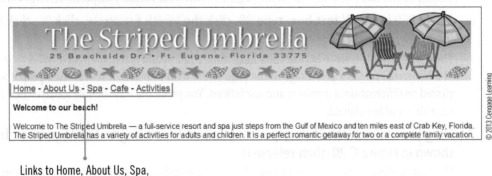

Home - About Us - Spa - Cafe - Activities

Welcome to our beach!

Welcome to The Striped Umbrella — a full-service resort and spa just steps from the Gulf of Mexico and ten miles east of Crab Key, Florida. The Striped Umbrella has a variety of activities for adults and children. It is a perfect romantic getaway for two or a complete family vacation.

© 2013 Cengage Learning

Links to Home, About Us, Spa, Cafe, and Activities pages

FIGURE C-17: Email Link dialog box

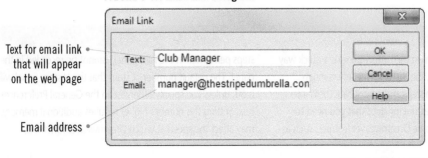

Text for email link that will appear on the web page

Email Link

Text: Club Manager

Email: manager@thestripedumbrella.con

OK

Cancel

Help

Email address

Developing a Web Page

Using the History Panel

The **History panel** shows the steps that you have performed while editing and formatting a document in Dreamweaver. To **edit** a page means to insert, delete, or change content by, for example, inserting a new image, adding a link, or correcting spelling errors. Remember that formatting, in contrast, means to change just the appearance of page elements. The History panel records all of the tasks that you perform and displays them in the order in which you completed them. If you make a mistake while editing or formatting a page, you can undo your previous steps. Simply drag the slider up next to the step you want to revert to, as shown in Figure C-18. This is a more efficient way to undo steps than using the Edit, Undo command. ░░░░░ You want to add a horizontal rule to divide the banner and menu bar from the rest of the page as well as use the History panel to undo the changes as you experiment.

1. **Click Window on the Menu bar, then click History**

   The History panel opens, and the steps you have already performed during this session, such as Make Hyperlink and Line Break, display in the panel window.

2. **Click the Panel menu ▤ on the History panel title bar, click Clear History, as shown in Figure C-18, then click Yes in the Dreamweaver warning box**

   The steps that were previously listed in the History panel are cleared and the panel is empty.

   > **QUICK TIP**
   > A horizontal rule can also be inserted by clicking Horizontal rule in the Common category on the Insert panel.

3. **Position the insertion point to the left of the words Welcome to our beach! heading, click Insert on the Menu bar, point to HTML, then click Horizontal Rule**

   A horizontal rule, or line, appears on the page above the first paragraph and remains selected.

   > **QUICK TIP**
   > The preferred way to format horizontal rules is with CSS. After you learn how to use CSS, you will use styles to format your horizontal rules.

4. **If "pixels" is not displayed in the width pop-up menu, click the width list arrow in the Property inspector, click pixels, type 950 in the W text box, then press [Enter] (Win) or [return] (Mac)**

   The width of the horizontal rule changes to 950 pixels wide and the step is recorded in the History panel.

5. **Click the Align list arrow in the Property inspector, then click Left**

   The horizontal rule is left-aligned on the page. Compare your Property inspector settings to Figure C-19.

6. **Select 950 in the W text box, type 80, click the Width list arrow, click %, click the Align list arrow, then click Center**

   The horizontal rule is set to 80% of the width of the window and is center-aligned. When you set the width of a horizontal rule as a percentage of the page rather than in pixels, it resizes itself proportionately when viewed on different-sized monitors and resolutions. You prefer the way the rule looked when it was wider, a set width, and left-aligned.

7. **Drag the slider on the History panel up until it is pointing to Set Alignment: left, as shown in Figure C-20, then release it**

   The bottom three steps in the History panel appear gray, indicating that these steps have been undone, and the horizontal rule returns to the left-aligned, 950-pixel width settings.

8. **Click File on the Menu bar, then click Save**

Using the History panel

Dragging the slider up and down in the History panel is a quick way to undo or redo steps. However, the History panel offers much more. It can "memorize" certain steps and consolidate them into one command. This is a useful feature for steps that you need to perform repeatedly. However, some Dreamweaver features, such as steps performed in the Files panel, cannot be recorded in the History panel. The default number of steps that the History panel will record is 50, unless you specify otherwise in the General Preferences dialog box. Setting this number higher requires additional memory, and may affect the speed at which Dreamweaver functions.

FIGURE C-18: **History panel**

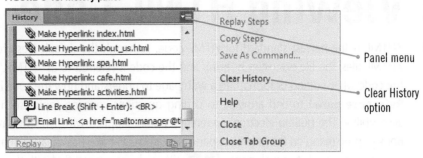

FIGURE C-19: **Property inspector settings for horizontal rule**

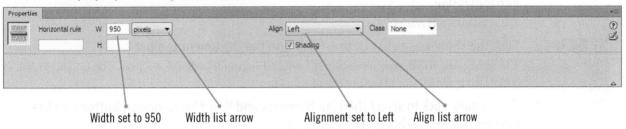

Width set to 950   Width list arrow   Alignment set to Left   Align list arrow

FIGURE C-20: **Resetting horizontal rule properties using the History panel**

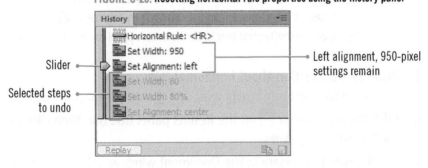

Slider

Selected steps to undo

Left alignment, 950-pixel settings remain

Checking your screen against book figures

To show as much of the Document window as possible, most figures appear with the Standard toolbar hidden. Keep in mind that Dreamweaver will "remember" the screen arrangement from the last session when it opens each time. This may mean that you would have to open, close, collapse, or expand the various

panels, toolbars, and inspectors to match your screens to the figures in the book. This is not really necessary unless you need a panel that is not open to complete a step. The rulers may also be displayed in figures in Design view. To turn this feature on or off, use the View > Rulers > Show command.

Viewing HTML Code

XHTML is the newest standard for HTML code. Although the default files created in Dreamweaver are XHTML files, the file extension is .html, and the code is referred to as "HTML." It is often helpful to view the code while editing or formatting a web page to understand how the code is working. You can use the **Reference panel** to find answers to coding questions covering topics such as HTML, JavaScript, and accessibility. The built-in electronic reference books supplied with Dreamweaver are available using the Book pop-up menu on the Reference panel. Dreamweaver also has a feature that tells you the last date that changes were made to a web page. Although you are satisfied with the placement of the horizontal rule on the page, you decide to use the Reference panel to research how to change its color. You also want to add a code so that the date will automatically update each time the page is saved.

1. **Click Window on the Menu bar, click History to close the History panel, then click the horizontal rule**

   The horizontal rule is selected.

QUICK TIP
[Ctrl] [P] (Win) or [command] [P] (Mac) prints the HTML code for an open page.

2. **Click the Show Code view button `Code` on the Document toolbar**

   The highlighted HTML code represents the selected horizontal rule on the page. The Coding toolbar is docked along the left side of the Document window.

3. **If necessary, click to select the Line Numbers and Word Wrap option buttons on the Coding toolbar, as shown in Figure C-21**

   The option buttons on the Coding toolbar appear with a black border when they are selected. The Line Numbers and Word Wrap options make it easier to navigate code. **Line numbers** provide a point of reference when locating specific sections of code. **Word wrap** keeps all code within the width of the Document window so you don't have to scroll to read long lines of code. It is easier for you to read and select the lines of code as you research the <hr> tag using the Reference panel.

4. **Click Window on the Menu bar, point to Results, click Reference, if necessary click the Book list arrow in the Reference Panel to select O'REILLY HTML Reference, click the Tag list arrow to select HR if necessary, as shown in Figure C-22**

   The HR tag appears in the Tag text box in the Reference panel menu bar; HR is the HTML code for horizontal rule tag.

5. **Read the information about horizontal rules**

   The color of rules can be changed by using CSS; this will be covered in Unit D.

QUICK TIP
You can also change the font size with the Results panel menu.

6. **Click the Panel menu on the Results panel title bar, then click Close Tab Group**

   The Results tab group closes.

7. **Scroll down if necessary in the Document window, select January 1, 2015, then press [Delete]**

   The date is deleted.

8. **Scroll down the Common category on the Insert panel until the Date object button appears, click Date to open the Insert Date dialog box, click March 7, 1974, in the Date format options list, click the Update automatically on save check box if necessary to select it, as shown in Figure C-23, then click OK**

   The Insert date dialog box closes and the JavaScript code for the date is added to the page. The current date will be placed on the page each time the page is opened and saved.

9. **Click the Show Design view button `Design` on the Document toolbar, then save your work**

   The index page appears in Design view in the Document window.

FIGURE C-21: Code view options

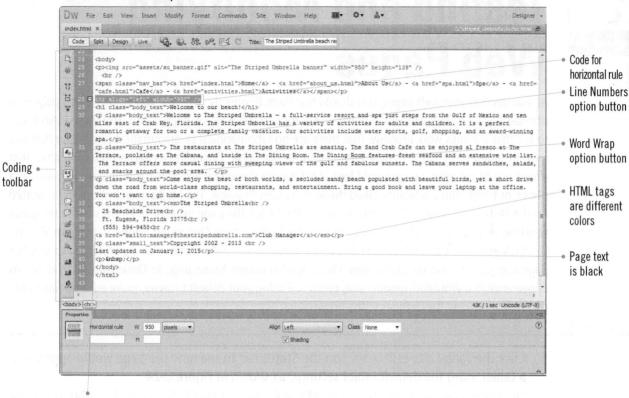

- Code for horizontal rule
- Line Numbers option button
- Word Wrap option button
- HTML tags are different colors
- Page text is black

Coding toolbar

HTML tag that begins a link

FIGURE C-22: `<HR>` tag information displayed in the Reference panel

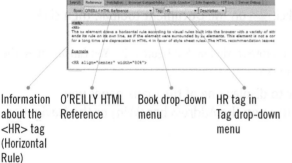

Information about the `<HR>` tag (Horizontal Rule)

O'REILLY HTML Reference

Book drop-down menu

HR tag in Tag drop-down menu

FIGURE C-23: Insert Date dialog box

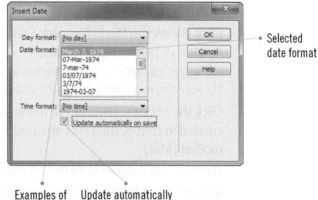

- Selected date format

Examples of date formats

Update automatically on save check box

Design Matters

Using Code view to edit pages

Some designers prefer to make changes to their pages by typing directly into the code, rather than working in Design view, because they feel that this gives them more precise control. Some features, such as JavaScript functions, are often added to pages by copying and pasting code into the existing page's HTML code. **JavaScript** is code that adds interaction between the user and the web page, such as rollovers or interactive forms. **Rollovers** are screen elements that change in appearance as the pointer rests on them. You can view the HTML code in Dreamweaver by using Code view or Code and Design view. This enables you to view the HTML code and the page content in different colors, highlight HTML code that contains errors, and **debug**, or correct, HTML errors.

Testing and Modifying Web Pages

As you develop your web pages, you should test them frequently. The best way to test a web page is to preview it in a browser window to make sure it appears the way you expect it to. You should also check to see that the links work properly, that there are no typographical or grammatical errors, and that you have included all of the necessary information for the page. Dreamweaver has a preview feature that allows you to see what a page would look like if it were viewed on a mobile hand-held device, such as a phone or tablet. This is a feature called the **Multiscreen Preview**. The Multiscreen button 🖳 is located on the Document toolbar. This button allows you to see the page in three different sizes in the same window, or you can choose one size to preview in the whole Document window. You can also use the Mobile size 🔲, the Tablet size 🔲, or the Desktop size 🖥 buttons on the Status bar to simulate page size. 🔳🔳🔳 You decide to view The Striped Umbrella home page in Dreamweaver to check its appearance in a simulated window size, preview it using your default browser, make adjustments to the page, then preview the changes in the browser.

1. **Click the Tablet size button 🔲 on the Status bar to see how the page would appear on a tablet using the default tablet settings, as shown in Figure C-24**

   The page is resized to simulate what it would look like in the default Tablet size, (768 × 1024). The Mobile size 🔲 and Desktop size 🖥 buttons are on either side of the Tablet size button 🔲 and are used to view a page in a simulated mobile and desktop screen.

2. **Click the Desktop size button 🖥, scroll down if necessary and highlight the period after the "...go home" text, then type !**

   An exclamation point replaces the period after "...go home".

3. **Click File on the Menu bar, click Save, click 🌐 on the Document toolbar, then click Preview in [your default browser]**

   The Striped Umbrella home page displays in your browser window. See Figure C-25. You can also press the F12 key (Win) to preview a page in the default browser.

4. **Click the About Us link on the menu bar to display one of the blank pages you created in Unit B, then click the Back button on the Address bar (Win) or the Navigation toolbar (Mac)**

   The index page reappears in the browser window.

5. **Repeat Step 4 to test the Spa, Cafe, and Activities links**

   Each link opens a corresponding blank page in the browser window since you haven't placed any text or images on them yet.

6. **Click the Club Manager link**

   The default mail program on your computer opens with a message addressed to manager@thestripedumbrella.com.

7. **Close the email message dialog box, close the browser window, close the index page, then click Exit on the File menu (Win) or Quit on the Dreamweaver menu (Mac) to close the Dreamweaver program**

FIGURE C-24: Using Tablet size to view the page

Multiscreen button

Page viewed in default tablet size

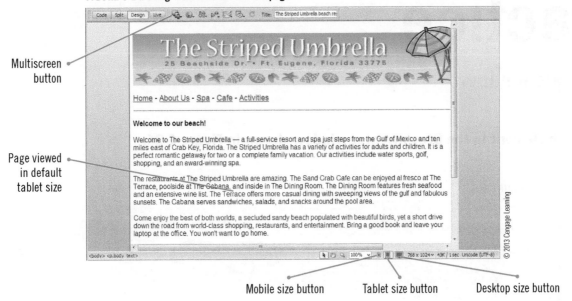

© 2013 Cengage Learning

Mobile size button   Tablet size button   Desktop size button

FIGURE C-25: The finished page

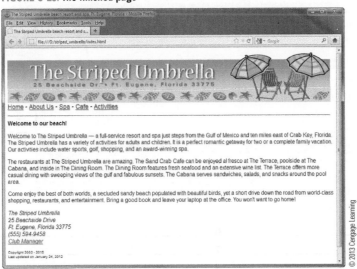

© 2013 Cengage Learning

Using smart design principles

As you view your pages in the browser, take a critical look at the symmetry of the page. Is it balanced? Are there too many images for the amount of text, or too few? Does everything "heavy" seem to be on the top or bottom of the page, or do the page elements seem balanced, with the weight evenly distributed between the top, bottom, and sides? Use design principles to create a site-wide consistency for your pages. **Horizontal symmetry** means that the elements are balanced across the page. **Vertical symmetry** means that they are balanced down the page. **Diagonal symmetry** balances page elements along the invisible diagonal line of the page. **Radial symmetry** runs from the center of the page outward, like the petals of a flower.

These principles all deal with balance; however, too much balance is not good, either. Sometimes it adds interest to place page elements a little off center to have an asymmetrical layout. Color, white space, text, lines, shapes, forms, textures, and images should all complement each other and provide a natural flow across and down the page. The **rule of thirds**—dividing a page into nine squares like a tic-tac-toe grid—states that interest is increased when your focus is on one of the intersections in the grid. The most important information should be at the top of the page where it is visible without scrolling— "above the fold," as they say in the newspaper business. Other design principles include the use of emphasis, movement, unity, proximity, and repetition to place elements attractively on a page.

Developing a Web Page

Practice

Concepts Review

Label each element in the Dreamweaver window shown in Figure C-26.

FIGURE C-26

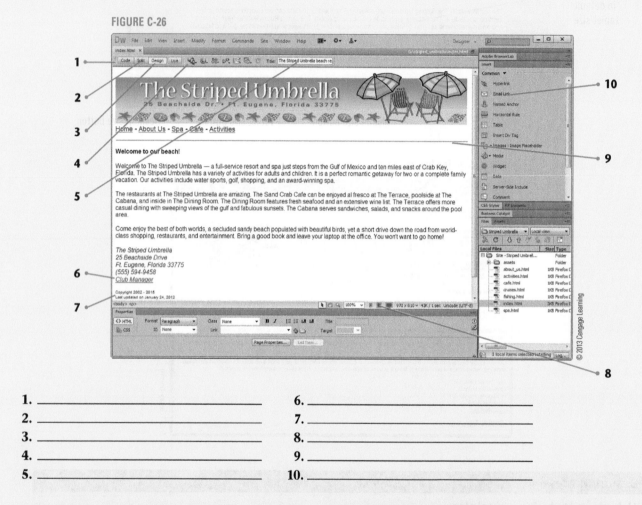

1. _____
2. _____
3. _____
4. _____
5. _____
6. _____
7. _____
8. _____
9. _____
10. _____

Match each of the following terms with the statement that best describes its function.

11. **Style**
12. **Head section**
13. **Body section**
14. **Page Properties dialog box**
15. **Heading 1**
16. **Heading 6**
17. **Edit a page**
18. **Format a page**

a. The part of a web page that includes text, graphics, and links

b. A named group of formatting characteristics

c. Includes the default web page settings

d. The smallest heading size

e. Make adjustments in the appearance of page elements

f. Insert, delete, or change page content

g. The largest heading size

h. The part of a web page that includes the page title and meta tags

Select the best answer from the following list of choices.

19. The head section of a web page can include:
   a. keywords.
   b. descriptions.
   c. Meta tags.
   d. all of the above.

20. Links that have been previously clicked are called:
   a. active links.
   b. links.
   c. visited links.
   d. broken links.

21. The button that is used to display a web page in Design view in three different sizes is the
_____ button.
   a. Multiscreen
   b. Mobile display
   c. Simulated screens
   d. Media

22. The _____ on the History panel is used to undo or redo several steps.
   a. scroll bar
   b. pointer
   c. slider
   d. Undo/Redo tool

23. An example of a point of contact is a:
   a. heading.
   b. title.
   c. mailto: link.
   d. keywords.

24. The Dreamweaver default color palette is the:
   a. Continuous Tone.
   b. Color Cubes.
   c. Windows OS.
   d. Mac OS.

Skills Review

Important: If you did not create the websites used in the preceding exercises in Unit B, you need to create a local site root folder for each website and define the websites using files your instructor provides. See the "Read This Before You Begin" section for more detailed instructions.

1. Plan the page layout.

    a. Using a word processor or a piece of paper, list three principles of good page design that you have learned, then list them in order of most important to least important, based on your experiences.

    b. Explain why you chose these three concepts and why you selected the order you did.

2. Create the head content.

    a. Start Dreamweaver.

    b. Use the Files panel to open the Blooms & Bulbs website.

    c. Open the index page, then view the head content.

    d. Use the Head button list arrow to insert the following keywords: **Blooms & Bulbs, garden, plants, nursery, flowers, landscape design**, and **greenhouse**.

    e. Insert the following description: **Blooms & Bulbs is a premier supplier of garden plants and trees for both professional and home gardeners.**

    f. Switch to Code view to view the HTML code for the head section.

    g. Switch to Design view.

    h. Save your work, then hide the head content.

3. Set web page properties.

    a. View the page properties.

    b. Change the background color to a color of your choice, then apply it to the page, leaving the dialog box open.

    c. Change the background color to white.

    d. Save your work.

4. Create and format text.

    a. Replace the hyphens in the current menu bar with a split vertical bar (the top of the backslash key) to separate the items.

    b. Place the insertion point at the end of the last sentence in the second paragraph, then add a paragraph break.

    c. Type the following text, inserting a line break after each line.

        Blooms & Bulbs

        Hwy 43 South

        Alvin, Texas 77511

        555-248-0806

    d. Delete the date in the "Last updated" line, then replace it with a date that will update automatically each time the page is saved, using the March 7, 1974 format.

    e. Using the HTML Property inspector, italicize the copyright statement and last updated statement.

    f. Save your work.

5. Add links to web pages.

    a. Link the word *Home* on the menu bar to index.html.

    b. Link *Our Plants* to plants.html.

    c. Link *Newsletter* to newsletter.html.

    d. Link *Workshops* to workshops.html.

    e. Link *Tips* to tips.html.

    f. Using the Insert panel, create an email link under the telephone number with a line break between them; type **Customer Service** in the Text text box and **mailbox@blooms.com** in the Email text box.

Skills Review (continued)

6. Use the History panel.

  a. Open and clear the History panel.

  b. Using the Insert menu, insert a horizontal rule right before the first paragraph.

  c. Using the Property inspector, left-align the rule and set the width to 950 pixels.

  d. Edit the horizontal rule to center-align it with a width of 70%.

  e. Use the History panel to change the horizontal rule back to left-aligned with a width of 950 pixels.

  f. Close the History panel.

  g. Save your work.

7. View HTML code.

  a. Use Code view to examine the code for the horizontal rule properties, the email link, and the date in the "Last updated" statement.

  b. Return to Design view.

8. Test and modify web pages.

  a. Using the Preview buttons on the status bar, view the page at two different preview sizes.

  b. Preview the page in your browser.

  c. Verify that all links work correctly, then close the browser.

  d. Add the text **We are happy to deliver or ship your purchases.** to the end of the first paragraph.

  e. Save your work, preview the page in your browser, compare your screen to Figure C-27, then close your browser.

  f. Close the page, then exit Dreamweaver.

FIGURE C-27

Important: *If you did not create the websites used in the exercises in Unit B, you need to create site root folders for each website and define the websites using files your instructor provides. See the "Read This Before You Begin" section for more detailed instructions.*

Independent Challenge 1

You have been hired to create a website for a river expedition company named Rapids Transit, located on the Buffalo River in Arkansas. In addition to renting canoes, kayaks, and rafts, they have several types of cabin rentals for overnight stays. River guides are available, if requested, to accompany clients on float trips. The owner's name is Mike Andrew.

a. Use the Files panel to open the Rapids Transit website.

b. Open the index page.

c. Create the following keywords: **Rapids Transit, river, rafting, Buffalo River, Arkansas, kayak, canoe,** and **float**.

d. Create the following description: **Rapids Transit is a river expedition company located on the Buffalo River in Arkansas.**

e. Change the page title to **Rapids Transit – Buffalo River Outfitters**.

f. Edit the menu bar below the Rapids Transit banner by changing **Our Guides** to **River Guides**.

g. Enter a line break under the address, then enter the telephone number **(555) 365-5228**.

h. Italicize the company copyright and last updated statements, then, after the phone number, enter a line break and create an email link, using **Mike Andrew** for the text and **mailbox@rapidstransit.com** for the email link.

i. Add links to the entries in the menu bar, using the files index.html, guides.html, rates.html, lodging.html, and before.html in the rapids site root folder. (Recall that these files don't have any content yet, but you can still link to them. You will add content to the pages as you work through the remaining units of the book.)

j. Delete the horizontal rule.

k. Delete the date in the last updated statement and change it to a date that will be automatically updated when the page is saved, using the March 7, 1974 data format. Reformat the date to match the rest of the line if necessary.

l. View the HTML code for the page, noting in particular the code for the head section.

m. View the page in Design view in two different screen sizes, save your work, then test the links in your browser, as shown in Figure C-28.

n. Close the browser, close the page, then exit Dreamweaver.

FIGURE C-28

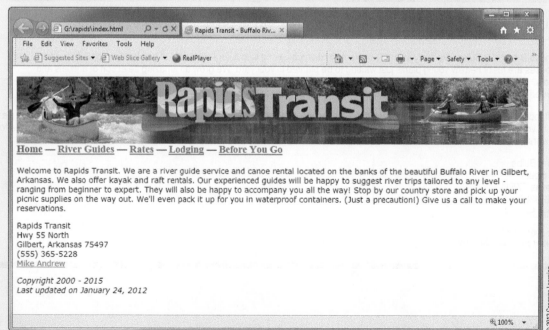

Independent Challenge 2

Your company is designing a new website for a travel outfitter named TripSmart. TripSmart specializes in travel products and services. In addition to selling travel products such as clothing, luggage, and accessories, they promote trips and offer travel advice. Their clients range from college students to families to vacationing professionals. The owner, Thomas Howard, has requested a dynamic website that conveys the excitement of traveling. Refer to Figure C-29 as you work through the following steps.

a. Open the TripSmart website, then open its index page.

b. Create the following keywords: **TripSmart, travel, traveling, tours, trips, vacations**.

c. Create the following description: **TripSmart is a comprehensive travel store. We can help you plan trips, make the arrangements, and supply you with travel gear.**

d. Change the page title to read **TripSmart: Serving all your travel needs**.

e. Change the menu bar below the banner to read **Home - Tours - Newsletter - Services - Catalog**.

f. Add links to the menu bar entries, using the files index.html, tours.html, newsletter.html, services.html, and catalog.html. (Recall that these files don't have any content yet, but you can still link to them. You will add content to the pages as you work through the remaining units of the book.)

g. Replace the date in the "Last updated" statement with a date that will update automatically when the file is saved.

h. Add the following contact information between the last paragraph and copyright statement using line breaks after each line: **TripSmart**, **1106 Beechwood**, **Fayetteville**, **AR 72604**, **555-848-0807**.

i. Immediately beneath the telephone number, place an Email link using **Contact us** as the text and **associate@tripsmart.com** for the link.

j. Insert a horizontal rule that is 950 pixels wide and left-aligned above the contact information.

k. View the HTML code for the page, noting in particular the head section code.

l. View the page in two different screen sizes, save your work, then test the links in your browser window.

m. Close the page and exit Dreamweaver.

FIGURE C-29

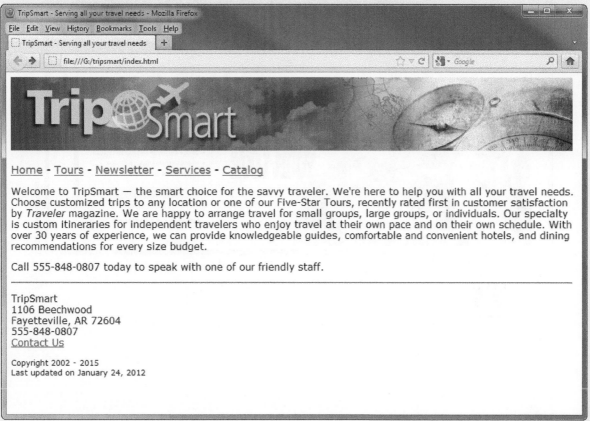

Angela Lou is a freelance photographer. She is searching the Internet for a particular type of paper to use in printing her digital images. She knows that websites use keywords and descriptions to increase traffic from search engines such as Google and Bing. She is curious as to how keywords and descriptions work with search engines. Write your answers to these questions on paper or using your word processor.

a. Connect to the Internet, then go to snapfish.com to see the Snapfish website's home page, as shown in Figure C-30.

b. View the page source by clicking View on the menu bar, then clicking Source (Internet Explorer) or Tools > Web Developer > Page Source (Mozilla Firefox). (*Hint*: Press the Alt key if the menu is hidden.)

c. Can you locate a description and keywords?

d. How many keywords do you find?

e. How many words are in the description?

f. In your opinion, is the number of keywords and words in the description about right, too many, or not enough?

g. Use a search engine such as Google (google.com), type the words **photo quality paper** in the Search text box, then press [Enter] (Win) or [Return] (Mac).

h. Choose a link in the list of results and view the source code for that page. Do you see keywords and a description? Do any of them match the words you used in the search? (You may have to scroll down quite a bit to find the keywords. Try using the Find feature to quickly search the code.)

i. If you don't see the search words in keywords or descriptions, do you see them in the body of the pages?

j. Save your work, then exit all programs.

FIGURE C-30

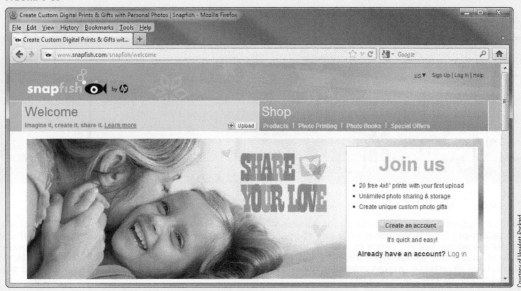

Real Life Independent Challenge

This assignment will continue to build on the personal website that you created in Unit B. In this lesson, you will work with your home page.

a. Insert a brief description and a list of meaningful keywords for your home page in the appropriate locations.

b. Insert an effective title for your home page.

c. Format the home page attractively, creating a strong contrast between your page background and your page content.

d. Add links from the home page to your other pages.

e. Insert an email link.

f. Insert a "Last updated" statement that includes a date that updates automatically when you save the file.

g. Preview the home page in your browser, verifying that each link works correctly.

h. Check the page for errors in content or format and edit as necessary.

i. Save your work, close the page, and exit the program.

Visual Workshop

Your company has been selected to design a website for a catering business named Carolyne's Creations. You are now ready to add content to the home page and apply formatting options to improve the page appearance, using Figure C-31 as a guide. Open your Carolyne's Creations website and modify the index page to duplicate Figure C-31. You can use **carolyne@carolynescreations.com** as the email link. (*Hint*: Remember to add an appropriate description and keywords, and revise the last updated statement so it will automatically update when the page is saved.)

FIGURE C-31

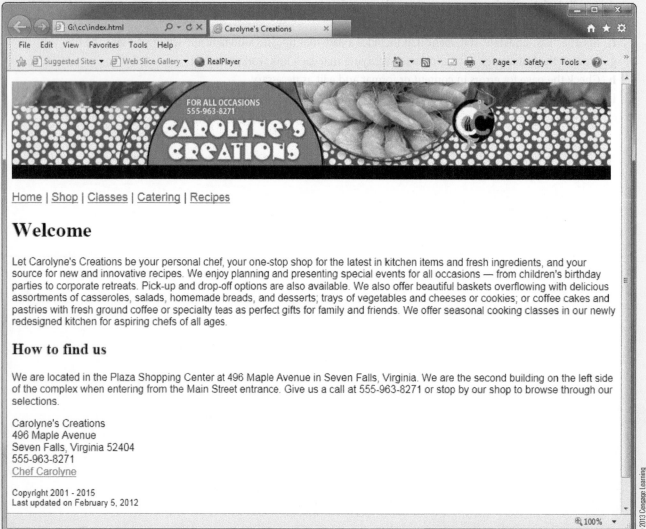

Working with Text and Cascading Style Sheets

Files You Will Need:

To view a list of files needed for this unit, see the Data Files Grid in the back of the book.

The content of most web pages is text-based. Because text on a computer screen can be more tiring to read than text on a printed page, you should strive to make your web page text attractive and easy to read. Dreamweaver has many options for enhancing text, including HTML properties for paragraphs and lists, as well as Cascading Style Sheets (CSS). CSS are used to assign sets of common formatting characteristics to page elements, such as paragraph text, lists, and table data. ▓▓▓ You decide to group content on the spa page for The Striped Umbrella website using lists to make the page more readable. Using lists to format text is also considered to be more accessible for users using screen readers. You want to use CSS to make these types of formatting changes consistent throughout the website.

OBJECTIVES

Create a new page

Import text

Set text properties

Create an unordered list

Understand Cascading Style Sheets

Create a rule in a new Cascading Style Sheet

Apply and edit a rule

Add rules to a Cascading Style Sheet

Attach a Cascading Style Sheet to a page

Check for spelling errors

Creating a New Page

You use the New Document dialog box to create a new page in Dreamweaver. You can create a blank page, a blank template, a fluid grid template, a page from a template, or a page from a sample layout. You have the option of several page types you can create, for example, HTML, CSS, XML, and ASP. Each page type has layout option choices. The HTML page type layouts include one column, two columns, and three columns. The new HTML5 layouts include two or three column layouts. ▰▰▰▰ You are ready to create a new page that will replace the placeholder spa page. You decide to use the HTML page type with no preset layout. After you create the page you insert the banner and the spa logo.

STEPS

1. **Start Dreamweaver, click the Site list arrow (Win) ▾ or ▾ (Mac) on the Files panel, then click The Striped Umbrella, if it isn't already selected**
   The Striped Umbrella website opens in the Files panel.

2. **Click File on the Menu bar, click New, click Blank Page (if necessary), click HTML in the Page Type column, click <none> in the Layout column, click the DocType list box, click HTML 5, as shown in Figure D-1, click Create, then click the Show Design view button** Design **if necessary**
   A new blank page opens in the Document window.

3. **Click File, click Save As, navigate to your Striped Umbrella local site root folder, then save the file as spa.html, overwriting the existing (blank) spa.html file**

4. **Click the Insert bar menu, click Common, click the Images list arrow, then click Image**
   The Select Image Source dialog box opens, as shown in Figure D-2.

QUICK TIP
You can also drag the banner image from the Files panel onto the page since it is already saved in the website assets folder.

5. **Browse to and open the website assets folder, double-click su_banner.gif, type The Striped Umbrella banner in the Alternate text box in the Image Tag Accessibility Attributes dialog box, then click OK**
   The banner appears at the top of the new page. You will learn more about the Image Tag Accessibility Attributes dialog box in Unit E.

6. **Click to the right of the banner to deselect it, press [Enter] (Win) or [Return] (Mac), repeat Step 4 to open the Select Image Source dialog box, then navigate to the assets folder in your unit_d Data Files folder**

7. **Double-click sea_spa_logo.png, type The Sea Spa logo in the Alternate text box in the Image Tag Accessibility Attributes dialog box, then click OK**

8. **Click to the right of the logo to place the insertion point on the spa.html page**
   The Sea Spa logo appears under the banner, as shown in Figure D-3.

FIGURE D-1: **Creating a new HTML document with the New Document dialog box**

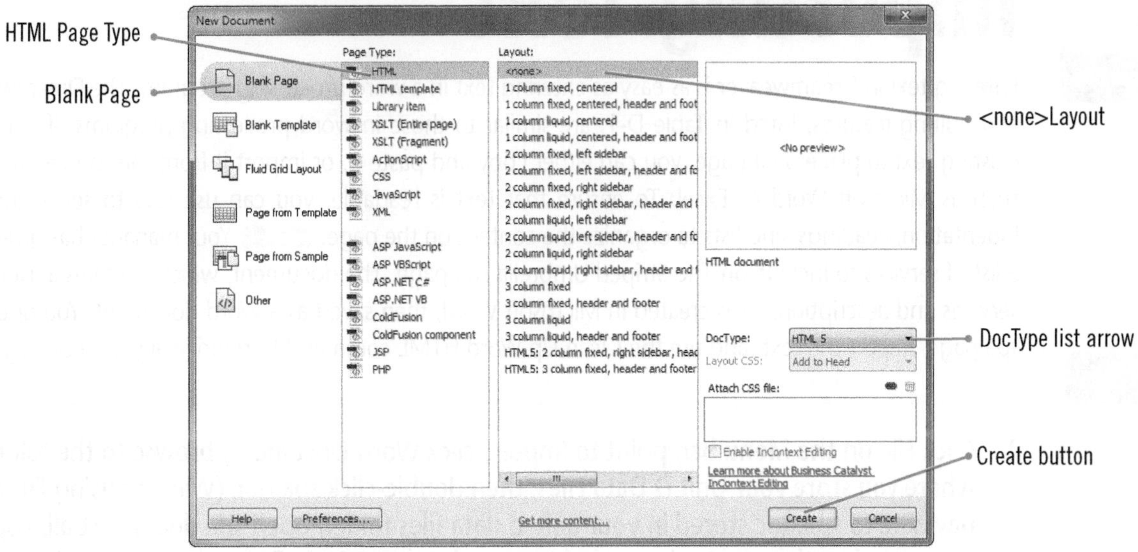

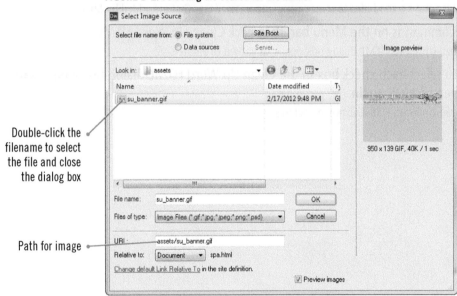

HTML Page Type

Blank Page

<none>Layout

DocType list arrow

Create button

FIGURE D-2: **Selecting the source for the banner**

Double-click the filename to select the file and close the dialog box

Path for image

FIGURE D-3: **Image file added to the Striped Umbrella assets folder**

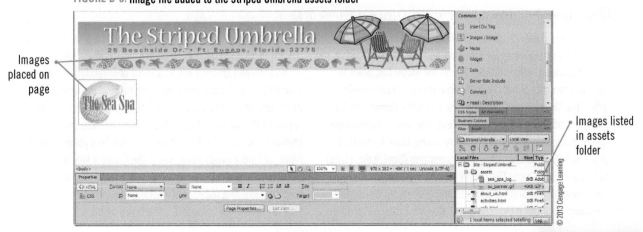

Images placed on page

Images listed in assets folder

© 2013 Cengage Learning

Working with Text and Cascading Style Sheets

Importing Text

Entering text in Dreamweaver is as easy as entering text in a word processing program. The Dreamweaver text editing features, listed in Table D-1, are similar to those in word processing programs. If you have existing text to place on a page, you can either copy and paste it, or import it from the source program, such as Microsoft Word or Excel. To ensure that text is readable, you can use CSS to set alignment, indentation, headings, and lists to organize the content on the page.  Your manager has given you a list of services to include on The Striped Umbrella spa page. The document, which contains a list of spa services and descriptions, was created in Microsoft Word, then saved as a Word document. You open the spa page, import the text, and use the Clean Up Word HTML command to remove any unnecessary tags.

1. **Click File on the Menu bar, point to Import, click Word Document, browse to the folder where you store your Unit D Data Files, then double-click spa.doc (Win); or using Finder, navigate to spa.doc stored in your unit_d data files folder, open spa.doc, select all, copy, close spa.doc, then paste the copied text on the spa page in Dreamweaver (Mac)**

   Mac users cannot use the Import > Word command. The text from the Word file is placed beside and wraps under the logo, as shown in Figure D-4. Although you may not see evidence of unnecessary code on the page, it is always a good idea to remove any unnecessary tags that are added by Microsoft Word.

2. **Click Commands on the Menu bar, then click Clean Up Word HTML**

   The Clean Up Word HTML dialog box opens, as shown in Figure D-5.

3. **Click to select each check box in the Clean Up Word HTML dialog box if necessary, click OK, then click OK again**

   The Clean Up Word HTML dialog box closes.

Importing and linking Microsoft Office documents

Adobe makes it easy to transfer data between Microsoft Office documents and Dreamweaver web pages. To import a Word or Excel document with a PC, click File on the Menu bar, point to Import, then click either Word Document or Excel Document. Select the file you want to import, then click the Formatting list arrow to choose among importing Text only; Text with structure (paragraphs, lists, and tables); Text, structure, basic formatting (bold, italic); or Text, structure, full formatting (bold, italic, styles) before you click Open. The option you choose depends on the importance of the original structure and formatting. Always use the Clean Up Word HTML command after importing a Word file.

On a Mac, open the file you want to import, copy the text, then paste it to an open page in Dreamweaver in Design view.

You can also create a link to a Word or Excel document on your web page. Simply drag the Word or Excel document from its current location to the place on the page you want the link to appear; if the document is located outside the site, you can browse for it using the Site list arrow on the Files panel, Explorer (Win), or Finder (Mac). Next, select the Create a link option button in the Insert Document dialog box, then save the file in your local site root folder so it will be uploaded when you publish your site. If it is not uploaded, the link will be broken.

FIGURE D-4: **Spa page with text imported**

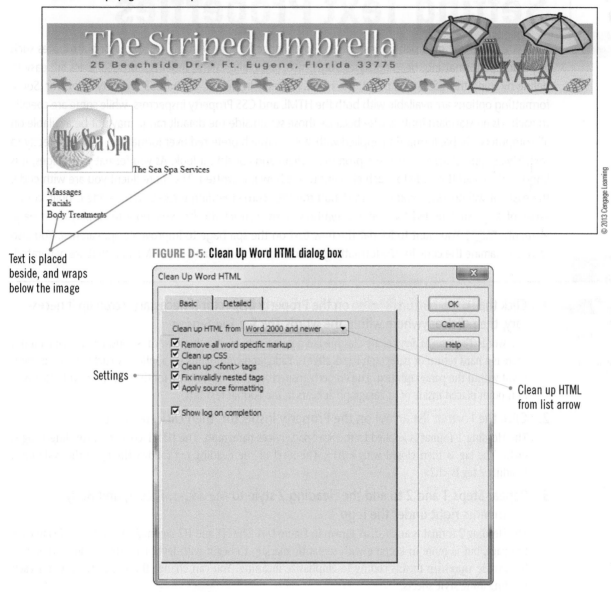

Text is placed
beside, and wraps
below the image

FIGURE D-5: **Clean Up Word HTML dialog box**

Settings

Clean up HTML
from list arrow

TABLE D-1: **Dreamweaver text editing features**

feature	menu	function	feature	menu	function
Find and Replace	Edit	Finds and replaces text on the current web page, the entire website, or in selected files	**Font families**	Modify	Selects font combinations for a browser or allows you to create custom font combinations
Indent and Outdent	Format	Indents selected text to the right or left	**Style**	Format	Sets various styles, such as bold and italic
Paragraph Format	Format	Sets paragraph, H1 through H6, and preformatted text	**CSS Styles**	Format	Provides options for applying a rule, creating a new CSS rule, attaching a style sheet, converting or moving rules, and applying Design-Time Style Sheets
Align	Format	Aligns text with the left or right margin, justifies it, or centers it on the page	**Color**	Format	Sets text color
List	Format	Creates unordered, ordered, or definition lists	**Check Spelling**	Commands	Runs a spell check on the page

Working with Text and Cascading Style Sheets

Setting Text Properties

After you place text on a page, you format it to enhance its appearance. Text formatting attributes such as paragraph formatting, heading styles, fonts, size, color, alignment, indents, and CSS styles are easy to define by using the CSS Styles panel, the HTML Property inspector, or the CSS Property inspector. Some formatting options are available with both the HTML and CSS Property inspectors, while some are specific to each. Using standard fonts is wise because those set outside the default range may not be available on all computers. Global formatting applied with styles is much preferred over formatting applied directly to text. Styles applied across a website promote a clean and consistent look. As you format your pages, it is important to read the code for each element to see how it is written. The more fluent you are with code, the easier it will be when you have to debug the site (correct coding errors). HTML code is built from a series of **tags** surrounded by < and > symbols. Tags instruct the browser how to display each page element. You want to format the new text on the spa page to improve its appearance. You also want to examine the code for the formatting commands to understand the HTML tags that are generated.

STEPS

QUICK TIP
To apply character formats such as bold and italic, you must select the paragraph rather than click within the text.

1. **Click the HTML button `<> HTML` on the Property inspector if necessary, scroll up if necessary, then click anywhere within the words** *The Sea Spa Services*

   The words *The Sea Spa Services* are classified as a paragraph; even a single word is considered a paragraph if there is a hard return or paragraph break after it. Paragraph commands are applied by clicking the insertion point within the paragraph text. The Property inspector shows the settings for the paragraph with the insertion point placed inside of it; Paragraph appears in the Format text box.

2. **Click the Format list arrow on the Property inspector, then click Heading 1**

   The Heading 1 format is applied to the Sea Spa Services paragraph. The HTML code for a Heading 1 tag is <h1>. The tag is then closed with </h1>. The level of the heading tag follows the h, so the code for a Heading 2 tag is <h2>.

3. **Repeat Steps 1 and 2 to add the Heading 2 style to Massages, Facials, and Body Treatments right under the logo**

   The Heading 2 format is applied, as shown in Figure D-6. The H1 and H2 tags make the text a little large for the page, but is more in keeping with semantic markup to begin with level 1 headings and work down. **Semantic markup** means coding to emphasize meaning. You can change the size of the text for each heading using style sheets.

TROUBLE
Mac users may notice that the insertion point does not match when viewing Code and Design view.

4. **Click after the word "Treatments", insert a line break, click the Show Code and Design views button `Split` on the Document toolbar**

   The HTML code for the headings displays in the left window, as shown in Figure D-7. The first tag in each pair begins the code and the last tag ends the code.

5. **Click the Show Design view button `Design` on the Document toolbar, then save your work**

   The spa page redisplays in Design view with its changes saved.

FIGURE D-6: Applying paragraph formats

Text with the Heading 1 format applied

Text with the Heading 2 format applied

Format list arrow

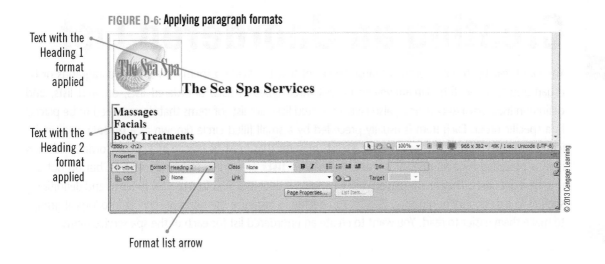

© 2013 Cengage Learning

FIGURE D-7: Show Code and Design views

Show Code and Design views button

The code that is displayed in Code view reflects the position of the insertion point on the page

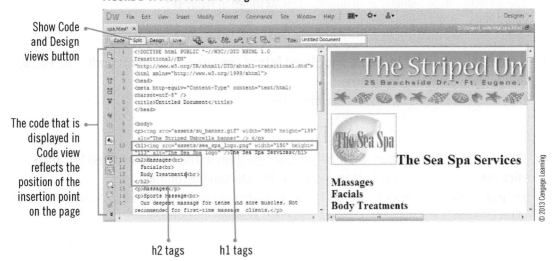

© 2013 Cengage Learning

h2 tags   h1 tags

Working with Text and Cascading Style Sheets

Creating an Unordered List

You can break up the monotony of large blocks of text by dividing them into smaller paragraphs or by organizing them as lists. Dreamweaver utilizes three types of lists: unordered lists, ordered lists, and definition lists. **Unordered lists**, also called bulleted lists, are lists of items that do not need to be placed in a specific order. Each item is usually preceded by a small filled circle (known as a **bullet**) or a similar icon. Numbered lists, or **ordered lists**, are lists of items that must be placed in a specific order, and each item is preceded by a number or a letter. **Definition lists** are similar to unordered lists, but do not use numbers or bullets. They are displayed with a hanging indent and are often used with terms and definitions, such as in a dictionary or glossary. ▓▓▓▓▓ You decide to organize the types of services into logical groups to make them easier to read. You want to create an unordered list for each of the spa service items.

STEPS

1. **Select the three spa service items and their descriptions under the Massages heading**
   Sports Massage, Swedish Massage, and Hot Stone Massage and their descriptions are selected.

2. **Click the Unordered List button ▤ on the HTML Property inspector, then deselect the text**
   The spa service items redisplay as an unordered list, as shown in Figure D-8.

3. **Repeat Steps 1 and 2 to create unordered lists of the spa service items under the Facials and Body Treatments headings**
   Each group of services redisplays as an unordered list.

4. **Click to place the insertion point before the first item in the first unordered list, then click the Show Code view button ⬚ Code on the Document toolbar**
   The page displays in Code view. The HTML tags surrounding the unordered list are <ul> and </ul>. Each of the list items is surrounded by <li> and </li> tags, as shown in Figure D-9.

5. **Click the Show Design view button ⬚ Design on the Document toolbar to return to Design view, then save your work**

FIGURE D-8: Creating an unordered list

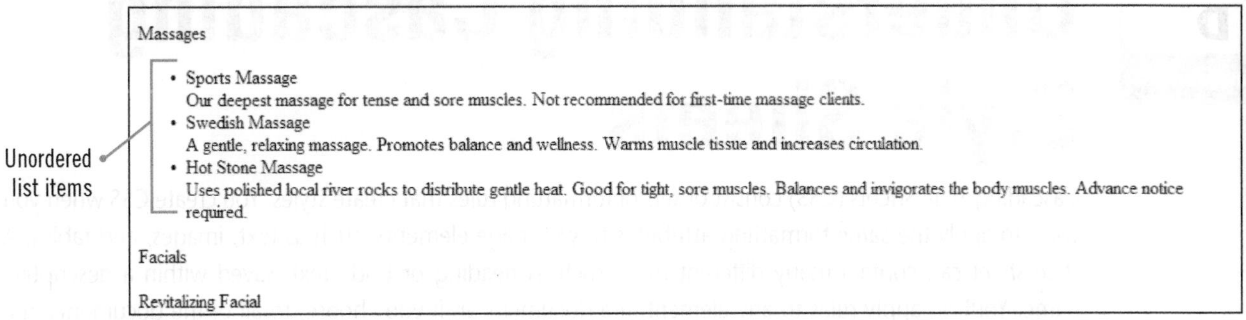

Massages

Unordered list items

- Sports Massage
  Our deepest massage for tense and sore muscles. Not recommended for first-time massage clients.
- Swedish Massage
  A gentle, relaxing massage. Promotes balance and wellness. Warms muscle tissue and increases circulation.
- Hot Stone Massage
  Uses polished local river rocks to distribute gentle heat. Good for tight, sore muscles. Balances and invigorates the body muscles. Advance notice required.

Facials

Revitalizing Facial

FIGURE D-9: Viewing an unordered list in Code view

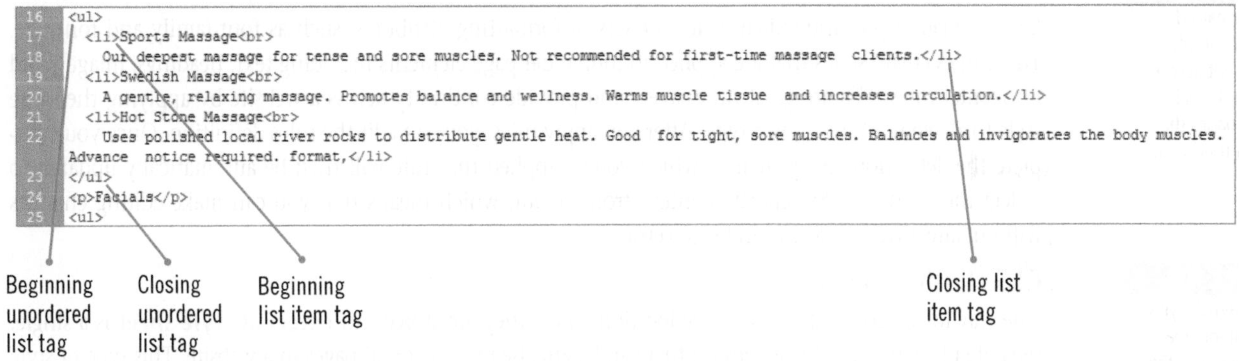

```
16  <ul>
17   <li>Sports Massage<br>
18    Our deepest massage for tense and sore muscles. Not recommended for first-time massage  clients.</li>
19   <li>Swedish Massage<br>
20    A gentle, relaxing massage. Promotes balance and wellness. Warms muscle tissue  and increases circulation.</li>
21   <li>Hot Stone Massage<br>
22    Uses polished local river rocks to distribute gentle heat. Good  for tight, sore muscles. Balances and invigorates the body muscles. Advance  notice required. format,</li>
23  </ul>
24  <p>Facials</p>
25  <ul>
```

Beginning unordered list tag

Closing unordered list tag

Beginning list item tag

Closing list item tag

Design Matters

Coding for the semantic web

You read several pages back about semantic markup and have previously heard the term *semantic* web. The word *semantics* refers to the study of word or sentence meanings. So the term **semantic web** refers to the way page content, such as paragraph, text, or list items, can be coded to emphasize their meaning to users. HTML tags such as the <p> tag, used for marking paragraphs, and the <ul> tag, used for marking unordered

lists, provide a clear meaning of the function and significance of the paragraphs or lists. **Semantic markup**, or coding to emphasize meaning, is a way to incorporate good accessibility practice. CSS styles affect the appearance of web page content while semantic markup enhances the meaning of the content. Both techniques work together to provide well-designed web pages that are attractive and easy to understand.

Using ordered lists

Ordered lists contain numbered or lettered items that need to appear in a particular order, such as listing the steps to accomplish a task. For example, if you followed directions to drive from point A to point B, each step would have to be executed in order or you would not successfully reach your destination.

For this type of sequential information, ordered lists can add more emphasis than bulleted ones. Dreamweaver uses several options for number styles, including Roman and Arabic. The HTML tags that surround ordered lists are <ol> and </ol>.

Understanding Cascading Style Sheets

Cascading Style Sheets (CSS) consist of sets of formatting rules that create styles. You create CSS when you want to apply the same formatting attributes to web page elements, such as text, images, and tables. A style sheet can contain many different rules, such as heading or body text, saved within a descriptive name. You can apply rules to any element in a document or, if you choose, to all of the documents in a website. If you edit an existing rule, all the page elements you have formatted with that rule will automatically update. ▓▓▓▓ You decide to research the ways CSS can save you time and provide your site with a more consistent look.

DETAILS

As you plan to use CSS in a website, keep in mind the following:

- **Advantages of using CSS**
  CSS are made up of individual **rules**, or sets of formatting attributes, such as font-family and font-size. These rules create styles that are applied to individual page elements including text, headings, images, and horizontal rules. CSS are great time-savers and provide continuity across a website by applying the same style to all elements of a given type. After you apply rules, you can edit the rules definition. Once you complete the definition, every item to which you've applied that rule will then be automatically updated to reflect the changes. CSS separate content from layout, which means that you can make editing changes without affecting formatting and vice versa.

- **CSS classified by location**
  One way to categorize styles is by the location where they are stored. An **external style sheet** is a single, separate file with a .css file extension that can be attached to one or all pages in a website. This type of style sheet determines the formatting for various page elements and can contain many individual styles. If you have an external style sheet with 10 styles, you would only need to create one file with 10 styles defined within it, rather than 10 separate style sheet files. You can then attach this style sheet file to all of the pages in the same website (or to pages in other websites) to apply all of the specific styles. **Internal style sheets** are in the code for an individual web page and can either be embedded or inline styles. An **embedded style** consists of code that is stored in a page's head content while an **inline style** is stored in a page's body content. While you are learning, you will create styles of each type. In a work environment, however, you will probably use external styles.

- **CSS classified by function**
  Another way to classify CSS is by their function. A **Class style** can be used to format any page element, such as a paragraph of text or an image. An **HTML style** is used to redefine an HTML tag, such as changing the color of a horizontal rule or the font size for a heading tag. An **Advanced** or **Compound style** is used to format combinations of page elements. For example, you could define an Advanced style that determines how all images are displayed inside a div tag.

- **The CSS Styles panel**
  You use the CSS Styles panel to create, edit, and apply rules. The panel has two views: All (Document) Mode and Current Selection Mode. Figure D-10 shows the CSS Styles panel in All (Document) Mode, which lists all attached and embedded styles. When you select a rule in the All Rules pane, that rule's properties appear in the Properties pane at the bottom of the panel. Figure D-11 shows the CSS Styles panel in Current Selection mode, which shows the properties for the page element at the current position of the insertion point. You can edit the properties for the rule in the Properties pane. The small pane between the Summary for Selection pane and the Properties pane in Current mode is called the Rules pane, which shows the location of the current selected rule in the open document.

Working with Text and Cascading Style Sheets

FIGURE D-10: **CSS Styles panel in All (Document) Mode**

Switch to All (Document) Mode button

External CSS styles

All Rules pane

Properties for selected style are displayed in Properties pane

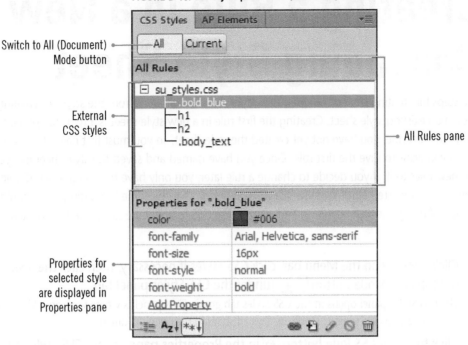

FIGURE D-11: **CSS Styles panel in Current Selection Mode**

Switch to Current Selection Mode button

Summary for Selection pane

The insertion point on the page is in a paragraph with the body_text rule applied

Rules pane

Properties for selected rule are displayed in Properties pane

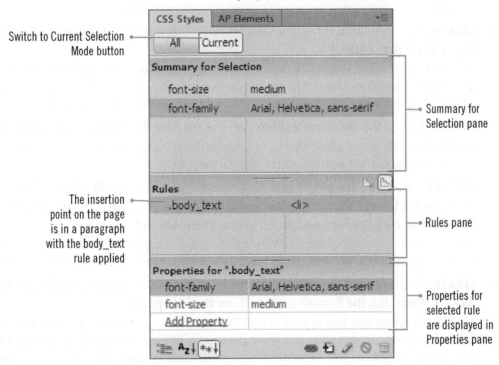

Using the CSS and HTML Property inspector

You apply CSS rules using either the CSS or HTML Property inspectors. You first select the element on the page, then apply a rule from the Property inspector. In the HTML Property inspector, you select a rule from the Class list box. In the CSS Property inspector, you select a rule from the Targeted Rule list box. You change back and forth between the two Property inspectors by clicking the HTML button **<> HTML** or CSS button **Bᴵ CSS**.

Working with Text and Cascading Style Sheets

Creating a Rule in a New Cascading Style Sheet

The steps for creating the first rule in a new style sheet are different from the steps for creating additional rules in an existing style sheet. Creating the first rule in a new style sheet is a two-step process. When you create the first rule, you have not yet created the style sheet, so you must first name the style sheet file in which you want to save the first rule. Once you have named and saved the style sheet file, you can then add new rules to it. If you decide to change a rule later, you only have to change the CSS rule and all the items will be updated automatically. You decide that the same formatting style should be applied to each of the spa service headings. You want to use CSS to apply the same rule to each item.

1. **Click Window on the Menu bar, click CSS Styles if necessary, then click the Switch to All (Document) Mode button** `All` **under the CSS Styles panel tab**

   The CSS Styles panel opens in the CSS Styles tab group. This panel is where you can add, delete, edit, and apply styles. All (Document) Mode displays all styles in the open document.

2. **Click the New CSS Rule button** 🔲 **in the Properties pane on the CSS Styles panel, click the Selector Type list arrow in the New CSS Rule dialog box, if necessary, to select Class (can apply to any HTML element), then type bold_blue in the Selector Name text box**

   The Class option creates a new custom rule that can apply to any HTML tag.

3. **Click the Rule Definition list arrow, click (New Style Sheet File), compare your screen to Figure D-12, then click OK**

   The Save Style Sheet File As dialog box opens, prompting you to name the Cascading Style Sheet file and store it in the website's root folder. The name of the new rule is bold_blue. The New Style Sheet File option makes the CSS style available for use in the entire website, not just the current document.

4. **Type su_styles in the File name text box (Win) or the Save As text box (Mac), then click Save**

   The CSS Rule Definition for bold_blue in su_styles.css dialog box opens. This dialog box allows you to choose attributes, such as font color and font size, for the CSS rule.

5. **Click the Font-family list arrow, click Arial, Helvetica, sans-serif; click the Font-size list arrow, click 14, leave the size measurement unit as px, click the Font-style list arrow, click normal; click the Font-weight list arrow, then click bold**

   The font-family, size, style, and weight settings are updated. Keeping the measurement at pixels (px) in the size measurement drop-down menu ensures that the text will be an absolute size when viewed in the browser.

6. **Click the Color box** 🔲 **to open the color picker, type #006, as shown in Figure D-13, click OK, then click the Refresh button** 🔁 **on the Files panel**

   The CSS rule named bold_blue appears in the CSS Styles panel, preceded by a period in the name. The Related Files toolbar displays under the file tab (Win) or file title bar (Mac) listing the style sheet filename su_styles.css. The Related Files toolbar, which displays the names of files related to the open document file, is used to quickly access files that are linked to the open document. The su_styles.css file appears in the file listing for the website, as shown in Figure D-14, with a different file extension from the HTML files. You may have to scroll down to see the su_styles.css file listed.

7. **Click the Show Code view button** `Code` **on the Document toolbar**

   The HTML code linking to the su_styles.css file appears in the Head section, as shown in Figure D-15. The bold_blue rule appears indented under the file su_styles.css in the CSS Styles panel.

8. **Click File on the Menu bar, then click Save All**

FIGURE D-12: Adding a new CSS Rule in the New CSS Rule dialog box

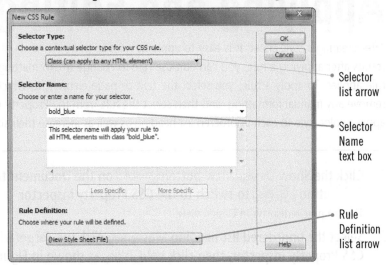

Selector list arrow

Selector Name text box

Rule Definition list arrow

FIGURE D-13: CSS Rule Definition for .bold_blue in su_styles.css dialog box

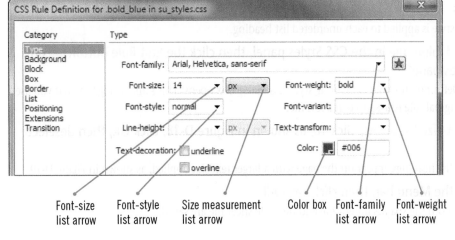

Font-size list arrow

Font-style list arrow

Size measurement list arrow

Color box

Font-family list arrow

Font-weight list arrow

FIGURE D-14: The Striped Umbrella site with the su_styles.css file listed

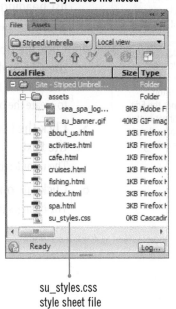

su_styles.css style sheet file

FIGURE D-15: Code view showing link to style sheet file

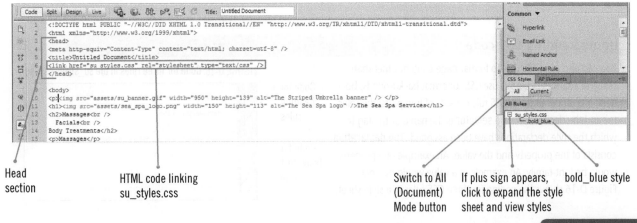

Head section

HTML code linking su_styles.css

Switch to All (Document) Mode button

If plus sign appears, click to expand the style sheet and view styles

bold_blue style

Working with Text and Cascading Style Sheets

Applying and Editing a Rule

After creating a style sheet, it is easy to apply its rules to page elements. If you are not satisfied with the results after applying a rule, you can edit the rule to change the formatting of all elements to which that rule applies. To apply a rule, you select the text or page element to which you want to apply the rule, remove any manual formatting, and then select the rule from the Property inspector. ▓▓▓▓ You want to apply a color style to each unordered list heading as well as increase their size to make them stand out.

STEPS

QUICK TIP

You can also click the Class list arrow in the HTML Property inspector to apply the bold_blue rule.

1. **Click the Show Design view button** `Design` **on the Document toolbar, then click the CSS button** `CSS` **to switch to the CSS Property inspector**

   The spa page redisplays in Design view.

2. **Select the unordered list heading Massages, click the Targeted Rule list arrow on the CSS Property inspector, then click bold_blue, as shown in Figure D-17**

   The bold_blue style is applied to the Massages heading. The Font-family, Font-size, Font-weight, Color, and Font-style text boxes on the Property inspector all reflect the bold_blue settings.

QUICK TIP

You can press [Ctrl][Y] (Win) or [command] [Y] (Mac) to redo (repeat) an action.

3. **Repeat Step 2 to apply the bold_blue style to the Facials and Body Treatment unordered list headings**

   The bold_blue style is applied to each unordered list heading.

QUICK TIP

If a rule is not selected, the Edit Rule button becomes the Edit Style Sheet button and opens the css file for editing.

4. **Click the bold_blue rule in the CSS Styles panel, then click the Edit Rule button** 🖉 **on the CSS Styles panel**

   The CSS Rule Definition for bold_blue in su_styles.css dialog box opens. This same dialog box that you used to create the original rule is used to edit a .css file.

5. **Click the Font-size list arrow, click 16, as shown in Figure D-18, click OK, then deselect the text**

   The unordered list headings appear on the page with a larger text size applied, as shown in Figure D-19.

6. **Click File on the Menu bar, then click Save All**

   The changes to both the spa document file and the style sheet file are saved.

Understanding CSS code

You can also use CSS rules to format page content other than text. For example, you can use CSS to format backgrounds, borders, lists, and images. A CSS rule consists of two parts: the selector and the declaration. The **selector** is the name or the tag to which the style declarations have been assigned. The **declaration** consists of the property and the value. An example of a property would be font-family. An example of a value would be Arial. Figure D-16 shows the coding for three CSS rules in a style sheet.

Code for heading rules

Code for .body_text rule

FIGURE D-16: **Code for three rules in the su_styles.css file**

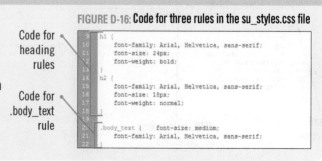

```
9   h1 {
10      font-family: Arial, Helvetica, sans-serif;
11      font-size: 24px;
12      font-weight: bold;
13  }
14  h2 {
15      font-family: Arial, Helvetica, sans-serif;
16      font-size: 18px;
17      font-weight: normal;
18  }
19
20  .body_text {    font-size: medium;
21      font-family: Arial, Helvetica, sans-serif;
22  }
```

FIGURE D-17: **Applying a rule to text**

Text is selected

CSS Property Inspector button

Targeted Rule list arrow

bold_blue rule

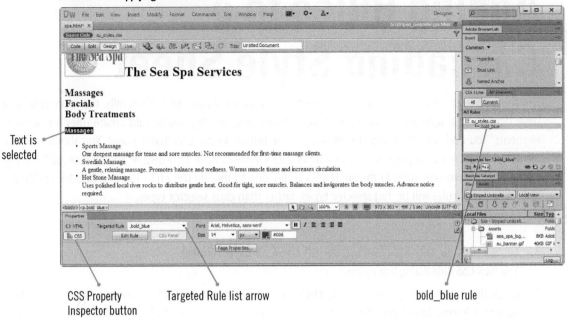

FIGURE D-18: **Editing the bold_blue rule**

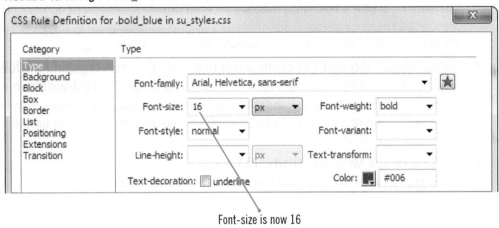

Font-size is now 16

FIGURE D-19: **Viewing text after editing the Font-size property**

Unordered list headings with larger font-size and color formatting applied

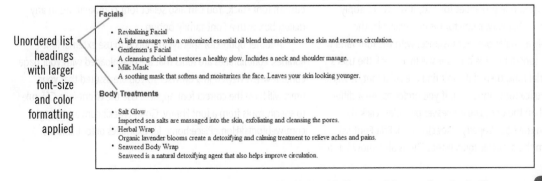

Working with Text and Cascading Style Sheets

Adding Rules to a Cascading Style Sheet

Once you have created a style sheet, it is easy to add additional rules to it. Generally, the more rules you have defined in a Style Sheet, the more time you can save. Ideally, you should create rules for all page elements. You add rules by using the New CSS Rule button in the CSS Styles panel. You should use the same style sheet for each page to ensure that all your elements have a consistent appearance. You decide to add two new rules in the su_styles.css file, one to modify the <h1> tag and one to modify the <h2> tag. These rules will be Tag selector types, rather than class selector types.

STEPS

1. **Click the** New CSS Rule button 🔳 **on the CSS Styles Panel**
   The New CSS Rule dialog box opens.

2. **Click the** Selector Type list arrow, **click** Tag (redefines an HTML element), **type** h1 **in the Selector Name text box, click the** Rule Definition list arrow, **click** su_styles.css, **as shown in Figure D-20, then click** OK
   The CSS Rule Definition for h1 in su_styles.css dialog box opens.

3. **Click the** Font-family list arrow, **click** Arial, Helvetica, sans-serif, **click the** Font-size list arrow, **click** 24, **click the** Font-weight list arrow, **then click** bold, **as shown in Figure D-21, then click** OK
   The font is set to a 24px, bold, Arial, Helvetica, sans-serif font-family. Notice that the heading "The Sea Spa Services" has changed appearance. Since it was originally formatted with the Heading 1 paragraph format, the new <h1> rule properties have been automatically applied to this heading.

   > **QUICK TIP**
   > If you click the insertion point within text or select text that has an applied rule, that rule appears in the Class list box in the HTML Property inspector, or the Targeted Rule list box in the CSS Property inspector.

4. **Repeat Steps 1 through 3 to create a rule to modify the** <h2> **tag using the following settings: Font-family:** Arial, Helvetica, sans-serif; **Font-size:** 18; **Font-weight:** normal
   The headings "Massages", "Facials", and "Body Treatments" have changed appearance. Since they were formatted with a Heading 2 paragraph format, the new <h2> rule properties have been automatically applied, as shown in Figure D-22.

5. **Click** File **on the Menu bar, then click** Save All
   The changes are saved to both the spa document file and the style sheet file.

Using font combinations in styles

When you are setting rule properties for text, it is wise to apply font combinations. That way, if one font is not available, the browser will apply a similar one. For instance, with the font family "Arial, Helvetica, sans-serif," the browser will first check the user's system for the Arial font, then, if it can't find the Arial font, it will look for the Helvetica font, and so on. If you prefer to use a different set of fonts than the ones Dreamweaver provides, click the Font list arrow on the CSS Property inspector, click Edit Font list, then choose from the available fonts listed. This is also known as a custom font stack. You can also select font combinations in any dialog box with a Font-family option.

Another option for specifying fonts is to use external font libraries. Font libraries are fonts that are downloaded with your page content when viewed in a browser so you are assured that your users will have the correct font applied. Use the @font-face CSS rule to specify fonts from a font library. Go to typekit.com and google.com/webfonts#HomePlace:home for examples of font libraries.

FIGURE D-20: Creating a new CSS rule to define the <h1> rule

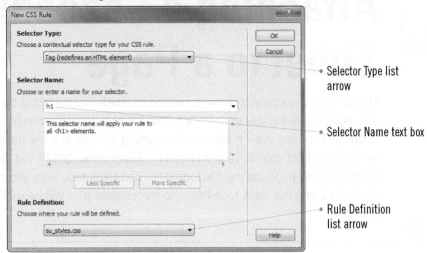

- Selector Type list arrow
- Selector Name text box
- Rule Definition list arrow

FIGURE D-21: Setting the properties for the <h1> rule

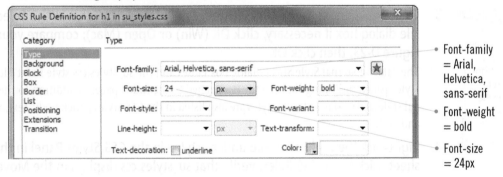

- Font-family = Arial, Helvetica, sans-serif
- Font-weight = bold
- Font-size = 24px

FIGURE D-22: New <h1> and <h2> properties applied to headings

<h1> rule properties applied

<h2> rule properties applied

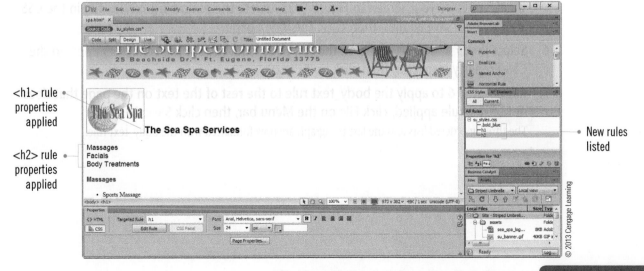

- New rules listed

© 2013 Cengage Learning

Working with Text and Cascading Style Sheets

Attaching a Cascading Style Sheet to a Page

After creating an external style sheet, you should attach it to the rest of the pages in your website to utilize the full benefit. Being able to define a rule and apply it to page elements across all the pages of your site means that you can make hundreds of formatting changes in a few minutes. Style sheets create a more uniform look from page to page and lead to cleaner code. ██████ You decide to attach the su_styles.css file to the home page and use it to format the paragraph text. Since you already have an internal style on the index page, you want to delete it so the external style will be used to format the paragraph text instead.

STEPS

QUICK TIP

(Win) To switch between open documents, click the tab for the document you wish to view, or press [Ctrl][Tab].

1. **Open the index.html page**

   Since an external style sheet has yet to be linked to the index page, the external style sheet is not listed in the CSS Styles panel. In order to use an external style sheet with other pages in the website, you must first attach the style sheet file to each page.

2. **Click the Attach Style Sheet button 📎 on the CSS Styles panel**

   The Attach External Style Sheet dialog box opens.

QUICK TIP

If you don't see your styles listed, click the plus sign (Win) or right-pointing triangle (Mac) next to su_styles.css in the CSS Styles panel.

3. **Click Browse next to the File/URL text box, click su_styles.css in the Select Style Sheet File dialog box if necessary, click OK (Win) or Open (Mac); compare your screen to Figure D-23, then click OK**

   The Attach External Style Sheet dialog box closes and the su_styles.css style sheet file appears in the CSS Styles panel, indicating that the file is attached to the index page. In addition to the su_styles.css external style sheet, some internal styles are also listed in the CSS Styles panel: body_text, nav_bar, small_text, and body.

4. **Right-click the body_text rule under <style> in the CSS Styles Panel in the internal style sheet, click Move CSS Rules, verify that su_styles.css displays in the Move to External Style Sheet dialog box, as shown in Figure D-24, then click OK to close the Move to External Style Sheet dialog box**

   The internal body_text style is moved to the external style sheet, so it can now be used to format the text on all other pages in the website.

5. **Repeat Step 4 to move the nav_bar, small_text, and body rules to the external style sheet, compare your screen to Figure D-25, delete the remaining <style> tag in the CSS Styles panel, save all files, then close the index page**

6. **Select the first unordered list on the spa page, click the Targeted Rule text box on the CSS Property inspector, then click body_text.**

7. **Repeat Step 6 to apply the body_text rule to the rest of the text on the page that does not have a rule applied, click File on the Menu bar, then click Save All**

   The three unordered lists and the last paragraph are now formatted with the body_text rule.

FIGURE D-23: Attaching the su_styles.css file to the index page

Name of external style sheet to attach to the page

Browse button

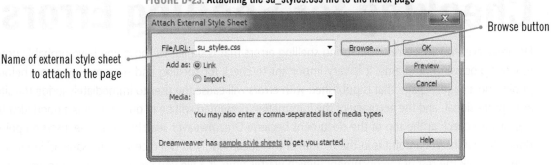

FIGURE D-24: The Move to External Style Sheet dialog box

su_styles.css is selected for the destination file

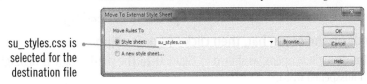

FIGURE D-25: The internal rules moved to the external style sheet

Select and delete this tag in Step 5

Internal rules are moved to the external style sheet

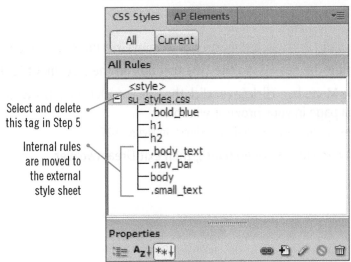

Design Matters

The evolution of CSS3

The use of Cascading Style Sheets has evolved over the years from CSS Level 1 to the present CSS Level 3. Cascading Style Sheets revisions are referenced by "levels" rather than "versions." Each new level builds on the previous level. CSS Level 1 is obsolete today. CSS Level 2 is still used, but CSS Level 3 is the latest W3C (World Wide Web Consortium) standard. With CSS3, several properties are available that promote website accessibility such as the @font-face rule. This rule in CSS2 provided the ability to embed fonts in documents using the WOFF format. WOFF stands for Web Open Font Format and was proposed to the W3C to be a standard format for all web browsers to use. Currently, Firefox Version 3.6 and up, Internet Explorer Version 9 and up, Google Chrome Version 5 and up, and Safari Version 5.1 and up support the WOFF format. The @font-face rule now is used to download a specific font from a font library to render text on a web page if the user does not have that font installed on their system. Examples of font libraries are typekit.com. and google.com/webfonts. For more information about CSS3, go to w3.org/TR/CSS/.

Checking for Spelling Errors

Dreamweaver has a feature for checking spelling errors that is similar to those you have probably used in word processing programs. It is very important to check for spelling and grammatical errors before publishing a page. A page that is published with errors will cause the user to immediately judge the site as unprofessional, and the accuracy of the information presented will be in question. It is a good idea to start a spell check at the top of the document because Dreamweaver searches from the insertion point down. If your insertion point is in the middle of the document, you will receive a message asking if you want to check the rest of the document, which wastes time. If a file you create in a word processor will be imported into Dreamweaver, make sure to run a spell check in the word processing program before you import it. ⬛⬛⬛ You want to check the spelling on the spa page and correct any errors.

STEPS

QUICK TIP
You can also press [Ctrl][Home] to move the insertion point to the top of the document. (Mac users may not have a [home] key depending on their keyboard.)

1. **Place the insertion point in front of The Sea Spa Services heading**

2. **Click Commands on the Menu bar, then click Check Spelling**

   The Check Spelling dialog box opens, as shown in Figure D-26. The word *masage* is highlighted on the spa page, indicating a misspelled word.

3. **Click massage. in the Suggestions list if necessary, click Change, then click Ignore if it stops on any other words that you know are spelled correctly**

   The Check Spelling dialog box closes and a Dreamweaver dialog box opens stating that the Spell check is complete.

4. **Click OK**

   The Dreamweaver dialog box closes and the spa page redisplays with the word *massage* spelled correctly.

5. **Add the page title The Sea Spa to the Title text box on the Document toolbar**

6. **Click File on the Menu bar, click Save, click the Preview/Debug in browser icon 🌐, then preview the spa page in your browser window**

   The spa page opens in your browser window as shown in Figure D-27.

7. **Close your browser, close all open pages, then exit Dreamweaver**

Using Find and Replace

Another useful editing command is Find and Replace, which is located on the Edit menu. You can use this command to make individual or global text edits in either Design or Code view. It is similar to Find and Replace commands in word processing programs, except that there is an added advantage in Dreamweaver. You can use Find and Replace to easily search through code if you are trying to locate and correct coding errors. For example, if you want to find a tag that formats a font with a specific color, you can search for that color number in the code. If you are searching for internal links that are incorrectly set as absolute links, you can enter the search term *src = "file"* to help you to locate them. You will learn more about absolute links in Unit F.

Working with Text and Cascading Style Sheets

FIGURE D-26: **Using the Check Spelling command**

Spa page

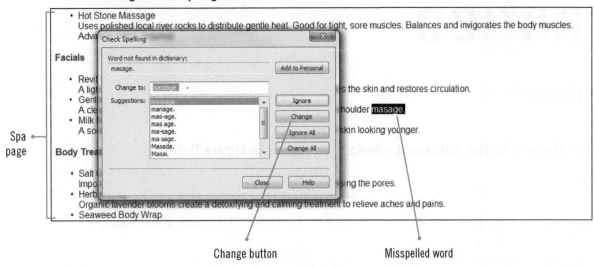

Change button

Misspelled word

FIGURE D-27: **The finished product**

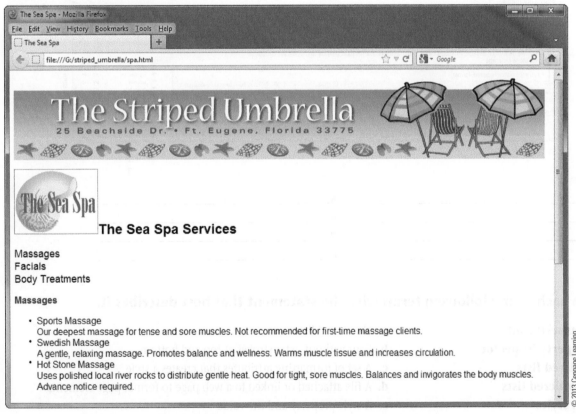

© 2013 Cengage Learning

Practice

Concepts Review

Label each element in the Document window, as shown in Figure D-28.

FIGURE D-28

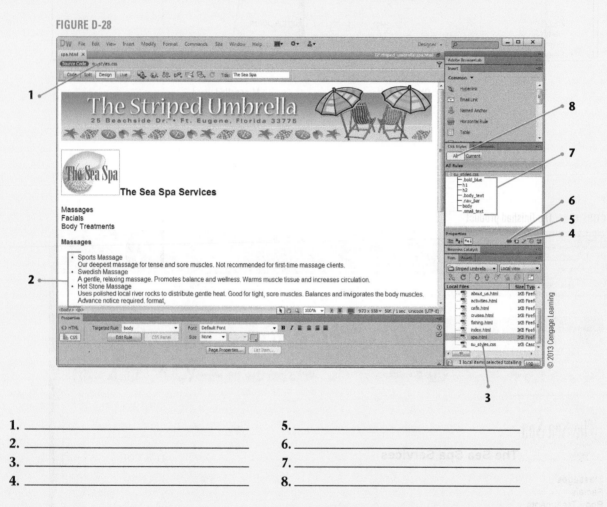

© 2013 Cengage Learning

1. _____
2. _____
3. _____
4. _____

5. _____
6. _____
7. _____
8. _____

Match each of the following terms with the statement that best describes it.

9. **Sans-serif font**

10. **Property inspector**

11. **Ordered lists**

12. **Unordered lists**

13. **CSS styles**

14. **CSS Rule**

15. **External style sheet**

16. **Selector**

17. **Declaration**

18. **Serif font**

a. Numbered lists

b. Font without extra strokes at top and bottom

c. A set of formatting attributes that creates a style

d. A file attached or linked to a web page to format page elements

e. A style property and the value

f. Bulleted lists

g. A panel used for formatting page elements

h. The name or tag to which style declarations have been assigned

i. Font with extra strokes at the top and bottom

j. Sets of formatting attributes to format page elements

Select the best answer from the following list of choices.

19. The button used to select color is:

a.

b.

c.

d.

20. External CSS files are saved with the filename extension:

a. .css

b. .cas

c. .stl

d. .csf

21. A CSS Class Style name in the Styles panel is preceded by a:

a. pound sign.

b. period.

c. dash.

d. number.

22. Styles that are part of the head content of a web page are called:

a. external styles.

b. embedded styles.

c. inline Styles.

d. HTML styles.

23. The type of style used to redefine an HTML tag in the New CSS Rule dialog box is called:

a. an Advanced style.

b. a Class style.

c. a Tag style.

d. a Compound style.

Skills Review

Important: *If you did not create this website in Unit B and maintain it in Unit C, you will need to create a local site root folder for this website and define the website using files your instructor will provide. See the "Read This Before You Begin" section of this book for more detailed instructions.*

1. **Create a new page.**
   a. Start Dreamweaver.
   b. Open the Blooms & Bulbs website.
   c. Create a new HTML file and save it as **tips.html** in the Blooms & Bulbs website, overwriting the existing blank file.
   d. Add the page title **Blooms & Bulbs** in the title text box.
   e. Insert the banner from your website assets folder at the top of the page, add appropriate alternate text, then enter a paragraph break after the banner.
   f. Insert the file butterfly.jpg from the assets folder in the drive and folder where you store your Unit D Data Files, then add appropriate alternate text.

2. **Import text.**
   a. With the insertion point to the right of the butterfly image, import (Win) or copy and paste (Mac) the Word document gardening_tips.doc from the drive and folder where you store your Unit D Data Files.
   b. Use the Clean Up Word HTML command on the tips page, then save the tips page.

3. **Set text properties.**
   a. Select the Seasonal Gardening Checklist heading, then format the text with the Heading 1 format.
   b. Select the Basic Gardening Tips heading and format it with a Heading 1 format.
   c. Save your work.

4. **Create an unordered list.**
   a. Select the items under the Seasonal Gardening Checklist.
   b. Format the list of items as an unordered list. (*Hint*: Be sure *not* to select the return at the end of the last line or you will accidentally create a fifth item.)
   c. Select the items under Basic Gardening Tips, then format them as an ordered list. (*Hint*: If you have extra line breaks, you will need to delete them to have only six items in your list.)

5. **Understand Cascading Style Sheets.**
   a. Using a word processor or piece of paper, list the types of CSS categorized by their location in a website.
   b. Using a word processor or piece of paper, list the types of CSS categorized by their function in a website.

6. **Create a Style in a new Cascading Style Sheet.**
   a. Open the CSS Styles panel, if necessary.
   b. Create a new Class style named **bold_gray** in a new style sheet file.
   c. Save the new style sheet file with the name **blooms_styles.css** in the blooms folder.
   d. Set the Font-family for the bold_gray style as Arial, Helvetica, sans-serif.
   e. Set the Font-size as small, the Font-weight as bold, then the Color as #333.
   f. Save all files.

7. **Apply and edit a style.**
   a. Apply the bold_gray style to the words *Fall*, *Winter*, *Spring*, and *Summer*.
   b. Edit the style to increase the text size to medium.
   c. Save all files.

Skills Review (continued)

8. Add styles to a Cascading Style Sheet.

a. Create a new Tag selector for the Heading 1 tag in the blooms_styles.css file.

b. Set the Font-family as Arial, Helvetica, sans-serif.

c. Set the Font-size as large, the Font-style as normal, then the Color as #000.

d. Save all files.

9. Attach a Cascading Style Sheet to a page.

a. Open the index page in the Blooms & Bulbs website.

b. Attach the blooms_styles.css file to the index page.

c. Move each of the internal styles to the external style sheet, delete the remaining <style> tag, then save all files and close the index page.

d. On the tips page, apply the body_text rule to all of the text on the page that is not formatted with either a heading format or CSS rule, then save your work.

10. Check for spelling errors.

a. Run a spell check on the tips page, correcting any misspelled words found, then save your work.

b. Preview the page in your browser, then compare your screen to Figure D-29.

c. Close your browser, then Exit (Win) or Quit (Mac) Dreamweaver.

FIGURE D-29

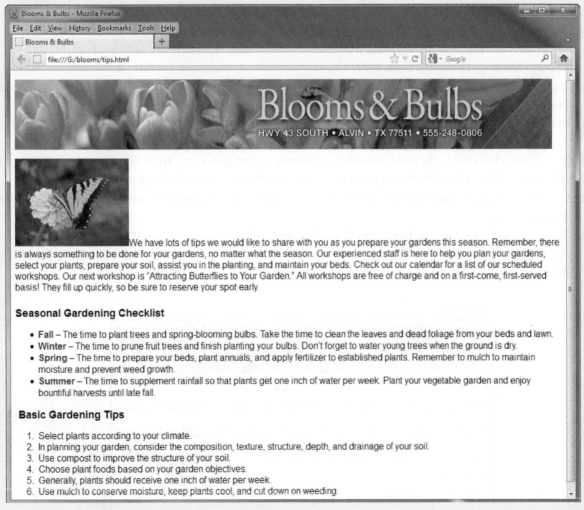

© 2013 Cengage Learning
Original photos courtesy of Sherry Bishop

Important: *If you did not create the following websites in Unit B and maintain them in Unit C, you will need to create a local site root folder for the websites in the following exercises and define the websites using files your instructor will provide. See the "Read This Before You Begin" section in this book for more detailed instructions.*

Independent Challenge 1

You have been hired to create a website for a river expedition company named Rapids Transit, located on the Buffalo River in Arkansas. In addition to renting canoes, kayaks, and rafts, they have several types of cabin rentals for overnight stays. River guides are available, if requested, to accompany clients on float trips. The clients range from beginners to experienced floaters. The owner's name is Mike Andrew. Mike has asked you to add a page to the site that will describe the lodge, cabins, and tents that are available to their customers.

a. Start Dreamweaver.

b. Open the Rapids Transit website.

c. Open the file dwd_1.html from the drive and folder where you store your Unit D Data Files, then save it as **lodging.html** in the Rapids Transit website, replacing the existing file, but not updating links.

d. Close dwd_1.html, then verify that the rapids banner path is set to the assets folder in the website.

e. Create an unordered list from the four types of lodging and their rates.

f. Create a new Tag Selector rule that modifies the Heading 1 tag, then save it in a new style sheet file named **rapids_transit.css** using the following settings: Font-family, Arial, Helvetica, sans-serif; Font-size, 16; Font-weight, bold; Color, #003.

g. Apply the Heading 1 format to the navigation bar text and the first sentence on the page.

h. Create a second Tag selector rule to modify the Heading 2 tag in the rapids_transit.css style sheet.

i. Format the <h2> rule with the following settings: Font-family Arial, Helvetica, sans-serif; Font-size 14; Font-style normal; Font-weight bold; and Color #003.

j. Open the index page, attach the rapids_transit.css file, move the internal body_text rule to the external style sheet, then delete the <style> tag in the CSS Styles panel.

k. Save all files, then on the lodging page, apply the Heading 2 format to the text "Rates are as follows:" and the body_text rule to the rest of the text on the page that is not formatted with a heading format.

l. Create a new class style in the rapids_transit.css style sheet named **contact_info** using Arial, Helvetica sans-serif; italic style; size 14, color #000; then apply it to the contact information on the index page.

m. Apply the Heading 1 format to the navigation bar text on the index page, then save your work using the Save All command on the File menu.

n. Preview the index page in your browser window, click the Lodging link, compare your screen to Figure D-30, close your browser window, close all files, then exit Dreamweaver. (*Hint:* Depending on whether you have clicked other links, your link colors may not match the links in the figure.)

FIGURE D-30

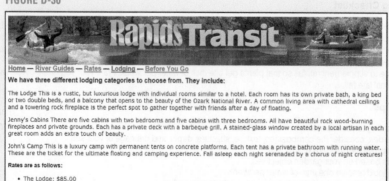

Independent Challenge 2

You are a marketing specialist for a travel outfitter named TripSmart. TripSmart specializes in travel products and services. In addition to selling luggage and accessories, they sponsor trips and offer travel advice. Your company is designing a new website and your job is to update the newsletter page on the current website with some timely travel tips.

a. Start Dreamweaver, then open the TripSmart website.

b. Open the file dwd_2.html and save it as **newsletter.html** in the TripSmart website, replacing the existing file, but not updating links, then close dwd_2.html.

c. Verify that the banner path is set to the assets folder of the website.

d. Create an ordered list from the 10 items on the page, starting with Be organized.

e. Create a new Tag Selector rule to modify the Heading 1 format, then save it in a new style sheet named **tripsmart_styles.css**.

f. Choose a font, size, style, color, and weight of your choice for the <h1> rule.

g. Apply the Heading 1 format to the Ten Tips for Stress-Free Travel paragraph heading.

h. Type **TripSmart - Serving all your travel needs** in the document title text box, then save your work.

i. Open the index page, delete the horizontal rule, attach the style sheet, then move the three internal rules to the external style sheet and delete the <style> tag left from the internal styles in the CSS Styles panel.

j. Create another class style in the tripsmart_styles.css style sheet named **contact_info** with settings of your choice, apply it to the contact information on the page, save your work, then close the page.

k. Apply the body_text rule to the two remaining paragraphs without styles applied, preview the newsletter page in your browser window, then compare it to Figure D-31 as an example for a possible solution.

l. Close your browser, close the file, then exit Dreamweaver.

FIGURE D-31

Our staff recently conducted a contest to determine ten top travel tips for stress-free travel. We compiled over forty great tips, but the following were selected as the winners. We hope you will find them useful for your next trip!

Ten Tips for Stress-Free Travel

1. Be organized.
   Make a list of what you want to pack in each bag and check it as you pack. Take this inventory with you in the event your bags are lost or delayed. Then use the list again when you repack, to make sure you haven't left anything behind.
2. Carry important information with you.
   Keep your important travel information in easy reach at all times. Include a list of your flight numbers, confirmation numbers for your travel and hotel reservations, and any car rentals. And don't forget printouts of your itinerary and electronic tickets. Remember to bring your passport, and keep a photocopy of it in another piece of baggage. Be sure to have copies of prescriptions, emergency phone numbers, telephone numbers and addresses of friends and relatives, complete lists of medications, and credit card information. It's not a bad idea to email this information to yourself as a backup if you will have email access.
3. Pack smartly.
   You know the old saying: lay out everything on your bed you plan to take with you, then remove half of it. Pack the remainder and carry your bags around the block once to make sure you can handle them yourself. If in doubt, leave it out! Use packing cubes or zip-top bags to organize your personal items, such as underwear and socks. Make distinctive-looking luggage tags with your name and address for easy identification, and be sure to include the same information inside your luggage.
4. Include basic medical necessities.
   Besides your prescription drugs, take a basic first aid kit with the basics: bandages, anti-nausea medications, anti-diarrhea medications, aspirin, antibiotics, and prescription drugs.
5. Wear comfortable shoes.
   Blisters can ruin a wonderful trip. Wear comfortable shoes and socks. Your priority should be comfortable, dry, warm feet — not fashion. Don't buy new shoes without breaking them in first.

Independent Challenge 3

Dr. Chappel is a government historian who is conducting research on the separation of church and state. He is using the Library of Congress website to find relevant information. Write your answers to the questions below on paper or using your word processor.

a. Connect to the Internet, then go to The Library of Congress website at www.loc.gov, shown in Figure D-32.

b. Is the content well organized?

c. What font or fonts are used on the pages for the main text? Are the same fonts used consistently on the other pages in the website?

d. Are there any ordered or unordered lists on the website? If so, how are they used?

e. View the source to see if CSS styles are used on the pages in the website.

f. Use a search engine to find another website of interest. Compare and contrast the use of text formatting on this site to that used on the Library of Congress website.

FIGURE D-32

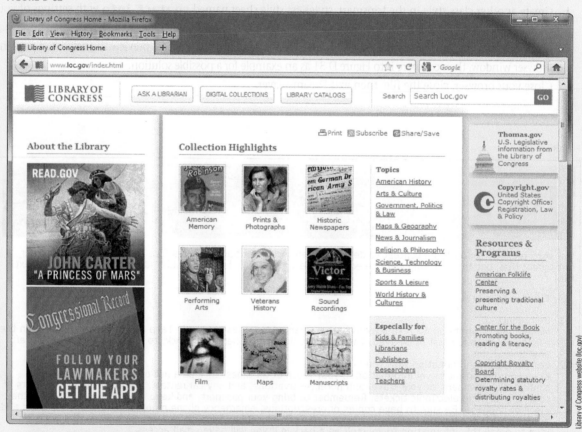

Library of Congress website (loc.gov)

Real Life Independent Challenge

This assignment will continue to build on the personal website that you created in Unit B and modified in Unit C. You have created and developed your index page. In this lesson, you will work with one of the other pages in your website.

a. Consult your wireframe, then decide which page you would like to develop in this lesson.

b. Create content for this page, then format the text attractively on the page using settings for font, size, text color, style, and alignment.

c. Format some of the text on the page as either an ordered or unordered list.

d. Create a style sheet with a minimum of two rules, then apply a rule to all text on the page.

e. Attach the style sheet to any of the pages you have already developed, then apply rules to all text.

f. Save the file, then preview the pages in your browser window.

After you are satisfied with your work, verify the following:

a. Each completed page has a page title.

b. All links work correctly.

c. The completed pages appear correctly using at least two screen resolutions.

d. All images are properly placed with a path to the assets folder of the website.

e. A style sheet is used to format all text.

Visual Workshop

Your company has been selected to design a website for a catering business named Carolyne's Creations. Open the Carolyne's Creations website, open the file dwd_3.html, then save it as **recipes.html** in the Carolyne's Creations website, replacing the original file, and not updating the links. Close dwd_3.html, then format the page using styles so it looks similar to Figure D-33. (The text may wrap slightly different depending on the size of your browser window.) Save the file pie.jpg from the drive and folder where you store your Unit D Data Files to your website assets folder (*Hint*: Use the following styles and settings to match the figure, and save them in a CSS file named cc_styles.css. The small_text rule was not used on the recipes page, but for the copyright and last updated statements on the index page.)

.nav_bar	.body_text	.small_text
Font-family: Arial, Helvetica, sans-serif	Font-family: Arial, Helvetica, sans-serif	Font-family: Arial, Helvetica, sans-serif
Font-size: large	Font-size: medium	Font-size: small
h1	**h2**	**.ingredients_list**
Font-family: Verdana, Geneva, sans-serif	Font-family: Verdana, Geneva, sans-serif	Font-family: Arial, Helvetica, sans-serif
Font-size: 18px	Font-size: 16px	Font-size: medium
Font-weight: bold	Font-weight: bold	Text-indent: 30px
Color: #333	Color: #333	List style-type: none

If you have not maintained this website from the previous unit, then contact your instructor for assistance.

FIGURE D-33

Home | Shop | Classes | Catering | Recipes

Caramel Coconut Pie

This is one of our most requested desserts. It is simple, elegant, and refreshing. It is easy to make in advance, because you keep it frozen until just before serving. It makes two pies — one to eat and one to give away!

Ingredients:

¼ cup butter
7 oz. dried coconut
½ cup chopped pecans
1 package (8 oz.) cream cheese, softened
1 can (14 oz.) sweetened condensed milk
1 container (16 oz.) whipped topping, thawed
1 jar (12 oz.) caramel ice cream topping
2 pie shells (9 in.), baked

Using and Managing Images

Web pages with images are more interesting than pages with just text. You can position images on your web pages, then resize them, add borders, and customize the amount of space around them. You can also use images as a web page, table, or CSS layout block background. In this unit you learn how to incorporate images into a website and how to manage them effectively using the Assets panel. 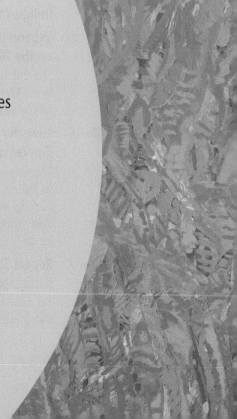 A photographer recently did a photo shoot of The Striped Umbrella property for some new brochures. You decide to incorporate several of the images on the about_us page so that the beauty of the resort comes across.

OBJECTIVES

Insert an image

Align an image

Enhance an image

Use alternate text and set Accessibility preferences

View the Assets panel

Insert a background image

Delete image files from a website

Create and find images for a website

Examine copyright rules

Inserting an Image

Images you import into a website are automatically added to the Assets panel. The **Assets panel**, located with the other panels on the right side of your workspace, lists the assets of the website, such as images and colors. As you add images to a web page, the page **download time** (the time it takes to transfer the file to a user's computer) increases. Pages that download slowly discourage users from staying on the site. To add an image to a page, you can either use the Insert, Image command on the Menu bar, use the Images button in the Common category on the Insert panel, or drag an image from the Assets panel onto the page. You want to place several photos of the resort on the about_us web page and check the file size of each in the Assets panel.

STEPS

TROUBLE

Your download time shown may vary according to the Connection Speed preferences set for your Status bar. To change your settings, click Edit (Win) or Dreamweaver (Mac) on the Menu bar, click Preferences, then click Status Bar.

1. **Start Dreamweaver, switch to Design view if necessary, open The Striped Umbrella website, open dwe_1.html from the drive and folder where you store your Unit E Data Files, save it as about_us.html in the striped_umbrella root folder, overwriting the existing file and not updating the links, then close dwe_1.html**

   The about_us page displays in Design view in your workspace. The Status bar displays the download time for the current web page, as shown Figure E-1.

2. **Click the Attach Style Sheet button** [icon] **in the CSS Styles panel, attach the su_styles.css style sheet, apply the nav_bar rule to the menu bar, the Heading 1 paragraph format to "Welcome guests!", and the body_text rule to all of the paragraph text on the page**

   The style sheet for the website is attached to the about_us page, and three rules are applied to the menu bar, heading, and two paragraphs.

3. **Click to the left of the word *When* in the first paragraph to place the insertion point, select the Common category on the Insert panel if necessary, scroll down and click the Images list arrow on the Insert panel, then click Image**

   The Select Image Source dialog box opens. This is the same dialog box you have been using to copy images from the Data Files folder to your site assets folder when you save new pages with images.

QUICK TIP

The Image Tag Accessibility Attributes dialog box contains Dreamweaver accessibility features, which you will learn about later in the unit.

4. **Navigate to the drive and folder where you store your Unit E Data Files, double-click club_house.jpg from the assets folder, type Club House as the Alternate text in the Image Tag Accessibility Attributes dialog box if prompted, then click OK**

5. **Expand the assets folder in the Files panel, if necessary, then click the Refresh Button** [icon] **on the Files panel toolbar if necessary**

   The club house image appears at the beginning of the first paragraph, as shown in Figure E-2. As indicated in the Files panel list, the club house image is located in the website assets folder. This is the location that will be used to load the image in the browser when the page is viewed.

QUICK TIP

You need to select club_house.jpg to see the thumbnail.

6. **Save the file, click the Assets panel tab, click the Images button** [icon] **on the Assets panel if necessary, then click** [icon] **at the bottom of the Assets panel, if necessary**

   The three images you added to The Striped Umbrella website—club_house.jpg, sea_spa_logo.jpg, and su_banner.gif—are listed in the Assets panel. When the Images button is selected, the Assets panel displays the images in the current website which, as shown in Figure E-3, is split into two panes. The lower window lists all of the images in the website, while the top window displays a thumbnail of the image currently selected in the list. The Dimensions column lists the height and width of each image.

TROUBLE

If the file names don't appear in the Files or Assets panels, click the Refresh button [icon], or click [icon] while you hold down the [Ctrl] key.

7. **Repeat Steps 3 and 4 to insert the boardwalk.png image at the beginning of the second paragraph, if prompted use Boardwalk to the beach as alternate text, then save your work**

   The boardwalk image appears on the page at the beginning of the second paragraph and boardwalk.png is added to the list of images in the Assets panel. The Assets panel lists the four images shown in Figure E-4.

FIGURE E-1: Status bar displaying page download time

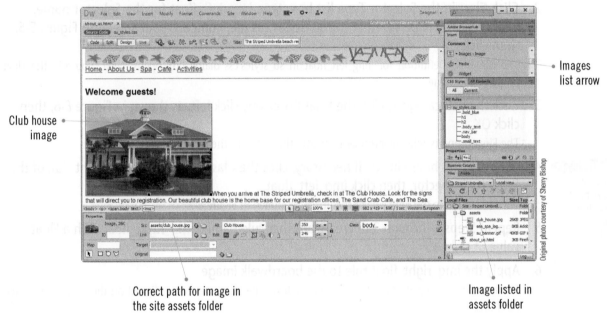

provides a safe route to the beach for both our guests and the native vegetation. The sea oats and other flora are tender. Please do not step on them or pick them. A lifeguard is on duty from 9:00 a.m. until sunset. Check the flag each time you head for the beach for the status of current swimming conditions and advisories. Jellyfish can be a problem at times, so be careful when you are walking along the beach, especially as the tide is retreating from high tide. We have beach chairs, umbrellas, and towels available to our guests. Check with the attendant on duty. Water, juices, and soft drinks are also available for purchase at the end of the boardwalk. Don't forget your sunglasses, hat, and sunscreen! A sunburn is sure way to ruin a nice vacation. The gift shop in The Club House is a

Your screen size
might differ

Page download time (yours
might differ, depending on
connection speed)

FIGURE E-2: About_us page with image inserted

Club house
image

Correct path for image in
the site assets folder

Images
list arrow

Image listed in
assets folder

FIGURE E-3: Assets panel listing for The Striped
Umbrella website

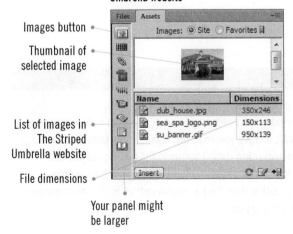

Images button

Thumbnail of
selected image

List of images in
The Striped
Umbrella website

File dimensions

Your panel might
be larger

FIGURE E-4: Assets panel with boardwalk.png
image included

Four images
now listed

Using and Managing Images

Aligning an Image

Like text, images can be positioned on the page in relation to other page elements. Positioning an image is called **aligning** the image. Use CSS to align images. You can use a global rule to modify the <img> tag, or you can create separate rules for individual images. When you first place an image on a page, it has the **Default** alignment which aligns the bottom of the image with the text **baseline**—the bottom of a line of text, not including descending portions of characters such as y or g. You should experiment with CSS rule properties to find the best alignment for your images. ██████ After experimenting with several alignment options, you decide to stagger the alignment of the images on the page to make it appear more balanced.

STEPS

1. **Click the New CSS Rule button ⊞ in the CSS Styles panel**

   The New CSS Rule dialog box opens. You will create a new rule to align images to the left of other page content.

2. **Click Class in the Selector Type list box, type img_left_float for the Selector name, verify that it will be saved in the su_styles.css file, compare your screen to Figure E-5, then click OK**

   The CSS Rule Definition for .img_left_float in su_styles.css dialog box opens. Next, you add the Float property and value.

3. **Click the Box category, click the Float list arrow, click left, as shown in Figure E-6, then click OK**

   The Float property tells the browser to "float" the image to the left of other page content.

QUICK TIP

You can also right-click an image, point to CSS Styles, then click the rule you want to apply.

4. **Click the club house image if necessary, click the Class list arrow on the right side of the Property inspector, then click img_left_float**

   The text moves to the right side of the image, as shown in Figure E-7.

5. **Repeat Steps 1 through 3 to create another rule named img_right_float with a Float value of right**

6. **Apply the img_right_float rule to the boardwalk image**

   The boardwalk image floats to the right of the text. The images are now aligned on the page in staggered positions.

7. **Click File, Save All to save your work**

Design Matters

Using dynamic images

To make a page even more interesting, you can place images on the page that change frequently, such as a group of several images that are set to automatically cycle on and off the page, called **dynamic images**. You can use dynamic images to display multiple items with a similar layout. For example, a website for a retail store might display images of current sale items in one window on a web page, one item at a time. To insert dynamic images, you must first create a Spry Data Set to store the images using the [+] button in the Bindings panel. You then insert the images on the page using the Data sources option, rather than the File system option, in the Select Image Source dialog box.

FIGURE E-5: New CSS Rule dialog box

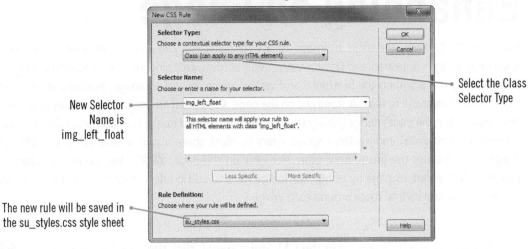

Select the Class Selector Type

New Selector Name is img_left_float

The new rule will be saved in the su_styles.css style sheet

FIGURE E-6: CSS Rule Definition for img_left_float in su_styles.css dialog box

Select the Box category

Select the left Float value

FIGURE E-7: Club house image with img_left_float rule applied

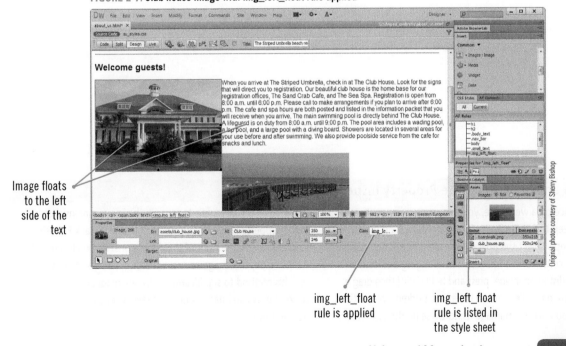

Image floats to the left side of the text

img_left_float rule is applied

img_left_float rule is listed in the style sheet

Original photos courtesy of Sherry Bishop

Enhancing an Image

After you select, place, and align an image on a web page, you can enhance its appearance. You can improve an image's appearance in Dreamweaver using borders, cropping, resizing, adjusting its brightness and contrast, and adjusting the horizontal and vertical space around an image. **Borders** are like frames that surround an image to make it stand out on the page. **Cropping** an image removes part of the image, both visually (on the page) and physically (the file size). A cropped image is smaller and takes less time to download. **Horizontal** and **vertical space** refers to blank space above, below, or on the sides of an image that separates the image from other elements on the page.  You decide to enhance the images on the about_us page by using your image rules to add borders around the images, and adjust the horizontal and vertical space around each image.

STEPS

1. Click the img_left_float rule in the CSS Styles panel, click the Edit Rule button 🖉, click the Border Category, enter the rule properties shown in Figure E-8, then click OK

2. Repeat Step 1 to add a border to the img_right_float rule
   Both images now have a thin border around them.

3. Edit the img_left_float rule again to add vertical and horizontal space by unchecking the "Same for all" check box under Margin in the Box category, then setting the Box Right Margin to 10 px as shown in Figure E-9, then click OK
   The text is more evenly wrapped around the image and is easier to read, because it is not so close to the edge of the image.

4. Using Step 3 as a guide, add a border and a 10 px left margin to the img_right_float rule, then compare your screen to Figure E-10

5. Save your work, open the spa page, then apply the img_left_float rule to the spa logo
   The headings wrap to the right side of the spa logo and look much better on the page.

6. Click File, Save All, to save all files, then close the spa page

> **QUICK TIP**
> You can use the Brightness and Contrast ◑, Crop ◳, and Sharpen △ buttons to slightly adjust images. To perform more complicated adjustments, such as significantly resizing an image, click the Edit button **Ps** to open the image in an editing program such as Adobe Photoshop or Fireworks if they are installed on your computer. Your Edit button will differ in appearance according to your default image editor.

Resizing an image using the Property inspector

To save space on a web page, you can crop an image. If you prefer to keep the entire image, you can resize it on the page instead. Simply select the image, then drag a selection handle toward the center of the image. Since dragging a selection handle can distort an image, press and hold [Shift] then drag a corner selection handle to retain the image's original proportions. (You can also enlarge an image using these methods.) After you drag an image handle to resize it, the image dimensions in the Property inspector appear in bold and a black Refresh icon appears to the right of the dimensions. If you click the Refresh icon, the image reverts to its original size. Do not use this method to significantly resize an image. Instead resize it using an image editor and save a copy of it with the new settings.

FIGURE E-8: CSS Rule Definition for img_left_float dialog box

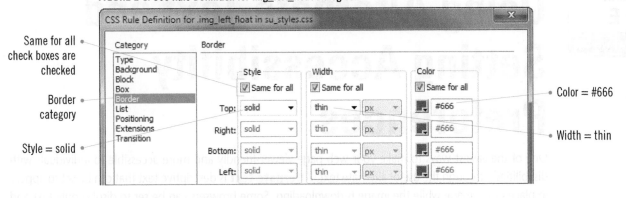

Same for all
check boxes are
checked

Border
category

Style = solid

Color = #666

Width = thin

FIGURE E-9: CSS Rule Definition for img_left_float dialog box

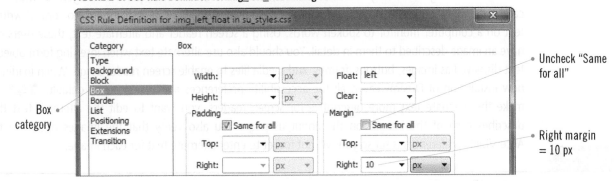

Box
category

Uncheck "Same
for all"

Right margin
= 10 px

FIGURE E-10: Viewing the images with borders and margins

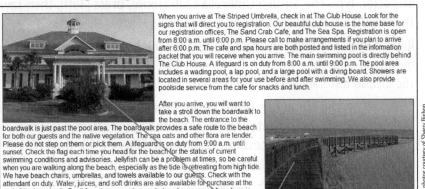

Original photos courtesy of Sherry Bishop

Both images have borders and horizontal space separating them from the text

Design Matters

Resizing images using an external editor

Each image on a web page takes a certain amount of time to download, depending on the size of the file and the speed of the user's Internet connection. Larger files (in terms of kilobytes, not width and height) take longer to download than smaller files. Many designers feel that an ideal page should download in less than five or six seconds; to ensure that your page downloads quickly, your images should have the smallest file size possible while maintaining the necessary level of image quality. If you need to significantly resize an image, use an external image editor instead of resizing it in Dreamweaver; resizing in Dreamweaver affects how an image appears onscreen, but does not alter the image file itself. Cropping an image in Dreamweaver, however, *will* modify the image file and decrease its overall size. As a general rule, it is better to crop your images using an external editor when you are making a significant change. Always save a copy of the original file before you crop it, then use the copy of the file to make your edits. This will always keep the original file intact in case you need it later.

Using Alternate Text and Setting Accessibility Preferences

One of the easiest ways to make your web page viewer-friendly and more accessible to individuals with disabilities is through the use of alternate text. **Alternate text** is descriptive text that can be set to appear in place of an image while the image is downloading. Some browsers can be set to display only text and to download images manually. In such instances, alternate text is used in place of images. Alternate text can be read by a **screen reader**, a device used by individuals with visual impairments to convert written text on a computer monitor to spoken words. Using a screen reader and alternate text, these users can have an image described to them in detail. You should also use alternate text when inserting form objects, text displayed as images, buttons, frames, and media files to enable screen reader usage. When loading a new installation of Dreamweaver, all the accessibility preferences are turned on by default. To make the alternate text more descriptive for screen readers, you want to edit the alternate text that describes each of the images on the about_us page. You also verify that the Images option in the Accessibility preferences is set so you will not forget to enter alternate text for each image.

STEPS

1. **Click the club house image to select it, select the text in the Alt text box in the Property inspector, type The Striped Umbrella Club House, press [Tab], then save the file**
   The alternate text is entered for the image, as shown in Figure E-11.

2. **Repeat Step 1 to edit the alternate text for the boardwalk image to read Boardwalk to our private beach**
   The alternate text is entered for the image, as shown in Figure E-12.

> **QUICK TIP**
> Once you set the Accessibility preferences, they will be in effect for all of your websites. You will not have to set each website separately.

3. **Click Edit on the Menu bar, (Win) or the Dreamweaver menu (Mac), click Preferences, click Accessibility in the Category list, click the Show attributes when inserting check boxes to select them if necessary, as shown in Figure E-13, then click OK**
   With these options selected, Dreamweaver will prompt you to enter alternate text for new objects you add to the website, including images.

> **QUICK TIP**
> If your Save option is not active, you do not need to save your file. However, you can use the Save All command in the File menu to make sure any changes you have made to an open page are saved.

4. **Save your work**

FIGURE E-11: Editing the alternate text for the club house image

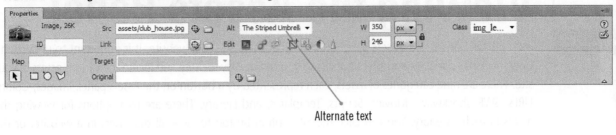

Alternate text

FIGURE E-12: Editing the alternate text for the boardwalk image

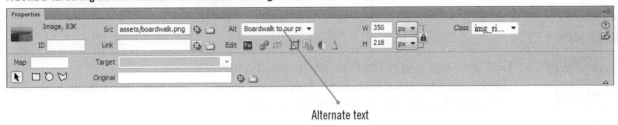

Alternate text

FIGURE E-13: Accessibility Preferences dialog box

Accessibility preferences category

Mac users may not see these options

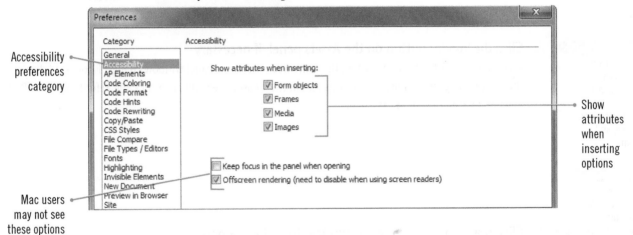

Show attributes when inserting options

Design Matters

Providing for accessibility with alternate text

The use of alternate text is the first checkpoint listed in the web content Accessibility Guidelines (WCAG), Version 2.0, from the World Wide Web Consortium (W3C). It states that a website should "provide text alternatives for any non-text content so that it can be changed into other forms people need, such as large print, Braille, speech, symbols, or simpler language." The twelve WCAG guidelines are grouped together under four principles called the POUR principles: perceivable, operable, understandable, and

robust. To view the complete set of accessibility guidelines, go to the Web Accessibility Initiative page (w3.org/WAI). A general rule is that if you need to enter more than 50 characters of alternate text, you should create a separate file with the information you want to convey. Enter the location of the file in the Long Description text box that appears under the Alternate Text text box in the Image Tag Accessibility Attributes dialog box that opens when you insert a new image.

Viewing the Assets Panel

As you have learned, the Assets panel displays all of the assets in a website. It is important to understand how the Assets panel organizes your assets so you can quickly identify and locate the various assets in your site. There are nine categories of assets, each represented by a button on the Assets panel: Images, Colors, URLs, SWF, Shockwave, Movies, Scripts, Templates, and Library. There are two options for viewing the assets in each category. You can click the Site option button to view all the assets in a website, or the Favorites option button to view those assets that you have designated as **favorites**—assets that you expect to use repeatedly while you work on the site. For more information about this topic see the *Using favorites in the Assets panel* Clues to Use box in this lesson. You can also use the Assets panel to insert images on your page by either dragging an asset to the page, or by selecting the image and clicking the Insert button. So far, your website includes several images and colors. You explore the Assets panel to understand how Dreamweaver organizes the image files and keeps track of the colors used in the site.

STEPS

QUICK TIP

Make sure that the page you have open is in the current website. If you open a page outside the current website, the Assets panel will not display the assets associated with the open page.

1. **Click the Assets tab in the Files Tab group, if necessary**

   The first time you use the Assets panel, it displays the Images category; after that, it displays the category that was selected during the last Dreamweaver session.

QUICK TIP

You can click the column headings in the Assets panel to sort the files by Name, Dimensions, Size, Type, and Full Path.

2. **Click the Images button on the Assets panel, if necessary**

   Each time you click a category button, the contents in the Assets panel window change. Figure E-14 displays the Images category, and lists the four images in the website. Remember to click the Refresh button 🔄 if you don't see all of your assets listed.

TROUBLE

If you see another color listed, click the Refresh button 🔄 to remove it. If you still see additional colors, you can either leave them or search for them in Code view and remove them.

3. **Click the Colors button ▦ to display the Colors category**

   Three colors are listed in the website, as shown in Figure E-15. They are gray, blue, and white. The gray and blue colors are used for formatting text and images and are located in the external style sheet. The white color formats the page background color. The Type column shows that each color is listed as Websafe. You learned about websafe colors in Unit C.

Using the terms *graphics* and *images*

In discussing design, people often use the terms **graphics** and **images**. This text uses the term *graphics* to refer to most non-text items on a web page, including photographs, logos, menu bars, Flash animations, graphs, background images, and illustrations. Any of these can be called a **graphic** or a **graphic file**. *Images* is a narrower term, referring to pictures or photographs. **Image files** are referred to by their file type, or file format, such as **JPEG** (Joint

Photographic Experts Group), **GIF** (Graphics Interchange Format), or **PNG** (Portable Network Graphics). See Table E-1 on page 119 for descriptions for each of these formats. This text refers to the pictures that you see on the pages as images. But don't worry too much about which term to use; many people use one term or the other according to habit, region, or type of business, or use them interchangeably.

FIGURE E-14: **Assets panel showing Images category**

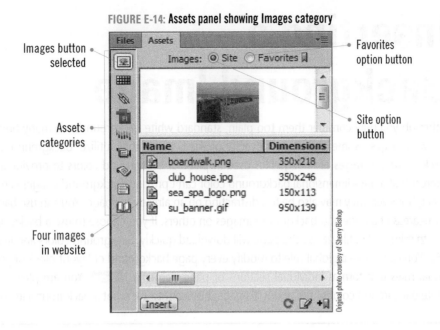

Images button selected

Favorites option button

Assets categories

Site option button

Four images in website

Original photo courtesy of Sherry Bishop

FIGURE E-15: **Assets panel showing Colors category**

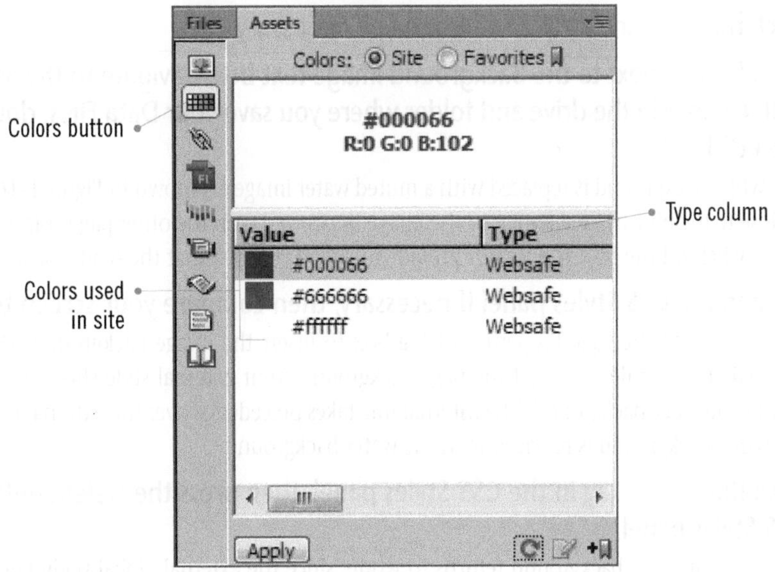

Colors button

Type column

Colors used in site

Using Favorites in the Assets panel

For assets such as images that you plan to use repeatedly, you can place them in the Favorites list in the Assets panel to make them readily available. There are a few ways to add favorites to the Favorites list in the Assets panel. You can right-click an image in Design view, then click Add to Image Favorites. When you subsequently click the Favorites option button in the Assets panel, the image will display in the list. You can also right-click the name of an image in the Site list (when the Site option is selected in the Assets panel), then click Add to Favorites. In addition, you can create a folder for storing assets by category by clicking the Favorites option in the Assets panel, clicking the Files panel options list arrow on the Files panel group, then clicking New Favorites Folder. You can give the folder a descriptive name, then drag assets from the Favorites list to move them to this folder. You can create nicknames for assets in the Favorites list by right-clicking (Win) or [ctrl]-clicking (Mac) the asset in the Favorites list, then clicking Edit Nickname.

Inserting a Background Image

Although you may consider them too plain, standard white backgrounds are many times the best choice for web pages. Some pages, however, look best when they utilize background colors or images. **Background images** are image files used in place of background colors to provide a depth and visual interest that a one-dimensional background color can't provide. Background images can create a dramatic effect; however, they may also be too distracting on an already full page. You can use background color for some areas of a page and background images on others. If you choose to use a background image, select one that is small in file size so the page will download quickly. Background colors and images are set using CSS. You can create a global rule to modify every page background or layout block or you can create individual rules that format individual sections or page elements.  You are pleased with the current white background color of the about_us page, but want to see what a background image would look like.

1. **Click Modify on the Menu bar, then click Page Properties**

   The Page Properties dialog box opens where you can add a background image to a web page by adding a link to the background image filename.

2. **Click the Appearance (CSS) category, if necessary**

3. **Click Browse next to the Background image text box, navigate to the assets folder in the unit_e folder in the drive and folder where you save your Data Files, double-click water.jpg, then click OK**

   The white background is replaced with a muted water image, as shown in Figure E-16. The color of the water is close to the blue in the banner, so the image fits in well with the other page colors. However, since it flows directly behind the text, it does not provide the good contrast that the white background did.

4. **Expand the CSS Styles panel if necessary, then compare your screen to Figure E-17**

   Since you used the Page Properties dialog box to insert the image background, Dreamweaver created an internal <body> rule to format the page background. Your external style sheet also has a <body> rule that sets a white page background. The internal rule takes precedence over the external rule, so for this page only, the white background is replaced with the water background.

   QUICK TIP
   Even when you remove an image from a web page, it remains in the assets folder in the local site root folder of the website.

5. **Click the <style> tag in the CSS Styles panel, then press the Delete button 🗑 on the CSS Styles panel**

   The about_us page background returns to white, since the external global body tag is again formatting the page background. The internal style is removed from the list in the CSS Styles panel, as shown in Figure E-18.

FIGURE E-16: about_us page with a background image

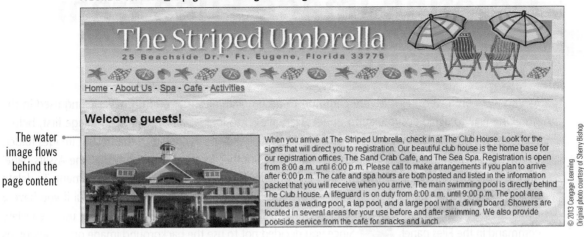

The water image flows behind the page content

© 2013 Cengage Learning
Original photo courtesy of Sherry Bishop

FIGURE E-17: **The CSS Styles panel with the new embedded body rule added**

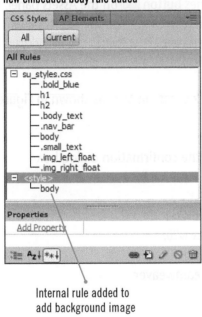

Internal rule added to add background image

FIGURE E-18: **The CSS Styles panel with the embedded body rule deleted**

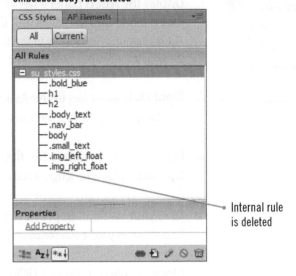

Internal rule is deleted

Integrating Photoshop and Fireworks with Dreamweaver CS6

Dreamweaver has many functions integrated with Photoshop CS6. For example, you can copy and paste images directly from Photoshop into Dreamweaver. Dreamweaver will prompt you to optimize the image by choosing a file format and settings for using the image in a web browser. Then it will paste the image on the page. If you want to edit the image later, select the image, then click the Edit button in the Property inspector to open the image in Photoshop. (The appearance of the Edit button will change according to the default image editor you have specified.) When you edit an image in Photoshop, you can export an updated Smart Object instantly. **Smart Objects** are layers with image source information that allow an image to be modified nondestructively without losing the original data. Photoshop users can set Photoshop as the default image editor in Dreamweaver for specific image file formats. Click Edit on the Menu bar, click Preferences (Win), or click Dreamweaver, click Preferences (Mac), click File Types/Editors, click the Extensions plus sign button, select a file format from the list, click the Editors plus sign button, use the Select External Editor dialog box to browse to Photoshop (if you don't see it listed already), then click Make Primary. Search the Adobe website (adobe.com) for a tutorial on Photoshop and Dreamweaver integration. Fireworks is another commonly used default image editor. Use the same steps to select it rather than Photoshop.

Deleting Image Files from a Website

As you work on a website, it is very common to accumulate files that end up never being used in the site. One way to avoid accumulating unnecessary files is to look at and evaluate an image first, before you copy it to the default images folder. If the file has already been copied to the default images folder, however, you should delete it (or at least move it to another location) to ensure that the Assets panel only lists the assets actually used in the site. This practice is considered good site management. To delete a file from the Assets panel, you can access the Locate in Site command, which is useful if you have a large number of images to search. If you just have a single file to delete, it's faster to just use the Delete command in the Files panel.  Since you decided not to use the background image on the about_us page, you want to delete it from the assets folder.

STEPS

QUICK TIP

 will not appear on the Assets panel when the Favorites option is selected.

1. **Display the Assets panel if necessary, click the Images button 🔳 on the Assets panel, verify that the Site option is selected, then click the Refresh button 🔄 on the Assets panel**
   The background file remains in the Images list on the Assets panel. Even though you have deleted it from the body rule, you have not yet deleted them in the website assets folder.

TROUBLE

If the file is not listed, click 🔄.

2. **Right-click water.jpg in the Assets panel, then click Locate in Site, as shown in Figure E-19**
   The Files panel opens with the water.jpg file selected.

3. **Press [Delete] to delete the file, then click Yes in the confirmation dialog box**
   The water.jpg file is no longer listed in the Assets panel because it has been deleted from the site.

4. **Save your work, then preview your file in your browser**
   Your about_us page is completed and should resemble Figure E-20.

5. **Close the page, then Exit (Win) or Quit (Mac) Dreamweaver**

Inserting files with Adobe Bridge

You can manage project files, including video and Camera Raw files, with a file management tool called Adobe Bridge that is included with Dreamweaver. Bridge provides an easy way to view files outside the website before bringing them into the website. It is an integrated application, working with other Adobe programs, such as Photoshop and Illustrator. You can also use Bridge to add meta tags and search text in your files. To open Bridge, click the Browse in Bridge command on the File menu or click the Browse in Bridge button on the Standard toolbar.

FIGURE E-19: Using the Assets panel to locate a file in a site

water.jpg

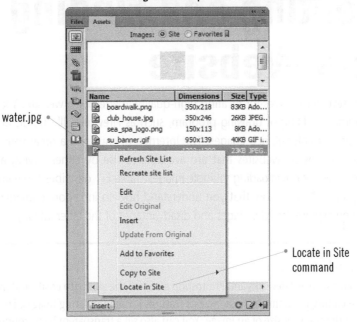

Locate in Site command

FIGURE E-20: The finished page

© 2013 Cengage Learning
Original photos courtesy of Sherry Bishop

Creating and Finding Images for a Website

There are several resources for locating high-quality images for a website. You can create original images using an image editing or drawing program, such as Fireworks, Illustrator, or Photoshop, or use original photographs for colorful, rich images. The Internet, of course, is a great source for finding images. Stock photos are photos on websites that are available to use by either paying a single fee per photo or a subscription fee for downloading multiple images. Table E-1 describes three image types that can be used on web pages.  Now that you understand how to incorporate images into The Striped Umbrella website, you explore the advantages and disadvantages of the different ways to accumulate images.

DETAILS

- **Original images**

  Programs such as Fireworks and Photoshop give you the ability to create and modify original artwork. These image editing programs have numerous features for manipulating images. For example, you can adjust the color, brightness, or size of an image. You can also set a transparent background for an image. **Transparent backgrounds** contain transparent pixels, rather than pixels with color, resulting in images that blend easily on a page background. Only certain file types can be used to create transparent images, such as gifs and pngs. Illustrator is a drawing program that is used to create original vector graphics, which can then be converted to a usable format for the web, such as jpg, gif, or png files.

- **Original photography**

  High-quality photographs can greatly enhance a website. Fortunately, digital cameras and scanners have made this venture much easier than in the past. Once you scan a photograph or shoot it with a digital camera, you can further enhance it using an image editing software program, such as Photoshop or Fireworks. Photographs taken with digital cameras often have large file sizes, so be sure to create resized copies using an image editing program such as Photoshop before placing them on web pages. If you don't have Photoshop or another image editor, many digital cameras come with their own basic software that you can use to resize and enhance images.

- **The Internet**

  There are many websites from which you are able to find images, but look carefully for copyright statements regarding the legal use of images. Stock photos sites, such as iStockphoto, are excellent resources used by many professional designers. To use these sites, you first sign up to become a member, then you either purchase images as you need them, or purchase a subscription, which allows you to pay a set price for the number of files you expect to download each year. There are many collections of images online that are free, but some sites require that you credit them on your website with either a simple statement or a link to their website. Images that are labeled as public domain are free to use without restrictions. Figure E-21 is an example of a source for public domain images. If you are uncertain about whether you may use an image you find on a website, it's best to either contact the site's owner or find another image to use. *If you copy and paste images you find while accessing other websites and use them for your own purposes, you may be violating copyright laws.*

FIGURE E-21: Example of a website with public domain images

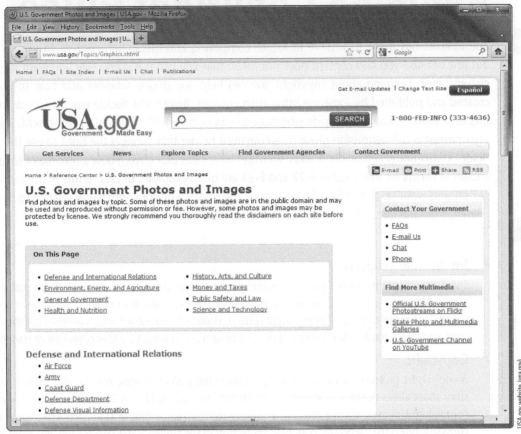

USA.gov website (usa.gov)

TABLE E-1: Common image file formats for images for web publication

format (file extension)	stands for	details
.jpg, .jpeg	Joint Photographic Experts Group	Pixel-based; a web standard. Can set image quality in pixels per inch (ppi), which affects file size. Supports millions of colors. Use for full-color images, such as photographs with large tonal range and those with lifelike artwork. This format is a good choice when targeting mobile devices.
.png	Portable Network Graphics	Can be compressed for storage and quicker download, without loss of picture quality. Supports variable levels of transparency and control of image brightness on different computers. Used for small graphics, such as bullets, as well as for complex photographic images. This format is also a good choice for targeting mobile devices. Not all browsers support the .png file format.
.gif	Graphics Interchange Format	Limited to 256 colors. Low color quality and limited detail are not suitable for printing. Small file size means faster transmission. Suitable for images with only a few colors, such as cartoons, simple illustrations, icons, buttons, and horizontal rules. This format is used for transparent images.

Examine Copyright Rules

The Internet has made it possible to locate compelling and media-rich content to use on websites. But just because you find content does not mean that you can use it however you want or under any circumstance. Learning about copyright law can help you decide whether and how to use content created and published by someone other than yourself. Before you decide whether to use media you find on a website, you must decide whether you can comply with its licensing agreement. A **licensing agreement** is the permission given by a copyright holder that conveys the right to use the copyright holder's work under certain conditions. Websites have rules that govern how a user may use its content, known as **terms of use**. Figures E-22 and E-23 are good examples of clear terms of use for the Library of Congress website. You decide to do some research on copyright law in relation to downloaded content from the Internet. There are several concepts to understand.

DETAILS

- ### Intellectual property

  Intellectual property is a product resulting from human creativity. It can include inventions, movies, songs, designs, clothing, and so on. The purpose of copyright law is to promote progress in society—not expressly to protect the rights of copyright owners. However, you should always assume that the majority of work you might want to download and use in a project is protected by either copyright or trademark law.

- ### Copyright

  A **copyright** protects the particular and tangible expression of an idea, not the idea itself. If you wrote a story about aliens crashing in Roswell, New Mexico, no one could copy or use your specific story without permission. However, anyone could write a story using a similar plot or characters—the actual idea is not copyright-protected. Generally, copyright protection in the United States lasts for the life of the author plus 70 years (most countries have similar regulations). A copyright attaches to a work as soon as it is created; you do not have to register it with the U.S. Copyright Office.

- ### Trademark

  A **trademark** protects an image, word, slogan, symbol, or design used to identify goods or services. For example, the Nike swoosh and the Google logo are images protected by trademark. Trademark protection lasts for 10 years, with 10-year renewal terms; it can last indefinitely provided the trademark is in active use.

- ### Fair use

  The law builds in limitations to copyright protection. One limitation to copyright is fair use. **Fair use** allows limited use of copyright-protected work. For example, you could excerpt short passages of a film or song for a class project. Determining if fair use applies to a work depends on the purpose of its use, the nature of the copyrighted work, how much you want to copy, and the effect on the market or value of the work. There is no clear formula on what constitutes fair use. It is always decided by the courts on a case-by-case basis. Except in cases of fair use, you must obtain permission from the copyright holder to use the work.

- ### Derivative work

  A **derivative work** is a work based on another pre-existing work, such as a movie adaptation of a book or a new musical arrangement of an existing song. Derivative works are included in the six rights of a copyright owner: reproduction (including downloading), creation of derivative works, distribution to the public, public performance, public display, and public performance by digital audio transmission of sound recordings. By default, only a copyright holder can create a derivative work of his or her original work.

- ### Public domain

  Work that is not protected by copyright is said to be in the public domain. Anyone can use it however they wish for any purpose, free of charge. In general, photos and other media on federal government websites are in the public domain, but some may have third-party ownership, so it's best to verify before you use them. For instance, there could be a photograph on the page that has a copyright restriction attached to it by the photographer. Websites will often state if their images or other content are in the public domain.

FIGURE E-22: Example of a website with a legal policy statement

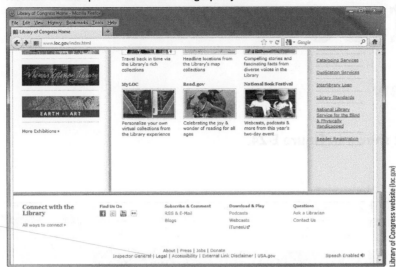

Link to legal policy statement

Library of Congress website (loc.gov)

FIGURE E-23: Library of Congress legal policies

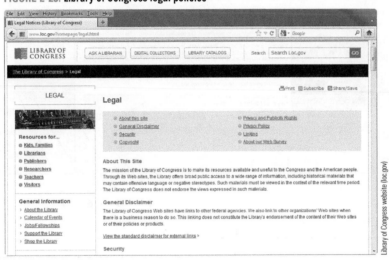

Library of Congress website (loc.gov)

Using proper methods to cite content

The familiar © symbol (or the word *Copyright*) is no longer required to indicate copyrighted materials, nor does it automatically register your work, but it does serve a useful purpose. When you post or publish the copyright term or symbol, you are stating clearly to those who may not know anything about copyright law that this work is claimed by you and is not in the public domain. If someone violates your copyright, your case is made even stronger if your notice is clearly visible. That way, violators can never claim ignorance of the law as an excuse for infringing. Common notification styles include using the word *Copyright* with the year, as in "Copyright 2013, Course Technology," or by using the copyright symbol ©, as in "© 2013 Course Technology."

You must provide proper citation for materials you incorporate into your own work. The following source was used for this lesson content and is referenced as follows:

- Waxer, Barbara M., and Baum, Marsha L. 2006. *Internet Surf and Turf – The Essential Guide to Copyright, Fair Use, and Finding Media*. Boston: Thomson Course Technology.

In addition to words that you quote verbatim, copyrights apply to ideas that you summarize or paraphrase. One prominent set of guidelines for how to cite material found in print or on the web (including text, images, sound, video, blogs, email and text messages, and so forth) is produced by the American Psychological Association (APA). To view these guidelines in detail, go to the APA website at apastyle.org. Other widely used guidelines are available from the Modern Language Association (mla.org) and the Chicago Manual of Style (chicagomanualofstyle.org).

Practice

Concepts Review

Label each element shown in Figure E-24.

FIGURE E-24

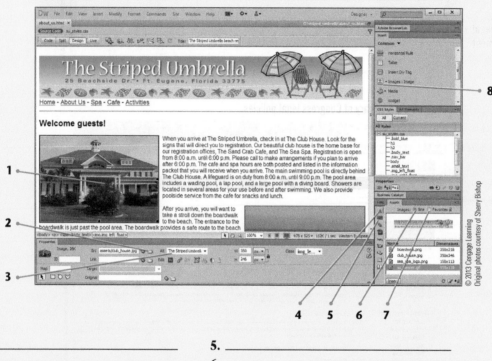

© 2013 Cengage Learning
Original photos courtesy of Sherry Bishop

1. _____	5. _____
2. _____	6. _____
3. _____	7. _____
4. _____	8. _____

Match each of the following terms with the statement that best describes it.

9. **Assets panel**

10. **JPG**

11. **Aligning an image**

12. **Derivative work**

13. **Favorites list**

14. **Refresh button**

15. **Trademark**

16. **Copyright**

17. **Alternate text**

18. **Border**

a. Positioning an image on a page

b. Updates the current list of assets in the Assets panel

c. Includes only those assets designated as Favorites

d. Protects an image, word, slogan, symbol, or design used to identify goods or services

e. A work based on another pre-existing work

f. Used by screen readers to describe an image

g. A frame placed around an image

h. An image file format

i. Protects the particular and tangible expression of an idea, not the idea itself

j. Lists all the assets of the website, including favorites

Select the best answer from the list of choices.

19. The following category is not found on the Assets panel:
- **a.** URLs
- **b.** Colors
- **c.** Tables
- **d.** Movies

20. When you no longer need files in a website, you should:
- **a.** leave them in the Assets panel.
- **b.** drag them off the page to the Recycle bin.
- **c.** place them in the Site list.
- **d.** delete them from the site.

21. Background images:
- **a.** are never appropriate.
- **b.** are always appropriate.
- **c.** should be used carefully.
- **d.** cannot be added with a CSS rule.

22. The following image file format is not appropriate to use for web publication:
- **a.** jpg.
- **b.** gif.
- **c.** png.
- **d.** bmp.

Skills Review

Important: *If you did not create this website in Unit B and maintain it during the preceding units, you will need to create a local site root folder for this website and define the website using files your instructor will provide. See the "Read This Before You Begin" section in this book for more detailed instructions.*

1. **Insert an image.**
   a. Start Dreamweaver.
   b. Open the Blooms & Bulbs website.
   c. Open dwe_2.html from the drive and folder where you store your Unit E Data Files, then save it as **plants.html** in the Blooms & Bulbs website, overwriting the existing plants.html file but not updating the links.
   d. Close dwe_2.html.
   e. Insert the rose_bud.jpg file from the assets folder in the drive and folder where you store your Unit E Data Files, in front of the words *Who can resist....* (Enter alternate text, if prompted.)
   f. Insert the rose_bloom.jpg file in front of the words *For ease of growing....* (Enter alternate text, if prompted.)
   g. Insert the two_roses.jpg file in front of the words *The Candy Cane....* (Enter alternate text, if prompted.)
   h. Attach the blooms_styles.css file to the plants page.
   i. Apply the body_text style to all of the paragraph text on the page.
   j. Apply the HTML Heading 1 format to the text *Featured Spring Plant: Roses!*
   k. Save your work.

2. **Align an image.**
   a. Add a new class rule named img_left_float that adds a float property with a left value.
   b. Add another class rule named img_right_float that adds a float property with a right value.
   c. Apply the img_left_float rule to the rose_bud and two_roses images.
   d. Apply the img_right_float rule to the rose_bloom image, then save your work.

3. **Enhance an image.**
   a. Edit the img_left_float rule to add a border to all sides of an image with the following settings: Style=solid; Width=thin; Color=#333.
   b. Edit the Box Margin property to add a 10px margin to the right side only, then save your changes.
   c. Repeat Step a to add the same border to the img_right_float rule.
   d. Edit the Box Margin property of the img_right_float rule to add a 10px margin to the left side only, then save your changes.
   e. Save your work, preview it in the browser, then compare your screen to Figure E-25.

4. **Use alternate text.**
   a. If you did not add alternate text in Step 1 above, select the rose_bud.jpg image, then use the Property inspector to enter **Rose bud on bird bath** as alternate text.
   b. If necessary, add the alternate text **Rose bloom** for the rose_bloom.jpg image, and **Candy Cane Floribunda** for the two_roses.jpg image.
   c. If necessary, edit the website preferences to set the Accessibility prompt for images.
   d. Save your work.

5. View the Assets panel.

   a. Display the Assets panel, if necessary.

   b. View the Images list to verify that there are five images in the list. Refresh the Images list, if necessary.

   c. View the Colors list to verify that there are three websafe colors.

6. Insert a background image.

   a. Use Page Properties to insert the lady_in_red file as a background image and refresh the Assets panel. (This file is in the assets folder in the drive and folder where you store your Unit E Data Files.)

   b. Save the page, then view it in your browser.

   c. Close the browser window.

   d. Remove the lady_in_red.jpg image from the background by deleting the internal body rule it created, then save your work.

7. Delete image files from a website.

   a. Delete the lady_in_red.jpg file from the Files panel.

   b. Refresh the Files panel and verify that the lady_in_red.jpg file has been removed from the site. (You may have to re-create the site cache.)

   c. Preview the page in the browser, compare your screen with Figure E-25, and close the browser. (Your text may wrap differently.)

   d. Close the page, Exit (Win) or Quit (Mac) Dreamweaver.

FIGURE E-25

Blooms & Bulbs
HWY 43 SOUTH • ALVIN • TX 77511 • 555-248-0806

Featured Spring Plant: Roses!

Who can resist the romance of roses? Poets have waxed poetically over them throughout the years. Many persons consider the beauty and fragrance of roses to be unmatched in nature. The varieties are endless, ranging from floribunda to hybrid teas to shrub roses to climbing roses. Each variety has its own personality and preference in the garden setting. Pictured on the left is a Summer Breeze Hybrid Tea bud. This variety is fast growing and produces spectacular blooms that are beautiful as cut flowers in arrangements. The enchanting fragrance will fill your home with summer sweetness. They require full sun. Hybrid teas need regular spraying and pruning, but will reward you with classic blooms that will be a focal point in your landscaping and provide you with beautiful arrangements in your home. They are well worth the effort!

For ease of growing, Knock Out® roses are some of our all-time favorites. Even beginners will not fail with these garden delights. They are shrub roses and prefer full sun, but can take partial shade. They are disease resistant and drought tolerant. You do not have to be concerned with either black spot or dead-heading with roses such as the Knock out®, making them an extremely low-maintenance plant. They are also repeat bloomers, blooming into late fall. The shrub can grow quite large, but can be pruned to any size. The one you see on the right is Southern Belle. Check out all our varieties as you will not fail to have great color with these plants.

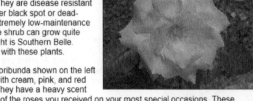

The Candy Cane Floribunda shown on the left is a beautiful rose with cream, pink, and red stripes and swirls. They have a heavy scent that will remind you of the roses you received on your most special occasions. These blooms are approximately four inches in diameter. They bloom continuously from early summer to early fall. The plants grow up to four feet tall and three feet wide. They are shipped bare root in February.

© 2013 Cengage Learning
Original photos courtesy of Sherry Bishop

Important: *If you did not create the following websites in Unit B and maintain them during the preceding units, you will need to create a local site folder for the websites in the following exercises and define the sites using files your instructor will provide. See the "Read This Before You Begin" section for more detailed instructions.*

Independent Challenge 1

You have been hired to create a website for a river expedition company named Rapids Transit, located on the Buffalo River in Arkansas. In addition to renting canoes, kayaks, and rafts, they have lodging for overnight stays. River guides are available, if requested, to accompany clients on float trips. The clients range from experienced floaters to beginners. The owner's name is Mike Andrew. Mike has asked you to develop the page that introduces the Rapids Transit guides available for float trips. Refer to Figure E-26 as you work on this page.

a. Start Dreamweaver and open the Rapids Transit website.

b. Open dwe_3.html from the drive and folder where you store your Unit E Data Files and save it in the Rapids Transit website as **guides.html**, overwriting the existing file but not updating links.

c. Close dwe_3.html.

d. Check the path for the Rapids Transit banner and reset the path to the assets folder for the website, if necessary.

e. Attach the rapids_transit.css style sheet, then save your work.

f. Insert the image river_guide.jpg at an appropriate place on the page. (This file is in the assets folder in the drive and folder where you store your Unit E Data Files.)

g. Create alternate text for the river_guide.jpg image, then create a rule to add an image border, float, and margins with settings of your choice, then apply the new rule to the image.

h. Apply the Heading 1 format to the menu bar and the body_text style to the paragraph text.

i. Add a heading above the first paragraph and apply the Heading 2 rule to it.

j. Save your work, preview the page in the browser, then compare your workspace to Figure E-26. (Your image location, border size, and vertical and horizontal space settings may differ.)

k. Close the browser and Exit (Win) or Quit (Mac) Dreamweaver.

FIGURE E-26

Our Guides

We have four of the best river guides you will ever find — Buster, Tucker, Max, and Scarlett. Buster has been with us for fourteen years and was born and raised here on the river. Tucker joined us two years ago "from off" (somewhere up north), but we've managed to make a country boy out of him! Max and Scarlett are actually distant cousins and joined us after they graduated from college last year. They're never happier than when they're out on the water floating and fishing. Each of our guides will show you a great time on the river.

Our guides will pack your supplies, shuttle you to the put-in point, maneuver the raging rapids for you, and then make sure someone is waiting at the take-out point to shuttle you back to the store. They haven't lost a customer yet! Give us a call and we'll set up a date with any of these good people. Here's a photo of Buster showing off his stuff. The river is always faster and higher in the spring. If you want to take it a little slower, come visit us in the summer or fall. Leave your good camera at home, though, no matter what the time of the year. You may get wet! Life jackets are provided and we require that you wear them while on the water. Safety is always our prime concern.

© 2013 Cengage Learning
Original photos courtesy of Sherry Bishop

Independent Challenge 2

Your company is designing a new website for TripSmart, a travel outfitter. TripSmart specializes in travel products and services. In addition to selling travel products, such as luggage and accessories, they sponsor trips and offer travel advice. Their clients range from college students to families and vacationing professionals. You are now ready to work on the destinations page. Refer to Figure E-27 as you work through the following steps.

a. Start Dreamweaver and open the TripSmart website.

b. Open dwe_4.html from the drive and folder where you store your Unit E Data Files and save it in the TripSmart website as **tours.html**, overwriting the existing tours file but not updating links.

c. Close dwe_4.html.

d. Check the path for the TripSmart banner and reset the path to the assets folder for the website, if necessary.

e. Attach the tripsmart_styles.css file to the page, then apply the HTML Heading 1 format to the Destination: The Galapagos heading and the body_text style to the rest of the text on the page. (*Hint*: You probably formatted your styles differently from the example, so your text may look different than Figure E-27.)

f. Change the site preferences to prompt you to add alternate text as you add new images to the website, if necessary.

g. Insert the images iguana_and_lizard.jpg and blue_footed_booby.jpg at the appropriate places on the page, adding alternate text for each image. (These files are in the assets folder in the drive and folder where you store your Unit E Data Files.)

h. Create a new CSS rule to format each image, then apply one to each image.

i. Save your work, preview the page in the browser, then compare your page to Figure E-27 for one possible design solution.

j. Close the browser and Exit (Win) or Quit (Mac) Dreamweaver.

FIGURE E-27

Destination: The Galápagos

We have a really special trip planned for next February. We have reserved ten cabins on the ship *The Wanderer* to explore the Galápagos Islands. The departure date is February 5 and the return date is February 21. This trip of a lifetime begins in Guayaquil, Ecuador. Guayaquil is a seaport on the southern coast of Ecuador. You will find it a vibrant center for business and tourism with lots of sites to explore. Stroll along the riverfront to enjoy colorful shops, lush parks, and street entertainment. After a night's rest, you will board your flight to Baltra Island in the Galápagos archipelago.

After arriving at Baltra's airport, you will board a bus for a short ride to the dock. Here you will find a welcoming committee of iguanas and sea lions. These natives love to sun on the docks and don't seem to mind sharing them with you as long as you don't come too close! *The Wanderer* is an exquisite touring ship licensed to explore the Galápagos by the Ecuadoran government. Tourism to the Galápagos is strictly regulated for the protection of the land, waters, and wildlife. You will use pangas for wet and dry landings to observe the wonderful variety of species of flora and fauna unique to the Galápagos, including the famous blue-footed booby. You will also have opportunities to swim, snorkel, and kayak with penguins. When your time on the ship ends, you will fly to Quito, the second-highest capital city in the world. Quito is a UNESCO World Heritage Site with beautiful colonial architecture. We recommend taking an extra day to explore its rich history and sample Ecuadoran cuisine.

To provide the finest in personal attention, this tour will be limited to no more than twenty people. The price schedule is as follows: Land Tour and Supplemental Group Air, $5,500.00; International Air, $1,350.00; and Single Supplement, $1,000.00. Entrance fees, hotel taxes, and services are included in the Land Tour price. Ship gratuities are also included for the Wanderer crew and guides. A deposit of $500.00 is required at the time the booking is made. Trip insurance and luggage insurance are optional and are also offered for an extra charge. A passport and visa will be required for entry into Ecuador. Call us at 555-555-0807 for further information and the complete itinerary from 8:00 a.m. to 6:00 p.m. (Central Standard Time).

ⓓ Independent Challenge 3

Donna Stevens raises and shows horses professionally. She is learning how to use Dreamweaver to be able to create a website to showcase her horses. She would like to look at some other websites about horses to get a feel for the types of images she may want to use in her site. Use a word processor or paper to answer the questions below.

a. Connect to the Internet and go to USHorse.biz (ushorse.biz), as shown in Figure E-28.

b. How are background colors used? Would you have selected different ones? Why, or why not?

c. Evaluate the images used in the site. Do they add interest to the pages? Was alternate text used for any or all of the images?

d. How long did the home page take to download on your computer?

e. Are there too few images, too many, or just enough to add interest?

f. Go to Google (google.com) or Yahoo! (yahoo.com) to find another horse website.

g. Compare the site you found to the USHorse.biz site by answering questions b through e above.

FIGURE E-28

Website courtesy of USHorse.biz

Real Life Independent Challenge

This assignment will continue to build on the personal website that you created in Unit B. You have created and developed your index page. You have also added a page with either an ordered or an unordered list, and a CSS Style Sheet with a minimum of two rules. In this lesson, you work with one of the other pages of your site.

a. Consult your storyboard and decide which page you would like to develop in this lesson.

b. Create content for this page and format the text attractively on the page using CSS rules for all formatting.

c. Set the Accessibility option to prompt you for alternate text for new images added to the website, if necessary.

d. Add at least two images with appropriate alternate text. Resize the images in an image-editing program if they are too large to place on the page.

e. Use CSS rules to enhance the images to place them attractively on the page.

f. Document the source for the images and print some proof that they are in the public domain. Use your own photographs or drawings if you have difficulty obtaining public domain images.

g. Document the estimated download time for the page and the setting you used to estimate download time.

h. Save the file and preview the page in a browser.

After you are satisfied with your work, verify the following:

a. Each completed page has a page title.

b. All links work correctly.

c. The completed pages look good using a screen resolution of 1024 × 768.

d. All images are properly set showing a path to the assets folder of the website.

e. All images have alternate text and are legal to use.

Visual Workshop

Your company has been selected to design a website for Carolyne's Creations, a small catering business. Open your Carolyne's Creations website. Chef Carolyne has asked you to create a page that displays featured items in the kitchen shop. Open dwe_5.html from the drive and folder where your Unit E Data Files are stored. Save the file as **shop.html** in the Carolyne's Creations website, then add the peruvian_glass.jpg image from the drive and folder where you store your Unit E Data Files to create the page shown in Figure E-29. (*Hint*: You will need to attach the cc_styles.css style sheet to the page.) Apply the nav_bar rule to the menu bar, the body_text style to the paragraphs, and the Heading 1 HTML format to the heading "June Special: Peruvian Glasses". Use a CSS rule to add horizontal space and a border to the peruvian_glass image.

FIGURE E-29

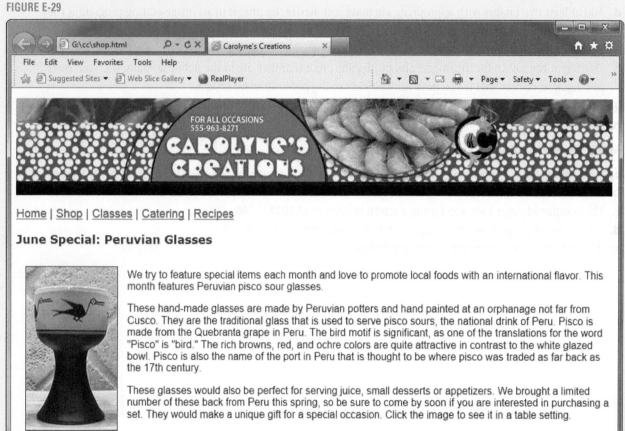

Creating Links and Menu Bars

Files You Will Need:

To view a list of files needed for this unit, see the Data Files Grid in the back of the book.

As you learned in Unit C, links are the real strength of a website, because they give users the freedom to open various web pages as they choose. You created a menu bar using a group of text links that helps users to navigate between pages of a website. In this unit, you will learn how to create a Spry menu bar and another type of link called an image map. A **Spry menu bar** is one of the preset widgets in Dreamweaver that creates a dynamic, user-friendly menu bar. A **widget** is a piece of code that allows users to interact with the program interface. An **image map** is an image with clickable areas defined on it that, when clicked, serve as links to take the user to another location.  You begin working on the link structure for The Striped Umbrella website. You add links to area attractions on the activities page, create a menu bar that will be used on all pages in the website, create an image map, and run some site management reports.

OBJECTIVES

Understand links and paths

Create an external link

Create an internal link

Insert a named anchor

Create internal links to named anchors

Create a Spry menu bar

Add menu bar items

Format a menu bar

Copy a menu bar to other pages

Create an image map

Manage website links

Understanding Links and Paths

You can use two types of links (hyperlinks) on web pages. **Internal links** are links to web pages within the same website, and **external links** are links that connect to pages in other websites or to email addresses. Internal and external links both have two important parts that work together. The first part of a link is what the user actually sees and clicks, such as a word, an image, or a button. The second part of a link is the path, which is the name and physical location of the web page file that opens when the link is clicked. A link is classified as internal or external based on the information in its path. External paths reference links with a complete web address, while internal paths reference links with a partial address, based on the relation of the destination page to the page with the link. A link that returns an error message, or a broken link, occurs when files are renamed or deleted from a website, the filename is misspelled, or the website is experiencing technical problems. The majority of the time now you do not have to enter "http://" or "www" before a website URL when you are moving from site to site on the Internet. ░░░░ You spend some time studying the various types of paths used for internal and external links.

TROUBLE
The figures illustrating paths on page 133 are for illustrative purposes only. They are not intended to be working links.

- **Absolute paths**

  Absolute paths are used with external links. They reference links on web pages outside the current website, and include "**http**" (hypertext transfer protocol) and the **URL** (Uniform Resource Locator), or address, of the web page. When necessary, the web page filename and the folder hierarchy are also part of an absolute path. Figure F-1 shows an example of an absolute path.

- **Relative paths**

  Relative paths are used with internal links. They reference web pages and graphic files within one website and include the filename and the folder hierarchy where the file resides. Figure F-2 shows an example of a relative path. Relative paths are further classified as root-relative (relative to the local site root folder) and document-relative (relative to the current document).

- **Root-relative paths**

  Root-relative paths are referenced from a website's local site root folder. As shown in Figure F-3, a root-relative path begins with a forward slash, which represents the website's local site root folder. This method is used when several websites are published to one server, or when a website is so large that it uses more than one server.

- **Document-relative paths**

  Document-relative paths reference the path in relation to the web page that appears, and do not begin with a slash. A document-relative path includes only a filename if the referenced file resides in the same folder as the current web page. For example, index.html and spa.html both reside in the local site root folder for The Striped Umbrella. So you would simply type spa.html to link to the spa page from the index page. However, when an image is referenced in the assets folder, since the assets folder is a subfolder of the local site root folder, you must include the word assets/ (with the slash) in front of the filename, for example, assets/the_spa.jpg. See Figure F-4 for an example of a document-relative path.

  In the exercises in this book, you will use document-relative paths because it is assumed that you will not use more than one server to publish your websites. For this reason, it is very important to make sure that the Relative to text box in the Select File dialog box is set to Document, rather than Site Root, when creating links. This option can also be set in the Site Setup dialog box.

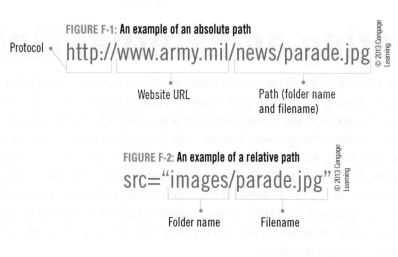

FIGURE F-1: An example of an absolute path

Protocol

http://www.army.mil/news/parade.jpg

© 2013 Cengage Learning

Website URL

Path (folder name and filename)

FIGURE F-2: An example of a relative path

src="images/parade.jpg"

© 2013 Cengage Learning

Folder name

Filename

FIGURE F-3: An example of a root-relative path

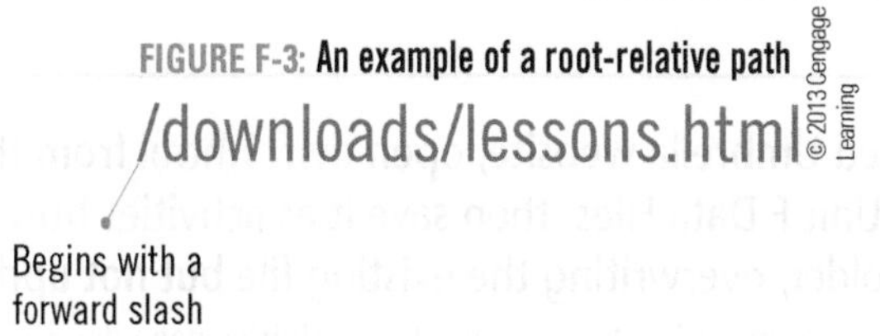

/downloads/lessons.html

© 2013 Cengage Learning

Begins with a forward slash

FIGURE F-4: An example of a document-relative path

downloads/lessons.html

© 2013 Cengage Learning

Begins with either a folder name or a filename

Design Matters

Ensuring error-free URLs

It is easy to make mistakes when you type long and complex URLs. One way to minimize errors is to copy and paste the URL of the web page that you would like to include as an external link in your website. To do this, open the web page then copy the link information in the Address text box (Internet Explorer) or the Location bar (Mozilla Firefox). Next, select the link text on your web page, then paste the link information in the Link text box in the HTML Property inspector. When you hear that text is "case sensitive," it means that the text will be treated differently when it is typed using uppercase letters rather than lowercase letters, or vice-versa. With some operating systems, such as Windows, it doesn't matter which case you use when you enter URLs. However, with other systems, such as UNIX, it does matter. To be sure that your links will work with all systems, use lowercase letters for all URLs. This is another good reason to select and copy a URL from the browser address bar, and then paste it in the Link text box or Dreamweaver code when creating an external link. You won't have to worry about missing a case change.

Creating an effective navigation structure

When you create a website, it's important to consider how your users will navigate from page to page within the site. A menu bar is a critical tool for moving around a site, so it's important that all text, buttons, and icons you use on a menu bar have a consistent look across all pages. If you use a complex menu bar, such as one that incorporates JavaScript or Flash, it's a good idea to include plain text links in another location on the page for accessibility. Otherwise, users might become confused or lost within the site.

A navigation structure can include more links than those included on a menu bar, however. For instance, it can contain other sets of links that relate to the content of specific pages. They can be placed at the bottom or sides of a page in a different format. No matter how you decide to design your navigation structure, make sure that every page includes a link back to the home page.

Other good navigation strategies that promote accessibility include adding keyboard equivalents for navigation elements, labeling all links, and incorporating jump menus to enable users to skip to links.

Creating an External Link

As you have learned, external links use absolute paths, which must include the complete name and path of the web address to link to the destination web page successfully. Because the World Wide Web is a constantly changing environment, you should check external links frequently. Websites may be up one day and down the next. If a website changes server locations or shuts down because of technical difficulties, the links to it may become broken. An external link can also become broken when an Internet connection is not working properly. Broken links, like misspelled words on a web page, indicate that the website is not being maintained diligently. ▓▓▓▓ Guests staying at The Striped Umbrella often ask for information about family activities in the surrounding area. Links to interesting attractions are helpful not only to currently registered guests, but to attract potential ones as well. You decide to create external links on the activities page that link to two websites for area attractions.

STEPS

1. **Open The Striped Umbrella website, open** dwf_1.html **from the drive and folder where you store your Unit F Data Files, then save it as** activities.html **in the striped_umbrella local site root folder, overwriting the existing file but not updating links**

   The new activities page opens in Design view. The activities page describes two popular area attractions of interest to resort guests. There are two broken image placeholders that represent images that must be copied to the website.

2. **Close** dwf_1.html

TROUBLE

If you don't see the image in the data files folder, remember to browse to the Unit F Data Files assets folder to locate the family_sunset.jpg image.

3. **Select the** first broken image placeholder, **click the Browse for File button** 📁 **next to the Src text box in the Property inspector, select** family_sunset.jpg **from the assets folder in the location where you store your Unit F Data Files, click OK (Win) or Open (Mac) to save the image in your assets folder, then click to the right of the placeholder**

   The family_sunset image is copied to the website assets folder and now appears on the page.

4. **Select the** second broken image placeholder, **then repeat Step 3 to place the second image,** two_dolphins.jpg **on the page**

5. **Attach the** su_styles.css **file, then apply the** body_text **style to the paragraphs of text on the page (not to the menu bar)**

6. **Apply the img_left_float rule to the first image and the img_right_float rule to the second image**

7. **Scroll to the bottom of the page if necessary, then select the** Blue Angels **text in the second to the last paragraph on the page**

   You use the Blue Angels text to create an external link to the Blue Angels website.

8. **Click the** Link text box **in the HTML Property inspector, type** http://www.blueangels.navy.mil, **compare your screen to Figure F-5, then press [Tab]**

   The Blue Angels text is now a link to the Blue Angels website.

TROUBLE

If your link does not work correctly, check for typing errors in the link path. If the link is typed correctly, the site may be down and you should remove the link until you can verify that it is working correctly.

9. **Click** File **on the Menu bar, click** Save, **click the** Preview/Debug in browser button 🌐, **click** Preview in [your browser], **click** Blue Angels **on the web page, verify that the link works, then close your browser window**

10. **Scroll to the bottom of the page if necessary, select the** USS Alabama **text in the last paragraph on the page, then repeat Step 8 to create the link for the USS Alabama text, using the URL** http://www.ussalabama.com

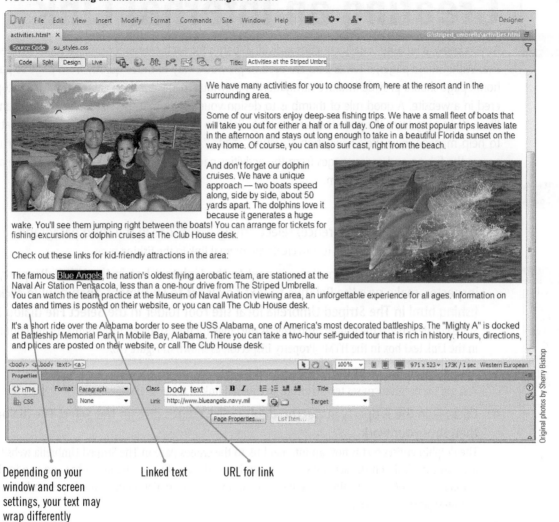

Depending on your
window and screen
settings, your text may
wrap differently

Linked text

URL for link

Design Matters

Understanding The Web Accessibility Initiative - Accessible Rich Internet Applications Suite

The Web Accessibility Initiative - Accessible Rich Internet Applications Suite (WAI-ARIA) is a resource for applying best practices when adding advanced user interface controls to a website. Functions such as drag-and-drop or browsing through a menu can be very difficult for users who rely on assistive devices to navigate a site. WAI-ARIA, at w3.org/WAI, provides guidelines and techniques for planning and implementing accessible content. It also provides presentations, handouts, and tutorials for developers who are interested in learning how to provide content that can be easily navigated by all users, such as providing alternative keyboard navigation for web objects primarily designed to function using mouse clicks. The information offered through WAI-ARIA is developed by the Protocols and Formats Working Group (PFWG), a part of the World Wide Web Consortium (W3C).

Creating an Internal Link

As you know, a website usually contains individual pages for each category or major topic covered in the site. Within those pages, internal links are used to provide a way to move quickly from page to page. The home page should provide intuitive navigation to individual pages for each category or major topic covered in a website. A good rule of thumb is to design your site so that users are never more than two or three clicks away from the page they are seeking. Refer to your wireframe frequently as you create pages to help manage your site's navigation structure.  You want to create an easy way for users to access the fishing and cruises pages from the activities page, so you create internal links on the activities page that will link to each of them.

STEPS

1. **Using Figure F-6 as a reference, select fishing excursions in the third paragraph**
   You use the fishing excursions text to create an internal link to the fishing page.

QUICK TIP
You can also select the file to which you want to link in the Files panel and drag it to the Link text box or use the Point to File button in the Property inspector to create an internal link.

2. **Click the Browse for File button next to the Link text box in the HTML Property inspector, make sure the Relative to text box is set to Document, then double-click fishing.html in The Striped Umbrella local site root folder in the Select File dialog box**
   Since you designated the fishing.html page as the target for the fishing excursions link, fishing.html is listed in the Link text box in the HTML Property inspector, as shown in Figure F-6.

3. **Select dolphin cruises in the same sentence**
   You use the dolphin cruises text to create an internal link to the cruises page.

4. **Click in the Property inspector, double-click cruises.html in the Select File dialog box, then save your work**
   The dolphin cruises text is now an internal link to the cruises page in The Striped Umbrella website. There are now nine links on the activities page: seven internal links (five on the menu bar and two in the paragraph text linking to the fishing and cruises pages), and two external links (the Blue Angels and USS Alabama websites), as shown in Figure F-7.

5. **Close the activities page**

Design Matters

Linking to the home page

Every page in your website should include a link to the home page so a user who has become "lost" in your site can quickly go back to the starting point without relying on the Back button. Don't make users rely on the Back button on the browser toolbar to find their way back to the home page. It's possible that the user's current page might have opened as a result of a search and clicking the Back button will take the user out of the your website, which is not a good thing.

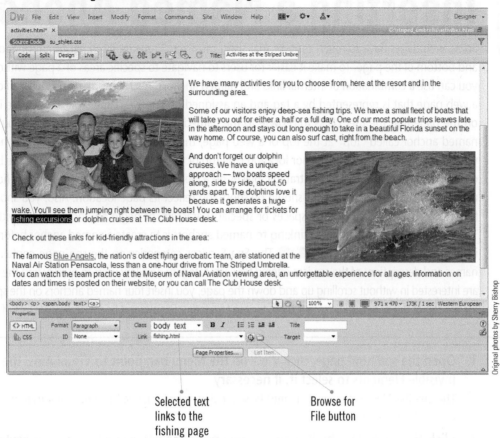

Selected text
used for the
link

Selected text
links to the
fishing page

Browse for
File button

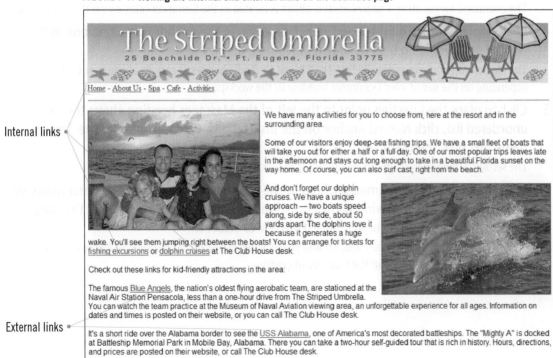

Internal links

External links

Inserting a Named Anchor

Some web pages have so much content that users must scroll repeatedly to get to information at the top and bottom of the page. To make it easier for users to navigate to specific areas of a page without scrolling, you can use a combination of internal links and named anchors. A **named anchor** is a specific location on a web page that is represented by a tag and an assigned descriptive name. You then create internal links on the page that the user clicks to browse to the named anchor location. For example, you can insert a named anchor called "top" at the top of a web page, then create a link at the bottom of the page that, when clicked, will display the anchor location (the top of the web page) when viewed in the browser. You can also insert named anchors at strategic places on a web page, such as before paragraph headings. The name chosen for a named anchor should be short and reflect its page location. Also, you should use only lowercase characters; do not use spaces or special characters, or begin an anchor name with a number. The logical order for creating and linking to named anchors is to create a named anchor before you create its link to avoid possible errors. The Spa Services categories on the spa page contain lists of the names and descriptions of the services offered for each category. To allow users to quickly find the services they are interested in without scrolling up and down the page, you insert four named anchors on the spa page: one for the top of the page and the other three for the Massages, Facials, and Body Treatments lists of services.

STEPS

1. **Open the spa.html page, click View on the Menu bar, point to Visual Aids, then click Invisible Elements to select it, if necessary**

   The Invisible Elements menu item must be selected in order for named anchor locations to be visible on the page in Design view.

2. **Click The Striped Umbrella banner, then press the left arrow key on your keyboard**

   The location for the first named anchor is positioned at the top of the page directly before the banner.

3. **Click the Common category on the Insert panel, if necessary**

   The command for inserting a named anchor object is located in the Common category on the Insert panel.

> **TROUBLE**
> If you don't see the Named Anchor icon on the page, make sure that Invisible Elements is selected in the Visual Aids menu.

4. **Click Named Anchor on the Insert panel, type top in the Anchor name text box in the Named Anchor dialog box, as shown in Figure F-8, then click OK**

   The Named Anchor icon appears before The Striped Umbrella banner. It may be above it or to the left of it depending on the size of your Document window in the workspace.

5. **Click to place the insertion point to the left of the Massages heading above the first unordered list, click Named Anchor on the Insert panel, type massages in the Anchor name text box, then click OK**

   The second named anchor appears before the Massages heading.

6. **Repeat Step 5 to insert named anchors to the left of the Facials and Body Treatments list headings, using the following names: facials and body_treatments, deselect the text, then click the body_treatments named anchor to select it**

   Named anchors appear blue when selected and yellow when not selected, as shown in Figure F-9. The name of the selected anchor appears in the Property inspector.

7. **Save your work**

FIGURE F-8: Named Anchor dialog box

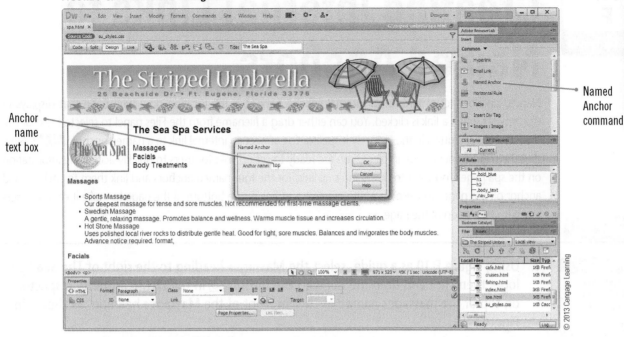

Anchor name text box

Named Anchor command

FIGURE F-9: Named anchor icons

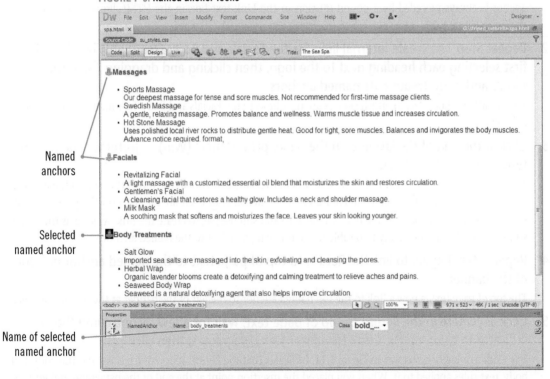

Named anchors

Selected named anchor

Name of selected named anchor

Using Visual Aids

The Visual Aids submenu on the View menu gives you several choices for displaying page elements in Design View, such as named anchor icons. Named anchor icons are considered invisible elements. When you check the Invisible Elements option, you will see the named anchor icons on the page. The icons do not appear when the page is viewed in a browser. Turning on visual aids makes it easier to edit the page. Other options in the Visual Aids menu are Fluid Grid Layout Guides, CSS Layout Backgrounds, CSS Layout Box Model, CSS Layout Outlines, AP Element Outlines, Table Widths, Table Borders, Frame Borders, and Image Maps. The Hide All option hides all of these page elements.

Creating Internal Links to Named Anchors

Named anchors act as targets for internal links. A **target** is the location on a web page that displays in the browser when a link is clicked. You can either drag a filename from the Files panel to selected text or use the Point to File button in the Property inspector to connect an internal link to a named anchor. Now that the named anchors are in place, you are ready to set up links for users to quickly access the information on the spa page. You want to create internal links for the four named anchors and link them to each named anchor on the page. You also decide to create a text link at the bottom of the page to make it easy for users to return to the top of the page.

TROUBLE

The line pointing from the Point to File button to the Massages heading may differ slightly in appearance depending on whether you are using a Mac or Windows.

1. **Using Figure F-10 as a guide, select the Massages heading to the right of The Sea Spa logo, then click and drag the Point to File button 🎯 in the HTML Property inspector on top of the massages named anchor in front of the Massages heading, as shown in Figure F-10**

   The named anchor, massages, is the target for the massages link. When viewing the spa page in the browser, the list of massages will display at the top of the window when Massages is clicked. The name of a named anchor is always preceded by a pound (#) sign in the Link text box in the HTML Property inspector, as shown in Figure F-10.

2. **Repeat Step 1 to create internal links for the Facials and Body Treatments headings by first selecting each heading next to the logo, then clicking and dragging 🎯 to the facials and body_treatments named anchors**

   The Facials and Body Treatments headings are now links to the Facials and Body Treatments unordered lists of services.

3. **Click at the end of the last line on the page, press [Enter] (Win) or [return] (Mac), then type Return to top of page**

   The Return to top of page text will be used to link to the named anchor at the top of the page. If the text you want to use for a link to a named anchor and the named anchor itself are far apart on the page, you can scroll up or down the page as much as you need to and still use 🎯 to create the link. As long as the text is still selected, it is not necessary to be able to see it when you point to the named anchor.

4. **Repeat Step 1 again to link the Return to top of page text to the named anchor in front of the banner**

   The top of page text is now a link to the top named anchor to the left of the banner at the top of the page.

QUICK TIP

To enable or disable the Code Navigator, click View on the Menu bar, click Code Navigator, then click the Disable check box. It takes a second or two for the Code Navigator to appear.

5. **Click anywhere in the Return to top of page text, wait for a few seconds until the Click indicator to bring up the Code Navigator icon 🌸 appears, then click 🌸**

   The Code Navigator, as shown in Figure F-11, indicates that the Return to top of page text has the body and body_text rules applied to it. When you placed the insertion point at the end of the paragraph and entered a paragraph break, the formatting was retained for the Return to top of page text.

6. **Save your work, preview the spa page in your browser, test each link, then close your browser**

   The page can only scroll as far as there is text on the page, so you may not see much change depending on your window size.

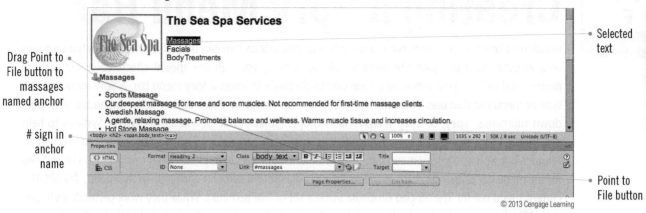

Selected text

Drag Point to File button to massages named anchor

sign in anchor name

Point to File button

© 2013 Cengage Learning

FIGURE F-11: Code Navigator displaying rule name

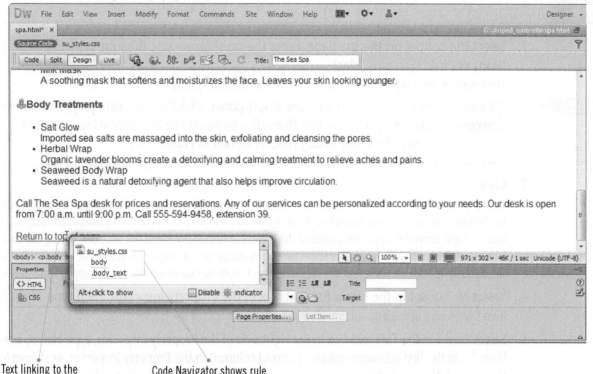

Text linking to the top of the page

Code Navigator shows rule name and location

Using the Code Navigator

When you click on a page element either in Code view or in Design view, wait a second or two; the Click indicator to bring up the Code Navigator icon ▒ will appear (you can also [Alt]-click (Win) or [Ctrl]-click (Mac) to display it instantly). Clicking ▒ will open a pop-up window called the Code Navigator. As you recall from Unit C, the Code Navigator lists the CSS rule name linked to the page element, along with the name of the style sheet that contains the rule. Pointing to the rule name will display the properties and values of the rule, as shown in Figure F-12. This is a quick way to view the rule definition. If you click the rule name, the code for the rule will open in Code and Design views, where you can then edit it.

FIGURE F-12: Code Navigator displaying rule properties

Pointing to the rule displays its properties and values

Mac users will see Cmd+Opt+click to show

Creating a Spry Menu Bar

Recall from Unit C that a menu bar is a set of text or image links that can be used to navigate between pages of a website. To make your site more visually appealing, you can use special effects to create a more professional look for your menu bars. One way to do this is to insert a Spry menu bar. A Spry menu bar is a type of menu bar that uses unordered lists, CSS, and Javascript to create an interactive menu bar with pull-down submenus. **Spry**, or **Spry framework**, is open source code developed by Adobe Systems to help designers quickly incorporate dynamic content on their web pages. Each link in a Spry menu bar is called an **item**. When you add a Spry menu bar, by default it first appears with placeholder text and generic settings for the menu bar properties, such as the width and background color for each item in the menu. The current menu bar for The Striped Umbrella site is a set of five text links. While they work perfectly well, you would like a more professionally designed look. You begin by creating a Spry menu bar that will contain five items: home, about us, cafe, spa, and activities.

STEPS

1. **Select the** banner **on the spa page, press the** right arrow key, **then press** [Shift] [Enter] **(Win) or** [Shift] [return] (Mac)
   The insertion point is positioned between the banner and the spa logo.

QUICK TIP
The Spry Menu Bar button is also in the Layout category on the Insert panel.

2. **Click the** Insert panel list arrow **on the Insert panel, click the** Spry **category, scroll down, if necessary, to click** Spry Menu Bar, **then click to select the** Horizontal layout option button **in the Spry Menu Bar dialog box, as shown in Figure F-13**
   The Horizontal layout option specifies that the menu bar will be placed horizontally on the page.

3. **Click** OK
   The Spry menu bar, which will be referred to from now on simply as the menu bar, displays selected under the banner. The menu bar contains four items by default and each item contains placeholder text, such as Item 1. Right above the upper left corner of the menu bar is the Spry menu bar label containing the default label name: MenuBar1. The Property inspector shows the menu bar properties. It lists the default items and submenu items, along with text boxes for linking each item and submenu item to the appropriate pages.

4. **Select** MenuBar1 **in the Menu Bar text box in the Property inspector, then type** MenuBar
   Item 1 is selected in the Item column (first column on the left) in the Property inspector.

5. **Select** Item 1 **in the Text text box in the right side of the Property inspector, type** Home, **select** Item 1.1 **in the first submenu column (second column) in the Property inspector, as shown in Figure F-14, then click the** Remove menu Item button — **above the first submenu column**
   Item 1 is renamed Home and the default submenu item Item 1.1 is deleted.

QUICK TIP
You can add submenu items by clicking the Add menu item button +.

6. **Click** — **two more times**
   The remainder of the default submenu items—Item 1.2 and Item 1.3—for the Home item are deleted as well.

7. **Click the** Browse for File button **next to the Link text box in the Property inspector, double-click** index.html **in the local site root folder, then compare your Property inspector to Figure F-15**
   The Home item is linked to the home page.

QUICK TIP
If you have a gap between the banner and the menu bar, go to Code view to see if you have a <p> tag around the banner. If you do, delete the beginning and ending tag and the space will be removed.

8. **Click to place the insertion point to the right of the menu bar, enter a line break, compare your screen to Figure F-16, save your file, click** OK **to close the Copy Dependent Files dialog box, then refresh the Files panel if necessary**
   The menu bar displays with the first item named Home linked to the home page. The supporting files that are needed to format the Spry menu bar and make it function properly are added to the local site root folder. A new SpryAssets folder is added that contains a JavaScript file, a CSS file, and some images that are used in the Spry menu bar.

FIGURE F-13: Spry Menu Bar dialog box

Horizontal layout
option button

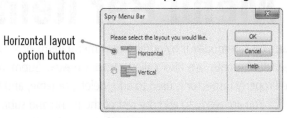

FIGURE F-14: Property inspector with Menu Bar properties

Menu Bar
text box

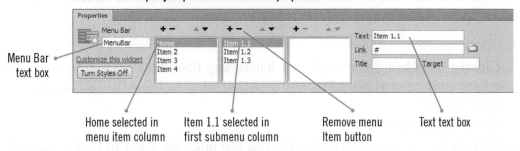

Home selected in
menu item column

Item 1.1 selected in
first submenu column

Remove menu
Item button

Text text box

FIGURE F-15: Home item for the menu bar

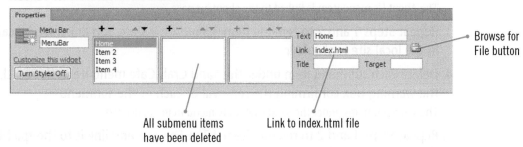

Browse for
File button

All submenu items
have been deleted

Link to index.html file

FIGURE F-16: The Spry Menu bar on the spa page

The named anchor icon may appear beside the banner, depending on the width of the window

Spry Menu Bar label

Item 1 is renamed "Home"

© 2013 Cengage Learning

Inserting a Fireworks menu bar

Another option for adding a menu bar to your page is to create a menu bar in Adobe Fireworks, open Dreamweaver, then import the menu bar onto the web page. Once you've created the Fireworks menu bar, you export the Fireworks file to a Dreamweaver local site root folder. This file contains the HTML code that defines the menu bar properties. Next, open the appropriate web page in Dreamweaver where you want to insert the menu bar, then use the Insert > Image Objects > Fireworks HTML command to add the HTML code to the page. You can also use Dreamweaver to import rollover images and buttons created in Fireworks.

Adding Menu Bar Items

After you create a menu bar, you can modify it by adding new menu items or submenu items or deleting those that you do not need. Submenus are also called **child menus**. Submenu items can also have submenus under them. The Property inspector is used to add, delete, rename, and link Spry menu items to pages in your website.  You are ready to add the rest of the menu and submenu items to the menu bar so users will have access to each of the main pages from the menu bar. You want to rename the rest of the default menu items, add one additional menu item, then add two submenu items under the activities item for the cruises and fishing pages.

STEPS

1. **Click the Spry Menu Bar: MenuBar tab if necessary, then click Item 2 in the Item menu column (first column) in the Property inspector, select Item 2 in the Text text box, then type About Us**

   Item 2 is renamed About Us.

2. **Click the Browse button 🗀 next to the Link text box, click about_us.html in the local site root folder, then click OK (Win) or Open (Mac) or double-click about_us.html**

   The About Us menu item is linked to the about_us page.

3. **Repeat Steps 1 and 2 to rename Item 3 Sand Crab Cafe and link it to the cafe.html page in the local site root folder**

4. **Delete each submenu item under the Sand Crab Cafe menu item, then click OK to close the warning box confirming the removal of each of the submenus**

   The submenu items under the Sand Crab Cafe menu item are deleted.

5. **Repeat Steps 1 and 2 to rename Item 4 The Sea Spa and link it to the spa.html page in the local site root folder**

   The Sea Spa menu item is linked to the spa page and remains selected in the Property inspector.

6. **Click the Add menu item button ➕ above the Item menu column (first column), select Untitled Item, in the Text text box type Activities, then link it to the activities.html page**

   The new menu item, Activities, is linked to the activities page and remains selected in the Property inspector.

7. **Click ➕ above the first submenu column (second column), select Untitled Item, type Cruises in the Text text box, then link it to the cruises.html page**

   A new submenu item, Cruises, is added under the Activities menu item that will link to the cruises page.

8. **Repeat Step 7 to add another submenu item named Fishing, link it to the fishing.html page, save your work, then compare your screen to Figure F-17**

   A second submenu item is added under the Activities menu item that will link to the fishing page.

9. **Create a new Tag rule in the su_styles.css file to modify the <img> tag, then set the Block Vertical-align to bottom**

   This rule will prevent a gap between the banner and menu bar.

10. **Click the Switch Design View to Live View button ⟨Live⟩ on the Document toolbar, view the menu bar, then compare your screen to Figure F-18**

    Live View shows you what the page will look like when opened in a browser. Not only is it a faster way to view your page than previewing it in a browser but it shows the interactive elements functioning. For more information about Live View read the Clues to Use box *Viewing your page in Live View*.

11. **Click ⟨Live⟩ again**

    The spa page redisplays in your workspace in Design view without the interactive elements being functional.

TROUBLE

If a message appears that you need to install the Flash plug-in, go to adobe.com to download the plug-in or this feature will not work.

FIGURE F-17: Adding menu items and submenu items to the menu bar

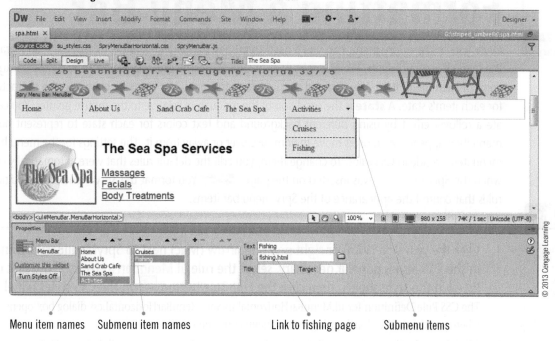

Menu item names   Submenu item names   Link to fishing page   Submenu items

FIGURE F-18: Viewing the spa page in Live View

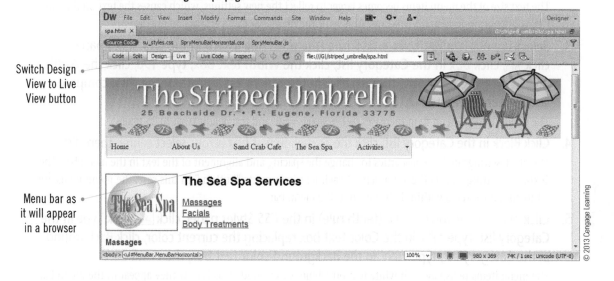

Switch Design View to Live View button

Menu bar as it will appear in a browser

Viewing your page in Live View

When you view your web pages in Dreamweaver, the page elements appear similar to the way they will look when viewed in a web browser. Live View gives you a more accurate picture of what the page will actually look like in a browser, with interactive elements active and functioning. You use the Switch Design View to Live View button on the Document toolbar to enable Live View. Next to this button is the Shows the Live View source in code view button, which displays the code. The code remains as read-only until you click the Shows the Live View source in code view button again. When the Switch Design View to Live View button is active, the Shows the Live View source in code view button can be toggled on or off. If Live View is not active, selecting the Shows the Live View source in code view button will turn it on. When you first click the Live View button, you may see a message that you need to install the Flash plug-in from the Adobe website, adobe.com. Once you download the plug-in, your pages can then be viewed using Live View.

Formatting a Menu Bar

Once you create a Spry menu bar, you'll need to modify the default settings to adjust the appearance of the menu bar and its items. For example, you can adjust their height and width or specify the background color of each menu item. You can add special effects for menu bar items by changing the characteristics for each item's state. A **state** is the condition of the menu item relative to the mouse pointer. You can create a rollover effect by using different background and text colors for each state to represent how the menu item appears when users move their mouse over or away from it. The settings for the menu bar and menu items reside in CSS rules. To change them, you edit the default rules that were automatically created when the Spry menu bar was inserted on the page. ▓▓▓▓ You format the Spry menu bar by editing the rules that control the appearance of the Spry menu bar items.

STEPS

TROUBLE
If you don't see the rule listed, click the Switch to All (Document) Mode button All in the CSS Styles panel.

1. **Click the plus sign (Win) or right pointing arrow (Mac) next to SpryMenuBarHorizonal.css in the CSS Styles panel if necessary, select the rule ul.MenuBarHorizontal (the first rule listed in the style sheet), then click the Edit Rule button ✎ on the CSS styles panel**

   The CSS Rule Definition for ul.MenuBarHorizontal in SpryMenuBarHorizontal.css dialog box opens. This is where you define the global settings for all menu and submenu items.

2. **Click Type in the Category list, click the Font-family list arrow, click Arial, Helvetica, sans-serif, click the Font-size list arrow, click 14, click the Font-size unit of measure list arrow, click px, compare your screen to Figure F-19, then click OK**

   The text size of the menu items becomes larger to reflect the new settings, which causes the text on the Sand Crab Cafe button to wrap to two lines. You want the menu bar to revert back to one line.

3. **Select the ul.MenuBarHorizontal li rule (the third rule listed) in the CSS Styles panel, click ✎, click Box in the Category list, click the Width text box, type 190, click the Width unit of measure list arrow, click px, click in the Height text box, type 25, then compare your screen to Figure F-20**

   The width of each menu item increases to 190 pixels wide and the height is set to 25 pixels.

4. **Click Block in the Category list, click the Text-align text box arrow, select center, then click OK**

   The block settings include properties to change the spacing and alignment of the text in the menu bar. The Text-align setting adjusts the alignment of each text item on its "button." In this case, the menu items are set to appear centered within their button in the menu bar.

TROUBLE
If you don't see the u.MenuBarHorizontal a rule listed in the CSS Styles panel, click the Switch to (All) Document Mode button All.

5. **Click ul.MenuBarHorizontal a (tenth rule) in the CSS Styles panel, click ✎, click Type in the Category list, type #FFF in the Color text box replacing the current color, click Background in the Category list, type #09C in the Background-color text box, then click OK**

   The menu items redisplay with white text on a blue background. This is how they appear in the menu bar when the mouse is *not* positioned over them.

QUICK TIP
To locate this rule, which is the longest rule, place your mouse over each rule name to see the extended names. You can also temporarily expand the CSS Styles panel width to see the entire name.

6. **Click ul.MenuBarHorizontal a.MenuBarItemHover, ul.MenuBarHorizontal a.MenuBarItemSubmenuHover, ul.MenuBarHorizontal a.MenuBarSubmenuVisible (twelfth rule) in the CSS Styles panel, then click ✎**

7. **Click Type in the Category list, type #630 in the Color text box, click Background in the Category list, type #FC9 in the Background-color text box, then click OK**

   The property values for the menu items and submenu items change to a sand background with brown text. This is how they appear when the mouse is positioned over them.

8. **Click File on the Menu bar, click Save All, preview your page in the browser, compare your screen to Figure F-21, test each link to ensure that each works correctly, then close the browser**

   The button background colors are blue with white text when the pointer is not placed over them and sand-colored with brown text when the pointer is positioned over them.

Creating Links and Menu Bars

FIGURE F-19: **Adding properties for the .ulMenuBarHorizontal rule**

Type category •

Font-size list arrow

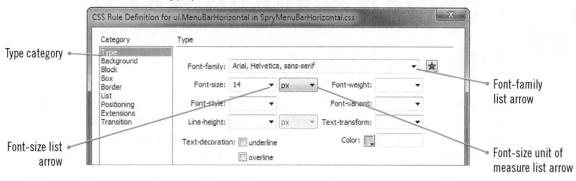

Font-family list arrow

Font-size unit of measure list arrow

FIGURE F-20: **Modifying properties for the ul.MenuBarHorizontal li rule**

Box category •

Width text box •

Height text box •

Width unit of measure list arrow

FIGURE F-21: **Spa page viewed in the browser with the updated menu bar**

© 2013 Cengage Learning

Menu items and submenu items are blue with white text when the pointer is not placed over them

Menu items and submenu items are sand colored with brown text when the pointer is placed over them

Creating Links and Menu Bars

Copying a Menu Bar to Other Pages

When you create a menu bar for one page in a website, you should copy it to all of the other pages in the site. This practice provides continuity in the navigation structure and makes it easy for users to navigate comfortably through pages in your site.  The new Spry menu bar is an improvement over the menu bar with plain text links. You decide to replace all existing menu bars on the pages in the website with this menu bar to improve each page's design and promote consistency. You copy the menu bar to the about_us, index, and activities pages in The Striped Umbrella website.

STEPS

1. **Click the Spry Menu Bar:MenuBar tab above the top left corner of the menu bar, as shown in Figure F-22, click Edit on the Menu bar, then click Copy**
   The menu bar is ready to be pasted on other pages in the website.

> **QUICK TIP**
> When you work on multiple open pages, use the file-name tabs at the top of the Document toolbar or press [Ctrl] [Tab] to move quickly between pages (Win).

2. **Double-click activities.html on the Files panel**
   The activities page opens.

3. **Select the original menu bar on the page, click Edit on the Menu bar, click Paste, click to the right of the menu bar, add a line break, delete the horizontal rule, compare your screen to Figure F-23, then save the page**
   The new menu bar appears on the page in place of the previous one and the new styles are added to the page.

> **TROUBLE**
> If you have trouble with the alignment and spacing between the banner and the menu bar, look at the break tag after the banner. If it is on a separate line under the banner, move it to the end of the line of code for the banner.

4. **Open the index page, delete the current menu bar, delete any <p> tags around the banner, click the banner to select it, press the right arrow key, paste the Spry menu bar on the page, delete the horizontal rule, then insert a line break after the menu bar**
   The menu bar is pasted on the index page and the spacing after the menu bar is adjusted to match the other two pages.

5. **Open the about_us page, replace the current menu bar with the new menu bar, add a line break, delete the horizontal rule, then apply the body_text rule to the heading "Welcome guests!"**
   The menu bar is pasted on the about_us page, the horizontal rule is deleted, and the page heading is formatted to match the home, spa, and activities pages.

> **QUICK TIP**
> View the pages at a high resolution to ensure that the menu bars do not break into two lines.

6. **Click File on the Menu bar, click Save All, then preview each page in the browser**
   The menu bar appears consistently on the index, about_us, spa, and activities pages of The Striped Umbrella website. Although the cafe, fishing, and activities pages are not designed yet, you see that the links all work correctly. If the spacing between the menu bar and the rest of the page content is not consistent, add or remove <br> tags if necessary to adjust the spacing on each page.

7. **Hold the pointer over the Activities link, as shown in Figure F-24, close the browser, then close all open pages except the about_us page**
   When the pointer is placed over the Activities link, the submenu drops down with the two submenu links visible and active.

FIGURE F-22: **Selecting the Spry menu bar on the spa page**

Spry Menu
Bar:
MenuBar tab

© 2013 Cengage Learning

FIGURE F-23: **Pasting the Spry menu bar on the activities page**

Spry Menu
bar copied to
activities
page

© 2013 Cengage Learning
Original photo courtesy of Sherry Bishop

FIGURE F-24: **Viewing the activities submenu items in the browser**

Submenu
items for
Cruises
and Fishing
pages

© 2013 Cengage Learning
Original photo courtesy of Sherry Bishop

Creating an Image Map

Another way to create navigation links for web pages is to create an image map. An image map is an image that has one or more hotspots placed on top of it. A **hotspot** is an active area on an image that, when clicked, links to a different location on the page or to another web page. For example, a map of the world could have a hotspot placed on each individual country so that users could click a country to link to more information. Hotspots are not visible in the browser window, but when users place their pointer over the hotspot, the pointer changes to a pointing finger, indicating the presence of a link. To create a hotspot, select the image on which you want to place the hotspot, draw the hotspot with one of the shape hotspot tools in the Property inspector, then add the link information, alternate text, and target information in the text boxes in the Property inspector. You want to create an image map on the activities page to provide another way for users to link to the index page.

STEPS

1. **Click The Striped Umbrella banner on the about_us page to select it, then double-click a blank area on the right side of the Property inspector to expand it, if necessary**

   The Property inspector displays the drawing tools for creating hotspots on an image in the lower-left corner.

   TROUBLE
   If you don't see the blue rectangle, click View, point to Visual Aids, then click Image Maps to select it.

2. **Click the Rectangle Hotspot Tool button ▢ on the Property inspector, drag to create a rectangle that encompasses The Striped Umbrella name on the banner, release the mouse button, click OK to close the Dreamweaver dialog box, then compare your screen to Figure F-25**

   A shaded blue rectangle appears within the area that you outlined. This blue rectangle is the hotspot. The dialog box reminds you to add to the alternate text for the hotspot.

3. **Drag the Point to File button ⊕ next to the Link text box in the Property inspector to index.html in the Files panel**

   The hotspot is linked to the index.html file. If the hotspot is clicked, the index file opens.

   TROUBLE
   If you don't see the Map text box in the Property inspector, click the image map object on the banner to select it.

4. **Select Map in the Map text box in the Property inspector, then type home**

   The image map is named home. Each image map should have a unique name, especially if a page contains more than one image map.

5. **Click the Target list arrow in the Property inspector, then click _self**

   The _self target directs the browser to display the home page in the same browser window as the activities page, rather than opening a separate window. When the hotspot is clicked, the home page opens in the same browser window. See the Clues to Use box *Setting targets for links* to learn more about how the _self property, along with other property options, are used to set targets for links.

   QUICK TIP
   You should always assign a unique name for each image map to make them more accessible to users utilizing screen readers.

6. **Type Link to home page in the Alt text box in the Property inspector, as shown in Figure F-26**

   The descriptive information placed in the Alt text box provides a brief clue to the user about what further information awaits if the hotspot is clicked. The alternate text is also read by screen readers to tell users what will happen if they click the image map.

7. **Switch to Code view, locate the <br> tag that has been added below the ending </map> tag, then delete it**

   QUICK TIP
   This additional code will prevent a border appearing around the banner in Internet Explorer.

8. **Place the insertion point right before the closing image tag for the banner, then type style="border:0"**

9. **Return to Design view, save your work, preview the page in your browser window, test the link on the image map, then close the browser**

   The hotspot is not visible in the browser, but if you place the mouse over the hotspot, you will see the pointer change to 🖑 to indicate a link is present.

FIGURE F-25: Drawing a hotspot on The Striped Umbrella banner

Hotspot

Rectangle Hotspot Tool

Pointer Hotspot Tool

Circle Hotspot Tool

Polygon Hotspot Tool

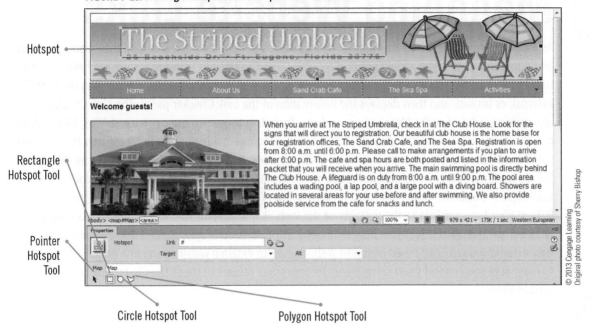

© 2013 Cengage Learning
Original photo courtesy of Sherry Bishop

FIGURE F-26: Adding a link, a target, and alternate text to a hotspot

Link text box

Target text box

Alt text box

Setting targets for links

You can set targets to determine how a new window will display in a browser when links on pages or in frames are clicked. A **frame** is a fixed region in a browser that can display a web page and act independently from other pages displayed in other frames within the browser. When you set a target for a link or frame, you have four options for how the new window will open after the link is clicked. These targets are set by clicking the Target list arrow in the HTML Property inspector and selecting the target

you want. The _blank target displays the destination page in a separate browser window and leaves the original window open. The _parent target displays the destination page in the parent window or frameset, replacing the original window or frameset. The _self target displays the destination page in the same window or frame. The _top target displays the destination page in the whole browser window.

Design Matters

Creating and modifying hotspots

In addition to the Rectangle hotspot tool, there are two other helpful shape tools: a Circle hotspot tool and a Polygon hotspot tool. These tools can be used to create any shape hotspot that you need. For instance, the Polygon hotspot tool could be used to draw an outline around each state on a map of the United States. Hotspots can be easily changed and rearranged on an image using the Pointer hotspot tool. First, select the hotspot you would like to edit, then drag one of the hotspot selector handles to change the size or

shape of a hotspot. You can also move the hotspot by dragging it to a new position on the image. It is a good idea to limit the number of complex or irregularly shaped hotspots in an image because the code can become too lengthy for the page to download in a reasonable amount of time. You should also make the hotspot boundaries a little larger than they need to be to cover the area you want to set as a link. This allows a little leeway for users when they place their mouse over the hotspot by creating a larger target area for them.

Managing Website Links

As your website grows, so will the number of links on it. Checking links to make sure they work is a crucial and ongoing task that you should perform regularly. The Check Links Sitewide feature is a helpful tool for managing your links. It checks your entire website for the total number of links, categorizing them as OK, external, or broken, and then displays the information in the Link Checker panel. The Link Checker panel also provides a list of all the files used in a website, including those that are **orphaned files**, files that are not linked to any pages in the website. If you find broken internal links (links to files within the website), you should carefully check the code entered in the Link text box for errors. You can either use the Browse for File button in the Link Checker panel to correct the link, or type the correction in the Link text box in the Property inspector. You check broken external links (links to files outside the website) by testing the links in your browser. Due to the volatility of the web, it is important to check external links routinely as websites are often under construction or undergoing address changes. ![icon] You have created three new external links in The Striped Umbrella website: two to external websites and one email link. You want to make sure you entered them correctly, so you run some reports to check the site for any broken links or orphaned files.

STEPS

TROUBLE
If any links are listed under the Broken Links category, click Site on the Menu bar, point to Advanced, click Recreate Site Cache, then run the report again.

1. **Click Site on the Menu bar, then click Check Links Sitewide**

   The Link Checker panel in the Results Tab group opens. By default, the Link Checker panel initially displays any broken internal links found in the website. The Striped Umbrella website has no broken links, as shown in Figure F-27.

QUICK TIP
To view all of the links without scrolling, you can float the Results Tab group.

2. **Click the Show list arrow in the Link Checker panel, click External Links, then compare your screen with Figure F-28**

   Two files are listed: the activities page and the index page. The activities page has two external links listed: one to the Blue Angels website and one to the U.S.S. Alabama website. The index page has an email link listed.

TROUBLE
If any orphaned files are listed under the Files category, click Site on the Menu bar, point to Advanced, click Recreate Site Cache, then run the report again.

3. **Click the Show list arrow, then click Orphaned Files**

   There are no orphaned files displayed in the Link Checker panel for the website, as shown in Figure F-29.

TROUBLE
If you don't see the links, click the Refresh button ![icon].

4. **Close the Results Tab Group, click the Assets tab on the Files Tab Group, then click the URLs button ![icon] on the Assets panel**

   The list of external links in the Striped Umbrella website displays in the Assets panel. See Figure F-30.

5. **Close the about_us page, then Exit (Win) or Quit (Mac) Dreamweaver**

FIGURE F-27: Link Checker with Broken Links results displayed

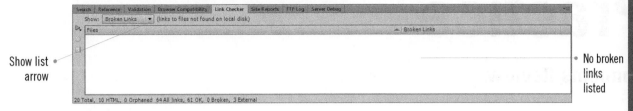

Show list arrow

No broken links listed

FIGURE F-28: Link Checker with External Links results displayed

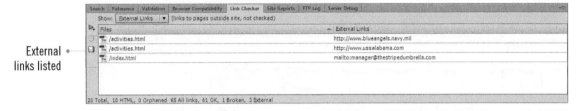

External links listed

FIGURE F-29: Link Checker with Orphaned Files results displayed

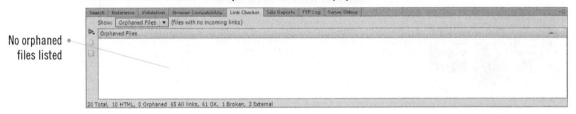

No orphaned files listed

FIGURE F-30: Assets panel with website external links displayed

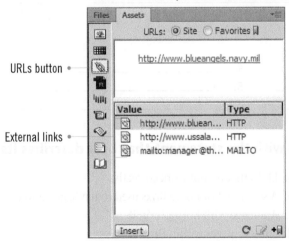

URLs button

External links

Design Matters

Designing for easy navigation

As you work on the navigation structure for a website, you should try to limit the number of internal links on each page. You should also provide visual clues on each page to let users know where they are, much like a "You are here" marker on a store directory at the mall, or a bread crumbs trail. A **bread crumbs trail** is a list of links that provides a path from the initial page you opened in a website to the page that you are currently viewing. Many websites provide a list of all the site's pages, called a **site map**. A site map is similar to a table of contents; it lets users see how the information is divided between the pages and helps them to locate the information they need quickly.

Creating Links and Menu Bars

Practice

Concepts Review

Label each element in the Dreamweaver window shown in Figure F-31.

FIGURE F-31

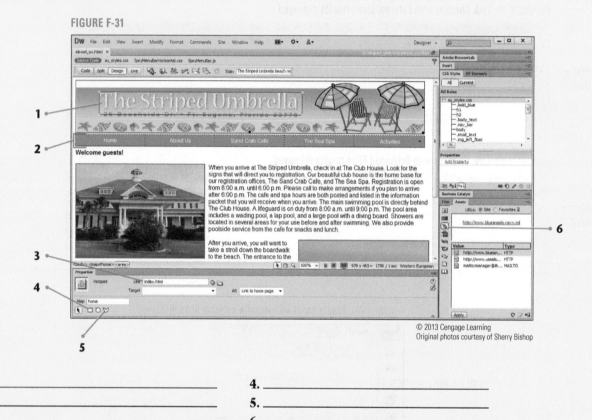

© 2013 Cengage Learning
Original photos courtesy of Sherry Bishop

1. _____   4. _____
2. _____   5. _____
3. _____   6. _____

Match each of the following terms with the statement that best describes its function.

7. **Internal links**   a. Links that do not work correctly
8. **External links**   b. A set of text or image links used to navigate between pages of a website
9. **Broken links**   c. An image with hotspots on it
10. **Named anchor**   d. Links to pages within the website
11. **Menu bar**   e. Active area on an image that serves as a link
12. **Target**   f. A location on a web page that browsers will display when a link is clicked
13. **Image map**   g. A specific location on a web page, represented by a special icon, that will fully
14. **Hotspot**   display in the browser window when a user clicks the link tagged to it
15. **Orphaned file**   h. A file that is not linked to any pages on a website
                             i. Links to pages outside the website

Select the best answer from the following list of choices.

16. Which type of path begins with a forward slash?

a. Document-relative

b. Root-relative

c. Absolute

d. Image-relative

17. Which button in the Property inspector do you use to connect an internal link to a named anchor?

a. Point to File

b. Point to Anchor

c. Anchor to File

d. Point to Named Anchor

18. The four target options for how a window will display in a browser when a link is clicked are:

a. _blank, _parent, _self, _top.

b. _blank, _child, _self, _top.

c. _blank, _parent, _child, _top.

d. _blank, _parent, _self, _new.

19. To see all links in a website, you click which button on the Assets panel?

a. Links

b. Paths

c. URLs

d. Anchors

20. Which dialog box shows you a list of orphaned files?

a. Orphaned Files

b. Link Checker

c. Check Links Sitewide

d. Assets

Skills Review

Important: *If you did not create this website in Unit B and maintain it during the preceding units, you will need to create a local site root folder for this website and define the website using files your instructor will provide. See the "Read This Before You Begin" section for more detailed instructions.*

1. Understand links and paths.

a. Write an example of an absolute path for a link.

b. Write an example of a relative path for a link.

c. Write a sentence explaining the difference between a document-relative path and a root-relative path.

2. Create an external link.

a. Start Dreamweaver, then open the Blooms & Bulbs website.

b. Open dwf_2.html from the drive and folder where you store your Unit F Data Files, save it as **newsletter.html** in the blooms local site root folder, replacing the existing file and not updating links, then close dwf_2.html.

c. Click the first broken image placeholder for the ruby_grass.jpg file browse to the drive and folder where you store your Unit F Data Files to copy it to your assets folder, then apply the img_left_float rule to it.

d. Repeat Step c to replace the next two broken image placeholders for the trees.jpg and plants.jpg files, apply the img_right_float rule to the trees image and the img_left_float rule to the plants image.

e. Scroll to the bottom of the page, then link the National Gardening Association text to **http://www.garden.org**.

f. Link the Organic Gardening text to **http://www.organicgardening.com**.

g. Link the Southern Living text to **http://www.southernliving.com/southern**.

h. Save the file, then preview it in your browser window.

i. Test the links to make sure they all work correctly, then close the browser.

3. Create an internal link.

a. Select the text "gardening tips" in the last sentence in the Gardening Issues paragraph.

b. Use the Point to File button to link the text to the tips.html page.

c. Change the page title to **Gardening Matters**.

d. Create a new Tag rule in the blooms_styles.css style sheet that modifies the <h2> tag as follows: font-family: Arial, Helvetica, sans-serif font; font-size: medium; font-weight: bold; color: #000.

Skills Review (continued)

e. Create a new Tag rule in the blooms_styles.css style sheet that modifies the <h3> tag as follows: font-family: Arial, Helvetica, sans-serif; font-size: medium; font-weight: bold; color: #060.

f. Save all files, test the link in your browser, then close the browser.

g. Open the plants page, then add a new paragraph to the bottom of the page: **In addition to these marvelous roses, we have many annuals, perennials, and water plants that have just arrived.**

h. Apply the body_text rule to the paragraph if necessary.

i. Use the Files panel to create three new blank files in the local site root folder named: annuals.html, perennials.html, and water_plants.html.

j. Link the "annuals" text in the new paragraph to the annuals.html file, link the "perennials" text to the perennials.html file, then link the "water plants" text to the water_plants.html file.

k. Save your work, test the links in your browser, then close the browser. (*Hint*: These pages do not have content yet, but are serving as placeholders.)

4. Insert a named anchor.

a. Switch to the newsletter page, then show the invisible elements if necessary.

b. Insert a named anchor in front of the Grass subheading, then name it **grass**.

c. Insert a named anchor in front of the Trees subheading, then name it **trees**.

d. Insert a named anchor in front of the Plants subheading, then name it **plants**.

e. Save the file.

5. Create an internal link to a named anchor.

a. Using the Point to File button in the Property inspector, create a link from the word grass in the Gardening Issues paragraph to the grass named anchor.

b. Create a link from the word trees in the Gardening Issues paragraph to the trees named anchor.

c. Create a link from the word plants in the Gardening Issues paragraph to the plants named anchor.

d. Save the file, then test the links in your browser window.

6. Create a Spry menu bar.

a. Enter a line break after the banner on the newsletter page.

b. Use the Spry category on the Insert panel to insert a Spry menu bar with a horizontal layout under the banner.

c. Replace MenuBar1 in the Menu Bar text box in the Property inspector with the name **MenuBar**.

d. Replace the name Item 1 in the Text text box with **Home**, then remove all submenu items from the Home item.

e. Link the Home item to the index.html file.

f. Switch to Code view, place your insertion point right after the ending tag for the unordered list, switch back to Design view, insert two line breaks, then save the file, copying the dependent files.

7. Add menu bar items.

a. Rename the Item 2 menu item **Newsletter**, then link it to the newsletter page.

b. Rename the Item 3 menu item **Plants**, then link it to the plants page.

c. Rename the Item 4 menu item **Tips**, then link it to the tips page.

d. With the Tips menu item selected, add a new menu item with the name **Workshops**, then link it to the workshops page.

e. With the Plants menu item selected, rename submenu Item 3.1 **Annuals**, then link it to the annuals.html page.

f. With the Plants menu item selected, rename submenu Item 3.2 **Perennials**, then link it to the perennials.html page.

g. With the Plants menu item selected, rename submenu Item 3.3 **Water Plants**, then link it to the water_plants.html page.

h. With the Annuals submenu item selected, delete its two submenu items, then save your work.

8. Format a menu bar.

a. Expand the SpryMenuBarHorizonal.css style sheet in the CSS Styles panel, then edit the rule ul.MenuBarHorizontal with the following settings: Font-family: Arial, Helvetica, sans-serif; Font-size: 14 px.

b. Edit the ul.MenuBarHorizontal li rule with the following settings: Box Width: 190 px; Box Height: 25 px; Block Text-align: center.

c. Edit the following rule: ul.MenuBarHorizontal a with the following settings: Type Color: #030; Background-color: #99F.

d. Edit the following rule: ul.MenuBarHorizontal a.MenuBarItemHover, ul.MenuBarHorizontal a.MenuBarItemSubmenuHover, ul.MenuBarHorizontal a.MenuBarSubmenuVisible with the following settings: Type Color: #FFC; Background-color: #030.

e. Create a new Tag rule in the blooms_styles.css file to modify the <img> tag as follows: Block Vertical-align:bottom.

f. Save your work, then test the menu bar on the page in the browser to make sure everything works correctly.

9. Copy a menu bar to other pages.

a. Select and copy the menu bar, then open the index page.

b. Select the banner, press the right arrow key, click the Format list arrow in the HTML Property inspector, then click None if necessary.

c. Paste the menu bar at the insertion point, then delete the existing menu bar created with text links and the horizontal rule.

d. Switch to Live View to view the placement of the menu bar on the page.

e. Return to Design view; when you are satisfied with the page, save your work, then close the index page.

f. Switch to the plants page, add a line break after the banner, paste the menu bar under the banner, then add another line break.

g. Switch to Live view to check the placement of the menu bar, then return to Design view and save and close the page.

h. Repeat Step f to add a menu bar on the tips page, apply the img_left_float to the butterfly image, then save the tips page. (*Hint*: If you see a space between the banner and the menu bar, go to Code view and look for <p> tags around the banner. If you see any, delete them.)

i. Preview all pages in the browser window, checking the spacing for each page to ensure a uniform look, then close the browser. (*Hint*: The workshops, annuals, perennials, and water_plants pages are serving as placeholder pages and do not have content yet.)

10. Create an image map.

a. On the newsletter page, create a rectangle hotspot over the words *Blooms & Bulbs* on the Blooms & Bulbs banner.

b. Name the image map **home**, then link it to the index page.

c. Set the target as _top.

d. Enter the alternate text **Link to home page**.

e. Switch to Code view, locate the <br> tag that has been added below the ending </map> tag, then delete it.

f. Place the insertion point right before the closing image tag for the banner, then type this code: **style="border:0"**.

g. Save all pages, then preview the newsletter page in the browser, testing all links. Refer to Figure F-32 to check your work.

FIGURE F-32

Blooms & Bulbs
HWY 43 SOUTH • ALVIN • TX 77511 • 555-248-0806

Home   Newsletter   Plants   Tips   Workshops

Gardening Matters

Welcome, fellow gardeners. My name is Cosie Simmons, the owner of Blooms & Bulbs. My passion has always been my gardens. Ever since I was a small child, I was drawn to my back yard where all varieties of beautiful plants flourished. A lush carpet of thick grass bordered with graceful beds is truly a haven for all living creatures. With proper planning and care, your gardens will draw a variety of birds and butterflies and become a great pleasure to you.

Gardening Issues

There are several areas to concentrate on when formulating your landscaping plans. One is your grass. Another is the number and variety of trees you plant. The third is the combination of plants you select. All of these decisions should be considered in relation to the climate in your area. Be sure and check out our gardening tips before you begin work.

Grass

Lawn experts classify grass into two categories: cool-climate and warm-climate. The northern half of the United States would be considered cool-climate. Examples of cool-climate grass are Kentucky bluegrass and ryegrass. Bermuda grass is a warm-climate grass. Before planting grass, whether by seeding, sodding, sprigging, or plugging, the ground must be properly prepared. The soil should be tested for any nutritional deficiencies and cultivated. Come by or call to make arrangements to have your soil tested. When selecting a lawn, avoid letting personal preferences and the cost of establishment be the overriding factors. Ask yourself these questions. What type of lawn are you expecting? What level of maintenance are you willing to provide? What are the site limitations?

Trees

Before you plant trees, you should evaluate your purpose. Are you interested in shade, privacy, or color? Do you want to attract wildlife? Attract birds? Create a shady play area? Your purpose will determine what variety of tree you should plant. Of course, you also need to consider your climate and available space. Shape is especially important in selecting trees for ornamental and shade purposes. Abundant shade comes from tall trees with long spreading or weeping branches. Ornamental trees will not provide abundant shade. We carry many varieties of trees and are happy to help you make your selections to fit your purpose.

Plants

There are so many types of plants available that it can become overwhelming. Do you want border plants, shrubs, ground covers, annuals, perennials, vegetables, fruits, vines, or bulbs? In reality, a combination of several of these works well. Design aspects such as balance, flow, definition of space and focalization should be considered. Annuals provide brilliant bursts of color in the garden. By selecting flowers carefully to fit the conditions of the site, it is possible to have a beautiful display without an unnecessary amount of work. Annuals are also great as fresh and dry cut flowers. Perennials can greatly improve the quality of your landscape. Perennials have come and gone in popularity, but today are as popular as ever. Water plants are also quite popular now. We will be happy to help you sort out your preferences and select a harmonious combination of plants for you.

Further Research

These are some of my favorite gardening links. Take the time to browse through some of the information they offer, then give me a call at (555) 248-0806 or e-mail me at cosie@blooms&bulbs.com.

National Gardening Association
Organic Gardening
Southern Living

Skills Review (continued)

11. Manage website links.

a. Recreate the Site Cache, then use the Check Links Sitewide command to view broken links, external links, and orphaned files.

b. Refresh the Site list in the Files panel if you see broken links or orphaned files. If any exist, locate them, analyze them, then correct any errors you find.

c. View the external links in the Assets panel. Exit (Win) or Quit (Mac) Dreamweaver.

Important: If you did not create the following websites in Unit B and maintain them during the preceding units, you must create a local site root folder for the websites in the following exercises and define the websites using files your instructor will provide. See the "Read This Before You Begin" section for more detailed instructions.

Independent Challenge 1

You have been hired to create a website for a river expedition company named Rapids Transit, located on the Buffalo River in Gilbert, Arkansas. In addition to renting canoes, kayaks, and rafts, they have lodging available for overnight stays. River guides are available to accompany clients on float trips. The owner's name is Mike Andrew. Mike has asked you to create a new web page that lists helpful links for his customers. Refer to Figure F-33 as you work on this page.

a. Start Dreamweaver, then open the Rapids Transit website.

b. Open dwf_3.html in the drive and folder where you store your Unit F Data Files, then save it as **before.html**, replacing the existing file and without updating the links. You need to save the young_paddler.gif file (the photo) in the assets folder of the Rapids Transit website, then correct the path for the banner if necessary.

c. Close the dwf_3.html file.

d. Create the following links for the links listed on the page:

Buffalo National River	http://www.nps.gov/buff/
Arkansas, the Natural State	http://www.arkansas.com/
Buffalo River Floater's Guide	http://www.ozarkmtns.com/buffalo/index.asp

e. Attach the rapids_transit.css style sheet, apply the body_text style to all text on the page, then apply the img_left_float rule to the young_paddler image.

Independent Challenge 1 (continued)

f. Design a Spry menu bar for the page using your choice of settings. The menu bar should include the following items: Home, Our Guides, Rates, Lodging, and Before You Go. Link the menu items to the appropriate files in your Rapids Transit site. Delete all submenus. (Remember to create a new Tag rule in the rapids_transit.css file to modify the <img> tag as follows: Block Vertical-align:bottom.)

g. Copy the completed menu bar to the guides, index, and lodging pages. Preview each page in the browser window to make sure the menu bar doesn't "jump," or shift position, when you move from page to page. (*Hint*: If you are having problems with spacing issues, look for stray <p>, <br>, or heading tags on your pages and remove them if necessary.)

h. Save your work, then test all links in your browser window.

i. Run reports for locate any broken links or orphaned files, then correct any that exist.

j. Exit your browser, then close all files and exit Dreamweaver.

FIGURE F-33

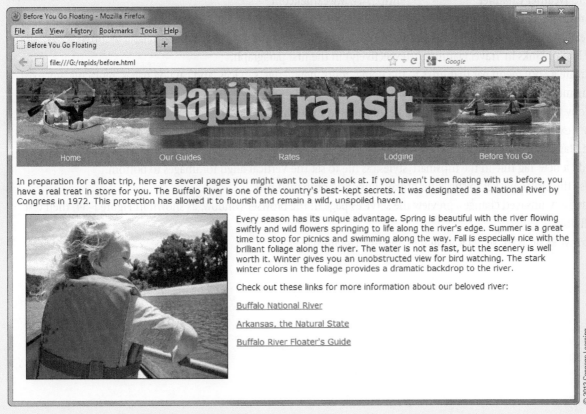

© 2013 Cengage Learning
Original photos courtesy of Sherry Bishop

Independent Challenge 2

Your company is designing a new website for TripSmart, a travel outfitter. TripSmart specializes in travel products and services. In addition to selling travel products, such as luggage and accessories, they sponsor trips and offer travel advice. Their clients range from college students to families to vacationing professionals. You are now ready to work on the services page. This page will include several helpful links for clients to use when planning trips.

a. Start Dreamweaver, then open the TripSmart site.

b. Open the file dwf_4.html from the drive and folder where you store your Unit F Data Files, save it as **services.html** in the tripsmart local site root folder, replacing the existing file but not updating the links, then close dwf_4.html.

c. Apply the Heading 1 format from the attached style sheet to the four paragraph headings, then apply the body_text style to the rest of the text on the page.

d. Create the following links using the text in the unordered list at the bottom of the page:

CNN Travel Channel	http://www.cnn.com/TRAVEL
US Department of State	http://travel.state.gov
Yahoo! Currency Converter	http://finance.yahoo.com/currency-converter
The Weather Channel	http://www.weather.com

e. Create named anchors called **reservations**, **outfitters**, **tours**, and **links** in front of the respective headings on the page, then link each named anchor to "Reservations," "Travel Outfitters," "Escorted Tours," and "Helpful Links in Travel Planning" (respectively) in the first paragraph.

f. Create a Spry menu bar that links to the home, tours, newsletter, services, and catalog pages, replacing any existing menu bars. Delete all submenus.

g. Copy the menu bar to the other completed pages in the website: index, newsletter, and tours pages, replacing any existing menu bars. (*Hint*: If you are having problems with spacing issues, look for stray <p>, <br>, or heading tags on your pages and remove them if necessary.)

h. Add a new Tag rule in the tripsmart_styles.css file to set the Vertical-align for images to bottom.

i. Use the Link Checker to check for broken links and orphaned files.

J. Save any unsaved changes, preview the services page in the browser window, as shown in Figure F-34, then test all links.

k. Exit your browser, then close all files and exit Dreamweaver.

FIGURE F-34

TripSmart has several divisions of customer service to assist you in planning and making reservations for your trip, shopping for your trip wardrobe and providing expert guide services. Give us a call and we will be happy to connect you with one of the following departments: Reservations, Travel Outfitters, or Escorted Tours. If you are not quite ready to talk with one of our departments and would prefer doing some of your own research first, may we suggest beginning with our Helpful Links in Travel Planning.

Reservations

Our Reservations Department is staffed with five Certified Travel Agents, each of whom is eager to assist you in making your travel plans. They have specialty areas in Africa, the Caribbean, South America, Western Europe, Eastern Europe, Asia, Antarctica, and Hawaii and the South Pacific. They also specialize in Senior Travel, Family Travel, Student Travel, and Special Needs Travel. Call us at *(555) 848-0807* extension 75 or e-mail us at *Reservations* to begin making your travel plans now. We will be happy to send you brochures and listings of Internet addresses to help you get started. We are open from 8:00 a.m. until 6:00 p.m. CST.

Travel Outfitters

Our travel outfitters are seasoned travelers that have accumulated a vast amount of knowledge in appropriate travel clothing and accessories for specific destinations. Climate and seasons, of course, are important factors in planning your wardrobe for a trip. Area customs should also be taken in consideration so as not to offend the local residents with inappropriate dress. When traveling abroad, we always hope that our customers will represent our country well as good ambassadors. If they can be comfortable and stylish at the same time, we have succeeded! Our clothing is all affordable and packs well on long trips. Most can be washed easily in a hotel sink and hung to drip-dry overnight. Browse through our on-line catalog, then give us a call at *(555) 433-7844* extension 85. We will also be happy to mail you a catalog of our extensive collection of travel clothing and accessories.

Escorted Tours

Our Escorted Tours department is always hard at work planning the next exciting destination to offer our TripSmart customers. We have seven professional tour guides that accompany our guests from the United States point of departure to their point of return.

Our current feature package tour is to Spain. Our local escort is Don Eugene. Don has traveled Spain extensively and enjoys sharing his love for this exciting country with others. He will be assisted after arrival in Spain with the services of archeologist JoAnne Rife, anthropologist Christina Elizabeth, and naturalist Iris Albert. Call us at *(555) 848-0807* extension 95 for information on the Spain trip or to learn about other destinations being currently scheduled.

Helpful Links in Travel Planning

The following links may be helpful in your travel research. Happy surfing!

- CNN Travel Channel - News affecting travel plans to various destinations
- US Department of State - Travel warnings, passport information, and more
- Yahoo! Currency Converter - Calculate the exchange rate between two currencies
- The Weather Channel - Weather, flight delays, and driving conditions

Independent Challenge 3

Dr. Joan Sullivent's patients often ask her questions about the current treatment protocol for Parkinson's disease, a debilitating neurological disease. She would like to post some helpful links in her clinic website to provide information for her patients. She begins her research at the National Institutes of Health website.

a. Connect to the Internet, then go to the National Institutes of Health website at nih.gov.

b. What do you like or dislike about the menu links?

c. Note the placement and appearance of the menu bar. Does it use text, images, or a combination of the two to form the links?

d. Using your favorite search engine, locate at least five helpful links that Dr. Sullivent should consider for her site, including the National Institutes of Health site pictured in Figure F-35.

FIGURE F-35

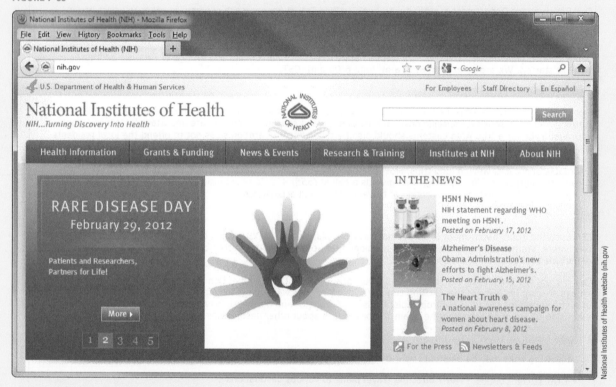

National Institutes of Health website (nih.gov)

Real Life Independent Challenge

This assignment will continue to build on the personal website that you created in Unit B. In Unit C you created and developed your index page. In Unit D you added a page with either an ordered or an unordered list, and a CSS style sheet with a minimum of two styles. In Unit E you added a page that included at least two images. In this lesson, you work with one of the other pages in your site.

a. Consult your wireframe and decide which page you would like to develop in this lesson.

b. Create content for this page and format the text attractively on the page using styles.

c. Add at least three external links to this page.

d. Think about a creative use for an image map, then add it to the page.

e. Add at least one named anchor and link to it.

f. Design a menu bar linking to the main pages of your site, then copy it to all of the main pages.

g. Save the file, then preview the page in the browser window.

After you are satisfied with your work, verify the following:

a. Each completed page has a page title.

b. All links work correctly.

c. The completed pages display correctly using a screen resolution of 1024 × 768.

d. All images are properly set showing a path to the website assets folder.

e. All images have alternate text and are legal for you to use.

f. The Link Checker shows no broken links or orphaned files. If there are orphaned files, note your plan to link them.

Visual Workshop

You are continuing your work on the Carolyne's Creations website that you started in Unit B and developed in subsequent units. Chef Carolyne has asked you to create pages describing her cooking classes offered every month. Use the following files for the tasks noted: dwf_5.html to replace the classes.html page; dwf_6.html to create a new children.html page; and dwf_7.html to create a new adults.html page. (Remember not to update the links when prompted.) Copy all new images, including the new banner, cc_banner_with_text.jpg, to the assets folder in the website. Next, create an image map at the bottom of the banner on the classes page with hotspots for each link, add the code **style="border:0"** to the image tag for the banner to prevent a blue outline appearing around the banner in Internet Explorer, and copy it to all pages in the website, replacing all existing menu bars. Create an email link on the classes page using the text "Sign me up!" and carolyne@carolynescreations.com for the link. Create links in the last sentence to the adults' and children's pages, as shown in Figure F-36. Refer to Figures F-36, F-37, and F-38 as you complete this project. Check that each completed page uses styles from the cc_styles.css file, and attach and apply these styles if you find pages without styles. The second image in Figure F-36 was aligned by creating a new rule based on the rule you created in Unit E, but with a different float property. (*Hint*: Remember to remove any formatting around the banners to prevent any pages from appearing to "jump.") Check for broken links and orphaned files. You will see that the former banner, cc_banner.jpg, is now an orphaned file.

FIGURE F-36

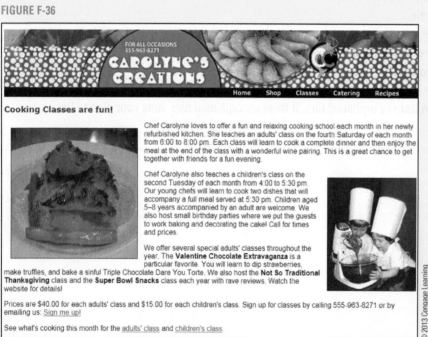

FIGURE F-37

© 2013 Cengage Learning
Original photo courtesy of Sherry Bishop

FIGURE F-38

© 2013 Cengage Learning
Original photo courtesy of Sherry Bishop

Using CSS and Tables to Position Content

Files You Will Need:

To view a list of files needed for this unit, see the Data Files Grid in the back of the book.

You have learned how to position elements on a web page using alignment and paragraph settings. These settings let you create simple web pages, but they limit your design choices. The preferred method to position page elements is to use Cascading Style Sheets (CSS). You have already learned to use CSS to format individual page elements. Now you will learn to use CSS to place your content on pages using divs. With CSS layouts, you use blocks of content formatted with CSS rules to place information on web pages. Once you've completed this book, you will have the skills and understanding to efficiently design sites built entirely with CSS. You will also learn to use CSS to position data in tables. 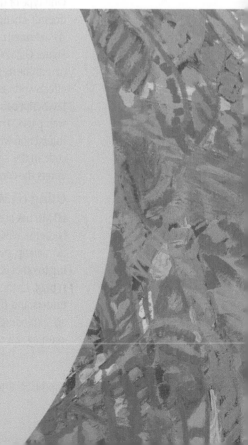 In this unit, you use a predesigned CSS layout with divs to create the cafe page for The Striped Umbrella website. You will add a table to the page to list the restaurant hours.

OBJECTIVES

Understand CSS layouts

Create a page using CSS layouts

Add content to CSS layout blocks

Edit content in CSS layout blocks

Edit CSS layout properties

Understand table modes

Insert a table and set table properties

Merge and split table cells

Insert and align images in table cells

Add text

Format and modify cell content

Format cells

Understanding CSS Layouts

Web pages built with Cascading Style Sheets use div tags to place and format page content. **Div tags** are HTML code segments that set the appearance and position of blocks of web page content. Think of div tags as building blocks. To build a web page with a layout based on CSS, you begin by placing div tags on the page to set up the framework to position the page content. Divs, the page elements created with div tags, can also be referred to as layout blocks, elements, or containers. Next, you add content and format the divs to position them on the page. For beginning designers, the predesigned CSS layouts that are available with Dreamweaver CS6 make creating pages based on CSS easy. You simply choose a predesigned CSS layout, and Dreamweaver places the div tags in the page code for you. You spend some time researching how style sheets are used for page layout.

DETAILS

Before using CSS layouts for page layout, you review the following concepts:

- **Using CSS vs. tables for page layout**

  Table were used previously by designers to position content on web pages. With CSS, designers have moved to positioning most page content with CSS layouts. Tables are still used for some layout purposes, such as placing tabular data on a page. Divs generate pages that are more compliant with current accessibility standards.

QUICK TIP

The Dreamweaver predesigned layouts have been tested using several different browsers.

- **Using Dreamweaver CSS page layouts**

  Dreamweaver offers 18 predesigned layouts in the New Document dialog box, as shown in Figure G-1. These layouts are a great way to learn how to create page layouts based on CSS. As you select each option, a preview of the layout appears on the right side of the New Document dialog box with a description below it. Once you select a layout, you can modify it to fit your needs. The two newest HTML5 page layouts use either a two column or three column layout. These layouts include new HTML tags to support semantic markup such as <section>, < header>, <footer>, <article>, and <aside>. Divs used for page layout are identified by an ID, or name. When the div tag is selected, the ID displays in both the HTML code for the div tag in the Property inspector, and in the CSS Styles panel. In Code view, the code for a div tag named header would be <div id="header">.

- **Using AP divs**

  One type of div is an AP div. AP stands for absolutely positioned, so an **AP div** has a specified position that doesn't change even when viewed in different-sized windows. An AP div creates a container called an **AP element**. You create an AP div by drawing the container with the Draw AP Div button, as shown in Figure G-2. When you create an AP div, a CSS rule is automatically created to apply the property values that determine its size and appearance on the page. You can stack AP divs on top of each other to create interesting effects such as animations. You can also use them to show or hide content on the page by using them with JavaScript behaviors. **JavaScript behaviors** are action scripts that allow you to add dynamic content to your web pages. **Dynamic content** is content that changes either in response to certain conditions or through interaction with the user. For example, the user might enter a zip code to display a local weather forecast. The code in the JavaScript behavior would direct the AP element with the correct forecast to appear after the user enters the corresponding zip code in a text box.

- **Using HTML5 and CSS**

  HTML has been in existence since the 1990s, but it wasn't until 1997 that the then current version, HTML4, became a W3C recommendation. HTML5 introduced new ways to add interactivity and tags that support semantic markup, such as the <nav> tag used for navigation links. Semantic markup refers to coding to convey meaning to other computer programs such as search engines. Semantics, or the meanings of words, when used with syntax, or the actual words and sentence structure, allows the computer to no longer just "read" words, but understand the meaning behind the words. HTML5 also introduces markup for Web applications (apps), an exploding sector of Web development. Other HTML5 tags include <header>, <footer>, <article>, <audio>, <section> and <video>. HTML5 is still a work in progress, but most modern browsers support it.

FIGURE G-1: **New Document dialog box**

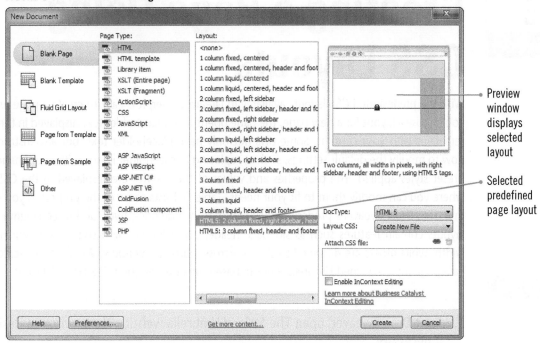

FIGURE G-2: **Inserting an AP div Tag using the Draw AP Div button**

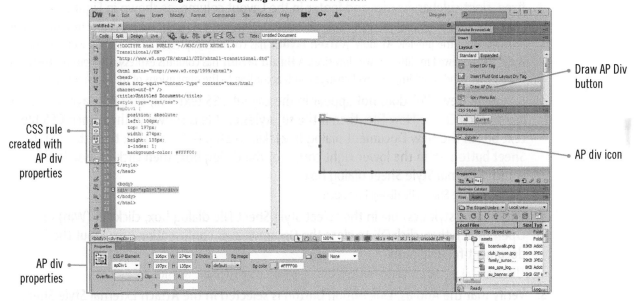

Using Dreamweaver sample pages

You can use either the Welcome Screen or the New Document dialog box, shown in Figure G-1, to create several different types of pages. The predesigned CSS page layouts make it easy for you to design accessible web pages using CSS without being an expert in HTML code. In the Page from Sample category, CSS Style Sheet and Mobile Starters are options that create pages you can use as starting points to develop pages for mobile devices and style sheets. Another choice in the New Document dialog

box is the **Fluid Grid Layout**. This layout is used for designing adaptive websites based on a single fluid grid. It is worth the time to explore each category to understand what is available to you as a designer. Once you have selected a sample page, you can customize it to fit your needs and the site design. You can also find a variety of sample pages, or templates, on the Internet. Some sites offer templates free of charge, while others make templates available for purchase.

Creating a Page Using CSS Layouts

With the predesigned CSS layouts available in Dreamweaver, it is easy to create a page using CSS. After you choose a layout for a new page, the page opens with placeholder text displayed in the divs until you replace it with your content. Some divs not only have placeholder text, but also instructional text on how to modify the default settings, such as replacing a placeholder image with your image. Each div has preset styles applied. The properties and values of these styles are displayed in the CSS Styles panel, where you can modify them to fit your needs. Table G-1 lists some of the properties you can use to format divs. Dreamweaver's predesigned CSS layouts include one-, two-, and three-column layouts. Some layouts contain features such as sidebars, headers, and footers, and some are designed with a fixed width, while others are designed to stretch across a browser window. ██████ You decide to create the cafe page for the Striped Umbrella website based on a predesigned CSS HTML5 layout.

1. **Start Dreamweaver, open The Striped Umbrella website, then switch to Design view if necessary**

2. **Click File on the Menu bar, click New, verify that Blank Page is highlighted in the left section, click HTML in the Page Type column if necessary, then click HTML5: 2 column fixed, right sidebar, header and footer in the Layout column, as shown in Figure G-3**
   The layout description confirms that this is a fixed layout, measured in pixels. The preview of this page layout is displayed in the preview window. A **fixed layout** has columns expressed in pixels and will not change width when viewed in different window sizes. A **liquid layout** has columns expressed as percents based on the browser window width, so it will change width according to the dimensions of the browser window.

3. **If "Create New File" does not appear in the Layout CSS text box, click the Layout CSS list arrow, click Create New File, then if the su_styles.css file is shown in the Attach CSS file text box in the New Document dialog box, skip to Step 6. If not, click the Attach Style Sheet button ▦ in the lower-right corner of the dialog box, then click Browse in the Attach External Style Sheet dialog box**
   The Select Style Sheet File dialog box opens.

4. **Click the su_styles.css file in the Select Style Sheet File dialog box, click OK (Win) or Open (Mac), then click OK to close the Dreamweaver confirmation box about the document-relative path**
   The links will not be document-relative until the page is saved in the website.

5. **Verify that the Add as: Link option button is selected in the Attach External Style Sheet dialog box, then click OK**
   The su_styles.css file is attached to the new page, as shown in Figure G-4.

6. **Click Create in the New Document dialog box, verify that the HTML5_twoColFixRtHdr.css file will be saved in the striped_umbrella local site folder in the Save Style Sheet File As dialog box, then click Save to close the Save Style Sheet File As dialog box. Open the CSS Styles panel if necessary, then expand the HTML5_twoColFixRtHdr.css and su_styles.css style sheets**
   A new page opens based on the predesigned CSS layout with blocks of placeholder content as shown in Figure G-5. It contains two columns, as well as a header and footer. Heading formats have been applied to the placeholder headings. There are two style sheets in the CSS Styles panel: the su_styles.css file you imported and the HTML5_twoColFixRtHdr.css style sheet file that was created to format the predesigned page layout.

7. **Save the file as cafe.html, overwriting the existing file**

Using CSS and Tables to Position Content

FIGURE G-3: Predefined layout selected for new page

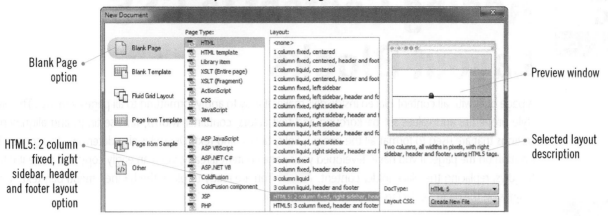

- Blank Page option
- HTML5: 2 column fixed, right sidebar, header and footer layout option
- Preview window
- Selected layout description

FIGURE G-4: The su_styles.css file attached to the new page

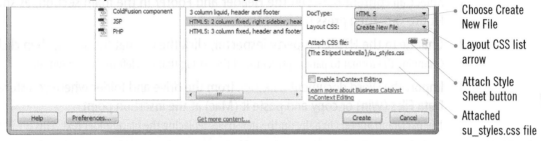

- Choose Create New File
- Layout CSS list arrow
- Attach Style Sheet button
- Attached su_styles.css file

FIGURE G-5: New page based on CSS HTML5 layout with placeholder content

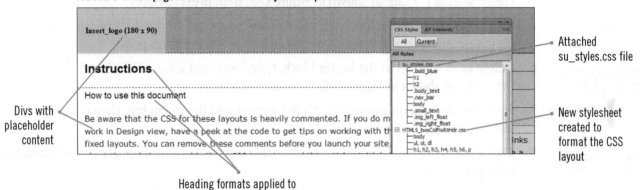

- Insert_logo (180 x 90)
- **Instructions**
- How to use this document
- Be aware that the CSS for these layouts is heavily commented. If you do m... work in Design view, have a peek at the code to get tips on working with th... fixed layouts. You can remove these comments before you launch your site.
- Attached su_styles.css file
- New stylesheet created to format the CSS layout
- Divs with placeholder content
- Heading formats applied to placeholder headings

TABLE G-1: Div tag properties

property	function
ID	Displays the name used to identify the div in the code
Class	Displays the class style currently applied to the div
Float	Sets the float, or position, of the div in relation to adjacent elements as left, right, none, or inherit
Position	Sets the position of the div as absolute, fixed, relative, static, or inherit
Top	Sets the div position in relation to the top of the page or parent element
Right	Sets the right position of the div as either auto or inherit
Bottom	Sets the bottom position of the div as either auto or inherit
Left	Sets the div position in relation to the left side of the page or parent element
Width	Sets the width of the div, in pixels by default
Height	Sets the height of the div, in pixels by default
Overflow	Controls how the div will appear in the browser if the content is larger than the div

Adding Content to CSS Layout Blocks

A page built with all content placed inside divs makes it easy to apply formatting to all page elements. The div style properties and values set background and text colors, container widths, font settings, and alignment settings that are used to format all the images, links, tables, and text. Div styles also determine the content's position on the page. If you have developed your page content already, you can easily copy and paste it into the divs, replacing the placeholder content. ▰▰▰ You are ready to place the banner, menu bar, text, and images on the page, replacing the placeholder content.

STEPS

1. **Select all content between the Header and Footer in the main section, as shown in Figure G-6, then press [Delete]**

2. **Change to the HTML Property inspector, click the Format list arrow, then click Paragraph**
   Changing the format to paragraph removed the h1 tag that was left in the content div.

3. **Import the Word document cafe.doc from the drive and folder where you store your Unit G Data Files (Win) or copy and paste it (Mac) at the insertion point**
   The paragraph appears in a div on the new page, replacing the placeholder text. This div is named content.

> **QUICK TIP**
> Be careful not to delete the beginning and ending div tags.

4. **Switch to Code view, select the code between the beginning and end of the <div class="sidebar1"> tag, as shown in Figure G-7, then press [Delete]**

5. **Return to Design view, then type Reservations are recommended for Beach 25 (our main dining room) during the peak summer season. at the insertion point**

> **QUICK TIP**
> Press [Ctrl][Tab] to switch between two open pages.

6. **Delete all of the text in the footer block, type Copyright 2002 - 2015 The Striped Umbrella, as shown in Figure G-8, then save your work**

7. **Open the index page and copy both the banner and the menu bar, then close the index page**

> **QUICK TIP**
> If you struggle with the placement of the banner and menu bar, use Code view to copy the code from the index page then paste it into the code for the cafe page.

8. **Click the placeholder logo image on the cafe page, then paste the banner and menu bar in its place**

9. **Place the insertion point at the end of the paragraph ending with "poolside.", enter a paragraph break, insert cafe_photo.jpg from the assets folder in the drive and folder where you save your Unit G Data Files, then type Sand Crab Cafe photo for the alternate text**
   The content is placed on the page, replacing all placeholder content, as shown in Figure G-9.

Design Matters

Understanding selector types

When you have a mixture of style classifications—embedded styles, external styles, and styles-redefining HTML tags—there is an order of precedence that is followed. Styles are ranked in order of precedence as they are applied to page elements, thus the name "cascading style sheets." The first order of precedence is to find declarations that match the media type being used, such as a computer monitor. The second order of precedence is by importance and origin. The third order of preference is by specificity of the selector. **Pseudo class styles**, styles that determine the appearance of a page element when certain conditions are met, are considered as normal class styles. Sometimes styles with common formatting properties are grouped together to help reduce the size of style sheets. These styles are called **group selectors**.

Another type of selector is called a **descendant selector**. A descendant selector includes two or more selectors that form a relationship and are separated by white space.

FIGURE G-6: Selected placeholder text in the new cafe page

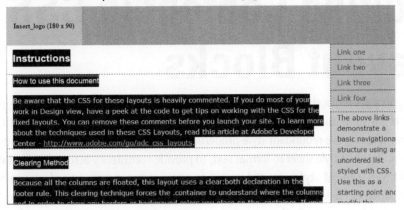

FIGURE G-7: Deleting the sidebar placeholder text

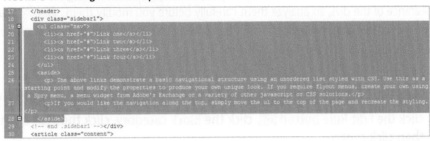

FIGURE G-8: New text for content, sidebar, and footer divs

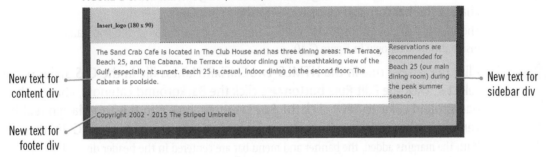

New text for content div

New text for sidebar div

New text for footer div

FIGURE G-9: Content added to cafe page

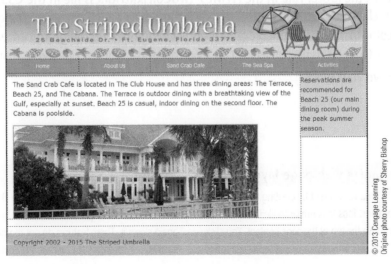

Editing Content in CSS Layout Blocks

After you replace placeholder content in divs with your website's content, you will probably want to adjust some of the formatting. Styles that you have previously applied might conflict with the div styles, so you may want to remove redundant style properties, such as font and alignment settings. It is generally better to use an external style sheet to format text, to provide consistency across the site. External style sheets use global styles. **Global styles** are styles used to apply common properties for certain page elements, such as text, links, or backgrounds. When you have styles that are defined in both the external style sheet that you created for your site and an external style sheet that was imported into your site after you created a new page based on a predesigned layout, you should evaluate which styles makes the most sense to use, based on the content each is intended to format. The styles for the div tags determine the placement and appearance of the divs, so analyze them carefully before you modify them. ░░░░ You continue to work on the new cafe page. You edit the rules for some of the divs to improve the appearance of the content within the divs.

STEPS

1. **Click the .sidebar1 rule in the HTML5_twoColFixRtHdr.css file in the CSS Styles panel, click the Edit Rule button** 🖉**, click the Block category, click the Text-align list arrow, then click center**

   You can also double-click a rule name to open the rule for editing.

QUICK TIP

You can enter either #FFFFFF or #FFF (the shorthand version).

2. **Click the Box category, change the Float from right to left, click the Background category, change the background color to #FFF, then click OK**

   The sidebar background changes to white, it moves to the left side of the page, and the text is centered inside the div, as shown in Figure G-10.

QUICK TIP

You can edit rule properties in either the CSS Styles Properties pane or by opening the CSS Rule definition dialog box.

3. **Click the header rule in the HTML5_twoColFixRtHdr.css file in the CSS Styles panel to select it, click the Edit Rule button** 🖉**, click the Background category, change the background color to #FFF, click the Box category, type 5 in the Top Margin text box, verify that the Same for all check box is checked, as shown in Figure G-11, then click OK**

   With the margins added, the banner and menu bar are centered in the header div and the div background is now white.

4. **Click the footer rule in the HTML5_twoColFixRtHdr.css file in the CSS Styles panel to select it, click the Edit Rule button** 🖉**, click the Background category, change the background color to #FFF, click the Block category, change the Text-align to center, then click OK**

   The footer text is now centered in the footer div with a white background, as shown in Figure G-12.

5. **Save your work**

Using CSS to organize web page layout

You can also use CSS3 to organize content by creating tabs, drop-down menus, and accordions. **Tabs** look similar to file folder tabs and are used for navigation above the top of the page content. You click a tab to display information. **Accordions**, also used for navigation, are buttons that, when clicked, open up like an accordion to display information that drops down below the button. Clicking the button again closes it. These features do not require images or JavaScript to work, but incorporate the animation capabilities of CSS3.

FIGURE G-10: Editing the properties of the .sidebar1 rule

The Sand Crab Cafe is located in The Club House and has three dining areas: The Terrace, Beach 25, and The Cabana. The Terrace is outdoor dining with a breathtaking view of the Gulf, especially at sunset. Beach 25 is casual, indoor dining on the second floor. The Cabana is poolside.

Reservations are recommended for Beach 25 (our main dining room) during the peak summer season.

© 2013 Cengage Learning

Sidebar moves to left side of the page, has a white background, and the content is centered

FIGURE G-11: Modifying the header rule

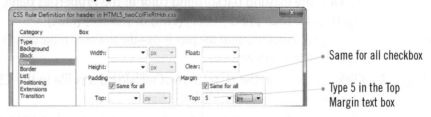

Same for all checkbox

Type 5 in the Top Margin text box

FIGURE G-12: Viewing the footer after editing the footer rule

Banner and menu bar are centered using margin settings for the header rule

Reservations are recommended for Beach 25 (our main dining room) during the peak summer season.

The Sand Crab Cafe is located in The Club House and has three dining areas: The Terrace, Beach 25, and The Cabana. The Terrace is outdoor dining with a breathtaking view of the Gulf, especially at sunset. Beach 25 is casual, indoor dining on the second floor. The Cabana is poolside.

Copyright 2002 - 2015 The Striped Umbrella

© 2013 Cengage Learning
Original photo courtesy of Sherry Bishop

Footer text is centered with a white background

Using Visual Aids to work with divs

There are several options for viewing your divs in Design view. You can choose to show or hide outlines, temporarily assign different background colors to each individual div, or view the **CSS Layout Box Model** (padding and margins included) of a selected layout. To change these options, use the View > Visual Aids menu, and then select or deselect the CSS Layout Backgrounds, CSS Layout Box Model, or CSS Layout Outlines menu choice. You can also use the Visual Aids button on the Document toolbar.

Editing CSS Layout Properties

It is unlikely that you will find a predesigned CSS page layout that is exactly what you have in mind for your website. However, once you have created a page with a predesigned CSS layout, it is easy to modify the properties for individual rules to better fit your needs. Ideally, every page element should be formatted using style sheets rather than by applying individual formatting properties with the Property inspector. You can apply the rules in attached external style sheets to format individual page elements with global styles, such as text or horizontal rules. The styles generated by the CSS page layout control the formatting of the divs, including the div width and background color, but, as you have seen, they can also include formatting for the page elements within the divs.  You continue working on the new cafe page by changing more div properties and the page properties.

TROUBLE
You may need to expand the Properties pane to be able to see the properties.

1. **Select the body rule in the HTML5_twoColFixRtHdr.css file in the CSS Styles panel, click to select the existing background color in the Properties pane, type #FFF as shown in Figure G-13, then press [Enter] (Win) or [return] (Mac)**
   The body tag is used to format the page body—the area outside the divs. The body tag for the page is set to display a white background.

QUICK TIP
You can also open the CSS Rule definition dialog box by double-clicking a rule name on the CSS Styles panel.

2. **Click .container in the HTML5_twoColFixRtHdr.css file in the CSS Styles panel, click the Edit rule button 🖉, then click the Border category**
   A border around the page sets it off from the extra space around it when it is viewed in a browser.

3. **Click the Top list arrow in the Style column, click solid, click the Top list arrow in the first text box in the Width column, click thin, click in the First color text box in the Color column, type #033, verify that the Same for all check box is selected in each of the three columns, compare your screen to Figure G-14, then click OK**
   The border properties for the container are set to include a thin solid line with a dark gray color.

4. **Type The Striped Umbrella Beach Resort and Spa, Ft. Eugene, Florida in the Title text box on the Document toolbar**

5. **Click to place the insertion point in front of the word "Reservations" in the sidebar, then enter a line break**

6. **Save your work, preview the page in the browser, compare your screen to Figure G-15, then close the browser**

FIGURE G-13: Editing the properties for the body rule

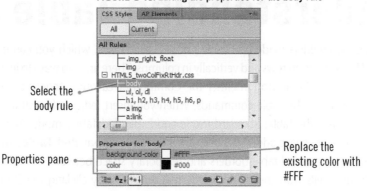

Select the body rule

Properties pane

Replace the existing color with #FFF

FIGURE G-14: Editing the properties for the container rule

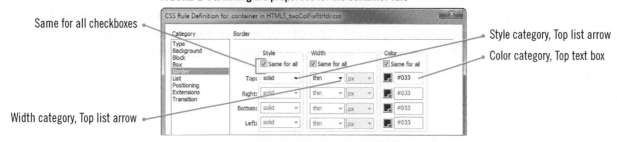

Same for all checkboxes

Style category, Top list arrow

Color category, Top text box

Width category, Top list arrow

FIGURE G-15: Viewing the new cafe page in the browser

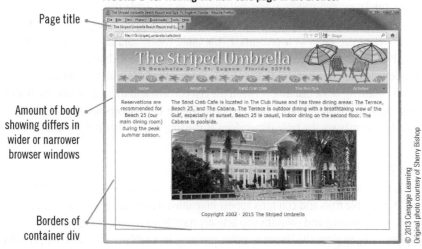

Page title

Amount of body showing differs in wider or narrower browser windows

Borders of container div

© 2013 Cengage Learning
Original photo courtesy of Sherry Bishop

Design Matters

Using the Adobe CSS Advisor and Adobe BrowserLab for cross-browser rendering issues

You can use the **Browser Compatibility Check (BCC)** feature to check for problematic CSS features that may render differently in multiple browsers. The BCC flags and rates code on three levels: an error that could cause a serious display problem; an error that probably won't cause a serious display problem; or a warning that unsupported code is present, but won't cause a serious display problem. Each bug is linked to the **CSS Advisor**, a part of the Adobe website that offers solutions for that particular bug and other helpful information for resolving any issues with your pages. To use the BCC feature, use the File > Check Page > Browser Compatibility command. Adobe also

has an online service called **Adobe BrowserLab** that is a useful tool for cross-browser and cross-platform compatibility testing. Since Adobe BrowserLab is an online service, you can access it from any computer with an Internet connection, but you must have an Adobe ID to use the service. There is no charge to create an Adobe ID. To connect to Adobe BrowserLab, open the Adobe BrowserLab panel, then click Preview. The Adobe BrowserLab panel is located above the Insert panel. The panel contains two buttons: one to connect to the service to preview your pages, and one to choose whether you want to preview the local or server version of your pages.

Using CSS and Tables to Position Content

Understanding Table Modes

Tables are placeholders made up of small boxes called **cells**, which you can use to insert data. Cells are arranged horizontally in rows and vertically in columns. There are two ways to insert a table in Dreamweaver. You can use the Table button in either the Common or Layout category on the Insert panel or use the Menu bar to access the Table commands. When you insert, edit, or format a table, you have a choice of two ways to view the table: Standard mode and Expanded Tables mode. **Standard mode** displays the table with no extra space added between the table cells. **Expanded Tables mode** is similar to Standard mode but has expanded table borders and temporary space between the cells to make it easier to work with individual cells. You choose the mode that you want by clicking the Standard mode button or the Expanded Tables mode button in the Layout category on the Insert panel. It is common to switch between modes as you work with tables in Dreamweaver. Expanded Tables mode is used most often when you are doing precise work with small cells that are difficult to select or move between. You can also use the Import Tabular Data command on the Insert > Table Objects menu to place an existing table with its data on a web page. You review the two modes for inserting and viewing tables using the Standard and Expanded Tables modes.

- **Inserting a table in Standard mode**

  To insert a table in Standard mode, you click the Standard mode button in the Layout category on the Insert panel, then click the Table button. You then enter values for the number of rows and columns, the table width, border thickness, cell padding, and cell spacing in the Table dialog box. The **width** refers to the distance across the table, which is expressed either in pixels or as a percentage of page width. This difference is significant. When expressed as a percentage, the table width adjusts to the width of the page in the browser window. When expressed in pixels, the table width does not change, regardless of the size of the browser window. The **border** is the outline or frame around the table and the individual cells. It is expressed in pixels. **Cell padding** is the distance between the cell content and the **cell walls**, the lines inside the cell borders. **Cell spacing** is the distance between cells. Figure G-16 shows an example of a table viewed in Standard mode. You may see the table dimensions at the top, rather than at the bottom, of the table on the open page.

- **Viewing a table in Expanded Tables mode**

  Expanded Tables mode lets you view a table with expanded table borders and temporary cell padding and cell spacing. Since table rows and columns appear magnified when viewed on the page, this mode makes it easier to see how many rows and columns you actually have in your table. It is often difficult, especially after splitting empty cells, to place the insertion point precisely in a table cell, because empty cells can be such small targets. The Expanded Tables mode lets you see each cell clearly. After you select a table item or place the insertion point, it's best to return to Standard mode to maintain the WYSIWYG environment. WYSIWYG is the acronym for "What You See Is What You Get." This means that your web page should look the same in the browser as it does in the web editor. You can toggle between the Expanded Tables mode and Standard mode by pressing [Alt] [F6] (Win) or [option][F6] (Mac). Figure G-17 shows an example of a table in Expanded Tables mode. You can also use the View > Visual Aids > command to hide or show table borders.

Using HTML table tags

When formatting a table, you should understand the basic HTML tags used to define it. The tags that define a table are `<table>` and `</table>`. The tags that define table rows are `<tr>` and `</tr>`. The tags that define table data cells are `<td>` and `</td>`. Dreamweaver places the   code into each empty table cell at the time it is created. The   code inserts a **nonbreaking space**; this is a space that appears in a fixed location to keep a line break from separating text into two lines or, in the case of table cells, to keep an empty cell from collapsing. Some browsers collapse an empty cell, which can ruin the look of a table. The nonbreaking space appears in the cell by default until it is replaced with content.

FIGURE G-16: Table viewed in Standard mode

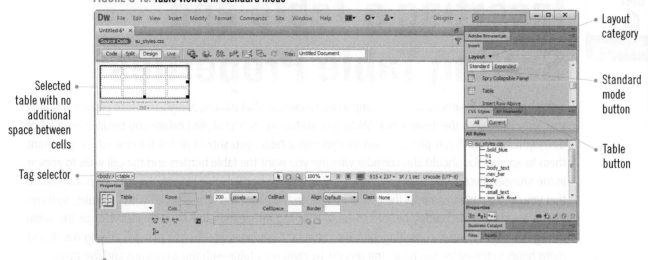

Selected table with no additional space between cells

Tag selector

Property inspector expanded to access cell properties

Layout category

Standard mode button

Table button

FIGURE G-17: Table viewed in Expanded Tables mode

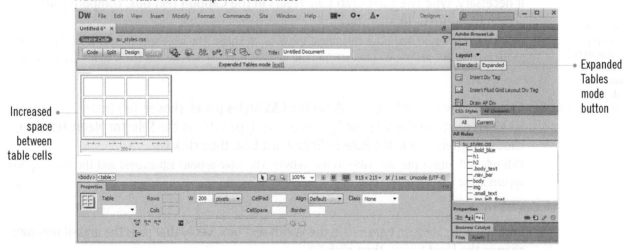

Increased space between table cells

Expanded Tables mode button

Inserting a Table and Setting Table Properties

Before you begin creating a table, it is important to decide what information you want to convey and how you want to achieve the desired look. Writing or sketching an overall plan before you begin saves a lot of development time. If you plan to insert images into a table, you should first determine where you want them to appear. You should also consider whether you want the table borders and the cell walls to appear in the browser. If you make a table "invisible" by setting the border value to zero, the user will not be aware that you used a table to arrange the text or images on the page. You format tables with CSS rules, so if you decide to add a table border, be sure to use a style tag rather than the Property inspector or the Table dialog box.  After consulting with the restaurant manager, you have a plan for adding the dining room hours to the page. You begin the process by creating a table with three columns and five rows.

STEPS

QUICK TIP
The Table command is also located in the Layout category of the Insert panel.

1. **With the insertion point to the right of the cafe photo, enter a paragraph break, then click Table in the Common category of the Insert panel**
   The Table dialog box opens.

QUICK TIP
The Table dialog box will retain settings from the last table that was inserted, so be sure to delete any settings that remain in the dialog box that you do not want to use.

2. **Type 5 in the Rows text box, 3 in the Columns text box, click Top in the Header section if necessary, type The Sand Crab Cafe Hours in the Caption text box, compare your screen to Figure G-18, then click OK**
   A table with five rows and three columns displays on the page. The table appears very small because the width for the table has not yet been set. You will define a new Tag Selector rule to use to format the table.

3. **Click the New CSS Rule button 🔁 in the CSS Styles panel, choose Tag (redefines an HTML element) in the Selector Type text box, type table in the Selector Name text box, choose su_styles.css in the Rule Definition list box, then click OK**
   This rule will format the only table in the website. The table appears left-aligned and the table caption appears at the top of the table by default.

4. **Click the Box category, type 600 in the Width text box, verify that px is the unit of measure, change the Float to left, then click OK**
   The <table> rule modified the table by setting the width and alignment on the page, as shown in Figure G-19.

Selecting a table

There are several ways to select a table in Dreamweaver. You can click the insertion point in the table, click Modify on the Menu bar, point to Table, then click Select Table. You can also select a table by moving the pointer slowly to the top or bottom edge of the table, then clicking the table border when the pointer changes to ⬚. Finally, if the insertion point is inside the table, you can click `<table>` on the tag selector.

FIGURE G-18: Table dialog box

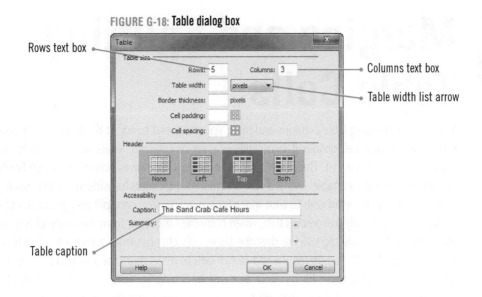

Rows text box

Columns text box

Table width list arrow

Table caption

FIGURE G-19: Table inserted and aligned in the div

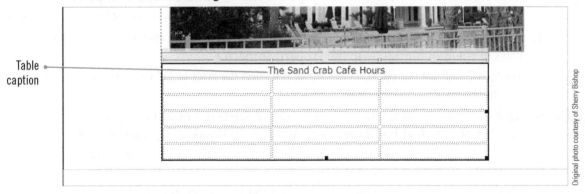

Table caption

Original photo courtesy of Sherry Bishop

Merging and Splitting Table Cells

In addition to resizing table columns and rows, you may need to adjust the table cells by splitting or merging them. **Splitting** a cell divides it into multiple rows or columns, while **merging** cells combines multiple adjacent cells into one cell. The ability to split and merge cells gives you more design flexibility for inserting images or text into your table. Merged cells are good placeholders for wide images or headings. For example, you could merge a row of cells to allot space for a heading. You can split merged cells and merge split cells. However, you can only merge cells that, when combined together, form the shape of a rectangle. When cells are merged, the HTML tag used to describe these cells changes from a width size tag to a column span or row span tag. ▰▰▰▰▰ You merge the top row of cells to make room for a heading across the table. You then split one cell to make room for a new image and its descriptive text in the first column. Finally, you merge four cells to create a larger area that will be used to describe room service availability.

STEPS

1. **Click to place the insertion point in the first cell in the top row, then drag the pointer to the right to select all three cells in the top row**

   A black border surrounds the cells, indicating that they are selected.

2. **Click the** Merges selected cells using spans button 🔳 **in the Property inspector**

   The three cells are merged into one cell, as shown in Figure G-20. The heading will display nicely in this area.

3. **Place the insertion point in the first cell in the fifth row, then click the** Splits cell into rows or columns button 🔲 **in the Property inspector**

   The Split Cell dialog box opens. This is where you select the Rows or Columns option, then specify the number of rows or columns you want as a result of the split.

4. **Click the** Split cell into: Rows option button **to select it if necessary, type 2 in the Number of rows text box if necessary, as shown in Figure G-21, then click** OK

   The dialog box closes, and the bottom-left cell is split into two rows. These rows will eventually contain the photograph of the featured dessert and its description.

5. **Click the** Show Code view button Code **on the Document toolbar**

   The code for the split and merged cells displays, as shown in Figure G-22. Table row and table column tags denote the column span and the nonbreaking spaces ( ) inserted in the empty cells. The tag <th colspan="3"> refers to the three top header cells that have been merged into one cell.

6. **Click the** Show Design view button Design **on the Document toolbar, select and merge the first cells in rows 2, 3, 4, and 5 in the left column, deselect the cell, compare your screen to Figure G-23, then save your work**

   With the table framework completed, the table is now ready for content.

Using nested tables

Inserting another table inside a cell within another table creates what is called a **nested table**. Nested tables can be used effectively when you want parts of your table data to contain both visible and invisible borders. For example, you can nest a table with red borders inside a table with invisible borders. The process of creating a nested table is similar to the one used to add a new row or column to a table. Simply click to place the insertion point inside the cell where you want the nested table to appear, click Insert on the Menu bar, then click Table, or click the Table button on the Insert panel. A nested table is separate from the original table so you can format it however you wish. The more nested tables you add, however, the more complicated the coding becomes, making it challenging to select and edit each table. You may be able to achieve the same results by adding rows and columns or splitting cells instead of inserting a nested table.

FIGURE G-20: Merging selected cells into one cell

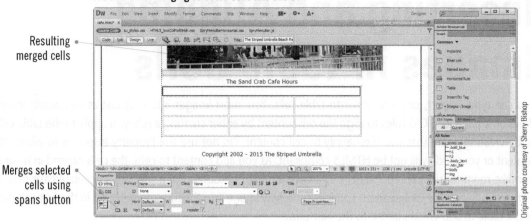

Resulting merged cells

Merges selected cells using spans button

FIGURE G-21: Split Cell dialog box

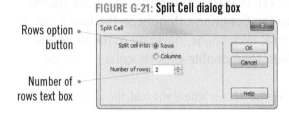

Rows option button

Number of rows text box

FIGURE G-22: Viewing the code for the merged and split cells

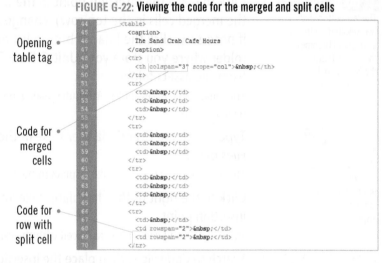

Opening table tag

Code for merged cells

Code for row with split cell

FIGURE G-23: Viewing the table after splitting and merging cells

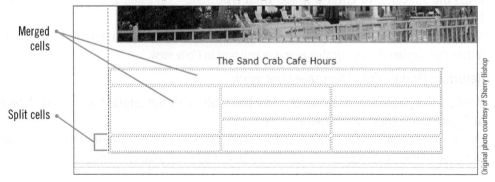

Merged cells

Split cells

Adding and deleting rows and columns

As you add new content to your table, you may find that you have too many or not enough rows or columns. You can add or delete one row or column at a time or add several at once, using commands on the Modify menu. When you add a new column or row, you must first select an existing column or row to which the new column or row will be adjacent. The Insert Rows or Columns dialog box lets you choose how many rows or columns you want to insert and specify where you want them placed, relative to the selected row or column. To add a new row to the end of a table, simply press [Tab].

Using CSS and Tables to Position Content

Inserting and Aligning Images in Table Cells

You can type, import, or paste text into table cells. You insert images into cells just as you would insert them on a page. Use CSS rules to align the cell content by either creating a rule you apply to the table cell or by creating a rule that you then apply to cell content. Do not use the Property inspector to align cell content or your code will not be HTML5 compliant. As you add content to cells, the cells expand in height to make room for the content.  You have a great photograph of a specialty chocolate cake that is featured in two of the dining areas. You insert the new image into the four merged cells in the first column of the table to add visual interest to the cafe page.

STEPS

QUICK TIP

The last button that was selected on the Insert panel becomes the default button that's used until you select another one.

1. **Click to place the insertion point in the first cell in the second row of the table (below the merged cells in the top row), change to the Common category on the Insert panel, if necessary, click the Images button list arrow, click Image, navigate to the drive and folder where you store your Unit G Data Files, then double-click chocolate_cake.jpg from the assets folder**

   The Image Tag Accessibility Attributes dialog box opens. This is where you add the alternate text for screen readers.

TROUBLE

If you do not see an alternate text dialog box, type the text in the Alt text box in the Property inspector.

2. **Type Chocolate Grand Marnier Cake in the alternate text box, click OK, then refresh the Files panel**

   The image of the chocolate cake displays in the merged cells and is saved in the website assets folder.

3. **Click to the right of the chocolate_cake image in the same cell to place the insertion point**

   You will now add code to the table cell with the cake image to center-align the contents of the cell.

TROUBLE

Be sure to click before the ending bracket>.

4. **Switch to Code view, then place the insertion point right after the code "<td rowspan="4"**

   This is the table cell that will be modified by adding a style to center-align the contents.

5. **Press the Spacebar to enter a space, then type style="text-align:center" as shown in Figure G-24**

   Notice how Dreamweaver helps you add code by providing **code hints**. Code hints is an auto-complete feature that displays lists of tags that appear as you type in Code view.

6. **Return to Design view, then save your work**

7. **Preview the page in your browser, view the table with the aligned image, as shown in Figure G-25, then close the browser**

   The image is still not in the exact position you intended. After you add more content to the table, the image will adjust to the correct position. You can also add rules to set the column widths in a table.

Using Live View to check pages

Live View is another option for previewing your pages. It is a quick way to see how your page will look without previewing the page in a browser window. Live View renders the page as though it were being viewed in a browser window with any active objects (such as a Spry menu bar) functioning. To use Live View, open a page in Design view, then click the Switch Design View to Live View button [Live]. Remember, a page cannot be edited in Live View. You must exit Live View to be able to make changes to the page content.

FIGURE G-24: Aligning the contents of a single cell

```
45          <caption>
46              The Sand Crab Cafe Hours
47          </caption>
48          <tr>
49              <th colspan="3" scope="col"> </th>
50          </tr>
51          <tr>
52              <td rowspan="4" style="text-align:center"> <img src=
        "assets/chocolate_cake.jpg" width="110" height="84" alt="Chocolate Grand Marnier
        Cake"></td>
53              <td> </td>
54              <td> </td>
55          </tr>
```

Code added to
align table cell

FIGURE G-25: Viewing the table in a browser window

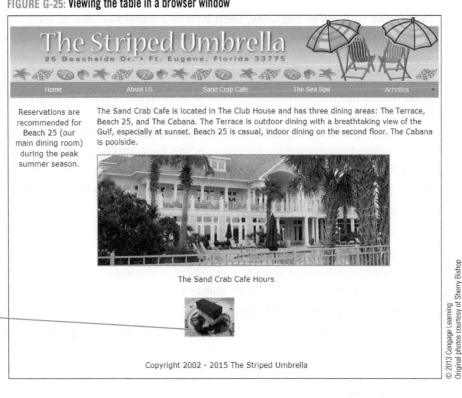

The table
borders are not
visible in the
browser

© 2013 Cengage Learning
Original photos courtesy of Sherry Bishop

Adding Text

You can enter text in table cells by typing it in the cell, copying it from another source and pasting it into the cell, or importing it into the cell from another program. You can then format the text for readability and appearance with CSS. If you import text from another program, you should use the Clean Up HTML or Clean Up Word HTML command to remove unnecessary code.  You add a heading to the table and a caption for the chocolate cake image. You also add the hours of operation for the three dining areas in the second column. Finally, you include a short description of room service options as well.

STEPS

TROUBLE
If you can't see the last lines you typed, click the `<div.container>` tag on the Tag selector to refresh the container size on the screen, resize the Dreamweaver application window, or close and reopen the page.

1. **Click in the first cell in the last row (below the chocolate cake image), type** Chocolate, **press [Shift] [Enter] (Win) or [shift] [return] (Mac) to add a line break, type** Grand Marnier, **add another line break, then type** Cake

   The text appears in the first cell in the last row below the chocolate cake image. The cell widths will change as you fill them with content. Don't be concerned about matching the figures exactly until you have completed inserting all content and set the table width.

2. **Click in the top row of the table, then type** Our individual dining areas are listed below:

   The header text appears centered and boldfaced in the table. Note that a header row in a table appears boldfaced and centered by default. Recall that the top row header was selected when the table was created. The caption appears above the table.

QUICK TIP
You can press [Tab] to move your insertion point to the next cell in a row, and press [Shift] [Tab] to move your insertion point to the previous cell.

3. **Enter the names for each dining area and its hours in rows 1 through 3, as shown in Figure G-26**

   The dining room areas and respective hours are listed in the table with the font properties from the body tag applied to them through the rules of inheritance. This means that if formatting is not specified for a child tag inside a parent tag, the parent tag properties and values will format the child tag content.

4. **Merge the second and third cells in the last row, then type the room service information from Figure G-26 with a line break after 12:00 a.m.**

   The room service hours are displayed at the bottom of the table.

TROUBLE
As you add content to the table, the data may not display correctly on the page. Clicking the `<table>` tag or resizing the screen refreshes the display and corrects this.

5. **Click the** `<table>` **tag on the Tag selector**

   The Room service information wraps to a second line, which looks a bit awkward. The width of the table could be extended to the right where there is more room.

6. **Click the** table rule **in the CSS Styles panel, click the** Edit rule button ✏, **click the** Box category, **change the Box width to** 635 px, **click** OK, **then compare your screen to Figure G-27**

   The table is resized to 635 pixels wide, allowing room for the lengthy sentence to remain on one line.

7. **Save your work**

FIGURE G-26: Table with data entered

Top row header

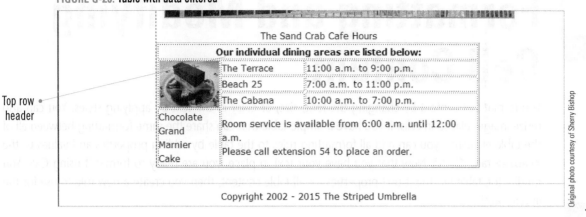

Original photo courtesy of Sherry Bishop

FIGURE G-27: Increasing the width of the table to accommodate data

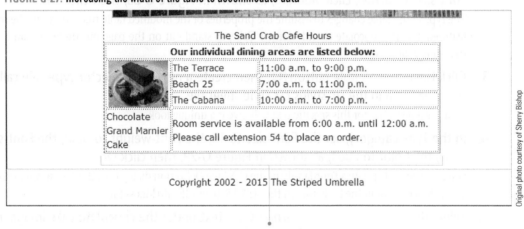

Table width has increased

Original photo courtesy of Sherry Bishop

Importing and exporting tabular data

You can import and export tabular data into and out of Dreamweaver. **Tabular data** is data that is arranged in columns and rows and separated by a **delimiter**, such as a comma, tab, colon, semicolon, or similar character, that tells Dreamweaver where to break the data into table cells. **Importing** means to bring data created in another software program into Dreamweaver, and **exporting** means to save data that was created in Dreamweaver in a different file format so that other programs can read it. Files containing tabular data that are imported into Dreamweaver must first be saved as delimited text files. Programs such as Microsoft Word and Excel offer many file formats for saving files, including saving as delimited text. To import a delimited file, click File on the Menu bar, point to Import, then click Tabular Data. The Import Tabular Data dialog box opens, offering you choices for the resulting table that will appear on the web page. To export a table that you created in Dreamweaver, click File on the Menu bar, point to Export, then click Table. The Export Table dialog box opens, letting you choose the type of delimiter and line breaks you want for the delimited file when you save it.

Formatting and Modifying Cell Content

You format cell content by changing the font, size, or color of the text by applying styles. You can also resize images placed in cells. If you have a simple table that can share the same formatting between all of the table elements, you can add all formatting rules to the table by adding properties and values to the `<table>` tag. ▓▓ Now that you have your text in place, you are ready to format it using CSS. You modify the table tag to set text properties for all table content, then you create a new rule to use for the image caption.

STEPS

1. **Expand the CSS Styles panel group if necessary**
   Formatting the text in the table cells will make the cafe page look more professional.

2. **Click the table rule in the CSS Styles panel, click the Edit Rule button 🖉, click the Type category, click the Font-family list arrow, click Arial, Helvetica, sans-serif, click the Font-size list arrow, click medium, as shown in Figure G-28, then click OK**
   The type in the table changes to assume the properties of the modified table rule. You want the name of the featured dessert, Chocolate Grand Marnier Cake, to stand out on the page but there isn't an existing rule that suits your needs.

3. **Click the New CSS Rule button 🖭, then create a new class selector type rule called featured_item in the su_styles.css style sheet file**
   Creating a new style for this specific text will give it a unique look.

4. **In the Type category, set the Font-size to 14, the Font-weight to bold, the Font-style to italic, the Color to #003, as shown in Figure G-29, then click OK**
   Since you did not specify a Font-family in the CSS Rule Definition dialog box, the font will remain the same, as it is inherited from the body rule in the HTML5_twoColFixRtHdr.css file.

5. **Select the Chocolate Grand Marnier Cake text under the chocolate cake image, click the CSS button 🖳 CSS in the Property inspector, then apply the featured_item rule to the text**
   All text on the page now has a rule applied.

6. **Click after the word Cake in the bottom-left cell, then press [Tab]**
   A new row is added. Pressing the Tab key while the insertion point is in the last cell of the table creates a new row. Even though it appears as if the cell with the room service information is the last cell, it is not because of the merged cells.

7. **Merge the cells in the new row, click in the merged cells, click Insert on the Menu bar, point to HTML, then click Horizontal Rule**
   A horizontal rule is displayed in the merged cells in the last row. Horizontal rules are used frequently to set off or divide sections on a page.

8. **Save your work, preview the cafe page in your browser, compare your screen to Figure G-30, then close your browser**
   The page looks much better with the formatted text.

FIGURE G-28: Modifying the table rule

FIGURE G-29: Creating the .featured_item rule

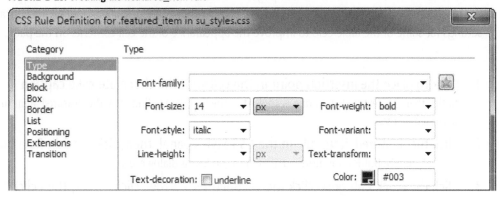

FIGURE G-30: Rules applied to text and horizontal rule added

body_text rule applied

featured_items rule applied

Horizontal rule added in new row

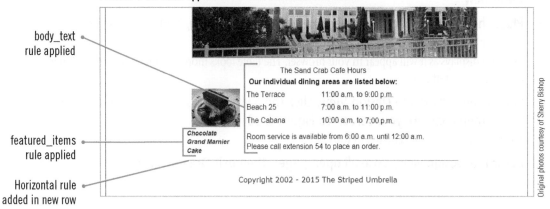

Original photos courtesy of Sherry Bishop

Design Matters

Setting accessibility preferences for tables

You can make tables more accessible to individuals with disabilities by adding table captions or table headers that can be read by screen readers. A table caption will appear at the top of the table in the browser window and adds to table accessibility. Another way to provide accessibility is by using a **table header**, which is an option used by screen readers to help users identify the content of a table. Table headers are automatically centered, boldfaced, and placed in the top row and/or left column. You create table captions and headers using the settings found in the Table dialog box.

Formatting Cells

Formatting a cell can include setting properties that visually enhance the cell's appearance, such as setting a cell width, assigning a background color, or setting global alignment properties for the cell content. To format a cell, with code that is HTML5 compliant, you can use tags to define a column group style <colgroup>, which will format all cells in a particular column. You can also use the column tag <col> to apply formatting styles to singular cells in a column. Once you have created your rules, you add them to the code for the appropriate columns or cells you wish to format. You can also add code to the tag for an individual cell. Formatting cells is different from formatting cell contents. When you format cell contents, you must select the contents and then apply a rule. See the Clues to Use *Using inherited properties to format cells and cell content* at the bottom of this page for more information. ![icon] You decide to experiment with the placement and alignment of the current page content. You change the horizontal and vertical alignment settings for some of the table cells to improve the appearance of the cell contents on the page.

STEPS

1. **Click to place the insertion point in the cell with the chocolate cake caption**

   Notice that the .featured_item rule is applied to the text. You will modify the .featured_item rule to add an alignment value.

2. **Click the .featured_item rule in the CSS Styles panel, then click the Edit Rule button** ![pencil icon]

   The CSS Rule Definition for .featured_item in su_styles.css dialog box opens.

3. **Click the Block Category, click the Text-align list arrow, click center, then click OK**

   The cake text is now centered in the cell, as shown in Figure G-31. Next you will align the contents of the cell describing room service. Since there is not a separate rule applied to this text, you modify the cell tag code to align the cell contents.

4. **Place the insertion point in the cell with the room service information, then switch to Code view**

5. **Place the insertion point at the end of the opening td tag, type** `style="text-align: center"`, **as shown in Figure G-32**

   The page displays as it will appear in your browser. The table looks more organized and professional with the new alignment settings.

6. **Save all files, switch to Design View, click the Switch Design View to Live View button** `Live`, **then compare your screen to Figure G-33**

   The room service text is centered in the cell.

7. **Return to Design view, close all open pages, then exit Dreamweaver**

Using inherited properties to format cells and cell content

If a table is inside a CSS layout, you can simply let the properties from the existing CSS rules format the content, rather than applying additional rules. This is called inheritance. When a tag is placed, or nested, inside another tag (the parent tag), the properties from the parent tag are inherited by any tags nested within that tag. For example, if you set the Font-family property in the body tag, all content on the page inherits and displays that same font family unless you specify otherwise.

FIGURE G-31: Setting horizontal cell alignment

Cell contents are centered

Original photos courtesy of Sherry Bishop

FIGURE G-32: Adding an align property to a cell tag

Add to the code for the cell tag to set the cell alignment to center

```
59        </tr>
60        <tr>
61          <td>The Cabana</td>
62          <td>10:00 a.m. to 7: 00 p.m.</td>
63        </tr>
64        <tr>
65          <td colspan="2" rowspan="2" style="text-align:center">Room service is available from 6:00 a.m. until 12:00 a.m.<br>
66            Please call extension 54 to place an order.</td>
67        </tr>
68        <tr>
69          <td class="featured_item">Chocolate<br>
70            Grand Marnier<br>
71            Cake</td>
72        </tr>
```

FIGURE G-33: The finished product

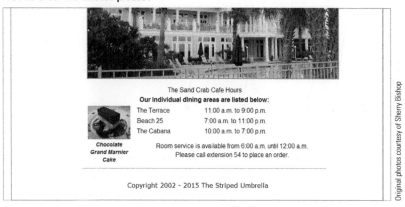

Original photos courtesy of Sherry Bishop

Using grids and guides for positioning page content

The View menu offers a number of options to help you position your page content more precisely. **Grids** consist of horizontal and vertical lines resembling graph paper that fill the page. You can edit the colors of the lines, the distance between them, whether they are displayed using lines or dots, and whether or not objects "snap" (automatically align) to them. **Guides** are horizontal or vertical lines that you place on the page yourself, by clicking and dragging onto the page from the vertical and horizontal rulers. Unlike grids, which fill the page, you can have as many or as few guides as you need. Both grids and guides are used to position page elements using exact measurements.

You can edit both the color of the guides and the color of the **distance,** a screen tip that shows you the distance between two guides when you hold down the control key (Win) or command key (Mac) and place the mouse pointer between the guides. You can lock the guides so you don't accidentally move them, and you can set them either to snap to page elements or have page elements snap to them. To display grids or guides, click View on the Menu bar, point to either Grid or Guides, then select an option from the displayed menu. Grids and guides only appear in Dreamweaver—they do not display when viewed in the browser.

Practice

Concepts Review

Label each element shown in Figure G-34.

FIGURE G-34

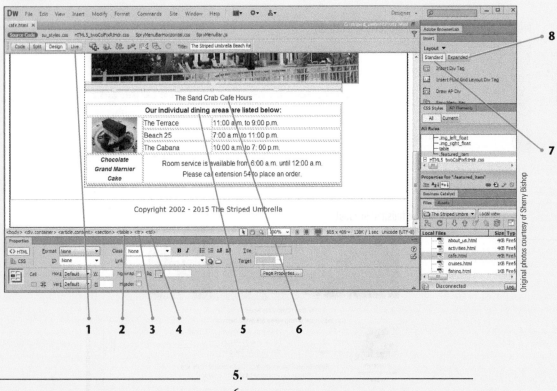

1. _____
2. _____
3. _____
4. _____
5. _____
6. _____
7. _____
8. _____

Match each of the following terms with the statement that best describes its function.

9. Cells
10. Standard mode
11. div tags
12. Import
13. Fixed layout
14. CSS page layouts
15. Deprecated tags
16. CSS Layout box model
17. Export
18. Dynamic content

a. Small boxes arranged in columns and rows

b. Pages built using div tags and CSS

c. Save data that was created in Dreamweaver with a different file format

d. Tags that are no longer considered to be the current standard

e. Page content that changes either in response to certain conditions or through interaction with the user

f. A layout with the width of content blocks based on pixels

g. The mode that does not include temporary cell padding and spacing

h. Bring data into Dreamweaver from another program

i. A view that displays padding and margins for divs

j. HTML tags that determine the appearance and position of containers of content

Skills Review

(If you did not create this website in Unit B and maintain it during the preceding units, you will need to create a local site root folder for this website and define the website using files your instructor will provide. See the "Read This Before You Begin" section for more detailed instructions.)

1. **Create a page using CSS layouts.**
   a. Start Dreamweaver, then open the Blooms & Bulbs website.
   b. Create a new blank HTML5 page with the 2 column fixed, right sidebar, header and footer layout, then attach the blooms_styles.css file to the page and save the new stylesheet file, HTML5_twoColFixRtHdr.css, in the blooms local site folder.
   c. Add the page title **Blooms & Bulbs – Your complete garden center** in the Title text box.
   d. Save the file as **workshops.html**, overwriting the existing workshops page.

2. **Add content to CSS layout blocks.**
   a. Open the index page, then copy the banner and menu bar. (Hint: Select the banner, hold down your Shift key, then click directly under the menu bar to select both.)
   b. Close the index page, then on the workshops page, delete the logo placeholder in the header and paste the banner and menu bar in the header block.
   c. Delete the footer placeholder text, then type **Copyright 2001 – 2015 Blooms & Bulbs** in the footer block.
   d. Delete the placeholder content from the content block.
   e. Type **New Composting Workshop!**, enter a paragraph break, then import the composting.doc file from the drive and folder where you store your Unit G Data Files.
   f. Enter a paragraph break after the last paragraph, then insert the chives.jpg file from the drive and folder where you store your Unit G Data Files. Add the alternate text **Even chives can be beautiful** to the image when prompted.
   g. Save your work.

3. **Edit content in CSS layout blocks.**
   a. Select the footer rule in the CSS Styles panel, then change the Text-align property in the Block category to center.
   b. Select the heading "New Composting Workshop!" and format it using the Heading 1 paragraph format if necessary.

4. **Edit CSS layout properties.**
   a. Select the header rule in the CSS Styles panel and change its background color to #FFF.
   b. Repeat Step a to change the background color of the sidebar1 rule to #FFF and the footer rule to #AFA19E.
   c. Edit the header rule so that the header has a 5-pixel margin on all sides.
   d. Edit the body rule in the HTML5_twoColFixRtHdr.css file to change the Font-size to 14 pixels.
   e. Edit the sidebar1 rule Float to left.
   f. Save your work.

5. **Insert a table and set table properties.**
   a. Delete the placeholder text in the sidebar, including the links, then insert a table with a header at the top of the table, eight rows, and two columns.
   b. Edit the sidebar1 rule to center-align the contents.
   c. Create a new Tag selector in the blooms_styles.css file to modify the table tag by setting the table Box width property to 180 pixels.
   d. Save your work.

Skills Review (continued)

6. Merge and split cells.

   a. Merge the two cells in the first row.

   b. Merge the two cells in the last row.

   c. Save your work.

7. Insert and align images in table cells.

   a. Use the Insert panel to insert gardening_gloves.gif from the drive and folder where you store your Unit G Data Files in the last row of the table. Add the alternate text **Gardening gloves** to the image when prompted.

   b. Save your work.

8. Add text.

   a. Type **Currently Scheduled Workshops** in the merged cells in the first row, using a line break after "Scheduled".

   b. Type the names and dates for the workshops from Figure G-35 in each row of the table.

   c. Save your work.

9. Format and modify cell content.

   a. Edit the table rule to center-align the contents.

   b. Save your work.

10. Format cells.

   a. Edit the table rule to add a left padding of 5 pixels.

   b. Place the insertion point in the top cell, switch to Code view, and add the following code to the end of the opening table data tag: **style="background-color:#C8DBB5"**. (Hint: When you finish editing the code it will read: <th colspan="2" scope="col" style="background-color:#C8DBB5">)

   c. Save your work, preview the workshops page in the browser, then compare your screen to Figure G-35.

   d. Close the browser and close all open pages.

Skills Review (continued)

FIGURE G-35

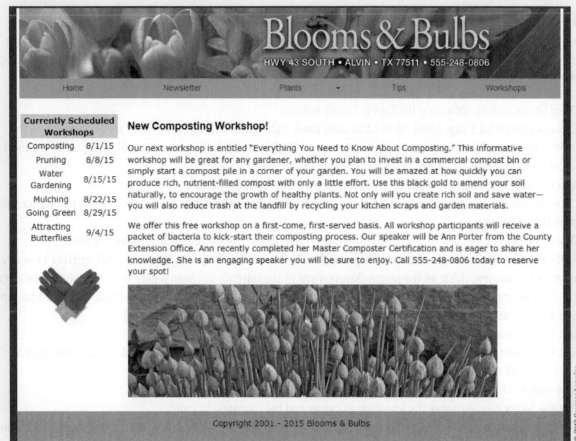

Important: *If you did not create the websites used in the following exercises in Unit B, you need to create a local site root folder for each website and define the websites using files your instructor provides. See the "Read This Before You Begin" section for more detailed instructions.*

Independent Challenge 1

You continue your work on the Rapids Transit website. After studying Cascading Style Sheets, you decide to experiment with predesigned CSS layouts. You create a new rates page based on a CSS HTML5 layout and add a table to list the equipment rental rates.

a. Open Dreamweaver, then open the Rapids Transit website.

b. Create a new HTML5 page based on the 2 column fixed, right sidebar, header and footer layout, and attach the rapids_transit.css file to the page. Verify that the new HTML5_twoColFixRtHdr.css file will be copied to the local site folder, then save it as rates.html, replacing the blank placeholder page.

c. Add the page title **Rapids Transit – Buffalo River Outfitters**.

d. Copy the banner and menu bar from the index page to the new, untitled page, replacing the logo placeholder, then close the index page.

e. Delete the placeholder text in the main content div, then import the file rentals.doc to take its place.

f. Replace the footer placeholder text with **Copyright 2001 - 2015 Rapids Transit. All rights reserved**.

g. Switch to Code view, delete all the placeholder content in the sidebar1 div, switch back to Design view, then insert girl_floating.jpg from the drive and folder where you store you Unit G Data Files. Add alternate text when prompted.

h. Edit the sidebar1 rule to change the box width to 240 pixels and the background to #FFF.

i. Edit the content rule to change the box width to 720 pixels.

j. Edit the header div to change the background color to #FFF, the text align to center, and add a box margin of 5 pixels on all sides.

k. Save your work.

l. Edit the footer rule to change the text-align to center and the font-style to italic.

m. Place the insertion point at the end of the last paragraph after the word "float" and insert a table with a top header, six rows, and four columns.

n. Create a new Tag Selector rule to modify the table tag with the following settings: Box width: 600 pixels, Box left margin: 60 pixels, Block text-align: left.

o. Merge the cells in the top row and type **Rental Rates per Day**.

p. Enter the rental information listed in Figure G-36 in the next three rows.

q. Merge the third and fourth cells in the fifth row, then insert the image rt_logo.gif. Add alternate text when prompted.

r. Merge the cells in the last row, then insert a horizontal rule.

s. Switch to Code view, then edit the header cell tag by adding following code: `style="text-align:center"`.

t. Edit each of the four cells under the header tag by adding the following code: `style="width:25%"`. (*Hint:* you will not see the column widths change to 25 percent unless you view the page in Live view or in a browser.)

u. Save your work, preview the page in Live view or the browser, compare your screen to Figure G-36, make any spacing adjustments to improve the appearance if necessary, then close all pages and exit Dreamweaver.

Independent Challenge 1 (continued)

FIGURE G-36

| Home | Our Guides | Rates | Lodging | Before You Go |

You may be wondering why we charge to use our equipment when we are already charging a fee for the float. We do this because we have many repeat customers who have invested in their own gear. We want to be able to charge them a lower price than we charge those who don't own equipment. Therefore, the more you bring along with you, the less your float will cost! Our basic float price is $20.00 without equipment. Add the amounts on the table for the equipment you will need to the basic price, and you will have the total price of the float. We also take an action shot of you on the water that is included in the price of the float.

Rental Rates per Day

Canoe	$15.00	Life jacket	$3.00
Kayak	$19.00	Helmet	$2.00
Two-man raft	$22.00	Dry Packs	$1.00

Copyright 2001 - 2015 Rapids Transit. All rights reserved.

Independent Challenge 2

You continue your work on the TripSmart website. You are ready to begin work now on a page featuring a catalog item. You plan to use a CSS HTML5 layout with a table to place the data about the item.

a. Open Dreamweaver, open the TripSmart website, then create a new page based on the HTML5: three column fixed, header and footer CSS layout. Attach the tripsmart_styles.css file, verify that the new style sheet file that formats the page layout will be saved in the tripsmart local site root folder, then save the file as catalog.html, replacing the placeholder catalog page in the website.

b. Open the index page, copy the banner and menu bar, then close the index page.

c. Delete the logo image placeholder in the header, then paste the banner and menu bar in the header block.

d. Replace the placeholder text in the footer rule with **Copyright 2002 – 2015**, then edit the footer rule in the HTML5_thrColFixHdr.css style sheet to center align the content and set the background color to #FFF.

e. Edit the header rule to change the background to #FFF and add margins of 5 pixels to each side.

f. Edit the body rule in the HTML5_thrColFixHdr.css style sheet to change the Font-family to Arial, Helvetica, sans-serif, the Font-size to 14 pixels, and the background color to #FFF.

g. Save your work.

h. Delete the placeholder content in the content block, then type **This Week's Featured Catalog Item**.

i. Delete the placeholder text in the sidebar1 div (first column) and type **These are the lengths available for order:**. (Hint: Remember it is much easier to select all of the placeholder content in Code view.)

j. Delete the placeholder text in the aside div (third column) then type **Special Shipping Offer**, enter a paragraph break, type **Order two or more walking sticks this week and your shipping is free. Enter the code twosticks when you check out to receive free shipping.** then apply the Heading 2 format to the Special Shipping Offer text.

k. Create a new Tag rule in the tripsmart_styles.css style sheet that modifies the Heading 2 tag as follows: Font-family: Arial, Helvetica, sans-serif; Font-size: 16 pixels; Type Color: #54572C, then create a new Tag rule in the tripsmart_styles.css file to modify the Heading 1 tag with settings of your choice.

l. Create a new Class rule called centered_text in the tripsmart_styles.css style sheet and set the Text-align property to center. Select the Special Shipping Offer heading and apply the centered_text rule.

m. Enter a paragraph break after the heading in the second column, then insert the image walking_stick.jpg from the drive and folder where you store your Unit G Data Files, adding appropriate alternate text.

n. Create a new class rule named catalog_images in the tripsmart_styles.css file that will add a border of your choice around the image, set the float to left, and add a margin to all sides with settings of your choice. Apply the catalog_images rule to the walking stick image.

o. Edit the sidebar1 rule and the aside rule to set the background color for each rule to #FFF.

p. Edit the footer rule to add a top border of your choice.

q. Edit the container rule to add a border with your choice of settings around all sides.

r. Edit the content rule to change the width to 580 pixels, 10-pixel padding for all sides, and the file tripsmart_gradient.jpg for a background image.

s. Place the insertion point to the right of the walking stick image, then import the file walking sticks.doc from the drive and folder where you store your Unit G Data Files.

t. Insert a table under the text "These are the lengths available for order." with the following settings: rows: 8, columns: 2, Header: top.

u. Create a rule in the tripsmart_styles.css file to modify the table tag as follows: Box width: 175 px; border: solid; border width: thin; border color: #BABD9F, text-align: center.

v. Insert the data for the table using the information in the table in Figure G-37.

w. Add the page title **TripSmart - Serving all your travel needs.**

x. Save your work, preview the page in the browser, and compare your screen to Figure G-37.

y. Close the browser, close all open pages, then exit Dreamweaver.

Independent Challenge 2 (continued)

FIGURE G-37

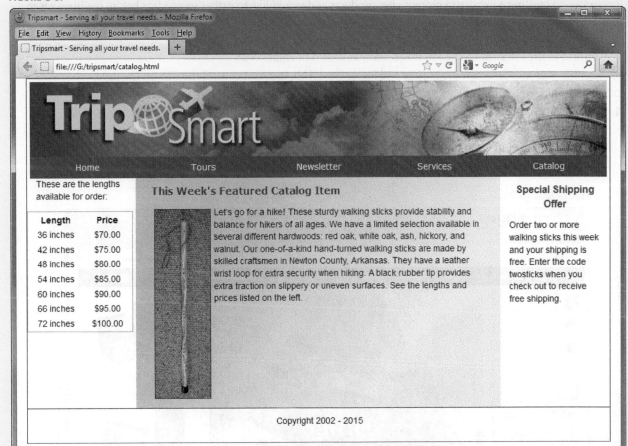

Independent Challenge 3

Dell Patterson has opened a new shop called CollegeFandz, an online source for college students' clothing and collectibles. She is considering creating a website to promote her products and would like to gather some ideas before she hires a web designer. She decides to visit websites to look for design ideas, and asks you for your help.

a. Connect to the Internet, then go to sfbags.com, as shown in Figure G-38.

b. View the source code for the index page and locate the HTML tags that control the CSS on the page.

c. How is CSS used on this site?

d. List at least five div IDs that you find on the index page.

e. Use the Reference panel in Dreamweaver to look up two sets of code used in this site for page layout that you don't understand.

FIGURE G-38

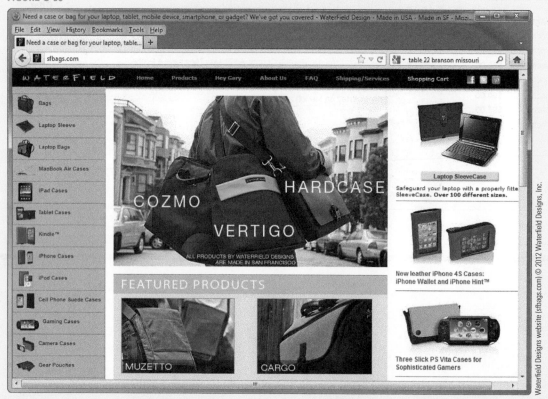

Waterfield Designs website (sfbags.com) © 2012 Waterfield Designs, Inc.

Real Life Independent Challenge

For this assignment, you will continue to work on the website that you have been developing since Unit A. You are building this website from unit to unit, so you must do each Real Life Independent Challenge to complete your website. There are no Data Files supplied. You will continue building your website by designing and completing a page that uses CSS for page layout.

a. Consult your wireframes to decide which page to create and develop for this unit. Draw a sketch of the page to show how you will use CSS to lay out the content.

b. Create the new page for the site using one of the predesigned CSS layouts. Add or edit the divs on your page, making sure to name each one.

c. Add text, images, or background colors to each div.

d. Copy the menu bar from an existing page to the new page.

e. Update the menu bar, if necessary, to include a link to the new page.

f. Consider using the new page as an example to redesign the existing pages with CSS.

g. Save your work, preview each page in your browser, then make any necessary modifications to achieve a clean, consistent, attractive design for each page.

h. Consult your wireframe to see if you have a need to incorporate a table into one of the pages.

i. If you decide to add a table, create rules to format the table elements.

j. Add the data in your plan to the table cells, modifying the appearance as necessary.

k. View your table in a browser, close your browser, close all open pages, then exit Dreamweaver.

Visual Workshop

Use Figure G-39 as a guide to continue your work on the Carolyne's Creations website. Create a new catering page based on the HTML5: 2 column fixed, right sidebar, header and footer page layout. Remember to attach the website style sheet to the page and save the HTML5_thrColFixHdr.css file in the local site root folder. The image, marshmallows.jpg, is found in the assets folder in the drive and folder where you store your Unit G Data Files. Experiment with your CSS settings to create your unique design for the page.

FIGURE G-39

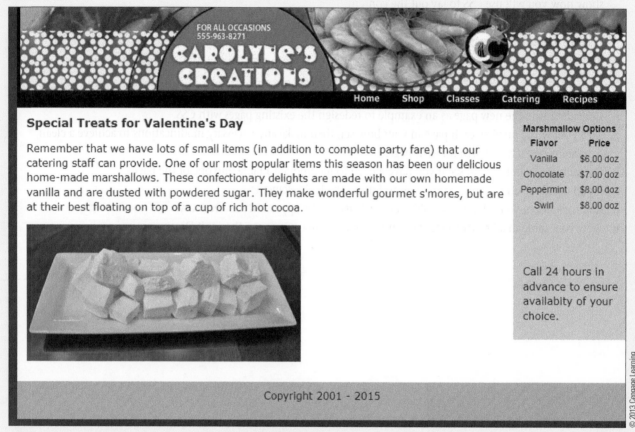

Adding Media and Interactivity

Files You Will Need:

To view a list of files needed for this unit, see the Data Files Grid in the back of the book.

There are many ways to make a website more compelling for users. Most users would rather feel that they are interacting with a site, rather than passively reading information. Adding media objects, such as rollover images, behaviors, Flash video, Flash movies, and sound, provides more interest than static text and images. You decide to add more interactivity to The Striped Umbrella website. You begin by exploring the various options available to you as a designer.

OBJECTIVES

Understand media objects

Add Flash objects

Add behaviors

Edit behaviors

Add rollover images

Add video

Add sound

Update files

Incorporate Web 2.0 technology

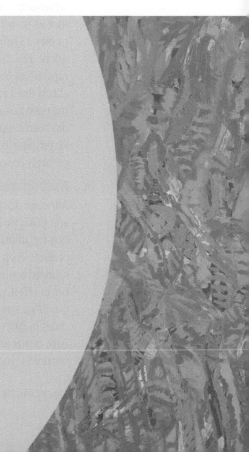

Understanding Media Objects

While a website with text and static images is adequate for presenting information, you can create a much richer user experience by adding movement and interactive elements. You can use Dreamweaver to add media objects created in other programs to the pages of your website. The term *media object* can have different meanings, depending on the industry it is applied to. For our purposes, **media objects** are combinations of visual and audio effects and text used to create an interactive experience within a website.  You want to add interest to The Striped Umbrella site by including media objects. You begin by learning about media objects and how they can help you achieve your remaining website goals.

DETAILS

• **Role of media objects**

The role of a media object is to enhance the user's experience while visiting a website. Thus, each media object that you add should provide a specific purpose that could not be achieved as well without it. As with the use of images, there is a fine balance between providing a rich experience for users, cluttering your page, and not adding enough interesting detail. Too many media objects on a page can slow the time it takes the page to load and be a problem for users with slow connection speeds. Strive to use the smallest possible file size for your media objects to keep download time at a minimum. Also, provide accessibility by using alt or title tags when you insert media objects. Figure H-1 shows an example of the NASA website, which uses video, rollovers, and audio files.

• **Types of media objects**

You can use Dreamweaver to insert a variety of media effects into your web pages, including Flash movies, video, and a series of built-in JavaScript behaviors, such as sounds, rollover images, drop-down menus, Go to URLs, and menus. **Go to URLs** direct the browser to use a link to open a different window. Some of the external media file types include Adobe Fireworks menu bars, rollover images, and buttons; video, sound, and animation; Flash Paper; Director and Shockwave movies and presentations; Java applets; ActiveX controls; server-side controls; and a variety of plug-ins. A **plug-in** (also called an **add-on**) is a small computer program that works with a host application, such as a web browser, to enable it to perform certain functions. In order to play a Flash SWF file in a web browser, you would need to install the Flash Player plug-in. In order to read Adobe PDF files, you would need to install the Adobe Reader plug-in. Plug-ins allow you to extend the capabilities of the browser to display content, letting you create complex, interactive websites with media effects that can be viewed within the pages themselves. Another advantage of plug-ins is that they eliminate the need to load an external document player, such as Windows Media Player. The future of Flash technology has been a topic of discussion recently. Some devices, such as the iPhone and iPad, do not support the Flash Player plug-in. With the development of HTML5, CSS3, Adobe Edge, Adobe Air, and Adobe Flex, we will probably be seeing some shifting in the methods we have used in the past to create animation and motion.

• **Adding media objects with HTML5**

Although Adobe Flash is still the premier tool used for creating animation, with the development of HTML5 and CSS3, we have new ways available now for incorporating motion and animation. HTML5 includes new tags for animation and video such as the <audio> tag and the <video> tag with attributes such as autoplay, controls, loop, and src. With CSS3, there are new styles for enhancing appearance of page objects such as rounded corners and gradients. Adobe Edge, a new program introduced by Adobe, combines the new capabilities of HTML5, CSS3, and JavaScript but uses a program interface similar to Flash. Like Flash, a stage, timeline, playhead, symbols, frames, and layers are used to manipulate text, shapes, and images. Unlike Flash, Edge codes in JSON (JavaScript Object Notation), a subset of JavaScript rather than ActionScript. This means that Edge creates animation that is coded entirely with HTML and JavaScript, so browsers that support HTML5 will not need a plug-in to play the animations. Edge also integrates with font services such as Typekit or FontSquirrel.

Using Adobe Flash Player to view Flash content

To view Flash movies, you need to install Adobe Flash Player. This program is included in the latest versions of Internet Explorer, Mozilla Firefox, Safari, and Opera. If you are using an older browser that does not support the version of Flash used to create your movie, you can download the latest Flash Player from the Adobe website, located at adobe.com. Almost all browsers use Adobe Flash Player. However, the mobile and touch markets are not as supportive. Internet Explorer 10 Metro and Apple iOS devices do not support the Flash plug-in. When you use the Insert panel to add Flash content to a web page, the code that links and runs the content (such as detecting the presence of Flash Player and directing the user to download it if necessary) is embedded into the page code.

Adding Flash Objects

Flash is a program that allows you to create low-bandwidth, high-quality animations and interactive elements called Flash movies that you can place on your web pages. **Low-bandwidth** animations are animations that don't require a fast connection to work properly. These animations use a series of vector-based graphics to create short movies that download quickly. **Vector-based graphics** are scalable graphics that are built using mathematical formulas, rather than pixels. When you use the Insert panel to add Flash content to a web page, the code that links and runs the content is embedded into the page code. Thus, the presence of a Flash player can be identified by the computer, which will then provide a prompt to the user to download the player if it is not detected. The original Flash file is stored as a separate file in the local site root folder. Flash movies have the .swf file extension. ![icon] The cafe logo displayed at the top of the cafe page is an attractive image. However, an animated logo would add movement and more interest to the page. You decide to replace the current logo image with a Flash movie.

STEPS

1. **Start Dreamweaver, switch to Design view if necessary, open the cafe page in The Striped Umbrella website, then place the insertion point in the sidebar to the left of the word "Reservations"**

   You will insert a Flash movie above the reservations sentence.

2. **Click the Media button list arrow in the Common category on the Insert panel, then click SWF**

   The Select SWF dialog box opens. You use this dialog box to locate the Flash movie.

   > **QUICK TIP**
   > If you already have a Flash .swf file in your local site root folder, you can drag and drop it from the Assets panel or Files panel instead of using the Insert panel or Insert menu.

3. **Navigate to the drive and folder where you store your Unit H Data Files, click crabdance.swf, click OK (Win) or Open (Mac), click Yes in the Dreamweaver dialog box, then click Save**

   The movie is copied and saved in the local site root folder of The Striped Umbrella website. An Object Tag Accessibility Attributes dialog box opens. This is where you add a title for screen readers.

4. **Type Cafe logo animation in the Title text box, click OK, select FlashID in the ID text box in the Property inspector, type crabdance, then press [Enter] Win or [return] Mac**

   A Flash movie placeholder appears on the page, as shown in Figure H-2. The title and ID provide accessibility for the Flash movie. The Loop check box in the Property inspector is currently selected, which means that the Flash movie will play continuously (loop) by default while the page is viewed.

   > **QUICK TIP**
   > Mac users do not have a Play button on the Property inspector.

5. **With the placeholder selected, click the Play button in the Property inspector, then click Stop (Win), or skip to Step 6 (Mac)**

   The movie plays in a continuous loop until you stop it.

   > **QUICK TIP**
   > You may have to refresh your Files panel to see the new Scripts folder.

6. **Click the Loop check box to deselect it, save your work, then click OK to close the Copy Dependent Files dialog box**

   Two supporting files, expressInstall.swf and swfobject_modified.js, are copied to a new Scripts folder. These files are necessary for the movie to play in the browser correctly. Deselecting the Loop check box stops the Flash movie from playing continuously.

   > **QUICK TIP**
   > If your Flash movie is too close to the menu bar, insert a line break between them.

7. **Click the Switch Design View to Live View button ⌷Live⌷, then compare your screen to Figure H-3**

   The page is displayed in Live View, with all active content functioning. As it will do when viewed in a browser, the Flash movie plays one time and then stops.

8. **Click ⌷Live⌷, then close the cafe page**

FIGURE H-2: The Flash movie inserted on the cafe page

Flash movie placeholder

Loop check box

ID text box   Name of Flash file   Play button (Mac users do not have a Play button)   Media button list arrow

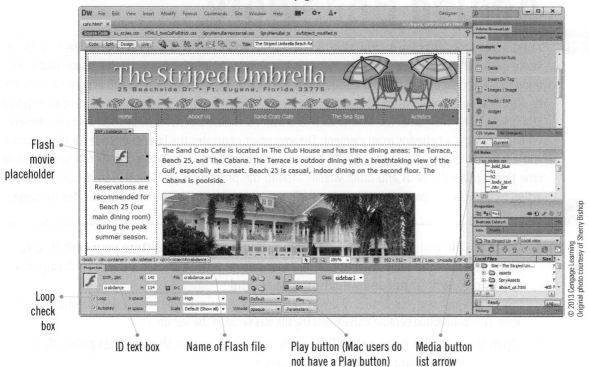

© 2013 Cengage Learning
Original photo courtesy of Sherry Bishop

FIGURE H-3: Viewing the Flash movie with Live View

Switch Design View to Live View button

Flash movie

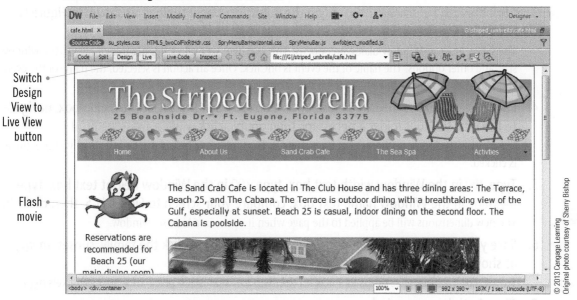

© 2013 Cengage Learning
Original photo courtesy of Sherry Bishop

Using Flash movies

Using Flash, you can create Flash movies that include multimedia elements, such as audio files (both music and voice-overs), animated objects, scripted objects, and clickable links. You can use Flash movies to add content to your existing website or to create an entire website. To add a Flash movie to a web page, click SWF from the Media menu in the Common category on the Insert panel to open the Select SWF dialog box, and then choose the Flash movie you want to insert. As with images, always add a title tag when inserting Flash content to provide accessibility. You also need to include code that will instruct the browser to check for and load a Flash player so the user can view the Flash content on the page. To preview your Flash movies, you can either use Live view or preview them in a browser window. See "Using Adobe Flash Player to view Flash content" at the bottom of page 203 for an additional way to add Flash content without using the Flash player.

Adding Behaviors

You can make your web pages come alive by adding interactive elements, such as special effects, to them. These special effects are called **actions**. For example, you could attach an action to an image that would result in a descriptive drop-down message when the mouse is rolled over it. You add actions to elements by attaching behaviors to them. **Behaviors** are sets of instructions that tell the page element to respond in a specific way when an event occurs, such as when the mouse pointer is positioned over the element. When you attach a behavior to an element, Dreamweaver generates the JavaScript code for the behavior and inserts it into your page code.  The Striped Umbrella staff would like guests to know ahead of time that feeding the birds and other wildlife around the property is prohibited. You decide to add an action to the activities page that will automatically open a new browser window with a related message.

STEPS

1. **Open the file dwh_1.html from the drive and folder where you store your Unit H Data Files, save it in the local site root folder as wildlife_message.html without updating links, then close dwh_1.html and wildlife_message.html**
    The wildlife_message page is already linked to the su_styles.css style sheet and coded with the body_text style. (The connection became active when the file was saved to the website.)

2. **Open the activities page, select the family_sunset image on the activities page, click Window on the Menu bar, then click Behaviors**
    The Tag Inspector panel opens with the Behaviors tab selected. With the family_sunset image selected, any action that is selected will apply to the image.

    > **QUICK TIP**
    > An event can be changed by clicking it and choosing a different event.

3. **Click the Add behavior button ⊞ on the Behaviors panel toolbar, as shown in Figure H-4, then click Open Browser Window**
    The Open Browser Window dialog box opens. This is where you select the file to be opened, the window size, and other options. The name of the event is onClick. Once an action is selected, the name of the event will appear by default in the left column of the Behaviors.

4. **Click Browse next to the URL to display text box to open the Select File dialog box, navigate to the local site root folder if necessary, then double-click wildlife_message.html**
    You identify the location where the message resides. The message will display when the family_sunset image is clicked.

5. **Type 300 in the Window width text box, type 300 in the Window height text box, type message in the Window name text box, compare your screen to Figure H-5, then click OK**
    The new dimensions will be applied to the page when it opens in a browser window.

    > **QUICK TIP**
    > The information bar at the top of the window will display specific instructions for your browser type.

6. **Save your work, preview the page in your browser, then click the family_sunset image, as shown in Figure H-6**
    The wildlife_message page opens in a new browser window that is 300 pixels wide and 300 pixels high.

7. **Close both browser windows**

Using the Behaviors panel to add Actions

You can use the Behaviors panel to insert a variety of JavaScript-based behaviors on a page. For instance, you can automate tasks, respond to user selections and mouse movements with drop-down menus, create games, go to a different URL, or add automatic dynamic effects to a web page. To insert a behavior, click the Add behavior button on the Behaviors panel to open the Actions menu, then click an action from the menu. Actions are triggered by events. For instance, if you want the user to see a page element slide across the page when the element is clicked, you would attach the Slide action using the **onClick** event to trigger the action. Other examples of events are onMouseOver and onLoad. The **onMouseOver** event will trigger an action when the mouse is placed over an object. The **onLoad** event will trigger an action when the page is first loaded in the browser window.

FIGURE H-4: **Behaviors panel with the Actions menu displayed**

Add behavior button

Actions menu

Open Browser Window action

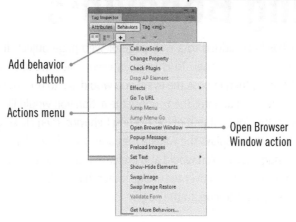

FIGURE H-5: **Setting Open Browser Window options**

URL to display text box

Window width text box

Window name text box

Window height text box

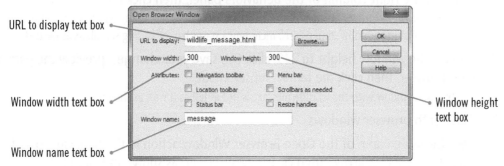

FIGURE H-6: **Viewing the wildlife message in a browser**

Wildlife message displayed in new browser window

Clicking the family_sunset image triggers the event

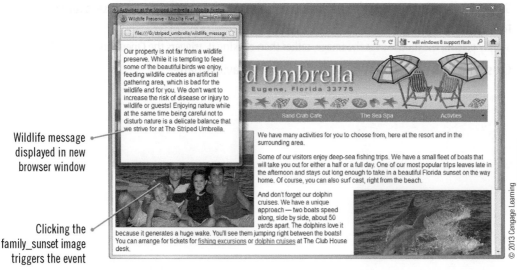

© 2013 Cengage Learning
Original photos courtesy of Sherry Bishop

Using the Spry framework

Some of the behaviors that you can add to web pages use a JavaScript library called the **Spry framework for AJAX**. **Asynchronous JavaScript and XML (AJAX)** is a method for developing interactive web pages that respond quickly to user input, such as clicking a map. The JavaScript library contains **spry widgets**, which are prebuilt components for adding interactivity to pages, and **spry effects**, which are screen effects, such as fading and enlarging page elements. When you add a spry effect to a page element, Dreamweaver automatically adds a **SpryAssets folder** to the local site root folder with the supporting files located inside the folder.

Editing Behaviors

Once a behavior has been added to a web page or web page object, it is easy to modify the action or event by using the Behaviors panel. To change an event, click the left column in the Behaviors panel to display the list of events, then choose the event you would like to use. To change the action, click the right column to display the list of actions, then choose the action you would like to use. You can edit an existing behavior by clicking the right column of the existing behavior, then clicking Edit Behavior. ██████ The current browser window that displays the wildlife message is a little too large. You want to resize the window so it will fit the message better. You would also prefer that the event for this behavior opens a new window when the mouse is simply placed over the image rather than clicked. You decide to use the Behaviors panel to make the necessary adjustments to the page.

1. **Click the** family_sunset image **if necessary, right-click (Win) the** Open Browser Window **action in the right column of the Behaviors panel, then click** Edit Behavior

   The Open Browser Window dialog box opens. This is where you adjust the window properties and settings, such as establishing window dimensions, including a status bar, or adding scrollbars as needed.

   QUICK TIP

   Your window may appear slightly different depending on the browser you are using to view the page.

2. **Change the window height to** 245, **click** OK, **save your changes, preview the page in your browser, then click the** family_sunset image

   The browser window with the wildlife message is not as tall as it was, as shown in Figure H-7.

3. **Close both browser windows**

4. **Click the** left column **of the Open Browser Window action in the Behaviors panel, click the** events list arrow, **then click** onMouseOver, **as shown in Figure H-8**

   The onMouseOver selection specifies that the event of placing the mouse over an image triggers an action. The Open Browser Window action remains the same.

   TROUBLE

   If you see a message that pop-ups are disabled in your browser, click the prompt to temporarily allow popups.

5. **Save your work, preview the page in the browser, then move the mouse over the** family_sunset image

   Simply placing the mouse over the image, rather than clicking it, triggers the Open Browser Window action.

6. **Close the browser windows, then close the Behaviors panel**

Using the Server Behaviors panel

In addition to the Behaviors panel, Dreamweaver also has a Server Behaviors panel, which is located in the Dynamic Content Tab group with the Databases, Bindings, and Components panels. The **Server Behaviors** panel is used to add server behaviors. Server behaviors are tools that write server-side code, such as ASP, PHP, or ColdFusion. For example, you can add code to create a login page or create a page that is password protected. You can also build search pages that will enable users to search a website for specific content. After you have created a server behavior and enabled Dreamweaver to display live data, you can add, edit, or delete the server behavior while you are in Design view, but viewing the page in Live View.

Reduced
window
size with
wildlife
message
displayed

© 2013 Cengage Learning
Original photos courtesy of Sherry Bishop

FIGURE H-8: Editing the event for the Open Browser Window action

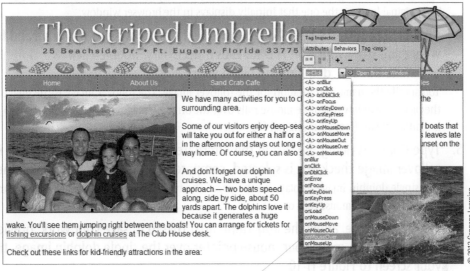

onMouseOver event

© 2013 Cengage Learning
Original photos courtesy of Sherry Bishop

Adding Rollover Images

A **rollover image** is an image that changes its appearance when the mouse pointer is placed over it in a browser. A rollover image actually consists of two images. The first image is the one that displays when the mouse pointer is not positioned over it, and the second image is the one that displays when the mouse pointer is positioned over it. Rollover images are often used to help create a feeling of action and interest on a web page. When a rollover image is inserted into a page, Dreamweaver automatically adds two behaviors: a Swap Image behavior and a Swap Image Restore behavior. A **Swap Image behavior** is JavaScript code that directs the browser to display a different image when the mouse is rolled over an image on the page. A **Swap Image Restore behavior** restores the swapped image back to the original image when the mouse is moved away from the image. You have a photograph of a dolphin that would be perfect on the activities page. To add some interactivity to the page, you decide to include the photograph as a rollover image for the current image of two dolphins.

STEPS

1. **Select the image of the two dolphins, then delete it**

   The rollover image will be placed in the same position on the page as the deleted two_dolphins image.

2. **Click the Images list arrow in the Common group on the Insert panel, then click Rollover Image**

   The Insert Rollover Image dialog box opens. This is where you specify the name of the image and link to the images you will use for both the original image and the rollover image.

3. **Type dolphins in the Image name text box, click Browse next to the Original image text box, browse to the drive and folder where you store your Unit H Data Files, open the assets folder, then double-click one_dolphin.jpg**

   You specify the image name for the rollover and identify the name and location for the original image. The original image is the one that initially displays in the browser window.

QUICK TIP

To prevent one of the images from being resized during the rollover, both images should be the same height and width.

4. **Click Browse next to the Rollover image text box, browse to the drive and folder where you store your Unit H Data Files if necessary, double-click two_dolphins.jpg, then overwrite the two_dolphins.jpg file in your website assets folder**

   You specify the name and location for the rollover image. The rollover image is the image that displays in the browser window when the mouse rolls over the original image. This version of the two_dolphins image is a different size from your original file.

QUICK TIP

The Preload rollover image option ensures that the rollover image displays without a delay.

5. **Type Dolphins riding the surf in the Alternate text text box, verify that the Preload rollover image check box is selected, compare your screen to Figure H-9, then click OK**

   The single dolphin image displays on the page. The two_dolphins image will only appear in the browser window when the mouse rolls over it.

TROUBLE

If you don't see the rollover image, temporarily direct your browser to allow blocked content.

6. **Select the image, apply the img_right_float rule to it, save your work, preview the page in your browser, move your mouse pointer over the single dolphin image, then compare your screen to Figure H-10**

   The image is aligned to the right of the paragraph with a left margin of 10px. When you point to the image, the single dolphin image is swapped with the two-dolphin image. When you move the mouse away from the image, it is swapped again.

7. **Close the browser, then click the Show Code view button [Code]**

   The code for the swap image behavior displays, as shown in Figure H-11. The code directs the browser to display the image with one dolphin "onmouseout"—when the mouse is not over the image. It directs the browser to display the image with two dolphins "onmouseover"—when the mouse is over the image.

8. **Click the Show Design view button [Design]**

FIGURE H-9: **Setting rollover image properties**

Image name text box

Original image text box

Rollover image text box

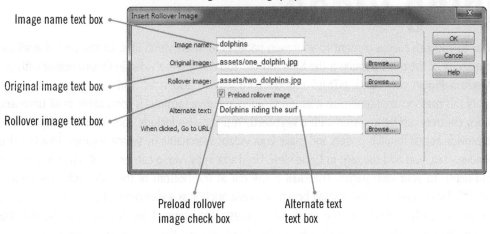

Preload rollover
image check box

Alternate text
text box

FIGURE H-10: **Viewing the rollover image in a browser**

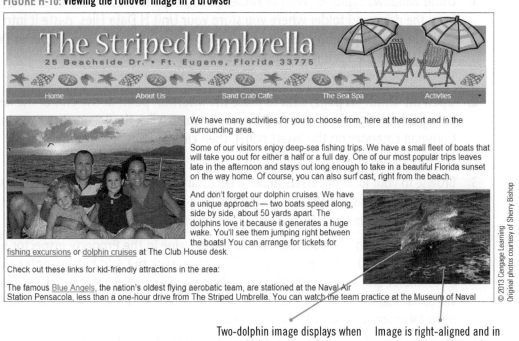

© 2013 Cengage Learning
Original photos courtesy of Sherry Bishop

Two-dolphin image displays when
mouse pointer rests on image

Image is right-aligned and in
same position as former image

FIGURE H-11: **Viewing the code for the rollover image**

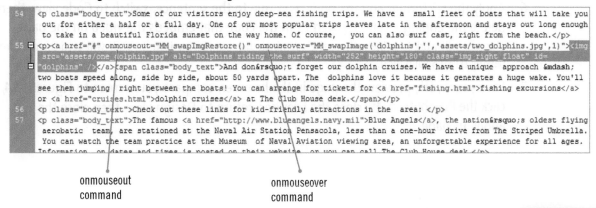

onmouseout
command

onmouseover
command

Adding Media and Interactivity

Adding Video

Another way to add rich media content to your web pages is to insert video files. Of the several available video formats, one of the most popular is the MP4 format. You can insert a video in Dreamweaver with the Insert > Media > Plugin command. HTML5 introduced a way to add video with the <video> tag. The advantages of this method are numerous: it supports video in native formats, is compatible in all browsers, and the video controls can be accessed with a keyboard. You can also include code to link multiple video formats to provide access for all browsers and make your videos searchable by search engines. To add video with the <video> tag, you add the tags in Code view. Used sparingly, video can be an effective way to add interest and depth to your web pages. The **skin** is the bar at the bottom of the video with the control buttons. Every guest is given a small beach umbrella anchor as a welcome gift, which then can be used to secure a beach umbrella in the sand. Since guests sometimes have trouble figuring out this procedure, you decide to add a short Flash video to the about_us page that demonstrates the process.

STEPS

1. **Using Windows Explorer (Win) or Finder (Mac), copy the file** umbrella_anchor_video.mp4 **from the drive and folder where you store your Unit H Data Files, paste it into the assets folder in The Striped Umbrella local site root folder, close Windows Explorer (Win) or Finder (Mac), then return to Dreamweaver**

   The file is copied to the local site assets folder and ready to insert in the page.

2. **Open the about_us page, click to place the insertion point at the end of the last paragraph on the page, enter a paragraph return, click the** Media list arrow **in the Common category on the Insert panel, then click** Plugin

   The Select File dialog box opens. This is where you enter the name of the video.

3. **Browse to your local site assets folder if necessary, double-click** umbrella_anchor_video.mp4, **then enter four paragraph breaks after the plug-in placeholder**

   The video plug-in placeholder is inserted on the page, as shown in Figure H-12.

4. **Select the plug-in placeholder, change the W value in the Property inspector to** 220, **and the H value to** 200, **click the** Parameters button, **click the** Add button, **enter** autostart **for a Parameter and** false **for the Value, as shown in Figure H-13, then click** OK

   The placeholder for the plug-in now fits the size of the video plus a little extra for the controls. The video will not start until the user clicks the play button.

5. **Place the insertion point to the right of the video placeholder image, type** Visit us at the front desk to pick up your complimentary Umbrella Anchor! **using line breaks as shown in Figure H-14, then apply the** img_left_float **rule to the plug-in placeholder.**

   The explanatory text helps guests understand the purpose of the video.

6. **Apply the** H3 **format and the** body_text **rule to the sentence, switch to Code view, then delete the ending** < /embed> **tag from the code that embeds the video on the page**

   The code will work just fine without the < /embed> tag, but leaving it in the code will keep the page from passing HTML5 validation.

7. **Save your work, preview the page in the browser, compare your screen to Figure H-14, click the** Play button ▶, **close the browser, return to Design view, then close the about_us page**

FIGURE H-12: Inserting a video on the activities page

Video placeholder inserted on page

Original photos courtesy of Sherry Bishop

FIGURE H-13: Editing the settings for the video

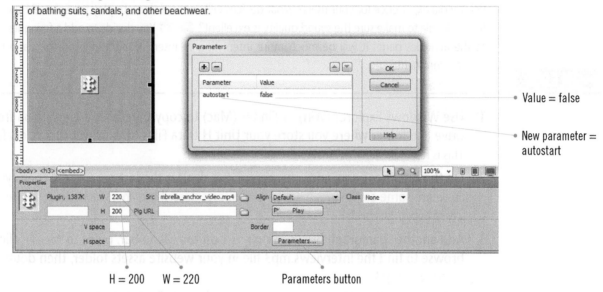

Value = false

New parameter = autostart

H = 200   W = 220

Parameters button

FIGURE H-14: Viewing the video in a browser

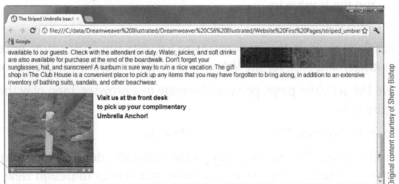

Play button becomes pause button while video is playing

Original content courtesy of Sherry Bishop

Comparing video file formats

There are several file format choices for publishing video files. Among them are **AVI** (Audio Visual Interleave), a Microsoft format; **MOV** (Apple QuickTime); **MP4** (a digital video compression standard); **FLV** (Adobe Flash Video); **WebM** (Google developed open-source format); and **Ogg** (Ogg Theora), an open-source format developed by Xiph.org. Of these file formats, MP4, WebM, and Ogg are the three HTML5 supported video formats.

Adding Sound

There are several ways to incorporate sound into a website. Sound files are relatively small in file size and easy to add to a page. You can embed them as a background sound, embed them on a page with visible sound controls, link them to a page, or add them to a page with the new <audio> tags introduced in HTML5. A few audio file formats do not require a plug-in to play, such as the wav (Waveform Extension) and aif or aiff (Audio Interchange File Format) file formats. Files that do require a plug-in are mp3 or MPEG (Motion Picture Experts Group) files, which can be played using QuickTime, Windows Media Player, or RealPlayer plug-ins. As with incorporating video, when you incorporate sound files, you should provide more than one audio format if possible to make sure all browsers will have a format they can play. Before you decide to add a sound to a page, think about the purpose you have in mind. Will the sound add to a rich media experience for your users? What devices will your users use to play the sound? Have you tested the audio file to make sure the sound quality is excellent? ▨▨▨▨ You decide to add a few guest comments to the activities page. It will be much more interesting to insert an audio file on the page rather than printed comments.

STEPS

1. **Use Windows Explorer (Win) or Finder (Mac) to copy the file** interviews.mp3 **from the drive and folder where you store your Unit H Data Files to your website assets folder**
   This is the audio file with the recorded guest comments.

2. **On the activities page, add a paragraph break after the last paragraph, then type**
   Here are some comments from recent guests describing their favorite activities at The Striped Umbrella.

3. **Add another paragraph break, click** Insert **on the Menu bar, point to** Media, **click** Plugin, **browse to find the interviews.mp3 file in your website assets folder, then double-click** interviews.mp3
   A plug-in icon placeholder appears on the page, as shown in Figure H-15. You create a rule to modify the placeholder appearance.

4. **Select the plug-in placeholder, then use the Property inspector to change the W value to** 200 **and the H value to** 20
   The plug-in placeholder image is longer.

5. **Click** Parameters **in the Property inspector, click the** Add button, **enter** autostart **for a Parameter and** false **for the Value, as shown in Figure H-16, then click** OK

6. **Save the activities page, preview the page in a browser, then play the file, as shown in Figure H-17**

7. **Close the browser, then switch to Code view**

8. **Scroll to locate the** <embed> **tag for the audio file, delete the ending** < /embed> **tag at the end of the line, then save your work, switch back to Design view, and close the page**
   The code will work just fine without the < /embed> tag, but leaving it will keep the page from passing HTML5 validation.

> **QUICK TIP**
> If the file won't play in your browser, it's possible that you are missing a plug-in. Contact your technical support for instructions.

FIGURE H-15: Inserting a sound file on the activities page

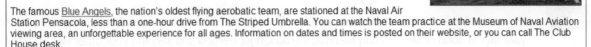

Check out these links for kid-friendly attractions in the area:

The famous <u>Blue Angels</u>, the nation's oldest flying aerobatic team, are stationed at the Naval Air Station Pensacola, less than a one-hour drive from The Striped Umbrella. You can watch the team practice at the Museum of Naval Aviation viewing area, an unforgettable experience for all ages. Information on dates and times is posted on their website, or you can call The Club House desk.

It's a short ride over the Alabama border to see the <u>USS Alabama</u>, one of America's most decorated battleships. The "Mighty A" is docked at Battleship Memorial Park in Mobile Bay, Alabama. There you can take a two-hour self-guided tour that is rich in history. Hours, directions, and prices are posted on their website, or call The Club House desk.

Here are some comments from recent guests describing their favorite activites at the Striped Umbrella:

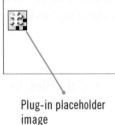

Plug-in placeholder image

FIGURE H-16: Adding a parameter to the sound object

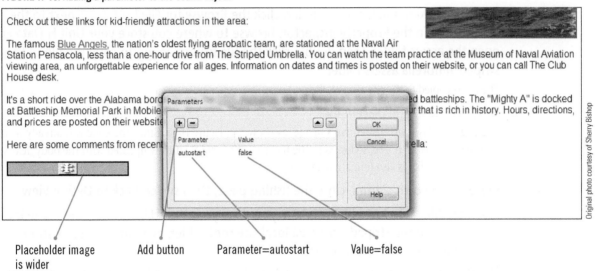

Check out these links for kid-friendly attractions in the area:

The famous <u>Blue Angels</u>, the nation's oldest flying aerobatic team, are stationed at the Naval Air Station Pensacola, less than a one-hour drive from The Striped Umbrella. You can watch the team practice at the Museum of Naval Aviation viewing area, an unforgettable experience for all ages. Information on dates and times is posted on their website, or you can call The Club House desk.

It's a short ride over the Alabama bord...

Placeholder image is wider   Add button   Parameter=autostart   Value=false

---

FIGURE H-17: Viewing the sound file on the activities page

love it because it generates a huge wake. You'll see them jumping right between the boats! You can arrange for tickets for <u>fishing excursions</u> or <u>dolphin cruises</u> at The Club House desk.

Check out these links for kid-friendly attractions in the area:

The famous <u>Blue Angels</u>, the nation's oldest flying aerobatic team, are stationed at the Naval Air Station Pensacola, less than a one-hour drive from The Striped Umbrella. You can watch the team practice at the Museum of Naval Aviation viewing area, an unforgettable experience for all ages. Information on dates and times is posted on their website, or you can call The Club House desk.

It's a short ride over the Alabama border to see the <u>USS Alabama</u>, one of America's most decorated battleships. The "Mighty A" is docked at Battleship Memorial Park in Mobile Bay, Alabama. There you can take a two-hour self-guided tour that is rich in history. Hours, directions, and prices are posted on their website, or call The Club House desk.

Here are some comments from recent guests describing their favorite activites at the Striped Umbrella:

The skin will vary in appearance depending on the browser used

Updating Files

As your website grows and you have additional folders and files to keep track of, it is imperative to keep your files in good order. Deleting files that are no longer needed and keeping your other files updated are important to insure quality websites. In Unit F, you learned to run reports to identify broken links and orphaned files. When you are using incomplete pages as placeholder pages, they will not show up as orphaned files if they contain links from other pages. Before publishing your site to a web server, however, be sure to complete all pages; publishing incomplete pages is considered unprofessional. ▓▓▓▓▓ You are ready to finalize the fishing and cruises pages. You replace the placeholder pages with completed pages so that all of the pages are up to date.

STEPS

1. **Open the file dwh_2.html from the folder where you store your Unit H Data Files, then save it as fishing.html in the striped_umbrella local site root folder, overwriting the existing fishing page but not updating links**

   Although the page is saved, the image will continue to display as a broken link on the fishing page until the image is saved in the website.

2. **Click the broken graphic placeholder, click the Browse for File button 🗀 next to the Src text box in the Property inspector, browse to where you store your Unit H Data Files, open the assets folder, then double-click the file fisherman.jpg to copy the file to the striped_umbrella assets folder**

   The file is copied to the site assets folder.

3. **Deselect the image placeholder**

   The page displays with fisherman's image, as shown in Figure H-18. Since the code was already in place on the page linking the su_styles.css to the file, the text is automatically updated with the body_text style. The Spry Menu bar is also formatted correctly.

4. **Close the file dwh_2.html, close the fishing page, then switch back to Design view**

5. **Open the file dwh_3.html from where you store your Unit H Data Files, then save it as cruises.html in the striped_umbrella local site root folder, overwriting the existing cruises page but not updating links**

   The page is saved, but the image link remains broken because the image has not been saved in the website.

6. **Close the dwh_3.html page, click the broken graphic placeholder, click 🗀 next to the Src text box in the Property inspector, browse to where you store your Unit H Data Files, open the assets folder, double-click the file boats.jpg, click Yes to copy the file to the striped_umbrella assets folder, then click Save**

   The file is copied to the site assets folder.

7. **Deselect the image placeholder**

   The image displays on the page, as shown in Figure H-19. Since the code was already in place on the page linking to the su_styles.css style sheet, the text is automatically updated with the body_text style.

8. **Save and close the page, then exit Dreamweaver**

FIGURE H-18: Fishing page updated

We have several boats available for fishing trips that can be rented by the hour, half day, or full day. You may choose to go out to sea several miles for deep-sea fishing, or fish in one of several bays not far from the resort. Call the front desk to schedule your trip and let them know the fishing gear you will need us to provide. Bring your catch back and our chefs will be happy to prepare it to your specifications for dinner!

Be sure to apply sunscreen liberally before you arrive at the dock. A large hat with a tie is highly recommended to protect your head and neck while you are on the open water. We will provide a cooler with bottles of water, but you will need to provide your own snacks or lunch. The Sand Crab Cafe will be happy to prepare these for you if you call several hours in advance.

© 2013 Cengage Learning
Original photo courtesy of Sherry Bishop

FIGURE H-19: Cruises page updated

This is the Dolphin Racer at dock. We leave daily at 4:00 p.m.and 6:30 p.m. for 1-1/2 hour cruises. There are snacks and restrooms available on board. We welcome children of all ages. Our ship is a U.S. Coast Guard approved vessel and our captain is a former member of the Coast Guard. Call The Club desk for reservations.

If you plan to join us, please apply sunscreen liberally before you leave. A hat that can be securely tied to your head is a must. Be sure to bring your video camera because you will not want to miss the opportunity to take some great footage of the dolphins at play.

© 2013 Cengage Learning
Original photo courtesy of Sherry Bishop

Using HTML5 compliant media tags

As HTML5 gains support across all browsers, you will want to use HTML5 tags to insert and format your media content. For example, to insert a Flash SWF file, while the code you used in this unit works fine in all browsers that support the Flash plug-in, you will want to use code that will be supported by those browsers that support HTML5 media tags rather than plug-ins like Flash. As you learned, you can use this code to insert the crabdance.swf file: `<object width="140" height="114" data="crabdance.swf"></object>`. To insert video files, use `<video>` tags, to insert audio, use `<audio>` tags.

Incorporating Web 2.0 Technology

The term **Web 2.0** describes the recent evolution of web applications that facilitate and promote information sharing among Internet users. These applications not only reside on computers, but on cell phones, in cars, on portable GPS devices, and in game devices. **GPS (Global Positioning System)** devices are used to track your position through a global satellite navigation system. They are regularly used for assistance with driving directions, hiking locations, and map making. Web 2.0 applications do not simply display information; they enable users to actively direct or contribute to the web page content.  Web 2.0 technology could potentially transform The Striped Umbrella website from a strictly informative site to one that is interactive and fully engaging. You decide to research Web 2.0 technology and analyze which web applications could be incorporated into the current site.

DETAILS

- ## RSS feeds and podcasts
  RSS feeds are an easy way to share information with users. **RSS (Really Simple Syndication)** feeds are regularly scheduled information downloads used by websites to distribute news stories, information about upcoming events, or announcements. Web users can subscribe to RSS feeds to receive regular releases of information from a site. Users can also download and play the digitally broadcasted files called **podcasts** (which stands for **Programming On Demand**) using devices such as computers or MP3 players. Many news organizations and educational institutions publish both audio and video podcasts. Video podcasts are also sometimes referred to as **vodcasts** or **vidcasts**.

- ## Social networking
  Web 2.0 also includes the ever-increasing use of social networking. **Social networking** refers to any web-based service that facilitates social interaction among users. One example of a social networking site is **Facebook**, which allows users to set up profile pages and post information for others to view. Facebook pages often contain lots of text, images, and videos. To fully view and post to an individual's page, you must be accepted by that person as a "friend," which lets them control who has access to page content.

- ## Wikis
  The term **wiki** (named for the Hawaiian word for "quick") refers to a site where a user can use simple editing tools to contribute and edit the page content in a site. A good example is **Wikipedia**, an online encyclopedia. Wikipedia allows users to post new information and edit existing information on any topic. Although people have different opinions about the reliability of the information on Wikipedia, it is generally viewed as a rich source of information. Proponents argue that its many active and vigilant users maintain its accuracy.

- ## Blogs
  Blogs are websites where the website owner regularly posts commentaries and opinions on various topics. Content can consist of text, video, or images. Users can respond to the postings and read postings by other users as well. **Twitter** is a website where users post short messages, called tweets. Twitter is considered a **micro blog**, because you cannot enter more than 140 characters in each post. To use Twitter, you must first join by creating a free account. Then you can post messages about yourself, "follow" other people's tweets, and invite others to follow you. It is a quick and easy way to exchange short bits of information.

- ## Video sharing applications
  There are many video sharing applications, such as Skype, Google Video Chat, and YouTube. **Skype** and **Google Video Chat** are free applications that you use to communicate live through video conferencing, using a high-speed Internet connection and a digital video camera connected to your computer, called a **webcam**. You can also use Skype or Google Chat to make regular telephone calls over the Internet. **YouTube** is a website where you can view or upload videos. To upload videos, you need to register with the site.

Peace Corps website (peacecorps.gov)

Links to the social networking pages

Design Matters

How to incorporate Web 2.0 components

Most websites today engage their users with one or more Web 2.0 component applications. The Peace Corps website, shown in Figure H-20, has links to Facebook, Twitter, flickr, YouTube, Tumblr, and LinkedIn. When you are designing a site, one of the decisions you must make is not if but how you will incorporate technology to fully engage users. To incorporate one of these applications into your website, first register to set up an account on the social networking site, then place a link on one of your site's pages (usually the home page) that links to the social networking site and opens your page. For example, if your Twitter account is located at twitter.com/your_name, add this link to your home page using the Twitter logo as a graphic link. You can download social networking sites' logos from their websites. You can also enter plain text links if you prefer, but most people are familiar with the logos and used to seeing them used for links.

Practice

Concepts Review

Label each element in the Dreamweaver window shown in Figure H-21.

FIGURE H-21: Concepts review

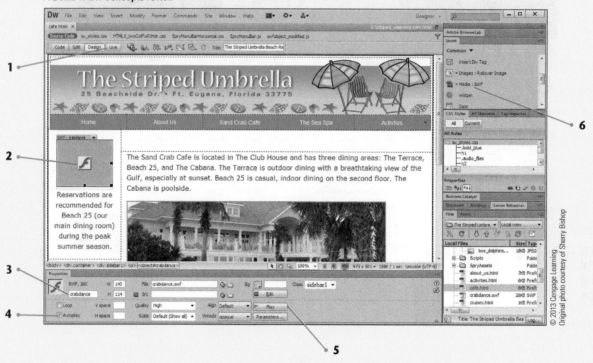

1. _____	4. _____
2. _____	5. _____
3. _____	6. _____

Match each of the following terms with the statement that best describes it.

7. **Skin**

8. **Low-bandwidth animation**

9. **Media objects**

10. **Plug-in**

11. **Vector graphic**

12. **Rollover image**

13. **Behavior**

a. Combinations of visual and audio effects and text used to create a fully engaging experience with a website

b. A scalable graphic that is built using mathematical formulas rather than pixels

c. A set of instructions that is attached to page elements and tells the page element to respond in a specific way when an event occurs

d. The bar at the bottom of a video with the control buttons

e. An image that changes its appearance when the mouse pointer is placed over it in a browser

f. A small computer program that works with a host application to enable certain functions

g. Does not require a fast connection to work properly

Select the best answer from the following list of choices.

14. The file extension for a Flash video file is:

a. .vid.

b. .fla.

c. .swf.

d. .flv.

15. The panel that is used to add JavaScript functions to page elements is:

a. the Behaviors panel.

b. the Server Behaviors panel.

c. the JavaScript panel.

d. the Functions panel.

16. Which event will trigger an action when a mouse is placed over a page element?

a. onMouseOut

b. onMouseOver

c. onLoad

d. onClick

17. Web 2.0 technology includes:

a. wikis.

b. blogs.

c. podcasts.

d. all of the above

18. When you add a Spry effect to a page element, which folder is automatically created?

a. SpryAssets folder

b. Spry folder

c. SpryEffects folder

d. Effects folder

Skills Review

Important: *If you did not create this website in Unit B and maintain it during the preceding units, you will need to create a local site root folder for this website and define the site using files your instructor will provide. See the "Read This Before You Begin" section for more detailed instructions.*

1. Understand Media objects.

  a. List three different types of media objects that you can add to a web page.

  b. Write a short paragraph that explains how to make media objects accessible and HTML5 compliant.

  c. Write a few sentences that explain what a plug-in does. Give two examples.

2. Add Flash objects.

  a. Start Dreamweaver, switch to Design view if necessary, open the Blooms & Bulbs website, then open the workshops page.

  b. Add a paragraph break after the last paragraph, then insert the garden_quote.swf Flash movie from the drive and folder where you store your Unit H Data Files at the insertion point.

  c. Type **Garden quote** in the Object Tag Accessibility Attributes dialog box, then add eight block quotes in front of the Flash object.

  d. Play the garden_quote.swf movie in Dreamweaver (Win), save your work, click OK to close the Copy Dependent Files dialog box, preview the page in your browser, compare your screen to Figure H-22, then close your browser.

  e. Close the workshops page.

FIGURE H-22

knowledge. She is an engaging speaker you will be sure to enjoy. Call 555-248-0806 today to reserve your spot!

One who plants a garden
plants happiness.
Chinese Proverb

Copyright 2001 - 2015 Blooms & Bulbs

Original photos courtesy of Sherry Bishop

3. Add Behaviors.

    a. Open the file dwh_4.html from the drive and folder where you store you Unit H Data Files, save it in the blooms root folder as **annuals.html**, overwriting the existing annuals page, but not updating links, then close the dwh_4.html file.

    b. Select the broken image placeholder, then browse to select the coleus.jpg file in the Unit H Data Files assets folder and save it in the website assets folder.

    c. Select the coleus image, then use the Behaviors panel to add the Appear/Fade effect so that the image will fade from 100% to 50% when clicked, select the Toggle effect check box, click OK, then save the page. (*Hint:* Dreamweaver will add the SpryEffects.js supporting file to the SpryAssets folder.)

    d. Preview the page in the browser, then close the browser. (*Hint:* Click the image to test the behavior. The image will alternate between 100% and 50% opacity each time you click the mouse.)

4. Edit Behaviors.

    a. Edit the behavior to onMouseOver, then save your work.

    b. Preview the page in the browser. (*Hint:* Place the mouse over the image twice to test the behavior.)

    c. Close the browser, then close the annuals page.

5. Add Rollover images.

    a. Open the tips page, then delete the butterfly image at the top of the page.

    b. Verify that your insertion point is still positioned at the deleted butterfly graphic location.

    c. Insert a rollover image from the drive and folder where you store your Unit H Data Files (*Hint:* Click Insert on the Menu bar, point to Image Objects, then click Rollover Image.) Type **butterfly_rollover** as the image name, insert butterfly1.jpg from where you store your Data Files as the original image, insert butterfly2.jpg from where you store your Data Files as the rollover image, type **Butterflies** as the alternate text, then click OK. Save each image in the site's assets folder.

    d. Apply the img_left_float rule to the rollover image.

    e. Save your work, preview the page in the browser to test the rollover, close the browser, then close the tips page.

6. Add video.

    a. Open the plants page, click at the end of the last sentence on the page, then insert two paragraph breaks.

    b. Insert the hanging_baskets.mp4 file from drive and folder where you store your Unit H Data Files folder and save it in your local site assets folder.

    c. Type **Join us Saturday at 9:00 for a class on hanging baskets.** after the last sentence on the page.

    d. Use the Property inspector to set the width of the video placeholder to **250**, the height to **200**, and add a new parameter to set autostart to false.

    e. Place the insertion point to the left of the placeholder, switch to Code view, click to the left of > at the end of the opening embed tag, then enter **style="margin-left:400px"** after the opening < /embed> tag, then delete the ending < /embed> tag.

    f. Save your work, preview the page and play the movie in the browser, then compare your screen to Figure H-23.

    g. Close the plants page.

FIGURE H-23

pruned to any size. The one you see on the right is Southern Belle. Check out all our varieties as you will not fail to have great color with these plants.

The Candy Cane Floribunda shown on the left is a beautiful rose with cream, pink, and red stripes and swirls. They have a heavy scent that will remind you of the roses you received on your most special occasions. These blooms are approximately four inches in diameter. They bloom continuously from early summer to early fall. The plants grow up to four feet tall and three feet wide. They are shipped bare root in February.

In addition to these marvelous roses, we have many annuals, perennials, and water plants that have just arrived. Join us Saturday at 9:00 for a class on hanging baskets.

Original content courtesy of Sherry Bishop

Skills Review (continued)

7. Add sound.

   a. Copy the file seeds_audio.mp3 from the drive and folder where you save your Unit H Data Files to your website assets folder.

   b. Open the tips page, place the insertion point after the last tip listed, enter two paragraph breaks to end the list, then type **Tip of the Week: Starting seeds for your vegetable garden**, then apply the H1 tag.

   c. Enter a paragraph break, then click Insert on the Menu bar, point to Media, click Plugin, browse to and select the file seeds_audio.mp3, then copy it to the site assets folder.

   d. Select the plug-in placeholder, then use the Property inspector to change the W value to **200** and the H value to **20**.

   e. Add a parameter to set autostart to false.

   f. Delete the ending < /embed> tag from the code for the audio file.

   g. Save the tips page and test the audio file in the browser, comparing your screen to Figure H-24.

   h. Close the browser and close the tips page.

FIGURE H-24

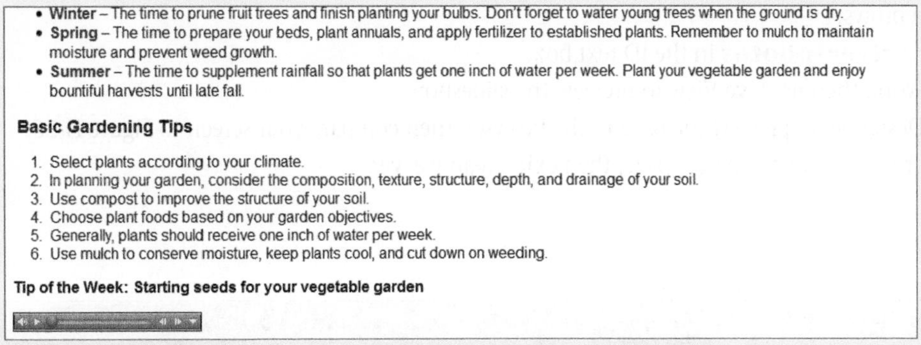

- **Winter** – The time to prune fruit trees and finish planting your bulbs. Don't forget to water young trees when the ground is dry.
- **Spring** – The time to prepare your beds, plant annuals, and apply fertilizer to established plants. Remember to mulch to maintain moisture and prevent weed growth.
- **Summer** – The time to supplement rainfall so that plants get one inch of water per week. Plant your vegetable garden and enjoy bountiful harvests until late fall.

Basic Gardening Tips

1. Select plants according to your climate.
2. In planning your garden, consider the composition, texture, structure, depth, and drainage of your soil.
3. Use compost to improve the structure of your soil.
4. Choose plant foods based on your garden objectives.
5. Generally, plants should receive one inch of water per week.
6. Use mulch to conserve moisture, keep plants cool, and cut down on weeding.

Tip of the Week: Starting seeds for your vegetable garden

8. Update files.

   a. Open the file dwh_5.html from the drive and folder where you store your Unit H Data Files, then save it as **perennials.html**, overwriting the blank placeholder page in the blooms local site root folder, but do not update links. Close dwh_5.html.

   b. Save the file fiber_optic_grass.jpg from the unit_h/assets folder in the blooms assets folder, then save and close the perennials page.

   c. Repeat Steps a and b to replace the blank placeholder water_plants page with the file dwh_6.html and save the file water_lily.jpg in the blooms assets folder.

   d. Save your work, then close all open files and exit Dreamweaver.

Important: *If you did not create this website in Unit B and maintain it during the preceding units, you will need to create a local site root folder for this website and define the website using files your instructor will provide. See the "Read This Before You Begin" section for more detailed instructions.*

Independent Challenge 1

You have been hired to create a website for a river expedition company named Rapids Transit, located on the Buffalo River in Northwest Arkansas. You have completed the main pages in the site, but would like to add a slideshow of some river photographs to the guides page. You have selected seven photographs to use and plan to place them on the page, replacing the existing image, as shown in Figure H-25.

a. Start Dreamweaver, then open the Rapids Transit website.

b. Open the before page, then select and delete the young_paddler image on the page.

c. Insert the file river_scenes.swf from the drive and folder where your Unit H Data Files are stored at the insertion point, adding **River Scenes** as the title.

d. Assign the rule img_left_float to the swf placeholder.

e. Use the Property inspector to uncheck the Loop check box so the file will only play through one time when it's viewed in a browser.

f. Enter the ID **river_photos** in the ID text box.

g. Save your work, then use Live View to preview the slideshow.

h. Return to Design view, preview the page in the browser, then compare your screen to Figure H-25.

i. Close the browser, close the before page, then exit Dreamweaver.

FIGURE H-25

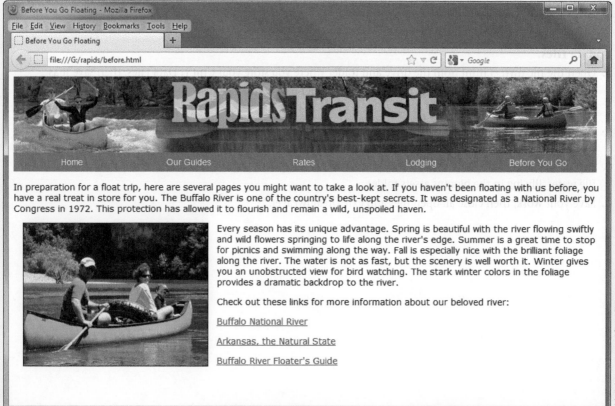

Independent Challenge 2

In this exercise, you will continue your work on the TripSmart website. You are ready to work on the tours, Peru, and Galapagos pages. You add content to the tours, Peru and Galapagos pages, and update all pages with a revised menu bar that includes links to the Peru and Galapagos pages. You also add a video to the Galapagos page.

a. Start Dreamweaver, open the TripSmart website, then open the file dwh_7.html from the drive and folder where you store your Unit H Data Files, then save it as **peru.html** in the tripsmart local site root folder. Do not update links.

b. Click the broken image placeholder, browse to the drive and folder where you store your Unit H Data Files, select the machu_picchu_from_high.jpg file in the assets folder, and then copy it to the local site's assets folder without updating the links.

c. Repeat Step b to replace the next broken image placeholder with the file llama.jpg.

d. Close the file dwh_7.html.

e. Use your existing styles or create new ones to format and position the text and images on the page, then save the Peru page.

f. Open the tours.html page from your local site root folder, then save it as **galapagos.html**.

g. Close the tours page, then create a page to replace your current tours page using the file dwh_8.html from the drive and folder where you store you Unit H Data Files. Save the files sea_lions_in_surf.jpg and machu_picchu_ruins.jpg in your local site assets folder.

h. Notice that the menu bar on the new tours page includes submenus for the Peru and Galapagos pages. Use this menu bar to replace the menu bars on all other pages.

i. Save your work, then use the navigation links to preview each page in the browser. Make any spacing adjustments you feel would improve the appearance of each page.

j. Close all pages except the Galapagos page.

k. Insert the file sealions_video.mp4 from the drive and folder where you store your Unit H Data Files after the last paragraph on the page, then delete the ending < /embed> tag.

l. Type a short introduction to the video similar to Figure H-26.

m. Use the Property inspector to set the Width and Height of the video to 400 × 240, then add a parameter to keep the movie from playing automatically.

n. Add any additional settings to improve the appearance of the page, save your work, preview the page in the browser, close the browser, then close all open pages.

FIGURE H-26

Galápagos, including the famous blue-footed booby. You will also have opportunities to swim, snorkel, and kayak with penguins. When your time on the ship ends, you will fly to Quito, the second-highest capital city in the world. Quito is a UNESCO World Heritage Site with beautiful colonial architecture. We recommend taking an extra day to explore its rich history and sample Ecuadoran cuisine.

To provide the finest in personal attention, this tour will be limited to no more than twenty people. The price schedule is as follows: Land Tour and Supplemental Group Air, $5,500.00; International Air, $1,350.00; and Single Supplement, $1,000.00. Entrance fees, hotel taxes, and services are included in the Land Tour price. Ship gratuities are also included for the Wanderer crew and guides. A deposit of $500.00 is required at the time the booking is made. Trip insurance and luggage insurance are optional and are also offered for an extra charge. A passport and visa will be required for entry into Ecuador. Call us at 555-555-0807 for further information and the complete itinerary from 8:00 a.m. to 6:00 p.m. (Central Standard Time).

This is a sea lion family out for the day. It's amazing how close you can come to the wildlife. They have very little fear of people, as they have been protected so well by the government regulations for visiting them.

Independent Challenge 3

Angie Wolf is an amateur astronomer. She would like to design a website about planets. She would like to use Dreamweaver to build her site and incorporate Flash elements, rollovers, and video to the site.

a. Connect to the Internet then go to the United States Navy website at www.navy.mil, as shown in Figure H-27.

b. Search for ".swf" and ".mp4" in the code for several pages to locate media objects.

c. Do you see any objects in the site that are made with rollover images?

d. How has adding Flash effects improved the appearance of this site?

e. Do you see any links to Web 2.0 applications that are being used? If so, list them.

f. Create a sketch of Angie's site that contains at least five pages. Indicate in your sketch what media elements you would insert in the site, including where you would add Flash objects, rollover images, and video.

FIGURE H-27

United States Navy website (navy.mil)

Real Life Independent Challenge

This assignment will continue to build on the personal website that you created in Unit B. In Unit C, you created and developed your index page. In Unit D, you added a page with either an ordered or an unordered list, using CSS with a minimum of two styles. In Unit E, you added a page that included at least two images. In Unit F, you added a page that included several links and an image map. In Unit G, you redesigned the index page based on CSS. In this lesson, you will continue building your site by designing and completing a page that contains rich media content or by adding media content to existing pages. After completing your site, be sure to run appropriate reports to test the site.

- **a.** Evaluate your wireframes, then choose a page or series of pages to develop in which you will include Flash objects as well as other media content, such as rollover images, video, and behaviors.
- **b.** Plan the content for your new page so that the layout works well with both the new and old pages in your site. Sketch a plan for your wireframes for the media content you wish to add, showing which media elements you will use and where you will place them.
- **c.** Create or find the media you identified in your sketch, choosing appropriate formatting.
- **d.** Add the rollover images to the page.
- **e.** Add a video to the page.
- **f.** Add a behavior to a page element, then specify the action you would like to use with it.
- **g.** Run a report on your new page(s) to ensure that all links work correctly.
- **h.** Preview the new page or pages in your browser and test all links. Evaluate your pages for content and layout.
- **i.** Make any modifications that are necessary to improve the page.

After you are satisfied with your work, verify the following:

- **a.** Each completed page has a page title.
- **b.** All links work correctly and styles are used consistently for all content.
- **c.** The completed pages are attractive using screen resolutions of 1024 × 768.
- **d.** All images are properly linked to the assets folder of the website.
- **e.** All images have alternate text and are legal to use.
- **f.** All media content works as you intended and downloads quickly.
- **g.** The link checker shows no broken links or orphaned files. If there are orphaned files, note your plan to link them.
- **h.** Run reports for untitled documents and missing alternate text. Make any corrections necessary.

Visual Workshop

Use Figure H-28 as a guide to continue your work on Carolyne's Creations. You thought it might be fun to add an effect to the photo of the two young boys cooking on the children page. After you have added your choice of effects, preview the page in the browser and test the effect.

© 2013 Cengage Learning
Original photo courtesy of Sherry Bishop

FIGURE H-28

Collecting Data with Forms

Files You Will Need:

To view a list of files needed for this unit, see the Data Files Grid in the back of the book.

Forms are a way to add interactivity and collect information on a web page, by presenting users with a series of options for collecting and entering information. Dreamweaver lets you easily create forms by adding form objects to the page, such as check boxes and option buttons. The form then sends information that users enter to the host web server to be collected and processed. Forms are useful for such things as ordering merchandise, responding to requests for customer feedback, and requesting information.  The Striped Umbrella Marketing Department wants interested guests to be able to request information about the fishing and dolphin cruises online. You decide to design and add this type of form to the activities page to collect the name and address of guests who make inquiries, along with their response to an offer to send them a quarterly newsletter.

OBJECTIVES

Understand forms and form objects

Create and insert a form on a page

Add a text form field

Add a radio group

Add a check box group

Insert a submit and a reset button

Format and test a form

Understanding Forms and Form Objects

Forms are a convenient and efficient way to obtain information from website users. A form can either be a page by itself, collecting several pieces of information from a user with numerous form objects, or it can take up only a small part of a page. **Form objects** are the individual form components that accept individual pieces of information. They include check boxes, radio buttons, text fields, and buttons. Many web pages include a form with only two form objects, such as a text box and a submit button. See Figures I-1 and I-2 for examples of long and short types of forms. You can insert tables in more complex forms to help organize the objects into rows and columns. Pages can have more than one form. However, you cannot place a form inside a form.  Before you begin work on the form, you review the various form objects you might use to collect information from guests.

DETAILS

As you create forms, you can choose from the following objects:

- **Form fields**

  A **field** is a form area into which users can insert a specific piece of data, such as their last name or address. Form fields include text fields, hidden fields, and file fields. **Text fields** can accept both numbers and letters, known as **alphanumeric** data. A text field can contain single or multiple lines of data. **Hidden fields** store information about the user and can be used by the company originating the form at a later time, such as the next time the user visits its website. **File fields** allow users to browse to a file on their computer and **upload** it to the form host web server. To upload a file means to transfer a copy of the file to a server.

- **Radio buttons**

  Radio buttons are option buttons that appear as small empty circles on a form that users click to select a choice. A selected radio button has a black fill. Radio buttons in a group are mutually exclusive, meaning that the user can select only one choice at a time.

- **Check boxes**

  Check boxes are small squares on a form. To select a choice, users click to place a check mark inside the box. In contrast to a group of radio buttons, with a series of check boxes it is possible to select more than one check box.

- **Lists and menus**

  Lists and menus provide the user with a list or menu of choices to select. Lists display the choices in a scrolling format while menus display the choices in a pop-up set of choices. Lists and menus provide a fast method of entering information that may be tedious for the user to type.

- **Buttons**

  Buttons (not to be confused with radio buttons) are usually small rectangular objects containing a text label. When a user clicks a button, a task is performed, such as submitting or clearing a form. To **submit** a form means to send the information on the form to the host web server for processing. Clearing or **resetting** the form means to erase all form entries and set the values back to the default settings.

Design Matters

Planning form layout

Before you begin creating your form, you should take the time to write down the information you want to collect and the order in which you want it to appear on the form. It's also a good idea to make a sketch of the form to make sure that all of the form objects are placed in a logical order that will make sense to the user. Position the most important information at the top of the form to make it more likely that users will complete it.

FIGURE I-1: **Example of a long form**

Menu

Text boxes

Radio buttons

Menu

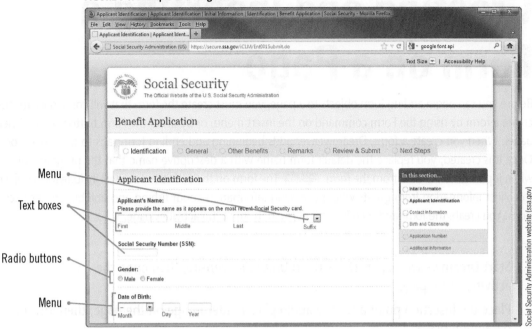

Social Security Administration website (ssa.gov)

FIGURE I-2: **Example of a short form**

Text box

Search button is
the Submit button

Federal Bureau of Investigation website (fbi.gov)

Creating and Inserting a Form on a Page

Before you can begin adding form objects to a page, you must create the form that will contain them. You create a form by using the Form command on the Insert menu, or by using the Form button on the Insert panel. When you create a form, Dreamweaver adds beginning and ending form tags to the HTML code. Once it is created, you replace the default form name with a descriptive name that the program will use when it processes the data from the form. The form on the activities page will include form objects to collect information from guests who are seeking information about fishing and dolphin cruises excursions. You create the form and then insert it at the bottom of the activities page.

STEPS

1. **Start Dreamweaver, open The Striped Umbrella website, then open the activities.html page**

2. **Place the insertion point after the audio placeholder image on the page, then insert a paragraph break**

    The insertion point is positioned where you want the form to reside, at the bottom of the page.

    > **TROUBLE**
    > If a message appears about needing to view invisible elements to see the form outline on the page, click View on the Menu bar, point to Visual Aids, then click Invisible Elements.

3. **Click the Form button in the Forms category on the Insert panel**

    The form displays as a red dotted outline (Win) or red solid outline (Mac), on the page. Although the Property inspector displays the form properties, the form objects won't display until you insert them.

4. **Click to place the insertion point in the Form ID text box in the Property inspector, type feedback, press [Tab], then compare your screen to Figure I-3**

    The form ID text box now contains the name *feedback* and the Tag selector shows the form tag with the name of the form <form#feedback>. The rest of the form properties identify how the information users enter will be processed on the host server. The Action and Target fields, for example, should remain blank unless your instructor provides you with the appropriate information. (The programming involved in processing a form is beyond the scope of this book.)

5. **Click the Show Code view button** `Code`

    The form code appears, as shown in Figure I-4. The form is surrounded by beginning and ending form tags as well as the attributes for the form ID, form name, form method, and form action. The form method information directs the way that the data will be sent to the server.

6. **Click the Show Design view button** `Design`

    Your page redisplays in Design view.

Design Matters

Creating user-friendly forms

When a form contains several required fields—fields that must be filled out before the form can be processed—it is a good idea to provide visual clues to alert the user. Adding asterisks in different font colors with an accompanying note is an easy way to increase the visibility of required fields. An asterisk is often placed right next to a required field with a corresponding note at either the top or the bottom of the form explaining that all fields marked with asterisks are required. This encourages users to complete these fields initially, rather than submitting the form and then receiving an error message asking them to complete required fields that were left blank.

FIGURE I-3: Form on the activities page

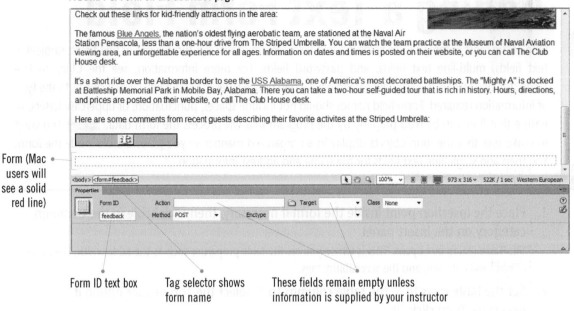

Form (Mac users will see a solid red line)

Form ID text box

Tag selector shows form name

These fields remain empty unless information is supplied by your instructor

FIGURE I-4: HTML code for the form on the activities page

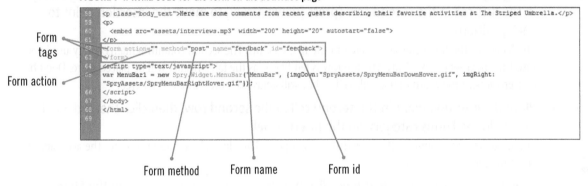

Form tags

Form action

Form method

Form name

Form id

Processing forms

An attractive, user-friendly form serves no purpose without a way to process and store the information. Sending emails with form information is not a time efficient or effective process. It is more practical to send form information directly to a server to read, store, and process the data. The data collection stage of form processing is called **front-end processing**, which denotes the beginning of the processing cycle. The data processing stage is accordingly called **back-end processing**, as it references the end of the processing cycle. Forms are processed according to the properties specified in the form action attribute. The **form action attribute** is the part of the form tag that specifies how the data in

the form will be processed. If you do not need to save the data that a user enters on a form, it is better to use **client-side scripting**. This means that the form is processed on the user's computer. An example of this is a mortgage calculator that allows you to estimate mortgage payments. **Server-side scripting** is used if data entered on a form needs to be stored and processed on the form's host web server. An example of this is ordering books on a bookstore website. Client-side scripting is written with programming languages such as JavaScript or VBScript. Server-side scripting is written with programming languages, such as Common Gateway Interface (CGI).

Adding a Text Form Field

One of the most common form fields is a text field. Dreamweaver has three types of text fields: single-line text fields, multi-line text fields, and password fields. For more information, see the Clues to Use *Understanding text fields*. Each field should have a descriptive label so users have a visual clue as to the type of information required. Form field names should not include spaces, punctuation, or uppercase letters, to ensure that they can be read properly by the program that will process the form data.  You want to make sure that the form objects display in an organized manner so you place a table inside the form. You then add single-line text fields for the name and address information.

STEPS

1. **Place the insertion point inside the form if necessary, then click Table in the Common category on the Insert panel**

   The Table dialog box opens. This is where you set the table properties such as the table width, the number of rows and columns, and the accessibility tags.

2. **Set the table rows to 8, the table columns to 3, select the Top header option if necessary, then click OK**

   The Table dialog box closes and the table is inserted inside the form, ready for placement of the form fields. The table is formatted with the table rule in the su_styles.css file that you defined earlier. This rule specifies the font, font size, table width, and left float.

3. **Using Figure I-5 as a guide, enter the labels for your text fields into the table beginning in the first cell in the second row (press [down arrow] to move the insertion point to each position)**

   The labels for the text fields are entered in the first column. The second column remains empty until you insert the next set of text fields. The top row is left blank, as the table header will be placed there. Don't be concerned with the width of the table cells. They will adjust as more content is entered.

4. **Place the insertion point in the second cell in the second row, then click the Text Field button in the Forms category on the Insert panel**

   The Input Tag Accessibility Attributes dialog box opens. This dialog box is used to enter the accessibility attributes for the form field.

5. **Type first_name in the ID text box, click the No label tag option button in the Style section to select it, click OK, type 30 in the Char width text box in the Property inspector, then type 60 in the Max chars text box**

   The text field for the First Name label is placed on the form with a black dotted outline. The Property inspector displays the text field ID first_name. The Char width and Max chars settings set the size of the text field and limit the number of characters that can be input in the field.

6. **Repeat Steps 4 and 5 to enter additional single-line text fields, using the information in Table I-1**

   All text fields are placed in the form with labels, IDs, settings for the character width that will display in the text field and the maximum characters the user can enter in each field.

7. **Click the first_name field to select it, save your work, then compare your screen to Figure I-6 (You are only selecting this field to be able to compare your field properties with the figure.)**

   The form field properties for the first_name field are displayed in the Property inspector.

FIGURE I-5: Adding form labels for text fields

It's a short ride over the Alabama border to see the USS Alabama, one of America's most decorated battleships. The "Mighty A" is docked at Battleship Memorial Park in Mobile Bay, Alabama. There you can take a two-hour self-guided tour that is rich in history. Hours, directions, and prices are posted on their website, or call The Club House desk.

Here are some comments from recent guests describing their favorite activites at the Striped Umbrella:

First Name
Last Name
Street
City
State
Zip Code

FIGURE I-6: Text form fields added to the feedback form

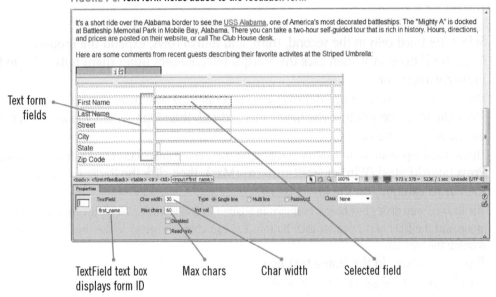

Text form fields

TextField text box displays form ID

Max chars

Char width

Selected field

TABLE I-1: Form field attributes for the feedback form

label	ID	char width	max chars
First Name	first_name	30	60
Last Name	last_name	30	60
Street	street	30	60
City	city	30	60
State	state	2	2
Zip Code	zip_code	10	10

Understanding text fields

Single-line text fields are useful for small pieces of data, such as a name or telephone number. **Multi-line text fields**, also called **Text area fields**, are useful for entering comments that may take several sentences to complete. **Password fields** are unique fields that display asterisks or bullets in place of text on the screen, to prevent others from viewing the data as it is entered. There are three ways to create a Multi-line text field. You can click the Text Field button in the Forms category on the Insert panel, select the field, then click the Multi line option on the Property inspector. Or you can create a Text area field by clicking the Text area button in the Forms category on the Insert panel. You can also use the Insert, Form submenu on the Menu bar. To create a Password field, create a text field, select the field, then select the Password option in the Property inspector.

Adding a Radio Group

Radio buttons let users select options. Two or more radio buttons together are called a **radio group**. When used in a group, radio buttons are mutually exclusive; if a user tries to select two radio buttons in the same group, the first one becomes deselected when the second one is selected. Radio buttons are useful in situations where you want users to select only one choice from a group of possible choices. For example, on a shoe order form, radio buttons could represent the different shoe sizes. To order one pair of shoes, users would select only one size. It is important to include labels to help users understand how to complete each item in the form. It is also important to set an appropriate default value to form objects. A default value will prevent users from unintentionally skipping over items or mistakenly sending unintentional information when they submit the form. You continue working on the form by adding a group of two radio buttons for users to indicate whether they would like to receive newsletters.

STEPS

1. **Select the third cells in the second, third, and fourth rows, expand the Property inspector if necessary, then click the** Merges selected cells using spans button ▣ **in the Property inspector**

   Merging these cells provides a good-sized location to position the radio group.

2. **Place the insertion point in the newly merged cell, then type** Would you like to receive our quarterly newsletters?

   This text will appear above the radio button group so the user will understand the significance of this group.

3. **Press [Shift][Enter] (Win) or [shift][return] (Mac), then click the** Radio Group button **in the Forms category on the Insert panel**

   The Radio Group dialog box opens, as shown in Figure I-7. This is where you specify the name of the radio group and the label and value for each button. You can choose whether to use line breaks or a table to position the buttons.

4. **Type** newsletters **in the Name text box**

   The radio group is assigned the name *newsletters*.

5. **Click** Radio **in the first row of the Label column to select it, type** Yes, **then press [Tab]**

   "Yes" will display as the label for the first radio button. The default value for the first radio button is selected.

6. **Type** positive

   "positive" is set as the value that, after users select the "Yes" option, will be sent to your script or program when the form is processed.

7. **Repeat Steps 5 and 6 for the second row of the Label and Value columns and enter the label** No **with a value of** negative **to create the second radio button**

TROUBLE
If you see empty space displayed at the bottom of the table, click the Table tag in the Tag selector to close it up.

8. **If necessary, click the** Lay out using: Line breaks (
 tags) **option button to select it, compare your screen to Figure I-8, then click** OK

   The radio group appears on the form.

9. **Save your work, click to the right of the form, then compare your screen to Figure I-9**

Design Matters

Creating good form field labels

Because labels are so important in identifying the information that the form collects, you must use form field labels that make sense to your users. For example, First Name and Last Name are good form field labels because users understand clearly what information they should enter. A generic label, such as Name, isn't as specific. If creating a simple and obvious label is impossible, include a brief preceding paragraph that describes the information that should be entered into the form field. You can add labels to a form using one of three methods: type a label in the appropriate table cell of your form; use the Label button in the Forms category on the Insert panel to link the label to the form object; or use the Input Tag Accessibility Attributes dialog box. The Input Tag Accessibility Attributes dialog box will prompt you to add a label if you have set your preferences to provide accessibility attributes for form objects.

FIGURE I-7: Radio Group dialog box properties

Radio Group name text box •

Delete Radio button •

Add Radio button •

Label column •

Click to change the button order •

Value column •

Lay out using option buttons •

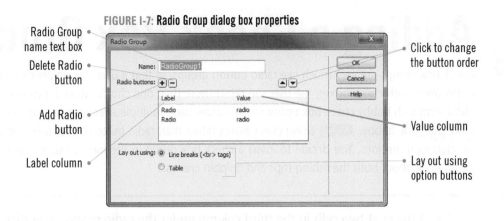

FIGURE I-8: Radio Group properties for newsletters radio group

Name of radio group •

Radio button labels •

Lay out using Line breaks (
 tags) option button •

Radio button values •

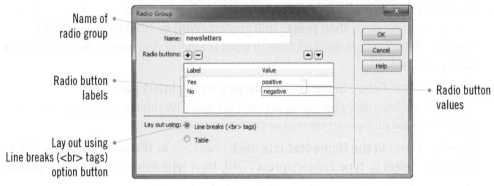

FIGURE I-9: The radio group added to the form

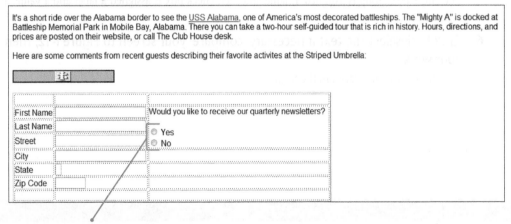

Radio group buttons and labels •

Design Matters

Using lists and menus

Often a form will include a field where the user is asked to select only one item, but there are so many items from which to choose that radio buttons would take too much space on the form. In those cases, lists or menus are the more appropriate choice for a form object. This form object can either take the form of a scrolling list or a shortcut menu. Lists differ from menus in that they allow form users to make multiple selections. Menus only allow one selection. Both make efficient use of space on a form.

Adding a Check Box Group

Check box groups are very much like radio button groups, in that a user can simply click one to select it. However, with check boxes, the user can select more than one choice when appropriate. For example, a form with hobby check box options would allow users multiple selections since many people have more than one hobby.  Using check boxes rather than radio buttons gives users the opportunity to select both options. You decide to insert a check box group in the form so users can request more information about both the fishing trips and dolphin cruises.

STEPS

1. **Select the next two cells in the third column under the radio group, then click the Merges selected cells using spans button 🖵 in the Property inspector**
   Merging these cells provides a good location to position the check boxes.

2. **Place the insertion point in the newly merged cell, type Please select the materials you would like to receive:, then press [Shift][Enter] (Win) or [shift][return] (Mac)**
   This text will display above the check boxes. It serves as a user prompt to direct the response for the check boxes on the form.

3. **Click Checkbox Group in the Forms category on the Insert panel**
   The Checkbox Group dialog box opens, as shown in Figure I-10. This is where you enter the name, labels, and values. These attributes are essential for creating an accessible form.

4. **Type brochures in the Name text box, click Checkbox in the first row of the Label column to select it, type Fishing, press [Tab], then type fishing in the value column**

5. **Click Checkbox in the second row of the Label column to select it, type Cruises, press [Tab], type cruises in the Value column, click the Lay out using: Line breaks (
 tags) option button if necessary, compare your screen to Figure I-11, then click OK**
   The check box group is assigned a name and each check box is assigned a label and a value, as shown in Figure I-11.

6. **Click to deselect the text if necessary, compare your screen to Figure I-12, then save your work**
   The check boxes are placed in the form.

Design Matters

Creating accessible HTML form objects

When users enter information in form fields, they use [Tab] to move the insertion point from field to field. By default, the insertion point moves through fields from left to right across the page and screen readers read from left to right. However, you can set your own tab order to override the default. For example, regardless of where the fields for First Name and Last Name are placed on the form, you can direct the insertion point to move directly from the First Name field to the Last Name field, even if there are other fields between them. To change an existing form object's tab order, right-click the form object (Win), or [Ctrl] + click the form object (Mac). Click Edit Tag <input>, click the Style Sheet/Accessibility category in the Tag Editor – input dialog box, then change the Tab index number. To assign the subsequent fields to move to after the user presses [Tab], type the number 2 in the Tab index box to denote the second field; type 3 to assign the third field, and so forth. You can also assign Tab Index values in the Input Tag Accessibility Attributes dialog box when you create the tag. Tab orders will only work if each tab is assigned an index number.

FIGURE I-10: **Checkbox Group dialog box properties**

Name text box

Label column

Lay out using
option buttons

Value column

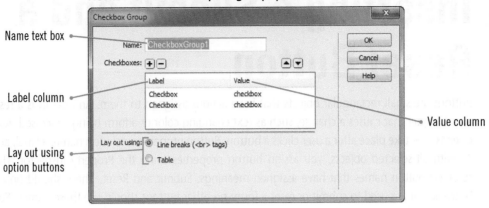

FIGURE I-11: **Checkbox Group properties for brochures checkbox group**

Name of
Checkbox Group

Check box labels

Lay out using Line
breaks (
 tags)
option button

Check box values

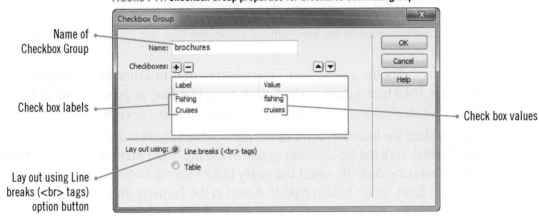

FIGURE I-12: **Viewing the check boxes**

User prompt text

Check boxes

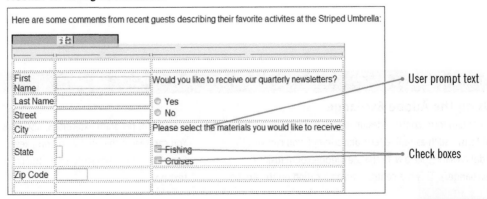

Inserting a Submit and a Reset Button

Buttons are small rectangular objects that have actions assigned to them. An **action** is a response to an event trigger that causes a change, such as text changing color or a form being processed. Actions trigger **events** that take place after a user clicks a button. Button properties include a name, a label, and an action. As with all selected objects, you assign button properties using the Property inspector. There are two reserved button names that have assigned meanings: Submit and Reset. These should only be used for buttons that are used to submit or reset a form; no other buttons should use these names. Submit means to send the form data to the processing program or script for processing. **Reset** means to clear the form fields to the original values. You want to add two buttons to the form: one that will submit the form for processing and another to clear the form in case the user needs to erase the information and start over.

1. **Place the insertion point in the third column of the next to last row**

2. **Click Button in the Forms category on the Insert panel, click the No label tag option button in the Style section of the Input Tag Accessibility Attributes dialog box, then click OK**

   A Submit button appears on the form, without a label next to it, and the Property inspector displays its properties.

3. **If necessary, click the Submit form option button next to Action in the Property inspector, then type Submit in the Button name text box, as shown in Figure I-13**

   When a user clicks this Submit button, the information in the form is sent to the server for processing.

4. **Click to place the insertion point to the right of the Submit button, click Button on the Insert panel, click the No label tag option in the Input Tag Accessibility Attributes dialog box if necessary, click OK, select the newly placed Submit button if necessary, then click the Reset form option button next to Action in the Property inspector**

   The second Submit button changes to a Reset button. When a user clicks this Reset button, the form will clear any information he or she has typed.

5. **Verify that the Button name text box and the Value text box contain Reset, compare your screen to Figure I-14, then save your work**

Design Matters

Using the Adobe Exchange

To obtain form controls designed for creating specific types of forms, such as online tests and surveys, you can visit the Adobe Marketplace & Exchange (adobe.com/cfusion/exchange/). This is a central storage location on the Adobe website for program extensions, also known as **add-ons**. You can search the site by entering keywords in a standard Search text box, similar to using the Dreamweaver Help Search text box.

FIGURE I-13: Inserting a Submit button

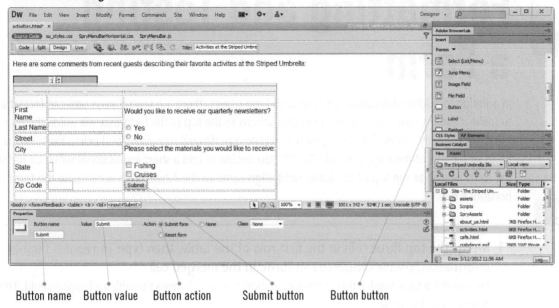

Button name   Button value   Button action   Submit button   Button button

FIGURE I-14: Inserting a Reset button

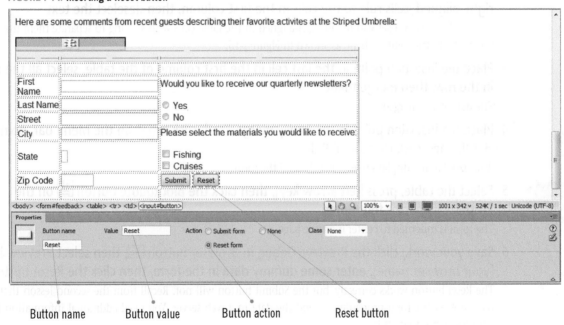

Button name   Button value   Button action   Reset button

Setting the Form Properties

Once you've inserted a form, you can then assign the properties for the application that you want to process the form information and the method you want it transmitted to the processing application. The **Action property** in the Property inspector specifies the application or script that will process the form data. The **Method property** specifies the protocol used to send the form data to the web server.

The **Get method** specifies that the data collected in the form be sent to the server as appended to the URL of the web page in the Action property. The **Post method** specifies that the data be sent to the processing script as a binary or encrypted file, allowing you to send the data securely. This information must be obtained from your instructor in order to be able to process the form.

Collecting Data with Forms

Formatting and Testing a Form

In addition to adding descriptive labels to each form object, there are several ways you can format a form to make it easier to use. You can add brief instructions to the top of the form that will guide the user in filling it out correctly. Simple formatting such as adding a horizontal rule above and below the form can set it off from the rest of the page content. ▓▓▓▓▓ You decide to add a short instructional sentence to serve as the form header at the top of the form, right-align some of the labels, then accentuate the form with a horizontal rule.

STEPS

1. **Merge the top three cells in the first row of the table, then type** To request further information, please complete this form. **in the merged cell**

   Because it is a table header, this text is automatically centered across the table and appears bold. The table rule is applied as well.

2. **Click the** New Rule button 🔲 **in the CSS Styles panel, then create a new Class rule named** right_aligned_cells **in the su_styles.css style sheet with the following properties: Block Text-align:** right; **Box Width:** 120px; **Box Padding: Right:** 10px, **apply the** right_aligned_cells **rule to the cells in the first column, then deselect the text**

   The labels are now a set width and right-aligned in the table cells with spacing to separate them from the text boxes to the right of them, as shown in Figure I-15.

3. **Place the insertion point in the last cell in the first column of the table, select all the cells in the row, then merge them**

   The new row is merged.

4. **Place the insertion point in the newly merged cell, click** Insert **on the Menu bar, point to** HTML, **then click** Horizontal Rule

   A horizontal line displays selected at the end the form.

QUICK TIP
Recall that you can click the table tag in the tag selector to select a table.

5. **Select the table, press [left arrow key], then click the** Blockquote button 📑 **on the Property inspector four times**

   The form is indented to center it on the page.

6. **Save your work, click the** Preview/Debug in Browser button 🌐, **then select** Preview in [your browser name], **enter some dummy data in the form, then click the** Reset button

   The Reset button works correctly, but the Submit button will not. Recall from the second lesson that you have not set the form properties to send the data to a web server. You need additional information from your instructor to do this.

7. **Compare your finished project to Figure I-16, then close your browser window**

8. **Run reports on the Entire Current Local Site to check for Missing Alt Text and Untitled Documents**

   There are no pages with missing alternate text or missing page titles.

9. **Recreate the site cache, then run reports for broken links and orphaned files**

   There are no broken links or orphaned files.

10. **Close the page, then exit Dreamweaver**

FIGURE I-15: **Formatting text field labels with CSS**

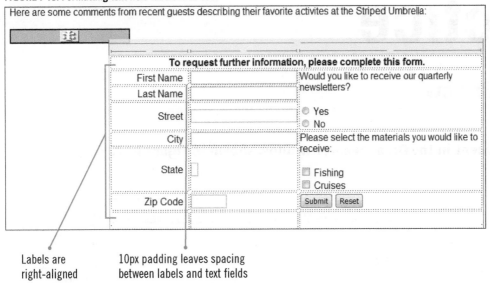

Labels are
right-aligned

10px padding leaves spacing
between labels and text fields

FIGURE I-16: **The finished project**

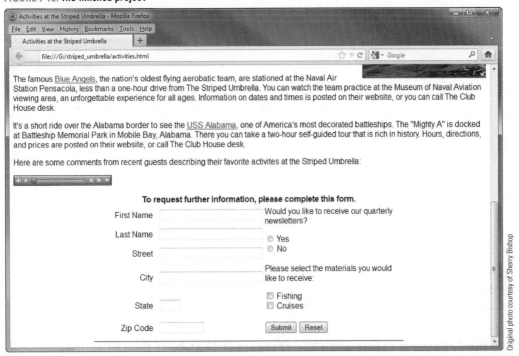

Original photo courtesy of Sherry Bishop

Practice

Concepts Review

Label each element in the Dreamweaver window shown in Figure I-17.

FIGURE I-17

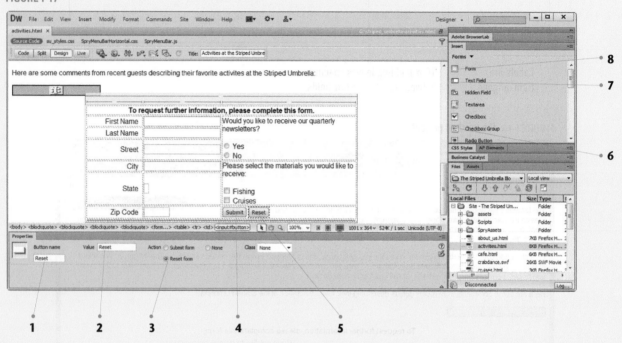

1. _____   5. _____
2. _____   6. _____
3. _____   7. _____
4. _____   8. _____

Match each of the following terms with the statement that best describes it.

9. **Check boxes**	**a.** Set(s) the form object values to the default settings
10. **Radio buttons**	**b.** Are mutually exclusive; only one in each group can be selected
11. **Submit button**	**c.** What happens after a button is clicked
12. **Reset button**	**d.** Display(s) data as asterisks or bullets
13. **Event**	**e.** Send(s) the data to be processed
14. **Password fields**	**f.** Contain(s) space for more than one line of data
15. **Multi-line text fields**	**g.** More than one can be selected

Select the best answer from the following list of choices.

16. Which of the following is not classified as a form field?

a. text field

b. hidden field

c. default field

d. file field

17. Button properties include:

a. a name, a field, and an action.

b. a name, a label, and an action.

c. a name, a label, and a value.

d. a name, a value, and an action.

18. Server-side scripting means that:

a. the form is processed on the user's computer.

b. the form is processed by a JavaScript program.

c. the form is processed on the form's host server.

d. b and c.

Skills Review

Important: If you did not create this website in Unit B and maintain it during the preceding units, you will need to create a local site root folder for this website and define the website using files your instructor will provide. See the "Read This Before You Begin" section for more detailed instructions.

1. **Understand forms and form objects.**

   a. Refer to Figure I-18 to locate a text field, a check box, a radio button, and a Submit button.

2. **Create and Insert a form on a page.**

   a. Start Dreamweaver and open the tips.html page in the Blooms & Bulbs website.

   b. Place the insertion point after the audio file placeholder image on the page and a paragraph break.

   c. Insert a form.

   d. Name the form **tips**.

   e. View the HTML code for the form.

   f. Return to Design view.

   g. Save your work.

3. **Add a text form field.**

   a. Place the insertion point inside the form and insert a table with 10 rows, 3 columns, and a Top header.

   b. Using Figure I-18 as a guide, enter labels that will be used for Single line text fields in the first column, beginning in row 2.

FIGURE I-18

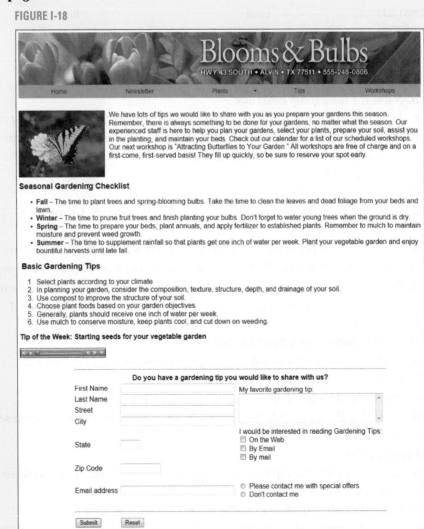

Skills Review (continued)

c. Use the information in Table I-2 to add text fields with no label tags in the column next to the labels, beginning in row 2.

d. Save your work.

e. Merge the second through fifth rows in the third column.

f. Type **My favorite gardening tip:** in the resulting merged cell.

g. Create a line break after the text and insert a Multi-line text field (or a Textarea field) with no label.

h. Name the new Textarea field **my_tips**, then set the Char width to **40** and the Num lines to **4**.

i. Click the table tag to remove any empty space displayed in the table, then save your work.

TABLE I-2: Form field attributes for the tips form

label	form field ID	char width	max chars
First Name	first_name	40	40
Last Name	last_name	40	40
Street	street	40	40
City	city	40	40
State	state	2	2
Zip Code	zip_code	10	10
Email Address	email	40	40

4. Add a radio group.

a. In the third column in the third-to-the-last row, insert a radio group.

b. Name the radio group **contact**.

c. Enter the label **Please contact me with special offers** for the first radio button, then enter a value of **yes**.

d. Enter the label **Don't contact me** for the second radio button, then enter a value of **no**.

e. Use line breaks to lay out the radio group.

f. Save your work.

5. Add a check box group.

a. In the cell below the My favorite gardening tip text area, type **I would be interested in reading Gardening Tips:**.

b. In the same cell, below the text, insert a check box group with the name **tips**.

c. Enter the label **On the Web** for the first check box, then enter a value of **web**.

d. Enter the label **By Email** for the second check box, then enter a value of **email**.

e. Add another check box, enter the label **By mail**, then add the value **mail**.

f. Save your work.

6. Insert a Submit and a Reset button.

a. Insert a Submit button with no label tag in the first column of the last row.

b. Change the button name to **Submit**.

c. Insert a Reset button in the second column of the last row.

d. Verify that **Reset** is the button name, **Reset** is the value, and the action is set to **Reset form**.

e. Save your work.

7. Format a form.

a. Merge the cells in the top row of the table, type **Do you have a gardening tip you would like to share with us?**.

b. Merge the cells in the row above the Submit and Reset buttons.

c. Place a horizontal rule in the new row and another one above the header in the top row.

Skills Review (continued)

d. Create a new Class rule in the blooms_styles.css file named **form_table** using the following properties: Type: Font-family: Arial, Helvetica, sans-serif; Font-size: medium; Block: Text-align: left; Box: Width: 750px.

e. Select the table, then apply the form_table rule.

f. Enter three Blockquotes in front of the table to space the table more to the center of the page.

g. Switch to Code view, then add the following code to the <th> tag for the table header: **style="text-align:center"** to center the table header. (The form_table rule left-aligned the header.)

h. Save your work, preview the page in the browser, compare your screen to Figure I-18, test all fields, then test the Reset button.

i. Close the browser, close all open files, then exit Dreamweaver.

Important: *If you did not create these websites in Unit B and maintain them during the preceding units, you will need to create a local site root folder for these websites and define the websites using files your instructor will provide. See the "Read This Before You Begin" section for more detailed instructions.*

Independent Challenge 1

You have been hired to create a website for a river expedition company named Rapids Transit, located on the Buffalo River in Northwest Arkansas. Mike Andrew, the owner of Rapids Transit, has asked you to add a form to the page that describes the three categories of lodging available. The purpose of this form will be to allow clients to request brochures for each lodging category.

    a. Start Dreamweaver, then open the Rapids Transit website.

    b. Open the page lodging.html.

    c. Place a paragraph break after the last sentence on the page and insert a form called **lodging**.

    d. Insert a table inside the form with 7 rows and 3 columns, and a Top header.

    e. Enter text labels in the first column beginning with the second row, using Figure I-19 as a guide.

FIGURE I-19

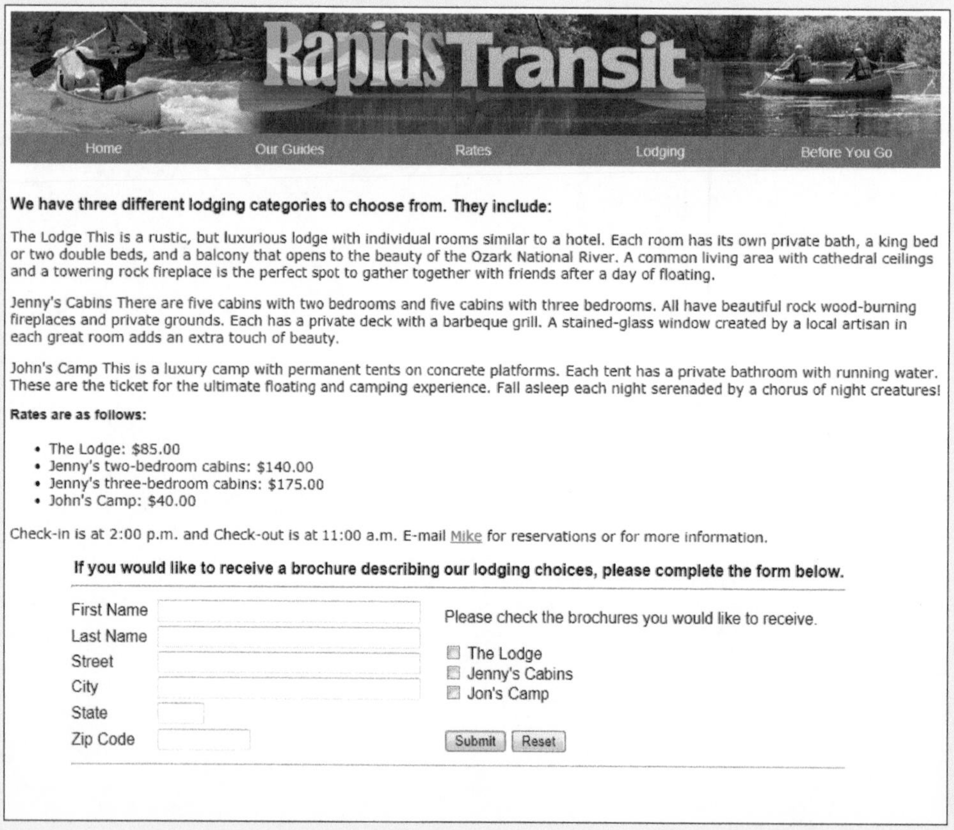

Independent Challenge 1 (continued)

f. Add Single line text fields with no label tags in the column next to the text labels using 40 characters for both the character width and maximum characters for all text fields except for the state and zip code; use a width of 2 for the state and 10 for the zip code. Name the fields appropriately.

g. Merge the third cells in the second, third, fourth, fifth, and sixth rows.

h. In the merged cells, type **Please check the brochures you would like to receive.**

i. Enter a line break after the sentence, then insert a check box group named **brochures**.

j. Enter the label **The Lodge** for the first check box, then enter a value of **lodge**.

k. Enter the label **Jenny's Cabins** for the second check box, then enter a value of **jenny**.

l. Enter the label **Jon's Camp** for the third check box, then enter a value of **jon**.

m. Insert a Submit button in the third column of the last row.

n. Insert a Reset button to the right of the Submit button in the same cell, and change the Action to **Reset form**, the button value to **Reset**, and the Button name to **Reset**.

o. Create a new class rule in the rapids_styles.css style sheet named form_table with the following properties: Font-family: Arial, Helvetica, sans-serif; Font-size: medium; Box Width: 800px. Apply the new form_table rule to the table, then indent the table using three block quotes.

p. Merge the cells in the top row, then type **If you would like to receive a brochure describing our lodging choices, please complete the form below.**

q. Insert a new row at the end of the table and merge the cells in the new row. (*Hint:* Place the insertion point in the last cell in a table, then press the [Tab] key to insert a new row at the end of the table.)

r. Insert a horizontal rule.

s. Insert another horizontal rule in the cell with the header, but under the header.

t. Preview the page in the browser, compare it to Figure I-19, then test the text fields and the Reset button.

u. Make any adjustments to improve the page, then save your work.

v. Run reports for broken links, orphaned files, untitled documents, and missing alternate text, correcting any errors that you find.

w. Close the page, then exit Dreamweaver.

Independent Challenge 2

In this exercise you will continue your work on the TripSmart website. The owner, Thomas Howard, wants you to create a form to collect data from users who are interested in receiving more information about one or more of the featured trips.

a. Start Dreamweaver, open the TripSmart website, then open the tours page.

b. Insert a paragraph break after the last sentence on the page, then insert a form named **tours**.

c. Insert a table in the form that contains 11 rows, 2 columns, and a Top header.

d. Merge the cells in the top row, type **Please complete this form for additional information on these tours.**

e. Beginning in the second row, type the following labels in the cells in the first column: **First Name**, **Last Name**, **Street**, **City**, **State**, **Zip Code**, **Phone**, **Email**, and **I am interested in:**.

f. Insert single-line text fields in the first eight cells in the second column beginning with row 2 and assign the following names: **first_name**, **last_name**, **street**, **city**, **state**, **zip_code**, **phone**, and **email**; setting the Char width to **40** and the Max Chars to **100** for each of these text fields. (*Hint*: To save time create the first_name field, then use copy and paste to create the other fields, changing the name of each pasted field in the Property inspector.)

g. In the second cell of the tenth row, insert a check box group with the name of **tours**.

h. Enter the label **Peru** for the first check box, then enter a value of **peru**.

i. Enter the label **The Galapagos** for the second check box, then enter a value of **galapagos**.

j. Create a new class rule in the tripsmart_styles.css style sheet named form_table with the following properties: Font-family: Verdana, Geneva, sans-serif; Font-size: medium; Block Text-align: left; Box Width: 650px. (Add the inline rule to modify the table header tag to center it if you wish.)

k. Apply the form_table rule to the table.

l. Insert a Submit button and a Reset button in the second cell of the eleventh row with appropriate names, values, and actions.

m. Insert a new merged row at the bottom of the table, then insert a horizontal rule, then use Blockquotes to indent the table to a position of your choice.

n. Run reports for untitled documents, missing alternate text, broken links, and orphaned files.

o. Save your work, preview the page in your browser, test the form, compare your screen to Figure I-20, close your browser, then close the tours page. (*Note:* the table border in the example is inherited from the table rule in the style sheet.)

FIGURE I-20

Destinations: The Galápagos and Peru

We are featuring two new trips for the coming year. The first is to the Galápagos. We will depart on February 5 and arrive in Lima, Peru. After arriving, we will stay at the Miraflores Park Hotel and enjoy the sights for two days in Lima. Next, we will fly to Guayaquil, Ecuador and stay overnight at the Hilton Colón before continuing on to Baltra Island in the Galápagos archipelago. After landing in Baltra, we will take a van to the dock and board the ship to begin our wonderful adventure. Our course will take us to several islands. The Galápagos archipelago consists of thirteen large islands and six small ones, along with over forty islets. The Galápagos is where Charles Darwin visited in 1835 and wrote his book "The Origin of Species." It is home to a variety of wildlife unlike anywhere else in the world. The expert local guides and naturalists will introduce you to the incredible Galápagos wildlife as you explore the islands and attend informative lectures each day.

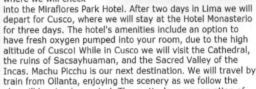

The second trip we are featuring is to Peru. Our Peru trip will depart on May 5 and last for ten days. We will arrive in Lima, where we will check into the Miraflores Park Hotel. After two days in Lima we will depart for Cusco, where we will stay at the Hotel Monasterio for three days. The hotel's amenities include an option to have fresh oxygen pumped into your room, due to the high altitude of Cusco! While in Cusco we will visit the Cathedral, the ruins of Sacsayhuaman, and the Sacred Valley of the Incas. Machu Picchu is our next destination. We will travel by train from Ollanta, enjoying the scenery as we follow the Urubamba River to Machu Picchu. Our time at Machu Picchu will be simply magical. The meticulous preservation of the site helps you to envision the lives of those who lived here centuries ago.

Please complete this form for additional information on these tours.

First Name
Last Name
Street
City
State
Zip Code
Phone
Email

I am interested in:
☐ Peru
☐ The Gálapagos

[Submit] [Reset]

Independent Challenge 3

Paul Patrick and his partner Donnie Honeycutt have a construction business in Southern California. They have recently published a website for their business and would like to add a search form to help their customers quickly find the data they are looking for. They begin this task by researching other website search pages on the Internet.

a. Connect to the Internet, then go to the Internal Revenue Service site at irs.gov.

b. Click the Advanced Search link to search the IRS site, as shown in Figure I-21.

c. How is the search form organized?

d. What form objects were used?

e. Click the Search Tips link. What information did you find to help users search the website?

f. Find one more example of a site that uses a search page and explain which of the two sites you prefer and why.

FIGURE I-21

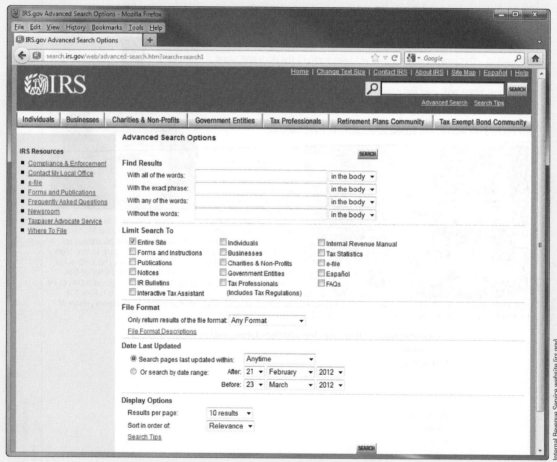

Internal Revenue Service website (irs.gov)

Real Life Independent Challenge

This assignment will continue to build on the personal website that you created in Unit B. In Unit C, you created and developed your index page. In Unit D, you added a page with either an ordered or an unordered list, using CSS with a minimum of two styles. In Unit E, you added a page that included at least two images. In Unit F, you added a page that included several links and an image map. In Unit G, you redesigned the index page based on CSS. In Unit H, you added some media elements. In this lesson, you will add a form to one of the pages in your website.

a. Consult your wireframe and decide which page you would like to develop in this lesson.

b. Sketch a layout for your page to place the form objects you would like to use.

c. Create the form using at least three different form objects. Include clear instructions that will help users fill out the form correctly.

d. Add text labels to each form object.

e. Add a Submit and Reset button and format them appropriately.

f. Format the form with CSS to help it stand out on the page.

g. Save the file and preview the page in the browser, testing the Reset button to make sure it works correctly.

h. Make any adjustments that are necessary to improve the appearance of your form.

After you are satisfied with your work, verify the following:

1. Each completed page has a page title.

2. All links work correctly.

3. The completed pages look good using a screen resolution of 1024 × 768.

4. All images are properly linked to the assets folder of the website.

5. All images have alternate text and are legal to use.

6. The link checker shows no broken links or orphaned files. If there are orphaned files, note your plan to link them.

7. All main pages have a consistent navigation system.

8. The form is attractive and easy to understand and use.

Visual Workshop

Use Figure I-22 as a guide to continue your work on the Carolyne's Creations website. You are adding a form to the classes page that will allow customers to sign up for a class. Since the customers are faxing their forms, there is no need for a Submit button. You can add a Reset button if you wish. Use form properties and settings of your choice. Use a table to lay out the form and create a new class rule to format the table. Run reports for missing alt text, untitled documents, broken links, and orphaned files. If cc_banner.jpg is listed as an orphaned file, delete it, as you no longer need it. (*Hint*: To match the figure, edit the text in the last paragraph before inserting the form.)

FIGURE I-22

Cooking Classes are fun!

Chef Carolyne loves to offer a fun and relaxing cooking school each month in her newly refurbished kitchen. She teaches an adults' class on the fourth Saturday of each month from 6:00 to 8:00 pm. Each class will learn to cook a complete dinner and then enjoy the meal at the end of the class with a wonderful wine pairing. This is a great chance to get together with friends for a fun evening.

Chef Carolyne also teaches a children's class on the second Tuesday of each month from 4:00 to 5:30 pm. Our young chefs will learn to cook two dishes that will accompany a full meal served at 5:30 pm. Children aged 5–8 years accompanied by an adult are welcome. We also host small birthday parties where we put the guests to work baking and decorating the cake! Call for times and prices.

We offer several special adults' classes throughout the year. The **Valentine Chocolate Extravaganza** is a particular favorite. You will learn to dip strawberries, make truffles, and bake a sinful Triple Chocolate Dare You Torte. We also host the **Not So Traditional Thanksgiving** class and the **Super Bowl Snacks** class each year with rave reviews. Watch the website for details!

Prices are $40.00 for each adults' class and $15.00 for each children's class. Sign up for classes by calling 555-963-8271, by emailing us, or by faxing the form below to 555-963-8272.

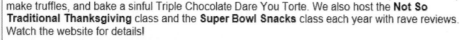

March Class Registration	
Please check which class you are signing up for:	
Adult: Peruvian Cuisine	☐
Child: Oven chicken fingers, chocolate chip cookies	☐
First Name	
Last Name	
Contact number or Email address	

Presenting and Publishing a Website

Files You Will Need:

To view a list of files needed for this unit, see the Data Files Grid in the back of the book.

There are many items to verify and tests to run before a website is ready to be finalized, presented to a client for approval, and published on the web. For instance, you need to confirm that all issues that could be affected by end-user technical factors have been resolved so that all page elements will work well under most operating environments. As recommended, testing your website should be an ongoing process that happens throughout the development cycle. It is much easier to make incremental corrections rather than last minute corrections.  You review the many factors that contribute to successful project completion.

OBJECTIVES

Collect feedback

Run site reports

Validate HTML and CSS markup

Test for browser compatibility

Use media queries

Evaluate and present a website to a client

Set up remote access

Publish a site

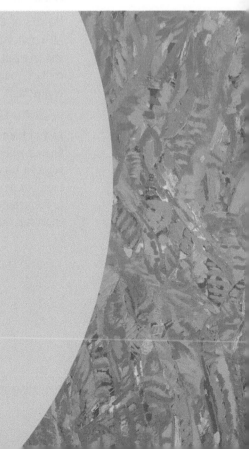

Collecting Feedback

Although you may be satisfied with the website that you have designed and developed, it is important to ask for and receive constructive feedback before you present it to the client and publish. Feedback is most helpful when it is solicited from a variety of sources, such as other content contributors, clients, and objective participants who are not connected to the project. Feedback should be solicited both during the project cycle and after the website is published. ▰▰▰ You decide to identify some of the methods you can use to collect final feedback on your website.

- **Site usability tests**

  Once you have at least a prototype of the website ready to evaluate, it is a good idea to conduct a **site usability test**. This process involves obtaining website feedback from users who are not connected to the project. Usability test participants, often selected from external marketing sources, are instructed to objectively evaluate the site based on a standard set of directions. A comprehensive usability test will include pretest questions, participant tasks, a posttest interview, and a posttest survey. The goal of this test is to obtain much-needed information as to how usable the site is to those unfamiliar with it. Typical questions include: "What are your overall impressions?", "What do you like the best and the least about the site?", and "How easy is it to navigate around the site?". It is helpful to have a test monitor observe the testers as they navigate the site to record the time it takes for them to locate information. For more detailed information about this topic, go to w3.org and search for "site usability test."

- **Surveys**

  Once the website is published, surveys are a great way to collect user feedback. A well-designed survey with articulate and pertinent questions can provide you with valuable feedback regarding issues about the website itself or regarding the company's products or services. You can request feedback with email solicitations sent to the company's clients or request feedback from the users while they are using a website. Users who complete surveys are often interested in supplying helpful information to a company. However, incentives such as discounts or promotional gifts are also used to increase levels of participation. The US Navy website, shown in Figure J-1, solicits user feedback on their website with a survey that the user is asked to complete and submit.

- **Points of contact**

  All websites should have several points of contact. A physical address, a mailing address, a telephone number, and an email address are all good points of contact. By providing your clients' users with multiple points of contact, you give them a choice as to how they would like to contact your client when they have problems or questions.

- **Web 2.0 Technology**

  As you learned in Unit H, many websites today are incorporating some form of Web 2.0 technology to interact with their users. Blogs and other social networking sites function as valuable communication tools between companies and their target audiences. For example, posts on such applications as Twitter or Facebook provide instant information as well as allow users the opportunity to post feedback directly back to the website. The White House website, shown in Figure J-2, has links to several Web 2.0 applications to encourage sharing information and gathering feedback.

FIGURE J-1: The US Navy website with form for feedback

Paragraph requesting feedback from users

Form for user feedback

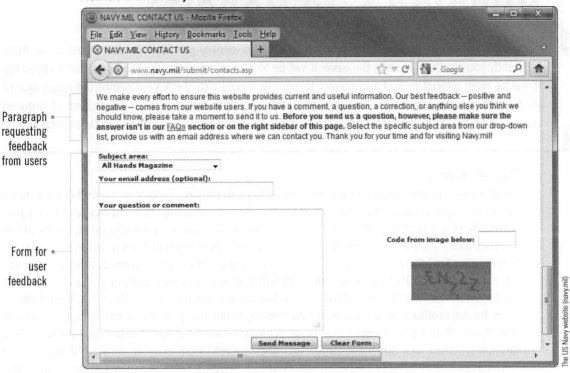

The US Navy website (navy.mil)

FIGURE J-2: The White House website with social networking links

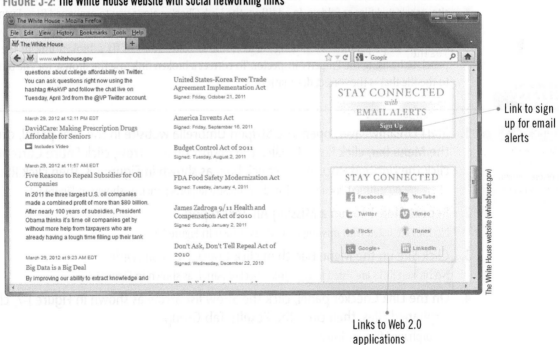

Link to sign up for email alerts

Links to Web 2.0 applications

The White House website (whitehouse.gov)

Running Site Reports

Dreamweaver has several helpful reports you can run to identify problems in your website. The more frequently you run these reports, the easier it will be to correct any errors. If you allow errors to build up, it will be more difficult to find and correct them. You should also check your completed pages against your wireframes to make sure that you have followed the design plan and included all required components. ▰▰▰▰ You want to review and run some of the site reports available in Dreamweaver.

DETAILS

- **Run site reports**

  Dreamweaver is capable of running any type of report as frequently as you want, as required by your project needs. The Reports command on the Site menu provides a list of reports that you can generate for your website. You can generate reports for the current document, the entire local site, selected files in the site, or a selected folder. These reports are grouped by type. The first type of report includes three categories of work-flow reports. **Workflow reports** are useful when working in a team environment. For instance, you can run a workflow report that enables you to see files that other designers are using or produce a report that will list all files that have been modified recently. You can also generate a report that lists **Design Notes**—notes directed to other content creators who are working on different parts of your site. In addition to work-flow reports, there are five categories of **HTML reports**: Combinable Nested Font Tags, Missing Alt Text, Redundant Nested Tags, Removable Empty Tags, and Untitled Documents. The Missing Alt Text and the Untitled Documents reports are especially important for website accessibility. After you run a report, you can save it as an XML file in a database, spreadsheet, or template for subsequent use.

- **Check links**

  The Link Checker in the Results panel provides you with a way to check external and internal links in your website. Link Checker alerts you to any broken internal links and helps you repair them; although it does list external links, it does not verify their validity. You can either check the links on a single page, the entire site, or selected files or folders. In addition, the Link Checker alerts you to orphaned files. Even if you are not ready to link these files, routinely running a list of orphaned files will remind you of the work you must complete in preparation for linking them to the website. You can fix a broken link in the Link Checker panel, or by using the Property inspector. To correct a broken link, use the Browse for File button to browse to the file that is the correct destination.

STEPS

QUICK TIP

It is a good idea to recreate the site cache before running reports to refresh the file listing.

1. **Start Dreamweaver, open The Striped Umbrella website in the Files panel, click** Site **on the Menu bar, click** Reports, **click the** Report on list arrow, **click** Entire Current Local Site, **click the** Untitled Documents check box, **as shown in Figure J-3, then click** Run

   There are no untitled documents listed in the Site Reports panel, as shown in Figure J-4.

2. **Repeat Step 1 to run a Missing Alt Text report**

   No files are listed with missing alt text, as shown in Figure J-5.

3. **Click** Site **on the Menu bar, then click** Check Links Sitewide

   No broken links are listed in the Link Checker panel, as shown in Figure J-6.

4. **On the Link Checker panel, click the** Show list arrow **as shown in Figure J-7, click** Orphaned Files, **then close the Results Tab Group**

   No orphaned files are listed.

FIGURE J-3: **Reports dialog box**

Specify the scope of the report to run from this list

Select check box to run a workflow report

Select check box to run an HTML report

Report on list arrow

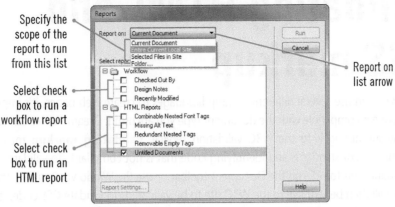

FIGURE J-4: **Site Reports panel displaying no pages without titles**

No untitled documents are listed

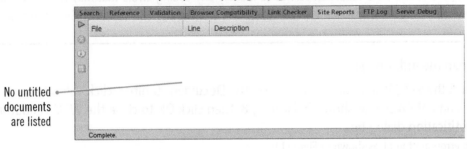

FIGURE J-5: **Site Reports panel displaying no pages with missing alt text**

No files are listed with missing alt text

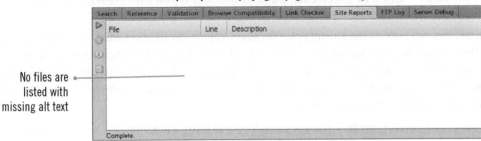

FIGURE J-6: **Link Checker displaying no files with broken links**

No broken links are listed

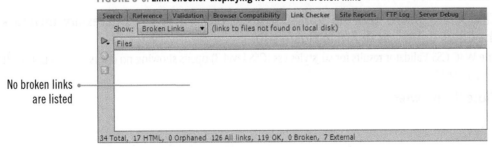

FIGURE J-7: **Link Checker displaying no orphaned files**

No orphaned files are listed

Show list arrow

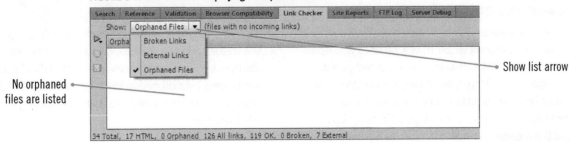

UNIT J
Dreamweaver CS6

Validating HTML and CSS markup

Because you can use several different markup languages to create web pages, it's important to make sure that the code is compatible with the document type you are using. Dreamweaver can validate your markup (code) by submitting it to the W3C validation service. **Validating markup** means comparing code against the current standards and identifying code that is not compliant. To validate HTML code, use the W3C Validation button 📄 on the Document toolbar or use the Window > Results > Validation command. The code will then be sent live to the W3C site to be validated. To validate CSS code, go to jigsaw.w3.org/css-validator and upload the style sheet you want to validate. 🔧 You submit the pages in The Striped Umbrella site to the W3C validation service to identify any coding errors that may need correcting. You then submit the style sheets to the CSS Validation Service using the CSS Validation Service website.

STEPS

1. **Open the index page**

2. **Click the W3C Validation button 📄 on the Document toolbar, click Validate Current Document (W3C), as shown in Figure J-8, then click OK to close the W3C Validator Notification dialog box**

   No errors are found, as shown in Figure J-9.

3. **Repeat Steps 1 and 2 to check each page in the site. If you find errors, evaluate and correct them**

   You will find one error on the activities page because you probably have not added an action to your form on the page. It is flagging this code to remind you to add one when you have the information available. You will find three errors on the about us page because the swf file is not inserted according to HTML5 standards. After the Flash technology issues are all settled, this can be corrected, but meanwhile, the existing code will work in most desktop browsers with no problems.

   > **TROUBLE**
   > Depending on the browser you are using, you may see a Choose button instead of a Browse button.

4. **Open your browser, go to jigsaw.w3.org/css-validator, click the By file upload tab, click the Browse button, browse to The Striped Umbrella local site root folder, then double-click su_styles.css**

5. **Click More Options, click the Profile list arrow, click CSS level 3 if necessary, then click the Check button, as shown in Figure J-10**

   The W3C CSS Validator results for su_styles.css (CSS level 3) opens showing no errors were found, as shown in Figure J-11.

6. **Close the browser**

The Evolution of HTML5

HTML has been in existence since the early 1990s, but it wasn't until 1997 that the then current version, HTML4, became a W3C recommendation. Many HTML4 attributes such as body background, align, cellpadding, and hspace are now added using CSS3. HTML5 introduced new ways to add interactivity and tags that support semantic markup, such as the <nav> tag used for navigation links. In Unit D you learned about using semantic markup to incorporate meaning with your HTML markup. Other semantic HTML5 tags include <header>, <footer>, <article>, <audio>, <hgroup>, <figure>, <embed>, <wbr>, <canvas>, <section> and <video>. HTML5 is still a work in progress, but most modern browsers support it. HTML5 also introduces markup for web applications (apps), an exploding sector of web development.

FIGURE J-8: Validating the index page

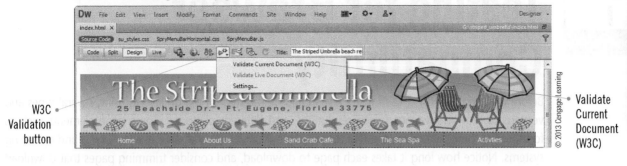

W3C
Validation
button

Validate
Current
Document
(W3C)

FIGURE J-9: The index page with no errors found

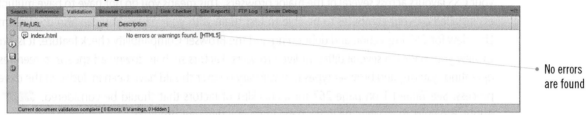

● No errors
are found

FIGURE J-10: The W3C Validation Service website

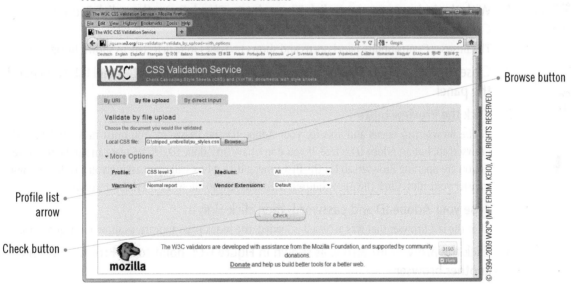

● Browse button

Profile list ●
arrow

Check button ●

FIGURE J-11: The su_styles.css file with no errors found

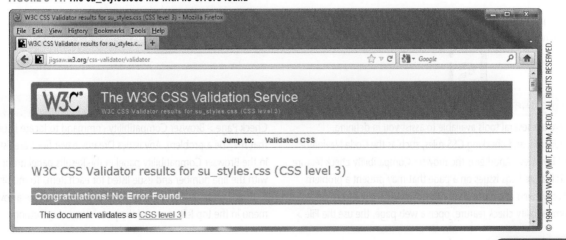

Presenting and Publishing a Website

Testing for Browser Compatibility

Before finalizing a website, each web page should be retested for design layout, using several types and versions of browsers, various screen resolutions, and different platforms. Some page elements such as fonts, colors, horizontal rules, and CSS div properties do not look the same in all browsers and operating systems. Notice how long it takes each page to download, and consider trimming pages that download slowly. You learned in Unit G about Adobe BrowserLab, the Adobe online service is that can be used to test your CSS layouts across several of the major browsers. This means you do not have to have multiple browsers installed on your computer to be able to test them with your pages. You can also use Dreamweaver's Live view for CSS inspection and debugging and the Browser Compatibility check feature. It is a good idea to view your pages in several different live browsers. Factors such as download speeds, screen resolutions, operating systems, and browser types that will vary by user should have been included in the development process. See Table J-1 on page 267 for a checklist of factors that should be considered. **You use** Adobe BrowserLab to view the index page in several different browsers.

STEPS

QUICK TIP
To see which browsers are being checked, click the Check Browser Compatibility button ▷ in the Browser Compatibility panel, then click Settings.

1. **With the index page open, click File, point to Check Page, then click Browser Compatibility**

   The Browser Compatibility panel opens and shows no issues were detected, as shown in Figure J-12.

2. **Close the Results Tab Group, then click the Adobe BrowserLab panel tab to expand the panel**

3. **Click the Preview button**

   Adobe BrowserLab opens and asks for your Adobe ID and password. You must have an Adobe ID to use BrowserLab, but an Adobe ID is free. If you don't have an Adobe ID, click Create an Adobe ID to create one. (If you are opening BrowserLab for the first time, a dialog box will open asking you to allow BrowserLab to transfer your files. Click the Allow button, then click OK to allow BrowserLab to work.)

4. **Type your Adobe ID and password, then click Sign In**

   After the last browser that was accessed is loaded, the index page appears, as shown in Figure J-13.

QUICK TIP
You can also view two browsers simultaneously, either side by side or one on top of the other (Onion Skin) by clicking the View list arrow, then making a selection.

5. **Click the Browser list arrow, as shown in Figure J-14, point to All Browsers, then choose another browser**

6. **Close the browser to close Adobe BrowserLab**

Using the Browser Compatibility check to manage styles

There are several tools available to assist you in defining, modifying, and checking CSS rules, such as the Code Navigator and Live view. Another is the Browser Compatibility check feature. This feature flags issues on a page that may present a problem when viewed in a particular browser. To use the Browser Compatibility check feature, open a web page, the use the File > Check Page > Browser Compatibility command to locate issues that may be a problem. Any issues Dreamweaver finds are listed in the Browser Compatibility panel in the Results panel group with the line number and issue listed for each item. To modify the settings to add additional versions of browsers, click the arrow menu in the top left corner of the panel, then click Settings.

FIGURE J-12: The Browser Compatibility panel with no browser compatibility errors found

Check browser compatibility button

No errors detected

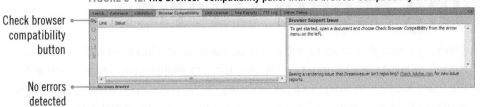

FIGURE J-13: Viewing the index page in Adobe BrowserLab

Internet Explorer 9.0 is the current browser shown (yours may differ)

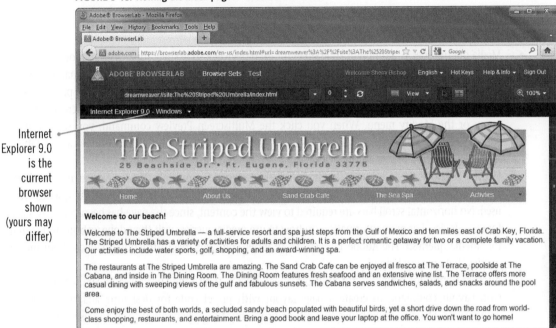

© 2013 Cengage Learning
Courtesy of Adobe Systems, Inc.

FIGURE J-14: Choosing another browser in Adobe BrowserLab

Browser list arrow

Point to All Browsers

Select a browser from the list

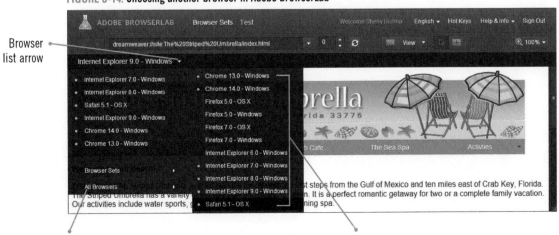

© 2013 Cengage Learning
Courtesy of Adobe Systems, Inc.

Using Media Queries

Today it is no longer enough to design a web page that that looks and functions well on a desktop monitor alone. Users will expect to be able to access your site using multiple mobile devices, such as tablets and smart phones, so you'll have to design your pages so they display correctly on all of them. To do this, you'll find media queries to be a great tool. **Media queries**, a new feature introduced in Dreamweaver 5.5, are style sheet files that specify set parameters for displaying pages on separate devices, such as tablets or smart phones. Media queries, combined with the new features of CSS3, enable you to create pages with content that can be modified to fit different sized devices.  You decide to learn more about media queries and how they might be used to modify the content in The Striped Umbrella website.

DETAILS

- **Using Media Queries**

  - Media queries specify a different style sheet for each device: a style sheet for a desktop monitor, a style sheet for a tablet, and a style sheet for a smart phone. Dreamweaver has a function named Media Queries that, like a traffic policeman, directs each device to the correct style sheet so the page will display correctly on that device. You can find the Media Queries command on the Multiscreen Preview menu or the Modify menu. When you click the Multiscreen Preview command, you see the page content rendered on three different simulated screens such as a laptop, a cell phone, and a tablet, sometimes referred to as a 3-up preview.

  - Figure J-15 shows the index page that has not been designed for multiple devices. Notice how you have to scroll horizontally to see the content. Figure J-16 shows the index page after media queries were used. No horizontal scroll bars are required to view the content, since the page has been correctly sized for each device. For more information on how to use media queries, visit the Adobe website and search for "media queries." The Adobe TV website, tv.adobe.com, has free instructional videos about media queries that are very helpful.

  - Another option for designing for multiple screen sizes is to use the Dreamweaver File > New > Fluid Grid Layout command to create a page layout with preset code for designing adaptive websites. **Adaptive websites** are websites that adjust or modify the page content to fit the user's needs and device type used to view the site. This grid contains three CSS layouts and typography presets based on a single fluid grid. You can save the styles Dreamweaver creates automatically in your existing style sheet.

FIGURE J-15: Multiscreen Preview before using media queries

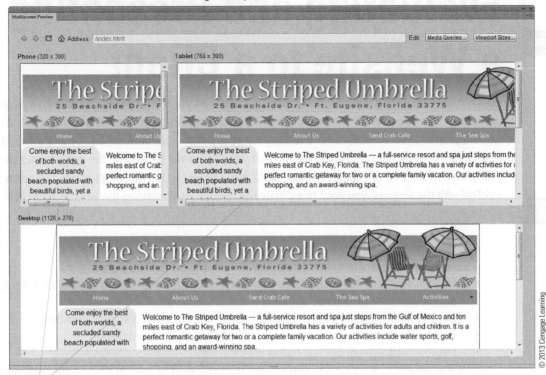

Horizontal scroll
bars are needed to
read content

FIGURE J-16: Multiscreen Preview after using media queries

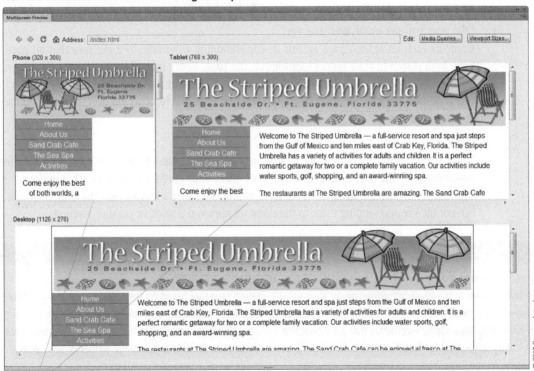

Horizontal scroll
bars are not needed
to read content

© 2013 Cengage Learning

Evaluating and Presenting a Website to a Client

Even if you create a great website, poor communication can put the project at risk. Ideally, a prototype of the website was approved at the beginning of the process. Before you present a website to a client as a finished product, you should answer a few key questions. If you are satisfied with your answers, it is time to present the project to your client. The method you choose will depend on the project, your client, and your preferred method of communication. You review a checklist of questions and when you are satisfied with the answers, you want to evaluate the options for presenting the work to your client.

DETAILS

- **Are you ready to present your work?**

  After running the battery of technical tests, you should answer the following questions:
  - Do all of your final design and development decisions reflect your client's goals and requirements and meet the needs of the intended audience?
  - Did you follow good web development practices and current accessibility standards?
  - Did you check your pages against your wireframes as you developed them?
  - Did your final delivery date and budget meet the goals?

  If your answer to the final question is "no," then you need to determine the reason why before your presentation. If you find that you did spend more time on the site than you expected, determine if it was because you underestimated the amount of work it would take, ran into unforeseen technical problems, or because the client changed the requirements or increased the scope of the project as it went along. If you underestimated the project or ran into unexpected difficulties, you usually cannot expect the client to make up the difference without a prior agreement. Any time there are budget and time considerations, it is best to communicate frequently with status updates during the project.

- **Did you follow your wireframe?**

  Compare each completed page against its corresponding wireframe to make sure that all page elements have been placed in their proper locations on the page. Verify that all specified links have been included and test them to make sure that they work correctly. You might also consider hiring site-usability testers to test your site navigation. A site-usability test provides impartial feedback on how intuitive and user-friendly your site is to use.

- **How should you present your work?**

  The best option for presenting the final project is to invite the client to your office and perform a full walkthrough of the site, if at all feasible. This offers your client a chance to ask questions. Alternately, consider publishing the site to a server and sending the client a link to view the completed site. Creating PDFs of the site and sending them to the client for approval is another possible method.

Design Matters

Using wireframes for planning, development, and presentation

You may have chosen to use low-fidelity wireframes, such as those created in Microsoft PowerPoint or Adobe Photoshop, or you may have used high-fidelity wireframes that are interactive and multi-dimensional, such as those created in OverSight, Protoshare, or Adobe Proto, shown in Figure J-17. Another popular method is BaseCamp, a professional web-based project collaboration tool that focuses on collaboration and communication between you and your client. You should

select your tool based on the size and complexity of the website, the budget, and your personal preferences. Used correctly, wireframes provide the basic framework of the site, the placement of the main page elements, and serve as a guide for all phases of development. They should be presented to the client for the initial project approval and used at the end of the project to document that the plan was executed as planned.

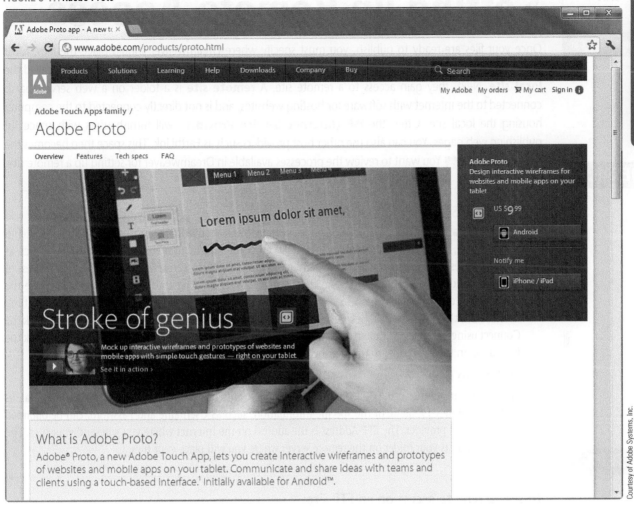

TABLE J-1: End-User Considerations for Development and Design

page element	design considerations
Tables	Are table widths sized for viewing in various screen resolutions? Are they sized to print correctly? Do they include summaries or headings?
Colors	Will users be able to successfully navigate the website in case the colors do not render exactly as intended? Do any page elements rely on the use of color alone?
Text	Are the font sizes large enough for users to read? Is the contrast between the text and the page background strong?
Media Objects	Has the embedded code been provided that searches for the appropriate plug-ins and prompts missing plug-ins to download? Are there too many media objects that will slow the download time appreciably? Do all media objects have a purpose in presenting the page content?
Images	Are all images as small in file size as possible? Do they all include alternate text?
Accessibility	Will the site pass the W3C Priority 1 Checkpoints and the W3C Priority 2 POUR principles for making a website accessible?

Setting up Remote Access

Once your files are ready to publish, you must specify where Dreamweaver should place the files. Most Dreamweaver users begin first by creating a local site root folder to store all of their website files, called the **local site**. Next, they gain access to a remote site. A **remote site** is a folder on a web server that is connected to the Internet with software for hosting websites, and is not directly connected to the computer housing the local site. Often the **ISP (Internet Service Provider)** will furnish users with space for publishing web pages. You can also use other host providers such as EarthLink. This space then becomes the remote site. 🖰🖰🖰 You want to review the processes available in Dreamweaver for setting up a remote site.

DETAILS

- **Using the Site Setup dialog box**

   When your pages are ready to publish, the files must be transferred from the local site to the remote site. In Dreamweaver, you use the Site Setup dialog box to enter the information about the remote server, such as the FTP address, root directory, username, and password. **FTP (File Transfer Protocol)** is the process of uploading and downloading files to and from a remote site. To open the Site Setup dialog box, use the Site > New Site; or Site > Manage Sites > Edit commands on the Menu bar. To enter the server information, click Servers, then click the Add new Server button. The choices for remote access appear when you click the Connect using list arrow, as shown in Figure J-18. After the remote site information is entered, you click the Put button in the Files panel to transfer the files.

- **Setting up FTP**

   Most users transfer files using FTP. If you select this file-transfer method, additional options will appear, as shown in Figure J-19. Some of the specific information, such as Username and Password, can be obtained from your host provider. The FTP Address is the address on the Internet where you will send your files. The Root Directory is your folder on the remote server where you will place your files.

STEPS

To set up remote access on an FTP site:

1. **Click** Site **on the Menu bar, then click** Manage Sites

2. **Click the** website name **in the Manage Sites dialog box, then click the** Edit the currently selected site button 🖉

3. **Click** Servers **in the Site Setup dialog box, click the** Add new Server button ➕**, type your** server name **in the Server Name text box, click the** Connect using list arrow, **then click** FTP **if necessary**

4. **Enter the** FTP Address, Username, Password, Root Directory, **and** Web URL **information in the dialog box**

5. **Click** Test

   The test button tests the connection between your computer and the server.

6. **Click** Save, **click** Save **again, click** OK **to recreate the cache, then click** Done

   The dialog boxes close.

To view a website on a remote server:

1. **Click the** View list arrow **in the Files panel, then click** Remote server

2. **Click the** Expand to show local and remote sites button 🖻

   The Remote site and the Local files panes display an expanded Files panel, as shown in Figure J-20.

3. **Click the** Collapse to show only local or remote site button 🖻**, click the** View list arrow, **then click** Local view

   Your window returns to Local view.

FIGURE J-18: Site Setup dialog box

Servers category •

Connect using options •

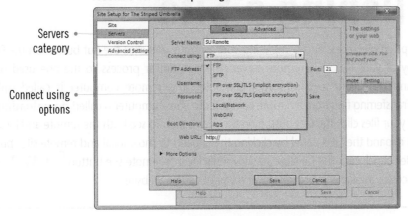

FIGURE J-19: Site Setup dialog box server settings

Server name •

Your host provider will furnish this information •

Root Directory name furnished by host provider •

• Test button

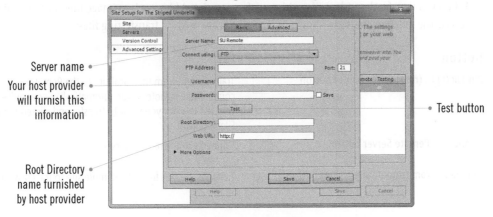

FIGURE J-20: Viewing the Remote Server and Local Files

• Collapse to show only local or remote site button

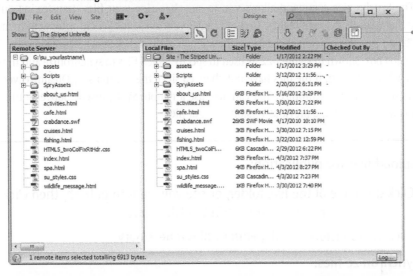

Choosing remote access options

Remote access choices include FTP, Local/Network, WebDAV, RDS, and Microsoft Visual SourceSafe. **Local/Network** refers to publishing a website on either the local drive (that is, your own hard drive) or a local network drive. **WebDAV (Web-based Distributed Authoring and Versioning)** is used with servers such as the Microsoft Internet Information Server (IIS) and Apache Web server.

RDS (Remote Development Services) is used with a remote folder running ColdFusion. Finally, **Microsoft Visual SourceSafe** is available under the Windows platform using Microsoft Visual SourceSafe Client. **Secure FTP (SFTP)** is an FTP option which lets you encrypt file transfers to protect your files, user names, and passwords.

Publishing a Site

After setting up remote access and completing your website, you click the Put button on the Files panel to transfer a copy of your files to a remote server. This is a similar process to the one used by FTP client programs. Transferring your files from your computer to a remote computer is called **uploading** or **publishing**. Transferring files from a remote computer to your computer is called **downloading**. To download a copy of your files click the Get button on the Files panel. To see both the remote and local versions of a site, you can expand the Files panel by clicking the Expand to show local and remote sites button 🔲. To collapse the Files panel, click the Collapse to show only local or remote site button 🔲. ▰▰▰ You want to review the processes available in Dreamweaver for publishing a website.

DETAILS

- **Using Put and Get**

  When you transfer dependent files; this transfers associated files, such as image files, in the local site to the server. The following buttons, shown in Figure J-21, are used for transferring files:

button		task
Put File(s) to (remote site name) button	⬆	Transfers files from the Local site to the Remote site; will connect to a remote server automatically once you've selected the files you want to transfer and clicked the Put File(s) button
Connect to Remote Server button	🔗	Connects to the remote server
Get File(s) from (remote site name) button	⬇	Transfers the files from the Remote site to the Local site.

- **Synchronizing files**

  The Synchronize command allows you to **synchronize** your files, transferring only the latest versions rather than all the website files. To synchronize your site, click Synchronize with (remote site name) button 🔄 on the Files panel or click Site on the Menu bar, then click Synchronize Sitewide. The Synchronize Files dialog box, shown in Figure J-22, is used to specify which files to synchronize and the direction in which to synchronize them. If the files have not changed since the last transfer, Dreamweaver notifies you that you do not need to synchronize. You can also use a remote SVN (Apache Subversion) repository to save and maintain current and previous versions of your files.

STEPS

To upload files for publication:

1. Click the name of the file, folder, or site you want to publish, then click the Put Files(s) to (remote site name) button ⬆ in the Files panel

2. Click Yes to include the dependent files if necessary

To synchronize files:

1. Click Site on the Menu bar, then click Synchronize Sitewide

2. Click the Synchronize list arrow, then click Entire '(Site name)' Site

3. Click the Direction list arrow, then click Put newer files to remote

4. Click Preview, then click OK

FIGURE J-21: **Files panel**

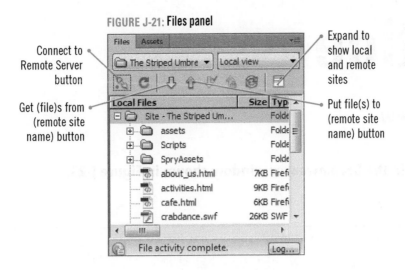

Connect to
Remote Server
button

Get (file)s from
(remote site
name) button

Expand to
show local
and remote
sites

Put file(s) to
(remote site
name) button

FIGURE J-22: **The Synchronize with Remote Server dialog box**

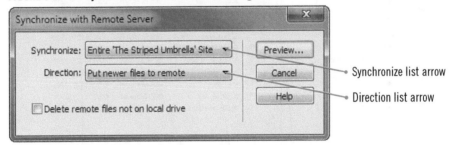

Synchronize list arrow

Direction list arrow

Cloaking files to exclude them from being uploaded to a server

There may be times when you want to exclude a particular file from being uploaded to a server. For instance, suppose you are not quite finished working on a particular web page. You can exclude a file by cloaking it. **Cloaking** is the process of marking a file or files for exclusion when the commands Put, Get, Synchronize, Check In, and Check Out are used. Cloaked files can also be excluded from site-wide operations such as checking for links or updating a template or library item. You can also cloak a folder or specify a type of file to cloak throughout the site. The cloaking feature is enabled by default. To cloak a file, select the file, click the Files panel Options button, point to Site, point to Cloaking, and then click Cloak.

Managing a website with a team

When you work on a large website, chances are that many people will be involved in developing and keeping the site up to date. Different individuals will need to make changes or additions to different pages of the site by adding, changing, or deleting content. If everyone had access to the same pages at the same time, problems could arise. Fortunately, Dreamweaver's collaboration tools eliminate such problems. For example, the **Check Out** feature enables only one person at a time to work on a file. This ensures that content contributors cannot overwrite each other's pages. To access the Check Out feature, you must first enable it in the Remote Info settings of the Site Setup dialog box. To check out a file, select the file name in the Files panel, then click the Check Out File(s) button on the Files panel. Another file management tool is Subversion control. A remote SVN (Apache Subversion) repository is used to maintain current and historical versions of your website files. It is used in a team environment to move, copy, and delete shared files. You can protect files from being accessed using the svn:ignore property to create a list of files that are to be ignored in a directory.

Practice

Concepts Review

Label each element in the Dreamweaver window shown in Figure J-23.

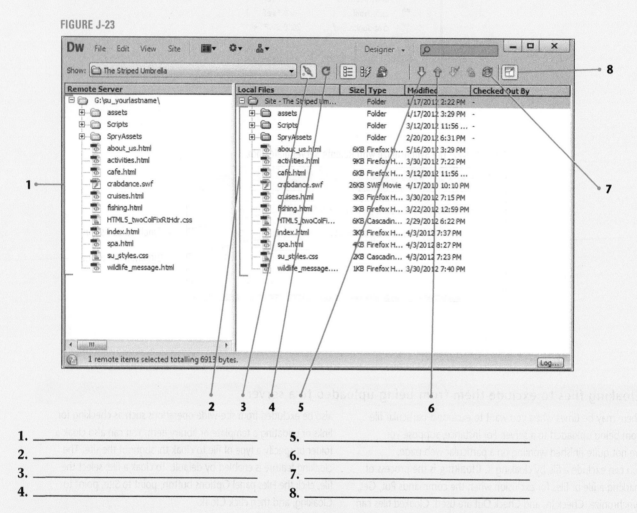

FIGURE J-23

1. _____
2. _____
3. _____
4. _____
5. _____
6. _____
7. _____
8. _____

Match each of the following terms with the statement that best describes it.

9. **Check out feature**
10. **Link Checker**
11. **Upload**
12. **Cloak files**
13. **Synchronize**
14. **Download**

a. To transfer files from your computer to a remote server
b. To transfer files from a remote server to your computer
c. A command that allows you to transfer only the latest versions of files
d. Allows a file to be used by only one user at a time
e. Used to check for orphaned files and broken links
f. To mark files for exclusion from several Commands, including Put, Get, Synchronize, check In, and check Out

Select the best answer from the following list of choices.

15. The process that involves requesting unbiased users who are not connected to the project to use to evaluate a site is called:

    a. a trial run.

    b. a test drive.

    c. a clinical trial.

    d. a site usability test.

16. What technology describes the recent evolution of Web applications that facilitate and promote information sharing among Internet users?

    a. Web 1.0 technology

    b. Web 2.0 technology

    c. Web 3.0 technology

    d. Virtual technology

17. A point of contact can include:

    a. A telephone number.

    b. An email address.

    c. A physical address.

    d. All of the above.

18. Which of the following is not an Html report?

    a. Untitled Documents

    b. Missing Alt Tag

    c. Design Notes

    d. Combinable Nested Font Tags

19. Which button is used to validate HTML code?

    a.

    b.

    c.

    d.

20. Media queries are used to:

    a. Identify the device that is being used to view a page.

    b. Direct which style sheet a page should use for a specific device.

    c. Prevent users from needing horizontal scroll bars to view page content.

    d. All of the above.

Skills Review

Important: *If you did not create this website in Unit B and maintain it during the preceding units, you will need to create a local site root folder for this website and define the website using files your instructor will provide. See the "Read This Before You Begin" section for more detailed instructions.*

1. **Collect feedback.**
   a. Start Dreamweaver, then open the Blooms & Bulbs website.
   b. Write a paragraph describing how a usability test would be conducted for a website.
   c. List three different methods for collecting feedback from website users.
   d. List four good points of contact that could be included on a website for website users to use to contact the company.
   e. Describe three social networking sites that you would consider using for a website to add interaction with users.

2. **Run site reports.**
   a. Run a site report for untitled documents.
   b. Add page titles to any pages you find without a title.
   c. Run a site report for missing alt text.
   d. Add alternate text to any page elements that are listed with missing alt text.
   e. Run a site report for orphaned files.
   f. If you see any orphaned files listed, evaluate whether they should be deleted or linked to a page.
   g. Run a site report for broken links, and repair any broken links that you find.

3. **Validate HTML and CSS markup.**
   a. Open the index page.
   b. Use the W3C Validation button to validate the HTML markup.
   c. Repeat Step b to validate each page in the site and note any errors that you find.
   d. Go to the W3C Validator at jigsaw.w3.org/css-validator, then validate the blooms_styles.css file against CSS level 3 standards.

4. **Test for browser compatibility.**
   a. With the index page open, use the Browser Compatibility panel to check for browser compatibility.
   b. Connect to Adobe BrowserLab, then preview the index page using three different browsers.
   c. Close Adobe BrowserLab.

5. **Use media queries.**
   a. With the index page open, use the Multiscreen preview to preview the page with the default settings.
   b. Write a plan to improve the appearance of the page so you can eliminate the need for horizontal scroll bars when the page is viewed on a tablet or smart phone.

6. **Evaluate and present a website to a client.**
   a. Check your pages against your wireframes to see if you developed each page according to plan.
   b. Write a plan to present the website to a client, including the software you will use.

7. **Set up remote access.**
   a. Open the Manage Sites dialog box, then add a new server using either FTP or Local/Network for the connection.
   b. If you don't have the information to use FTP, create a folder named **blooms_yourlastname** on your local computer to set up the Local/Network connection.
   c. Test the connection with the Test button. When you are successful, close the Manage Sites dialog box and view the Remote server in the Files panel.
   d. Return to Local view.

Skills Review (continued)

8. Publish a site.

  a. Use the Put File(s) button to upload the local site root folder to the remote server.

  b. Expand the Files panel to view both the remote site and the local site files, then compare your screen to Figure J-24.

  c. Collapse the Files panel, close all open files, then close Dreamweaver.

FIGURE J-24

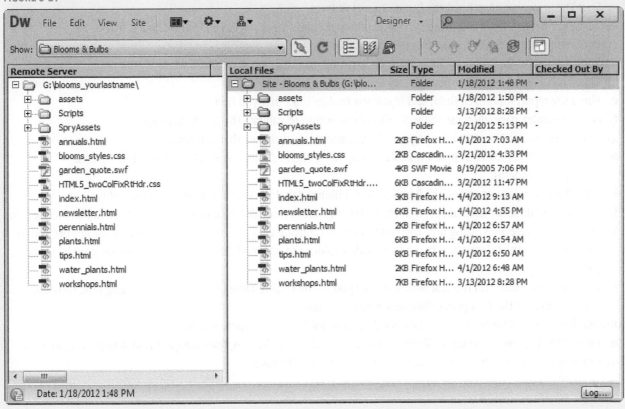

Important: *If you did not create the following websites in Unit B and maintain them during the preceding units, you must create a local site root folder for the websites in the following exercises and define the websites using files your instructor will provide. See the "Read This Before You Begin" section for more detailed instructions.*

Independent Challenge 1

You have been hired to create a website for a river expedition company named Rapids Transit. The owner's name is Mike Andrew. The website is almost complete and you are ready to run reports and conduct tests to make sure the site is ready to publish.

a. Start Dreamweaver, then open the Rapids Transit website.

b. Run a site report for untitled documents and add page titles to any pages you find without a title.

c. Run a site report for missing alt text and add alternate text to any page elements that are listed with missing alt text.

d. Run a site report for orphaned files. If you see any orphaned files listed, evaluate whether they should be deleted or linked to a page.

e. Run a site report for broken links, and repair any broken links that you find.

f. Open the index page, then use the W3C Validation button to validate the HTML markup.

g. Open and validate the rest of the pages in the site and note any errors that you find.

h. Go to the W3C Validator at jigsaw.w3.org/css-validator, then validate the rapids_transit.css file against CSS level 3 standards.

i. With the index page open, use the Browser Compatibility panel to check for browser compatibility.

j. Connect to Adobe BrowserLab, preview the index page using three different browsers, then close Adobe BrowserLab.

k. Open the Manage Sites dialog box, then add a new server using either FTP or Local/Network for the connection. If you don't have the information to use FTP, create a folder named **rapids_yourlastname** on your local computer to set up a Local/Network connection.

l. Test the connection with the Test button. When you are successful, close the Manage Sites dialog box, view the Remote server in the Files panel, then return to Local view.

m. Use the Put File(s) button to upload the local site root folder to the remote server.

n. Expand the Files panel to view both the remote site and the local site files, then compare your screen to Figure J-25.

o. Collapse the Files panel, close all open files, then close Dreamweaver.

FIGURE J-25

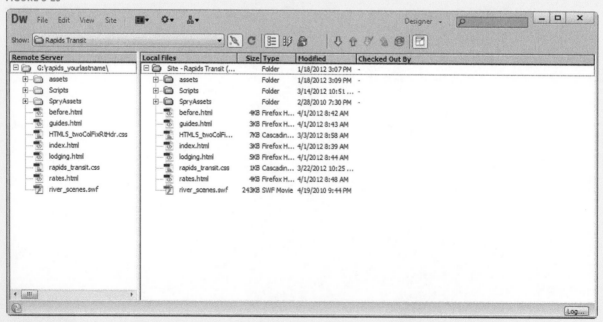

Independent Challenge 2

You are ready to do the final check on the TripSmart website before you present it to the owner, Thomas Howard, for his approval. You also set up the remote server information to upload the files after you receive the authorization.

a. Start Dreamweaver, then open the TripSmart website.

b. Run a site report for untitled documents and add page titles to any pages you find without a title.

c. Run a site report for missing alt text and add alternate text to any page elements that are listed with missing alt text.

d. Run a site report for orphaned files. If you see any orphaned files listed, evaluate whether they should be deleted or linked to a page.

e. Run a site report for broken links, and repair any broken links that you find.

f. Open the index page, then use the W3C Validation button to validate the HTML markup.

g. Open and validate the rest of the pages in the site and note any errors that you find.

h. Go to the W3C Validator at jigsaw.w3.org/css-validator, then validate the tripsmart_styles.css file against CSS level 3 standards.

i. With the index page open, use the Browser Compatibility panel to check for browser compatibility.

j. Connect to Adobe BrowserLab, preview the index page using three different browsers, then close Adobe BrowserLab.

k. Open the Manage Sites dialog box, then add a new server using either FTP or Local/Network for the connection. If you don't have the information to use FTP, create a folder named **tripsmart_yourlastname** on your local computer to set up a Local/Network connection.

l. Test the connection with the Test button. When you are successful, close the Manage Sites dialog box, view the Remote server in the Files panel, then return to Local view.

m. Use the Put File(s) button to upload the local site root folder to the remote server.

n. Expand the Files panel to view both the remote site and the local site files, then compare your screen to Figure J-26.

o. Collapse the Files panel, close all open files, then close Dreamweaver.

FIGURE J-26

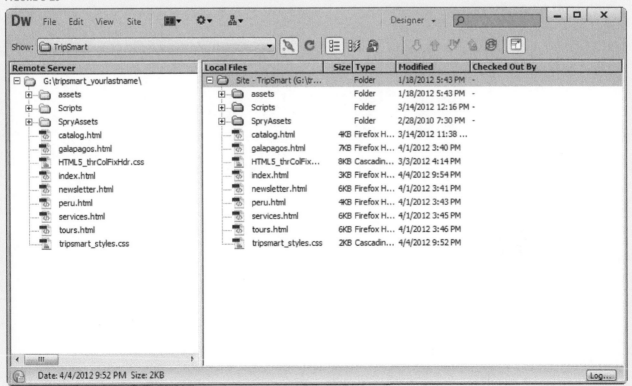

Independent Challenge 3

You are interested in learning more about designing websites for multiple devices. You would like to understand how media queries work and what other options besides media queries are available to you as a designer. You decide to visit several websites and view them on your desktop, a tablet, and a smart phone.

a. Connect to the Internet, then go to Table 22 at table22branson.com.

b. View the website on a desktop, then open it on a tablet or smart phone.

c. Figure 27 shows the website viewed on a desktop. Figure 28 shows the website viewed on an iPad. Notice how the pages are different in content and appearance.

d. View the page source to see if you can find any clues as to how this site adapts itself to the device being used to view it.

FIGURE J-27

FIGURE J-28

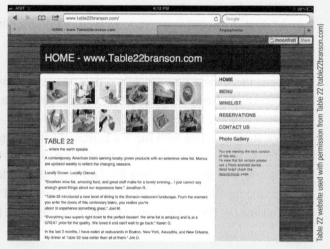

Real Life Independent Challenge

This assignment will continue to build on your personal website that you created in Unit B. In Unit C, you created and developed your index page. In Unit D, you added a page with either an ordered or an unordered list, and a style sheet with at least two rules. In Unit E, you added a page that included at least two images. In Unit F, you added a page that included several inks and an image map. In Unit G, you created a page based on a CSS layout with a small table for tabular data. In Unit H, you added a media file. In Unit I, you added a form to a page. In this unit, you will be checking your site for broken links, orphaned files, untitled documents, and missing alt text. You will check the files against HTML and CSS standards and use Adobe BrowserLab to view the pages using several different browsers.

    a. Run the following site reports: Untitled Documents and Missing Alt Text.

    b. Check for broken links and orphaned files.

    c. Use the W3C Validation button to validate the code for each page.

    d. Go to jigsaw.w3.org/css-validator/ and validate your style sheets.

    e. Set up your remote server and upload the website files.

After you are satisfied with your work, verify the following:

    a. The site does not have any pages without titles or media files without alternate text.

    b. The site does not have any broken links or orphaned files.

    c. The style sheets meet CSS3 compliance.

    d. Each page passes HTML validation.

    e. Each pages displays appropriately in at least three different browsers.

Visual Workshop

You are ready to do the final check on, and publish, the files in the Carolyne's Creations website. Run the appropriate site reports and verify that your links all work correctly. Validate your page code and your style sheets. View the pages on several browsers to verify that the content displays correctly. When you are finished, set up a remote server and upload all files. Compare your remote and local files lists to Figure J-29.

FIGURE J-29

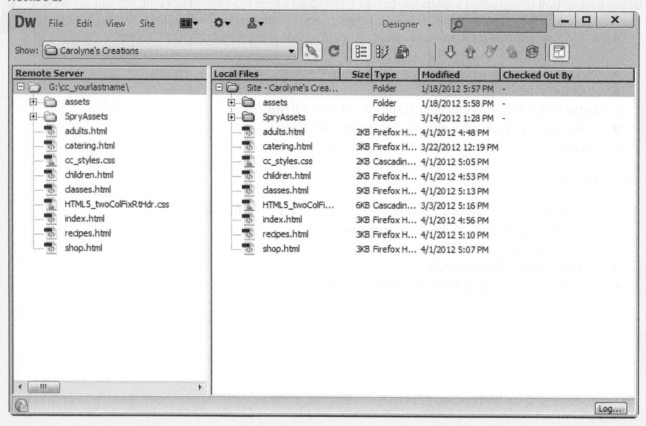

Getting Started with Photoshop CS6

Photoshop CS6 is the latest version of the revolutionary, best-selling photo editing software from Adobe. Photoshop offers a set of powerful tools and easy-to-use panels that let you perform all kinds of image editing, from simple to complex. In this unit, you will learn essential skills for viewing and navigating a document and investigate the basic building blocks of a Photoshop image. The information you learn in this unit will form an important foundation for everything else covered in the book.  MegaPixel is a graphic arts service bureau and design agency. Laura Jacobs, the owner of MegaPixel, has hired you as a production artist. Your job will involve using Photoshop CS6 to address a variety of image-processing issues to produce high-quality Photoshop files.

OBJECTIVES

Define photo editing software

Start Photoshop and view the workspace

Use the Zoom tool and the Hand tool

Save a document and understand file formats

Understand and change resolution

Change image size

Create a new document

Transform the canvas

Crop an image

Crop an image to a specific size

Defining Photo Editing Software

Photoshop CS6 is photo editing software. In a nutshell, Photoshop offers you a variety of tools, menu commands, and panels that allow you to edit and manipulate **digital images**—images that you get from a digital camera, scan from a photograph or a slide, or create from scratch. Photoshop CS6 allows you to edit images in a variety of ways in order to enhance or process them for different types of uses, such as for print or for the web.  Laura Jacobs invites you to her office for an orientation meeting on your first day at MegaPixel. The conversation turns to Photoshop, and you share with her some of your experiences with the many uses of the application.

The following are just some of the tasks you can use Photoshop CS6 to accomplish:

- **Acquire images from a variety of devices**

  Transfer images from CDs, DVDs, digital cameras, and scanners into Photoshop. Download images from the web and open them in Photoshop. With some digital cameras, you can use Photoshop to preview images from your camera before you open them in Photoshop.

- **Apply basic processing procedures**

  Crop an image to get rid of unwanted elements or to focus more dramatically on your subject. Rotate an image if it is upside down, on its side, or crooked. Resize an image so that it prints to fit the frame you just bought. All of these are essential and practical procedures that Photoshop can do quickly and efficiently.

- **Improve the color and quality of images**

  Photoshop has many sophisticated color tools that allow you to enhance the appearance of photographs. You can brighten images that are too dark, or darken images that are overexposed. Turn an otherwise plain image into something striking with a quick increase in contrast. Make the color more vivid or remove it entirely to create a dramatic black-and-white image.

- **Fix image flaws**

  Photoshop's retouching tools and production filters offer you many options for fixing flaws in an image, such as dust and scratches, graininess, and red eye. You can also retouch photos of your family and friends—best of all, retouch and restore old family photos and give them as gifts to be treasured. Figure A-1 shows an image with various effects applied.

- **Add special effects**

  If you can think of it, you can probably do it in Photoshop. Turn a brand-new photo into an old-looking photo, or take a typical black-and-white photo and make it look hand-tinted. Add grain effects or blur effects to give an ordinary photo a custom look. Distort photos by giving your friends big heads on little bodies or making your sister appear to be a giant 40-foot woman crashing her way down Fifth Avenue. Photoshop makes your imagination a reality.

- **Batch-process image files**

  Photoshop is also a production workhorse. For example, Photoshop can automatically process a batch of files for one type of output, such as professional printing, and then reprocess the same batch of files by reducing their physical size and file size, and changing their format for use on the web. And that's literally with the click of one button.

- **Output to various devices**

  You can use Photoshop to create graphics for slide shows, video presentations, and electronic billboards. Photoshop is used every day to create elements for on-screen animation projects. Photoshop comes complete with software you can use to save images for your cell phone or your iPod. Photoshop can even process a bunch of different-sized images into one contact sheet.

FIGURE A-1: Various effects with an old photo

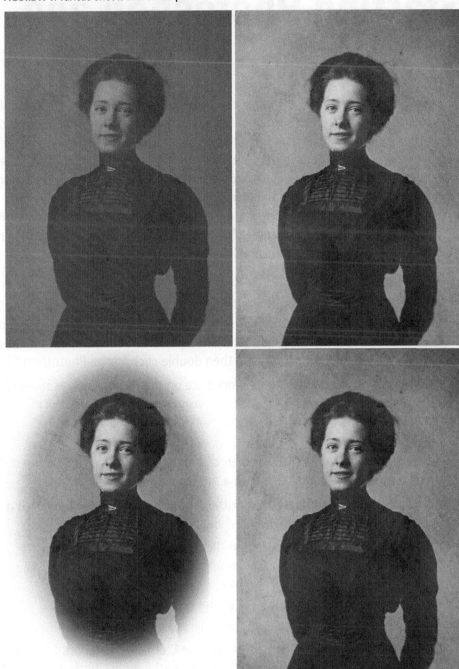

Understanding graphics programs

The term **graphics program** can refer to a wide range of software applications. Generally speaking, though, graphics programs fall into three basic categories: bitmap, vector, and animation. You can think of **bitmap graphics** (also called **raster graphics**) as very sophisticated mosaics. Instead of using colored tiles, bitmap graphics use **pixels**—colored squares that are so small that your eye perceives only the whole image, not the pixels themselves. All digital photographs are bitmap graphics, and all Photoshop images are bitmap graphics. **Vector graphics** are often created on a computer, not through scanning or downloading. Many times, vector-based programs are called **draw programs**, because vector graphics are created by drawing lines, creating objects, and filling them with color. Adobe Illustrator is a vector-based program. Finally, **animation programs**, such as Adobe Flash, use timeline structures to create sequences of graphics—both bitmap and vector—then create the illusion of motion and animation by presenting that sequence of images so quickly that your eye perceives movement.

Starting Photoshop and Viewing the Workspace

You start Photoshop by launching the program or by opening a Photoshop file that is already created. Once in Photoshop, before you open or create a new document, the **workspace** becomes available. The workspace consists of the Menu bar at the top of the screen, the Options bar below the Menu bar, the Tools panel on the left of the screen, and the dock of panels on the right of the screen. Most of the panels are expanded while a few others are closed and represented by thumbnail images. Clicking a panel thumbnail opens the panel. The Menu bar contains the Photoshop menus and the Minimize, Restore, and Close buttons. You can rearrange the elements of the workspace to your liking to create and save your own customized workspace. ██████ Laura has shown you your office and new computer. You start Photoshop and familiarize yourself with the workspace.

STEPS

1. **Click the Start button ⊕ on the taskbar, point to All Programs, click Adobe Design Standard CS6 (or the name of your specific Adobe Creative Suite package) if necessary, then click Adobe Photoshop CS6 (Win); or Open the Finder, double-click Applications, double-click Adobe Photoshop CS6, then double-click Adobe Photoshop CS6 (Mac)**

2. **Verify that Essentials is the chosen workspace on the Options bar, as shown in Figure A-2.**
   The Essentials workspace is one of many preset workspaces in Photoshop. Different workspaces are designed for different tasks. For example, the Painting workspace opens a number of panels that are very useful when painting.

3. **Note the Tools panel on the left, then click the double arrows at the top of the Tools panel repeatedly to toggle between a single and double row of tools**

4. **In the panels dock on the right, click the tabs of each panel to show each panel**
   These are the panels that are displayed when the Essentials workspace is chosen.

5. **Click Window on the Menu bar, then click Character**
   The Character panel opens. Note that by default it is grouped with the Paragraph panel. Use the Window menu to access all of the panels in Photoshop.

6. **Drag the Character panel name tab to the center of the workspace**
   The Character panel is separated from the Paragraph panel.

7. **Drag the Paragraph panel name tab over the Character panel until you see a light blue frame around the Character panel, then release the mouse button**
   The panels are grouped once again.

8. **Double-click the name tab of any visible panels in the panels dock**
   Double-clicking the name tab of an open panel minimizes the panel.

9. **Click the workspace list arrow on the Options bar, then click Reset Essentials**
   The panels are restored to their original locations.

FIGURE A-2: The Essentials workspace

Menu bar

Options bar

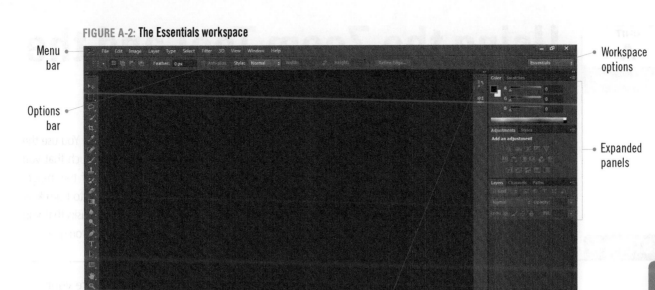

Workspace options

Expanded panels

Thumbnails of minimized panels

Getting help in Photoshop CS6

Whenever you have a question about what you're doing in Photoshop or want to learn more about a tool or a feature, remember that you always have the Help menu close at hand. Installing Photoshop on your computer automatically gives you access to Adobe's online help site.

To access Photoshop Help, click Help on the Menu bar, and then click Photoshop Online Help. The Photoshop Help page of the Adobe.com website opens in your browser. At the top of the page are help categories, such as What's new, Image adjustments, and Repair and restoration. Clicking a category brings you to that section of help and offers more specific topics within the chosen category. Clicking a topic opens a new web page with information about the chosen topic.

Managing the workspace

Think of the Photoshop workspace just as you would your own home or apartment; you want to have things how you like them and where you like them. For example, click the double arrows above the Tools panel to display the tools in one or two rows. Your biggest consideration with the workspace is always maximizing the room available to view the image you are working on. For this reason, managing the panels on the right of the window is important, because open panels can take up a lot of space in the Document window. Condensing panels by grouping them with other panels is a smart choice for maximizing working space. Minimizing panels is the best choice for keeping essential panels open but out of the way.

UNIT A

Photoshop CS6

Using the Zoom Tool and the Hand Tool

When you work with Photoshop files, you will often be viewing them from different perspectives. You use the Zoom tool to enlarge and reduce the image on your screen. When the image is enlarged so much that you can't see the whole image, you can use the Hand tool to scroll around to see other areas of the image. Because the Zoom and Hand tools are used so often when working in Photoshop, it's important to learn keyboard commands to access the tools. See Table A-1 for a list of useful quick keys. ▓▓▓▓▓ Laura asks that you open a file and demonstrate your abilities with using the Zoom and Hand tools and viewing the workspace.

STEPS

1. **Click File on the Menu bar, click Open, navigate to the location where you store your Data Files, click PS A-1.psd, then click Open**
   Figure A-3 shows the opened file in the default workspace. The name of the file appears in the document tab, which is located in the upper-left corner of the file.

> **QUICK TIP**
> Double-clicking the Hand tool on the Tools panel also fits the image on the screen.

2. **Click View on the Menu bar, then click Fit on Screen**
   This command resizes the view to fit the entire canvas on your screen. The current magnification is listed in the document tab and also in the lower-left corner of the document window.

> **QUICK TIP**
> The pixels are outlined in white. To hide the white outline, press [Ctrl][H] (Win) or [⌘][H] (Mac).

3. **Click the Zoom tool 🔍 on the Tools panel, position it over the bird's eye, then click the eye eight times to zoom in on the image**
   Each time you click, the image is enlarged. Note that the magnification level on the document tab changes to show the percentage at which you are viewing the image each time you click.

4. **Click the Hand tool ✋ on the Tools panel, then click and drag the Hand tool pointer over the image to see other areas of the bird**

5. **Double-click ✋, click 🔍, position it directly above the eye, drag the Zoom tool pointer to create a marquee as shown in Figure A-4, then release the mouse button**
   As you drag, a dotted rectangle, called a **marquee**, appears around the area that you drag over. When you release the Zoom tool pointer, the area inside the marquee is enlarged in the window. Dragging the Zoom tool on the image is called a **marquee zoom**. Make sure the Scrubby Zoom check box is not checked on the Options bar. If the Scrubby Zoom check box is checked, you will not be able to create a marquee zoom using the Zoom tool.

> **QUICK TIP**
> Press and hold [Ctrl] (Win) or [⌘] (Mac) then press [-] repeatedly to reduce the view. See Table A-1 for other useful quick keys.

6. **Press and hold [Alt] (Win) or [option] (Mac), then click ten times anywhere on the image**
   The image's magnification level is reduced. When you press and hold [Alt] (Win) or [option] (Mac), the Zoom tool shows a minus sign, indicating that it will reduce the view, rather than magnify it.

7. **Press and hold [Ctrl] (Win) or [⌘] (Mac) then press [+] repeatedly to enlarge the view**

8. **Click View on the Menu bar, then click Fit on Screen**

Accessing the Zoom and Hand tools

When you're working with various tools, you will find yourself having to continuously switch to the Zoom tool to enlarge your view or to the Hand tool to change your view. This will slow you down. Take time to practice and master the quick keys that allow you to temporarily switch to the Zoom or Hand tool while remaining in the current tool. Press and hold [Spacebar] to access the Hand tool. Press and hold [Spacebar] [Ctrl] (Win) or [Spacebar] [⌘] (Mac) to access the Zoom Plus tool. Press and hold [Spacebar] [Alt] (Win) or [Spacebar] [option] (Mac) to access the Zoom Minus tool. When you release the quick keys, the current tool is active again. These three keyboard commands will help you enormously in speeding up your workflow.

FIGURE A-3: Viewing the document in the Essentials workspace

FIGURE A-4: Creating a marquee with the Zoom tool

This area will be magnified

TABLE A-1: Useful quick keys

command	Windows	Macintosh
Open	[Ctrl][O]	⌘[O]
Fit on Screen	[Ctrl][0] (zero)	⌘[0] (zero)
Fit on Screen	Double-click Hand tool	Double-click Hand tool
Zoom In	[Ctrl][+]	⌘[+]
Zoom Out	[Ctrl][-]	⌘[-]
Access Zoom Plus tool	[Spacebar][Ctrl]	[Spacebar]⌘
Access Zoom Minus tool	[Spacebar][Alt]	[Spacebar][option]
Access Hand tool	[Spacebar]	[Spacebar]

Saving a Document and Understanding File Formats

File formats are specific types of computer code that you use to save an image for various types of output or use with other applications. Table A-2 shows a list of common file formats you can use with Photoshop. PSD stands for Photoshop Document and is the basic format for saving a Photoshop file. All other Adobe programs can open and/or place a file saved as a PSD. ████ You refresh your knowledge of file formats by saving the bird image as a PSD, a TIFF, and a JPEG.

1. **Click File on the Menu bar, click Save As, then navigate to the location where you store your Data Files**

2. **Type birdie_PS-A in the File name text box (Win) or the Save As text box (Mac), click the Format list arrow, click Photoshop (*.PSD, *.PDD), if necessary, then click Save**
   The filename in the document tab changes to birdie_PS-A.psd.

3. **If the Photoshop Format Options dialog box opens, click OK to close it**
   This dialog box is for maximizing the compatibility of the file with other programs. To prevent the dialog box from opening each time you save a document, click the Don't show again check box in the dialog box before clicking OK.

4. **Click File on the Menu bar, click Save As, click the Format list arrow, click TIFF (*.TIF, *.TIFF), then compare your dialog box to Figure A-5**

5. **Click Save, then click OK in the TIFF Options dialog box**
   TIFF is an acronym for Tagged Image File Format. TIFF is a standard file format for placing digital images for print in page layout programs.

6. **Click File on the Menu bar, click Save As, click the Format list arrow, click JPEG (*.JPG, *.JPEG, *.JPE), then click Save**
   The JPEG Options dialog box opens, as shown in Figure A-6. The JPEG file format is a lossy compression format often used for images on the web and for images that will be emailed. Because it compresses a file by removing data, the JPEG format always reduces an image's file size.

7. **Drag the Quality slider to 6**
   The file size is reduced to approximately 176 KB.

8. **Click OK, click File on the Menu bar, then click Close**

TABLE A-2: Standard file formats for Photoshop files

file format	extension	use
Bitmap	.bmp	Bitmap images, popular with Windows operating systems
CompuServe GIF	.gif	Web graphics
Photoshop EPS	.eps	Photoshop graphics with live type or shape layers
Photoshop PSD	.psd	Basic format for all Photoshop documents
JPEG	.jpg, .jpeg	Web graphics, images to be emailed
PICT	.pct, .pict	Graphics to be used in presentation programs, such as PowerPoint
PNG	.png	High-quality web graphics
TIFF	.tif, .tiff	Graphics to be used for print in page layout programs

FIGURE A-5: Save As dialog box

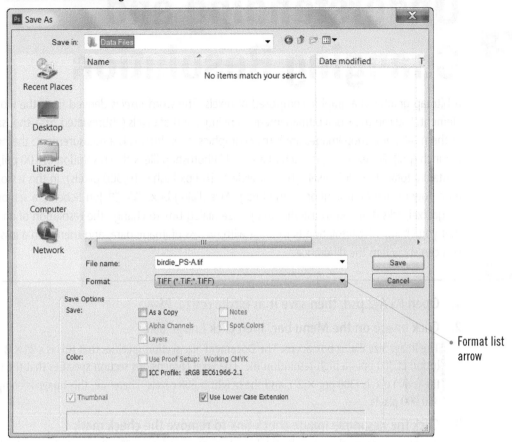

Format list arrow

FIGURE A-6: JPEG Options dialog box

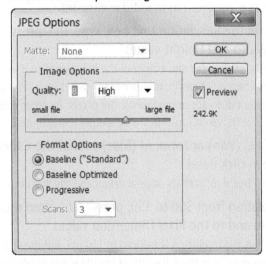

Choosing the right file format

In the real world, working with file formats is seldom challenging. You'll save the vast majority of your files as basic PSD documents, and if you're saving a file at work or for a client, usually you'll be told which format to choose. The key to choosing a file format is understanding what the file will be used for. For web graphics, you'll usually choose JPEG. For PowerPoint graphics, you'll usually choose PICT. With a little bit of experience, you will soon be comfortable knowing which file format to choose for a given output or to interface with another software package.

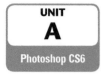

Understanding and Changing Resolution

A bitmap graphic is a graphic composed of pixels. The word *pixel* is derived from the words picture and element. You can think of a bitmap image as being a grid of pixels (abbreviated *px*)—thousands or millions of them. All Photoshop images are bitmap graphics. **Resolution** is a measurement: the number of pixels per inch (ppi). For example, if you had a 1" × 1" Photoshop file with a resolution of 100 ppi, that file would contain a total of 10,000 pixels (100 px wide × 100 px high = 10,000 pixels). In this lesson, you'll investigate how to change resolution in the Image Size dialog box. ▰▰▰ Jon Schenk, a senior art director at MegaPixel, asks that you to use the Image Size dialog box to change the resolution of an image. He asks that you change the resolution twice, first with no loss of image data, and then with a loss of data so that you can show him the difference.

STEPS

1. **Open PS A-2.psd, then save it as** birdie resize_PS-A

2. **Click** Image **on the Menu bar, then click** Image Size

   The Image Size dialog box opens. The Document Size section specifies that this is a 2" × 2" file with a resolution of 300 ppi—a high-resolution file. The Pixel Dimensions section specifies that the full width of the file is 600 pixels (300 ppi × 2"), and the height is 600 pixels. Therefore, this image is composed of exactly 360,000 pixels.

3. **Click the** Resample Image check box **to remove the check mark**

   Resampling means changing the total pixel count of an image. The Resample Image check box is perhaps the most important option in this dialog box. When the Resample Image check box is not checked, the total number of pixels in the image must remain the same. In other words, no matter how you resize the image or change the resolution, no pixels can be added or discarded.

4. **Double-click** 300 **in the Resolution text box, type** 100, **press [Tab], then note the changes in the Width and Height values**

   As shown in Figure A-7, the width and height of the file change to 6 inches. Because the pixel dimension of 600 pixels cannot change, when the number of pixels per inch is reduced to 100, the file must enlarge to 6" wide × 6" inches tall to accommodate all the pixels. In other words, no pixels were added or discarded with the change in resolution—they were simply redistributed.

5. **Press and hold [Alt] (Win) or [option] (Mac) so that the Cancel button changes to the Reset button, then click** Reset

   The Image Size dialog box returns to its original values and the Resample Image check box is checked.

6. **Change the resolution from** 300 **to** 150, **press [Tab], then note the changes to the Width and Height values and to the Pixel Dimension values**

   As shown in Figure A-8, the resolution is reduced to 150 ppi, but the width and height remain at 2 inches. The Pixel Dimensions show that the full width of the file is 300 pixels (150 ppi × 2") and the full height is 300 pixels. This means that, if you click OK, the total number of pixels will be 90,000. 75% of the original 360,000 pixels will be discarded because of the reduction in resolution from 300 to 150 ppi.

7. **Click** OK

   Though the image doesn't look much different on your screen, 75% of its original data has been discarded.

8. **Save your work, then close birdie resize_PS-A.psd**

FIGURE A-7: **Decreasing resolution without resampling**

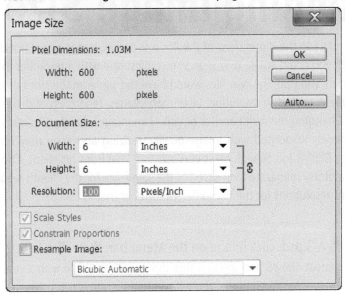

FIGURE A-8: **Decreasing resolution with resampling**

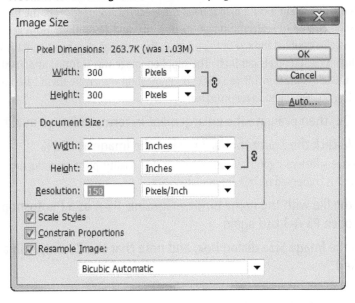

Understanding the difference between image size and file size

Try not to confuse the terms image size and file size. Image size refers to the physical dimensions of the image—its width and height. So if you say an image is 8" × 10", you are referring to its image size. File size refers to how big the file is in computer memory—how much storage space it takes up on your computer. If an image is 42 MB (megabytes), that is its file size. Remember that every pixel in an image increases the file size of the image. Therefore, resolution and image size both affect file size. The greater the resolution—the more pixels per inch—the greater the file size. The greater the image size—the more inches of pixels—the greater the file size. If you were printing an 8" × 10" color poster at 300 ppi, your file size would be somewhere close to 27 MB, and the image would be composed of more than 7 million pixels!

Getting Started with Photoshop CS6

Photoshop 11

Photoshop CS6

Changing Image Size

Image size refers to the dimensions of the Photoshop file. Image size is not dependent on resolution; in other words, you could create two 3" × 5" inch files, one with a resolution of 72 ppi and the other with a resolution of 300 ppi. The two files would have the same image size but different resolutions. Image size is, however, related to resolution: all bitmap images, regardless of their physical dimensions, have a resolution. Changing the width and/or height of an image will affect its resolution. Also, because resolution is so closely associated with image quality, resizing an image may have a negative effect on its appearance. Jon Schenk gives you a 2" × 2" file from his client. The file needs to be printed at 4"× 4" for a glossy magazine then saved at the same size for the client's website. You create two files at two different resolutions for the two different types of use.

1. **Open PS A-3.psd, click Image on the Menu bar, then click Image Size**

   The Document Size section specifies that this is a 2" × 2" file with a resolution of 300 ppi. The Pixel Dimensions section specifies that the full width of the file is 600 pixels (300 ppi × 2") and the height is 600 pixels. Thus, this image is composed of exactly 360,000 pixels.

2. **Verify that the Resample Image check box is checked**

   This file is 2"× 2" and you need it to be 4" × 4".

3. **Change the Width value to 4, then compare your dialog box to Figure A-9**

   In order to be used in a color magazine at the specified size of 4" × 4", the file must be 300 ppi at that size. Photoshop is able to scale the image to that size and resolution. However, note the pixel dimensions. Because we've doubled the size of the original, the new size now must contain 1,440,000 pixels to maintain a resolution of 300 pixels per inch. The supplied image was scanned at 360,000 total pixels. Where did all the new pixels come from? If you click OK, Photoshop will create them based on information from existing pixels in a process called **interpolation**.

4. **Click OK, then evaluate the enlargement in terms of image quality**

5. **Double-click the Zoom tool 🔍 to view the image at 100%**

   The image still looks good overall. However, for quality print reproduction, this image is unacceptable because it is composed of 75% interpolated data.

6. **Save the file with the name birdie magazine_PS-A as a Photoshop document, close it, then open PS A-3.psd again**

7. **Open the Image Size dialog box, and note that the Resample Image check box is checked**

   Now you will resize the file to be used on the client's website.

8. **Change the Width and Height values to 4, change the Resolution to 72, then compare your dialog box to Figure A-10**

   As shown in the Pixel Dimensions section, the file size will be reduced from 1.03 MB to 243KB. Even though the image was doubled in size, the reduction in resolution from 300 ppi to 72 ppi resulted in the need for fewer than 25% of the number of original pixels.

9. **Click OK, then evaluate the enlargement in terms of image quality**

   Viewed at 100%, the image looks great on screen, which is our goal, given that it will be used on a website. Even though Photoshop has discarded more than 75% of the original number of pixels, the reduced image contains only original data and no interpolated data.

10. **Save the file as a .jpg file with a Quality setting of 10 named birdie web graphic_PS-A, then close it**

FIGURE A-9: Increasing image size and resampling pixels

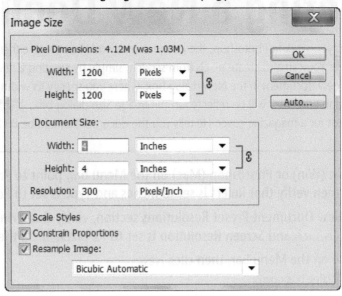

FIGURE A-10: Decreasing image size and resampling pixels

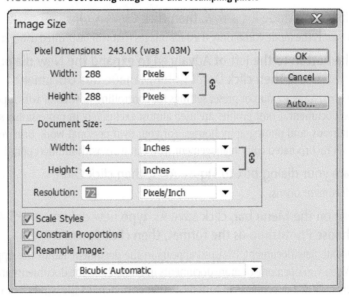

What is "hi-res" exactly?

Pixels must be small to create the representation of a photographic image—you want to see the image, not the pixels. 300 ppi is considered a high resolution for any file that will be professionally printed. For a home desktop printer, 150 ppi is generally enough resolution for a good-looking print. For the web and other "on-screen" graphics, the standard resolution is low—just 72 ppi. "Hi-res" is an abbreviation for "high-resolution", and generally speaking, a hi-res file pertains only to the world of printing. So when you think of hi-res, think of images—color or black-and-white—printing at a high quality, like in a magazine or a poster. This type of reproduction requires the industry standard of 300 pixels per inch.

Creating a New Document

Usually when you work in Photoshop, the image you're working on was either scanned or captured by a digital camera. You can also create pixels from scratch, simply by creating a new document in Photoshop. You create a new document in the New dialog box, where you specify its width, height, and its resolution. The information you enter will be reflected in the Image Size dialog box. ▄▄▄▄ Jon asks you to create a new document for a magazine cover. He tells you the document should be 8.125" × 11.25".

1. **Click** Edit **(Win) or** Photoshop **(Mac) on the Menu bar, point to** Preferences, **click** Units & Rulers, **then verify that Rulers is set to Inches and Type is set to Points**

2. **In the New Document Preset Resolutions section, verify that Print Resolution is set to 300 pixels/inch and Screen Resolution is set to 72 pixels/inch, then click OK**

3. **Click** File **on the Menu bar, then click** New

   The New dialog box opens.

4. **Click the** list arrow **next to Width, then click** Inches

5. **Change the Width value to** 8.125, **change the Height value to** 11.25, **then change the Resolution value to** 300

   You set the resolution to 300 ppi because you know in advance that the file will be used on a magazine cover.

6. **Click the** Color Mode list arrow, **then click** CMYK Color

   CMYK Color is the mode commonly used for images that will be printed using traditional printing methods.

7. **Click the button to the left of Advanced to expand the New dialog box, click the** Color Profile list arrow, **then click** Don't Color Manage this Document

   A **color profile** is a group of preset settings for controlling how color will appear on your monitor and in a printed document. Color profiles are used almost exclusively in professional settings such as ad agencies, service bureaus, and photography houses. For your own personal work, or if you're working for a business that hasn't incorporated color management, you can work without incorporating default color profiles.

8. **Compare your dialog box to Figure A-11, then click** OK

   A new document opens.

9. **Click** File **on the Menu bar, click** Save As, **type** new document_PS-A **in the File name text box, choose** Photoshop **as the format, then click** Save

   The filename new document_PS-A.psd appears in the document tab in the upper-left corner of the document. When you open one or more documents in Photoshop, the documents are docked together as tabbed documents. Click a document tab to activate that document in the window or rearrange the order of documents by dragging a document tab to a new location in the dock. You can undock a document from a group by pulling the document tab out of the group. The document will be in a free-floating window.

10. **Close the document**

Using the Revert command

The Revert command on the File menu is one of your best methods for undoing lots of moves. When you choose the Revert command, the file is reverted to the same status it was at when you last saved. This can be an enormous help if you've made more changes than you can undo with the Undo command. Simply click File on the Menu bar, click Revert, and you're back to where you were when you last saved. This is another reason to remember to save often when you work, preferably every 10 minutes.

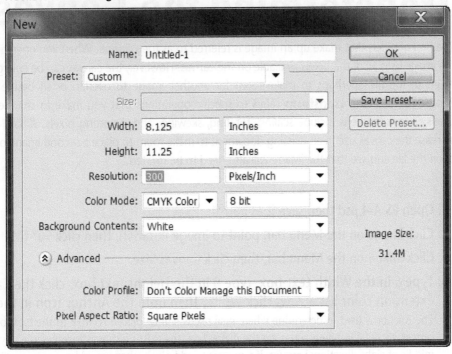

Introducing color models and color modes

A **color model** defines the colors we see and work with in digital images. RGB (red, green, blue), CMYK (cyan, magenta, yellow, black), and HSB (hue, saturation, brightness) are all color models, and each uses a different method for describing color.

In Photoshop, a document's **color mode** is listed on the Image menu. The color mode determines which color model is being used to display and print the image on which you are working. In most cases, you will be working in RGB Color for color images and Grayscale for black-and-white images. RGB Color is the standard color mode for working with color images. Choosing a color mode has an impact on which tools and file formats are available. All of Photoshop's tools and features are available to files in the RGB

Color mode. Many of them are not available to files in the CMYK Color mode. That's one of many reasons why it's best to do all of your color work in RGB, not CMYK.

All files that are printed professionally must at some point be CMYK files, so therefore it is likely that you will eventually switch to CMYK Color mode. However, most designers do all their color work in RGB Color then save a CMYK Color copy for printing. In other words, they use CMYK Color as part of the saving and output procedure, not part of the Photoshop design work itself. To change the color mode, click Image on the Menu bar, point to Mode, then click one of the color modes on the menu.

Transforming the Canvas

The bed of pixels that make up an image is referred to as the **canvas**. When you open an image, usually the image uses all of the pixels available on the canvas. However, the canvas can be enlarged to add more pixels to the file—perhaps to make room for another image to overlap or sit beside the original. In Photoshop, the term **transform** refers to specific operations that you make to change the location of pixels. Transformations include scaling, rotating, skewing, and distorting pixels. ░░░░ Jon asks you to increase the canvas size in an existing document to make room to place a second image over the first. You open the file and see that the image will also need to be rotated.

STEPS

1. **Open PS A-4.psd then save it as** parrots_PS-A

2. **Click** Image **on the Menu bar, point to** Image Rotation, **then click** 90° CW

3. **Click** Image **on the Menu bar, then click** Canvas Size

4. **Type** 6 **in the Width text box, type** 8 **in the Height text box, click the** Canvas extension color list arrow, **click** White, **then note the Anchor icon in the dialog box**

   The Anchor is used to determine where new pixels will be placed relative to the location of the existing canvas. By default, when you open the dialog box, the existing canvas is represented by the circle in the middle of eight directional arrows. If you were to add pixels, they would be evenly distributed on all sides of the existing canvas.

5. **Click the** lower-left arrow **in the grid**

   Clicking the lower-left arrow of the Anchor indicates that the new pixels will be positioned above and to the right of the existing canvas, as shown in Figure A-12.

6. **Click** OK, **then compare your canvas to Figure A-13**

   The canvas is enlarged to the new dimensions. White pixels are added above and to the right of the original canvas.

7. **Open PS A-5.psd, click** Image **on the Menu bar, point to** Image Rotation, **then click** Flip Canvas Horizontal

8. **Click** Select **on the Menu bar, click** All, **click** Edit **on the Menu bar, click** Copy, **then close the file without saving changes**

9. **Click** Edit **on the Menu bar, then click** Paste

   The image you copied is pasted into the parrots_PS-A.psd document.

QUICK TIP

For precise moves, use the arrow keys to move the image one pixel at a time. Press and hold [Shift] while pressing the arrow keys to move the image in 10-pixel increments.

10. **Click the** Move tool ▸⊕, **drag the** little parrot image **to the position shown in** Figure A-14, **save your work, click** OK **in the Photoshop Format Options dialog box, then close parrots_PS-A.psd**

"Res-ing up" when you have no choice

Inevitably, there will come a time when you have no other choice but to increase the resolution or the image size of a file and live with the results. In the working world, this often happens when a client delivers an original file at one size and wants you to use it at a much larger size. In that case, you'll want to be smart about how you increase the size or resolution of the image. Remember that Photoshop is running complex algorithms to create that new data. Don't make it more complicated by enlarging by odd numbers. For example, if you have a 3-inch square image that needs to print as a 5.75-inch square, double the image size to a 6-inch square. It's much easier for Photoshop to interpolate data with a simple doubling of the existing image size; this will result in a higher quality interpolation and a better result for your enlarged image. You can then import the image into your layout at 5.75".

FIGURE A-12: Canvas Size dialog box

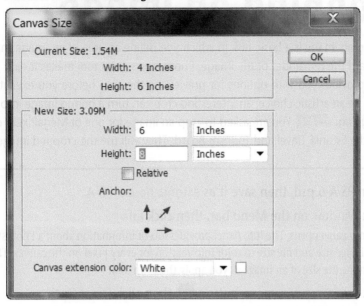

FIGURE A-13: Viewing new pixels added to the canvas

New white pixels
added to canvas

FIGURE A-14: Positioning a second image over the new pixels

Cropping an Image

Cropping an image is a basic task in which you define an area of an image that you want to keep and then discard the remainder of the image. Photoshop's Crop tool makes it easy to execute a simple crop and also provides you with options for previewing the crop before you execute it. Cropping an image can often be an artistic choice: an interesting crop can turn a boring image into something eye-catching and intriguing. You are asked to crop an image for one of MegaPixel's clients, the United States office of the Estonia Travel and Tourism Board. They will use the cropped image as an email postcard.

STEPS

1. **Open PS A-6.psd, then save it as** estonia house_PS-A

2. **Click** Window **on the Menu bar, then click** Info

    The Info panel opens. The Info panel provides lots of information about a Photoshop document, everything from image size and file size to color information for every pixel on the canvas. The Info panel can help you determine the size of an image as you apply the Crop tool.

3. **Click the** Info panel menu button ▦**, then click** Panel Options

    The Info Panel Options dialog box is where you choose what type of information you want to view about your document. By default, the Info panel does not display the document size or document dimensions.

    > **QUICK TIP**
    > Viewing document dimensions in the Info panel is faster than relying on the Image Size dialog box.

4. **Click the** Document Sizes **and the** Document Dimensions **check boxes to select them, if they are not already checked, then click** OK

    The document size (Doc) refers to the size of the file in megabytes. The document dimensions refer to the physical dimensions of the file. They are listed below "Doc" at the bottom of the Info panel.

    > **QUICK TIP**
    > Click the list arrow next to Unconstrained to choose from preset crop ratios.

5. **Click the** Crop tool ▦ **on the Tools panel**

    A dotted line, called a **crop marquee**, appears around the image with crop handles at each corner and at the horizontal and vertical centers. You can drag the crop handles to crop the image or use the Crop tool inside the marquee by dragging it over the image. The Options bar displays settings for the Crop tool, such as width, height, and ratio settings. The default ratio setting is Unconstrained which means that you can crop the image without being constrained by a specific width to height ratio.

6. **Verify that Unconstrained appears as the crop ratio setting on the Options bar.**

    Choosing Unconstrained removes the previously used settings for the Crop tool.

7. **Using Figure A-15 as a guide, drag the** Crop tool pointer **around the house so that only the house remains and the two other buildings are discarded, then release the Crop tool pointer**

    As you drag, the crop marquee is created. When you release the Crop tool, the dotted line changes to solid. The area inside the crop marquee is what will remain after the crop is executed. You can continue to adjust the marquee by dragging the crop handles to resize it.

    > **QUICK TIP**
    > You can also press [Enter] (Win) or [return] (Mac) to execute a crop. To remove a crop marquee from the canvas, click the Crop tool, then click Don't Crop or press [Esc].

8. **Double-click inside the** crop area, **then click outside the image to deselect**

    The image is cropped. The pixels outside the crop still remain even though you do not see them. If you crop the image again, the original image appears in its full size. If you would like to permanently discard the pixels outside of the crop area, click the Delete Cropped Pixels check box on the Options bar before you commit to the crop. The crop marquee remains active on the image unless you select another tool when you are done with the Crop tool.

9. **Compare your result to Figure A-16, save your work, then close estonia house_PS-A.psd**

FIGURE A-15: **Creating a crop marquee**

Click to
change ratio

Width setting

Height setting

Info panel

Crop border

Crop handles

FIGURE A-16: **The cropped image**

Setting opacity for the Crop tool

Opacity refers to how opaque something is. It is a term you will see used for a number of different Photoshop elements. When using the Crop tool, you can change the shield color and opacity of the area outside the crop using the Color and Opacity settings on the Options bar. Click the Set additional Crop options button ⚙ on the Options bar, then verify that the Enable Crop Shield check box is checked. To choose a new shield color, click the Color list arrow, then click Custom. The Color Picker dialog box opens. Choose a color, then click OK. You can also change the opacity by dragging the Opacity slider. This is a great option for

previewing the image as it would look if cropped, especially if you hide the crop marquee. The more you reduce the opacity, the more the pixels outside of the marquee will be visible, which is useful for seeing where your crop lines fall in the image and what would be discarded if you execute the crop. As a preview before cropping, many designers set the opacity to 50% while they're experimenting and then, when they think they've found a crop that they like, they increase the opacity to 100%. If you prefer to crop without using color or opacity, click the Enable Crop Shield check box to remove the check mark.

Cropping an Image to a Specific Size

The Crop tool has a number of options attached to it that enable the tool to execute more than just a simple crop. After you create a crop marquee, the Crop tool pointer becomes an arrow pointer when inside the marquee. Using the arrow, you can move the image to crop a different area. When the Crop tool pointer is outside of the crop marquee, it becomes a rotate pointer that allows you to rotate the image. You can also input specific width and height dimensions to create a crop marquee at a specific size. ■ A client of MegaPixel has provided you with an image they would like cropped vertically to 2.25" × 4". You crop the image and then rotate it in order to improve the appearance of the image.

STEPS

1. **Open PS A-7.psd, then save it as** hotel postcard_PS-A

QUICK TIP
Once you enter values in the Width and Height text boxes, you cannot drag the Crop tool pointer inside the crop marquee.

2. **Click the Crop tool** ⌗ **, type** 2.25 **in the Width text box on the Options bar, then type** 4 **in the Height text box**

3. **Drag any corner of the crop marquee to create a new crop marquee of any size**
   As you drag, the crop marquee is constrained proportionally to the values you input.

4. **Position the Crop tool pointer outside of the marquee**
   The pointer changes to a rotate pointer.

QUICK TIP
You can hide the marquee if you find it distracting by clicking [Ctrl][H] (Win) or ⌘[H] (Mac).

5. **Using Figure A-17 as a guide, drag the image to rotate it, then size and position it as shown, being sure that the crop marquee remains within the borders of the canvas**
   Note that the bottom of the marquee is parallel to the step that the girl is standing on.

6. **Execute the crop, then compare your result to Figure A-18**

7. **Save the document, then close hotel postcard_PS-A**

8. **Click File on the Menu bar, then click Exit (Win) or click Photoshop on the Menu bar, then click Quit Photoshop (Mac).**

Cropping, resolution, and image size

When you select the Crop tool, you can enter a specific width, height, and resolution to crop an image to. You can also enter a specific resolution in the Crop Image Size & Resolution dialog box. To access this dialog box, click the list arrow next to Unconstrained on the Options bar. It may occur to you that the options for the Crop tool make it function much like the Image Size dialog box. Think about it: in the Image Size dialog box, you modify width, height, resolution, or all three. The same is true in the Crop Image Size & Resolution dialog box. That being said, it's important that you don't mistakenly resample an image by using the Crop tool. The key to making sure this doesn't happen is to understand that if you input a new height or width value but leave the Resolution text box empty, the resolution cannot change. It's

like turning off the Resample Image option in the Image Size dialog box. No matter where you crop or what size crop marquee you create, new pixels cannot be added or deleted, only redistributed. Make no mistake, the Crop tool is not intended to be used as a practical alternative to the Image Size dialog box. However, the Crop tool options are most practical when you have a target size and resolution that you want as a result. For example, it's often the case that you will be given high-res files and asked to crop them to a specific size for use on a website. In that case, you could simply enter the specific width and height, enter a resolution of 72 ppi, and crop the image. Your result would be cropped to that size and resolution in one step.

FIGURE A-17: **Rotating the image**

FIGURE A-18: **The cropped, rotated, and resized image**

Practice

Concepts Review

Label the elements of the Photoshop screen shown in Figure A-19.

FIGURE A-19

Match each term with the statement that best describes it.

6. Pixel

7. Resolution

8. Image Size

9. File Size

10. Canvas

11. Menu bar

12. JPEG

13. Cropping

a. The bed of pixels in a Photoshop file

b. The physical dimensions of an image

c. Removing unwanted areas of an image

d. File format often used for web graphics

e. Picture element

f. The amount of memory a file takes up

g. Part of the workspace that contains menu items

h. The number of pixels per inch

Select the best answer from the list of choices.

14. What is the name of the tool that you use to enlarge and reduce the view of a document?

   a. Hand

   b. Window

   c. Zoom

   d. Control

15. Which dialog box do you use to change the resolution of a file?

   a. Image Size dialog box

   b. Canvas Size dialog box

   c. New dialog box

   d. Both a and b but not c

16. Which of the following can you not specify in the New dialog box?

   a. Resolution

   b. Units and Rulers

   c. Width and Height

   d. Color Mode

17. Which of the following can you use to change the size of an image after it has been created?

   a. Canvas Size dialog box

   b. Crop tool

   c. New dialog box

   d. Both a and b but not c

18. Which of the following occurs every time you enlarge an image?

   a. New pixels are added based on existing pixels

   b. Increase in file size

   c. Reduction in quality

   d. All of the above

19. When you enlarge an image and Photoshop creates pixels from existing pixels, what is that process called?

   a. Interpretation

   b. Intertranslation

   c. Interrelation

   d. Interpolation

Skills Review

1. Define photo editing software.

   a. List four tasks that you can accomplish with Photoshop CS6.

   b. If you were publishing a monthly magazine, what role would Photoshop play in the production of that magazine?

   c. If you have a box full of family photos, what could you use Photoshop to do with them?

   d. If you have an old photo that is torn and faded, what help would Photoshop be for that situation?

2. Start Photoshop and view the workspace.

   a. Click the Start button on the taskbar, point to All Programs, click Adobe Design Standard CS6 (or the name of your specific Adobe Creative Suite package) if necessary, then click Adobe Photoshop CS6 (Win) or open the Finder, then double-click Adobe Photoshop CS6, then double-click **Adobe Photoshop CS6**.

   b. Identify the Menu bar.

   c. Toggle the Tools panel between being a single and double row of tools.

   d. On the panels dock on the right, click the tabs of each panel to show each panel.

   e. Click the workspace list arrow on the Options bar, then click Painting.

   f. Click the workspace list arrow on the Options bar, then click Essentials.

   g. Click Window on the Menu bar, then click Character.

   h. Drag the Character panel to the center of the workspace, separating it from the Paragraph panel.

   i. Drag the Paragraph panel back over the Character panel name tab to group the two panels together.

   j. Double-click the name tab of any visible panels in the panels dock to minimize them.

   k. Click the workspace list arrow on the Options bar, then click Reset Essentials.

3. Use the Zoom tool and the Hand tool.

   a. Click File on the Menu bar, click Open, navigate to the location where you store your Data Files, click PS A-8.psd, then click Open.

   b. Click View on the Menu bar, then click Fit on Screen.

   c. Click the Zoom tool on the Tools panel, position it over the black steeple in the middle ground, then click five times to zoom in on the image.

Skills Review (continued)

d. Click the Hand tool on the Tools panel, then drag the Hand tool pointer over the image to see other areas of the image.

e. Double-click the Hand tool.

f. Click the Zoom tool, then click and drag a marquee around the same steeple.

g. Press and hold [Alt] (Win) or [option] (Mac), then click four times anywhere on the image.

h. Press and hold [Ctrl] (Win) or ⌘ (Mac), then press [+] repeatedly to enlarge the view.

i. Click View on the Menu bar, then click Fit on Screen.

4. Save a document and understand file formats.

a. Click File on the Menu bar, click Save As, then navigate to the location where you store your Data Files.

b. Type **tallinn_PS-A** in the File name text box, click the Format list arrow to see all the file formats available, click Photoshop (*.PSD, *.PDD) then click Save.

c. Click File on the Menu bar, click Save As, click the Format list arrow, then click TIFF (*.TIF, *.TIFF).

d. Click Save, accept the defaults in the TIFF Options dialog box, then click OK.

e. Click File on the Menu bar, click Save As, click the Format list arrow, click JPEG (*.JPG, *.JPEG, *.JPE), then click Save.

f. Drag the Quality slider so that the file size is less than 200 KB but greater than 100 KB.

g. Click OK, then close tallinn_PS-A.jpg.

5. Understand and change resolution.

a. Open PS A-9.psd, then save it as **eagle resize_PS-A**.

b. Click Image on the Menu bar, then click Image Size.

c. Click the Resample Image check box to remove the check mark.

d. Change the value in the Resolution text box to 100, press [Tab], then note the changes in the Width and Height values.

e. Press and hold [Alt] (Win) or [option] (Mac) so that the Cancel button changes to the Reset button, then click the Reset button.

f. Change the resolution from 300 to 150, press [Tab], then note the changes to the Width and Height values and to the Pixel Dimensions.

g. Click OK.

h. Click File on the Menu bar, then click Revert.

6. Change image size.

a. Click Image on the Menu bar, then click Image Size.

b. Note that the Resample Image check box is checked by default.

c. Change the Width value to 9.

d. Click OK, then evaluate the enlargement in terms of image quality.

e. Revert the file, open the Image Size dialog box, and note that the Resample Image check box is checked.

f. Change the Width value to 9, then change the resolution to 72.

g. Click OK, then evaluate the enlargement in terms of image quality.

h. Save changes, then close the file.

7. Create a new document.

a. Click Edit (Win) or Photoshop (Mac) on the Menu bar, point to Preferences, then click Units & Rulers.

b. Verify that Rulers is set to Inches and Type is set to Points.

c. In the New Document Preset Resolutions section, verify that Print Resolution is set to 300 ppi and Screen Resolution is set to 72 ppi.

d. Click OK, click File on the Menu bar, then click New.

e. Click the list arrow next to Width, then click Inches.

f. Change the Width value to 5, change the Height value to 7, then change the resolution to 300.

g. Click the Color Mode list arrow, then click CMYK Color.

Skills Review (continued)

h. Click the Advanced button to expand the New dialog box, if necessary, click the Color Profile list arrow, then choose Don't Color Manage this Document.

i. Click OK.

j. Save the file as **skills new_PS-A**, then close the file.

FIGURE A-20

8. **Transform the canvas.**
   a. Open PS A-10.psd, then save it as **title_PS-A**.
   b. Click Image on the Menu bar, point to Image Rotation, then click Flip Canvas Horizontal.
   c. Click Image on the Menu bar, then click Canvas Size.
   d. Type **4** in the Height text box.
   e. Click the lower-center arrow in the Anchor section, then click OK.
   f. Save your work, then close title_PS-A.psd.

9. **Crop an image.**
   a. Open PS A-11.psd, then save it as **email postcard_PS-A**.
   b. Click Window on the Menu bar, then click Info to show the Info panel, if necessary.
   c. Click the Info panel menu button, then click Panel Options.
   d. In the Status Information section, verify that both the Document Sizes and Document Dimensions check boxes are checked, then click OK.
   e. Click the Crop tool on the Tools panel.
   f. Verify that the ratio setting on the Options bar is set to Unconstrained.
   g. Drag the Crop tool anywhere on the canvas to create a crop marquee and note the width and height values on the Info panel as you drag.
   h. Drag the crop handles to define an area similar to that shown in Figure A-20.
   i. Click the Crop tool, verify that the Delete Cropped Pixels check box on the Options bar is checked, then click Crop.
   j. Save your work, then close email postcard_PS-A.psd.

Crop marquee

10. **Crop an image to a specific size.**
   a. Open PS A-12.psd, then save it as **san francisco_PS-A**.
   b. Click the Crop tool on the Tools panel.
   c. Verify that the ratio setting on the Options bar is set to Unconstrained.
   d. On the Options bar, type **6** in the Width field.
   e. Float your cursor outside of the marquee to see the rotate pointer, then rotate the image so that the sky-line is parallel to the bottom of the marquee.
   f. Drag the crop handles of the marquee so that all four are on the canvas.
   g. Execute the crop, then compare your result to Figure A-21.
   h. Save changes, then close san francisco_PS-A.psd.
   i. Click File on the Menu bar, then click Exit (Win) or click Photoshop on the Menu bar, then click Quit Photoshop (Mac).

FIGURE A-21

Independent Challenge 1

Your first client, the Estonia Travel and Tourism Board, has sent you three files that they want to put on their website to promote all the construction, development, and restoration going on in the city. Each image needs to be a 3" square with a file size less than 100 KB each.

a. Open PS A-13.psd.

b. Check the Image Size dialog box to verify that the image is larger than 3" × 3" and has a resolution higher than 72 ppi.

c. Click Image on the Menu bar, point to Mode, then click RGB Color.

d. Click the Crop tool, click the list arrow next to Unconstrained on the Options bar, then click Size & Resolution.

e. In the Crop Image Size & Resolution dialog box, type **3** in the Width and Height text boxes, type **72** in the Resolution text box, then click OK.

f. Crop the image in a way that you think is aesthetically pleasing.

g. Open the Image Size dialog box to verify the settings.

h. Open PS A-14.psd.

i. Using the same settings, crop PS A-14.psd in a way that the size and position within the frame of the subject's head and body are consistent with the cropped PS A-13.psd.

j. Open PS A-15.psd, then crop it in a way that is consistent with the two previous crops you executed.

k. Position the three documents side by side, then compare your screen to Figure A-22. (*Hint*: The sample in the figure shows the three heads on the same horizontal line and the subject's boot in the left photo is on the same baseline as his knee in the right photo.)

FIGURE A-22

PS A-13.psd   PS A-14.psd   PS A-15.psd

l. If you don't like the relationships between any of the three photos, revert the files and then recrop.

m. Save PS A-13.psd as a JPEG named **web graphic 1_PS-A**, then choose a compression setting that will compress the file to under 100 KB.

n. Save PS A-14.psd as a JPEG named **web graphic 2_PS-A**.

o. Save PS A-15.psd as a JPEG named **web graphic 3_PS-A**.

Advanced Challenge Exercise

- Verify that the web graphic 3_PS-A.psd file is active in the document window.
- Click Image on the Menu bar, point to Mode, then click CMYK Color. Click OK in the warning dialog box that follows, if necessary.
- Click Image on the Menu bar, point to Mode, then click Grayscale.
- Click OK in the dialog box that follows.

p. Close the three files without saving changes, then exit Photoshop.

Independent Challenge 2

The Estonia Travel and Tourism Board provides you with three images. They ask you to create one file with all three images displayed vertically. They ask that you leave 1/8-inch space between each image, and the space between should be black. You open the three Photoshop files. Each one is in RGB Color mode and has been cropped to 3" × 3" at 72 pixels per inch.

a. Open PS A-16.psd, PS A-17.psd, and PS A-18.psd.

b. Save PS A-16.psd as **triptych_PS-A**.

c. Open the Canvas Size dialog box.

d. Change the dimension of the canvas to accommodate the client's specifications.

e. triptych_PS-A.psd will be the topmost of the three images, so click the appropriate box in the Anchor section to accommodate the other two images.

f. Specify that the new pixels will be Black, then click OK.

g. In PS A-18.psd, select all, copy, then close the file.

h. Paste into the triptych_PS-A.psd file.

i. Click the Move tool, then use the arrow keys to move the image down to the bottom of the file.

j. Zoom in to be sure that the pasted image is at the very bottom of the file and no black pixels are showing beneath it.

k. Fit on screen.

l. Copy and paste PS A-17.psd into the file, then position it so that it is centered vertically between the other two images.

m. Close PS A-17.

n. Save triptych_PS-A.psd as a JPEG and choose a compression setting that will output the file at less than 200 KB.

o. Compare your result to Figure A-23, save and close triptych_PS-A.psd, then exit Photoshop.

Independent Challenge 3

The city zoo is planning on creating a series of animal bookmarks that they will sell in their gift shop. They want you to create a preliminary design for the first bookmark. The width must be between 1 and 2.5 inches and the height must be between 6 and 7.5 inches. They want the bookmark to be "interesting and unexpected." Since there's a range of acceptable sizes, you decide to first experiment with the Crop tool to find an interesting crop, then change the physical size after you crop. Because this is just a preliminary design, you're not worried about resolution or quality issues that might occur with resizing the file after you crop.

a. Open PS A-19.psd then save it as **bookmark_PS-A**.

b. Click the Crop tool, then verify that the ratio setting on the Options bar is set to Unconstrained.

c. Create a crop marquee of any size anywhere on the canvas.

d. Click the Set additional Crop options list arrow on the Options bar, then click the Enable Crop Shield check box to select it, if necessary.

e. Drag the Opacity slider to 100%.

f. Experiment with different crops of different sizes, being sure to stay within the parameters of between 1 and 2.5 inches in width and between 6 and 7.5 inches in height.

Independent Challenge 3 (continued)

Advanced Challenge Exercise

- Verify that you have an active crop marquee. Click the Set additional Crop options list arrow on the Options bar, then click the Enable Crop Shield check box, if necessary.
- Click the Color list arrow, then click Custom.
- Click in the red area of the Color Picker, then click OK.
- Drag the Opacity slider to 50%.

f. Decide on a crop that you feel is "interesting and unexpected", then execute the crop. (*Hint*: Remember that you can rotate the image, which could produce interesting results.)

g. Open the Image Size dialog box, then verify that the Resample Image check box is checked.

h. Change the Height value to 6 inches, note the new Width value, then click OK.

i. Compare your result to the sample shown in Figure A-24, save your work, then exit Photoshop.

FIGURE A-24

Real Life Independent Challenge

You have a digital camera, and you've just captured a great picture of your sister and her young daughter. You want to email it to your aunt and uncle who live on the opposite coast—just so they can see it. You know they don't have a high-speed Internet line, but you want it large enough for them to enjoy, and you want the image quality to be there, too. You decide to make the image 5 inches wide on its longest side and the resolution 150 ppi. Your goal is to get the image at that resolution and the size to be under 750 KB when saved.

a. Open PS A-20.psd, then save it as **mother's love_PS-A**.

b. Look at the image size and resolution of the file.

c. Click the Crop tool, then verify that the ratio setting on the Options bar is set to Unconstrained.

d. Crop the image (without changing the resolution) in a way that you think is aesthetically pleasing.

e. Open the Image Size dialog box to see the physical size you cropped the image to.

f. Change the width or the height—whichever is largest—to 5 inches.

g. Reduce the resolution to 150 ppi.

Real Life Independent Challenge (continued)

h. Check the before-and-after file size at the top of the dialog box to verify that the file size is being reduced, not enlarged.

i. Click OK, then compare your screen to Figure A-25 and Figure A-26. (*Hint:* The figures show two sample crops—the first is more of a standard crop. In the second, the very tight crop conveys a sense of the closeness of the mother and daughter.)

j. Save your file as a JPEG and choose a quality setting that produces a file size that's less than 750 KB.

k. Close mother's love_PS-A.psd, then exit Photoshop.

FIGURE A-25

FIGURE A-26

Visual Workshop

Open PS A-21.psd, then save it as **visual solution_PS-A**. Crop the image so that it resembles the one shown in Figure A-27.

Getting Started with Photoshop CS6

Selecting Pixels

Files You Will Need:

To view a list of files needed for this unit, see the Data Files Grid in the back of the book.

In order to modify specific pixels, you first need to select them. Making selections is one of the most fundamental procedures you'll do in Photoshop. The Tools panel houses three types of selection tools: the Marquee tools, the Lasso tools, and the Tolerance tools—the Magic Wand and Quick Selection tools. Making selections is just one component of working with selections. In this unit, you'll learn how to define a selection edge—with a feather, for example—how to save a selection, how to preview a selection in Quick Mask, and how to refine a selection's edge. You'll also gain an understanding of issues involved with moving pixels to a new location on the canvas. At MegaPixel, Laura has prepared a number of projects for you that will test your abilities with making selections, previewing them, saving them, and refining selection edges.

OBJECTIVES

Use the marquee tools

Use the lasso tools

Use the Magic Wand tool

Save and load selections

Work with and save alpha channels

Understand anti-aliased edges

Work with a feathered edge

Refine selection edges

Using the Marquee Tools

The Marquee tools are the most basic tools available for making selections in Photoshop. The Rectangular Marquee tool is used for making rectangular or square selections and the Elliptical Marquee tool is used for making oval or circular selections. You can add to an existing selection and remove pixels from a selection using simple quick keys. If you are not happy with a selection, you can deselect and start over. ██████ Laura has given you a Photoshop file which is a puzzle that the company uses to test new employees' understanding of basic selections. You use the Rectangular Marquee tool and the Elliptical Marquee tool to select the first four pieces of the puzzle.

STEPS

QUICK TIP

The white triangle on some tool icons indicates that there are more tools hidden beneath the current tool.

QUICK TIP

If you need to start over, deselect by pressing [Ctrl][D] (Win) or ⌘[D] (Mac) or click Select on the Menu bar, then click Deselect.

Before starting these steps, verify that only the Tools panel is open. Press [D] so that the foreground and background colors on the Tools panel are black over white. Use all the zooming and scrolling techniques you learned in Unit A.

1. **Open PS B-1.psd, save it as selections puzzle_PS-B, zoom in on the #1 piece, then click the Rectangular Marquee tool ▣**

2. **Position the center of the crosshair on the upper-left corner of the puzzle piece, drag downward until the center of the crosshair is on the lower-right corner, then release the mouse pointer**

3. **Click View on the Menu bar, then click Fit on Screen, click the Move tool ▶✛, drag the piece to the correct position on the hot air balloon image, as shown in Figure B-1, then deselect**

   You will be positioning puzzle pieces 2, 3, and 4 for the remainder of this lesson. Each time you select a puzzle piece, zoom in on the piece, select it, zoom out, move it to the correct position on the hot air balloon using the Move tool, then deselect. The point of this exercise is to practice making selections, adding to, and removing from selections. Do not worry if your selections include extra white pixels.

4. **Click ▣, select the top square in the #2 piece, press and hold [Shift], position the crosshair over the lower-right corner, drag a second marquee that overlaps the first, then release the mouse pointer**

   The entire piece is selected. Pressing and holding [Shift] when making a selection adds pixels to the existing selection.

QUICK TIP

To switch quickly between the marquee tools and the Move tool, press [M] to select the current marquee tool and [V] to select the Move tool.

5. **Select the outer square in the #3 piece, press and hold [Alt] (Win) or [option] (Mac), then select the white inner rectangle**

   The white inner rectangle is removed from the selection. Pressing and holding [Alt] (Win) or [option] (Mac) when making a selection removes pixels from the existing selection.

6. **Press and hold ▣, click the Elliptical Marquee tool ◯, then position the crosshair icon over the white pixel at the center of the #4 piece**

7. **Press and hold [Alt][Shift] (Win) or [option][Shift] (Mac), then drag to the edge of the circle to complete the selection**

   Pressing and holding [Alt] (Win) or [option] (Mac) when no pixels are selected creates a marquee selection that starts in the center and grows outward. Pressing and holding [Shift] while dragging a marquee tool constrains the marquee selection to a perfect circle or square. Don't worry if you have a slight white halo at the edge of your selection.

TROUBLE

If you're using a Macintosh computer and you see a dialog box asking what you want to use ⌘[H] for, click Hide Extras.

8. **Press [Ctrl][H] (Win) or ⌘[H] (Mac) to hide the marquee, then move the piece into position so that your canvas resembles Figure B-2**

9. **Deselect, then save your work**

FIGURE B-1: Positioning the first piece

FIGURE B-2: Positioning the circle piece

Circle piece in place

The Shift key: doing double duty

As you've seen in this lesson, the Shift key does two important things: it adds to an existing selection, and it constrains a selection to a perfect shape. What if you wanted to do both—to select two perfect squares? You would press and hold [Shift] while selecting the first square to make a square marquee. To select the second square, you would need to press [Shift] to add to the first selection. So how would you use the Shift key to add to the first square *and* constrain the shape of the second selection as a square? Release the Shift key while dragging, then press it again and it will constrain the selection.

Using the Lasso Tools

There are three types of Lasso tools in Photoshop: Lasso, Polygonal Lasso, and Magnetic Lasso. Lasso tools are also used for making free-form selections: simply click and drag anywhere on the canvas to create a section of pixels. When selecting a complex shape with the Lasso tool, you will usually find it easier to make small selections then add to them with the Shift key. The Polygonal Lasso tool functions like the Lasso tool, but it does so with straight lines. This makes the tool very effective for making quick selections or selecting areas of the canvas that are geometric in shape, as the tool's name implies. 　 Laura instructs you to move on to select the free-form pieces of the puzzle. You use the Lasso tool to select an organically shaped object and the Polygonal Lasso tool to select a multi-lateral object.

STEPS

1. Zoom in on the #5 piece, then click the Lasso tool 🔾

2. **Click and drag to select just an interior section of the piece, as shown in Figure B-3**
   Your selection may differ from the figure.

3. **Press [Shift] while using the Lasso tool to keep adding to the selection until the entire shape is selected**

4. **If necessary, press [Alt] (Win) or [option] (Mac) while using the Lasso tool to remove unwanted selected areas you might create outside of the shape**

5. **Move the piece into place in the puzzle, as shown in Figure B-4**
   Don't worry if the selection isn't perfect. This is just for practice with the Lasso tool; you will learn more precise methods for selecting these types of shapes.

6. **Zoom in on the #6 piece, click the Polygonal Lasso tool 📐, then press [Caps Lock] so that the Lasso tool icon is a precise crosshair**

7. **Position the crosshair at the tip of the upper-right point of the shape, click, release the mouse button, then move the mouse pointer to the next corner on the shape and click**

8. **Using the same method, move the mouse pointer around the shape, clicking on the next 12 corners of the shape**

9. **Float over the original point you clicked so that the Polygonal Lasso tool icon appears with a small "o" beside it, then click to close the selection**

10. **Move the piece into place in the puzzle, deselect, then compare your result to Figure B-5**

Working with the foreground and background colors

As shown in Figure B-15, the Foreground and Background colors are the colors that you paint with and fill selections with. You can click the Switch Foreground and Background Colors button or press [X] to switch the foreground and background colors. Click the Default Foreground and Background Colors button or press [D] to revert the foreground and background colors to black and white.

FIGURE B-15: Foreground and Background colors

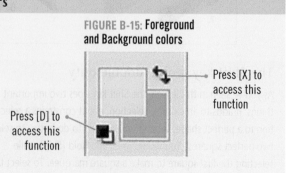

Press [X] to access this function

Press [D] to access this function

FIGURE B-3: Selecting the interior of the object

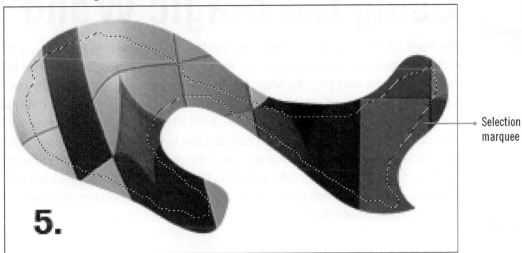

Selection
marquee

FIGURE B-4: Positioning piece #5

Piece #5 in place •——

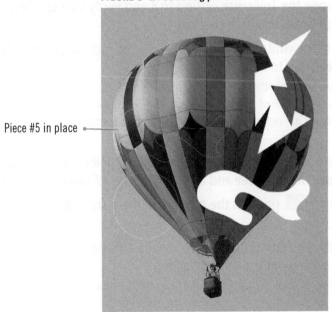

FIGURE B-5: Positioning piece #6

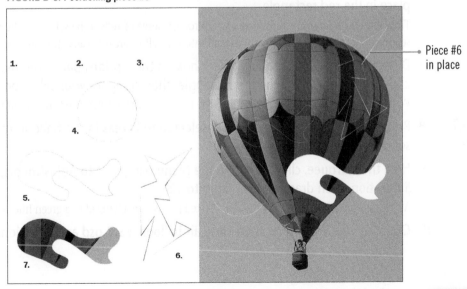

Piece #6
in place

Selecting Pixels

Using the Magic Wand Tool

The Magic Wand tool is a very powerful selection tool. Click any pixel on the canvas, and the Magic Wand tool selects other pixels based on tolerance—the similarity of their color. The greater the tolerance value you set for the tool, the more pixels the Magic Wand tool will select. By clicking the Contiguous check box on the Options bar, you can specify that the Magic Wand tool selects only pixels that are contiguous to (touching) the area where you click the image. Otherwise, it will select similar pixels throughout the image. For more information about the Magic Wand tool, see the Clues to Use, called *Understanding tolerance*, on the next page. As with any selection, once you select all of the pixels that you want, you can modify them in many ways, such as by changing their color in the Hue/Saturation dialog box. Laura tells you to complete the test using the Magic Wand tool, and then to show her a method for changing selected pixels' color using the Hue/Saturation dialog box.

STEPS

QUICK TIP

The Magic Wand tool may be hidden behind the Quick Selection tool .

1. **Release [Caps Lock] if it is activated, click the Magic Wand tool , then, on the Options bar, change the Tolerance setting to 8 and verify that the Anti-alias and Contiguous check boxes are both checked**

2. **Click anywhere in the white area that represents the missing piece in the puzzle, then compare your selection to Figure B-6**

   The Magic Wand tool selected other white and almost-white pixels, but did not select pixels of the balloon image because they are outside of tolerance. Because the Contiguous option was checked, the white pixels on the left of the canvas are not selected because they are not contiguous—they don't touch the area that you clicked.

QUICK TIP

Once the marquee is close to the #7 piece, zoom in and use the arrow keys to align it precisely.

3. **Float over the selected area so that the Magic Wand pointer changes to a white arrow, then drag to move the marquee and align it with the #7 piece on the left of the canvas**

4. **Click the Move tool , position the #7 piece in the puzzle, deselect, then save your work**

5. **Open PS B-2.psd, save it as air balloon_PS-B, click the Magic Wand tool , then click in the center red rectangle of the hot air balloon**

   Only a small selection is created because the tolerance setting is low, and there are a variety of red pixels in this area.

6. **Deselect, increase the Tolerance value on the Options bar to 48, then click the same place in the red rectangle**

   The increased tolerance value allows for a broader range of reds to be selected. The entire red rectangle is selected, but the selection does not extend into the yellow areas because they are out of tolerance.

7. **Deselect, click the Contiguous check box on the Options bar to remove the check mark, click the same place in the red rectangle, then compare your selection to Figure B-7**

   With the Contiguous option deactivated, the red pixels within tolerance throughout the image are selected.

QUICK TIP

Zooming in on areas of the image that you want to select always helps when making selections

8. **Press and hold [Shift], then click unselected red areas in the balloon to add them to the selection**

9. **Hide the marquee, click Image on the Menu bar, point to Adjustments, click Hue/Saturation, then drag the Hue slider to 126**

   All of the selected pixels—and only the selected pixels—are changed to a green hue, as shown in Figure B-8.

10. **Click OK, save your work, then close air balloon_PS-B.psd and selections puzzle_PS-B.psd**

Selected pixels

FIGURE B-7: Selecting pixels without the Contiguous option

FIGURE B-8: Results of changing the hue of selected pixels

Understanding tolerance

The Magic Wand tool and many other tools in Photoshop do their work based on the function of tolerance. The key to understanding tolerance is to understand that in every Photoshop file, every pixel has a number. The clearest example of that concept can be found in a grayscale image. In a grayscale image, each pixel can be one—and only one—of 256 shades of gray. Tolerance settings work and interact directly with those pixel numbers. For example, let's say you set the tolerance option for the Magic Wand tool to 10. Next, you click the Magic Wand tool on a pixel whose grayscale value is 75. The Magic Wand tool

would select all contiguous pixels whose grayscale value falls within the range of 65–85; ten grayscale values higher and lower than the pixel that you clicked. If the Contiguous option is not activated, the Magic Wand tool would select all the pixels throughout the image whose grayscale values were 65–85. Of course, you don't need to know the number of the pixel you are clicking. Your goal is simply to select pixels of similar color. All you need to do is experiment with different tolerance settings until you get the selection you want.

Saving and Loading Selections

Making selections can be some of the most complex and time-consuming work you'll do in Photoshop, so it makes sense that you can save selections with the Photoshop file. Saving a selection is always a smart idea because you never know when you might want to access the selection again in the future. ▰▰▰ You've been assigned to work on a design project for a client. Jon explains that the client wants to see color applied to a posterized image. You posterize the file, then create and save four selections in order to load them and fill them with four different colors.

Before starting these steps, open the Swatches and Color panels.

1. **Open PS B-3.psd, click** Image **on the Menu bar, point to** Adjustments, **then click** Posterize

   Posterize is a special effect that is created by reducing the number of colors available for the image.

2. **Drag the** Levels slider **to** 4, **then click** OK

   With the Posterize effect set to four, each pixel in the image can be one—and only one—of four available shades of gray: black, dark gray, light gray, or white.

3. **Click** Image **on the Menu bar, point to** Mode, **then click** RGB Color

   Changing the color mode to RGB Color will allow you to add color to the selections.

4. **Click the** Magic Wand tool ▨, **set the Tolerance to** 1 **on the Options bar, verify that the Anti-alias and the Contiguous check boxes are not checked, then click a white area of the image**

5. **Click** Select **on the Menu bar, click** Save Selection, **then type** White **in the Name text box**

   The Save Selection dialog box, shown in Figure B-9, shows that the new selection will be saved with the file PS B-3.psd when you save the file.

6. **Click** OK **to close the dialog box, then repeat Steps 4 and 5 to make three more selections, named** Light Gray, Dark Gray, **and** Black, **by clicking a light gray area, a dark gray area, and a black area with the Magic Wand tool, then saving each selection**

7. **Deselect the last selection by pressing** [Ctrl][D] **(Win) or** ⌘[D] **(Mac), click** Select **on the Menu bar, click** Load Selection, **click the** Channel list arrow, **click** Light Gray, **then click** OK

   The saved selection is loaded.

Press [Alt] [Delete] (Win) or [option] [delete] (Mac) to fill a selection with the foreground color and [Ctrl][Delete] (Win) or ⌘ [delete] (Mac) to fill a selection with the background color. Press [Delete] (Win) or [delete] (Mac) to open the Fill dialog box.

8. **Float the pointer over the Swatches panel, then click the swatch named** Pure Yellow Orange, **as shown in Figure B-10**

   Pure Yellow Orange becomes the foreground color on the Tools panel.

9. **Click** Edit **on the Menu bar, click** Fill, **click the** Use list arrow, **click** Foreground Color, **verify that the Opacity setting is** 100%, **click** OK, **then deselect**

   The Light Gray selection is filled with Pure Yellow Orange.

10. **Repeat Steps 7–9 to load the** White, Dark Gray, **and** Black **selections, filling each with a color of your choice on the Swatches panel**

    Figure B-11 shows one possible result.

FIGURE B-9: **Save Selection dialog box**

FIGURE B-10: **Pure Yellow Orange swatch on the Swatches panel**

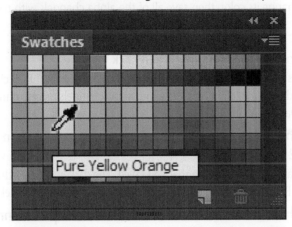

FIGURE B-11: **The image with different fill colors for each selection**

Saving color swatches

There are many ways to change the foreground and background colors. On the Swatches panel, for example, if you click a swatch, the foreground changes to that color. Press [Ctrl] (Win) or ⌘ (Mac) when you click a swatch to change the background color. You can also click the Eyedropper tool and sample any pixel from the image. Doing so changes the foreground color to the color of the pixel. You can also drag the sliders on the Color panel to modify the current foreground color. To save colors that you create, simply float the pointer over a dark gray area of the Swatches panel. The pointer changes to a paint bucket icon. Click and the color will be added as a new swatch. You're even given the option to name it. The new swatch will remain on the Swatches panel for every new file that you create from that point forward. To delete a swatch from the Swatches panel, press and hold [Alt] (Win) or [option] (Mac), then click to delete the swatch.

Working with and Saving Alpha Channels

Alpha channels are saved selections. To put it another way, when you save a selection, the selection is saved as an alpha channel. Alpha channels are listed on the Channels panel in Photoshop. They are displayed as black and white thumbnail images. The selected areas are represented by white, and the areas not selected are represented by black. You can save selections as you are working, but alpha channels are not automatically saved when you save the file. You must specify that they be saved when you save the file. ~~~~~ Now that you have four new alpha channels, you view them on the Channels panel. You load the Dark Gray alpha channel, change its color, then save all of the alpha channels with the file.

STEPS

1. **Click Window on the Menu bar, then click Channels**

   The Channels panel holds four default channels: the "composite" RGB channel, and one channel each for Red, Blue, and Green. In addition are the four alpha channels representing the selections you saved: White, Light Gray, Dark Gray, and Black.

   QUICK TIP

   Many users like to think of alpha channels as stencils and the white areas as that which has been "cut out" of the stencil.

2. **Click the Channel thumbnail on the Dark Gray channel, then compare your canvas to Figure B-12**

   The alpha channel is the selection that you saved. The dark gray pixels that you selected are represented by white pixels. Everything that wasn't selected is represented by black pixels.

3. **Click the Channel thumbnails for the other three alpha channels that you saved, then click the RGB channel thumbnail to see the composite image with all of its colors**

4. **Press and hold [Ctrl] (Win) or ⌘ (Mac), then click the Channel thumbnail of the Dark Gray alpha channel**

   The Dark Gray alpha channel is loaded as a selection. Pressing and holding [Ctrl] (Win) or ⌘ (Mac) while clicking a channel thumbnail is a quicker way to load a selection.

5. **On the Swatches panel, click Pure Yellow Green**

   Pure Yellow Green becomes the foreground color.

6. **Fill the selection with the foreground color, deselect, then compare your result to Figure B-13**

7. **Click File on the Menu bar, click Save As, type save selections_PS-B in the File name text box (Win) or the Save As text box (Mac), verify that the Alpha Channels check box is checked, as shown in Figure B-14, then click Save**

   All of the saved selections—the alpha channels—are saved with the file. Every time you save a selection and add a channel to a file, you are increasing the file size substantially. Delete alpha channels when you no longer need them.

8. **Close save selections_PS-B.psd**

FIGURE B-12: **The Dark Gray alpha channel**

FIGURE B-13: **Filling the loaded selection with a new color**

FIGURE B-14: **Save Alpha Channels option in the Save As dialog box**

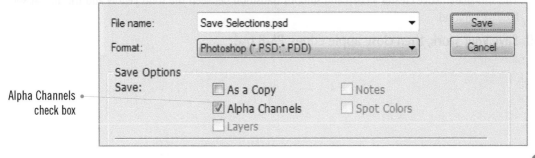

Alpha Channels •
check box

Selecting Pixels

Understanding Anti-Aliased Edges

The outline of a selection is called the **edge** of a selection; the type of edge that you choose will have a big impact on how your work appears. The edge of a selection is always either aliased or anti-aliased. An **aliased** edge is a hard edge—the hard "stair-stepped" pixels are very obvious. The edge is noticeably blunt. This is why aliased edges are seldom used. An **anti-aliased** edge is a crisp but smoother edge. With an anti-aliased edge, Photoshop creates a smooth transition between the edge and its background using many shades of the edge pixel color. ▆▆▆ Jon provides you with an image he needs for an educational poster. He asks you to try to improve the appearance of an apple against a blue background. You apply an aliased edge and an anti-aliased edge to compare the difference between the two.

STEPS

1. Open PS B-4.psd, then save it as apple edges_PS-B

2. Press and hold [Ctrl] (Win) or ⌘ (Mac), then click the yellow swatch (RGB Yellow) in the top row on the Swatches panel

   The background color changes to RGB Yellow.

QUICK TIP
You will need to make more than one selection to select the entire apple.

3. Click the Magic Wand tool ✦, set the Tolerance value to 72, verify that the Anti-alias check box is *not* checked and that the Contiguous check box *is* checked, then select the entire apple

4. Click the Move tool ⊹, drag the apple into the black area on the right, hide the marquee, then zoom in on the top edge of the apple

   Figure B-16 is an enlarged view of the top edge of the apple and shows the hard aliased edge; the square shapes of the pixels are clearly visible.

5. Double-click the Hand tool ✋ to fit the page in the window, then note on the left of the canvas that the yellow background color fills the remaining area after the move and has the same aliased edge

6. Click Edit on the Menu bar, click Undo Move, then deselect

QUICK TIP
You will need to make more than one selection to select the entire apple.

7. Click the Magic Wand tool ✦, click the Anti-alias check box on the Options bar, then select the apple

8. Click ⊹, drag the apple into the black area, hide the marquee, then zoom in on the top edge

   As shown in Figure B-17, the apple has an anti-aliased edge. Edge pixels of various shades of green create the illusion of a smooth edge where the apple meets the black background.

9. Click ✋, then move the canvas to the right so that you can examine the edge where the yellow fill meets the blue background

   The anti-aliased edge creates a crisp and smooth transition between the solid yellow and the almost-solid blue background.

10. Save your work, then close apple edges_PS-B.psd

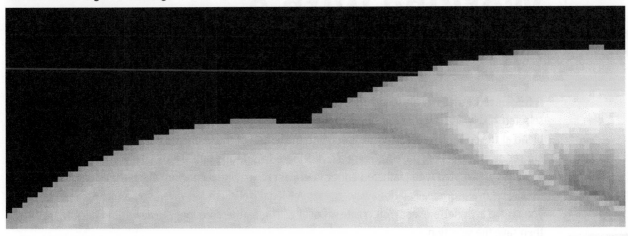

FIGURE B-17: Viewing the anti-aliased edge

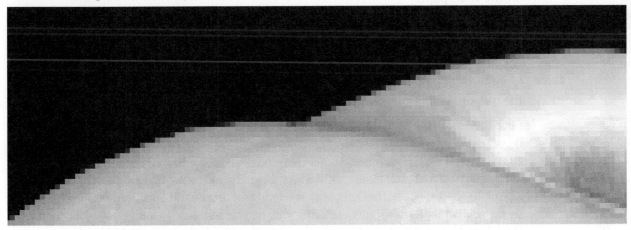

How anti-aliasing works

As has been said before, a Photoshop image is made up of pixels, and pixels are square. By definition, a square does not have a soft edge. So think about this: How do you create a soft edge for a curved object using only squares? The answer is that you can't create a soft edge with squares; squares have right-angle corners. All you can do is create the *illusion* of a soft edge. That's what an anti-aliased edge is: an illusion. Anti-aliasing manipulates the color of edge pixels in a selection to create a visual transition between the selected object and the background. So the soft edge is an optical illusion made by manipulating color—the color of square pixels.

Computer monitors and viewing edges

Your computer monitor acts as the middleman between you and the Photoshop image. Everything you are seeing is through your monitor. Monitors also use red, green, and blue pixels of transmitted light. Using these three colors, your monitor is able to show you millions of colors—more than your eye can differentiate. Monitors have resolution as well; most have a resolution of 72 pixels per inch. This fact has a big impact on how you view your Photoshop image, because at all times the monitor's resolution is trying to match the image's resolution. When you're viewing your image at less than 100%, your monitor is not giving you an accurate visual representation of the pixels in your image. When you're analyzing subtle components of your image—like selection edges!—be sure that you're viewing your canvas at least at 100%.

Working with a Feathered Edge

A **feathered edge** is a blended edge. Photoshop creates a blend at the edge of a selection between the selected pixels and the background image. Photoshop offers settings for controlling the length of the blend at the edge. The feather value is equal to the length of the feathered edge. When you apply a feathered edge to a selection, the edge is equally distributed inside and outside the selection edge. In Photoshop, vignettes are created with feathered edges. A **vignette** is a visual effect in which the edge of an image—usually an oval—gradually fades away. ░▒▓ A MegaPixel client has given you a picture and asked that you create a vignette effect. You create an oval with a feathered edge, preview it in Quick Mask Mode, then save the selection.

1. **Open PS B-5.psd,then click the** Default Foreground and Background Colors button ▣ **on the Tools panel**

The Rectangular Marquee tool and the Lasso tool also offer feather options.

2. **Click the** Elliptical Marquee tool ⬭**, type** 32 **in the Feather text box on the Options bar, then verify that the Anti-alias check box is checked**

3. **Position the mouse pointer on the jewelry at the woman's neck, press [Alt] (Win) or [option] (Mac), then draw an oval from the center that resembles the shape and size of the one shown in Figure B-18**

The Quick Mask in Figure B-19 uses the default red Quick Mask color. Your quick mask color and degree of transparency may differ.

4. **Click the** Edit in Quick Mask Mode button ▣ **on the Tools panel to preview the selection**
   Quick Mask Mode provides a preview of how the feathered edge will appear when you save the selection. The Quick Mask Mode feature shows the selected pixels and hides or "masks" unselected pixels. As shown in Figure B-19, the 32-pixel blend created a very soft and smooth edge that progressively fades out the edge of the selected image. The Quick Mask is very helpful because without it, you would not be able to see the result of the feathered edge until after you saved the selection. To learn more information about Quick Mask Mode, see the Clues to Use on the next page called *Understanding Quick Mask Mode*.

5. **Click the** Edit in Standard Mode button ▣ **to return to the Standard view**

6. **Click the** Select **menu, click** Save Selection**, save the selection as** Vignette**, then deselect**
   The selection is now an alpha channel saved on the Channels panel.

7. **Open the Channels panel, then click the** Vignette channel thumbnail **to view the saved selection**
   In this selection, which transitions gradually from selected pixels to unselected pixels, the alpha channel transitions gradually from white to black. See the Clues to Use called *Understanding gray pixels in alpha channels*.

Use the Select menu to load the selection.

8. **Click the** RGB channel thumbnail **on the Channels panel, then load the** Vignette selection

9. **Click the** Move tool ⯒**, drag the selected pixels into the green area on the right, then deselect**
   Figure B-20 shows the moved pixels with the feathered edge and also the feathered edge remaining after the move.

10. **Save the file with its alpha channels as** vignette_PS-B**, then close vignette_PS-B.psd**

FIGURE B-18: Drawing the feathered oval selection

FIGURE B-19: Previewing the selection in Quick Mask Mode

FIGURE B-20: The selected pixels relocated

Understanding Quick Mask Mode

Many graphic arts professionals refer to alpha channels as "masks" because the non-selected areas are "masked" by the black areas in the alpha channel. Quick Mask works with the same concept as alpha channels. Quick Mask is a visual aid that gives you a preview of your selection. It helps you to see your selection by "masking out" the areas that aren't selected and showing only the areas that are. You can increase or decrease the opacity of the Quick Mask by double-clicking the Edit in Quick Mask Mode button on the Tools panel. The Quick Mask Options dialog box opens. In this dialog box, you can change the color and the opacity as well as decide whether you want the color to indicate the masked area or the selected area. You can toggle between Quick Mask Mode and Standard Mode by pressing [Q].

Understanding gray pixels in alpha channels

How does Photoshop save a selection? By creating an alpha channel. Selected areas are white, and non-selected areas are black. But what if the selection has a feathered edge? The only way an alpha channel can render that is with gray pixels. This is the concept of opacity. Here's the easiest way to understand this concept in relation to alpha channels: The feathered edge makes the image fade away to nothing outside the selection. In the case of the previous lesson, the center of the oval is where the pixels have 100% opacity—they are fully visible, and they are represented by 100% white pixels in the alpha channel. The pixels completely outside the selection have 0% opacity—they are completely transparent, and thus represented by 100% black pixels in the alpha channel. In a feathered edge, the opacity fades from 100% to 0%, so in the alpha channel, that area fades from white to black. For example, the pixels smack in the middle of the feathered edge would be 50% black; in other words, gray. Pixels closer to the outer edge would be dark gray, almost black, and therefore fading out to nothing.

Refining Selection Edges

The Refine Edge dialog box offers you a number of useful options for viewing and refining the edge of a selection. The two key options in this dialog box are the Feather slider, which you can use to dynamically feather a selection while you preview the result, and the Shift Edge slider, which expands or contracts a selection marquee. The Contrast slider is especially useful for removing halos from the edge of a selection. Table B-1 on the next page offers useful keyboard commands for the Refine Edge dialog box. ██████ MegaPixel's city zoo client has asked that you create a preliminary design that involves a silhouette of a bird's head on a white background. You note immediately that this will be challenging because the background is so dark and the white head feathers are so numerous. You decide to make a quick selection and tweak it in the Refine Edge dialog box.

STEPS

1. **Open PS B-6.psd, then save it as** eagle silhouette_PS-B

2. **Press and hold the** Magic Wand tool ██, **click the** Quick Selection tool ██, **click the Brush Picker list arrow on the Options bar, then set the Size setting to** 10 px

   The Quick Selection tool is a selection tool that you use by dragging the tool pointer over the item you wish to select until you have all of it selected. The Quick Selection tool selects pixels based on their similarity, but there's no option to set a tolerance value. Instead, the Quick Selection tool offers you the Add to selection and Subtract from selection tools that you can use to either enlarge an existing selection or remove unwanted areas from a selection. In addition, you can reduce the brush size to select smaller or more specific areas.

3. **Position the Quick Selection tool pointer at the top of the eagle's head, then drag the brush slowly down over the eagle's white feathers and then down over the eagle's brown feathers**

   Compare your result to Figure B-21.

4. **Click** Select **on the Menu bar, then click** Refine Edge

   By default, the selection should appear against a white background.

5. **Click the** View list arrow, **sample all seven views, then choose** On White

6. **In the Edge Detection section, verify that the Smart Radius check box is not checked, drag the** Radius slider **to experiment with changing the size of the refinement area, then set the Radius value to** 30

   The Radius setting improves the selection of the long white feathers on the eagle's neck.

7. **Experiment with the** Smooth slider, **then set the Smooth value to** 3

   The Smooth option will reduce bumps and stair-stepping at the edges of the selection.

8. **Experiment with the** Contrast slider, **set the Contrast value to** 12, **then compare your Refine Edge dialog box to Figure B-22**

9. **Click** OK, **click** Select **on the Menu bar, then click** Inverse

   Everything outside of the eagle selection is selected.

10. **Click** Edit **on the Menu bar, click** Fill, **click the** Use list arrow, **click** White, **click** OK, **then deselect**

    The original background is now filled with white. The Refine Edge dialog box did a great job on the white feathers of the head, but the brown edges on the top and breast are unacceptable and would need to be corrected.

11. **Compare your canvas to Figure B-23, save your changes, then close eagle silhouette_PS-B.psd**

FIGURE B-21: Quick selection made from the Quick Selection tool

FIGURE B-22: Refine Edge dialog box

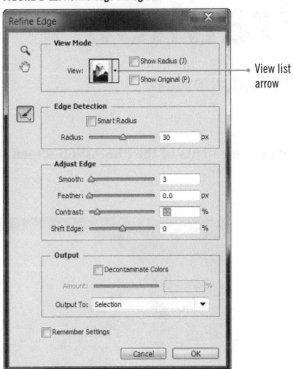

View list arrow

FIGURE B-23: The silhouette of the eagle against white

Refine Edge improved selection of feathers

Other areas are not acceptable

TABLE B-1: Useful keyboard commands for the Refine Edge dialog box (Win & Mac)

keyboard	action
[P]	Toggles the Preview option on and off
[F]	Cycles through the preview modes
[Shift][F]	Cycles backward through the preview modes
[X]	Temporarily displays the entire image

Selecting Pixels

Practice

Concepts Review

Label the elements of the Photoshop screen shown in Figure B-24.

FIGURE B-24

Match each term with the statement that best describes it.

8. Alpha channel
9. Quick Mask Mode
10. Aliased edge
11. Anti-aliased edge
12. Tolerance
13. Feather
14. Posterize
15. Vignette

a. Hard edge showing pixels stair-stepping
b. Setting that controls the Magic Wand tool
c. Useful for previewing selections
d. Blended edge
e. To reduce the colors in an image
f. Created whenever a selection is saved
g. Effect made with a feathered edge
h. Smooth and crisp edge

Select the best answer from the list of choices.

16. Which of the following offers the hardest edge for a selection?

　　a. Alias

　　b. Anti-alias

　　c. Feather

　　d. Tolerance

17. Which of the following would be the best tool for selecting an image of a stop sign?

　　a. Rectangular Marquee tool

　　b. Elliptical Marquee tool

　　c. Lasso tool

　　d. Polygonal Lasso tool

18. Which of the following is not true about saved selections?

　　a. Saving a selection creates an alpha channel

　　b. An alpha channel is a selection

　　c. Alpha channels are saved automatically when you save a file

　　d. Saving alpha channels increases file size

19. Which of the following is true about alpha channels?

　　a. White pixels represent selected pixels

　　b. Saving a selection with a feathered edge results in an alpha channel with gray pixels

　　c. The Load Selection command is the only way to load a saved selection

　　d. Both a and b but not c

20. Which of the following quick keys is used to fill a selection with the foreground color?

　　a. [Alt][Enter] (Win) or [option][return] (Mac)

　　b. [Alt][Backspace] (Win) or [option][Delete] (Mac)

　　c. [Shift][Enter] (Win) or [Shift][return] (Mac)

　　d. [Backspace] (Win) or [Delete] (Mac)

21. What are the default foreground and background colors in Photoshop?

　　a. Black over White

　　b. White over Black

　　c. Black over Black

　　d. White over White

Skills Review

1. Use the marquee tools.

　　a. Open PS B-7.psd, save it as **shapes_PS-B**, zoom in on the #1 piece, then click the Rectangular Marquee tool.

　　b. Press [D] to access the default colors on the Tools panel.

　　c. Position the center of the crosshair on the upper-left corner of the #1 puzzle piece, drag downward until the center of the crosshair is on the lower-right corner, then release the mouse pointer.

　　d. Click View on the Menu bar, click Fit on Screen, click the Move tool, drag the piece to the corresponding position in the puzzle on the right, then deselect. You will be positioning puzzle pieces 2, 3, and 4 for the remainder of this exercise. Each time you select a puzzle piece, zoom in on the piece, select it, zoom out, move it to the correct position on the puzzle on the right, then deselect.

　　e. Click the Rectangular Marquee tool, select the top square in the #2 piece, press and hold [Shift], position the crosshair over the lower-right corner, drag a second marquee that overlaps the first, then release the mouse pointer.

　　f. Select the outer square in the #3 piece, press and hold [Alt] (Win) or [option] (Mac), then select the blue inner rectangle so that it is removed from the selection.

　　g. Using the same method, click the Elliptical Marquee tool, verify that the Feather value on the Options bar is 0, press and hold [Alt] (Win) or [option] (Mac), then remove the circle from the selection.

　　h. Press [Ctrl][H] (Win) or [⌘][H] (Mac) to hide the marquee, then move the piece into position.

　　i. Deselect, then save your work.

2. Use the lasso tools.

　　a. Zoom in on the #4 piece, then click the Lasso tool.

　　b. Click and drag to select just an interior section of the piece.

　　c. Use the [Shift] key in conjunction with the Lasso tool to keep adding to the selection until the entire shape is selected.

　　d. Press [Alt] (Win) or [option] (Mac) while using the Lasso tool to remove unwanted selected areas you might have created outside of the shape.

Skills Review (continued)

   e. Move the piece into place in the puzzle on the right.

   f. Zoom in on the #5 piece, click the Polygonal Lasso tool, then press [Caps Lock] so that the Lasso tool icon is a precise crosshair.

   g. Position the crosshair at the tip of the upper-right point of the shape, click, release the mouse button, then move the mouse pointer to the next corner on the shape and click.

   h. Using the same method, move the mouse pointer around the shape, clicking on the remaining corners of the shape.

   i. Float over the original point you clicked so that the Polygonal Lasso tool icon appears with a small "o" beside it, then click to close the selection.

   j. Move the piece into place in the puzzle on the right, then deselect.

3. Use the Magic Wand tool.

   a. Verify that Caps Lock is not active, then click the Magic Wand tool.

   b. Change the Tolerance setting to 4.

   c. Verify that the Anti-alias check box is checked.

   d. Verify that the Contiguous check box is checked.

   e. Click anywhere in the #6 puzzle piece to select it.

   f. Click the Move tool, move the piece into position, and keep the piece selected.

   g. Hide the marquee, click Image on the Menu bar, point to Adjustments, click Hue/Saturation, then drag the Hue slider to -112.

   h. Click OK, then compare your screen to Figure B-25.

   i. Save your work, then close shapes_PS-B.psd.

FIGURE B-25

Skills Review (continued)

4. Save and load selections.

  a. Open PS B-8.psd.

  b. Click Image on the Menu bar, point to Adjustments, then click Posterize.

  c. Drag the Levels slider to 4, then click OK.

  d. Click Image on the Menu bar, point to Mode, then click RGB Color.

  e. Click the Magic Wand tool, set the Tolerance to 1, then verify that the Anti-alias check box is not checked and that the Contiguous check box is not checked.

  f. Click a white area of the image.

  g. Click Select on the Menu bar, click Save Selection, type **White** in the Name text box, then click OK.

  h. Repeat Steps f and g to save three new selections named **Light Gray**, **Dark Gray**, and **Black**.

  i. Click Select on the Menu bar, click Load Selection, click the Channel list arrow, click Light Gray, then click OK.

  j. Float your cursor over the Swatches panel so that it changes to the Eyedropper, then click Pure Yellow Orange to make it the foreground color.

  k. Click Edit on the Menu bar, click Fill, click the Use list arrow, click Foreground Color, then click OK.

  l. Repeat Steps i–k to load and fill the three other saved selections with different colors. Figure B-26 shows one possible result.

5. Work with and save alpha channels.

  a. On the Channels panel, click the Dark Gray channel thumbnail to view the channel itself.

  b. Click the thumbnails for the three other alpha channels that you saved, then click the RGB channel to return to the image on the canvas.

  c. On the Swatches panel, choose Pastel Violet Magenta as a new foreground color.

  d. Press and hold [Ctrl](Win) or ⌘ (Mac) then click the Dark Gray channel thumbnail.

  e. Fill the selection with the foreground color.

  f. Click File on the Menu bar, click Save As, type **clown posterize_PS-B** in the Name text box, then verify that the Alpha Channels check box is checked.

  g. Click Save, then close clown posterize_PS-B.psd.

FIGURE B-26

Skills Review (continued)

6. Understand anti-aliased edges.

    a. Open PS B-9.psd, then save it as **skills edges_PS-B**.

    b. On the Swatches panel, press and hold [Ctrl](Win) or ⌘ (Mac), then click the RGB Yellow swatch in the top row to make it the background color.

    c. Click the Magic Wand tool, set the Tolerance value to 4, verify that the Anti-alias check box is not checked and that the Contiguous check box is not checked, then click the center of any orange shape.

    d. Click the Move tool, then drag the selected pixels into the white area on the right.

    e. Hide the selection, then examine the edges of various shapes.

    f. Undo the move, deselect, click the Magic Wand tool, check the Anti-alias check box, then select all the shapes again.

    g. Move the selected pixels into the white area, then hide the selection marquee.

    h. Zoom in and examine the edges of various shapes.

    i. Examine the edges where the yellow fills meet the blue background on the left of the canvas.

    j. Undo the move, then save your work.

7. Work with a feathered edge.

    a. Verify that all pixels are deselected, then set the foreground and background colors on the Tools panel to the default colors.

    b. Click the Magic Wand tool, then click the center of any orange shape.

    c. Click Select on the Menu bar, point to Modify, then click Feather.

    d. Type **12** in the Feather Radius text box, then click OK.

    e. Click the Edit in Quick Mask Mode button on the Tools panel to preview the selection.

    f. Click the Edit in Standard Mode button to return to Standard view.

    g. Click the Move tool, then drag the selected pixels into the white area on the right.

    h. Hide the selection, then examine the edges of the shapes on the right and left.

    i. Compare your results with Figure B-27.

    j. Save your work, then close skills edges_PS-B.psd.

FIGURE B-27

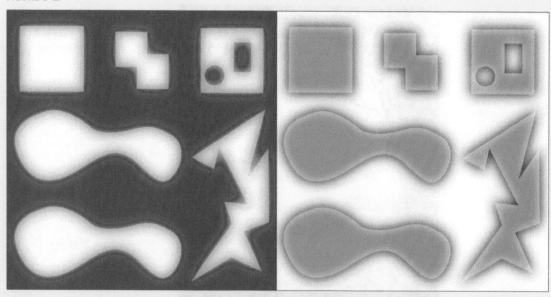

Skills Review (continued)

8. Refine selection edges.

  a. Open PS B-10.psd, then save it as **apple silhouette_PS-B**.

  b. Click the Quick Selection tool, click the Brush Picker list arrow on the Options bar, then set the Size setting to 10 px.

  c. Click and drag the brush slowly over the apple until the entire apple is selected.

  d. Click Select on the Menu bar, then click Refine Edge.

  e. Verify that Smart Radius is not checked, then drag the Radius slider to 3.

  f. Drag the Smooth slider to 25, then click OK.

  g. Click the Move tool, then move the selected pixels into the black space on the right part of the canvas.

  h. Deselect, compare your canvas to Figure B-28, save your work, then close apple silhouette_PS-B.psd.

FIGURE B-28

Independent Challenge 1

The Estonia Travel and Tourism Board has sent you a great image of a hot air balloon to promote sightseeing around Tallinn. They tell you that they love the image, but they don't like the colors of the balloon—they think the primary palette of yellow, red, and blue is "not exciting or magical." They ask that you change the colors of the balloon to something more interesting. You realize that you'll need to make a really good selection of the balloon so that the color changes won't show.

a. Open PS B-11.psd, then save it as **magic wand mask_PS-B**.

b. Click the Magic Wand tool.

c. Set the Tolerance to 20, then verify that the Anti-alias and Contiguous check boxes are both checked.

d. Use the Magic Wand tool to select the sky. (*Hint*: You will need to click multiple times with the Magic Wand tool to select the entire sky.)

e. Click Select on the Menu bar, then click Inverse.

f. Use the Lasso tool to remove the basket from the selection so that only the balloon is selected.

g. Click Select on the Menu bar, then click Refine Edge.

h. Click the View list arrow, then click On Black. (*Hint*: The selection is clearly outside of the edge of the balloon and is a very hard edge.)

i. Verify that the Smart Radius check box is not checked, then drag the Radius slider to 3.0.

j. Drag the Smooth slider to 9.

k. Drag the Contrast slider to 13, and note how the edge is improved.

l. Click OK, then hide the selection marquee.

m. Click Image on the Menu bar, point to Adjustments, then click Hue/Saturation.

n. Drag the Hue slider to -84, then click OK.

o. View the image at 100%, then scroll around to examine the edges.

p. Save your work, compare your screen to Figure B-29, then close magic wand mask_PS-B.psd.

FIGURE B-29

Independent Challenge 2

Your client has called, asking that you modify a file that shows balloons against the sky. They tell you that they would like you to posterize the balloons and change their color so that the yellow balloons are orange. They have created and saved a selection of the balloons to make your work easier.

a. Open PS B-12.psd, then save it as **orange balloons_PS-B**.

b. Posterize the image to 4 levels.

c. Open the Channels panel.

d. Press and hold [Ctrl](Win) or ⌘ (Mac), then click the Balloons channel thumbnail to load the selection.

e. Click Image on the Menu bar, point to Adjustments, then click Hue/Saturation.

f. Drag the Hue slider to -45, then click OK.

g. Deselect, then compare your result to Figure B-30.

h. Save your work, then close orange balloons_PS-B.psd.

FIGURE B-30

Independent Challenge 3

Your company has a client that specializes in online IQ tests. You've worked on producing more than 100 visual puzzles in the last month. Two of the puzzles have come back with requests for changes. The client has supplied two low-res examples of the changes for you to match.

a. Open PS B-13.psd, then save it as **iq test_PS-B**.

b. Open PS B-14.psd. (*Hint*: If you can, make room on your screen for both files. You need to make iq test_PS-B.psd match the small file.)

c. Use the Rectangular Marquee tool to draw one marquee around all four red boxes—be precise.

d. Draw one marquee around the four blue squares to deselect that entire area. (*Hint*: Use [Alt] (Win) or [option] (Mac) when drawing to deselect the area.)

e. Use the Magic Wand tool to remove the black squares from the selection with one click. (*Hint*: Deselect the Anti-alias and Contiguous check boxes on the Options bar and press [Alt] (Win) or [option] (Mac) when clicking a black square.)

f. Use the same method to remove the red squares from the selection.

g. Fill the remaining selection with the 50% gray swatch on the Swatches panel.

h. Deselect.

i. Click the first yellow swatch on the Swatches panel to make it the foreground color.

j. Use the Magic Wand tool to select only the white squares in the center, then fill them with yellow.

k. Use the Magic Wand tool to select the blue squares, then fill them with the first green swatch on the Swatches panel.

l. Select the four red squares, then fill them with the same yellow you used in Step j so that your screen resembles Figure B-31.

Advanced Challenge Exercise

- Expand the Swatches panel so that you can see all the swatches.
- Float your cursor in the gray area beneath the swatches so that your cursor turns into a paint bucket icon.
- Click the mouse pointer.
- Type **Yellow I Used** in the Name text box, then click OK.

m. Close PS B-14.psd.

n. Save your work, then close iq test_PS-B.psd.

FIGURE B-31

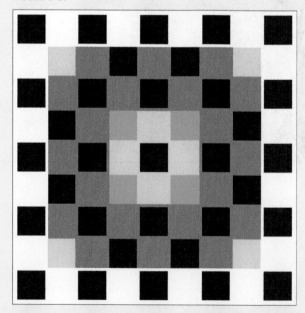

Real Life Independent Challenge

Your sister has just bought a new condo and has lots of wall space to fill. You have a great photo of her and decide to apply an "Andy Warhol" effect to the photo and give it to her to enlarge and frame.

   a. Open PS B-15.psd, then posterize the file to 6 levels.

   b. Click Image on the Menu bar, point to Mode, then click RGB Color.

   c. Open the Channels panel and keep it visible while you work.

   d. Click the Magic Wand tool, set the Tolerance to 8, then verify that the Anti-alias check box is not checked and that the Contiguous check box is not checked.

   e. Click the lightest gray area in the woman's cheek.

   f. Save the selection as **Lightest Gray**.

   g. Save three new selections named **Light Gray**, **Dark Gray**, and **Darkest Gray**. (*Hint*: Don't select any of the white areas or the black areas.)

   h. Use the Channels panel to load the Lightest Gray selection.

   i. Fill the selection with a color of your choice.

   j. Load and fill the three other saved selections with different colors. Figure B-32 shows one possible solution.

Advanced Challenge Exercise

- Load the Lightest Gray selection.
- Double-click the Edit in Quick Mask Mode button.
- Click the Color box and set the color to R255/G0/B0.
- Set the Opacity to 100%.
- Click OK.
- Click the Edit in Standard Mode button.

   k. Save the file with the alpha channels as **posterized woman_PS-B**.

   l. Close posterized woman_PS-B.psd.

FIGURE B-32

Visual Workshop

Open PS B-16.psd, then save it as **visual solution_PS-B**. Create a feathered selection so that the canvas resembles Figure B-33.

FIGURE B-33

Working with Layers

The Layers panel is one of Photoshop's greatest features because it allows you to segregate various art components onto different layers within a single document. Working with layers allows you to apply various effects, like drop shadows or glows, to individual art components without affecting others. Layers give you options for positioning artwork in relation to other artwork and allow you to move that artwork without affecting the content on other layers. At MegaPixel, you're given artwork for a print ad for a local jewelry retailer. The artwork involves a **montage**: multiple art components overlapping to create a single composition. You prepare yourself to work extensively with layers and the Layers panel.

OBJECTIVES

Work with the Layers panel

Merge layers and manipulate opacity

Duplicate, delete, and paste new layers

Scale artwork

Flip and rotate artwork

Add an Outer Glow layer style

Add a Drop Shadow layer style

Work with a layer mask

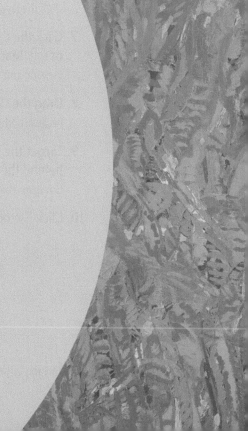

Working with the Layers Panel

The Layers panel houses all the layers in a document and offers you many options for manipulating those layers. Some basic operations you can do with the Layers panel and layered artwork are to hide or show various art components and move them independently of one another. ▓▓▓▓▓ Jon asks that you spend a few minutes examining the supplied document. He asks that you examine the layer structure and move items around just to get a sense of how the montage has been built.

STEPS

1. **Open PS C-1.psd, then save it as** roman holiday 1_PS-C

2. **Click the** Layers panel menu button ▤, **click Panel Options, click the** medium Thumbnail Size option button, **then click OK**

   The thumbnails in the figures throughout this unit are the medium size.

3. **Press and hold [Alt] (Win) or [option] (Mac), then click the** Indicates layer visibility button 👁 **on the Passport layer**

   Only the artwork on the Passport layer is visible. Pressing and holding [Alt] (Win) or [option] (Mac) and clicking the Indicates layer visibility button shows only that layer and hides all other layers.

   > **QUICK TIP**
   > You can make layers visible by clicking and dragging the mouse pointer over the empty gray squares on the Layers panel. The Indicates layer visibility buttons reappear.

4. **Click the** Indicates layer visibility button 👁 **on the Coin and Colosseum layers, then compare your screen to Figure C-1**

   The artwork on the two layers becomes visible.

5. **Make all the remaining layers visible**

6. **Click the** Move tool ⊹, **click the** Pen layer name **on the Layers panel, then click and drag the** pen artwork **to move it to the left side of the canvas**

   Only the artwork on the selected layer moves. Note that when you are directed to click or target a layer, click the layer name once. Only click the layer thumbnail when you are told to specifically.

   > **QUICK TIP**
   > Selecting a layer on the Layers panel is called targeting a layer.

7. **Click the** Couple layer name **on the Layers panel to target it, press and hold [Ctrl] (Win) or ⌘ (Mac), then click the** Couple Shadow layer name **so that both are selected**

   Pressing and holding [Ctrl] (Win) or ⌘ (Mac) allows you to select multiple layers on the Layers panel.

8. **Drag the** Couple **and** Couple Shadow **artwork to the upper-right corner of the canvas**

   Because both layers are selected on the Layers panel, the artwork on both layers moves as you drag.

9. **Target the** Coin layer, **then drag the** Coin artwork **down so that its bottom edge is behind the title**

   Compare your screen to Figure C-2. Your results will vary from the figure.

10. **Click File on the Menu bar, then click Revert**

FIGURE C-1: Viewing the visible layers

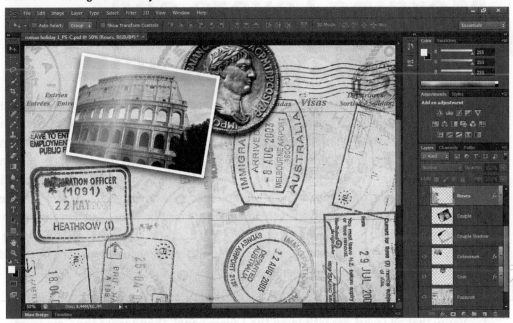

Three layers showing

FIGURE C-2: Canvas with repositioned artwork

Life without layers

It seems quite hard to believe now, but in the early versions of Photoshop, there were no layers! It was possible to overlap various components of artwork, but once you deselected, those components would become embedded in the canvas. So, if the montage we worked on in this lesson was created in Photoshop 2.0, all of the elements would have existed on one canvas, one bed of pixels. If you think about that for a moment, you get a real sense of the true benefit of working with layers: the options to edit, rethink, and redesign.

Merging Layers and Manipulating Opacity

On the Layers panel, artwork on a top layer appears in *front* of artwork on layers beneath it. Thus, artwork on the bottom layer would be behind the artwork on layers above it. You can use the Layers panel to reorder layers and also to merge layers. When you merge multiple layers, separate artwork on those layers is merged onto one layer and can no longer be manipulated individually. In Photoshop, the term opacity refers to how opaque artwork is. For example, if artwork has 100% opacity, it is completely opaque—no part of it is transparent. Conversely, artwork with 0% opacity is completely transparent and thus invisible. In between the two extremes, artwork with 50% opacity would be visible, but any artwork on a layer or layers beneath it would be visible *through* it. You decide to experiment with reordering the layers in hopes of improving the impact of the montage. You also experiment with merging layers and reducing the opacity of various artwork components.

STEPS

1. **Verify that all layers are visible on the Layers panel, then target the Coin layer**

2. **Drag the Coin layer above the Colosseum layer on the Layers panel until you see a horizontal gray line, as shown in Figure C-3, then release the mouse**

   The coin artwork appears in front of the Colosseum artwork.

3. **Click the Pen layer on the Layers panel, then drag it down below the Euros layer so that your canvas resembles Figure C-4**

QUICK TIP

When you merge artwork, the resulting merged layer takes on the name of the top of the original layers.

4. **Target both the Coin and the Colosseum layers, click the Layers panel menu button ☰, then click Merge Layers**

   The artwork is merged onto one layer as one piece of art. See the Clues to Use titled *Merging layers and memory* on the next page.

5. **Click the Move tool ▶✛, then click and drag to move the artwork in any direction**

   Both the Coin and Colosseum artwork move because they are now one piece of art on the same layer.

6. **Click Edit on the Menu bar, click Undo Move, then drag the Opacity slider on the Layers panel to 50%**

   The Coin and Colosseum artwork becomes 50% transparent. The Opacity slider can set a layer's opacity to any percentage between 0% and 100%.

7. **Target the Couple Shadow layer, then reduce its opacity to 75%**

QUICK TIP

With the Move tool or any selection tool selected, pressing [5] changes the opacity of a targeted layer to 50%, pressing [6] changes it to 60%, and so on. Pressing [0] results in 100% opacity.

8. **Verify that the Move tool is selected, target the Passport layer, then press [5]**

   The opacity of the Passport layer is reduced to 50%.

9. **Compare your canvas to Figure C-5, save your work, then close roman holiday 1_PS-C.psd**

FIGURE C-3: Moving the Coin layer above the Colosseum layer

Moving the layer

FIGURE C-4: Moving the Pen layer beneath the Euros layer

FIGURE C-5: Canvas with transparent artwork

Merging layers and memory

The more layers in a file, the larger the file size, and therefore merging layers reduces file size. Remember, though, that merging layers is a commitment: once artwork is merged onto a single layer, it can't be unmerged later on in the project (other than by undoing, reverting, or using the History panel). For example, if you merge two layers and then exit Photoshop, there will be no way to unmerge that artwork. Generally speaking, it's best to keep artwork segregated on different layers simply to keep your options open for any modifications you might need to make as your project evolves.

Duplicating, Deleting, and Pasting New Layers

Layers are created in Photoshop in a variety of ways. You can click the Create a new layer button on the Layers panel or use the New Layer command on the Layers panel menu. However, some of the most common ways that new layers are created are when you duplicate an existing layer or when you paste artwork copied from another file. Now that you've studied the layers in the document and made some changes to them, you decide to duplicate one layer to make a more interesting montage. Then Jon asks you to remove one piece of artwork and replace it with artwork from another file.

STEPS

1. **Open PS C-2.psd, save it as** roman holiday 2_PS-C, **target the** Coin layer, **click the** Layers panel menu button ▦, **then click** Duplicate Layer

2. **Type** Top Coin **in the As text box, then click** OK
   A duplicate of the original artwork is created in the same position on a layer immediately above the targeted layer.

3. **Use the Move tool** ▶⊕ **or the arrow keys to reposition the Top Coin artwork as shown in Figure C-6**

QUICK TIP
Pressing [Ctrl][J] (Win) or ⌘[J] (Mac) is the fastest and easiest way to duplicate a layer.

4. **With the Top Coin layer still targeted, press [Ctrl][J] (Win) or** ⌘**[J] (Mac)**
   The layer is duplicated.

5. **Double-click the** Top Coin copy layer name **on the Layers panel, type** Bottom Coin **to rename the layer, press [Enter] (Win) or [return] (Mac), drag the** Bottom Coin layer **beneath the Couple Shadow layer, then reposition the Bottom Coin artwork, as shown in Figure C-7**

QUICK TIP
Click the Don't show again check box in the warning dialog box if you don't want to be asked to confirm that you want to delete future layers.

6. **Target the** Colosseum layer, **click the Delete layer button** 🗑 **on the Layers panel, then click** Yes **to confirm that you want to delete the layer**

7. **Open Colosseum.psd, then view each layer separately to understand how the file was built**

8. **Show both layers, select all, click** Edit **on the Menu bar, then click** Copy Merged
   Clicking Copy Merged copies the visible image on the canvas as a single image. In other words, Copy Merged copies a combined, or "merged," result of all the visible layers.

9. **Close Colosseum.psd without saving changes, return to the roman holiday 2_PS-C.psd file, target the** Euros layer, **click** Edit **on the Menu bar, then click** Paste
   The artwork is pasted as a new layer, named Layer 1, directly above the targeted Euros layer.

10. **Name the new layer** Colosseum, **move it to the position shown in Figure C-8, then save your work**

FIGURE C-6: **Repositioning the Top Coin artwork**

FIGURE C-7: **Repositioning the Bottom Coin artwork**

FIGURE C-8: **Positioning the Colosseum artwork**

Pasting new layers

Whenever you copy artwork and then paste, the copied artwork is pasted onto a new layer, above the targeted layer on the Layers panel. This is a great feature in Photoshop, because you can always be confident that when you paste artwork, the new artwork will always be isolated on its own layer and will not directly affect any existing artwork in the file. If you use the Fit on Screen command on the View menu so that your entire canvas is visible before you paste, when you paste, the pasted artwork will be centered on the canvas. This knowledge can be very useful for alignment considerations.

UNIT
C
Photoshop CS6

Scaling Artwork

One of the preeminent features of Photoshop is the ability to **transform** artwork—moving, scaling, rotating, flipping, and distorting it. Transforming skills become important especially when creating a montage, because montages involve specific positioning relationships between elements. Resizing or **scaling** artwork is one of the most basic transformations, and one you'll use often. ▓▓▓▓▓ Now that the montage contains all of the elements that you want to work with, Jon asks you to reduce the size of the Colosseum and the Bottom Coin images.

STEPS

QUICK TIP
Throughout this lesson, keep an eye on the W and H text boxes on the Options bar to see the percentage of enlargement or reduction you are making to the width and height of the selected artwork.

1. **Verify that the Colosseum layer is targeted, click Edit on the Menu bar, point to Transform, then click Scale**

   The transform bounding box appears around the artwork. The bounding box has a square handle at each corner that you click and drag to transform artwork. The handles are sometimes referred to as resizing handles.

2. **Position the mouse pointer on the lower-right corner handle until a double-headed arrow appears, click and drag in many directions to modify the image, then release the mouse pointer**

   Clicking and dragging the corner handle allows you to enlarge, reduce, and/or distort the image.

3. **Undo your last step, position the mouse pointer on the lower-right corner handle, press and hold [Shift], click and drag in different directions, then release the mouse pointer**

   The [Shift] key constrains the scale proportionately. You can enlarge or reduce the artwork, but you can't modify the proportional relationship between the width and height.

4. **Undo the move, then note the crosshair icon in the middle of the bounding box**

   The crosshair icon is automatically positioned at the center of the bounding box and therefore at the center of the artwork.

QUICK TIP
If you activate the Maintain aspect ratio button (the link icon) between the W and H text boxes, any change you make to one will automatically be made to the other.

5. **On the Options bar, double-click the W text box, type 80, press [Tab], type 80 in the H text box, press [Tab], then compare your screen to Figure C-9**

   The artwork is scaled 80% at the crosshair, which is at the artwork's center point. By default, when you enter a scale value in the W and/or H text boxes on the Options bar, the artwork is scaled using the crosshair icon as the point of origin for the scale.

QUICK TIP
Press [Enter] (Win) or [return] (Mac) to apply a transformation quickly.

6. **Click the Move tool ⊹, then click Apply to apply the scale**

   You can press [Esc] to cancel a transformation.

7. **Target the Bottom Coin layer, press [Ctrl][T] (Win) or ⌘[T] (Mac), then drag the crosshair icon to the position shown in Figure C-10**

QUICK TIP
[Ctrl][T] (Win) or ⌘[T] (Mac) are the quick keys for accessing the Transform command.

8. **Press and hold [Shift][Alt] (Win) or [Shift][option] (Mac), position the mouse pointer over the lower-left handle, drag to experiment with resizing the coin artwork, then release the mouse pointer**

   Pressing and holding the [Alt] (Win) or [option] (Mac) key ensures that any transformation will be executed using the location of the crosshair as the point of origin. The [Shift] key is used in this step to constrain the width/height proportion of the artwork while scaling.

9. **Undo the move, double-click the W text box on the Options bar, type 67, press [Tab], type 67 in the H text box, press [Tab], then compare your screen to Figure C-11**

10. **Click ⊹, click Apply, then save your work**

FIGURE C-9: Using the Options bar to scale the artwork

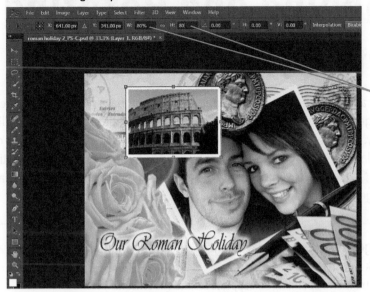

Width and
Height text
boxes on
Options bar

FIGURE C-10: Moving the crosshair icon

Crosshair icon
determines
the point of
origin for a
transformation

FIGURE C-11: Scaling the artwork from the relocated crosshair icon

Flipping and Rotating Artwork

Flipping and rotating are two transformations that can be very useful when creating a montage of various images. **Flipping** artwork creates a mirror image of the artwork. You can flip images horizontally or vertically. **Rotating** moves an object clockwise or counterclockwise around its center point, much like a windmill spins. You can rotate an image by hand or by entering a specific rotation value on the Options bar. Jon directs you to flip the main image in the montage and asks that you rotate the coins in the image so that it is not so obvious that they are duplicate images.

STEPS

1. **Target the** Colosseum layer, **click** Edit **on the Menu bar, point to** Transform, **then click** Rotate

   The transform bounding box appears around the artwork.

2. **Position the mouse pointer outside of the bounding box so that a curved double-arrow icon appears, click and drag to rotate the artwork to various rotations, then release the mouse pointer**

   QUICK TIP

   Entering a positive value in the Set rotation text box rotates artwork in a clockwise direction. Entering a negative value in the Set rotation text box rotates artwork in a counterclockwise direction.

3. **Undo the move, type** 17 **in the Set rotation text box on the Options bar, apply the transformation, then compare your result to Figure C-12**

   The image is rotated 17 degrees (clockwise) around its center point.

4. **Drag the** Colosseum layer **down on the Layers panel so that it is immediately above the** Passport layer

5. **Target both the** Couple **and the** Couple Shadow layers, **click** Edit **on the Menu bar, point to** Transform, **then click** Flip Horizontal

   The artwork on both layers is flipped horizontally.

6. **Verify that the Couple and Couple Shadow layers are still selected, add the** Bottom Coin layer **to the selection, then move the artwork down slightly to the position shown in Figure C-13**

   QUICK TIP

   Pressing and holding [Shift] when rotating rotates the artwork in 15 degree increments.

7. **Click the** Bottom Coin layer **so that it is the only targeted layer, press [Ctrl][T] (Win) or** ⌘[T] **(Mac), press and hold [Shift], then click and drag to rotate the bottom coin –45 degrees**

   The bottom coin is rotated and no longer appears as an obvious duplicate of the larger coin.

8. **Apply the rotation, then compare your artwork to Figure C-14**

9. **Save your work**

Rotating vs. flipping

Rotating and flipping are two very different transformations that produce different results. You can compare rotating artwork with the tire on your car turning on a specific point. By default, artwork in Photoshop is rotated around its center point unless you move the crosshair icon to a new location. When you flip artwork, you create a mirror image of the artwork. Photoshop offers you the ability to flip artwork horizontally (across an imaginary vertical axis) or vertically (across an imaginary horizontal axis). Flipping an image can produce odd results, especially when the image shows peoples' faces. Nobody's face is perfectly symmetrical, and flipping a face can yield unflattering results. Also remember, if there's text anywhere in an image when flipped, that text is going to read backwards, which is a dead giveaway that the image has been flipped! If you want to flip an image, target the layer that the image is on, click Edit on the Menu bar, point to Transform, then click Flip Horizontal or Flip Vertical.

FIGURE C-12: Rotating the Colosseum artwork

FIGURE C-13: Moving the artwork on three layers

FIGURE C-14: Rotating the bottom coin artwork

• Rotated coin

Adding an Outer Glow Layer Style

Layer styles are built-in effects that you can apply to layers; they include glows, shadows, bevels, embosses, and chiseled edges, among many others. When you apply a layer style to a layer, all the artwork on that layer inherits the layer style. Layer styles are listed on the Layers panel beneath the layer they've been applied to. Click the small black triangle to the right of the layer to expand or collapse the list of layer effects for that layer. ▓▓▓▓▓ Jon asks you to apply a gold outer glow to the pen artwork, similar to the glow around the bouquet of roses.

STEPS

QUICK TIP
Move the Layer Style dialog box to the side, if necessary, so that you can see the pen artwork on the canvas.

1. **Target the Pen layer, click Layer on the Menu bar, point to Layer Style, then click Outer Glow**

   The Layer Style dialog box opens. Note that on the left side is a list of all the available layer styles and that Outer Glow is checked and highlighted. The settings you see in the dialog box are settings for an outer glow.

2. **Enter the values shown in Figure C-15 and verify that the Preview check box is checked**

   As you change settings in the Layer Style dialog box, you will see changes made to the selected artwork in real time.

QUICK TIP
You can also choose a glow color by placing the mouse pointer over the canvas and then clicking a color with the eyedropper pointer when the Color Picker dialog box is open.

3. **Click the Set color of glow square, type 253 in the R text box, 226 in the G text box, and 162 in the B text box, click OK to close the Color Picker, then click OK to close the Layer Style dialog box**

4. **Compare your canvas and Layers panel to Figure C-16**

   The Outer Glow layer style is listed on the Layers panel as a component of the Pen layer; the Indicates layer effects icon appears on the layer, indicating a layer style has been applied to it.

5. **Click the Eye button 👁 on the Outer Glow layer style to hide and show the style**

6. **Double-click the Outer Glow layer style on the Layers panel to open the Layer Style dialog box**

   The Layer Style dialog box opens with the Outer Glow layer style settings.

7. **Drag the Opacity, Spread, and Size sliders to see the effect that each has on the outer glow effect, then click Cancel to close the Layer Style dialog box without saving the changes, then save your work**

Understanding the point of origin in a transformation

The point of origin defines the point from which a transformation occurs. For example, if you create a 2" × 2" square and then reduce it by 50% using its center point as the point of origin, all four sides of the square would move equally towards the center until the new size of the square was 1" × 1". Before you transform, move the crosshair icon to the point that you want to remain fixed, then transform the artwork using that point as the point of origin for the transformation.

Remember that the crosshair icon determines the point of origin automatically when you enter values on the Options bar. If you transform by hand by clicking and dragging the bounding box, you must press and hold [Alt] (Win) or [option] (Mac) to transform using the location of the crosshair as the point of origin.

FIGURE C-15: Settings for an Outer Glow layer style

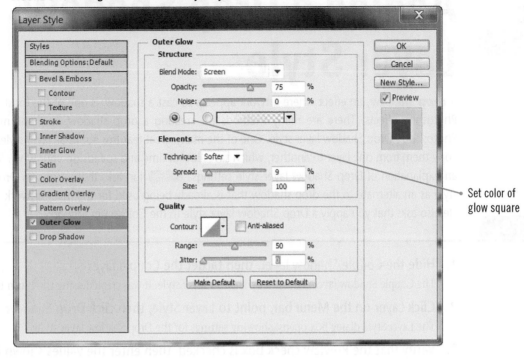

Set color of
glow square

FIGURE C-16: Viewing the layer style on the canvas and on the Layers panel

Indicates
layer effects
icon

Outer Glow
layer style
listed on
Layers panel

Adding a Drop Shadow Layer Style

A **drop shadow**, an effect where artwork appears to cast a shadow, is one of the most commonly used Photoshop effects. There are many methods for creating a drop shadow, and one method is to use Photoshop's Drop Shadow layer style. One of the many great features about all layer styles is that you can copy them from one layer to another, which saves lots of time and speeds up your work. See Table C-1 for an explanation of Drop Shadow layer style settings. Jon asks that you use a Drop Shadow layer style as an alternate to the drop shadow that is already being used for the main artwork in the montage. He also asks that you apply a Drop Shadow layer style to the Colosseum artwork.

STEPS

1. **Hide the** Couple Shadow layer, **then target the** Couple layer
   The Couple Shadow layer is not a drop shadow layer style. It was created using the Brush tool.

2. **Click** Layer **on the Menu bar, point to** Layer Style, **then click** Drop Shadow
   The Layer Style dialog box opens, showing settings for the Drop Shadow layer style.

3. **Verify that the Preview check box is checked, then enter the values shown in Figure C-17**

4. **Click** OK, **then compare your canvas to Figure C-18**

5. **Click the** Eye button 👁 **on the Drop Shadow layer style to hide and show the style**

6. **Press and hold** [Alt] **(Win) or** [option] **(Mac), drag the** Indicates layer effects icon _fx_ **to the Colosseum layer, then release the mouse pointer when a white frame surrounds the Colosseum layer**
   As shown in Figure C-19, the drop shadow appears behind the Colosseum artwork, and the Drop Shadow layer style is added to the Colosseum layer.

7. **Double-click the** Drop Shadow layer style **on the Colosseum layer to open the Layer Style dialog box, change the Spread value to** 12 **and the Size value to** 40, **then click** OK
   The drop shadow on the Colosseum artwork is updated.

8. **Save your work**

TABLE C-1: Drop Shadow layer style options

setting	purpose
Angle	Determines the lighting angle at which the effect is applied to the layer
Distance	Specifies the offset distance for the shadow—how far it is away from the artwork
Spread	Determines the size of the shadow effect before the edge blurs
Size	Controls the size of the blur at the edge of the effect

FIGURE C-17: Settings for a Drop Shadow layer style

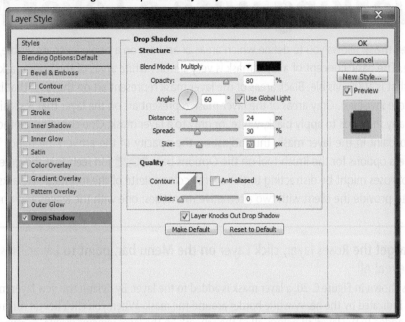

FIGURE C-18: Viewing the Drop Shadow layer style on the canvas and on the Layers panel

FIGURE C-19: Viewing the Drop Shadow layer style behind the Colosseum artwork and on the Layers panel

Working with Layers

Working with a Layer Mask

A **layer mask** allows you to define which areas of artwork on a single layer are visible, not visible, or partly visible. The basic concept of a layer mask is very simple: white areas of the layer mask represent art on the layer that is 100% visible. Black areas of the layer mask represent art on the layer that is 100% masked (and therefore invisible). Gray areas of the layer mask represent art on the layer that is semitransparent. You can use many methods to apply black, white, or gray to a layer mask. One common method is to use the Brush tool to paint in the layer mask, thus adjusting the opacity of the artwork by hand. You can set size and hardness options for the Brush tool on the Options bar. ▓▓▓▓ Jon feels that the green leaves on the bouquet of roses might be distracting to the overall color palette of the montage. He asks that you use a layer mask to provide the client with two alternative montages: one with the leaves and one without the leaves.

STEPS

1. **Target the Roses layer, click Layer on the Menu bar, point to Layer Mask, then click Reveal All**

   As shown in Figure C-20, a layer mask is added to the layer. By default the new layer mask is targeted, which is indicated by the heavy white border around the mask. When you click Reveal All, an all-white layer mask is added to the layer; therefore, all of the artwork on the layer remains visible, or revealed. The Hide All type of layer mask creates an all-black layer mask in which all of the artwork is hidden.

2. **Click the small gray triangle on the Roses layer to reveal the layer effects, then hide the Outer Glow layer style on the Roses layer**

3. **Click the Default Foreground and Background Colors button ▣ on the Tools panel, click the Switch Foreground and Background Colors button ▣ so that the foreground color is white, then click the Brush tool ✎**

4. **On the Options bar, verify that the Opacity setting is 100%, click the Brush Preset picker list arrow, set the Size to 15 px, then set the Hardness to 30%**

5. **Zoom in so that the top green leaf in the bouquet is large on your screen, then paint over the leaf until the entire leaf is no longer visible**

   The areas you paint become invisible because you are painting black in the layer mask, not on the canvas.

6. **Scroll, then paint to mask out the bottom leaf, as shown in Figure C-21**

7. **Press and hold [Alt] (Win) or [option] (Mac), click the layer mask thumbnail on the Layers panel, then compare your canvas and Layers panel to Figure C-22**

   Pressing and holding [Alt] (Win) or [option] (Mac) and clicking the layer mask thumbnail displays the layer mask on the canvas.

8. **Click the Roses Layer thumbnail to the left of the layer mask thumbnail**

   The canvas displays the artwork on the layer. The layer mask is no longer targeted, but it is still active.

9. **Press and hold [Shift], then click the layer mask thumbnail on the Roses layer**

   As shown in Figure C-23, the layer mask is inactive, and the green leaves are visible once again.

10. **Save your work, close roman holiday 2_PS-C.psd, then exit Photoshop**

Three Brush tool techniques

Practice these three techniques that will make you much more effective with the Brush tool:

1. Press the right bracket key repeatedly to increase the brush size.
2. Press the left bracket key repeatedly to decrease the brush size.

3. [Shift]-click the brush to cover large areas. Click the brush once anywhere on the canvas. Move the brush pointer to a different location. Press and hold [Shift], then click the brush at the new location. The Brush tool will paint from the first click and connect to the second click.

FIGURE C-20: **Layer mask added to the Roses layer**

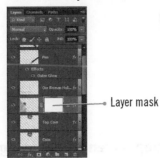

Layer mask

FIGURE C-21: **Artwork with both leaves masked out**

Masked pixels in the
layer mask and on
the artwork

FIGURE C-22: **Viewing the layer mask**

Masked areas
in the layer
mask

FIGURE C-23: **Deactivating the layer mask**

Leaf is visible because
layer mask is inactive

Red X indicates
layer mask is
inactive

Working with Layers

Practice

Concepts Review

Label the elements of the Photoshop screen shown in Figure C-24.

FIGURE C-24

Match each term with the statement that best describes it.

6. Transform
7. Layer style
8. Layer mask
9. Opacity
10. Flipping
11. Merging
12. Indicates layer effects icon

a. Used to affect image opacity in specific areas
b. Appears when layer styles are applied
c. Transformation that creates a mirror image
d. The measure of how opaque artwork is
e. Effects such as a drop shadow or an outer glow
f. Condensing layered artwork onto one layer
g. To move, scale, or rotate an image

Select the best answer from the list of choices.

13. Which of the following is not a benefit of using layers?

    a. Organization

    b. Segregation

    c. Editing ability

    d. Saving file space

14. Which of the following is not a layer style?

    a. Outer Glow

    b. Blur

    c. Drop Shadow

    d. Inner Shadow

15. Which of the following is not a transformation option?

    a. Rotate

    b. Blend

    c. Scale

    d. Move

16. Which of the following is not true about the Opacity slider?

    a. It can be applied to specific areas of a layer.

    b. It can be applied at 52%.

    c. It can be used to make pixels semitransparent.

    d. It is manipulated only on the Layers panel.

17. Which of the following is not true about a layer mask?

    a. It can be used to manipulate opacity in specific areas of a layer.

    b. One layer mask affects all areas of the layer.

    c. It is created by default when you create a new layer.

    d. It can be shown and hidden.

18. Which of the following is true about a layer mask?

    a. An all-black layer mask means all the artwork on the layer is visible.

    b. An all-white layer mask means all the artwork on the layer has 0% opacity.

    c. Pixels in a layer mask are either black or white.

    d. A light gray layer mask means all the artwork on the layer is semitransparent.

Skills Review

1. Work with the Layers panel.

    a. Open PS C-3.psd, then save it as **shining future 1_PS-C**.

    b. Click the Layers panel menu button, click Panel Options, choose the medium Thumbnail Size option button, then click OK.

    c. Press and hold [Alt] (Win) or [option] (Mac), then click the Indicates layer visibility button on the Flower layer.

    d. Click the Indicates layer visibility button on the Background and Flower Shadow layers.

    e. Make all the remaining layers visible.

    f. Click the Move tool, click the Moon layer on the Layers panel, then drag the moon artwork to move it to the right side of the canvas behind the flower.

    g. Click the Child layer to select it, press and hold [Ctrl] (Win) or ⌘ (Mac), then click the Child Shadow layer so that both are selected.

    h. Drag to move the Child and Child Shadow artwork up so that the child is "standing" in the water.

    i. Target the Type artwork, then move it to the left so it is outside of the flower's shadow.

    j. Save your work, then close shining future 1_PS-C.psd.

2. Merge layers and manipulate opacity.

    a. Open PS C-4.psd, then save it as **shining future 2_PS-C**.

    b. Verify that all layers are visible, then target the Moon layer on the Layers panel.

    c. Drag the Moon layer down below the Flower Shadow layer on the Layers panel.

    d. Click the Type layer, then drag it to the top of the Layers panel so that it is the top layer.

    e. Target both the Flower and the Purple Center layers, click the Layers panel menu button, then click Merge Layers.

    f. Click the Move tool, then drag the merged artwork to the right of the canvas.

Skills Review (continued)

g. Undo the move, target the Moon layer, then drag the Opacity slider on the Layers panel to 55%.

h. Target the Dolphin layer, then reduce the Opacity to 75%.

i. Verify that the Move tool is selected, then press [5].

j. Save your work, then close shining future 2_PS-C.psd.

3. Duplicate, delete, and paste new layers.

a. Open PS C-5.psd, save it as **bright shining future_PS-C**, target the Moon layer, click Layer on the Menu bar, then click Duplicate Layer.

b. Type **Middle Moon** in the As text box, then click OK.

c. With the Middle Moon layer still targeted, press [Ctrl][J] (Win) or ⌘[J] (Mac).

d. Double-click the Middle Moon Copy name, then rename the layer as **Little Moon**.

e. Target the Purple Center layer, click the Delete layer button on the Layers panel, then click Yes to confirm that you want to delete the layer.

f. Open Globe.psd, then note that the file has three layers.

g. Click Select on the Menu bar, click Load Selection, click the Channel list arrow, click Globe Only, then click OK.

h. Click Edit on the Menu bar, then click Copy Merged.

i. Close Globe.psd without saving changes, return to the bright shining future_PS-C.psd file, target the Flower layer, then paste.

j. Name the new layer **Globe**, move it to the position shown in Figure C-25, then save your work.

4. Scale artwork.

a. Target the Little Moon layer, click Edit on the Menu bar, point to Transform, then click Scale.

b. Position the mouse pointer over the lower-right corner handle until a double-headed arrow appears, click and drag in many directions to modify the image, then release the mouse pointer.

c. Undo the move, position the mouse pointer over the lower-right corner handle, press and hold [Shift], click and drag in different directions, then release the mouse pointer.

d. Undo the move, then note the crosshair icon in the middle of the bounding box.

e. On the Options bar, double-click the W text box, type **10**, press [Tab], type **10** in the H text box, then press [Tab].

f. Click the Move tool, then click Apply to apply the scale.

g. Target the Middle Moon layer, then press [Ctrl][T] (Win) or ⌘[T] (Mac).

h. Press and hold [Shift][Alt] (Win) or [Shift][option] (Mac), position the mouse pointer over the lower-right selection handle, click and drag to experiment with different sizes, then release the mouse pointer.

FIGURE C-25

Skills Review (continued)

i. Undo the move, double-click the W text box, type **28**, press [Tab], type **28** in the H text box, press [Tab], then click the Move tool to apply the scale.

j. With the Move tool, move the Little Moon and Middle Moon artwork to the positions shown in Figure C-26, then save your work.

5. Flip and rotate artwork.

a. Target the Middle Moon layer, click Edit on the Menu bar, point to Transform, then click Rotate.

b. Position the mouse pointer outside of the bounding box so that a curved double-arrow icon appears, click and drag to rotate the artwork to various rotations, then release the mouse pointer.

c. Undo the move, type **27** in the Set rotation text box on the Options bar, then apply the transformation.

d. Target both the Child and the Child Shadow layers, click Edit on the Menu bar, point to Transform, then click Flip Horizontal.

e. Target the Little Moon layer, press [Ctrl][T] (Win) or ⌘ [T] (Mac), press and hold [Shift], then drag the rotate pointer to rotate the artwork –45 degrees.

f. Apply the rotation, then save your work.

6. Add an Outer Glow layer style.

a. Target the Dolphin layer, click Layer on the Menu bar, point to Layer Style, then click Outer Glow.

b. Verify that the Preview check box is checked, set the Blend mode to screen, set the Opacity to 75%, set the Noise to 0, set the Spread to 27%, then set the Size to 40.

c. Click the Set color of glow square, type **255** in the R text box, **190** in the G text box, and **255** in the B text box, click OK to close the Color Picker, then click OK to close the Layer Style dialog box.

d. Hide and show the Outer Glow layer style on the Layers panel to hide and show the effect on the artwork.

e. Double-click the Outer Glow layer style on the Layers panel to open the Layer Style dialog box.

f. Drag the Opacity, Spread, and Size sliders to see the effect that each has on the outer glow effect, then click Cancel to close the Layer Style dialog box without applying the changes.

g. Save your work, then compare your screen to Figure C-27.

7. Add a Drop Shadow layer style.

a. Target the Type layer.

b. Click Layer on the Menu bar, point to Layer Style, then click Drop Shadow.

c. Verify that the Preview check box is checked, set the Blend Mode to Multiply, set the Opacity to 100%, set the Distance to 9, set both the Spread and Size to 0, then click OK.

d. On the Layers panel toggle the Drop Shadow layer style off and on to hide and show the effect.

e. Target the Dolphin layer, press and hold [Alt] (Win) or [option] (Mac), click and drag the Indicates layer effects icon to the Globe layer, then release the mouse pointer when a white frame appears around the Globe layer.

f. Save your work.

FIGURE C-26

FIGURE C-27

Skills Review (continued)

8. Work with a layer mask.

   a. Target the Moon layer, click Layer on the Menu bar, point to Layer Mask, then click Reveal All.

   b. Click the Default Foreground and Background Colors button on the Tools panel, click the Switch Foreground and Background Colors button, then click the Brush tool.

   c. On the Options bar, verify that the Opacity setting is 100%, click the Brush Preset picker list arrow, set the Size to 125 pixels, then set the Hardness to 40%.

   d. Paint over the bottom third of the moon so that it is no longer visible.

   e. Press and hold [Alt] (Win) or [option] (Mac), then click the layer mask thumbnail on the Layers panel to view the mask.

   f. Click the Moon layer thumbnail to the left of the layer mask thumbnail to view the artwork again.

   g. Press and hold [Shift], then click the layer mask thumbnail on the Moon layer to make it inactive.

   h. Press and hold [Shift], then click the layer mask thumbnail on the Moon layer to make it active.

   i. Compare your results to Figure C-27.

   j. Save your work, close bright shining future_PS-C.psd, then exit Photoshop.

Independent Challenge 1

The Web Design department at your advertising agency has asked you to create a drop shadow to create a "white on white" effect that they will be using for graphics on a website they are building.

   a. Open PS C-6.psd, then save it as **roman numerals_PS**-C.

   b. Hide the Background layer to see the contents of the XVII layer, show the Background layer again, then target the XVII layer.

   c. Click Layer on the Menu bar, point to Layer Style, then click Drop Shadow.

   d. Verify that the Preview check box is checked, set the Opacity to 80%, set the Distance to 34, set the Spread to 0, set the Size to 40, then click OK.

   e. Click Layer on the Menu bar, point to Layer Style, then click Stroke.

   f. Experiment with the Size slider to see the effect on the XVII artwork.

   g. Enter the values shown in Figure C-28 then click OK.

   h. Save your work, compare your result to Figure C-29, then close roman numerals_PS-C.psd.

FIGURE C-28

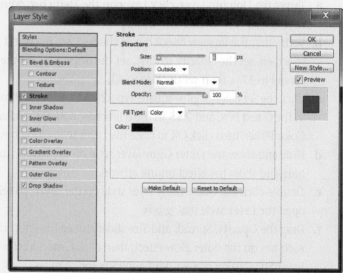

FIGURE C-29

Independent Challenge 2

The web design department at your advertising agency is designing a splash page for a website that shows an image of a dolphin in front of a large moon. You are asked to copy the dolphin image into the moon file, then use a layer mask to remove the background from the dolphin image.

a. Open PS C-7.psd, then save it as **dolphin moon_PS-C**.

b. Open Dolphin Sky.psd, select all, copy, then close Dolphin Sky.psd.

c. Return to dolphin moon_PS-C.psd, paste, then name the new layer **Dolphin**.

d. Click Layer on the Menu bar, point to Layer Mask, then click Reveal All.

e. Set the foreground color on the Tools panel to black.

f. Click the Brush tool, verify that the Opacity is set to 100%, change the Size to 40 pixels, then set the Hardness to 80% on the Options bar.

g. Paint over the big areas of blue sky to mask them out.

h. Zoom in on the dolphin's head, reduce the Master Diameter of the Brush to 7 px, then paint along the edges of the dolphin to remove the sky completely. (*Hint*: Use the Hand tool to scroll around the magnified image.)

i. Compare your result to Figure C-30, save your work, the close dolphin moon_PS-C.psd.

FIGURE C-30

Independent Challenge 3

You have been asked to take over the design of a splash page for an important client. You are given the artwork that the Web Design department has created so far, along with notes on how to finish the job.

a. Open PS C-8.psd, then save it as **double dolphins_PS-C**.

b. Drag the Green Moon layer beneath the Purple Moon layer.

c. Target the Dolphin layer, then duplicate the layer.

d. Rename the new layer **Small Dolphin**.

e. Click the Move tool, press and hold [Shift], then click and drag the Small Dolphin artwork straight down and center it over the Green Moon artwork.

f. Select both the Green Moon layer and the Small Dolphin layer.

g. Scale the artwork 50%.

h. Save your work, then compare your canvas to Figure C-31.

FIGURE C-31

Independent Challenge 3 (continued)

Advanced Challenge Exercise

- Target just the Small Dolphin layer.
- Rotate the small dolphin 180 degrees.
- Target the Dolphin layer.
- Flip it horizontally.

i. Close double dolphins_PS-C.psd, then exit Photoshop.

Real Life Independent Challenge

It's the end of the summer and you have some great photos to share with family and friends. Rather than just send out an individual photo, you decide to make a montage of three photos, two of them inset into a larger photo.

a. Open PS C-9.psd, then save it as **sisters postcard_PS-C**.

b. Open Jenny.tif, select all, copy, then close Jenny.tif.

c. Paste the artwork into sisters postcard_PS-C.psd, then rename the layer **Jenny**.

d. Open Annie.tif, select all, copy, then close Annie.tif.

e. Paste the artwork into sisters postcard_PS-C.psd, then rename the layer **Annie**.

f. Move the Jenny artwork to the upper-right corner.

g. Scale the Jenny artwork so that it fits into the upper-right corner without overlapping the girls in the main image.

h. Move the Annie artwork to the lower-left corner.

i. Scale the Annie artwork so that it fits into the lower-left corner over the girl's legs.

j. Add a light yellow outer glow layer style to the Jenny artwork.

k. Copy the layer style from the Jenny artwork to the Annie artwork.

l. Compare your result to Figure C-32, then save your work.

Real Life Independent Challenge (continued)

Advanced Challenge Exercise

- Double-click the Outer Glow layer on the Annie layer, then drag the Layer Style dialog box to the right so that you can see the canvas.
- Click the Set color of glow box in the Layer Style dialog box.
- Position the eyedropper pointer over the pink stripe in the little girl's dress, then click.
- Close the Color Picker dialog box, then close the Layer Style dialog box.

m. Close sisters postcard_PS-C.psd, then exit Photoshop.

FIGURE C-32

Visual Workshop

Open PS C-10.psd, then save it as **three glowing globes_PS-C**. Reorder the layers and move the globes to the position shown in Figure C-33. Add a gold Outer Glow layer style to the large gold globe. Copy the Outer Glow layer style from the Gold Globe layer to the Pink Globe and the Blue Globe layers. Change the color of the glow on the two smaller globes to match the figure. Close three glowing globes_PS-C.psd, then exit Photoshop.

FIGURE C-33

Improving Images with Adjustment Layers

Files You Will Need:

To view a list of files needed for this unit, see the Data Files Grid in the back of the book.

In our digital world, images can come from just about anywhere. Photoshop offers many practical **adjustment** operations to improve characteristics of images: their color, their contrast, their overall effect. An adjustment layer is called "non-destructive" because it exists as a layer on the Layers panel and allows you to apply adjustments to images without directly affecting the artwork. Brightness/Contrast, Levels, and Color Balance are three common, powerful, and highly useful adjustments for improving the overall appearance of an image. When you understand the basics of Grayscale and RGB color modes, then you're ready and able to dramatically improve your images with adjustments. Jon asks you to improve the appearance of a number of grayscale and RGB images using adjustments.

OBJECTIVES

Understand grayscale

Investigate a grayscale image

Use the Brightness/Contrast adjustment

Adjust black and white points with levels

Adjust the midpoint with levels

Investigate an RGB image

Use the Color Balance adjustment

Use the Vibrance adjustment

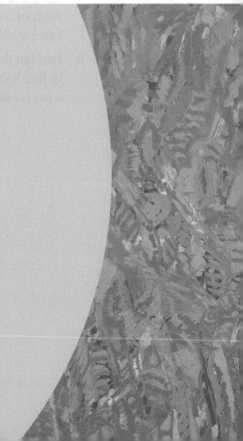

Understanding Grayscale

A **grayscale** image is a digital image in which each pixel can be one—and only one—of 256 shades of gray. With 256 shades of gray available per pixel, the illusion of a continuous tone image can be created. The grayscale range is 0–255. Pixels with a grayscale value of 0 are black. Pixels with a grayscale value of 255 are white. Any number in between 0 and 255 is gray—light gray or dark gray—with 128 being the middle point in the grayscale range. Jon tells you about a new client who will be supplying imagery that will require lots of analysis and correction for quality and color. He gives you a grayscale image and asks that you analyze it.

STEPS

1. Open PS D-1.psd, then save it as grayscale_PS-D

2. Click Image on the Menu bar, point to Mode, then note that Grayscale is checked

   This image has been saved in Grayscale mode, meaning that one of 256 shades of gray is available per pixel.

3. Click the Window menu, then click Info to open the Info panel, click the Info panel menu button ⊟, click Panel Options, enter the settings shown in Figure D-1, then click OK

   When you set the readouts on the Info panel to RGB, they indicate the grayscale value of each pixel, from 0–255. The three readouts—R, G, and B—will always be the same for a grayscale image; you can think of them as a single number.

> **QUICK TIP**
> Identifying pixel information on the Info panel is referred to as **sampling** pixels.

4. Click the Eyedropper tool 🖋, then position it over different areas of the image, noting the readouts on the Info panel

5. Position the Eyedropper tool at the very bottom of the gradient on the right, then move slowly to the top of the gradient

   The pixels in the gradient range from 0 at the bottom to 255 at the top.

6. Sample areas in the man's shoulder to see the grayscale information for the darker areas of the image, then see if you can find pixels with a value of 0, the darkest pixels in the grayscale range

7. Sample areas in the white stripe in the hat and parts of the hood to find mid-range areas of the image, then see if you can find pixels with a value near 128, which is the exact middle of the grayscale range

8. Position the Eyedropper tool over the man's cheek and the light area at the lower right to find light areas of the image

   Figure D-2 identifies some of the lightest pixels in the image.

FIGURE D-1: Info Panel Options dialog box

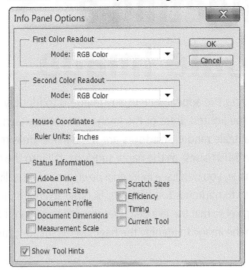

FIGURE D-2: Sampling the lightest pixels in the image

Very light pixels

Choosing settings on the Info panel

Why do you set the readouts on the Info panel to RGB if you are sampling a pixel in a grayscale image? Because the RGB readouts identify pixel values in grayscale, from 0–255. If you sampled pixels using the Grayscale setting on the Info panel, the readouts would identify pixels in ink percentages. In other words, the readouts would provide information for what would be a printed reproduction of the image. In a printed piece, a pixel with the value of 100% is a black printed dot. Zero percent means no ink, and on white paper, where there's 0% ink, that area remains white. So generally speaking, when adjusting an image, you'll want to use the RGB settings on the Info panel, because that setting presents pixels' grayscale values.

Improving Images with Adjustment Layers

Investigating a Grayscale Image

The first step in analyzing the appearance of any image is to identify the highlights, midtones, and shadows. **Highlights** are the lightest areas of the image and are represented by pixels whose value falls in the upper third of the grayscale range. **Shadows** are the darkest areas represented by pixels in the low third of the grayscale range. **Midtones**, as the name suggests, fall into the middle range of the grayscale. When you look at a digital image, you don't see individual pixels, you see the illusion of **continuous tone**: a smooth transition from shadows to midtones to highlights. In order to create this illusion, a sufficient number of grays must be available per pixel so that the eye perceives smooth transitions between tones. ▄▄▙▘ Jon asks you to continue working with the image to identify the basic overall shadow, midtone, and highlight areas.

1. Move the Info panel to the upper-left corner of the canvas, then close the Properties panel, if necessary

2. On the Layers panel, make the Chart layer visible, then compare your canvas to Figure D-3
   The chart uses a gradient to identify the shadow, midtone, and highlight areas of the grayscale image.

3. Look at the image of the man and try to see it not as a picture but as a range of tones from shadows to midtones to highlights

4. Using the chart as a guide, sample different areas of the image to identify shadows, midtones, and highlights

5. Target the Background layer on the Layers panel

QUICK TIP

The readouts on the Info panel now show before and after information. The number on the left refers to the original grayscale value of a given pixel, and the number on the right refers to the value with the posterize adjustment applied; this value can only be 0, 148, or 255.

6. Click the Image menu, point to Adjustments, click Posterize, drag the Levels slider to 3, and keep the Posterize dialog box open

7. Drag the Posterize dialog box out of the way, if necessary, then compare your image and the gradient on the right to Figure D-4
   At this posterize setting, only three shades of gray are available per pixel: 0, 148, and 255. Each pixel can be one and only one of these grayscale values. This image now has one color for highlights, one for midtones, and one for shadows. In the same way that those three shades are unable to render a smooth gradient on the right, they are unable to render the image as a smooth continuous-tone image.

8. Position the pointer over the image and note the readouts on the Info panel

QUICK TIP

The appearance of the gradient in this figure is called **stair-stepping**, which refers to the idea that you can see each step in the transition from black to white.

9. In the Posterize dialog box, change the Levels value to 16, then compare your result to Figure D-5
   At this setting, 16 shades of gray are available per pixel. The image has clearly improved, but not nearly enough to create the illusion of continuous tone. The effect on the gradient at the right of the window mirrors the effect of the image. Just as the gradient shows distinct steps between grays, the image shows the same effect, especially in the hood and in the image background areas on the right side. However, note that at a very quick glance, your eye might accept the appearance of the knitted hat and—to some degree—the man's face as continuous tone.

10. Change the Levels value to 200
    At this level—still inferior to the standard 256 levels available in a grayscale image—the eye cannot identify any stair-stepping effect in the image; it appears to be continuous tone. The gradient on the right, however, still shows some signs of stair-stepping.

11. Click Cancel, hide the Chart layer on the Layers panel, save your work, then close grayscale_PS-D.psd

FIGURE D-3: Shadows, midtones, and highlights identified on the gradient

FIGURE D-4: Image with three shades of gray available per pixel

Every pixel can be one of three shades of gray

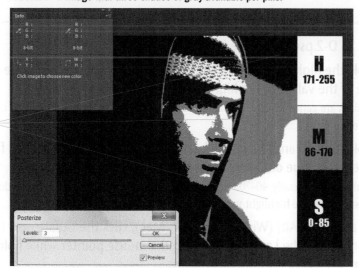

FIGURE D-5: Image with 16 shades of gray available per pixel

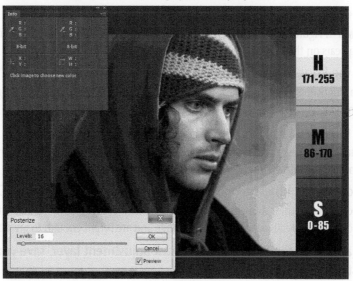

Background and gradient show stair-stepping

Improving Images with Adjustment Layers

Using the Brightness/ Contrast Adjustment

Adjustments are operations you do that affect the appearance of an image, such as manipulating brightness and contrast. You can make adjustments directly to pixels on a layer, but you can't go back and re-adjust at a later time. **Adjustment layers** are adjustments you make that exist as layers on the Layers panel. Once created, they affect the image, but they can be manipulated at a later time. You can hide an adjustment layer or show it, and you can delete it at any time.

The Brightness/Contrast adjustment, as the name suggests, affects the brightness and contrast in an image. **Brightness** is defined by a pixel's grayscale value: the higher the number, the brighter the pixel. **Contrast** is represented by the relationship between the highlights and shadows. When the highlights aren't bright enough and the shadows aren't dark enough, the image will lack contrast and appear "flat" in its tonal range. Good contrast is created when highlights and shadows are distinctly different in tonal range: bright vs. dark. Jon gives you an image that overall is too dark and has poor contrast. He asks that you use the Brightness/Contrast adjustment to improve the tonal range of the image.

STEPS

1. **Open PS D-2.psd, then save it as** adjust brightness contrast_PS-D

2. **Sample the highlight areas of the face, including the whites of the eyes, to get a general range of the values of the highlights in the image**

   The values are generally 140–170, far too low for highlights, which should be over 200. This image is not bright enough.

3. **Sample the hair and the image background area to the left of the face to get an idea of the general range of the shadows in the image**

   The values are generally 40–70, which puts them at the high end of the shadow range. The image lacks contrast because the highlight values are too close to the shadow values.

4. **Press and hold [Alt] (Win) or [option] (Mac), click the** Create new fill or adjustment layer **button** ◔ **on the Layers panel, drag the mouse pointer while holding down the mouse button, then click** Brightness/Contrast

   The New Layer dialog box and the Properties panel open. The Properties panel displays the settings for the current adjustment.

5. **Click** OK **to close the New Layer dialog box**

   As shown in Figure D-6, the Properties panel shows Brightness and Contrast sliders, and a Brightness/Contrast layer appears on the Layers panel.

6. **Drag the Brightness slider on the Properties panel to** 75

   With a Brightness value of 75, the pixels in the face fall into the 200–225 range. As shown in Figure D-7, with increased brightness, the appearance of the image improves dramatically.

7. **Drag the** Contrast slider **on the Properties panel to** 80

   The shadows darken and the highlights brighten. The shadows are improved dramatically, especially in the hair and the dark details of the face, like the pupils and the eyelashes.

8. **Reduce the Brightness to** 65**, then compare your result to Figure D-8**

   The reduced brightness deepens the shadows and increases the visible details of the face. Note the freckles. The face pixels still fall into the highlight range and are bright enough to give the image stunning contrast.

9. **Hide and show the Brightness/Contrast adjustment layer, save your work, then close adjust brightness contrast_PS-D.psd.**

Improving Images with Adjustment Layers

FIGURE D-6: Brightness/Contrast adjustment layer on the Layers panel

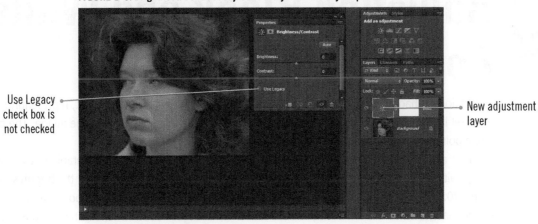

Use Legacy
check box is
not checked

New adjustment
layer

FIGURE D-7: Increasing the brightness

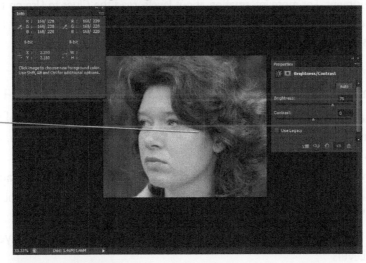

Face is brighter but
still shows detail

FIGURE D-8: Before and after the adjustment

Extreme working behavior

A key to making adjustments is to sometimes walk the fine line between going far enough to make the adjustment the best it can be and going too far. When making adjustments, the first thing many designers do is push the adjustment to the extreme to see what the adjustment looks like when it's too much. When you work this way, seeing what you don't want can make it easier to find what you do want. Experiment with adjustments to see them at their extreme first. You're training your eye to recognize when an image looks its best, and recognizing when an image looks *bad* is a big part of that training.

Adjusting Black and White Points with Levels

In addition to shadows, midtones, and highlights, every image has a **black point**, representing the darkest pixel in the image, and a **white point**, representing the brightest pixel in the image. The black and white points represent the start and the end of the tonal range of the image.

Black and white points have a substantial effect on contrast. Often, photographers will capture an image with settings defined that the darkest pixel be no darker than, say, 15, and the brightest no lighter than 240. This forces the camera not to make shadows too dark or highlights too white. It results in an image that has a smooth tonal range from shadow to highlight but still lacks contrast because the darkest shadows aren't dark enough and the whitest highlights aren't white enough. This can be fixed using a Levels adjustment. For more information about levels, read the Clues to Use on the next page titled *How the Levels adjustment works.* Jon gives you an image with poor contrast and says he suspects the problem is with the black and white points.

STEPS

1. **Open PS D-3.psd, then save it as** adjust white and black points_PS-D

2. **Take a moment to make a visual analysis of the image and its tonal range**

   The image looks good, with a smooth range from shadow to highlight. However, it has low contrast-it lacks "snap," and it's "flat."

3. **Sample the image to find the darkest and lightest pixels in the image**

   The darkest pixels are in the low 20s and the lightest pixels are around 230. No pixels have a grayscale value of 0–19 or 234–255.

4. **Click the** Create new fill or adjustment layer button ⬤ **on the Layers panel, then click** Levels

   The Properties panel displays settings for the Levels adjustment layer.

5. **Resize the Properties panel so that you can see all of it, as shown in Figure D-9**

   The histogram, shown on the panel, reflects exactly what you learned when sampling the image. The **histogram** is a visual reference of every pixel in the image, or in a selection if only part of the image is selected. The black point on the histogram is represented by the black triangle, and the white point is represented by the white triangle. The tonal range of the image does not use the entire grayscale, represented by the gradient ramp below the histogram. Note how far to the right of the black triangle the histogram begins, and how far it ends from the white triangle.

   QUICK TIP
   The repositioned black and white triangles determine the new range of the histogram. The pixels at the far left of the histogram now have a grayscale value of 0, and those at the far right now have a grayscale value of 255.

6. **Drag the** black triangle **immediately beneath the histogram towards the right to the beginning of the histogram, drag the** white triangle **towards the left to the end of the histogram, then compare your result to Figure D-10**

7. **Hide and show the Levels 1 adjustment layer on the Layers panel to see the before and after view of the image**

   The *lengthened* tonal range is a stunning improvement in overall contrast for the image.

8. **Save your work**

FIGURE D-9: **Properties panel with Levels adjustment layer settings**

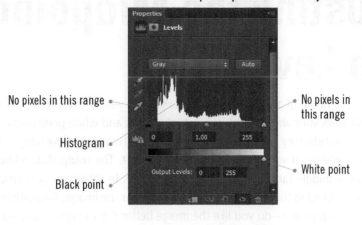

No pixels in this range •

• No pixels in this range

Histogram •

Black point •

• White point

FIGURE D-10: **Adjusting the black and white points**

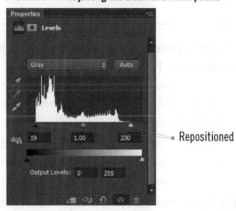

• Repositioned

How the Levels adjustment works

The Levels type of adjustment, shown in Figure D-11, is a powerful adjustment option for affecting the tonal range of images. The most striking component of the Levels adjustment is the histogram.

Imagine that the histogram has 256 slots, one for each of the 256 available colors in the grayscale image. The slot for the 0-value pixels is on the left, and the slot for the 255-value pixels is on the right. Now imagine that there are a total of 1000 pixels in the image with a grayscale value of 64. Using a black marble to represent each pixel, imagine that you drop 1000 marbles into the 64 slot on the slider. Next, imagine that the image contains 1500 pixels with a grayscale value of 72, and you drop 1500 black marbles into the 72 slot. Imagine that you do this for each of the 256 slots on the slider. Your result would be the histogram—exactly what you see on the Properties panel. The height of the histogram, from left to right, shows the relative number of pixels that the whole file—or a selection of pixels—has for each of the 256 grayscale values.

You adjust the image by manipulating the sliders at the bottom of the histogram. The black triangle represents the 0 on the grayscale. The white triangle represents 255 on the grayscale.

The gray triangle represents the 128 midpoint. When you move any of the triangles, you readjust how the histogram relates to the full grayscale range, from shadow to highlight.

FIGURE D-11: **Levels adjustment options on the Properties panel**

Improving Images with Adjustment Layers

Adjusting the Midpoint with Levels

Adjusting the tonal range of an image is a lot like knowing which fork to use in fine dining. You start at the outside and work your way in. First, you set your black and white points—the extremes. Then, you verify that there's satisfactory contrast between the highlight and shadow range. Once those are established, you are ready to—if you want—adjust the midpoint. The **midpoint** defines which areas of the image fall into the middle range of the available grayscale. In other words, it separates the bright half from the dark half. Moving the midpoint darkens or lightens the image. Interestingly, a midpoint adjustment is often only subjective—do you like the image better if it's brighter or darker? Jon thinks you've been very successful adjusting the black and white points. He tells you to "play" with the midpoint and "see what you come up with."

STEPS

1. **Take a moment to note the overall "feel" of the image, then relate that impression to the histogram on the Properties panel**

   Overall, the image has more dark areas than light areas. The hood is such a big part of the image and mostly falls into the mid-upper shadow range. This is represented in the histogram, which shows significantly more pixels to the left of the midpoint than to the right.

   QUICK TIP
   If you have trouble dragging to the exact value, you can double-click the text box, then type 1.20.

2. **Drag the gray midpoint triangle left until the text box reads 1.20**

   Moving the midpoint triangle left by definition places more of the histogram to the right of the midpoint. Now, pixels that were in the lower half of the histogram are being defined as the midpoint of the grayscale.

3. **Evaluate the feel of the adjusted image, then compare your image to Figure D-12**

   Brightened, the image feels less heavy, but it also has less tension overall. The midpoint adjustment also makes the face too bright.

4. **Drag the gray midpoint triangle right until the text box reads .70**

   Artistically, this was a much better move than brightening the midpoint. The darkening has given great intensity to the face and the eyes. But it has also made the shadow areas so dark that they no longer show any detail, and this is not acceptable.

5. **Set the foreground color to black, click the Brush tool , then on the Options bar set the Size to 300 px and the Hardness to 0%**

6. **Click the Opacity list arrow on the Options bar, then change the Opacity to 10%**

7. **Target the layer mask on the Levels adjustment layer, then paint to lighten the shoulders and darkest areas of the jacket**

   Because the opacity of the brush is set to only 10%, you are essentially painting with a light gray. You are masking the adjustment very gradually.

8. **When you are done masking, press and hold [Shift] then click the layer mask thumbnail on the Layers panel to hide it, then click again to show it**

9. **Compare your result to Figure D-13, save your work, then close adjust white and black points_PS-D.psd**

FIGURE D-12: **Brightening the midtones**

FIGURE D-13: **Masking areas of the image from the adjustment**

Adjustment is reduced in these areas

Using layer masks with adjustments

When you create an adjustment layer—a Levels adjustment layer, for example—it is created automatically with a layer mask. It's a smart idea to think of the layer mask as less of an option and more of an essential component of working with adjustment layers. Sometimes, you will make an adjustment that you can apply completely to the artwork beneath, but more often, you will want to use the layer mask to apply the adjustment selectively in different strengths to different areas of the artwork.

When you set a low percentage of opacity on the Brush tool and then paint in the layer mask, the brush has reduced impact. In other words, if you set the brush to 10% opacity and paint in the layer mask with a black foreground color, each stroke of the brush will mask the artwork very gradually. This allows you to show or mask the adjustment very subtly and to be very specific as to how you want to affect the artwork beneath. Some designers automatically mask the adjustment completely then use a low-opacity brush to paint white in the mask, thus "brushing in" the adjustment gradually in specific areas. The layer mask allows you to apply it in a way that is unique and expresses your artistic vision.

Investigating an RGB Image

There are certain things you need to know to work effectively in Photoshop. That starts with your monitor, which displays color with light. Like a TV screen, your monitor is a light source. Red, green, and blue are the **additive primary colors** of light. They can combine to produce all the other colors in the spectrum. The colors you see on your monitor—the purples, oranges, limes, yellows—are all created by mixing varying strengths and combinations of red, green, and blue.

In the early lessons in this unit, we examined grayscale in a black-and-white image as being 256 shades of gray available per pixel to render the image. To apply the concept to an RGB image, simply take that concept and multiply by three! In an RGB image, there are 256 shades of red, 256 shades of green, and 256 shades of blue available per pixel. Remember, the resulting pixel appears to be just one color—say, baby blue—but it is created by combining red, green, and blue. Jon tells you about a new client who will be supplying imagery that will require lots of analysis and correction for quality and color. He gives you an RGB image and asks that you analyze it.

STEPS

1. **Open PS D-4.psd, save it as rgb_PS-D, then click the** Default Foreground and Background Colors button **on the Tools panel**

2. **Click** Edit (Win) or Photoshop (Mac) **on the Menu bar, point to** Preferences, **click** Interface, **click the** Show Channels in Color check box **to activate it, if necessary, then click** OK

3. **Verify that the two readouts in the Info panel are set to RGB color, click the** Eyedropper tool **, then position it over different areas of the image**
   The Info panel shows different values of R (red), G (green), and B (blue) per pixel. Each pixel combines one of 256 shades of red, one of 256 shades of green, and one of 256 shades of blue.

QUICK TIP
Because only the Red channel is displayed, all three readouts on the Info panel show info for the Red channel.

4. **Click** Window **on the Menu bar, click** Channels, **then click the** Red channel thumbnail
   As shown in Figure D-14, the Red channel is displayed. Each pixel in the Red channel can be one of 256 shades of red, from 0 (black) to 255 (red).

QUICK TIP
You can think of the color cyan as being "minus red," because it is created by removing red.

5. **Click the** Green channel thumbnail **to see the Green channel, click the** Blue channel thumbnail **to see the Blue channel, then click the** RGB channel thumbnail **to see the color image**
   The RGB channel is called the **composite** channel because it is the result of combining the R, G, and B channels.

QUICK TIP
You can think of the color magenta as being "minus green," because it is created by removing green.

6. **Select the right half of the canvas, click** Edit **on the Menu bar, click** Fill, **click the** Use list arrow, **click** White, **then click** OK **to fill the selection with white**

7. **Deselect, then use the** Eyedropper tool **to sample the white pixels**
   Every white pixel is 255R/255G/255B.

8. **Click the** Red channel thumbnail, **fill the channel with black, click the** RGB thumbnail **to see the composite image, then compare your canvas to Figure D-15**
   The pixels on the right side of the canvas change to cyan because 0R + 255G + 255B = Cyan.

QUICK TIP
You can think of the color yellow as being "minus blue," because it is created by removing blue.

9. **Undo the fill to restore the Red channel, fill the Blue channel with black, then click the** RGB channel thumbnail
   As shown in Figure D-16, the pixels on the right side of the canvas change to yellow because 255R + 255G + 0B = Yellow.

10. **Save your work, then close rgb_PS-D.psd**

FIGURE D-14: Viewing the Red channel only

• Information on panel refers to the Red channel only

FIGURE D-15: Viewing the image with no red component

O red component in any • pixel on the canvas

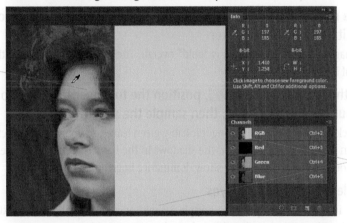

• Cyan = Minus Red

FIGURE D-16: Viewing the image with no blue component

O blue component in • any pixel on the canvas

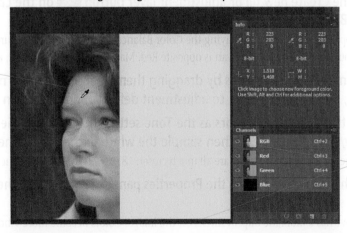

• Yellow = Minus Blue

About cyan, magenta, and yellow

If you've done any professional printing, you know that color printing is done using cyan, magenta, and yellow inks, plus black ink for shadows and detail, collectively called CMYK. In fact, cyan, magenta, and yellow are the primary colors for printing. However, it's important that you exclude that information from this discussion. We're looking at color on a monitor, a monitor is a light source, and the primary colors of light are red, green, and blue.

The role of cyan, magenta, and yellow—as per this lesson—is that each is created by removing one of the additive RGB primary colors. This point is the key to manipulating color and doing color corrections in Photoshop. Many of Photoshop's color adjustments manipulate color using RGB and CMY as their basis, which you'll see in the next lesson.

Improving Images with Adjustment Layers

Using the Color Balance Adjustment

Color Balance is an adjustment that allows you to control the balance of red, green, and blue in an image. It's a great tool for adjusting any color problems with an image. For example, many images from a digital camera are often too red. You can use the Color Balance adjustment to fix that. This lesson is closely related to what you learned in the previous lesson: when you work with the Color Balance adjustment, you'll see that you are manipulating the relationships between RGB and CMY. ▓▓▓▓ Jon asks you to open an image in Photoshop and improve the color by removing blue and green, using the Color Balance adjustment.

STEPS

1. Open PS D-5.psd, then save it as color balance_PS-D

2. **Take a moment to look at the image and get a feel for what it looks like, and how you think it could be made better**

   The image has good contrast but is "cold" overall. The colors are muted, and the flesh tone has underlying hints of blue and purple.

3. **Click the Eyedropper tool 🖊, position the tool over the background, note the RGB readouts on the Info panel, then sample the shadows in the hair**

   The background is a natural setting, probably green leaves, so you would expect to see larger concentrations of green in these pixels. However, the shadows in the hair also reflect this green: where the shadows in the hair should be neutral gray, they show dominance in green.

4. **Sample the whites in the eyes**

   Whites in eyes are great places to sample for midtones and highlights. The RGB values should all be relatively close; in this image, the whites show dominance in blue.

5. **Click the Create new fill or adjustment layer button 🔘 on the Layers panel, then click Color Balance**

   The Properties panel opens displaying the Color Balance options, shown in Figure D-17. The sliders represent what you learned in Lesson 6. Cyan is opposite Red, Magenta is opposite Green, and Yellow is opposite Blue.

6. **Experiment with the sliders by dragging them in each direction, noting the effect on the image, then click the Reset to adjustment defaults button 🔄 on the Properties panel**

7. **Verify that Midtones appears as the Tone setting on the Properties panel, drag the Yellow/Blue slider to –26, then sample the white of the eye on the left side of the screen**

   With the adjustment, the values are all much closer: 187R/197G/197B. Thus, the blue dominance is reduced.

8. **Click the Tone list arrow on the Properties panel, click Shadows, then drag the Magenta/Green slider left to –16**

   The move has a dramatic improvement on the image. Colors become more vibrant, and the face becomes a warmer pink because reducing green increases the magenta balance. Green is much less dominant in the shadows in the hair.

9. **Close the Properties panel, hide and show the Color Balance 1 adjustment layer to see the before and after view of the image as shown in Figure D-18, then save your work**

FIGURE D-17: **Color Balance adjustment**

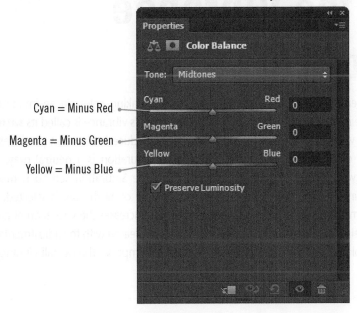

Cyan = Minus Red

Magenta = Minus Green

Yellow = Minus Blue

Properties

⚖ Color Balance

Tone: Midtones

Cyan ——— Red ——— 0

Magenta ——— Green ——— 0

Yellow ——— Blue ——— 0

☑ Preserve Luminosity

FIGURE D-18: **Before and after the adjustment**

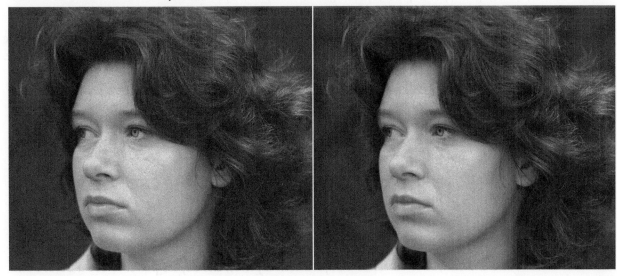

Looking for neutral grays

In an RGB file, color is created by an imbalance in the three channels. For example, when a pixel's red component is substantially greater than the green and blue components, the pixel's color will tend to fall into the red hue. However, when the three numbers are close in value, the pixel becomes neutral in color. Whenever the three components are the same, the pixel will have no color and can be only a neutral gray. For example, 20R/20G/20B would produce a dark gray, and 210R/210G/210B would produce a light gray.

Sampling an image for neutral grays can lead to many insights for improving color. If you sample areas that should be neutral—like shadows in hair—and they show a substantial dominance in one color, that's a good hint that you should reduce that color in the shadows.

On the other hand, if an area that should have vibrant color is grayish and neutral, that tells you that the color balance in that area is too close between the three and one or two need to be more dominant.

Improving Images with Adjustment Layers

Photoshop 99

Photoshop CS6

Using the Vibrance Adjustment

The Vibrance adjustment is a very useful method for quickly making colors in an image more vibrant. **Vibrance** refers to the intensity of a color. The measure of a pixel's vibrance is called its **saturation**. High saturation produces a vibrant color, like the red of a tomato. Reduced saturation produces a dull, more neutral color, like the dull red of a radish. A pixel with no saturation is a neutral gray. The Vibrance adjustment provides two settings: Vibrancy and Saturation. The Saturation setting is more of a blunt instrument; it simply increases or decreases the saturation value of all the pixels selected. The Vibrancy setting uses a more complex method for improving the image. It increases the saturation of pixels that need it without affecting pixels that are already saturated. Jon is pleased with the adjustments you made to the image with the Color Balance adjustment but asks that you improve the overall vibrancy of the color in the image.

STEPS

1. **Verify that the Color Balance 1 adjustment layer is targeted on the Layers panel, click the Create new fill or adjustment layer button [ ], then click Vibrance**
   The Properties panel opens with settings for the Vibrance adjustment.

2. **Drag the Saturation slider all the way to the left**
   The image is completely desaturated and resembles a black-and-white image. Even though the image appears black-and-white, the file is still an RGB file and all pixels still have an RGB component. In this case, all RGB values are all equal for all pixels.

3. **Drag the Saturation slider all the way to the right, then compare your result to Figure D-19**
   The image is oversaturated.

4. **Click the Reset to adjustment defaults button [ ], then drag the Vibrance slider all the way to the right**

5. **Hide and show the Vibrance 1 adjustment layer on the Layers panel to see a before and after view of the image**
   Even though the move is extreme, the result is very acceptable. The color is vibrant but not oversaturated.

6. **Click the Reset to adjustment defaults button [ ], then drag the Saturation slider to +37**

7. **Hide and show the Vibrance 1 adjustment layer on the Layers panel to see a before and after view of the image**

8. **Compare your result to Figure D-20**

9. **Save your work, then close color balance_PS-D.psd**

Using a group layer for adjustment layers

When you use multiple adjustment layers on the Layers panel, you will often want to see a before/after view of the image, with and without the adjustments. When you have many adjustment layers, it can be a little tricky to turn them all on and off simultaneously. For this reason, many designers place their adjustment layers in a group. A group is a new layer on the Layers panel with a folder icon. When you hide and show a group layer, you hide and show all the adjustment layers in the group. To create a group layer, click the Create a new group button [ ] on the Layers panel. Drag adjustment layers into the group layer, as necessary.

FIGURE D-19: **Oversaturating the image**

Note oversaturated "hot spots"

FIGURE D-20: **Before and after the adjustment**

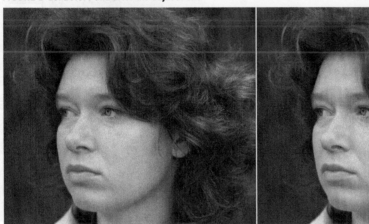

Doing a "super-undo" with the History panel

The History panel, shown in Figure D-21, offers lots of great features; one of them is the ability to quickly revert a file to its state when you first opened it, then to undo the revert to bring it back to its current state. As you work, the History panel records your steps and lists the last 20 of them, called **states**, in the panel. You can increase or decrease the default number of states in the Preferences dialog box. The last state in the list represents the last change you made to the file. You can click a state in the list to go back to that point of your work, and then continue working from that state. At the top of the panel is a thumbnail that represents the file the way that it looked when it was first opened. If you click the thumbnail you will undo all states in the panel. All of the states in the History panel are grayed out. Click any state to continue working from that particular state. For example, if you want to continue working with the file the way it was before you clicked the thumbnail image, click the last state before you continue working. If you undo all states and continue working by

accident, you can click File on the Menu bar, then click Revert. This will take you back to the status of the file when you last saved it. You may lose some of your work, but at least not *all* of your work.

FIGURE D-21 **The History panel**

Practice

Concepts Review

Label the elements of the Photoshop screen shown in Figure D-22.

FIGURE D-22

Match each term with the statement that best describes it.

6. **Grayscale mode**
7. **RGB mode**
8. **Shadow point**
9. **Cyan**
10. **Magenta**
11. **Yellow**
12. **Continuous tone**
13. **Vibrance**

a. Darkest pixels in an image
b. "Minus blue"
c. Intensity of a pixel's color
d. "Minus green"
e. 256 shades of gray available per pixel
f. "Minus red"
g. 256 shades available per pixel per channel
h. Smooth transition from shadows to highlights

Select the best answer from the list of choices.

14. **Which of the following is not an adjustment you can make in Photoshop?**
    a. Levels
    b. Bevel and Emboss
    c. Color Balance
    d. Vibrance

15. **Which of the following is not true of an RGB file?**
    a. It has three color channels.
    b. It is larger in file size than a grayscale version of the same file.
    c. Each pixel can be one of 256 shades of gray.
    d. The image can appear to be black-and-white.

16. **Which of the following is not true about a Levels adjustment?**
    a. A histogram is involved.
    b. You can use levels to adjust a color or a black-and-white image.
    c. You can choose a Tone setting so that the Levels adjustment will affect only shadows, midtones, or highlights.
    d. You can brighten the midpoint.

17. **Which of the following is not true about the Color Balance adjustment?**
    a. You can move a slider between Magenta and Cyan.
    b. You can move a slider between Blue and Yellow.
    c. You can move a slider between Cyan and Red.
    d. You can move a slider between Green and Magenta.

18. **Which of the following is not involved in assessing the appearance of an image?**
    a. Contrast
    b. Color balance
    c. Shadows
    d. Grayscale

Skills Review

1. **Understand grayscale.**
   a. Open PS D-6.psd, verify the Background layer is targeted, then save the file as **grayscale skills_PS-D**.
   b. Click the Background layer, click Image on the Menu bar, point to Mode, then note that Grayscale is checked.
   c. Open the Info panel, click the Info panel menu button, click Panel Options, then verify that First Color Readout and Second Color Readout are both set to RGB Color.
   d. Click the Eyedropper tool and position it over different areas of the image, noting the readouts on the Info panel.
   e. Position the Eyedropper tool at the very bottom of the gradient on the right, then move slowly to the top of the gradient, sampling as you go.
   f. Sample areas in the background to see grayscale information for the darker areas of the image.
   g. Sample areas in the flower at the center to find mid-range areas of the image.
   h. Sample the petals and try to find the lightest pixels in the image.

Skills Review (continued)

2. **Investigate a grayscale image.**

   a. On the Layers panel, make the Chart layer visible.

   b. Look at the flower image and the background and try to see it not as a picture but as a range of tones from shadows to midtones to highlights.

   c. Using the chart as a guide, sample different areas of the image to identify shadows, highlights, and midtones.

   d. Move the Info panel to the upper-left corner, click Image on the Menu bar, point to Adjustments, click Posterize, then drag the Levels slider to 3.

   e. Position the cursor over the image and note the before/after readouts on the Info panel.

   f. In the Posterize dialog box, change the Levels value to 16.

   g. Change the Levels value to 200.

   h. Click Cancel, then hide the Chart layer.

   i. Save your work, then close grayscale skills_PS-D.psd.

FIGURE D-23

3. **Use the Brightness/Contrast adjustment.**

   a. Open PS D-7.psd, then save it as **brightness contrast skills_PS-D**.

   b. Sample the highlight areas in the river and where sunshine strikes the rocks to get a general range of the values of the highlights in the image.

   c. Sample the dark areas of the rocks to get a general range of the shadows in the image.

   d. Click the Create new fill or adjustment layer button on the Layers panel, then click Brightness/Contrast.

   e. On the Properties panel, drag the Brightness slider and sample the image until the lightest pixels in the water fall into the 220–235 range.

   f. Drag the Contrast slider to 90.

   g. Reduce the Brightness to 58.

   h. Close the Properties panel.

   i. Hide and show the Brightness/Contrast 1 adjustment layer and compare your before and after appearance to Figure D-23.

   j. Save your work, then close brightness contrast skills_PS-D.psd.

Skills Review (continued)

4. **Adjust black and white points with levels.**

   a. Open PS D-8.psd, then save it as **levels skills_PS-D**.

   b. Take a moment to make a visual analysis of the image and its tonal range.

   c. Sample the image to find the darkest and lightest pixels in the image.

   d. Click the Create new fill or adjustment layer button on the Layers panel, then click Levels.

   e. Drag the black triangle toward the right to the beginning of the histogram, and drag the white triangle toward the left to the end of the histogram.

   f. Sample the image, trying to find shadow pixels that have a value of 10 or lower and highlight pixels that have a value of 240 or higher.

   g. Adjust the black and white triangles as necessary to produce the best shadow and highlight points.

   h. Hide and show the Levels 1 adjustment layer on the Layers panel to see the before and after view of the image.

   i. Save your work.

5. **Adjust the midpoint with levels.**

   a. Take a moment to note the overall feel of the image, then relate that impression to the histogram on the Properties panel.

   b. Click the Create new fill or adjustment layer button on the Layers panel, then click Levels to add a second Levels adjustment layer.

   c. Drag the gray midpoint triangle left until the text box reads 1.30.

   d. Evaluate the appearance of the adjusted image.

   e. Drag the gray midpoint triangle right until the text box reads .80.

   f. Hide and show the new Levels 2 adjustment layer to see the midpoint adjustment. (*Hint*: Be sure the Levels 2 adjustment layer is showing when you're done.)

   g. Set the Foreground color to black, click the Brush tool, then on the Options bar, set the Size to 175 px and the Hardness to 0%.

   h. Click the Opacity list arrow on the Options bar, then set the opacity to 30%.

   i. Target the layer mask on the Levels 2 adjustment layer, then paint to lighten the center of the flower slightly.

   j. Compare your result to Figure D-24, save your work, then close levels skills_PS-D.psd.

FIGURE D-24

Skills Review (continued)

6. Investigate an RGB image.

    a. Open PS D-9.psd, then save it as **color balance skills_PS-D**. (*Hint*: The file has been saved in RGB Color mode.)

    b. Click Edit (Win) or Photoshop (Mac) on the Menu bar, point to Preferences, click Interface, click the Show Channels in Color check box to add a check mark, if necessary, then click OK.

    c. Verify that the two readouts on the Info panel are set to RGB Color, click the Eyedropper tool, then position it over different areas of the image.

    d. Click Window on the Menu bar, click Channels, then click the channel thumbnail on the Red channel.

    e. Click the Green channel thumbnail to see the Green channel, click the Blue channel thumbnail to see the Blue channel, then click the RGB channel thumbnail to see the composite image.

    f. Select the right half of the canvas, fill the selection with white, deselect, then position the Eyedropper tool to sample the white pixels.

    g. Click the Red channel thumbnail, fill the channel with black, then click the RGB channel thumbnail to see the composite image.

    h. Undo the fill to restore the Red channel, fill the Green channel with black, then click the RGB channel thumbnail.

    i. Undo the fill to restore the Green channel, fill the Blue channel with black, then click the RGB channel thumbnail.

    j. Click File on the Menu bar, then click Revert.

7. Use the Color Balance adjustment.

    a. Take a moment to look at the image and get a feel for what it looks like, and how you think it could be made better. (*Hint*: Elephants are usually gray, not brown.)

    b. Click the Eyedropper tool, sample different areas of the image, and note the RGB readouts on the Info panel. (*Hint*: Red dominates almost every pixel in the image.)

    c. Sample the whites in the tusk.

    d. Click the Create new fill or adjustment layer button on the Layers panel, then click Color Balance.

    e. Take some time to experiment with the sliders, noting the effect on the image, then click the Reset to adjustment defaults button on the panel.

    f. Verify that the Midtones option button is selected, then drag the Cyan/Red slider to –34.

    g. Drag the Magenta/Green slider to –6, then drag the Yellow/Blue slider to +20.

    h. Click the Tone list arrow on the Properties panel, click Highlights, drag the Cyan/Red slider to –25, then drag the Magenta/Green slider to –12.

    i. Close the Properties panel, hide and show the Color Balance 1 adjustment layer to see the before and after view of the image, then save your work. (*Hint*: Note how the yellow flowers in the background remain yellow and vibrant. Note too how the grass/brush behind the elephant has a more natural and realistic color.)

Skills Review (continued)

8. Use the Vibrance adjustment.

   a. Verify that the Color Balance 1 adjustment layer is targeted on the Layers panel, click the Create new fill or adjustment layer button, then click Vibrance.

   b. Drag the Saturation slider all the way to the left.

   c. Drag the Saturation slider all the way to the right.

   d. Click the Reset to adjustment defaults button, then drag the Vibrance slider to +40.

   e. Hide and show the Vibrance 1 adjustment layer on the Layers panel to see a before and after view of the image.

   f. Drag the Saturation slider gradually to +12.

   g. Hide and show the Vibrance 1 adjustment layer on the Layers panel to see a before and after view of the image.

   h. Compare your result to Figure D-25. (*Hint*: The figure shows the image before and after all adjustments.)

   i. Save your work, then close color balance skills_PS-D.psd.

FIGURE D-25

Independent Challenge 1

You're designing a brochure of photos from your hometown and want to adjust an image to make it look its best.

a. Open PS D-10.psd, then save it as **hay bale_PS-D**.

b. Create a Brightness/Contrast adjustment layer.

c. Drag the Brightness slider to +35, then sample the brightest cloud in the sky.

d. Drag the Contrast slider to +60.

e. Sample the bright cloud again and verify that its values are somewhere between 200 and 225. (*Hint*: Because the cloud is very distant, you shouldn't make it too bright.)

f. Sample the shadows in the hay bale and on the ground to be sure they haven't become too black.

g. Create a Vibrance adjustment layer.

h. Drag the Vibrance slider all the way to the right.

i. Drag the Vibrance slider to +86, then compare your result to Figure D-26.

j. Save your work, then close hay bale_PS-D.psd.

Independent Challenge 2

You work for a boating magazine and are working on a photo you're going to use in a layout. The creative director tells you that the foreground of the image is great but that she'd like you to give the sky and the mountains in the distance "more weight for detail."

a. Open PS D-11.psd, then save it as **sailboat_PS-D**.

b. Create a Levels adjustment layer.

c. Drag the midpoint triangle right to .64.

d. Click the Brush tool.

e. Use various brush sizes and hardness values to mask the adjustment so that it affects only the sky and the mountain in the distance.

f. Save your work, compare your screen to Figure D-27, then close sailboat_PS-D.psd.

FIGURE D-27

Independent Challenge 3

You're a designer for a greeting card company. You download an image from an online stock photography website and decide to improve it with some adjustments.

a. Open PS D-12.psd, then save it as **color flowers_PS-D**.

b. Create a Levels adjustment layer.

c. Drag the black slider toward the right to where the histogram starts, then drag the white triangle toward the left to where the histogram ends.

d. Create a Brightness/Contrast adjustment layer, then drag the Contrast slider to +35.

e. Create a Color Balance adjustment layer.

f. Drag the Cyan/Red slider to +6, drag the Magenta/Green slider to –12, then drag the Yellow/Blue slider to –26.

g. Click the Levels 1 adjustment layer, then drag the midpoint triangle left until the text box reads 1.16.

h. Drag the black triangle right until the text box reads 40.

i. Target the Color Balance 1 adjustment layer on the Layers panel, then create a Vibrance adjustment layer.

j. Drag the Saturation slider to +30.

k. Compare your results to Figure D-28.

Advanced Challenge Exercise

- Click the Levels 1 adjustment layer.
- Slowly drag the white triangle left to see the white petals begin to lose detail and "blow out."
- Keep dragging left until the petals are entirely white with no detail.
- Drag the white triangle right and sample with the Info panel to find the point where the pixels in the petals are their brightest but not at 255.

l. Hide/show the adjustment layers to see before and after.

m. Save your work, then close color flowers_PS-D.psd.

Real Life Independent Challenge

You're a talented amateur photographer. You use great equipment, and so your photos download from your camera looking good without any editing. You just returned from your trip out west and are using Photoshop to tweak your photos from looking good to looking great.

a. Open PS D-13.psd, then save it as **canyon_PS-D**.

b. Create a Levels adjustment layer.

c. Drag the black triangle right to 12, then drag the white triangle left to 212.

FIGURE D-29

d. Drag the midpoint slider right to .90.

e. Create a Color Balance adjustment layer.

f. Drag the Cyan/Red slider to +5, then drag the Yellow/Blue slider to –10.

g. Create a Vibrance adjustment layer.

h. Drag the Vibrance slider to +62.

Advanced Challenge Exercise

- Open the History panel.
- Click the PS D-13 thumbnail at the top of the panel to see the image in its original state.
- Click the Modify Levels Layer state on the History panel.

i. Compare your results to Figure D-29, save your work, then close canyon_PS-D.psd.

Visual Workshop

Open PS D-14.psd, then save it as **visual solution_PS-D**. Apply adjustments to the image so that the canvas resembles Figure D-30.

FIGURE D-30

Improving Images with Adjustment Layers

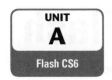

Getting Started with Adobe Flash Professional

Adobe Flash Professional CS6 is a multimedia program used to create applications, animations, games, and other user experiences. Its tools let you create content and control how users interact with it. Flash is an essential development tool in the Creative Suite at the core of the Adobe® Flash® Platform, a set of tools, applications, and technologies viewable across multiple devices and platforms. By learning and applying the essential skills presented in these units, your projects will create engaging and immersive user experiences. To work productively in Flash, you need to know some basic multimedia concepts, how to navigate in the program, how to play a movie, and how to plan and manage a project.  You have just started working at GreenWinds Eco-Cruise, an ecologically friendly travel agency specializing in oceanic vacations. As a marketing intern, you'll use Flash to create content for websites, online ads, and mobile applications. You prepare for your first project by familiarizing yourself with Flash.

OBJECTIVES

Understand Adobe Flash

Start Adobe Flash Professional CS6

View the Flash workspace

Arrange the workspace

Open a document and play a movie

Understand the Timeline

Add a layer and element

Plan and manage a project

Understanding Adobe Flash

Adobe Flash is a multimedia program that lets you create and organize media and then apply animation and other effects to them to create a file rich with media and functionality. **Multimedia** refers to content that integrates different types of elements such as text, graphics, video, animation, and sound. You can use Flash tools to arrange how media elements appear and function to create movies and applications that let users interact with them. ▓▓▓▓ You want to learn how Flash can help you in your work as a marketing intern.

DETAILS

You can use Adobe Flash to:

- ### Add applications to web pages and mobile devices

  You can use Flash tools to create animated content and applications for the web, such as banner ads, and for other devices, such as TV, smart phones, and desktop and laptop computers, and tablets and other mobile devices.

  Flash applications include weather and road conditions, games, and contests you use on a device, as well as larger uses, such as interactive museum, science center, or park exhibits. An **animation** is a series of still images that are played rapidly in a sequence, creating the illusion of movement. An animation can be one part of a web page or it can be a stand-alone file, such as an e-card, advertisement, game, or simulation. Figure A-1 shows a simple animation open in Flash.

  Flash applications use different media and graphic file formats, such as vector graphics, a type of graphic that reduces file size, and streaming video and audio. **Streaming** is an online method of playing media in your browser or mobile device before it has downloaded completely, thus saving time and storage space. You'll learn more about vector graphic files in Unit B.

  > **QUICK TIP**
  >
  > To ensure your content is accessible to all users, your design must plan for consistent design and navigation elements, mouse and keyboard controls, labels, audio, and visual captions.

- ### Create interactive content

  Flash lets you create **interactive content** that accepts and responds to human actions using multimedia elements or touch gestures for touch-based user interfaces, such as tablets or smartphones. A **touch gesture** performs an action, such as zooming, displaying a menu or option bar, or otherwise manipulating the screen. For mobile devices such as smart phones or tablets, you can create applications that respond to tap, rotate, swipe, and other touch gestures. One type of interactive content includes **navigational components** such as icons, menus, and similar items that help you navigate a banner ad or an application. You can use and reuse such elements to create a consistent user interface, which consists of items that help **users interact** with an application. Figure A-2 shows the result of a user changing a variety of facial features by clicking parts of the face.

  > **QUICK TIP**
  >
  > The Flash Player comes standard in the browser software installed in most new computers and is downloaded and installed millions of times each day around the world.

- ### Develop reusable content

  Flash is an **authoring tool**, which is a program that creators use to develop and package content for users. Flash files that you create are known as **documents**, and they have the **.fla** file extension. To create an output file for users, you save your document in the **.swf** file format. To play a SWF file in a web page, users must have the **Flash Player plug-in**, a free, easily downloadable program, installed in their browser. Other programs can also play SWF files.

FIGURE A-1: Viewing a Flash movie

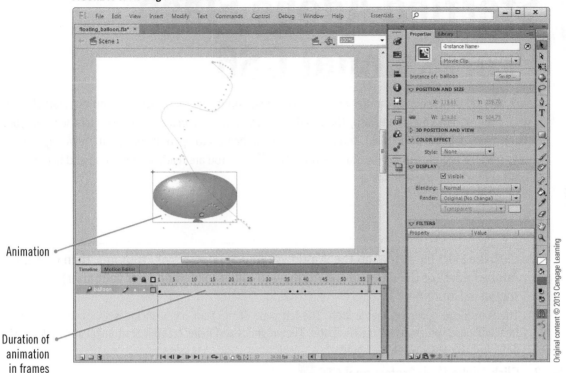

Animation

Duration of
animation
in frames

Original content © 2013 Cengage Learning

FIGURE A-2: Viewing an application created in Flash

monoface™

happy new year from all of us.

what do i do?
shuffle face
view gallery
screensaver

mono-1.com
©2007 mono LLC

Website courtesy mono-1.com

Design Matters

Understanding animation

Translating light into sight involves a nearly instantaneous exchange between our eyes and brain. Depending on the brightness of an image, we can retain its impression for less than 1/10th of a second. Our capacity to retain an image, even as a new image is "burned" on top of it, is known as **persistence of vision**. This overlap between images creates the illusion of movement. Because our eyes keep an image in our mind as it processes each new one, our brains are "tricked"

into seeing smooth motion. Theatrical release and digital movies typically play at 24 frames per second. At this speed, persistence of vision ensures that we never see that a film is essentially dark for much of the time. If you watch a silent movie from the early 20th century, however, which runs at only 16 frames per second, you will see a noticeable flickering. At this speed, you can actually perceive individual frames flashing on the screen.

Starting Adobe Flash Professional CS6

Depending on the type of computer or device you own and its operating system, you can start Flash in several ways. When you install Flash, the installation program may place a Flash shortcut icon on your desktop (Win) or in the dock (Mac). You can double-click the icon to open the program. However, you can always start the program using the Start menu (Win). You are ready to start Flash and begin familiarizing yourself with the workspace.

STEPS

WIN

1. **Click the** Start button ⊕ **on the Windows taskbar, point to** All Programs, **then click the** Adobe folder **(or the name of the Adobe CS6 folder loaded on your computer), as shown in Figure A-4**

   The Start menu opens on the desktop. The left pane of the Start menu includes shortcuts to the most frequently used programs on the computer. The programs and items on your Start menu and desktop will differ from those shown in the figure.

   > **TROUBLE**
   > If this is the first time you are using Flash, or if you are using a trial version, you might receive a prompt to register the program or create an Adobe ID.

2. **Click** Adobe Flash Professional CS6 ▣

   The Adobe Flash Professional CS6 Welcome Screen appears in the program window.

MAC

1. **Open the** Finder, **click the** hard drive icon, **if necessary, double-click** Applications, **then double-click the** Adobe folder **(or the name of the Adobe CS6 folder loaded on your computer); if there isn't an Adobe folder present, then click the** Adobe Flash CS6 folder, **as shown in Figure A-4**

   The items in your Finder window will differ from those shown in the figure.

   > **TROUBLE**
   > If this is the first time you are using Flash, or if you are using a trial version, you might receive a prompt to register the program or create an Adobe ID.

2. **Double-click** Adobe Flash CS6 ▣

   The Adobe Flash Professional CS6 Welcome Screen appears.

Understanding the Welcome Screen

In the top three panes of the Welcome Screen, you can create a file from several templates, open existing or recently used files, create new files of various file types, and link to Flash training. You can also access a link to the Flash Exchange website, where you can download extensions, plug-ins, and other components.

The lower-left corner of the Welcome Screen contains links to sites where you can learn about new features in Flash Professional CS6 and access other specific information and tutorials. The Macintosh Welcome Screen also has a link for a feature tour in the lower-right corner. To turn off the Welcome Screen so it does not open when you start Flash, click the Don't show again check box in the lower-left corner of the window. See Figure A-3.

FIGURE A-3: **Welcome Screen**

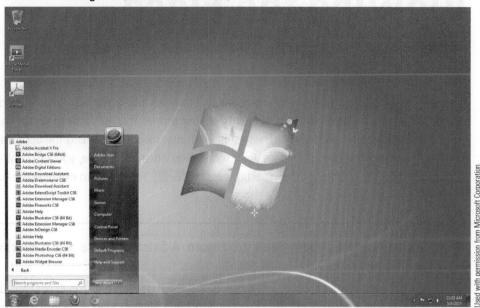

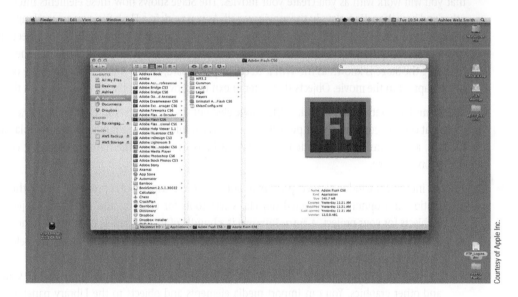

Creating self-running programs

You can use advanced features in Flash to create **Rich Internet Applications (RIA)**, which are mobile applications or web programs that work like desktop application programs, but the user doesn't need to install any software to run them. Instead, the Flash content contains the necessary functionality that allows the program to run. Examples of RIAs could include a web buying guide to help you select the features you want in a particular product, such as a digital camera, or a map that displays driving directions. RIAs often include interactive content as well, and they can be delivered on a mobile device, on your desktop, or on the web. RIAs are characterized by a consistent user interface (buttons, colors, menus, and fonts), which shortens the development time and improves the usability of your project or site. You'll learn more about creating consistent and reusable elements in a later unit. When planning an RIA application, your team needs to know the functional requirements, how the RIA will be used and by whom, and whether you should concentrate on design or data.

Viewing the Flash Workspace

The Flash interface consists of several components arranged into a workspace. The **workspace** is the screen area where you work with the elements of your movie. You use Flash to create applications and movies. A movie naturally includes characters; in Flash that means controlling the appearance of various media elements, such as objects, images, text, sound, and video. In a movie, you also control actions over time, determining how, when, and what actions occur. You decide to examine the Flash workspace to familiarize yourself with it.

DETAILS

When a document is open, refer to Figure A-5 to find the Flash workspace items described below:

QUICK TIP

The Project panel makes it easy to organize and view multiple files that belong to the same project.

- The most commonly used workspace components are the Stage, Timeline, panels, and Menu bar. The main area is the **Stage**, which contains the movie's elements—text, images, graphics, drawings, video, and sound—that you will work with as you create your movies. The Stage shows how these elements interact with each other and how the action plays in the movie overall. As you work in a Flash file, you are working on a **project**, which is the source Flash .fla file you create and modify. You can work on multiple Flash projects at one time; each file opens in its own Document window, represented by a tab at the top of the Stage. The gray area surrounding the Stage is known as the **work area**, or pasteboard, where you can place or store objects that do not yet appear in the movie. Objects that enter or exit the movie from offstage also appear on the work area.

- The **Timeline** controls and organizes the movie elements by using layers and frames. **Layers** are individual rows that contain content in your project. A **frame** is a single point in a movie. When you play a document in Flash, a red translucent bar called the **playhead** moves through the frames, displaying content in the frames on the Stage.

QUICK TIP

In the default view, panels are docked in the right half of the workspace.

- You use individual windows called **panels** to control crucial aspects of a project. You use them to display information and options for selected objects, select tools for creating and modifying objects, and store media objects for your project. A **panel group** is a bundle of related panels that open as one.
  - The **Properties panel** displays the attributes and available options for the selected element on the Stage or in the Timeline.
  - The **Library panel** contains the media that you'll use in a project, including video, sound, photos, and other graphics. You can import media elements and objects to the Library panel and then drag them to the Stage.
  - The **Tools panel** contains tools to draw, select, modify, and view graphics and text. The Tools panel is divided into sections: selection tools; drawing, painting, and text tools; retouching tools; navigation tools; color tools; and tool options. Tool options vary based on the tool selected.

QUICK TIP

The Essentials workspace is selected by default.

- The **Menu bar** contains Flash commands on the left and workspace and a Help search text box on the right. Note: The Flash workspace differs slightly for Mac users; menus on are the Application bar. You can click the **workspace switcher** to switch to a different preset workspace configuration. The currently selected workspace name appears on the workspace. Most are tailored to a specific task, such as Animator, Designer, and Developer. To select a workspace, click the workspace switcher on the Menu bar, then click a workspace name.

TROUBLE

If Flash quits unexpectedly, a dialog box appears when you restart, prompting you to open the auto-recover file, which has "RECOVER" in the filename.

You can select how often Flash saves a document as you're working, although this feature is not turned on by default. The Auto-Save options are available when you create a new document in the New Document dialog box. You can also adjust the settings in an existing document by clicking the Edit document properties button in the Properties panel to open the Document Settings dialog box. See Figure A-6.

FIGURE A-5: **Viewing the Flash workspace**

Menu bar (Win)

Document window

Edit bar

Work area

Stage

Playhead

Timeline

Layer

Workspace switcher

Library panel

Flash CS6

Tools panel

Frames

Properties panel

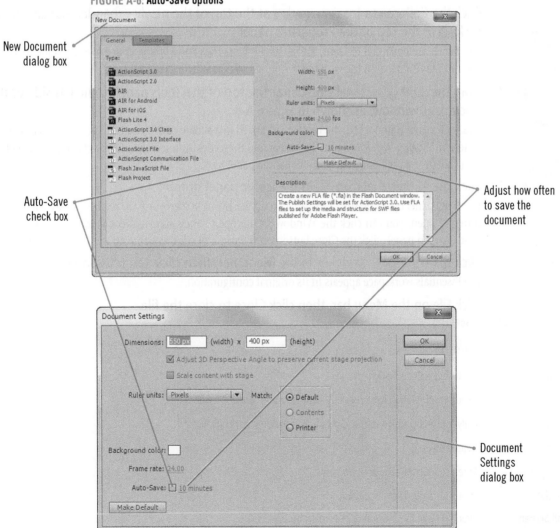

FIGURE A-6: **Auto-Save options**

New Document dialog box

Auto-Save check box

Adjust how often to save the document

Document Settings dialog box

Arranging the Workspace

Panels open by default in the selected workspace when you start Flash. See Table A-1 for a summary of the different workspace configurations you can select. You can think of panels as floating windows that you can arrange to maximize your on-screen "real estate." Flash lets you dock (group), undock, regroup, collapse, expand, and close panels or panel groups. You can collapse panels completely to **iconic view**. To open or close a panel, click Window on the Menu bar, then click the panel's name. To expand or collapse a panel or panel group, click the gray panel next to the tab or the panel title bar. To undock a panel group, drag the panel title bar; to undock a single panel, drag the panel name in the tab. You create a new file, then explore and modify the Flash workspace.

STEPS

1. **Click File on the Menu bar, click New, click the General tab if necessary, verify that ActionScript 3.0 is selected in the New Document dialog box, then click OK**

   A new blank document named Untitled-1 opens in the Document window. **ActionScript** is a programming language in Flash that lets you control interactivity and actions in a movie or website. You'll learn more about creating new files and ActionScript in a later unit. You explore collapsed panels in the workspace.

   > **QUICK TIP**
   > To increase the width of a panel, place the mouse pointer along its edge, then drag ⟺ left or right.

2. **Click the Expand Panels arrow ◄◄ above the Iconic panels on the Panel title bar next to the Properties panel**

   Several panels and panel groups expand, as shown in Figure A-7.

3. **Click the Collapse to Icons arrow ►► at the top of the newly expanded panels, then click ►► at the top of the Properties panel**

   The panels are collapsed to icons, although the Properties and Library icons have labels identifying them. You can move a panel in the workspace.

   > **QUICK TIP**
   > You can move undocked panels anywhere on the screen, even if the Flash program window is in Restore Down view.

4. **Drag the light gray panel title bar at the top of the Tools panel to the left side of the Document window, as shown in Figure A-8**

   The Tools panel is undocked, the tools are arranged in a square panel. You can also open or close individual panels by clicking Window on the Menu bar and then clicking a panel name, by clicking the Panel title bar on a collapsed panel, or by clicking a collapsed panel icon.

   > **QUICK TIP**
   > To dock a panel, drag a gray panel title bar to an area of the workspace; then when a blue bar or rectangle is visible and the panel appears translucent, release the title bar.

5. **Click the Align panel icon ▤ in the iconic panel group**

   The Align panel opens on top of its panel group, as shown in Figure A-9. To review quickly which panels are currently open, you can click the Window menu; open panels have a check mark next to their name. To close an open panel, click the Close button on the panel or click its name on the Window menu.

6. **Click the workspace switcher in the Menu bar, then click Reset 'Essentials'**

   The Essentials workspace appears in its original configuration.

7. **Click File on the Menu bar, then click Close to close the file**

TABLE A-1: Flash workspaces

workspace	function
Animator	Create and edit animation
Classic	Default configuration from previous Flash versions
Debug	Analyze object properties, the Timeline, and ActionScript code
Designer	Create artwork
Developer	Write ActionScript code and programs
Essentials	Default all-purpose configuration
Small Screen	Minimized panels for working in a small viewing area

FIGURE A-7: Viewing expanded panels

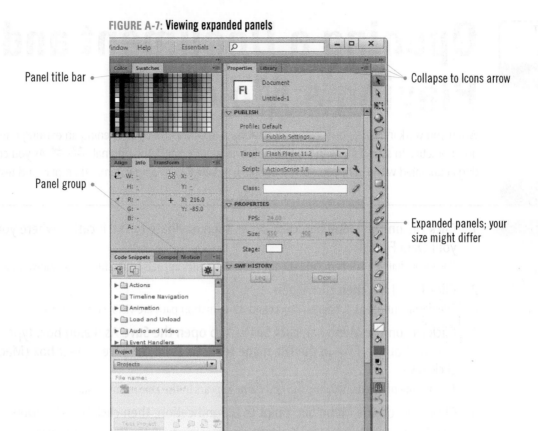

Panel title bar

Panel group

Collapse to Icons arrow

Expanded panels; your size might differ

FIGURE A-8: Undocked Tools panel

Drag gray panel title bar to move an undocked panel

Drag name tab to undock a panel

Tools panel undocked; your exact arrangement might differ

Iconic panel view

FIGURE A-9: Panel opened from collapsed icon

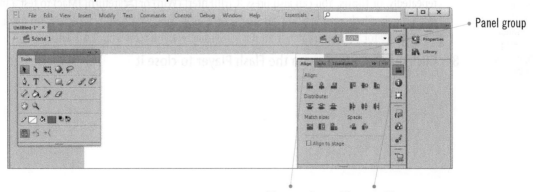

Panel group

Align panel

Align panel icon

Getting Started with Adobe Flash Professional

Opening a Document and Playing a Movie

When you work in Flash, you'll either be creating a new document or opening an existing one. It is always good practice to save a file with a different file name to protect the original. As you continue getting acquainted with Flash, you open a sample file, save it with a new name, then play and test the movie.

QUICK TIP

You can also click Open in the Welcome Screen, then press [Ctrl][O] (Win) or ⌘[O] (Mac) to open a file.

1. **Click File on the Menu bar, click Open, then navigate to the location where you store your Data Files**

   The Open dialog box opens, and the list of available files appears in the file list, as shown in Figure A-10.

2. **Click FL A-1.fla, then click Open**

   The document opens. A balloon object and its animation path are visible on the Stage.

3. **Click File on the Menu bar, click Save As to open the Save As dialog box, type balloon-bounce_FL-A in the File name text box (Win) or Save As text box (Mac), then click Save**

   The document is renamed, and the new name appears in the Document window.

4. **Click View on the Menu bar, point to Magnification, then click Fit in Window**

   The Stage is scaled to fit in the Document window. Objects off the Stage, such as the balloon, may not be visible. You can also click the View arrow at the top of the Document window to select a view option.

QUICK TIP

You can also open a floating Controller on the Window, Toolbars menu.

5. **Click Control on the Menu bar, then click Play**

   The balloon floats in and bounces a couple times. As the movie plays on the Stage, the playhead moves through the Timeline. Several commands on the Control menu are similar to playback buttons, such as Rewind or Step Forward One Frame. To quickly play or stop a movie, you can press [Enter] (Win) or [return] (Mac). You explore ways to control how to view a movie.

6. **Click the Step back one frame button ◀ in the Controller at the bottom of the Timeline, drag the playhead in the Timeline to frame 1, then drag it to frame 38**

   The playhead moves back one frame, then to the beginning of the movie, and then to the middle, as shown in Figure A-11. Playing a movie in Flash presents a general preview of the movie, but does not provide a way to fully test it, which is critical if the movie or application contains interactivity such as buttons or video. You can preview and test the movie using the Flash Player.

QUICK TIP

You can control the movie or turn off looping by clicking Control on the Menu bar in the Flash Player window, and then clicking Loop (Win) or Loop Playback (Mac).

7. **Click Control on the Menu bar, point to Test Movie, then click in Flash Professional**

   The movie plays in a Flash Player window, as shown in Figure A-12. You can increase the size of the Flash Player window as needed by clicking and dragging a corner of the window. By default, the movie plays repeatedly, or **loops**. You can also press [Ctrl][Enter] (Win) or ⌘[return] (Mac) to test a movie. When you test a movie, Flash automatically creates a .swf output file, which you can see if you open the file management utility for your computer, then navigate to where you store your Data Files.

8. **Click the Close button on the Flash Player to close it**

FIGURE A-10: **Open dialog box**

Your location
might differ

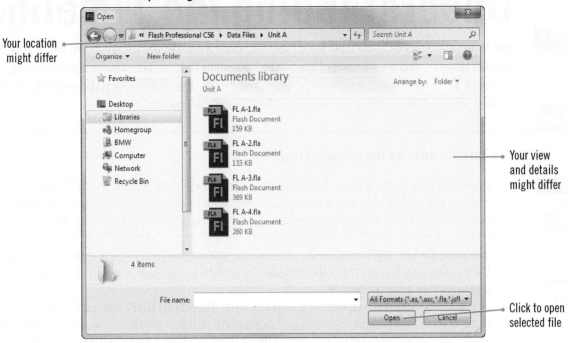

Your view
and details
might differ

Click to open
selected file

FIGURE A-11: **Playing a movie using the Controller**

Control menu

View arrow

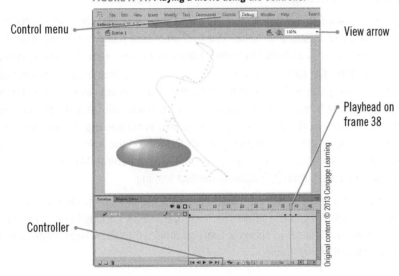

Playhead on
frame 38

Controller

Original content © 2013 Cengage Learning

FIGURE A-12: **Testing a movie in Flash Player**

Flash Player
window (Win)

Flash Player
menu (Mac
menus differ)

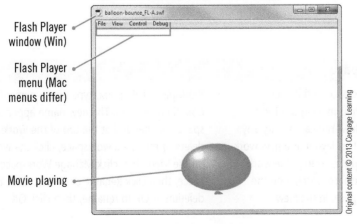

Movie playing

Original content © 2013 Cengage Learning

Getting Started with Adobe Flash Professional

Understanding the Timeline

The Timeline is a multipurpose tool divided into two main areas. On the left are layers, which appear in a column. Layers contain the elements of a movie and determine their position. On the right are frames, which appear in a row and show the elements in your project over time. As you continue to familiarize yourself with the Flash interface, you review the functions of the Timeline.

DETAILS

The Timeline includes the following features:

• **Layers section** Layers let you build depth and dimension into a project. In the Timeline, layers are arranged in a stack as they appear on the Stage, from front to back: The layer at the top of the stack is in front in the movie, and the layer at the bottom of the stack is in back in the movie. You can see this in Figure A-13, where the balloons are the objects in front, followed by the confetti, the Happy Birthday text, and finally the cake and banner. In the Timeline, the layers correspond to their appearance on the Stage: The balloons layer is at the top of the Timeline, the confetti and message layers are in the middle, and the cake banner layer is at the bottom.

  The Timeline offers several ways to manipulate layers. For existing layers, you can use buttons at the top of the layers section to show or hide a layer, lock it from editing, or display it as an outline. At the bottom of the layers section are buttons to add and delete layers or create a folder, where you can move related layers. Flash projects can become complex, and folders can be a useful organizing tool for your layers, just as they are with file management on your computer. See Figure A-14.

• **Frames section** You use frames to create animation; you create different effects by using different frame types, which you'll learn more about in a later unit. Each frame is a snapshot in time of an event on the Stage. Time in Flash is measured in frames, known as a **frame rate**, or frames per second—**fps**.

  You can view the status of a movie—the current frame, frame rate, and total elapsed time up to the selected frame—using indicators at the bottom of the Timeline, as shown in Figure A-14. The playhead shows the current frame playing in the movie. You can manually drag the playhead in the Timeline to play a group of frames on the Stage, in a process known as **scrubbing**. When creating animation, it is often beneficial to view a group of frames repeatedly to focus on the action. You can click the Loop button, select the frames you want to view, press [Enter] (Win) or [return] (Mac) to preview the selected framespan, then click the Loop button again to deselect looping.

• **Changing appearance** You can modify the Timeline as you can other panels: You can undock, move, resize, or close it. You can also adjust your view of frames by clicking the Panel menu button and selecting a frame size. Figure A-15 shows a Timeline modified to show large frames and Preview in Context, a small thumbnail of each frame.

Creating a custom workspace

You can arrange panels in a workspace to suit your individual work preferences, such as moving the Tools panel to the left side of the window. You can modify any preset workspace and then save that layout as a new workspace. To create a custom workspace, arrange the workspace as you wish, click the workspace switcher on the Menu bar, then click New Workspace. In the New Workspace dialog box, type a new name in the Name text box, then click OK. The new name appears on the workspace switcher and at the top of the Workspace menu. To delete or rename a workspace, click the workspace switcher on the Menu bar, click Manage Workspaces, select a workspace, then click Rename or Delete. Click Yes to confirm a deletion or OK to rename, then click OK.

FIGURE A-13: **Viewing layers**

Scene

Objects on Stage

Selected object

Layers in Timeline

Selected layer

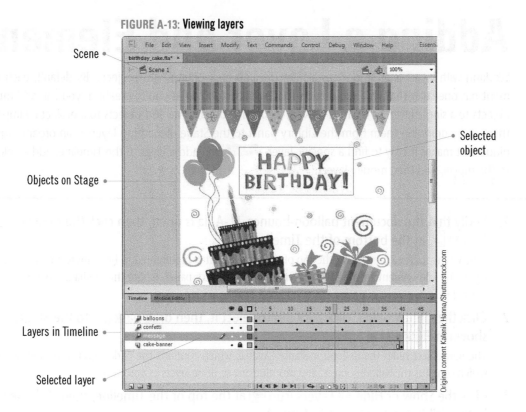

FIGURE A-14: **Viewing the Timeline**

Show or Hide All Layers icon

Lock or Unlock All Layers Icon

New Layer button

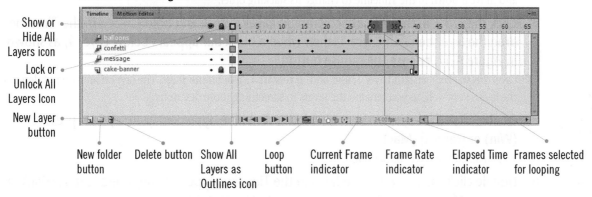

New folder button

Delete button

Show All Layers as Outlines icon

Loop button

Current Frame indicator

Frame Rate indicator

Elapsed Time indicator

Frames selected for looping

FIGURE A-15: **Modified Timeline**

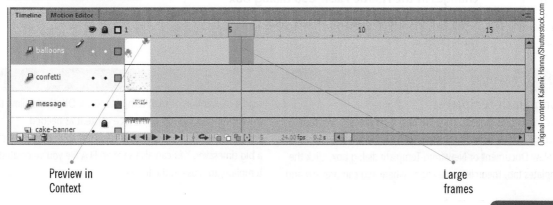

Preview in Context

Large frames

Getting Started with Adobe Flash Professional

Adding a Layer and Element

Working with layers is an important skill to develop for working with projects. By default, each document has one layer that you add objects to. Depending on what you're creating, you can add multiple objects to a single layer, or create a new layer for each object. You add objects to a project by importing them or by dragging them from the Library panel to the Stage. Renaming layers is an organizing technique that makes it easy to find a specific layer. You add a layer to the Timeline, add an element to the movie, and then modify layers.

STEPS

1. **Verify that the document balloon-bounce_FL-A.fla is open, then click the New Layer button** ⬛ **at the bottom of the Timeline**

   A new layer, Layer 2, appears at the top of the Timeline. It is highlighted in blue, indicating it is the active layer. You add content to the active layer using the Library panel, where the media assets for this movie are stored.

   TROUBLE
   Use the arrow keys to align the image on the Stage, if necessary.

2. **Click the Library panel, click park.jpg to select it, then drag park.jpg to the Stage, as shown in Figure A-16**

   The new object hides the balloon, because Layer 2, which contains the park object, is on top of Layer 1, which contains the balloon object. You can hide one or more layers as you work.

3. **Click the Show or Hide All Layers icon** 👁 **at the top of the Timeline, then click the red X in the visibility column next to Layer 1**

   All the layers are hidden when they all have a red "X," and Layer 2 is hidden after you display Layer 1. Although you can now see the balloon, you can't work with the new content, so you decide to show Layer 2 and move it down in the Timeline to change its stacking order.

4. **Click the red X in the visibility column on Layer 2, click and hold Layer 2 in the Timeline, drag the layer beneath Layer 1, then when a black bar appears below Layer 1, as shown in Figure A-17, release the mouse button**

   Layer 2 is stacked beneath Layer 1, and both layers are visible on the Stage. The layer names do not describe the layers very well, so you rename the layers to something more descriptive.

   QUICK TIP
   To expand the layer label so you can read a long layer name, place the mouse pointer over the gray vertical line before frame 1, then drag it to the right until the full name appears.

5. **Double-click the Layer 2 name label in the Timeline, type background, then press [Enter] (Win) or [return] (Mac)**

   You renamed the layer "background."

6. **Double-click the Layer 1 name label in the Timeline, type balloon, press [Enter] (Win) or [return] (Mac), then compare your screen to Figure A-18**

7. **Press [Ctrl][Enter] (Win) or ⌘[return] (Mac) to test the movie, then close the Flash Player**

8. **Click File on the Menu bar, click Close, then click Yes (Win) or Save (Mac) to save changes in the Adobe Flash CS6 dialog box**

   QUICK TIP
   You can also press [Ctrl][Q] (Win) or ⌘[Q] (Mac) to close the program.

9. **Click File on the Menu bar, then click Exit**

   Flash closes.

Design Matters

Using Flash templates

You can open or create different types of Flash files using the Welcome Screen or the New command on the File menu. In the New Document or New from Template dialog box, click the Templates tab, then click a category, where you can preview and read a description of each template. Click OK, then follow the directions if applicable, or replace content as needed. Predesigned templates contain ActionScript code, so they can be a big timesaver. You can also save an FLA file you've created as a template, to reuse in the future.

FIGURE A-16: Adding content to a new layer

Library panel

Thumbnail preview

Element on the Stage

Drag this element to the Stage

Newly added layer

New Layer button

FIGURE A-17: Moving a layer in the Timeline

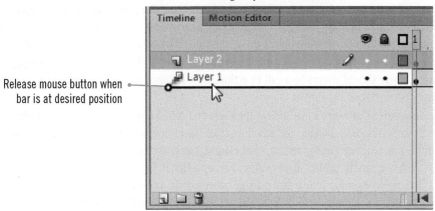

Release mouse button when bar is at desired position

FIGURE A-18: Viewing renamed layers

Getting Started with Adobe Flash Professional

Planning and Managing a Project

Developing a Flash project or application can involve working with multiple elements and multiple collaborators, so it easily becomes a complex process. To create a successful project, your plan should include communication, monitoring, and control. Many features in Flash help you organize your graphic and other media elements so you can work as efficiently as possible. 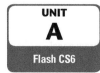 In order to better plan your Flash projects, you take a few minutes to learn more about project management.

DETAILS

Essential project management elements include:

- **Project teams**

  Typically, a team consists of designers, developers, artists, managers, and, of course, the client.

- **Project plans**

  When working with a team, it is essential to have clear, seamless communication about design and content. Investing time to develop a project plan with your team can help streamline your workflow, keep the focus on your goals, and troubleshoot problems. The process chart shown in Figure A-19 outlines the steps that can save time and help avoid time-consuming errors. Whether the final output is a banner ad, game, or mobile app, you should determine up front what you want to accomplish, who will use it, the look and feel, what content is included, and how it works. Specifically, how is the application arranged and how does it function?

  For example, in a banner ad or website side ad, you must determine and prioritize the user's engagement with the content. There should always be a call to action, such as filling out a form, replaying a video, or clicking through to a website.

  Project management provides a methodical approach that guides a project from start to finish. It controls the project's scope, resources, budget, and schedule. It also identifies the project's milestones through five phases: initiation, planning, executing, testing, and closing. Good project management detects common problems early, such as when the project scope begins to **creep**—that is, to shift in small ways that can lead to large changes over time. Planning also helps manage expectations; you should identify what your client receives in the final package, known as the **deliverable**. It starts with the goals of the project and the content that supports the goals. It could include all the specifications, prototypes and preparatory documents, copy writing, identity and content design, image selection and editing, deployment on multiple devices, maintenance, actual files (SWF, mobile, planning documents), and so on. Building in a common workflow and communication process ensures that everyone shares the same assumptions, evaluation criteria, and accountability.

  To ensure your content is accessible to all users, your application must plan for consistent design and navigation elements, gesture or mouse and keyboard controls, labels, audio, and visual captions.

QUICK TIP

The business contract with your client should also specify change control charges to manage scope creep, who owns all the design and content elements, and whether you can use them in your portfolio.

QUICK TIP

A quick way to determine whether you need to remove or redo a scene on your storyboard is if you cannot determine what is happening in the scene without reading the caption.

- **Planning applications with storyboards**

  Using a storyboard can be a great planning tool for an animation or a storyboard. A **storyboard** is a series of pictures containing captions that describe the action in a movie. Your most valuable production tool may be a storyboard. Basic storyboards should provide an organizational and page-level view. A good storyboard uses panels to map out the sequence and major action points and events of the animation. Often, each panel in a storyboard correlates to a keyframe in the animation, although it is also important to note transitions, sequencing and timing, navigation, images, text, audio, placement of Stage elements, and interactivity. A storyboard can be elaborately drawn or just a very simple sketch, as shown in Figure A-20. One benefit of creating a storyboard for any length of animation is that you and your clients can clearly see the beginning, middle, and end of the sequence, so you can correct or tweak it ahead of time.

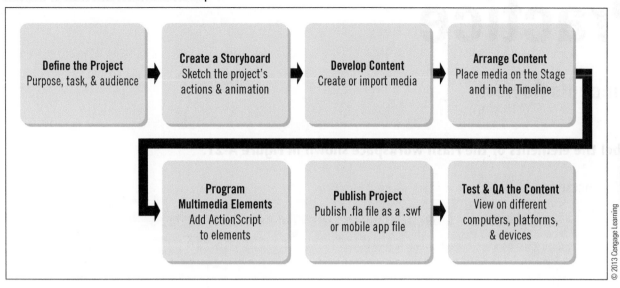

FIGURE A-20: Sample storyboard

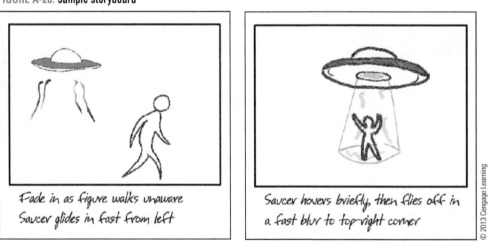

Fade in as figure walks unaware
Saucer glides in fast from left

Saucer hovers briefly, then flies off in
a fast blur to top-right corner

Using Help features

Flash includes an extensive online help system. To access it, click Flash Help on the Help menu, or press [F1]. In addition, you may find other commands on the Help menu useful. You can download extensions (user-created software that enhances Flash capabilities), access forums, and find additional support and training by clicking the Flash Support Center, Flash Exchange, Manage Extensions, and Adobe Online Forums links on the Help menu. Much of the support is free. You can post questions on specific help pages by signing in with your Adobe ID.

Practice

Concepts Review

Label the elements of the Flash workspace shown in Figure A-21.

FIGURE A-21

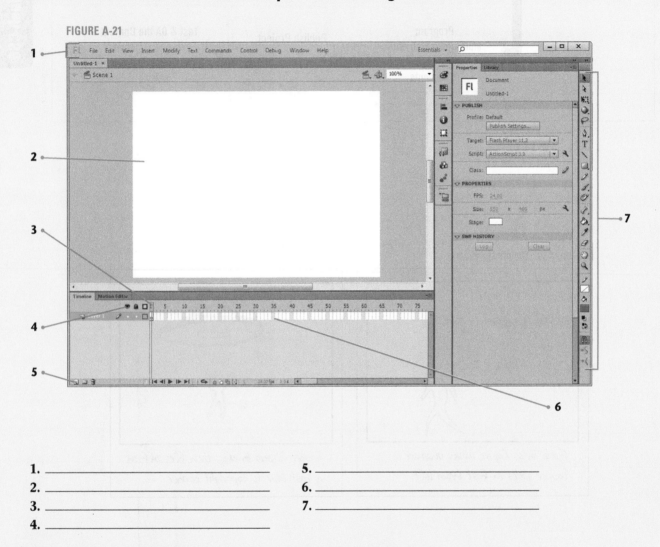

1. _____
2. _____
3. _____
4. _____
5. _____
6. _____
7. _____

Match each term with the statement that best describes it.

8. .fla
9. Stage
10. Workspace
11. Frame rate
12. Loops
13. Layer
14. .swf

a. Area containing movie's elements
b. To play repeatedly
c. Output file type of a Flash project for viewing on the web
d. Native Flash file project type
e. Measurement in time of a movie or Flash project
f. A row containing content for a Flash project
g. A configuration of the components in the Flash program window

Select the best answer from the list of choices.

15. **Which component shows a single snapshot of an event in a movie?**
    a. Properties panel
    b. Frame
    c. Layer
    d. Work area

16. **What happens when you reset a workspace?**
    a. You can name a custom workspace.
    b. You can no longer move components around.
    c. The currently open file closes.
    d. Components return to their default size and location.

17. **What is the area called where you can store assets that do not yet appear on the Stage?**
    a. Work area
    b. Library panel
    c. Properties panel
    d. Timeline

18. **Which command do you use to preview a movie in the Flash Player?**
    a. Preview Movie
    b. Test Movie
    c. Review Movie
    d. Watch Movie

19. **What happens on the Stage when you move a layer to the top of the stack in the Timeline?**
    a. The layer moves in front of all other layers.
    b. You should add animation to it.
    c. The first frame is selected.
    d. The layer moves behind all other layers.

20. **Which of the following is *not* available in the Timeline?**
    a. Step forward one frame button
    b. New Folder button
    c. Rename Name Label button
    d. Loop button

Skills Review

1. **Understand Adobe Flash.**
    a. Describe different interactive content you can create with Flash.
    b. Explain the difference between the Flash program and the Flash Player.

2. **Start Adobe Flash Professional CS6.**
    a. Start Flash.
    b. Describe two things you can do in the Welcome Screen.
    c. Open a new document.

3. **View the Flash workspace.**
    a. Identify the Stage.
    b. Identify the Timeline.
    c. Identify expanded and collapsed panels.
    d. Identify the Tools panel.

4. **Arrange the workspace.**
    a. Collapse the Tools panel to iconic view.
    b. Collapse the Properties panel and Library panel to iconic view.
    c. Undock the Tools panel from the other panels.
    d. Reset the Essentials workspace.
    e. Display the Small Screen workspace.
    f. Display the Essentials workspace, then close the open document.

Skills Review (continued)

5. **Open a document and play a movie.**

   a. Open the document FL A-2.fla from the location where you store your Data Files.

   b. Save the document as **abduction_FL-A.fla**.

   c. Change the view of the Document Window to Show All.

   d. Play the movie on the Stage.

   e. Use a button on the Controller to rewind the movie, then move the playhead to frame 3.

   f. Test the movie.

   g. Close the Flash Player.

6. **Understand the Timeline.**

   a. Describe the two main sections of the Timeline.

7. **Add a layer and element.**

   a. Verify that the document abduction_FL-A.fla is open, then click frame 1 in Layer 1.

   b. Display the Library panel, then drag saturn.jpg to right of center on the Stage.

   c. Play the movie.

   d. Hide and then show Layer 1, then move Layer 1 to the top of the Timeline.

   e. Rename Layer 1 **saturn**.

   f. Move the saturn layer to the bottom of the stack in the Timeline, use buttons on the Controller to move the playhead to frame 33, then compare your screen to Figure A-22.

   g. Test the movie, then close the Flash Player.

   h. Save and close the document abduction_FL-A.fla, then exit Flash.

8. **Plan and manage a project.**

   a. Describe three aspects of project management.

   b. Describe what a deliverable is and what it can contain.

   c. List three elements that a storyboard should include.

FIGURE A-22

NASA (nasa.gov); © 2013 Cengage Learning

Independent Challenge 1

You're helping a rescue shelter develop a digital persona for adoptions. The owners want to build interest in the shelter by adding some subtle animation to images in their mobile web presence. You begin with one of the newest additions.

a. Start Flash, open the file FL A-3.fla from the location where you store your Data Files, then save it as **wagmore_FL-A.fla**.

b. Show Layer 2 and the bone layer in the Timeline.

c. Move the playhead to frame 1, if necessary, then play the movie on the Stage.

d. Rename Layer 2 **tail**.

e. Rename Layer 3 **head**.

f. Add a new layer above the bone layer, then name it **dish**.

g. Display the Library panel, if necessary, undock it, then drag the dish_png object from the Library panel to the lower-left corner of the Stage.

h. Move the body layer above the dish layer in the Timeline.

i. Test the movie, then close the Flash Player.

j. Drag the playhead to frame 15, click the work area, then compare your screen to Figure A-23.

k. Reset the workspace, save your work, close the document, then exit Flash.

FIGURE A-23

© 2013 Cengage Learning

Independent Challenge 2

A friend started a blog about using music to heal from a broken heart. You take over this project from the person who created it. The previous author was experimenting with a couple of different effects, so you decide to keep the one that best fits the theme.

a. Start Flash, open the file FL A-4.fla from the location where you store your Data Files, then save it as **heart2heart_FL-A.fla**. (*Hint*: Click OK if you receive a prompt about a missing font.)

b. Show all layers.

c. Play the movie on the Stage.

d. Move Layer 2 above Layer 1.

e. Hide Layer 3, then play the movie on the Stage, noting that the hidden layer is not visible.

f. Test the movie. Compare playing the animation in the Flash Player to playing the movie on the Stage. (*Hint*: Layers hidden in the Timeline still play when the movie is tested in the Flash Player.)

g. Delete Layer 3. (*Hint*: Select the layer if necessary, then click the Delete button on the bottom of the Timeline.)

h. Rename Layer 1 **heart**, then rename Layer 2 **text**.

i. Drag the playhead to frame 45, click the work area, then compare your screen to Figure A-24.

j. Save the file, test the movie in Flash Professional, then close the Flash Player.

FIGURE A-24

© 2013 Cengage Learning

Advanced Challenge Exercise

- Create a new layer named **static heart**, then move it to the bottom of the stack in the Timeline.
- Show the Library, then drag pink-heart.png to the Stage at least twice, then arrange the hearts on the Stage as desired.
- Lock the heart layer. (*Hint*: Click the circle in the Lock or Unlock All Layers column.)
- Test the movie, close the Flash Player, then save the document.

k. Close the document.

l. Exit Flash.

Independent Challenge 3

Adobe's online support can help answer a question, provide troubleshooting tips, and direct you to more advanced techniques. You decide to go online and examine some of its features.

a. Start Flash.

b. Select Flash Support Center from the Help menu.

c. View or read an item that interests you. (*Hint*: Some features might be advanced.)

d. Print a page, then add your name to the printout.

Advanced Challenge Exercise

- Select Adobe Online Forums on the Help menu.
- Select at least one topic.
- Scroll through a couple pages of the forum, then print a topic that interests you. (*Hint*: You can also type a keyword in the Search Forums text box if you wish.)

e. Close the Help window and exit Flash.

Real Life Independent Challenge

You're interested in learning more about controlling applications and modifying panels in Flash. You begin by exploring different workspaces and features.

a. Start Flash, then open any of the saved documents you worked on in this unit.

b. Switch to the Designer workspace, then examine the open panels.

c. Use Help to look up the function of panels you are unfamiliar with.

d. Undock the Tools panel, then redock it on the right side of the program window. (*Hint*: Drag the panel to the right until a blue vertical line is visible, then release the mouse button.)

e. Reset the Designer workspace, then display the Essentials workspace.

f. In the Timeline, change the frame size to Tiny. (*Hint*: Use the Panel menu button.)

g. Use the Controller to play, stop, rewind, and move the movie frame by frame for a couple of frames.

h. Use commands on the Control menu to replicate the instructions in Step g.

i. Test the movie. In the Flash Player window, click Control on the Menu bar (Win) or menu bar (Mac) to replicate the instructions in Step g, then close the Flash Player.

j. Reset the frame size to Normal in the Timeline, reset the Essentials workspace, then close the document.

k. Exit Flash.

Visual Workshop

When you work in Flash, you can customize your workspace so that you can view and access the information you need. Start Flash, open the balloon-bounce_FL-A.fla file you created earlier, then arrange the workspace so that it matches the one shown in Figure A-25. When you are finished, press [Print Screen] (Win) or ⌘[Shift][4] to select the window using the mouse (Mac), paste the image into a word-processing program or program of your choice, add your name at the top of the document, then print or post the document. Please check with your instructor for assignment submission instructions. Close the word processor or other program without saving changes, then exit Flash without saving changes to the file.

FIGURE A-25

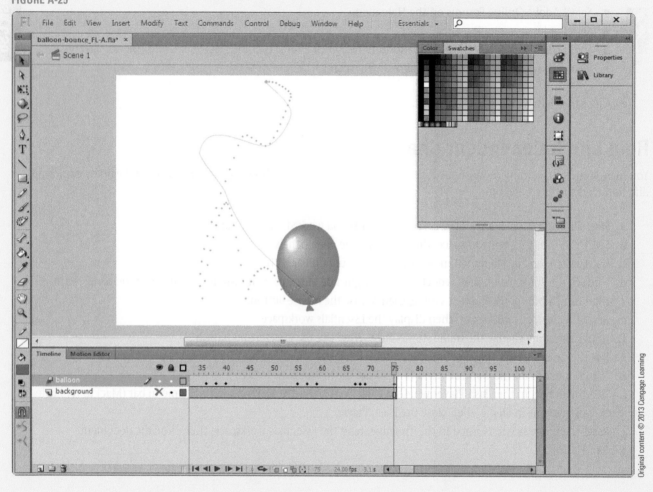

Creating Graphics and Text

Files You Will Need:

To view a list of files needed for this unit, see the Data Files Grid in the back of the book.

Creating objects in Flash is often the first step to creating dazzling animation or web elements. You use drawing tools such as the Rectangle tool, Oval tool, and PolyStar tool to create shapes, and the Pencil tool and Line tool to create lines. By drawing with these tools you create vector graphics. Along with bitmap graphics, which designers usually use to display photographs, vector graphics are prominent on the web and in applications. Designers use vector graphics to display illustrations. You use the Text tool to create text. Because text and shapes are vector objects, you can modify their attributes without affecting the quality of the image. You begin work on the GreenWinds Eco-Cruise logo using vector shapes and text.

OBJECTIVES

Understand Vector and Bitmap Graphics

Create a New Document

Set Tool Options and Create a Shape

Reshape an Object

Modify a Shape

Copy and Transform an Object

Use Design Panels

Create Text

Modify Text

Understanding Vector and Bitmap Graphics

Graphics are the core of your animations. Generally, two types of graphics are used on the web: vector and bitmap. Although you can import bitmap images into a Flash document, bitmap images are usually best used as a static design element or for limited animation. Most often in Flash, you work with vector graphics, and either create them using drawing tools on the Tools panel or import them from another graphic design program. Once you select a shape tool, you can choose between two types of drawing modes: merge drawing and object drawing. ********** Before drawing in Flash, you want to learn more about graphics and Flash drawing modes.

Review the following graphic types:

- **Vector graphics**

  A **vector graphic** is a mathematically calculated object composed of **anchor points** and straight or curved line segments, which collectively form a **path**. You can fill a path with a color, gradient, or pattern and outline it with a line known as a **stroke**. Vector graphics appear smooth, which makes them perfect for illustrations.

  Because they retain their appearance regardless of how you edit them, vector graphics offer far more flexibility than bitmap images. They keep their sharp, crisp-looking edges no matter how much you enlarge them. Figure B-1 compares the image quality of enlarged vector and bitmap images.

- **Bitmap graphics**

  A **bitmap graphic** displays a picture image as a matrix of dots, or pixels, on a grid. A **pixel** is the smallest square of color used to display an image on a computer screen. This is why most of the photographs and other images on a web page are bitmap images (also known as **raster images**). Pixels allow your computer screen to depict colors realistically in a photographic image. A bitmap image consists of a finite number of pixels. Therefore, when you resize the image, the existing pixels are stretched over a larger area, which causes distortion and loss of image quality. The shell image on the right side of Figure B-1 shows the jagged edges and blurry appearance typical of an enlarged bitmap graphic.

- **Resolution**

  Resolution describes the degree of clarity, detail, and sharpness of a displayed or printed image. Resolution is expressed by the number of pixels in a square inch of an image. The higher the resolution, the better the picture. On-screen resolution is usually 72 or 96 pixels per inch (ppi); print graphics require higher resolution, typically starting around 220 ppi.

- **Flash drawing modes**

  Flash has two drawing modes: Merge Drawing mode and Object Drawing mode. Deciding which drawing mode to use depends on your design goals and how you want objects to interact as you draw or arrange them. **Merge Drawing mode** assumes that the objects' paths (their strokes and fills) will combine in some fashion, such as using the outline of one object to create a shape in another. You can select, move, or delete an object's fill or stroke, or overlap multiple objects and then move the top one to punch or cut its shape through the bottom shape. **Object Drawing mode** treats the object as a whole. You can modify an object's attributes, such as fill or stroke color, and you can overlap multiple objects without affecting either object. The top object may obscure the bottom object, just as a top layer obscures a lower layer in the Timeline. Figure B-2 compares some of the features of Merge Drawing and Object Drawing.

FIGURE B-1: Comparing vector and bitmap images

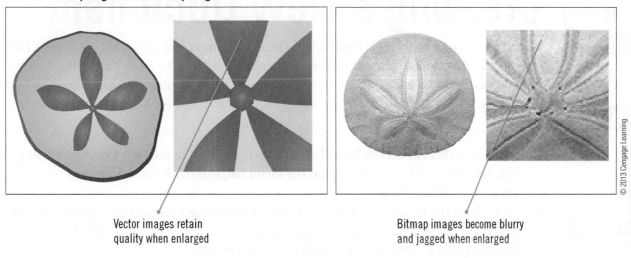

Vector images retain
quality when enlarged

Bitmap images become blurry
and jagged when enlarged

© 2013 Cengage Learning

FIGURE B-2: Comparing objects in Merge Drawing and Object Drawing modes

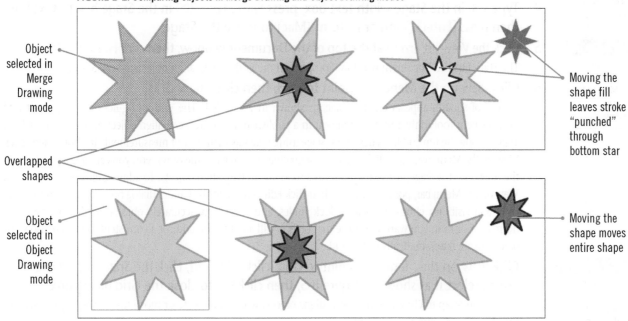

Object
selected in
Merge
Drawing
mode

Moving the
shape fill
leaves stroke
"punched"
through
bottom star

Overlapped
shapes

Object
selected in
Object
Drawing
mode

Moving the
shape moves
entire shape

Design Matters

Understanding guide layers

A **guide layer** is a layer that contains a shape you can use to trace or align objects, or to create a motion path for an animated object. First, you create the shape or path on the guide layer, then you use it as a template for objects in the layers above it. Because a guide layer appears in the Timeline but is not visible in a published movie, it is an efficient design tool. For example, say you want to show the curved path a spaceship takes before entering faster-than-light speed. You could add the spaceship graphic to one layer. You could then draw and modify an oval shape on a guide layer and then use that layer as the motion path of the spaceship graphic. You can also import or copy a graphic to a layer and then convert it to a guide layer. To create a guide layer, right-click (Win) or [control]-click (Mac) a layer in the Timeline, then click Guide. A guide layer icon appears on the layer.

Creating a New Document

You can create a new document in Flash and then modify document settings, such as size or color. Flash provides several methods to precisely measure and position objects on the Stage: You can display rulers, create guides, or display a grid. ▰▰▰▰ Your boss, Vanessa Mayes, wants you to begin developing the GreenWinds Eco-Cruise logo by creating the document, modifying the Stage size, and displaying the grid.

STEPS

1. **Start Flash, click File on the Menu bar, click New, click OK in the New Document dialog box, click the workspace switcher on the Menu bar, then click Reset 'Essentials'**
   A new untitled document opens.

2. **Click File on the Menu bar, click Save As to open the Save As dialog box, navigate to the location where you store your Data Files, type GreenWinds-logo_FL-B in the File name text box (Win) or Save As text box (Mac), then click Save**
   You begin by setting the size of the document.

   > **QUICK TIP**
   > To adjust additional properties, click the Edit document properties button 🔧 on the Properties panel to open the Document Settings dialog box.

3. **Click the expand section arrow ▷ next to Properties on the Properties panel, if necessary**
   Here you can modify the document's frame rate, size, and Stage color. See Figure B-3.

4. **Type 200 in the Stage width text box, press [Tab], type 200 in the Stage height text box, then press [Enter] (Win) or [return] (Mac) to resize the Stage**

5. **Click the View list arrow at the top of the Document window, then click Fit in Window**
   The Stage fills the Document window. You turn on the grid to help align objects on the Stage.

   > **QUICK TIP**
   > You can also press [Ctrl][2] (Win) or ⌘[2] (Mac) to fit the Stage in the window.

6. **Click View on the Menu bar, point to Grid, then click Show Grid**
   A **grid** of squares appears on the Stage, as shown in Figure B-4. The grid and guides are alignment and measurement tools only and do not appear in a published movie. You can align objects using **rulers**, which appear along the top and left sides of the Stage using pixels as their unit of measurement. To show rulers, click View on the Menu bar, then click Rulers. To align objects at an exact measurement, you can drag a **guide** from the ruler onto the Stage, where it appears as a solid line to help align objects. To adjust Guide properties, click View on the Menu bar, point to Guides, then click Edit Guides. In the Guides dialog box, you can adjust guide color and visibility, choose to clear or lock guides, and select how accurately objects snap to guides: close, normal, or distant. You want to ensure that objects will align to the grid for a consistent look. You also want objects to align automatically to the grid.

   > **QUICK TIP**
   > Objects will snap to the grid or guides even if they are not displayed; objects will snap to guide first if it falls between grid lines.

7. **Click View on the Menu bar, point to Grid, click Edit Grid, click the Snap to grid check box to select it as shown in Figure B-5, then click OK to close the Grid dialog box**
   Turning on Snap to Grid automatically aligns objects when you create or move them. The object snaps to the closest intersection on the grid.

8. **Click View on the Menu bar, point to Snapping, click Snap Align if necessary to add a check mark, then save the document**
   With Snap Align selected, dotted lines will appear on the Stage to aid in aligning objects.

Understanding view tools

In addition to adjusting magnification on the Stage using the View list arrow in the Document window, you can use the Zoom tool 🔍. You can zoom in or zoom out by selecting one of the zoom option buttons that appears at the bottom of the Tools panel when the Zoom tool is active, and then clicking the Stage. To focus in on a particular area, you can select the Zoom tool and drag a zoom bounding box around an area on the Stage and the magnification will increase based on the size of the selection box. To resize to 100% quickly, double-click the Zoom tool on the Tools panel. You can use the Hand tool 🖑 to move a particular part of a large or magnified object into view if the object is too large to fit completely in the current magnification. To switch to the Hand tool temporarily when another tool is selected, press [Spacebar]. Neither tool affects the actual size of objects in your document; they simply allow you to manipulate your view of the Stage.

FIGURE B-3: Document Properties on the Properties panel

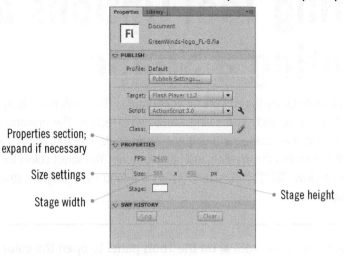

Properties section; expand if necessary

Size settings

Stage width

Stage height

FIGURE B-4: Viewing the grid turned on in a document

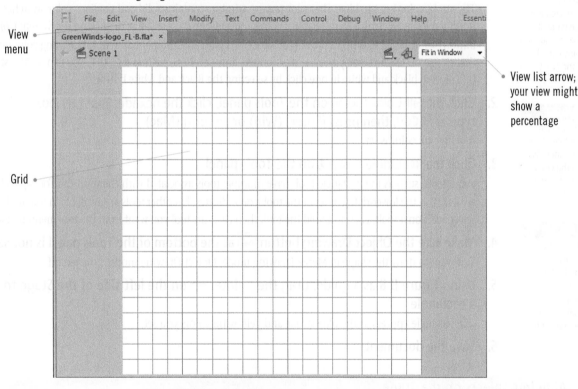

View menu

View list arrow; your view might show a percentage

Grid

FIGURE B-5: Grid dialog box

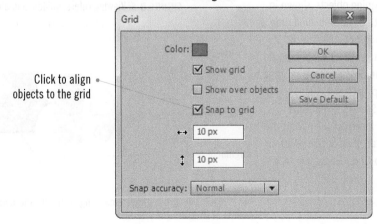

Click to align objects to the grid

Setting Tool Options and Creating a Shape

You use Flash tools to create the artwork for your projects. The Tools panel is separated into sections, each containing related tools, such as drawing, view, and selection. The drawing section contains tools for drawing or painting lines, shapes, and patterns. Many tools have tool options at the bottom of the Tools panel. Table B-1 describes the drawing and painting tools. You select colors for strokes and fills using the color pop-up window. You start work on the logo by setting the stroke and fill color and then creating a shape.

QUICK TIP

You can adjust the transparency of a color by decreasing the percentage of the Alpha setting, or not set any color by clicking the No Color icon ☑.

1. **Click the Stroke Color tool on the Tools panel to open the color pop-up window, then click the blue color swatch (#3300FF) shown in Figure B-7**

   The stroke color is set to blue. The color pop-up window contains solid and gradient color swatches. You can select a color by clicking a color swatch, typing a hexadecimal color value, or clicking the System Color Picker button 🔘 and then selecting a color. **Hexadecimal** is an alphanumeric system for defining color on the web that designates each color by a set of six numbers and/or letters, such as #3300FF. You can set the stroke and fill colors to black and white in one click by selecting the Black and white button.

TROUBLE

If the Rectangle tool is not visible on the Tools panel, click and hold the visible tool, then click the Rectangle tool.

2. **Click the Fill Color tool on the Tools panel, click the hexadecimal text box, type #FFCC00, then press [Enter] (Win) or [return] (Mac)**

   A yellow fill color is set.

3. **Click the Rectangle tool on the Tools panel**

   Some tools, such as the Rectangle tool, have multiple tools associated with them on the Tools panel. A small arrow ◢ in the lower-right corner of the tool icon indicates that other tools are available in that tool group. To select additional tools, click and hold the tool, then click the tool you want from the tool menu that appears.

QUICK TIP

To create a perfect square or circle, select the Rectangle tool or Oval tool, and then press and hold [Shift] as you draw the shape on the Stage.

4. **Make sure the Object Drawing button at the bottom of the Tools panel is not selected**

   You want to draw the shape in Merge Drawing mode, Object Drawing mode is turned off.

5. **Using Figure B-8 as a guide, drag the pointer + on the left side of the Stage to create a rectangle**

   The rectangle appears in the blue stroke and yellow fill colors you set.

6. **Save the document**

Aligning objects on the Stage

Flash provides several options for aligning objects, shown in Figure B-6. Snap Align displays a dotted line when you drag an object within a defined distance of another object or the Stage edge. Snap to Grid aligns an object's center or edge to a grid intersection. Snap to Guides aligns an object's center or edge to a guide dragged from the ruler. Snap to Objects snaps an object along another object's edge. Snap to Pixels moves objects one pixel at a time. To show Rulers, click View on the Menu bar, then click Rulers. To turn an align option on or off, click View on the Menu bar, point to Grid, Guides, or Snapping, then click an option.

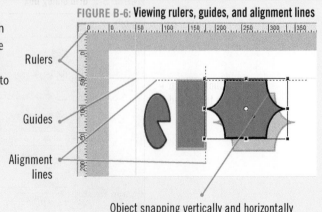

FIGURE B-6: Viewing rulers, guides, and alignment lines

Rulers
Guides
Alignment lines

Object snapping vertically and horizontally

FIGURE B-7: **Setting stroke color by clicking a color swatch**

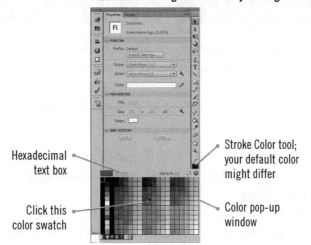

Hexadecimal text box

Click this color swatch

Stroke Color tool; your default color might differ

Color pop-up window

FIGURE B-8: **Creating a shape**

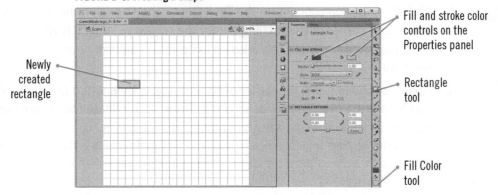

Newly created rectangle

Fill and stroke color controls on the Properties panel

Rectangle tool

Fill Color tool

TABLE B-1: **Drawing tools**

tool	tool name	description
	Pen tool	Creates paths and anchor points
	Text tool	Creates text
	Line tool	Creates straight lines
	Pencil tool	Creates freehand lines
	Brush tool	Paints fill shapes
	Spray Brush tool	Sprays in a specific fill pattern or shape
	Deco tool	Creates geometric patterns
Shape tools		
	Rectangle tool	Creates squares and rectangles
	Oval tool	Creates circles and ellipses
	Rectangle Primitive tool	Creates squares and rectangles with extra modifiable properties
	Oval Primitive tool	Creates circles and ellipses with extra modifiable properties
	PolyStar tool	Creates multisided shapes or multipointed shapes, such as stars

Reshaping an Object

You can change an object's shape using a variety of methods. The Selection tool allows you to manipulate the object's shape directly by dragging its border into a different contour. When you need to adjust your view of an object, you can use the Zoom tool to zoom in or out of the image. ▞▞▞▞ You work on the design elements of the logo by changing the rectangle to a triangle and then creating a curve.

STEPS

1. **Click the Zoom tool 🔍 on the Tools panel, move the Zoom In pointer ⊕ near the rectangle, then click the Stage until the object and grid are clearly visible on your screen, if necessary**

   The plus sign in ⊕ indicates that you are zooming in, or enlarging, your view of the object. To zoom out of an object, press and hold [Alt] (Win) or [option] (Mac), then when the pointer changes to ⊖ click the Stage.

   > **QUICK TIP**
   > You can deselect objects on the Stage by pressing [Ctrl][Shift][A] (Win) or [⌘][Shift][A] (Mac).

2. **Click the Selection tool ▶ on the Tools panel, then position the mouse pointer over the lower-right corner of the rectangle until the corner pointer ↳ is visible**

   Depending on where you place the Selection tool pointer, a different pointer appears. The corner pointer allows you to adjust corners.

3. **Drag ↳ to the upper-right corner of the rectangle, then when the dragged corner snaps and becomes a straight line, as shown in Figure B-9, release the mouse button**

   The rectangle is now a triangle. A snap ring is visible as you reshape the object. A **snap ring** is an alignment aide; the ring becomes larger as it nears a snapping point, in this case, a grid intersection. You want to move the lower-right point on top of the upper-right point to have one smooth line. Next, you add a curve to an edge of the triangle.

   > **TROUBLE**
   > If the curve pointer is not visible as you point to the edge of the triangle, redo Step 3 to create a perfectly straight line.

4. **Move the mouse pointer over the bottom edge of the triangle until the curve pointer ↳ appears**

5. **Click and drag ↳ toward the upper-left corner of the rectangle, then when the curve resembles Figure B-10, release the mouse button**

   The bottom edge of the triangle is now curved.

6. **Save the document**

Design Matters

Understanding the Elements of Design and Principles of Design

The **Elements of Design** are the basic ingredients that the artist uses separately or in combination to produce artistic imagery. *Lines* serve to illustrate or provide information. *Shapes* are areas that are contained within an implied line, or are identified because of color or value changes. Shapes have length and width, and can be geometric or free form. *Form* describes the volume and mass, or the three-dimensional aspects of objects that take up space. *Value* or color tone, refers to dark and light. *Color* communicates feeling and can make a statement. *Texture* influences the mood of the design and consequently that of the reader. *Space*, whether white or negative, binds sections, frames the design, and focuses attention.

The **Principles of Design** determine how the Elements of Design are used in a composition. *Balance* consists of how two different elements, such as type and shape, can offset each other to be perfectly formatted. It relates to symmetry, an even placement of visual weight in the design; asymmetry, the psychological or "felt" balance even if space and shapes are not evenly distributed; and radial balance, where images emit from a point like spokes on a wheel. Balance also covers the *rule of thirds*, where you divide an image area into thirds using two vertical and two horizontal lines so you have nine equal parts. You place important compositional elements along these lines. In addition, design should have *repetition* of visual movement, such as colors, shapes, or lines. *Pattern* uses the art elements in planned or random repetitions. *Movement* is used to direct the viewer's eye through the work, often to a focal area. *Contrast* is the difference in values, colors, textures, shapes, and other elements. *Emphasis* is also known as dominance in graphic design—the first thing the eye sees. Finally, there should be *unity*, the cohesive quality that makes an artwork feel complete and finished.

FIGURE B-9: Creating a triangle

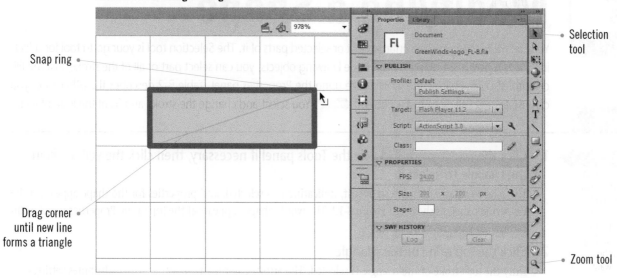

Snap ring •

Drag corner •
until new line
forms a triangle

Selection
tool

Zoom tool

FIGURE B-10: Creating a curve

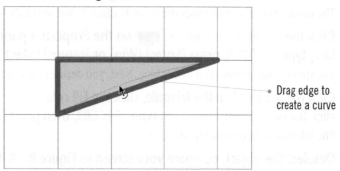

Drag edge to
create a curve

Understanding primitive tools

You can create the same shapes using Rectangle Primitive and Rectangle tools or the Oval Primitive and Oval tools. The difference lies in their shape type and editability after you create them. The shapes you draw with the primitive tools are separate objects, similar to objects you draw in Object Drawing mode using regular shape tools. With the regular shape tools, you set the shape options before you create the shape. After you create the shape,

you cannot alter shape options, such as corner radius value for a rectangle, and start and end angles and inner radius values for an oval. In contrast, you can edit any of these settings with a primitive shape, and reset the shape to default settings. See Figure B-11. With the Rectangle Primitive tool, you can even change a corner radius as you are creating it by dragging the mouse on the Stage. To do so, press the Up or Down arrow keys on the keyboard.

FIGURE B-11: Comparing primitive and regular shape tools options

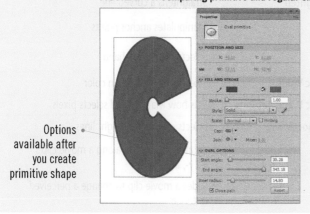

Options
available after
you create
primitive shape

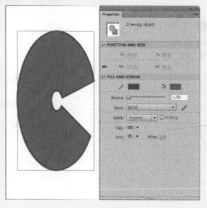

Options
unavailable
after you
create
regular
shape

Creating Graphics and Text

Modifying a Shape

You can make changes to an entire object or selected parts of it. The Selection tool is your go-to tool for selecting every aspect of an object. With Merge Drawing objects, you can select part or all of the stroke, just the fill, or both. You can change the fill or stroke using the Properties panel. Table B-2 describes the other tools you can use to select all or part of an object. ▓▓▓▓ You select and change the stroke and fill of the logo object.

STEPS

QUICK TIP

To quickly select an entire object or multiple objects, click the Selection tool ▸, then drag a selection bounding box around the objects you want to select.

1. **Click the Selection tool ▸ on the Tools panel if necessary, then click the yellow fill in the triangle to select it**

   The selection has a dot pattern over it, indicating it is selected, and properties for the shape appear on the Properties panel, as shown in Figure B-12. The word "Shape" appears at the top of the Properties panel, indicating that you are editing a shape.

2. **Click the top edge of the triangle**

   Only the top stroke of the triangle is selected. The Stroke color icon and other stroke attributes settings are active on the Properties panel, as shown in Figure B-13.

3. **Double-click the top edge of the triangle**

   The entire stroke that surrounds the shape is selected. You are ready to change the color of the stroke.

QUICK TIP

You can double-click any part of the stroke to select it in its entirety.

4. **Click the Stroke color icon 🖊️ ▬ on the Properties panel, click the hexadecimal text box, type #0000BA, press [Enter] (Win) or [return] (Mac), then click the work area**

   The stroke color changes to a darker blue. Next, you decide to change the fill color.

QUICK TIP

For objects created in Object Drawing mode, you can double-click the object and then individually select a fill or stroke.

5. **Click the yellow fill in the triangle, click the Fill color icon 🎨 ▬ on the Properties panel, click the hexadecimal text box, type #03CC03, then press [Enter] (Win) or [return] (Mac)**

   The fill color changes to a bright green.

6. **Deselect the object, compare your screen to Figure B-14, then save the document**

   The new stroke and fill colors also appear on the Tools panel.

TABLE B-2: Selection and 3D tools and tool options

tool	name	tool option	name	description
▸	Selection tool			Selects by clicking or dragging
		🧲	Snap to Objects	Aligns objects
		-S	Smooth	Smoothes a straight line
		-(	Straighten	Straightens a curved line
▸	Subselection tool			Manipulates anchor points
🔾	Lasso tool			Selects objects freehand
		🪄	Magic Wand	Selects pixels based on color
		🪄	Magic Wand Settings	Sets how Magic Wand selects pixels
		🔽	Polygon Mode	Selects objects in straight lines
🔮	3D Rotation tool			Rotates perspective along a movie clip's x-, y-, and z-axes
🔧	3D Translation tool			Slides a movie clip to change a perceived distance

FIGURE B-12: **Selecting a fill**

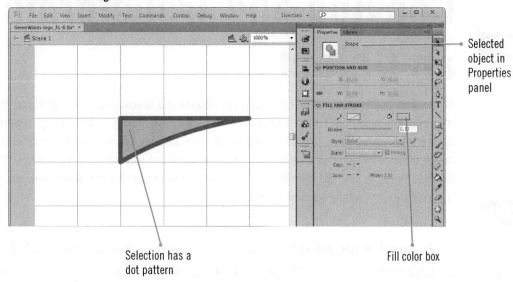

Selected
object in
Properties
panel

Selection has a
dot pattern

Fill color box

FIGURE B-13: **Selecting part of a stroke**

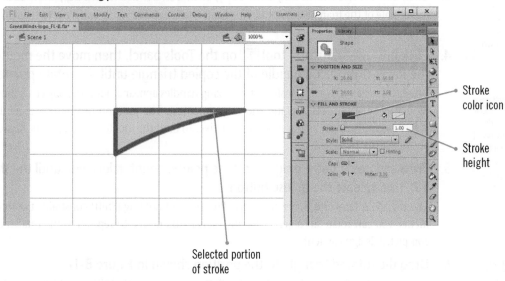

Stroke
color icon

Stroke
height

Selected portion
of stroke

FIGURE B-14: **Viewing edited colors in an object**

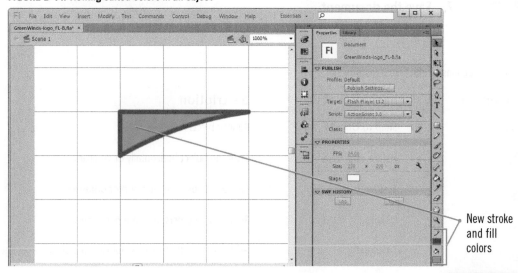

New stroke
and fill
colors

Copying and Transforming an Object

As you work in Flash, you save time if you copy objects and **transform**, or reconfigure, the copies instead of re-creating each object from scratch. You can transform an object by scaling, rotating, skewing, and distorting it. Flash offers a few different ways to copy an object from outside or within the program. You can reconfigure objects using options for the Free Transform tool. Options for the Free Transform tool are described in Table B-3. ⬛⬛⬛ Now that you have set the colors for the design element, you are ready to finalize it by copying and transforming the triangle.

STEPS

1. **Zoom out as needed so that more of the Stage is visible; approximately by half**

2. **Click the Selection tool ▶ on the Tools panel if necessary, drag a bounding box around the triangle to select both the stroke and the fill, then compare your image to Figure B-15**

3. **Click Edit on the Menu bar, click Copy, click Edit on the Menu bar, then click Paste in Center**
   A duplicate of the triangle is pasted in the center of the visible Stage. You want to rotate the copied object to create a design.

> **TROUBLE**
> Depending on your monitor and zoom level, your pasted object may be in a different location than the one shown in the figure.

4. **Click the Free Transform tool ▦ on the Tools panel, then move the mouse pointer near the lower-right sizing handle of the copied triangle until the rotate pointer ⤵ appears**
   When you select the Free Transform tool, sizing handles appear around the object, as shown in Figure B-16. By default, you can scale, rotate, and skew an object. The position of the mouse pointer on or near the object determines which option pointer is active. To limit the tool to a single function, click an option at the bottom of the Tools panel.

> **QUICK TIP**
> To flip objects horizontally or vertically or to rotate objects 90°, click Modify on the Menu bar, point to Transform, then click a flip or rotate command.

5. **Press and hold [Shift], drag the mouse pointer counterclockwise until the shape rotates 90°, then release the mouse button**
   The triangle rotates and snaps into place. Pressing and holding [Shift] constrains the rotation to 45° increments; you can rotate an object from any corner. You decide to reposition the rotated object to form the completed design element.

> **TROUBLE**
> You may need to drag slowly or increase magnification to see the line.

6. **Drag the rotated triangle to the position shown in Figure B-17**
   When the rotated triangle is left-aligned with the original, a dotted alignment line appears along the objects' left edges.

7. **Save the document**

TABLE B-3: Options for the Free Transform tool

tool option	name	description
🔘	Snap to Objects	Aligns objects
↻	Rotate and Skew	Slants an object horizontally or vertically
⬒	Scale	Resizes an object by side or proportionately
◹	Distort	Repositions corners to create perspective
▣	Envelope	Adds anchor points to allow for extreme distortion in lines and curves

FIGURE B-15: Copying a selection

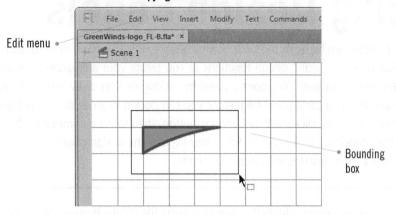

Edit menu •

• Bounding
box

FIGURE B-16: Positioning the rotate pointer

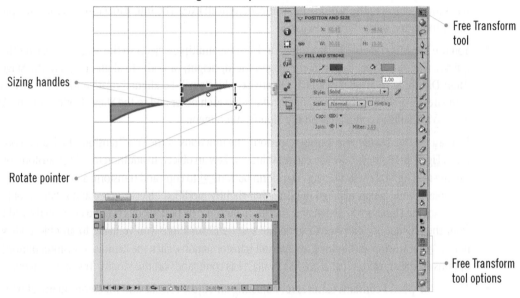

Sizing handles •

Rotate pointer •

• Free Transform
tool

• Free Transform
tool options

FIGURE B-17: Transformed and repositioned object

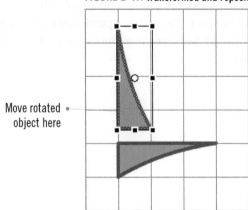

Move rotated •
object here

Understanding paste and drag options

After you copy an object, you can use commands on the Edit menu to paste it in various locations. Paste in Center—[Ctrl][V] (Win) or [⌘][V] (Mac)—pastes the object in the middle of the visible Stage. Paste in Place—[Ctrl][Shift][V] (Win) or [⌘][Shift][V] (Mac)—pastes the object directly on top of the original. You use Paste Special when you've copied a selection from another program, and Duplicate to paste a copy at a 10-pixel offset from the original. To use the keyboard to drag and copy a duplicate from the original, select the object(s), press and hold [Alt] (Win) or [option] (Mac), then drag the copy anywhere on the Stage.

Creating Graphics and Text

Using Design Panels

Now that you're familiar with the basic Flash interface, this is a good time to learn about several other panels that perform specific design functions as you create your animations: the Info, Align, Transform, Color, and Swatches panels. You open a panel by clicking its icon or by clicking its name on the Window menu. If you find you use a panel frequently, you can dock it in an existing panel group, or create a new panel group. To do so, click the Panel options button, then select a command. ▐▛▞▟ You have already noticed the abundance of features in Flash. You explore the design panels to see how they can improve your efficiency when working with movie elements.

DETAILS

- The **Info panel** shows information based on where the pointer is on the Stage, such as the color beneath the pointer, and the size, location, and color of a selected object, as shown in Figure B-18. You view coordinates for an object in the X (horizontal) and Y (vertical) axes. The Info panel displays the same property and size information as the Properties panel.

- You use the **Align panel** to size, align, or distribute multiple objects to the Stage or to each other. You can quickly resize an object to match the Stage's width, height, or both. To align objects to the Stage, click the Align/Distribute to Stage check box. Otherwise, objects will be aligned relative to each other. Figure B-18 compares several objects aligned and distributed to each other and to the Stage. Options on the Align panel are also available as commands on the Modify, Align menu.

- You can use the **Transform panel** to perform the functions of the Free Transform tool, and more. The sample in Figure B-19 shows how you can set values to skew an object. In addition to using transform options, you can use the Duplicate Selection and Transform button ⊞ to copy and transform a new object in one step. For example, if your design required duplicate but slightly modified objects, you could rotate an object 25° and then click the Duplicate Selection and Transform button. The pasted object would be rotated an additional 25° from the original. If you want to undo the size transformations you've made to an object, click the Reset button ⟲ at the top of the panel. To undo all transformations, click the Remove Transform button ⊡. Many options on the Transform panel are also available as commands on the Modify, Transform menu.

- The **Color panel** contains features for adjusting an object's stroke and fill colors, many of which are also available on the Properties panel. You can select solid or gradient color, hue, brightness, and **alpha** (transparency) of an object. The **Swatches panel** contains colors from the active color palette, or set, of available colors. You can add colors to the Swatches panel, and save a palette to share with other Flash users or in a format usable by other Adobe programs, such as Photoshop and Fireworks. Figure B-20 shows the Color and Swatches panels.

Using web-safe colors

The pop-up color window that appears when you change text, stroke, or fill color displays the colors included with your document. The default Flash color palette is the **web-safe color palette**, a set of 216 colors that appear consistent in web browsers and across platforms and devices designed for screens capable of displaying a maximum of 256 colors. Many consider the limited web-safe color palette a moot issue for most computers and mobile devices, given the improvement in standard video cards. Using web-safe colors is no longer considered critical because most mobile devices that have a camera automatically support tens of thousands of colors.

FIGURE B-18: Viewing the Info and Align panels

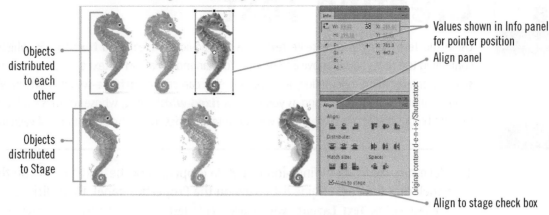

Objects
distributed
to each
other

Objects
distributed
to Stage

Values shown in Info panel
for pointer position

Align panel

Align to stage check box

Original content d-e-n-i-s/Shutterstock

FIGURE B-19: Skewing an object using the Transform panel

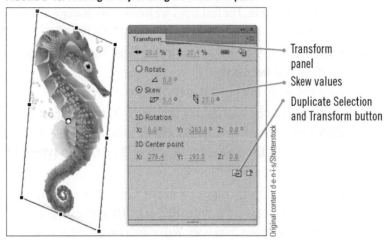

Transform
panel

Skew values

Duplicate Selection
and Transform button

Original content d-e-n-i-s/Shutterstock

FIGURE B-20: Viewing the Color panel and Swatches panel

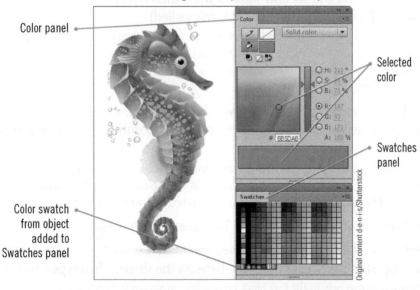

Color panel

Selected
color

Swatches
panel

Color swatch
from object
added to
Swatches panel

Original content d-e-n-i-s/Shutterstock

Resizing objects

To adjust a shape's size proportionately, make sure the Lock Constrain icon 🔗 on the Properties panel is active. To adjust a width or height size individually, click 🔗 to make the Unlock Constrain icon 🔗 active. The ScreenTip for both the Lock Constrain and Unlock Constrain icons is Lock width and height values together.

Creating Text

Using the Text tool, you can create text to use in movies by creating a **text block**, which is an object containing text that you can move and modify. You can modify a host of text attributes, including font, size, style, color, alignment, orientation, and spacing. You can create **variable-width text**, in which the text block continues to expand as long as you type, or **fixed-width text**, whose width is limited by the size of the text block. ▓▓▓ You experiment with both text modes to see the advantages of each in your logo.

STEPS

1. **Make sure that GreenWinds-logo_FL-B.fla is open, click the** Text tool T **on the Tools panel, click the** Text engine list arrow **on the Properties panel, then click** TLF Text

   The text engine, **Text Layout Framework (TLF)** text, provides flexible formatting features that can accommodate complex typographic requirements. You can create columns, wrap text around any object, and link text blocks. The text types are **Read Only** (cannot select or edit text), **Selectable** (can select but not edit text), or **Editable** (can both select and edit text). For this project, you want Read Only text.

2. **Click the** Text type list arrow **in the Text Tool section of the Properties panel, then click** Read Only **if necessary**

   Users will not be able to select or edit the text.

TROUBLE
If a section in the Properties panel is not expanded, click the expand section arrow ▷ on the section's title bar.

3. **Click the** Set the font family list arrow **in the Character section of the Properties panel, click** Times New Roman, **click the** Set the font style list arrow, **then if necessary, click** Regular, **click the** Select point size text box, **then type** 12 **if necessary**

   You decide to set a new text color.

4. **Click the** Text (fill) color box **in the Character section of the Properties panel, click the** hexadecimal text box, **type** #006600, **then press** [Enter] **(Win) or** [return] **(Mac)**

   A new dark green text color is set. You create a fixed-width text block to limit how much text fits on one line.

5. **Using Figure B-21 as a guide, drag a** text block **beneath the shapes on the Stage three grid squares tall and six grid squares wide, then type** GreenWinds ecocruise (*Note:* **The name of the company is deliberately misspelled)**

   A tab ruler appears above the fixed-width text block, which is not quite wide enough to accommodate the word "GreenWinds." See Figure B-22, but do not worry about the precise size of your text block. You can adjust the size so the word fits on one line. (You'll correct the lowercase "e" and "c" on "ecocruise" and add a hyphen in the next lesson.)

TROUBLE
If you inadvertently deselect the text, click it with the Text tool.

6. **Position the mouse pointer ↔ over the** small black square sizing handle **on the right side of the text block, then drag ↔ to the right until the word "ecocruise" fits on the top line**

   All the letters in the word "GreenWinds" are together on one line, but you would have to continue to adjust the text block to get it to fit precisely, which could be time-consuming if you have a text block to which you want to add or delete text. Instead, you delete this text box and create variable-width text.

7. **Click the** Selection tool ▶ **on the Tools panel, then press** [Delete]

QUICK TIP
To manually insert a line break in variable-width text, press [Enter] (Win) or [return] (Mac).

8. **Click T on the Tools panel, click the** Align to start button ▤ **in the Paragraph section of the Properties panel, click the** Stage **beneath the shapes, then type** GreenWinds ecocruise

   The words fit precisely in the text block on one line, as shown in Figure B-23.

9. **Save the document**

FIGURE B-21: **Creating a fixed-width text box**

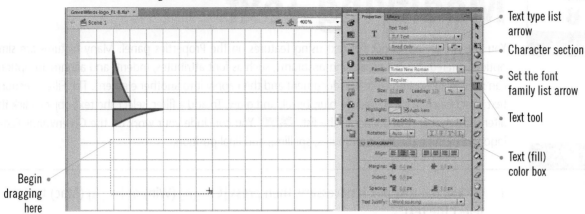

Text type list arrow

Character section

Set the font family list arrow

Text tool

Text (fill) color box

Begin dragging here

FIGURE B-22: **Viewing fixed-width text**

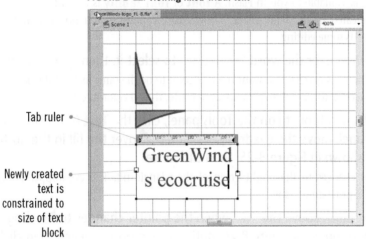

Tab ruler

Newly created text is constrained to size of text block

FIGURE B-23: **Creating variable-width text**

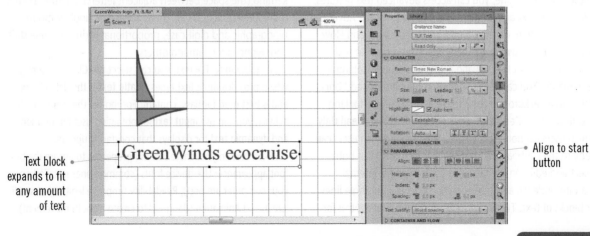

Align to start button

Text block expands to fit any amount of text

Creating Graphics and Text

Modifying Text

You can modify any aspect of text using features on the Properties panel. Many features are similar to options offered in word-processing programs, such as font attributes, indent, and alignment options. You can sample an existing color in a document and then apply it to another element. The Filters section offers text effects such as drop shadow, blur, bevel, and glow. To add a filter, select the text object, click the Add filter button, then click a filter in the list. ▓▓▓▓▓ You conclude your work on the GreenWinds Eco-Cruise logo by adjusting the text's attributes, spelling, and final position.

STEPS

1. **Click in the text box if necessary, then press [Ctrl][A] (Win) or ⌘[A] (Mac) to select the text**

TROUBLE
You may need to scroll down the list to the "G" section to locate the font, or if this font is not available, select another font. Some fonts might not have a bold option.

2. **Click the** Set the font family list arrow **on the Properties panel, click** Adobe Garamond Pro, **click the** Set the font style list arrow, **then click** Bold

   The font changes to Adobe Garamond Pro, bold style.

3. **Click the** Select point size text box, **type** 13, **then press [Enter] (Win) or [return] (Mac)**

   The font size increases, as shown in Figure B-24. When you create text, the current set of fonts installed on your computer is available to you in Flash. A **font** or **font family** is the entire array of letters, numbers, and symbols created in the same shape, known as a **typeface**. You notice that the company name, "ecocruise," needs some editing.

4. **Drag the** pointer **over the word** "ecocruise" **to select it, then type** Eco-Cruise

   The company name is correct. You want the text color to be the same as the fill color of the triangles. The easiest way to accomplish this is to pick up, or **sample**, the fill color directly.

5. **Click the** Selection tool ▶ **on the Tools panel, click the** Text (fill) color box **on the Properties panel, move the** eyedropper pointer ⌖ **over the fill in the bottom triangle in the logo, as shown in Figure B-25, then click once**

   The font color changes to the bright green of the triangle fill. The eyedropper pointer samples color anywhere in the program window.

QUICK TIP
Your text block might snap to a slightly different location.

6. **Click the** text block **above the "G," when the pointer changes to ▶⊹, drag the** text block **to the location shown in Figure B-26, notice a** snap ring **appears, then click outside the text block to deselect it**

7. **Save and close the document, then exit Flash**

Understanding Flash text engines

In the TLF text engine, you can access advanced text features, add a link to text and set advanced properties in the Advanced Character section, or set columns in the Container and Flow section. TLF text uses containers, which are similar to text blocks, to support text flowing across and around columns and images. You can resize and link containers and add borders and a background color to create professional-looking text flows. TLF offers three types of published text: **Read Only**, which users cannot select or edit, **Selectable**, which users can copy to the clipboard, and **Editable**, which users can both select and edit. On the tab ruler, you can adjust internal margins, indents, and tabs and choose to realign single lines or blocks of text. TLF also provides typographical control for kerning (the space between adjacent letters), ligatures (two or more letters, such as "fl," that appear as a single symbol), typographic and digit case, proportional width, baseline shift, and hyphenation, among others.

In addition to TLF text, you can select the Classic Text engine, which provides three text types. **Static text** is the default type and is best used for basic content. For movies that contain interactivity, you can use **input text** for obtaining user information, and **dynamic text** for displays that constantly update.

Both text engines share aliasing properties to ensure the best font appearance: Use device fonts (common ones installed on your computer are best), Readability (improve legibility at small sizes), and Animation (designed to create smooth movement).

FIGURE B-24: Editing text attributes

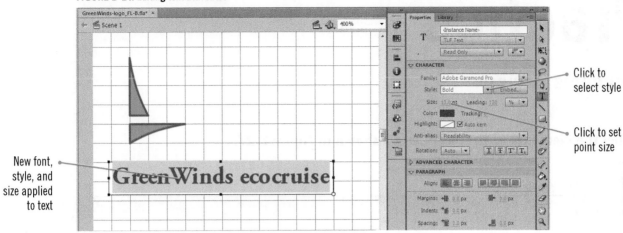

Click to select style

Click to set point size

New font, style, and size applied to text

FIGURE B-25: Sampling a color

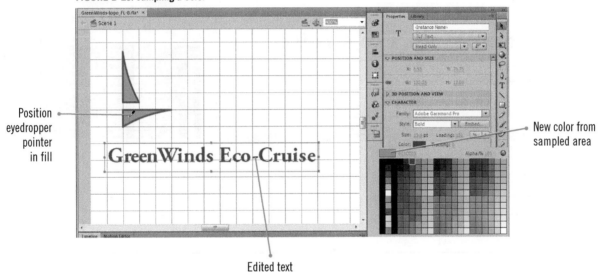

Position eyedropper pointer in fill

New color from sampled area

Edited text

FIGURE B-26: Aligning text

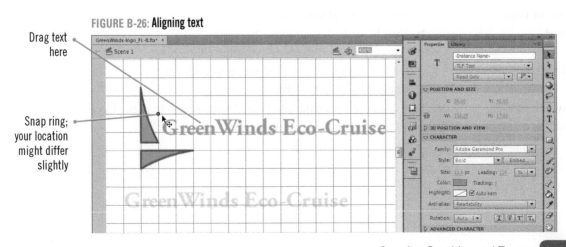

Drag text here

Snap ring; your location might differ slightly

Creating Graphics and Text

Practice

Concepts Review

Label the elements of the Flash screen shown in Figure B-27.

FIGURE B-27

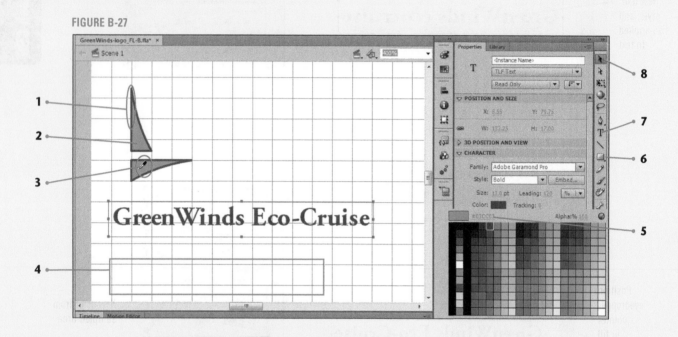

1. _____
2. _____
3. _____
4. _____

5. _____
6. _____
7. _____
8. _____

Match each term with the statement that best describes it.

9. **Free Transform tool**

10. **Anchor point**

11. **Sampling**

12. **Fixed-width text**

13. **Grid**

14. **Merge Drawing mode**

15. **Hexadecimal**

a. Text block created in a set size

b. Used to scale, skew, or rotate an object

c. Can merge new strokes and fills into existing ones

d. Used to define color in an alphanumeric system

e. Component of vector objects

f. A layout of horizontal and vertical squares used to align objects

g. To select a color by clicking an object

Select the best answer from the list of choices.

16. **From which menu can you open the Transform, Info, and Color panels?**
    a. Window
    b. Modify
    c. Edit
    d. View

17. **Which of the following are drawing modes in Flash?**
    a. Fixed-width Drawing and Merge Drawing
    b. Merge Drawing and Object Drawing
    c. Merge Drawing and Bitmap Drawing
    d. Bitmap Drawing and Vector Drawing

18. **What is the typical resolution for web images?**
    a. 72 or 96 ppi
    b. 24 or 72 ppi
    c. 150 or 200 ppi
    d. 150 or 96 ppi

19. **Which key(s) do you press to constrain a rotation to 45° increments?**
    a. [Alt] (Win) or [option] (Mac)
    b. [Ctrl] (Win) or [⌘] (Mac)
    c. [Shift][Tab]
    d. [Shift]

20. **Which of the following is *not* true when describing the grid?**
    a. You can adjust the size.
    b. You can adjust the grid color.
    c. Objects will snap to the grid if it is not displayed.
    d. You can view the grid in the published movie.

Skills Review

1. **Understand vector and bitmap graphics.**
   a. Describe the difference between vector and bitmap graphics.
   b. Give an example of how vector and bitmap graphics are used on the web and in applications.
   c. Explain what a pixel is in relation to a bitmap image.
   d. Describe one difference between Merge Drawing mode and Object Drawing mode.

2. **Create a new document.**
   a. Start Flash, then create a new document named **LightFootRecycling_FL-B.fla**.
   b. Make the stage width **300** px and leave the height at **400** px using size controls in the Properties panel.
   c. Show the grid and turn on Snap to Grid.
   d. Save the document.

3. **Set tool options and create a shape.**
   a. Select the Stroke Color tool on the Tools panel, then set the color to none. (*Hint*: Click the No color icon.)
   b. Select the Fill Color tool, click the hexadecimal text box, then set the color to #000099.
   c. Select the Rectangle tool, make sure that you are in Merge Drawing mode, create a rectangle of any size, select it, then adjust the size on the Properties panel to approximately W: 133, H: 38. (*Hints*: If necessary, expand the Position and Size section on the Properties panel. To size dimensions independently, click the Lock Constrain icon, then enter each value separately. The ScreenTip for both the Lock Constrain and Unlock Constrain icons is Lock width and height values together.)
   d. Click the Rectangle tool, press and hold [Shift], create a square elsewhere on the Stage, select it, then adjust its size to W: 48, H: 48.
   e. Save the document.

Skills Review (continued)

4. **Reshape an object.**
   a. Zoom in the Stage as needed.
   b. Select the Subselection tool, then drag the upper-right corner of the square inward until it snaps to form a triangle. (*Hint*: The Subselection tool is located beneath the Selection tool on the Tools panel.)
   c. Select the Free Transform tool, click the triangle, press and hold [Shift], then rotate the triangle 45° clockwise.
   d. Drag the rotated triangle to the left side of the rectangle, use the arrow keys to align it so it forms a left-pointing arrow, then click a blank area of the Stage, as shown in Figure B-28. (*Hint*: Be sure to align the triangle to the rectangle before deselecting it, as it will merge with the rectangle to form an arrow.)
   e. Save the document.

5. **Modify a shape.**
   a. Select the arrow shape, then select the arrow's fill.
   b. Change the fill color to #009900.
   c. Save the document.

6. **Copy and transform an object.**
   a. Select the arrow if necessary, move it lower on the Stage to become the bottom arrow shown in Figure B-28, then copy and paste it anywhere on the Stage to create a second arrow.
   b. Open the Transform panel, then use the Rotate control to rotate the second arrow 120°. (*Hint*: Click the icon in the iconic panels next to the Properties panel or use the Window menu to open the panel.)
   c. Move the second arrow to the left-most position shown in Figure B-28.
   d. Press and hold [Alt] (Win) or [option] (Mac), drag and copy the copied arrow to create a third arrow, rotate it 120°, then move the arrow to the right position shown in Figure B-28.
   e. Save the document.

7. **Use design panels.**
   a. List two pieces of information contained on the Info panel.
   b. Describe how selecting the Align/Distribute to stage button on the Align panel affects objects.

8. **Create text.**
   a. Select the Text tool, then if necessary set the Text engine to TLF Text, the Text type to Read Only, the font to Times New Roman (or another font), the style to Regular, and the font size to 40 pt.
   b. Create a fixed-width text block beneath the arrows that is half the width of the bottom arrow, then type **recycle**.
   c. Fit the text in the text block, then delete the text block.
   d. Click the Stage, then type **recycle**.
   e. Save the document.

9. **Modify text.**
   a. Select the text, then change the font to Arial or a similar font, the font style to Bold, the font size to 50, and the text fill color to black. (*Hint*: Click a color swatch in the first column.)
   b. Select the first letter, then type **R**.
   c. Position the text in the location shown in Figure B-28.
   d. Deselect all objects, then save the document.
   e. Exit Flash.

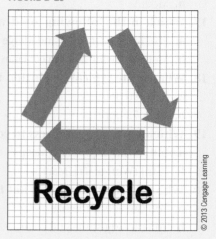

Independent Challenge 1

You work at CoasterWoop, an online source of news by, for, and about roller coaster enthusiasts. Your boss has asked you to redo the logo to something modern and minimalist. You begin by creating three circles in Flash and then transforming them in a creative way.

a. Start Flash, open a new file, then save it as **CoasterWoop_FL-B.fla**.

b. Make sure that Snap to Grid is turned off and that Snap Align and Snap to Guides are turned on.

c. Select the Oval tool on the tools panel, then select Object Drawing mode. (*Hint*: The Oval tool is in the Rectangle tool group.)

d. Set the stroke color to black with no fill color, then set a stroke height of 1 px, if necessary.

e. Draw a perfectly round circle, then modify it as follows: selection height and selection width 40 px, stroke color #FF0000, stroke height 5 px.

f. Open the Transform panel, select the Skew option, then change the Skew Horizontal value to 10.0°.

g. Draw a second perfect circle, then modify it as follows: selection height and selection width 65 px, stroke color #FFCC00, stroke height 7 px, skew horizontal 4.0°.

h. Draw a third perfect circle, then modify it as follows: selection height and selection width 85 px, stroke color #0000FF, stroke height 9 px, skew horizontal –17°. (*Hint*: To enter a negative value, drag the selected value to the left or type a hypen.)

i. Select the circles, then use a command on the Modify, Align menu to bottom-align them. (*Hint*: Be sure that the Align to Stage option is not selected.)

j. Zoom in the Stage as necessary, then drag the circles to the positions shown in Figure B-29. (*Hint*: Be sure to first create a selection box around the circles or double-click to select them; otherwise, you will modify the shape border when you drag.)

k. Select the Text tool, then if necessary, set the Text engine to TLF text, Text type to Read Only, set the font to Myriad Pro or another font, bold, 24 pt, black, then type **CoasterWoop** beneath the circles.

l. Select the Selection tool, drag the text to center it, deselect the text, then compare your image to Figure B-29. (*Hint*: Use the arrow keys to center the text.)

m. Save and close the document, then exit Flash.

FIGURE B-29

© 2013 Cengage Learning

Independent Challenge 2

As the new Program Director at Lingoroots, an educational website specializing in linguistics, you're constantly looking for exciting ways to engage new visitors. For the next feature, you'll compare the evolution of written Chinese across its 4,000-year history. The earliest written Chinese characters were pictures, which evolved to a more stylized and artistic writing form. You begin by using artwork a colleague sent you to trace a mountain.

a. Start Flash, open the file FL B-1.fla from the location where you store your Data Files, then save it as **lingoroots_FL-B.fla**. (*Hint*: The document contains a guide layer named mountain trace that you'll use to trace an object.)

b. Zoom in the Stage as necessary, then make sure that Layer 1 is selected in the Timeline.

c. Select the Line tool on the Tools panel, make sure you are in Merge Drawing mode (deselect the Object Drawing tool if necessary), change the fill color to none, then change the stroke color to #CC0000 and stroke height to 1 px.

d. Using Figure B-30 and the guide layer, draw a series of lines to form the mountain range and horizon. (*Hint*: To use the Line tool, drag in any direction on the Stage. Draw the left side of each mountain a little higher than the right side.)

Independent Challenge 2 (continued)

e. Select the Selection tool, then use the curve pointer to adjust the sides of the first and third peaks, as shown in the bottom part of Figure B-30.

f. Select the entire object, change the stroke height to 4.5 px, deselect the object, select just the left side (stroke) of each mountain, then change the stroke height to 6 px. (*Hint*: To repeat the previous action or command, press [Ctrl][Y] (Win) or ⌘[Y] (Mac).)

g. Select the Text tool, set the Text engine to TLF Text, Text type to Read Only, the font to Adobe Garamond Pro, 14 pt, color #666666, then type **Mountain-Ancient**.

h. Select the text, then change the font style to italic and move it beneath the object.

i. Align the text with the right side of the object, hide the guide layer, then compare your screen to Figure B-31.

Advanced Challenge Exercise

- Make a copy of the mountain object, then move it to a different part of the Stage.
- Resize the copied object, then change the stroke height, then change the color to a color of your choosing.
- Align the copied object on the Stage so it snaps when you align it to another object.

j. Save and close the document.

k. Exit Flash.

Independent Challenge 3

You work for ibRobotz, an online entertainment site. Users can download ibRobotz characters or create their own to insert in stories. You've been assigned to develop a character for younger users, so you begin building one using various Flash drawing tools.

a. Start Flash, create a new document, then save it as **ibrobotz_FL-B.fla**.

b. Change the background color to #0066FF. (*Hint*: Use the Stage color box on the Properties panel.)

c. On the Tools panel, set the stroke and fill colors to black and white respectively, select the Oval tool, set the stroke height to 4.5 px, then make sure you are in Merge Drawing mode.

d. Create a perfectly round circle that is 100 px round. (*Hint*: Be sure to select the entire object when resizing.)

e. Create a rectangle with the following dimensions: W: 100 px and H: 80 px. (*Hint*: Make sure the Break Link icon appears on the Properties panel.)

f. Using Figure B-32 as a guide, select the rectangle, then drag it to the middle of the circle, so that the circle looks like a dome when the rectangle intersects it.

g. Create two rectangles with the dimensions W: 100 px and H: 17 px, and W: 100 px and H: 15 px, then stack them beneath the first rectangle.

h. Color the strokes and fills of the objects as you wish, then use the Align panel to align the horizontal centers of all the objects, or show the grid and align them manually.

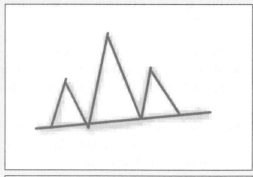

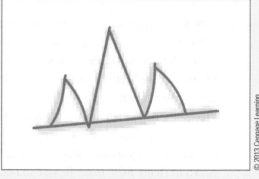

Mountain-Ancient

© 2013 Cengage Learning

Independent Challenge 3 (continued)

i. Select the Pencil tool, set the color to black and the stroke to 4.5 px, draw arms and legs, then reshape the appendages as you wish or as shown in Figure B-32 if desired.

j. Create eyes, hands, feet, and a mouth using the drawing tools of your choice, then reshape, transform, and color them.

k. Select the Text tool, set the font to Arial, regular, size 16 pt, position the cursor in the middle rectangle, then type **ibROBOTZ**.

l. Change the color of the letters "ib" to a different color than the rest of the text.

m. Create an antenna using the drawing tools of your choice, then align, reshape, transform, and color it as you wish.

n. Compare your screen to the sample shown in Figure B-32.

Advanced Challenge Exercise

■ Embellish the antenna using additional tools in the drawing section.

■ Using one or more tools described in Table B-1, change the shape and stroke of the hands.

■ Transform or reshape at least one object.

o. Save and close the document, then exit Flash.

Real Life Independent Challenge

You're interested in developing your own Flash project—it could be an animation for a mobile device, a logo for your company, and so on. You can pick the theme of your choice, such as something about a new business, music, film, friends, family, interests, and so on.

a. Begin planning your Flash project. (*Hint*: Use the planning chart in Unit A as a template.)

b. Start Flash, create a new document, then save it as **myproject_FL-B.fla**.

c. Set document settings as desired.

d. Use a minimum of three drawing tools to create multiple objects, set stroke and fill, and transform at least two of them. Identify the tools and tool options you used.

e. Show the grid, set snapping options, and/or use the Align panel to align objects. Identify which align options you found most useful.

f. Check your document for proper alignment and design consistency.

g. Save and close the document myproject_FL-B.fla, then exit Flash.

Visual Workshop

Visiting websites is a great way to get inspired for your own projects. Figure B-33 shows the site for the National Archives. Go to www.archives.gov or study the figure below and answer the following questions. For each question, include why or how you reached a conclusion. You can open a word processor or use the Text tool in Flash to complete this exercise. When you are finished, add your name to the document, save it, print it, then close the word processor or exit Flash.

a. What is the website's purpose and goal?

b. Who is the target audience? How does the design (look and feel) of the website fit the target audience?

c. Looking at the banner and navigation bar at the top of the page:

- How are vector and bitmap shapes used?

- Are there obviously drawn shapes? Which elements appear to have been created in Merge Drawing mode or Object Drawing mode?

- Do objects have clear strokes and fills?

- How do objects appear to have been modified or transformed?

- How is text used on this page? How many fonts are there?

d. What is animated on this page?

e. What is your overall opinion of the design, organization, and function of this page? How would you improve it?

f. Close your browser.

FIGURE B-33

Using Symbols and the Library Panel

In any creative project, you begin by considering the purpose of the piece. For example, in a print piece, you want photographs to have the highest visual quality. But for projects, including those for mobile devices, where users interact with Flash movies and performance is often critical, you need to strike a balance between visual quality and file size. Symbols are the key to creative and successful animation in Flash because they allow you to keep file size small. Flash stores symbols on the Library panel. You can create clones of symbols without adding to file size, and edit them as desired. 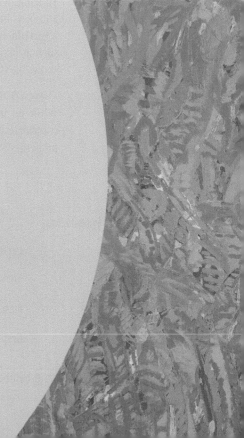 Your boss, Vanessa, wants you to work on an animation for the GreenWinds Eco-Cruise application. To prepare a document for animation, you convert objects to symbols, create symbols, and generate instances.

OBJECTIVES

Understand symbols and instances

Understand the Library panel

Create a symbol

Add instances to the Stage

Edit an instance

Edit a symbol

Organize the Library panel

Understanding Symbols and Instances

A Flash movie can quickly accumulate many elements, each of which increases file size. Some elements, such as video, can take up more space than others, such as simple text. Because elements appear in multiple frames, a movie's file size can grow even more. Fortunately, Flash allows you to create symbols, which offer a more space- and design-efficient way to reuse elements. ▰▰▰▰ You examine the way symbols operate in Flash so you can optimize the GreenWinds movie.

DETAILS

Before creating design elements, you review information about symbols and instances:

- **Symbols and instances**

  A **symbol** is a copy of an object, such as a graphic, that you can reuse in a project. You can convert an existing object to a symbol or create a new one from scratch. The advantage of using symbols is that you can use them multiple times in any project while keeping file size at a minimum. Technically, you use copies of symbols in projects. A copied symbol is known as an **instance**; you create an instance by dragging a symbol from the Library to the Stage. As soon as the copy of the symbol reaches the Stage, it becomes an instance and is linked to the symbol. Flash stores and manages symbols on the Library panel, and instances on the Stage. To preview a symbol, click the symbol's name in the Library. You can adjust the size of the preview pane as needed.

  You can modify the properties of an individual instance, although you are limited to editing its transformation and color effect properties. Editing instance properties does not affect the symbol's properties. However, if you edit the properties of a symbol, each instance is updated instantly on the Stage. Figure C-1 shows a shark symbol on the Library panel and several modified instances of the symbol on the Stage.

- **Symbol types**

  When you create a symbol, you can choose one of three types: graphic, movie clip, or button. Each serves a specific purpose and has a unique icon to help identify it in the Library panel, as shown in Table C-1. A **graphic symbol** is a static object usually used to create an animation spanning across frames in the Timeline. A **movie clip symbol** is a minimovie or animation within a Flash movie. It has its own Timeline and plays independently of the main movie's Timeline. You place it into a single frame of the main movie. A **button symbol** responds to users clicking or rolling over it, which activates a different part of the movie, such as playing a movie clip. You'll learn more about movie clips and buttons in later units. Figure C-2 shows the Convert to Symbol dialog box, where you can name a symbol and select its type.

- **How symbols help reduce file size**

  While an instance is an accurate representation of a symbol, only the symbol on the Library panel contributes to a document's file size, no matter how many instances you create. Flash adds the instance's properties to the file, but the amount of actual data added is minor.

TABLE C-1: Symbol icons

icon	type	description
🎬	Movie clip	Use for animations within a movie
👆	Button	Use for interactivity
🖼	Graphic	Use for static objects

FIGURE C-1: Viewing a symbol and its instances

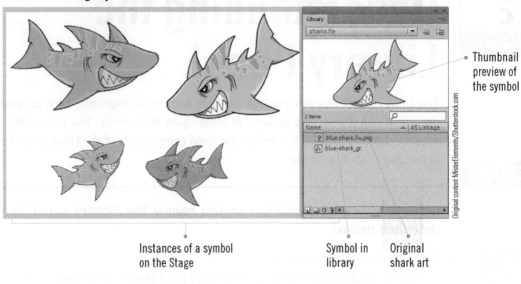

Original content MisterElements/Shutterstock.com

Instances of a symbol on the Stage

Symbol in library

Original shark art

Thumbnail preview of the symbol

FIGURE C-2: Using the Convert to Symbol dialog box to create a symbol

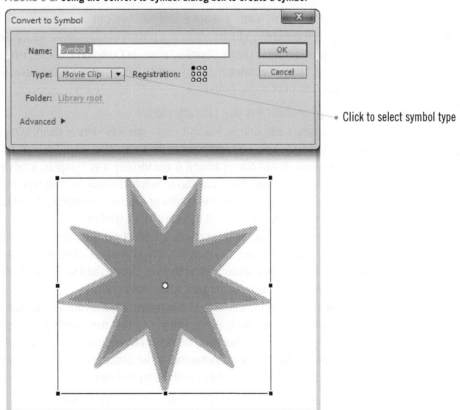

Click to select symbol type

Using the Break Apart command

In addition to using the Break Apart command to sever an instance from its symbol, you can break apart text to divide a word into its individual characters, and then break apart a character to convert it to an editable path.

If you break apart a bitmap, you can modify individual segments of the image. Depending on the source image, breaking apart an image can also reduce overall file size and load time.

Using Symbols and the Library Panel

Flash CS6

Understanding the Library Panel

The Library panel lets you manage symbols and media elements, such as sounds, in the current document and also access libraries in other open documents. You can create, edit, preview, and organize symbols. ✎✎✎ You review the main components of the Library panel and the importance of naming symbols properly.

Refer to Figures C-3 and C-4 as you review the Library panel tools and functions described below:

- **Using the Library panel**

  Flash automatically adds symbols to the Library panel as soon as you create or import them. You can access libraries from other open documents by clicking the Library panel list arrow and then clicking a document. To share an element or symbol from another movie, display the library that contains the element, then drag it to the Stage, to the Library panel, or copy and paste it.

  The Library panel is also a management tool you can use to organize symbols and other elements. For example, you can create a folder where you place related symbols. See Figure C-3.

  Flash provides three sample libraries, known as Common Libraries, where you can access preset buttons and sounds. To open a common library panel, click Window on the Menu bar, point to Common Libraries, then click Buttons, Classes, or Sounds.

- **Naming symbols on the Library panel**

  As you construct animations, you will create symbols—lots of them. When you create a symbol, you can name it whatever you wish. In practice, however, you should follow an effective naming convention. A symbol name should convey what it is and identify it as a graphic, a movie clip, or a button. Flash assigns unique icons to symbols, but it can also be helpful to indicate their type in your symbol names using short abbreviations. You can add these as a prefix or a suffix. For example, by adding the suffix "_gr" to the name, you can also tell immediately that this is a graphic symbol.

  Remember, too, that the more precise a symbol name is, the easier it will be to find later. For example, the Library panel in Figure C-3 contains several symbols relating to sharks. It may be tempting to name related symbols in a sequence, such as shark-1, shark-2, and so on, but as you can see, that would not help much if you were looking for the great white shark symbol.

  In addition to naming a symbol for convenience and accuracy, you must also follow file-naming conventions for web elements, such as beginning a symbol name with a lowercase letter. Just as a web browser cannot display a file it cannot read, the Flash Player cannot play a symbol it cannot read. Do not include spaces, tabs, brackets, slashes, punctuation, or the characters above the number keys. But you can add hyphens and underscores to make it easier to read the symbol name.

- **Understanding hyphens and underscores in names**

  Hyphens and underscores are great for making a long file name easier to read, but it's important to know that Flash sorts them differently. Flash sees a hyphen as a space separating the words, so it sorts by the first word. In contrast, it interprets underscores as being a part of the word and sorts the entire name string. It doesn't matter which you use in a symbol, as long as you are consistent. If you use underscores or hyphens consistently, the list is—and will appear to be—in alphabetical order. If you alternate using underscores or hyphens when you name related symbols, they will not appear to be in alphabetical order because Flash sorts underscores first. Figure C-4 compares how Flash sorts symbols with hyphens and underscores.

FIGURE C-3: Viewing symbols in the Library

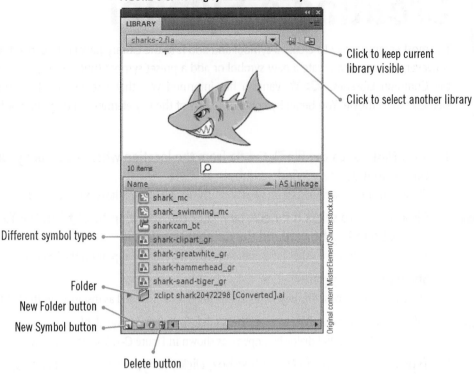

Click to keep current library visible

Click to select another library

Different symbol types

Folder

New Folder button

New Symbol button

Delete button

Original content MisterElement/Shutterstock.com

FIGURE C-4: Comparing the sort order of symbol names with underscores and hyphens

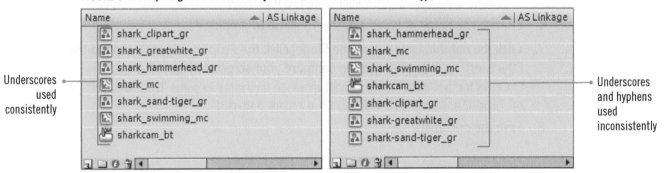

Underscores used consistently

Underscores and hyphens used inconsistently

Understanding transformation and registration points

Symbols and other objects have a **transformation point**, a small hollow circle that appears on an object when it is selected, which Flash uses to orient the object every time you transform or animate it. For example, when you rotate an object, it pivots around the transformation point. You can move the transformation point by selecting the Free Transform tool, dragging the transformation point to a new location, and then selecting the Transformation point button ⊞ on the Info panel.

The **registration point** ⊞ appears as a small plus sign and is the default point that positions an object on the Stage. You can adjust an object's registration point—and its relative position to the upper-left corner of the Stage—by adjusting its X and Y values in the Properties panel or Info panel. For symbols, text, and other objects, the default registration point is the upper-left corner. The

registration point is visible when you edit a symbol, and it is crucial when using ActionScript to move instances. Figure C-5 shows the transformation and registration points in a selected object.

FIGURE C-5: Transformation and registration points

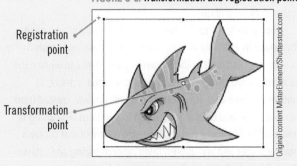

Registration point

Transformation point

Original content MisterElement/Shutterstock.com

Using Symbols and the Library Panel

Creating a Symbol

The most common way to create a symbol and add it to the Library panel is to convert an existing object. However, you can also create a new symbol or add a preset symbol (buttons and sounds, primarily) from the Common Libraries. ████ Vanessa has informed you that GreenWinds Eco-Cruise wants several elements in its movie. You begin by converting one of the key elements, a dolphin graphic, to a symbol.

STEPS

1. **Start Flash, open the file FL C-1.fla from the location where you store your Data Files, then save it as GreenWinds_symbols_FL-C.fla**

   The document contains objects on two layers. The light blue wave layer is locked to prevent accidental editing.

   > **QUICK TIP**
   > You can also click a frame on a layer to select an object.

2. **Click Layer 1 to select it if necessary, click the Selection tool ▶ on the Tools panel, then draw a bounding box around the dolphin to select it**

   The object is selected on the Stage, and properties for a Shape appear on the Properties panel.

   > **QUICK TIP**
   > You can also press [F8] to open the Convert to Symbol dialog box.

3. **Show the Library panel**

   The Library panel contains two symbols that are already inserted as instances in the light blue wave layer.

4. **Click Modify on the Menu bar, then click Convert to Symbol**

   The Convert to Symbol dialog box opens, as shown in Figure C-7. You name the symbol and set the type.

   > **TROUBLE**
   > Expand the height of the preview area by dragging the bottom of the window, if necessary.

5. **Type dolphin_gr in the Name text box, click the Type list arrow, click Graphic, then click OK**

   Flash converts the drawing to a symbol, and it appears on the Library panel, as shown in Figure C-8. Flash also automatically converts the dolphin object on the Stage to an instance of the dolphin symbol.

6. **Change the name of Layer 1 in the Timeline to dolphins**

7. **Click the dolphin instance on the Stage, click the Properties panel, expand the Color Effect section, if necessary, then compare your screen to Figure C-9**

   Properties for the instance of the symbol appear on the Properties panel. The Color Effect section replaces the Fill and Stroke section that appears when a shape is selected.

8. **Save the document**

Creating patterns from symbols with the Spray Brush tool

The Spray Brush tool 🖌 is a great time-saver for creating backgrounds or unique content. You can use this tool to spray in either dots or symbols.

The Spray Brush tool, located in the Brush tool group, paints by default in a shower of dots, whose color, scale, and brush angles you can adjust in the Properties panel. You can replace the dots with a symbol, and paint in instances of that symbol, as shown in Figure C-6. The group of red balloons was created from an oval shape and default Spray Brush tool settings. The group of multi-colored balloons was created using a symbol that contains several shapes and was applied using random scaling and rotation Spray Brush tool settings. To replace the default dot pattern with a

symbol, click the Edit button on the Properties panel to open the Select Symbol dialog box, click the desired symbol, then click OK.

FIGURE C-6: Content created with the Spray Brush tool

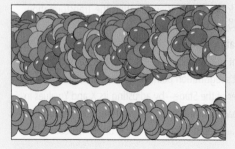

FIGURE C-7: Convert to Symbol dialog box

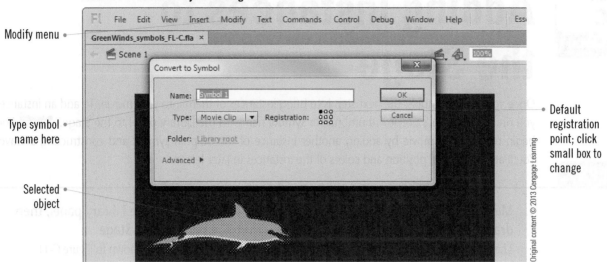

Modify menu •

Type symbol • name here

Selected • object

Default registration point; click small box to change

FIGURE C-8: Viewing a new symbol in the Library panel

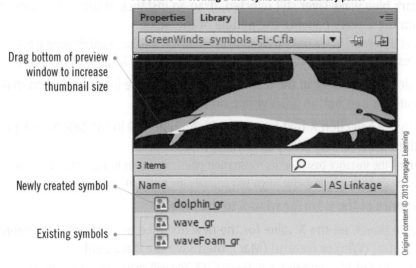

Drag bottom of preview • window to increase thumbnail size

Newly created symbol •

Existing symbols •

FIGURE C-9: Viewing instance properties

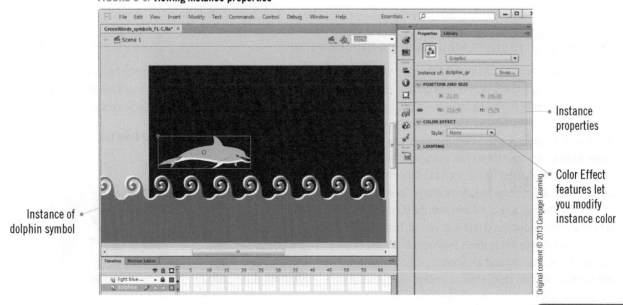

Instance of • dolphin symbol

Instance properties

Color Effect features let you modify instance color

Using Symbols and the Library Panel

Adding Instances to the Stage

Once you create symbols, the next step is to bring instances of them into your movie. To add an instance, you drag the symbol's preview thumbnail or symbol name on the Library panel to the Stage. You begin building the movie by adding another instance of the dolphin symbol and constructing a wave. You'll adjust the final position and colors of the instances in later lessons.

STEPS

1. **Make sure the dolphins layer is selected in the Timeline, show the Library panel, then drag an instance of the dolphin_gr symbol from the panel to the Stage**

   The dolphins layer now contains two instances of the dolphin_gr symbol, as shown in Figure C-11.

2. **Create a new layer in the Timeline, then name it dark blue wave**

   The new layer appears beneath the light blue wave layer.

   > **QUICK TIP**
   > If necessary, drag the layers section of the Timeline to the right to make the layer name visible.

3. **With the dark blue wave layer still selected, drag an instance of the waveFoam_gr symbol from the Library panel to the middle of the Stage**

   The instance of waveFoam_gr is a white wave pattern, which you will use to add dimension to the waves. To position the instance, you first need to open the Info panel, so you can keep the Library panel accessible.

4. **Click the Info panel icon ⓘ in the iconic panels to open the Info panel, then make sure the Registration point button ⊞ is visible on the panel**

   > **TROUBLE**
   > If the Registration point button ⊞ is not visible on the panel, click the Transformation point button ⊞ on the Info panel to show it.

5. **Type –110 in the Selection X text box, press [Tab], type 220 in the Selection Y position text box, then press [Enter] (Win) or [return] (Mac)**

   Flash repositions the instance based on its registration point, as shown in Figure C-12. The wave extends into the work area, which will be useful when you animate the waves in a later unit.

6. **Drag an instance of the wave_gr symbol to the Stage**

7. **Show the Info panel, set the X value for the new instance to –107, set the Y value to 222, press [Enter] (Win) or [return] (Mac), then save the document**

   You constructed the dark blue wave shown in Figure C-13. You will change its color in the next lesson.

Creating patterns from symbols using the Deco tool

You can create a variety of patterns with the Deco tool 🖌, which includes more than a dozen preset drawing effects that you can customize with symbols and other attributes. You can use the Deco tool's fills, brushes, and animations to draw nearly any of kind of pattern or effect, from minimalist to intricate. Some drawing effects are themselves animations, and automatically create content across frames, such as a burning fire or rising smoke. Others are complex textures or images, as shown in Figure C-10. The buildings are drawn with the Building Brush options and the foliage was drawn with various Tree Brush options. The cat's eye image shows Symmetry Brush and Grid Fill drawing effects. You can load the Symmetry Brush with up to four symbols and then choose how to arrange multiple instances

of it. The cat's eye sample shown is in the Rotate Around configuration. The background of the cat's eye image shows a grid fill comprised of instances of a single symbol.

FIGURE C-10: Content created with the Deco tool

Original content © 2013 Cengage Learning

FIGURE C-11: Dragging a second instance to a layer

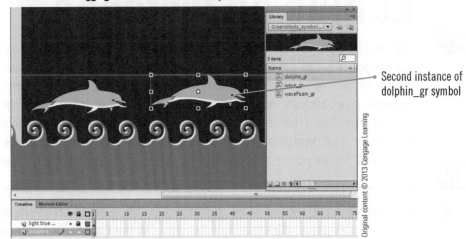

Second instance of
dolphin_gr symbol

Original content © 2013 Cengage Learning

FIGURE C-12: Positioning the waveFoam_gr instance

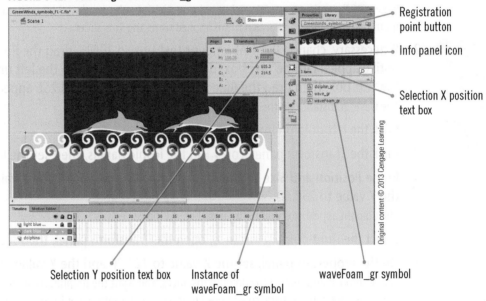

Registration
point button

Info panel icon

Selection X position
text box

Selection Y position text box   Instance of
                                        waveFoam_gr symbol

waveFoam_gr symbol

Original content © 2013 Cengage Learning

FIGURE C-13: Constructing an element using multiple instances

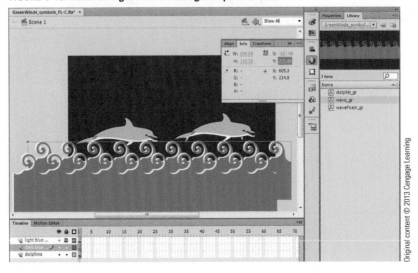

Original content © 2013 Cengage Learning

Editing an Instance

Once you have placed the instances for your animation on the Stage, you often want to change their color and position. You can edit instances using the Properties panel and the Transform panel (or by selecting options for the Free Transform tool). You change the color of an instance by applying an effect to it on the Properties panel. Each instance can have individual coloring, which you set in the Color Effect section. You can adjust brightness, tint, transparency, and advanced color options. ▰▰▰▰ Vanessa thinks the design would have more depth if the wave in the back were a darker blue. You decide to do this by applying a color effect. You also rotate and position the dolphin instances to heighten the effect.

STEPS

1. **Make sure the second wave_gr instance is still selected on the dark blue layer, show the Properties panel, click the Style list arrow in the Color Effect section, then click Tint**
   Options for the Tint style appear, as shown in Figure C-14. You can adjust the amount of tint by adjusting the Tint percentage. You can change the tint color in three ways: Click the Tint color swatch to open the color pop-up window and then click a color swatch, drag an RGB slider, or enter values in the RGB text boxes. **RGB (red, green, blue)** is a color model for color produced by emitted light, such as computer monitors. You adjust how much tint is applied using the Tint slider.

2. **If necessary, change the Tint amount text box to 100%, drag the Red slider 🔺 to the left until 0 appears in the text box, drag the Green slider 🔺 to the left until 0 appears in the text box, then drag the Blue slider 🔺 to the right until 255 appears in the text box**
   The wave_gr instance on the dark blue wave layer turns dark blue.

3. **Click the left dolphin instance on the Stage**

4. **Click the Transform panel icon ▦ in the iconic panels, then set the Rotate value to –27°**

5. **In the Position and Size section of the Properties panel, set the X value to –23.25 and the Y value to 252.60**
   The dolphin appears to be jumping from behind the waves.

6. **Select the right dolphin instance, open the Transform panel, then set the rotation to –30°**

7. **On the Properties panel, set the X value to 120.20 and the Y value to 242.80**
   You positioned and rotated the dolphin instances. You want the dolphins to appear to be jumping between the waves, not behind them, so you need to move the dolphins layer in the Timeline.

8. **Drag the dolphins layer between the light blue wave layer and the dark blue wave layer in the Timeline, then compare your screen to Figure C-15**

9. **Save the document**

FIGURE C-14: **Selecting a fill**

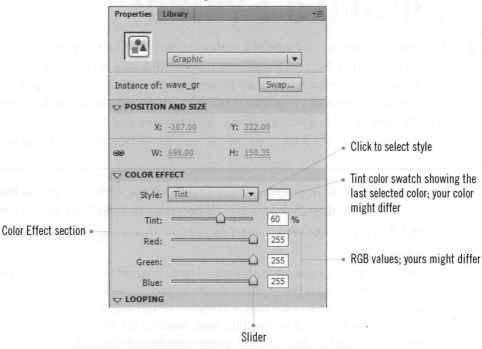

Click to select style

Tint color swatch showing the last selected color; your color might differ

Color Effect section

RGB values; yours might differ

Slider

FIGURE C-15: **Repositioned and transformed instances**

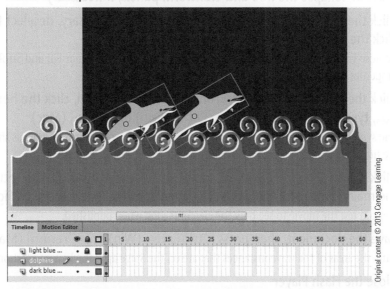

Original content © 2013 Cengage Learning

Design Matters

Understanding RGB color

RGB is the default color model used for computer monitors, smart phones and other mobile devices, television screens, and any other medium that emits the light itself. Red, green, and blue are the additive primary colors of light.

Additive primary colors combine to produce other colors, as shown in Figure C-16. RGB color values range from 0 to 255, representing all possible levels of red, green, or blue. Adding 100% of all three colors (255 red, 255 green, and 255 blue) produces white. A value of 0 red, 0 green, and 0 blue, which is the absence of light, produces black.

FIGURE C-16: **Additive primary colors**

Black is the absence of color

White is the combination of all three colors

Using Symbols and the Library Panel

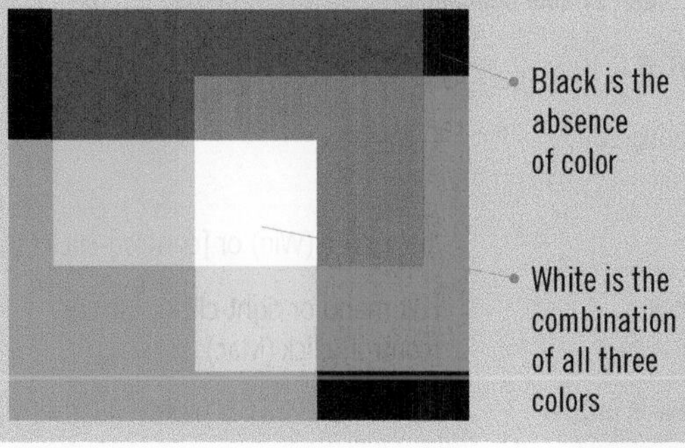

Editing a Symbol

As you work with multiple instances of a symbol, you may want to change their color or another aspect of their appearance. By editing the symbol instead of each individual instance, you change the appearance of every instance of the symbol automatically. Because changing a symbol can have a profound effect on a document, the Edit menu provides three ways to edit a symbol. You can also double-click an instance on the Stage or on the Library panel to open it for editing. ▰▰▰▰ Vanessa would like the dolphins to be a more realistic color. You change the color in the symbol so the new color will be applied to both instances on the Stage.

STEPS

1. **Select only the right dolphin instance on the Stage, click View on the Menu bar, point to Preview Mode, then click Anti-Alias, if necessary to make lines appear smoother**

2. **Click Edit on the Menu bar, click Edit in Place, then compare your screen to Figure C-17**

   The dolphin symbol is selected, and the symbol opens in an edit window in the Document window with its own Timeline. The top of the Document window contains the Back button, which you can click to return to Scene 1, and the **breadcrumb trail**, a navigation aid that displays a path showing an element's location in the document. Other elements on the Stage, including the other dolphin instance, are dimmed (they appear lighter in color). Additional edit symbol commands are described in Table C-2.

3. **Close or collapse the Info and Transform panels, if necessary**

4. **Click the Selection tool ▶ on the Tools panel if necessary, deselect the dolphin, then click the green body to select it**

   Because you are editing the symbol, which is a drawn shape, regular Fill and Stroke options appear on the Properties panel. You select a new color for the dolphin body.

5. **Click the Fill color icon ◇▭ on the Properties panel, click the hexadecimal text box, type #CCCCCC, then press [Enter] (Win) or [return] (Mac)**

   The symbol and both instances of dolphin_gr change to a realistic light gray, as shown in Figure C-18. You are finished editing the symbol, so you return to the Scene 1 window.

6. **Click the Back button ◁ at the top of the Document window to return to Scene 1 and the main Stage, click the work area, then compare your screen to Figure C-19**

   You can test the movie to see how the elements look when published.

7. **Save the document, then press [Ctrl][Enter] (Win) or ⌘[return] (Mac) to test the movie**

   Only the areas of the wave instances that are on the Stage appear when you test or publish the movie.

8. **Close the Flash Player**

TABLE C-2: Edit symbol commands

command	access it from	what it does
Edit Symbols, Edit Selected	Edit menu	Edits symbol within current Document window; other elements on Stage not visible
Edit	Right-click (Win) or [control]-click (Mac)	Edits symbol
Edit in Place	Edit menu or right-click (Win) or [control]-click (Mac)	Edits symbol within current Document window; other elements on Stage still visible
Edit in New Window	Right-click (Win) or [control]-click (Mac)	Edits symbol in separate Document window

FIGURE C-17: **Editing a symbol in place**

Edit menu

Back button

Symbol name in the
breadcrumb trail
indicates you are
editing a symbol

Breadcrumb trail

Selected symbol

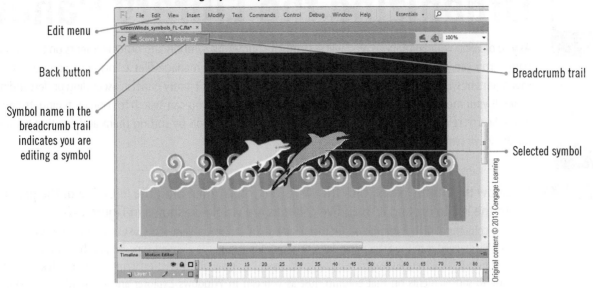

Flash CS6

FIGURE C-18: **Editing a symbol and its instances**

Changes
apply
automatically
to other
instance

New color

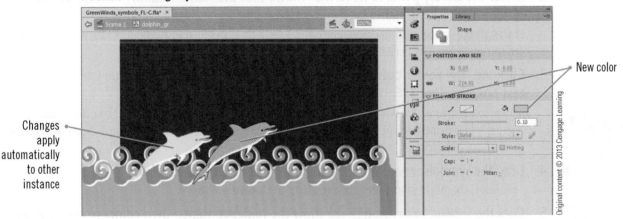

FIGURE C-19: **Viewing modified instances after editing symbol**

Dolphin
instances
are gray

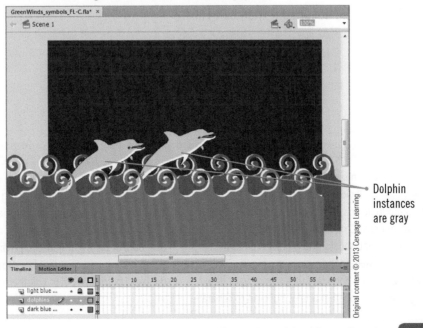

Using Symbols and the Library Panel

Organizing the Library Panel

As you develop your animations, you will accumulate numerous symbols and other elements on the Library panel. You can organize them by creating folders, just as you manage files using your computer's file management system. You can **sort**, or rearrange, elements on the Library panel in ascending or descending order. If your movie contains numerous symbols and elements, you can search for one by typing its name in the Search text box. ▓▓▓▓▓ You decide to organize the symbols by sorting them and creating a folder for the wave symbols.

STEPS

QUICK TIP

You can also press [Ctrl][L] (Win) or [⌘][L] (Mac) to open the Library panel.

1. **Show the Library panel, click the wave_gr symbol, then drag the left edge of the panel to the left to expand it so all five columns are visible, as shown in Figure C-20**

   The columns contain information for each element, including its Name, its Use Count (the number of times you've dragged it to the Stage), the date it was modified, and the element type. (It also has information on AS Linkage, an advanced feature relating to the asset being reusable in ActionScript.) You can click a column title to sort elements on that column, just as you can in Windows Explorer and many file management dialog boxes.

2. **Resize the Library panel to its former width, click the Name column header, observe the result, then click the Name column header again**

   Flash sorts the symbols first in descending order, from Z to A, and then in ascending order, from A to Z. You can sort any column in ascending or descending order.

3. **Click the New Folder button ▭ at the bottom of the Library panel, type Waves in the text box, then press [Enter] (Win) or [return] (Mac)**

   A new folder named "Waves" appears at the bottom of the Library panel, as shown in Figure C-21. Because folder names are not web documents, you can name them as you wish, using capital letters and nonstandard characters.

QUICK TIP

To select multiple symbols, press and hold [Shift], then click the symbols.

4. **Drag the symbols waveFoam_gr and wave_gr into the Waves folder**

   The folder is highlighted in green when you drag an element over it.

QUICK TIP

To delete a folder or element, select it, then click the Delete button 🗑 at the bottom of the Library panel.

5. **Click the Expand folder icon ▶ to show the folder contents, then compare your screen to Figure C-22**

   The symbols appear in the folder.

6. **Save the document, then exit Flash**

Grouping and ungrouping objects

Often, you may want to combine multiple shapes to form a single object. To manipulate multiple shapes or objects as one, you **group** them. To group objects, click Modify on the Menu bar, then click Group, or press [Ctrl][G] (Win) or [⌘][G] (Mac).

Deciding whether you should group objects or convert them to a symbol is based on their use in the movie. For example, if the objects are not a repetitive element, or if you just need to group them together briefly, but plan to separate them later in the movie, there is no need to convert them into a symbol. However, if you are going to animate the objects, it is always best practice to convert them to a symbol.

To ungroup objects, click Modify on the Menu bar, then click Ungroup, or press [Ctrl][Shift][G] (Win) or [⌘][Shift][G] (Mac). When editing a symbol that has grouped objects, first double-click the symbol to edit them, then ungroup the objects.

Using Symbols and the Library Panel

FIGURE C-20: Viewing columns in the Library panel

Click column ● to sort ascending or descending

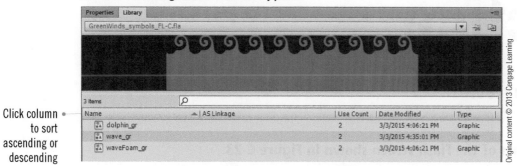

FIGURE C-21: Creating a folder in the Library panel

Folders add to the ● item count

Newly created folder ●

New Folder button ●

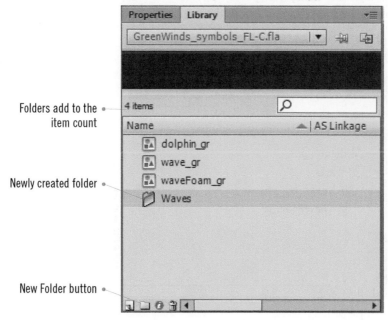

FIGURE C-22: Viewing symbols in a folder

Click to collapse folder ●

Symbols in folder ●

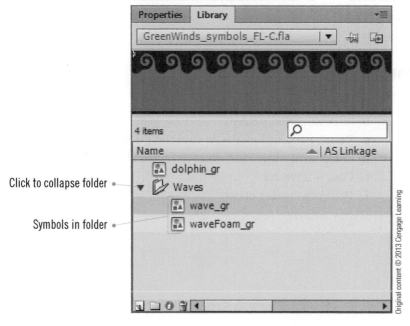

Practice

Concepts Review

Label the elements of the Flash screen shown in Figure C-23.

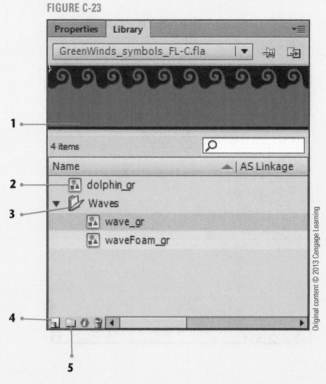

FIGURE C-23

1. _____   4. _____
2. _____   5. _____
3. _____

Match each term with the statement that best describes it.

6. **Instance**   a. Color model for emitted light
7. **RGB**   b. Reusable project element
8. **Symbol**   c. Default point that locates an object on the Stage
9. **Library panel**   d. Component where Flash stores symbols and other elements
10. **Registration point**   e. Copy of a symbol
11. **Symmetry Brush**   f. Deco tool drawing option

Select the best answer from the list of choices.

12. Which tool would you use to create a burning flame?

a. Spray Brush tool

b. Symmetry Brush tool

c. Direct Animation tool

d. Deco tool

13. Which symbol would you use to run an animation in one frame of a movie?

a. Graphic

b. Break Apart

c. Button

d. Movie clip

14. Which of the following is *not* a way to return to the main Stage after editing a symbol?

a. Click the Back button.

b. Double-click the symbol.

c. Click Scene 1 or the Back button.

d. Click Scene 1.

15. When adding a type to a symbol name, where is a good place to add the type?

a. Anywhere

b. At the beginning or the end

c. Only at the end

d. Only at the beginning

16. When editing the color of an instance, which option do you use to change its color?

a. Tint

b. Stroke color icon

c. Fill color icon

d. Either the Fill color or Stroke color icon

Skills Review

1. **Understand symbols and instances.**

   a. Describe the difference between a symbol and an instance.

   b. List three types of symbols.

   c. Briefly describe how symbols help reduce file size.

2. **Understand the Library panel.**

   a. Describe the main function of the Library panel.

   b. List two requirements and one recommendation for naming symbols.

   c. Briefly describe how you could use hyphens and underscores in symbol names.

   d. Briefly describe how Flash sorts hyphens and underscores.

3. **Create a symbol.**

   a. Start Flash, open the file FL C-2.fla from the location where you store your Data Files, then save it as **LightFootRecycling_symbols_FL-C.fla**.

   b. Show the Library panel.

   c. On the Stage, select the bag of newspapers object, then convert it to a graphic symbol named **bagNewspaper_gr**.

   d. In the Timeline, rename Layer 1 **newspaper**, then save the document.

4. **Add instances to the Stage.**

   a. Drag an instance of the recycleSymbol_gr symbol to the upper-right corner of the Stage on the newspaper layer. (*Hint*: You will adjust the instance later.)

   b. Create a new layer named **recycle bin back**.

   c. Drag an instance of the recycleBinBack_gr symbol to the middle of the Stage.

   d. Open the Info panel, make sure the Registration point icon appears, then set the X value to **150.8** and the Y value to **148.2**.

   e. Create a new layer named **recycle bin front**.

   f. Drag an instance of the recycleBinFront_gr symbol to the middle of the Stage, then roughly align its corners to the corners of the back of the bin.

   g. On the Info panel, set the X value to **147.9** and the Y value to **148.2**.

   h. Lock the two recycle bin layers, then save the document.

Skills Review (continued)

5. Edit an instance.
a. Hide the two recycle bin layers, then move the instance of the recycleSymbol_gr symbol on top of the newspaper bag.

b. Open the Transform panel, constrain the size if necessary, then transform the Scale Width and Scale Height to **40%**, and the skew horizontal to **6.0°**.

c. On the Info panel, set the X value to **295** and the Y value to **133**.

d. Save the document.

6. Edit a symbol.
a. Select the recycleSymbol_gr symbol on the Library panel, then double-click the preview thumbnail.

b. Change the fill color to white (#FFFFFF), then return to the Stage in Scene 1 using the breadcrumb trail.

c. Show the two recycle bin layers, then move the plastic bottles layer between the recycle bin front layer and the recycle bin back layer.

d. Using Figure C-24 as a guide, drag the plastic bottles in the bin.

e. Save the document.

7. Organize the Library panel.
a. On the Library panel, create a new folder named **bin**.

b. Move every symbol except recycleSymbol_gr and bagNewspaper_gr into the folder.

c. Expand the folder, then compare your screen to Figure C-24.

d. Save the document, then exit Flash.

FIGURE C-24

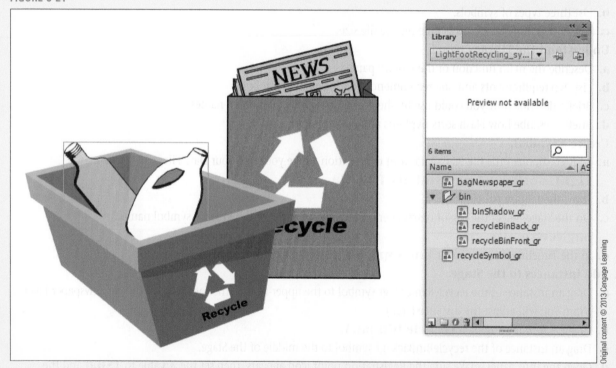

Independent Challenge 1

You work at CoasterWoop, an online source of news by, for, and about roller coaster enthusiasts. Your boss would like you to create an animation of a roller coaster for the application. You begin by creating and modifying the symbols you'll use in the movie.

a. Start Flash, open the file FL C-3.fla from the location where you store your Data Files, then save it as **CoasterWoop_symbols_FL-C.fla**.

b. Make sure that Snap to Grid is turned off and that Snap Align and Snap to Objects are turned on, then open the Info panel and zoom in as needed. (*Hint*: Use the View, Snapping menu.)

c. Convert the shape on Layer 1 to a graphic symbol named **foliageFront_gr**, then rename Layer 1 **foliage front**.

d. Convert the shape in Layer 2 to a graphic symbol named **foliageBack_gr**, rename Layer 2 **foliage back**, then move the layer to the bottom of the Timeline.

e. Drag an instance of the foliageBack_gr symbol to the Stage, then place it by changing the X value to **47.5** and Y value to **142.8**. (*Hint*: Use the Info panel or the Properties panel.)

f. Create a new layer named **rail1**, move it to the bottom of the Timeline, drag an instance of the rail1_gr symbol to the Stage, then place it by changing the X value to **49.8** and Y value to **84.5**.

g. Create a new layer named **rail2**, move it beneath the rail1 layer in the Timeline, drag an instance of the rail2_gr symbol to the Stage, then place it by changing the X value to **61.6** and Y value to **79.3**.

h. Create a new layer named **rail3**, move it beneath the rail2 layer in the Timeline, drag an instance of the rail3_gr symbol to the Stage, then place it by changing the X value to **120.3** and Y value to **93.2**.

i. Create a new layer named **rail4**, move it beneath the rail3 layer in the Timeline, drag an instance of the rail4_gr symbol to the Stage, then place it by changing the X value to **105.8** and Y value to **70.4**.

j. Select the foliage_Front_gr instance on the Stage, then use the Tint style in the Color Effect section of the Properties panel to change the color of the instance to **#3DAC4F**. (*Hint*: Click the Tint color swatch next to the Color styles list arrow.)

k. Edit the foliageBack_gr symbol, changing the fill color of the symbol to **#4F7500**, then return to Scene 1. (*Hint*: Use the Library.)

l. Click the work area, compare your screen to Figure C-25, save and close the document, then exit Flash.

FIGURE C-25

Original content © 2013 Cengage Learning

Independent Challenge 2

As the new Program Director at Lingoroots, an educational website specializing in linguistics, you're constantly looking for exciting ways to engage new visitors. For the next application feature, you'll compare the evolution of written Chinese across its 4,000-year history. The earliest written Chinese characters were pictures and evolved to a more stylized and artistic writing form. You want to show how Chinese calligraphy has changed over time, and begin constructing an animation using both original and modern versions of three characters.

a. Start Flash, open the file FL C-4.fla from the location where you store your Data Files, then save it as **lingoroots_symbols_FL-C.fla**. Make sure guides are visible in the document. (*Hint*: Substitute a font available on your computer if prompted.)

b. Create a new layer named **moon-ancient text** just above the calligraphy title text layer, drag an instance of the moonAncientTxt_gr symbol to the Stage, then use the green guides to align it under the original moon symbol on the left. (Hint: Make sure Snap to Guides and Snap Align are selected as snapping options and refer to Figure C-26.)

c. Create a new layer named **moon-current text**, drag an instance of the moonCurrentTxt_gr symbol to the Stage, then use the green guides to align it under the current moon character on the right.

d. Create a new layer named **sun-ancient text**, select the Text tool, show the Properties panel, select Classic Text as the Text engine, set the font to Adobe Garamond Pro, 14 pt, italic, color **#666666**, click under the original sun symbol, then type **Sun-Ancient**.

e. Use the guides to align the text object under the original sun character. (*Hint*: Use the Selection tool. Substitute a font such as Garamond if Adobe Garamond Pro is not available.)

f. Convert the text object to a graphic symbol named **sunAncientTxt_gr**.

g. Create a new layer named **sun-current text**, select the Text tool if necessary, click under the current sun symbol, then type **Sun-Current**.

h. Use the guides to align the text object under the current sun character.

i. Convert the text object to a graphic symbol named **sunCurrentTxt_gr**.

j. Create a new folder on the Library panel named **mountain**, then move the mountain symbols into that folder.

k. Click a blank part of the Library panel, create a new folder named **moon**, then move the moon symbols into that folder.

l. Click a blank part of the Library panel, create a new folder named **sun**, then move the sun symbols into that folder.

m. Hide the guides, save the document, then compare your screen to Figure C-26.

FIGURE C-26

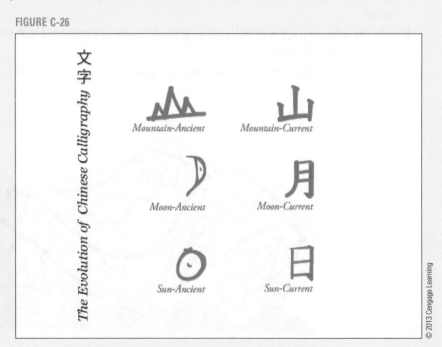

Independent Challenge 2 (continued)

Advanced Challenge Exercise

- Select the text instances in the ancient column on the Stage, open the Align panel, make sure the Align to stage check box is not selected, click the Align right edge button, then compare the command alignment to your manual alignment.
- Select the text instances in the current column on the Stage, right-align them using the method above, then compare the command alignment to your manual alignment.
- Break apart the instance of the calligraphyTxt_gr symbol, then delete it from the Library panel. (*Hint*: Use a command on the Modify menu or right-click (Win) or [control]-click (Mac) the instance, then click the command.)

n. Save and close the document, then exit Flash.

Independent Challenge 3

You work for ibRobotz, an online entertainment site. Users can download ibRobotz characters or create their own to insert in stories. You continue building a character using various Flash drawing tools.

a. Start Flash, open the file FL C-5.fla from the location where you store your Data Files, then save it as **ibrobotz_symbols_FL-C.fla**. (*Hint*: Substitute a font available on your computer if prompted.)

b. Select the entire pink square and black stroke that currently make up the robot's hand, convert it to a graphic symbol named **smPinkSquare_gr**, then add instances of the symbol as feet, the other hand, and the top of the antenna. Modify instances in minor ways as desired, such as rotating. (*Hint*: You can copy the instance on the Stage instead of dragging it from the Library.)

c. Add an instance of the greenRectangle_gr symbol to the Stage, then place it on the robot as the mouth. Add another instance as the horizontal part of the antenna, then modify that instance by adjusting the Selection width on the Properties panel. (*Hint*: The antenna should be about as wide as the robot body; refer to Figure C-27.)

d. Rename Layer 1 **ibROBOTZ**.

e. Create a new layer named **itzyBOTZ**, drag an instance of the itzyBotz_gr symbol to the Stage, then place it by changing the X value to **304** and the Y value to **205.8**. (*Hint*: Open the Info panel or show the Properties panel.)

f. Edit the itzyBotz_gr symbol if desired, return to Scene 1 if necessary, then drag an instance of the smPinkSquare_gr symbol to the Stage. Resize the instance to W: **11.3** and H: **11.3**, then using Figure C-27 as a guide, copy the instance to create the hands, feet, and antenna. Return to Scene 1. (*Hint*: To rotate the instance 45° for the hands, press and hold [Shift], then rotate an instance clockwise or counterclockwise.)

g. Create a new layer named **furnishings**, then drag an instance of the picture_gr symbol to the Stage, then place it by changing the X value to **375.4** and the Y value to **38.5**.

h. Edit the picture_gr symbol by changing the frame color to **#FFCC33**, then return to Scene 1.

i. Create a new layer named **wall & floor**, then drag an instance of the wallPaper_gr symbol to the Stage, then place it by changing the X value to **–9.1** and the Y value to **–4.1**.

j. On the wall & floor layer, drag an instance of the floor_gr symbol to the Stage, and place it by aligning the squares to the instance of the wallPaper_gr symbol. (*Hint*: Change the X value to **–25.1** and the Y value to **293.9**.)

Independent Challenge 3 (continued)

k. Move the wall & floor layer to the bottom of the Timeline.

l. On the Library panel, create a new folder named **wall & floor**, then move the wallPaper_gr and floor_gr symbols to it.

m. Save the document, test the movie using a keyboard command, then close the Flash Player.

n. Compare your screen to Figure C-27.

Advanced Challenge Exercise

- Change the color of the botPhone_gr symbol to a color of your choice. (*Hint*: Zoom in and change just the selected botPhone box.)
- Change the color of the instance of the floor_gr symbol to a color of your choice. (*Hint*: Select the floor instance on the Stage.)
- Add another instance of the picture_gr symbol, transform or reshape it, then modify it using two style settings in the Color Effect section of the Properties panel.

o. Close the document, then exit Flash.

FIGURE C-27

© 2013 Cengage Learning

Real Life Independent Challenge

This Independent Challenge will continue to build on the personal movie that you created in Unit B. Here, you create symbols and prepare elements to be animated.

a. Start Flash, open your myproject file, then save it as **myproject_symbols_FL-C.fla**.

b. Create symbols to represent the objects that you plan to animate, adding layers as needed.

c. Add instances to the Stage and reshape, modify, and transform them however you like.

d. Create folders on the Library panel for related items if necessary.

e. Check your document for proper alignment and design consistency.

f. Save and close the document myproject_symbols_FL-C.fla, then exit Flash.

Visual Workshop

Watching movies, animations, or rich graphics are great ways to get inspired for your own projects. Figure C-28 shows a frame from a NASA animation depicting how a black hole sends out "bullets" of ionized gasses. Open your browser, go to http://www.nasa.gov/multimedia/videogallery/index.html?media_id=128357901, watch the animation, and then answer the following questions. For each question, include why or how you reached a conclusion. You can open a word processor or use the Text tool in Flash to complete this exercise. When you are finished, press [Print Screen] (Win) or ⌘[Shift][4] to select the window using the mouse (Mac), paste the image into a word-processing program, add your name at the top of the document, then print or post the document. Please check with your instructor for assignment submission instructions.

a. What is the website's purpose and goal? What is the animation's purpose?

b. Who is the target audience? How does the design (look and feel) of the website fit the target audience and the topic it represents?

c. Looking at the animation:

- How are vector and bitmap shapes used?
- How many instances of symbols do you see?
- How do objects appear to have been modified or transformed?
- How could text be used effectively in this image? What kinds of fonts?

d. How is animation used?

e. What is your overall opinion of the design, organization, and function of this animation? How would you improve it?

f. Close your browser.

FIGURE C-28

Image NASA/Goddard Space Flight Center/CiLab

Creating Animation

Animation plays a huge role in the computer, advertising, marketing, and entertainment industries. It has become a distinctive—and sometimes notorious—feature of the online experience. Adding animation makes it easy to take your project to the next level. But remember that animation can easily annoy or overwhelm your audience if you overuse it or do not build in good design. Flash offers a few different ways to animate your projects, and, with a little practice, you can create effective animations that help communicate any online message.  Vanessa has reviewed the document for GreenWinds Eco-Cruise and has begun animating various elements. She's given you the go-ahead to finish the document using Flash animation methods.

OBJECTIVES

Understand animation

Use frames

Create a motion tween

Create and copy a motion path

Use easing

Create nested symbols

Animate nested symbols

Create frame-by-frame animation

Create a shape tween

Use shape hints

Create a mask

Understanding Animation

Creating animation in Flash involves object-based animation: creating and adjusting frames and the artwork that appears in them, determining the length of the animation, and setting a frame rate to control the animation's speed. You can animate many attributes or aspects of an object, such as its shape, size, color, and position. When working with frames, it is useful to refer to a group of frames as a **frame span**. Before animating objects in the GreenWinds Eco-Cruise project, you review the process of creating an animation.

To create an animation in Flash, you do the following:

- **Specify frames**

  Animation shows change over time, which, in Flash, is represented by frames in the Timeline. As the creator, you use frames to define when artwork appears and how it changes in a movie. When you open a new document, the Timeline contains a single frame, known as a **blank keyframe** ▫, indicating that there is currently no artwork on the Stage in that frame. When you add content, such as an instance, to a blank keyframe, it becomes a keyframe. A **keyframe** ▪ is a special frame that signals a change in a movie, such as adding or creating artwork on the Stage, or in an animation, such as a change in an object's appearance, location, or behavior.

QUICK TIP

In traditional hand-drawn film anima-tion, senior artists drew the anima-tion's major action points (which they named keyframes), and junior artists, having the monoto-nous job of drawing the frames in between, were known as *tweeners*.

- **Select animation methods**

  In Flash, you can create animation literally frame by frame or have Flash do some—or all—of the work for you. It's up to you to decide how much specific control you need to create the final result. Regardless of how you create an animation, you can always edit it.

  In **frame-by-frame animation**, Flash animates an object gradually over several consecutive frames. You can control the action in every frame, which may be necessary in a complex animation. Be aware, how-ever, that the more keyframes a movie contains, the larger the file size and the longer it will take users to view it on a web page. And, because you're creating each frame as you go along, frame-by-frame animation can be time consuming. Figure D-1 shows a sample of frame-by-frame animation, including a view of the previous and subsequent frames.

  With **tweened animation**, Flash automatically creates animation between two keyframes. You define the starting and ending keyframes, and then modify the object or symbol in the ending keyframe, to indicate the end result. "Tween," the term for this automatically created animation, comes from the phrase "in between," because Flash creates the animation between the two keyframes. The most common types of tweens in Flash are motion tweens and shape tweens.

  - **Motion tweens** show movement on the Stage as an instance moves from one position to another or changes properties such as color, size, or rotation. Because a motion tween uses symbols, it is an effi-cient way to animate objects. Figure D-2 shows a sample motion tween with a curved motion path.
  - **Shape tweens** change one shape to another, in a process known as morphing. You can control how the shape changes when you create the shape tween by adding and positioning transformation hints around the area of the shape that you want to preserve. Figure D-3 shows a shape tween morphing one shape into another.

QUICK TIP

To access options for viewing, selecting, or removing key-frames, right-click (Win) or [control]-click (Mac) a key-frame in a layer, then select an option in the list.

- **Understand tweens in the Timeline**

  When you create a tweened animation, Flash creates a frame span, called a **tween span**, on its Timeline layer in between two keyframes. Motion tween spans are blue, and shape tween spans are green. In a motion tween animation, Flash creates **property keyframes**, which contain the specific property values that change in that frame: position, scale, skew, rotation, color, or filter.

FIGURE D-1: Sample frame-by-frame animation

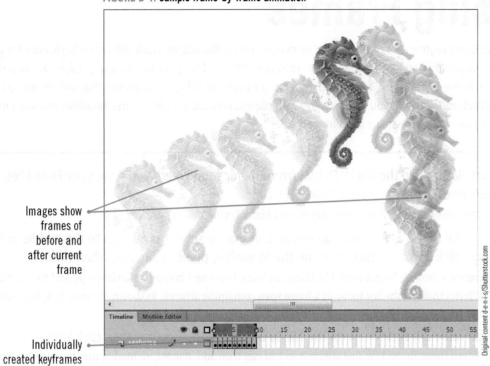

Images show frames of before and after current frame

Individually created keyframes

Original content d-e-n-i-s/Shutterstock.com

FIGURE D-2: Sample motion tween

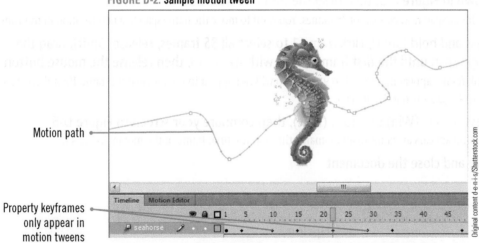

Motion path

Property keyframes only appear in motion tweens

Original content d-e-n-i-s/Shutterstock.com

FIGURE D-3: Sample shape tween

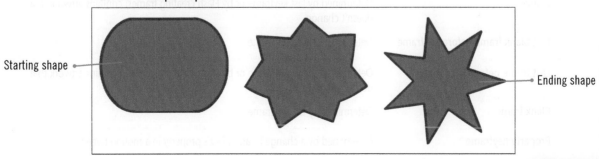

Starting shape

Ending shape

Creating Animation

Using Frames

You can insert keyframes in a document, or depending on the action, Flash will create keyframes for you. You can adjust the length of a frame span or move selected frames in the Timeline. Table D-1 describes different frame types. ▓▓▓▓ You and Vanessa go over the different elements that will appear in the GreenWinds movie. Since you'll be working with objects on various points in the Timeline, you learn more about frames and frame spans in a simple movie.

STEPS

QUICK TIP
You can also press [F5] to insert a frame.

TROUBLE
It's important to distinguish between frames not used in a movie, which are blank or empty and not part of a frame span, and blank frames, which are part of a movie in a frame span and intentionally do not contain artwork.

QUICK TIP
If you need to undo an action, press [Ctrl][Z] (Win) or ⌘[Z] (Mac).

1. **Start Flash, open the file FL D-1.fla from the location where you store your Data Files, then save it as GreenWinds_frames_FL-D.fla**

   The document does not have any content, so a blank keyframe ⊙ appears in frame 1.

2. **Show the Library panel, drag an instance of the cruiseShip_gr symbol to the middle of the Stage, click frame 15, click Insert on the Menu bar, point to Timeline, then click Frame**

   The movie is now 15 frames long. The blank keyframe in frame 1 becomes a keyframe ●, and the last frame ▯ indicates that it is the last frame in a frame span containing artwork, as shown in Figure D-4. You want to extend the length of the frame span by adding another frame in the Timeline.

3. **Click frame 24, click Insert on the Menu bar, point to Timeline, then click Frame**

   Clicking a frame in the Timeline selects it so you can then add, remove, or modify that frame. Flash inserts a new frame, which extends the frame span to 24 frames. You can also click and drag the last frame to extend the ending frame.

4. **Press and hold [Ctrl] (Win) or ⌘ (Mac), position the pointer ←→ over the last frame, as shown in Figure D-5, then drag the frame to frame 35**

   The frame span now consists of 35 frames. You want to move the frame span to a new location in the Timeline.

5. **Press and hold [Shift], click frame 1 to select all 35 frames, release [Shift], drag the frame span until the first frame aligns with frame 10, then release the mouse button**

   Blank frames appear in frames 1 to 9. The ship will not appear in the movie until frame 10; it then exits after frame 44, as shown in Figure D-6.

6. **Press [Enter] (Win) or return (Mac), then compare your screen to Figure D-6**

   The ship appears at frame 10 and remains through the final frame of the movie, frame 44.

7. **Save and close the document**

TABLE D-1: Frame types

icon	type	description
⊙	Blank keyframe	Determined by user to not contain artwork
●	Keyframe	Determined by user; contains artwork, signifies change
�	Frame	Determined by last keyframe or by Flash creating frames; contains artwork that doesn't change
▯	Last blank frame before keyframe	Determined by last keyframe
▯	Last frame before keyframe	Determined by last keyframe or by Flash creating frames; contains artwork that doesn't change
▢	Blank frame	Determined by last keyframe
▪	Property keyframe	Determined by a change to an object's property in a motion tween

FIGURE D-4: Viewing a frame span

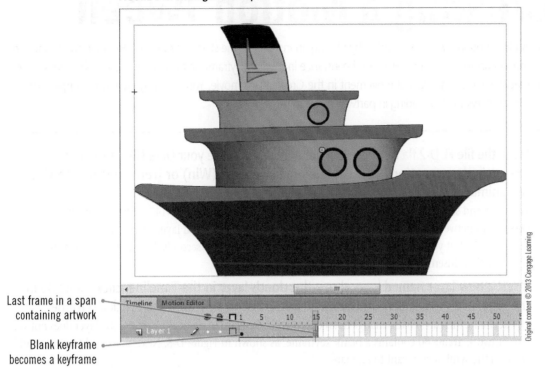

Last frame in a span
containing artwork

Blank keyframe
becomes a keyframe

Original content © 2013 Cengage Learning

FIGURE D-5: Extending a frame span by dragging

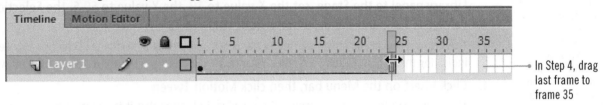

In Step 4, drag
last frame to
frame 35

Original content © 2013 Cengage Learning

FIGURE D-6: Moving a frame span

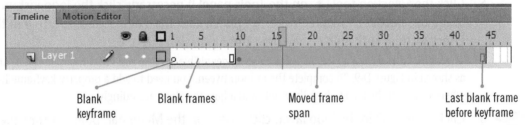

Blank
keyframe

Blank frames

Moved frame
span

Last blank frame
before keyframe

Using the Motion Presets panel

Flash includes several predesigned motion tweens you can apply to symbol instances. Open the Motion Presets panel from the Window menu, open the Default Presets folder, then select a preset. A preview of the preset appears at the top of the panel. To apply a preset, select the instance on the Stage, select a preset, then click Apply at the bottom of the panel. Figure D-7 shows a sample preset. To save any motion tween as a custom preset, right-click (Win) or [control]-click (Mac) a motion tween span in the Timeline, click Save as Motion Preset, type a name in the Preset name text box, then click OK to close the Save Preset As text box. The preset appears in the Custom Presets folder on the Motion Presets panel.

FIGURE D-7: Motion Presets panel

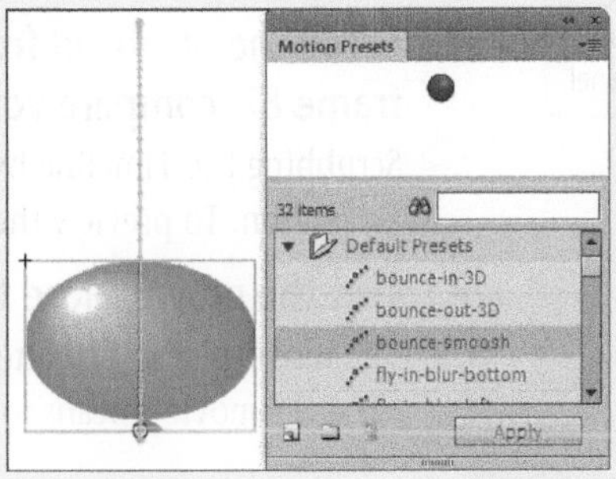

Original content © 2013 Cengage Learning

Creating a Motion Tween

You apply a motion tween to a symbol by placing an instance in the starting keyframe, and then modifying the position or transformation properties of the instance in the last keyframe of the animation. Vanessa tells you that she'd like to see lots of movement in the GreenWinds movie. You begin by creating a simple motion tween that shows the logo fading in partway through the movie.

STEPS

1. **Open the file FL D-2.fla from the location where you store your Data Files, save it as GreenWinds_animation_FL-D.fla, then press [Enter] (Win) or [return] (Mac) to view the animation**

    The wave and ship objects are animated with a motion tween in frames 1–147, indicated by the light blue tween span between the keyframes. All document objects are on locked layers. You want to insert the logo in the movie, but you want to delay the logo's appearance for a few seconds. You do this by creating a new layer and then inserting a keyframe in a later frame of the movie.

    QUICK TIP
    You can also press [F6] to insert a keyframe.

2. **Insert a new layer named logo above the clouds layer in the Timeline, click frame 80 in the logo layer, click Insert on the Menu bar, point to Timeline, then click Keyframe**

    The keyframe indicates that a change to an object will take place in frame 80. Because the layer does not yet have artwork, frame 80 contains a blank keyframe, as shown in Figure D-8. Next, you need to choose and position the symbol you want to animate.

    QUICK TIP
    Open or undock the Transform, Info, Library, and Properties panels as needed or switch to another workspace to make your work easier throughout this unit.

3. **Show the Library panel, drag an instance of the greenWindsLogo_gr symbol from the Library panel to the Stage, set the X value to 19, the Y value to 50.5, the Selection width value to 355.6, and the Selection height value to 109.4**

    The logo appears in the movie starting in frame 80, and the blank keyframe ▯ changes to a keyframe ▮, indicating that it now contains a symbol instance. Next, you instruct Flash to create a motion tween.

4. **Click Insert on the Menu bar, then click Motion Tween**

    The frame span to the right of frame 80 turns blue, indicating that it is a motion tween span. Next, you adjust the alpha setting for the logo at the beginning and end of the tween to achieve the fade-in effect.

5. **Click the Selection tool � on the Tools panel if necessary, click the logo instance on the Stage to select it, show the Properties panel, click the Color styles list arrow in the Color Effect section, click Alpha, then drag the Alpha slider △ to 0**

    The logo is still selected on the Stage but is no longer visible because you've set its alpha (transparency) to 0, as shown in Figure D-9. To complete the motion tween, you need to add a property keyframe in the frame where you want the logo to be fully visible and adjust the alpha accordingly.

    TROUBLE
    You must select an instance on the Stage to access properties for the instance; otherwise, properties for the animation appear on the Properties panel.

6. **Click frame 100 in the logo layer, click Insert on the Menu bar, point to Timeline, click Keyframe, click the logo instance on the Stage to select it if necessary, then drag the Alpha slider △ to 100 on the Properties panel**

    The logo is visible on the Stage, and a new property keyframe ▪ appears in the Timeline. You check to see that the logo fades in from frames 80 to 100, then remains visible for the rest of the movie.

7. **Scrub the playhead from frames 80 to 100 to view the animation, drag the playhead to frame 87, compare your screen to Figure D-10, then lock the logo layer**

    Scrubbing the Timeline by dragging the playhead over selected frames is a great way to quickly view an animation. To preview the final result, you test the movie.

8. **Test the movie, close the Flash Player, then save the document**

    The movie plays, then after a few seconds, the logo fades in. In future lessons in this book, the instruction "Test the movie" means to view the movie in the Flash Player, and, then close the Flash Player.

FIGURE D-8: Adding a keyframe to a layer

Blank keyframe

FIGURE D-9: Adjusting the value of a property keyframe

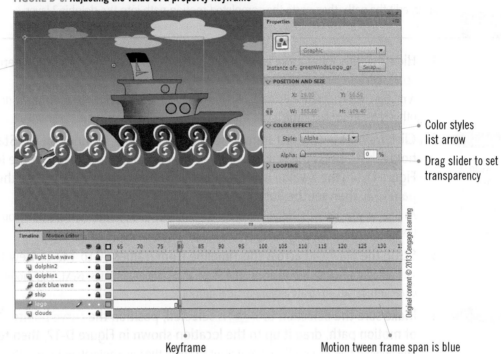

Instance is selected but not visible

Color styles list arrow

Drag slider to set transparency

Keyframe

Motion tween frame span is blue

FIGURE D-10: Viewing a motion tween

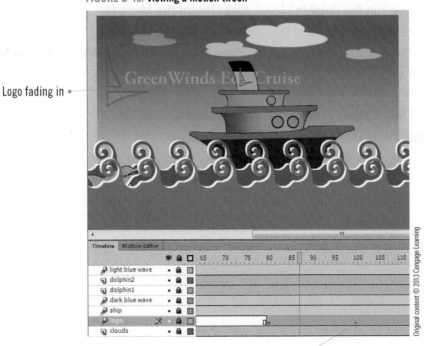

Logo fading in

Property keyframe

Creating Animation

Creating and Copying a Motion Path

After you create a motion tween and move an instance on the Stage, you create a motion path. You can copy and paste a motion tween on other layers to keep your animations consistent and save time. ▓▓▓▓▓ Vanessa wants the dolphins to look like they're jumping out of the water. You create a motion path in the dolphin1 layer, edit the path, then paste the completed motion path into the dolphin2 layer.

1. **Hide the light blue wave layer, unlock the dolphin1 layer, click anywhere in its frame span, click Insert on the Menu bar, then click Motion Tween**

   A motion tween is created in frames 1–147. You create a motion path by moving the dolphin instance to the other side of the Stage, which you will do using keyboard keys.

   > **QUICK TIP**
   > You can press [Shift][.] to move to the last frame in a movie or press [Shift][,] to move to frame 1.

2. **Click frame 147 (the last frame), select the dolphin1 instance on the Stage, press and hold [Shift], press the right arrow key until the dolphin appears in the location shown in Figure D-11 (the X value is approximately 380), release [Shift], show the Transform panel ▣, then set the Rotate value to 64.7°**

   As soon as you move the dolphin instance, Flash inserts a keyframe in frame 147. You have set the dolphin instance to move straight across the Stage and rotate, as if diving back in the water.

3. **Scrub the playhead across the Timeline from frames 80 to 147 to view the animation**

   The dolphin instance moves across the Stage and gradually rotates. Next, you modify the motion path to curve into an arc to create a more natural motion.

   > **QUICK TIP**
   > You can adjust the curves and the length of a motion path directly on the Stage using the Selection tool or Subselection tool.

4. **Make sure the Selection tool ▨ is selected, position the curve pointer ⬩ on the center of motion path, drag it up to the location shown in Figure D-12, then test the movie**

   The dolphin flies in a gentle arc. You want to apply the same animation to the other dolphin instance, so you copy the tween span in the dolphin1 layer to the dolphin2 layer.

5. **Click frame 1 in the dolphin1 layer, click Edit on the Menu bar, point to Timeline, then click Copy Motion**

6. **Unlock the dolphin2 layer, click anywhere in its frame span, click Edit on the Menu bar, point to Timeline, click Paste Motion, then show the light blue wave layer**

   The dolphin2 layer frame span turns blue, indicating that you have pasted the copied motion tween span there.

   > **QUICK TIP**
   > You can close the Flash Player after testing a movie.

7. **Test the movie, then compare your screen to Figure D-13**

8. **Lock the dolphin1 layer, then save the document**

FIGURE D-11: Creating a motion path

Motion path

Move the dolphin here

Original content © 2013 Cengage Learning

FIGURE D-12: Modifying a motion path

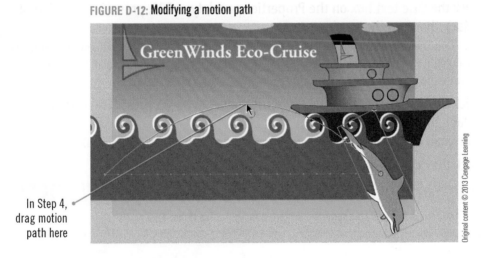

In Step 4, drag motion path here

Original content © 2013 Cengage Learning

FIGURE D-13: Viewing motion tweens

Dual motion paths

Original content © 2013 Cengage Learning

Creating Animation

Using Easing

When you play a motion tween, the animation moves at a uniform speed from beginning to end; this may not always provide a sense of realistic or organic movement. You can speed up or slow down the start or end of an animation by adjusting its **easing** on the Properties panel. When an object eases in, it starts out slow and then speeds up at the end. When it eases out, the opposite happens: it starts out fast, then slows down. When you use easing, you may have to experiment with different values to get the effect you want. 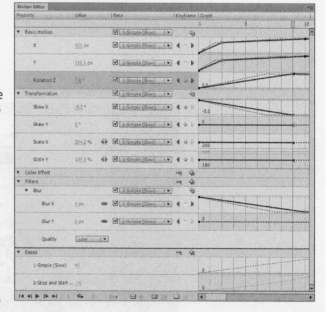 Currently, the dolphins look and move at the same speed throughout the movie. You use the easing setting to change the speed for one of the dolphins.

1. **Click the dolphin2 layer to select it, click the Ease text box in the Ease section of the Properties panel, type –100, then press [Enter] (Win) or [return] (Mac)**

   To ease an object in, you enter a negative value. The word "in" appears after the value.

2. **Test the movie**

   The dolphin in the dolphin2 layer lags significantly behind the first dolphin, as shown in Figure D-15. This is not the effect you wanted, so you ease out the motion tween.

3. **Click the Ease text box on the Properties panel, type 100, press [Enter] (Win) or [return] (Mac), then test the movie**

   The word "out" appears after the value. Now the dolphin enters the movie so quickly that its path crosses the dolphin1 path, as shown in Figure D-16. This effect detracts from the overall look of the movie, so you decrease the amount of easing out.

4. **Click the Ease text box on the Properties panel, type 20, press [Enter] (Win) or [return] (Mac), then test the movie**

   This setting adds enough variation without being distracting, as shown in Figure D-17.

5. **Lock the dolphin2 layer, then save the document**

Using the Motion Editor

Using the **Motion Editor**, you can control every property of object-based animation independently, including timing, motion paths, rotation, and color.

To use the Motion Editor, select a motion tween span, then open the Motion Editor from the Window menu or click the tab behind the Timeline. The values are shown both as numbers and as curves, as shown in Figure D-14. To expand a property and see your animation frame by frame, click a blank part of the property section. Use controls on the bottom of the panel to adjust the size of the layers and Timeline. The Motion Editor is divided into property sections: Basic Motion, Transformation, Color Effect, Filters, and Eases.

Each property has its own Timeline where you can adjust X and Y values, add keyframes, create custom easing, or apply a preset easing option.

When you select custom easing for an animation, you can control the timing in your animation by adjusting the animation line for that object. If you drag a keyframe, you create a Bezier curve and can then easily adjust the Bezier handles to create very smooth and realistic animation. The steeper the curve, the faster the animation plays in those frames.

FIGURE D-14: The Motion Editor

FIGURE D-15: Viewing animation at maximum easing in

Dolphins' paths are out of synch

Negative value eases an object in

FIGURE D-16: Viewing animation at maximum easing out

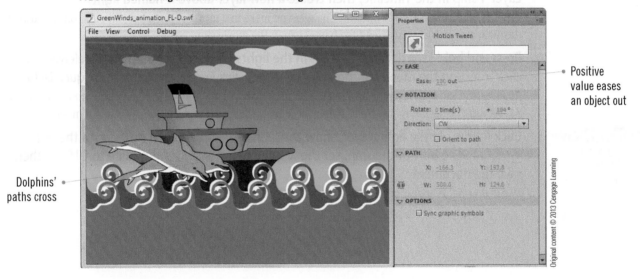

Dolphins' paths cross

Positive value eases an object out

FIGURE D-17: Corrected easing

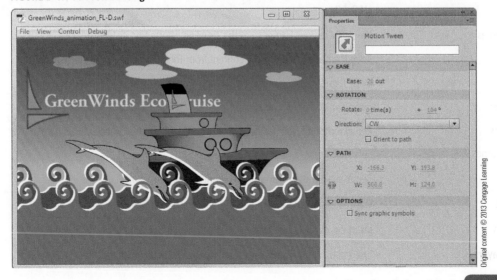

Creating Nested Symbols

Using a movie clip within a movie lets you add more complex motion within your movie. You can animate a single graphic or button symbol, or animate multiple symbols on several layers. Placing a symbol inside another symbol creates a **nested symbol** and is a great way to create a unique new symbol while preserving the individuality of the original symbols. Each movie clip has its own timeline; see Table D-2 for Timeline commands. ████ Vanessa wants you to add flashing lights to the bow of the ship. First you convert the ship graphic symbol to a movie symbol, then add (nest) instances of a light symbol to it.

STEPS

TROUBLE
If the ship graphic shrinks in size, click the Reset button ⟳ on the Transform panel.

1. **Unlock the** ship layer, **click** frame 1, **select the** ship instance **on the Stage, click** Modify **on the Menu bar, then click** Convert to Symbol **to open the Convert to Symbol dialog box**

2. **Type** shipWithLights_mc **in the Name text box, click the** Type list arrow, **click** Movie Clip, **compare your dialog box to Figure D-18, then click** OK

   Flash converts the graphic symbol into a new movie clip symbol, which appears on the Library panel.

QUICK TIP
Adjust the zoom as needed.

3. **Double-click the** ship instance **on the Stage to open the movie clip Timeline, rename Layer 1** ship **in the Timeline, then create a new layer above it named** lights

   The symbol opens in an edit window. Changes you make in a movie clip symbol will play continuously in the main movie. First, you extend the frame span in the movie clip.

4. **Press and hold** [Shift], **click** frame 24 **in the lights layer and the ship layer, release** [Shift], **click** Insert **on the Menu bar, point to** Timeline, **click** Frame, **then refer to Figure D-19**

   Adding frames to both layers means that the flashing lights animation will start in frame 1 and end in frame 24. Because the default frame rate is 24 fps, the action will be one second long in the main movie.

QUICK TIP
The light_gr symbol is nested in the movie clip.

5. **Click** frame 1 **in the lights layer, show the** Library panel, **drag an instance of the** light_gr symbol **to the bow of the ship, set the X value to** 262.6 **and the Y value to** 115.75, **then save the document**

   Two yellow lights appear on the ship's bow, as shown in Figure D-20.

TABLE D-2: Timeline commands on the Edit menu

command	use to
Remove Frames	Physically remove frames from the Timeline, shortening its length
Cut Frames	Keep the frames, but remove content from them and place it on the Clipboard
Copy Frames	Copy frames and content and place them on the Clipboard
Paste Frames	Insert copied frames and content
Clear Frames	Remove content from frames but do not place it on the Clipboard
Select All Frames	Select all frames in all layers
Cut Layers	Remove layer; places layer and content on the Clipboard
Copy Layers	Copy layer and content and place them on the Clipboard
Paste Layers	Insert cut or copied layers
Duplicate Layers	Insert copy of layer and content automatically in the Timeline

FIGURE D-18: Creating a Movie Clip symbol

FIGURE D-19: Extending a frame span to multiple layers in a movie clip

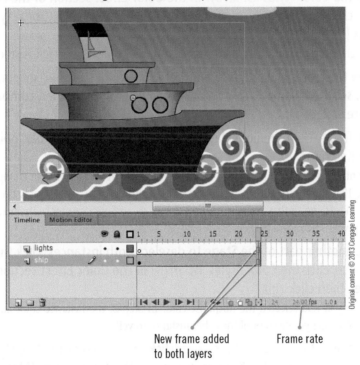

New frame added
to both layers

Frame rate

FIGURE D-20: Symbol nested in a movie clip

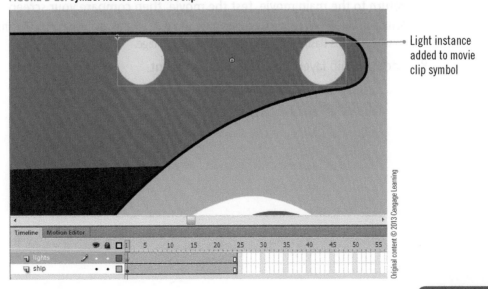

Light instance
added to movie
clip symbol

Creating Animation

Animating Nested Symbols

You can animate any part of a movie clip. Animating a nested symbol instead of animating part of the actual clip still allows you to reuse the symbol elsewhere in the movie, where it can be part of another animation. ▰▰▰▰ You create a series of flashing lights by aligning two instances of the light_gr symbol and then changing the instances' color in a later keyframe.

1. **Make sure that the edit window for the** shipWithLights_mc symbol **is open and the** light_gr instance **is selected**

TROUBLE
Drag the Tint slider ▲ to 100%, if necessary.

2. **Click the** Color styles list arrow **in the Color Effect section of the Properties panel, click** Tint, **click the** Tint color swatch, **click the** hexadecimal text box, **type** #00FFCB, **then press** [Enter] (Win) **or** [return] (Mac)

   The lights turn turquoise. You add a second instance of the lights symbol to the layer.

3. **Show the** Library panel, **drag another instance of the** light_gr symbol **to the bow of the ship, set the X value to** 249 **and the Y value to** 115.75, **then compare your screen to Figure D-21**

QUICK TIP
To move one frame at a time in the Timeline, press [.].

4. **Click** frame 12 **in the lights layer, click** Insert **on the Menu bar, point to** Timeline, **then click** Keyframe

   Currently, the movie clip shows yellow and turquoise lights that do not change. By adding a keyframe to frame 12, you can now change a property of the light instances. By changing the colors of the light instances in this keyframe so they change color every half second, you can make them appear to flash in alternating colors when the movie plays.

5. **Click another part of the Stage to deselect both instances, click the** left (yellow) instance, **click the** Color Styles list arrow **in the Color Effect section of the Properties panel, then click** Tint

   Because you had selected the turquoise color in Step 2, the instance color automatically changes to this color. You change the color of the other instance to yellow.

6. **Click the** right (turquoise) instance, **click the** Tint color swatch, **click the** hexadecimal text box, **type** #FFFF00, **then press** [Enter] (Win) **or** [return] (Mac)

   The colors of the lights in frames 12 to 24 are reversed, as shown in Figure D-22.

7. **Scrub the** playhead **across the Timeline to see the lights change color, click** Scene 1 **to return to the main movie, test the movie, then compare your screen to Figure D-23**

   Scrubbing the Timeline quickly shows the effect of the lights changing color. Testing the movie allows you to see the lights flash as the ship moves across the Stage.

8. **Lock the** ship layer, **then save the document**

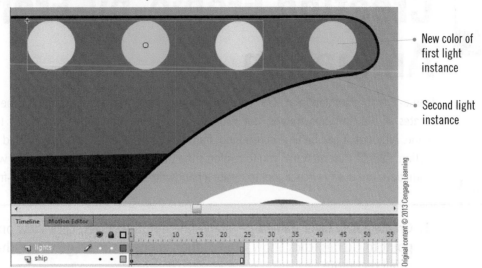

New color of
first light
instance

Second light
instance

Original content © 2013 Cengage Learning

FIGURE D-22: Modifying instances in a new keyframe

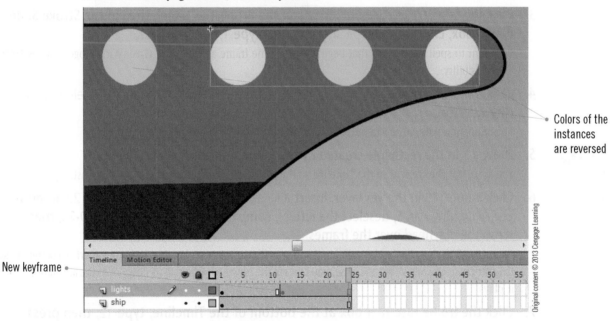

Colors of the
instances
are reversed

New keyframe

Original content © 2013 Cengage Learning

FIGURE D-23: Viewing a movie clip

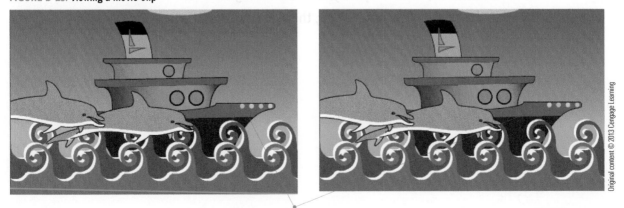

Lights flash in alternating colors

Original content © 2013 Cengage Learning

Creating Animation

Creating Frame-by-Frame Animation

Frame-by-frame animation in Flash comes closest to traditional animation techniques. In tweening, Flash creates all the transition frames, but with frame-by-frame animation, you create the content in every frame. Although it can be time consuming, frame-by-frame animation offers detailed control over the animation. ▓▓▓▓ Vanessa wants you to reinforce the GreenWinds Eco-Cruise message with a brief skywriting animation. You use the Pencil tool to create a handwritten message using frame-by-frame animation.

STEPS

1. **Create a new layer named** yes **above the dolphin2 layer, click** View **on the Menu bar, point to** Guides, **click** Show Guides, **then zoom in the Stage where the guides form a small rectangle**

2. **Click the** Pencil tool 🖉 **on the Tools panel, then set the following properties: Stroke color: #FFFFFF (white), Stroke height: 2, Stroke style: Dotted**

3. **Click the** Edit stroke style button 🖉 **on the Properties panel, then in the Stroke Style dialog box, click the** Dot spacing text box, **type** 1, **then click** OK

   You want to spell out a word that begins in the same frame as when the GreenWinds logo reaches 100% alpha visibility.

4. **Click** frame 100 **in the yes layer, click** Insert **on the Menu bar, point to** Timeline, **then click** Keyframe

   The animation will start at frame 100.

TROUBLE
You may need to undo and redraw a few times to get the look you want.

5. **Draw a Y in the rectangle created by the guides, as shown in Figure D-24**

   You space out the content in the Timeline so the letters do not appear in the movie too fast.

6. **Click** frame 110 **in the yes layer, insert a** keyframe, **draw an E, click** frame 120, **insert a** keyframe, **draw an S, deselect the letters, compare your screen to Figure D-25, then scrub the** playhead **over the frames**

   The word "YES" is spelled out one letter at a time, with the letters appearing 10 frames apart. To better evoke the spirit of a leisurely vacation cruise, you change the movie's frame rate to slow down the animation when it plays.

7. **Click the** frame rate text box **at the bottom of the Timeline, type** 12, **then press [Enter] (Win) or [return] (Mac)**

8. **Test the movie, then compare your screen to Figure D-26**

9. **Hide the guides, lock the** yes **layer, then save the document**

FIGURE D-24: **Drawing a letter in a frame**

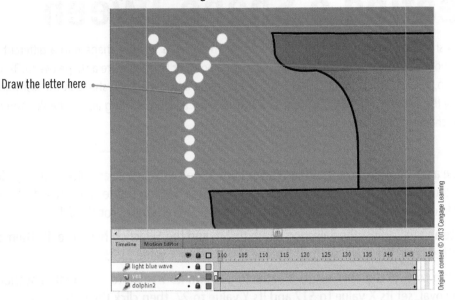

Draw the letter here

FIGURE D-25: **Completed frame-by-frame animation**

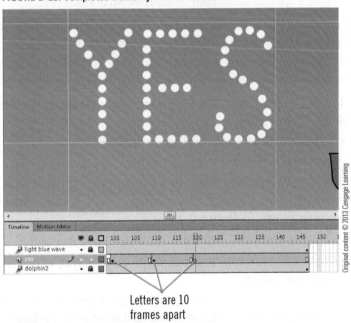

Letters are 10
frames apart

FIGURE D-26: **Viewing frame-by-frame animation**

Letters appear
one by one

Creating Animation

Creating a Shape Tween

Creating a shape tween in an animation changes, or **morphs**, a starting shape into a different ending shape. So, you use shapes instead of symbols, bitmap images, or text to create a shape tween. To create a shape tween, you place the starting shape in the first frame and the ending shape in the last frame, and then create the shape tween. ▨▨▨ Vanessa wants to show a cloud blowing across the sky. You create a cloud that changes shape as it moves across the Stage.

STEPS

1. **Create a new layer above the clouds layer named** cloud shape tween, **click** frame 1, **click the** Oval tool ⬭ **on the Tools panel, make sure Object Drawing mode is not selected, select the** No color icon ⊘ **for the stroke, then select** #FFFFFF (white) **for the fill**

TROUBLE
Make sure the Unlock Constrain icon 🔒 is active on the Properties panel.

2. **Create an** oval, **adjust the Selection width to** 110 **and the Selection height to** 40, **then place it near the top of the Stage with an X value of** 448 **and a Y value to** 33

3. **Create a** copy **of the oval, set its X value to** 505 **and its Y value to** 8.5, **create another** copy **of the oval, set its X value to** 512 **and its Y value to** 27, **then click the in the** work area
   The composite shape resembles a fluffy cloud, as shown in Figure D-27.

QUICK TIP
You can quickly see which frame is selected by looking at the current frame indicator.

4. **Select and copy the** cloud shape, **click** frame 147 **in the cloud shape tween layer, click** Insert **on the Menu bar, point to** Timeline, **then click** Blank Keyframe
   Because a shape tween requires two separate shapes, you must insert a blank keyframe before you create the ending shape. First you paste and reposition the cloud so it will appear to move across the Stage.

5. **Paste the** cloud shape **at frame 147, select it on the Stage if necessary, then set the X value to** –72 **and the Y value to** 8.5
   The cloud is now on the left side of the Stage, so the shape will move across the sky as it morphs. Next, you modify its ending appearance.

QUICK TIP
You can use a shape created by the Shape tools in Merge Drawing or Object Drawing, or you can use other vector objects in a shape tween.

6. **Show the** Transform panel, **make sure the** Unlock Constrain icon 🔒 **is selected, set the Scale Height to** 78%, **click the** Skew option button, **set the Skew Horizontal to** –68, **then compare your screen to Figure D-28**
   The cloud's ending shape looks flattened. Now you're ready to create the shape tween.

7. **Click in the** frame span **on the cloud shape tween layer, click** Insert **on the Menu bar, then click** Shape Tween
   The tween span turns green, indicating a shape tween. When you test the movie, you will see the cloud morph from fluffy to flattened as it moves from right to left across the Stage.

8. **Test the movie, compare your screen to Figure D-29, lock the** cloud shape tween layer, **then save and close the document**

Understanding and fixing tweening errors

You may discover that an animation it is not working properly or at all because you have not followed the rules for creating that particular animation. In some cases, Flash will prompt you for the fix, such as to convert an object to a symbol if you are trying to apply a motion tween to a shape. When created properly, a successful motion tween layer is blue and has diamond-shaped property keyframes, a shape tween layer is green and has a solid arrow, and a classic tween layer is purple with a solid arrow. If you break a rule, the tween will show as a dotted or dashed line instead, or the property keyframe in a motion tween will be a

circle, indicating that the tween is broken. To fix a broken shape tween or classic tween, check that you have added an ending keyframe. For a shape tween, also make sure that the ending object is a drawing object. If you added a symbol instead, you can apply the shape tween, but it will be broken and the top of the Properties panel will display a Mixed type icon. The easiest way to fix the tween is to click the symbol in the ending keyframe and then click the Break Apart command on the Modify menu. When you fix a broken tween, the line changes to a solid arrow.

FIGURE D-27: **Creating a cloud shape**

Shape composed of three ovals

Timeline | Motion Editor

logo

cloud shape tween

clouds

FIGURE D-28: **Transforming an object in a shape tween**

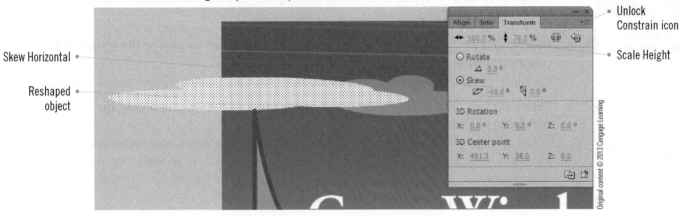

Skew Horizontal

Reshaped object

Unlock Constrain icon

Scale Height

FIGURE D-29: **Viewing a shape tween**

End tweened shape

Creating Animation

Using Shape Hints

Sometimes the way a shape morphs in Flash looks awkward or unrealistic. You can correct the appearance of a shape tween using shape hints. **Shape hints** mark specific points on the beginning and ending shapes in a shape tween that tell Flash how to transition one area into another. The more complex or asymmetrical the shape, the more shape hints you'll need. ▓▓▓ Vanessa has provided you with a shape animation she wants to use in a future movie. You decide to add some shape hints to improve the transitions.

STEPS

1. **Open the file FL D-3.fla from the location where you store your Data Files, save it as GreenWinds_shapehints_FL-D.fla, then test the movie**

   The animation shows a square turning into an "E," but the transition is rough and not particularly attractive. You add shape hints to control how the square morphs into the "E". To use shape hints, you place them on the shape in the first frame, then place them on the corresponding areas in the last frame. You can add new shape hints only in the first frame of the shape tween span.

2. **Click frame 1, click Modify on the Menu bar, point to Shape, then click Add Shape Hint**

   A shape hint lettered "a" appears in the middle of the square. You want to control how the corners morph.

3. **Drag the hint to the upper-left corner of the square**

4. **Repeat Step 2 three times, then drag the hints to the other corners of the square in a counterclockwise direction, as shown in Figure D-31**

   The hints are set in the beginning shape in the first frame. Next, you position the hints in the ending frame.

5. **Click frame 62, drag hint d to the upper-right corner of the "E", then drag the remaining hints so they resemble Figure D-32**

   At first, the hints in frame 62 are stacked on top of each other in the middle of the object in the order in which they were created and are red. When you move them close to their corresponding location in the starting shape, they snap into position and turn green, indicating that they are placed properly.

6. **Test the movie, then compare your screen to Figure D-33**

   The shape tween is much cleaner because you placed the shape hints on the areas you want Flash to preserve.

7. **Save and close the document**

> **QUICK TIP**
> You can also press [Ctrl][Shift][H] (Win) or ⌘[Shift][H] (Mac) to insert a shape hint.

> **QUICK TIP**
> Shape hints work most effectively when arranged in a clockwise or counterclockwise pattern.

> **TROUBLE**
> If the shape hints are not visible on the Stage, click View on the Menu bar, then click Show Shape Hints.

Animating using the Bone tool

You can use the Bone tool 🦴 to create **inverse kinematics (IK)**, or animated poses, to mimic natural movement. You first draw or import one or more objects, convert the objects to a symbol, and then use the Bone tool to click and draw hinged segments in the object(s).

Each segment serves as a bone, with the connections between them acting as hinges or joints. As you move one joint, other segments respond, creating a sense of natural movement. Once you create the bone segments, Flash creates a new layer, known as an Armature or pose layer, which you can then animate using a motion tween. You create a **pose** by adjusting the joints in each keyframe, as shown in Figure D-30.

FIGURE D-30: Viewing multiple armatures

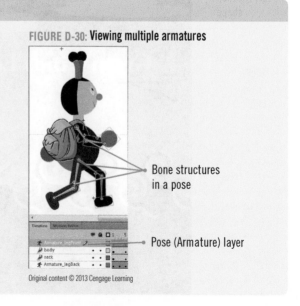

Bone structures in a pose

Pose (Armature) layer

Original content © 2013 Cengage Learning

FIGURE D-31: **Positioning shape hints on the starting shape**

Drag shape
hints to corners

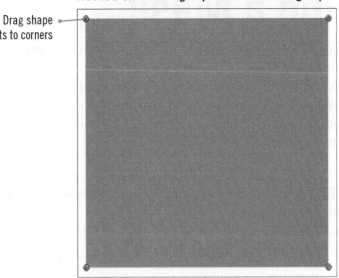

FIGURE D-32: **Positioned shape hints on the ending shape**

FIGURE D-33: **Improved shape tween**

Shape hints
improved transition

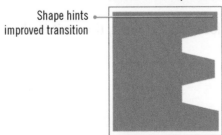

Adjusting IK animation

You can use controls in the Properties panel to control speed, pin a segment, and apply organic movement effects either to the IK as a whole or to individual segments. To adjust the overall movement of an IK animation, select a frame, then adjust the easing using the Strength setting or apply a preset easing from the Type list. To adjust a segment only, click a frame, then click a segment in the IK.

Creating a Mask

For a special transition or special effect that uses the shape of one object to reveal content in another shape, you can create a mask. A **mask** on one layer exposes content on the layer directly beneath it, but only within the confines of a particular shape. To create this type of animation, you first add content to the **masked layer**, the layer that will be revealed by the mask. Next, you create a shape on the **mask layer**, the layer above, through which content will be viewed. ◄▒▒▒▒ Vanessa has asked you to liven up an online ad. You decide to use a simple mask to enhance the animation.

QUICK TIP
You can choose any color for a mask shape; including transparency allows you to see exactly where to position the mask.

1. **Open the file FL D-4.fla from the location where you store your Data Files, then save it as GreenWinds_mask_FL-D.fla**
   In frame 1, the logo, title, and background layers are visible; the turtle layer is not visible until frame 50.

2. **Click frame 50 on the mask shape layer, click the work area, then compare your screen to Figure D-34**
   A transparent oval covers the turtle's face. You'll use this shape as the mask's starting shape. Next, you'll create the mask's ending shape.

QUICK TIP
It's OK if the shape extends into the work area.

3. **Click frame 74 on the mask shape layer, insert a keyframe, click the Free Transform tool 📐 on the Tools panel, then enlarge and shape the oval to completely cover the turtle**

4. **Click anywhere in frame 50–74 frame span, click Insert on the Menu bar, then click Shape Tween**
   The oval mask shape expands over the 24 frames. Next, you create the mask layer.

5. **Click Modify on the Menu bar, point to Timeline, then click Layer Properties**
   The Layer Properties dialog box opens. Here you can select the layer to become the mask or masked layer. You select Mask for the mask shape layer so the turtle will be visible in the oval.

6. **Verify that the Show check box is selected, click the Lock check box to select it, click the Mask option button, compare your dialog box to Figure D-35, then click OK**
   To complete the mask effect, you select the masked layer.

7. **Click the turtle layer, click Modify on the Menu bar, point to Timeline, click Layer Properties, click the Lock check box to select it, click the Masked option button, then click OK**

8. **Scrub the playhead over the shape tween frame span**
   The mask causes the turtle to be gradually revealed within the mask of the expanding oval shape, as shown in Figure D-36.

9. **Test the movie, save and close the document, then exit Flash**

FIGURE D-34: Viewing mask shape

Transparent oval •

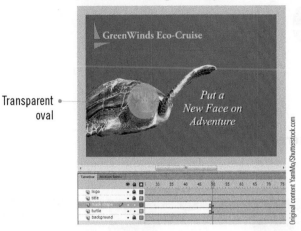

Original content YanMo/Shutterstock.com

FIGURE D-35: Selecting the Mask layer in the Layer Properties dialog box

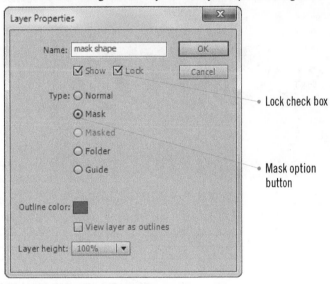

• Lock check box

• Mask option button

FIGURE D-36: Viewing a mask

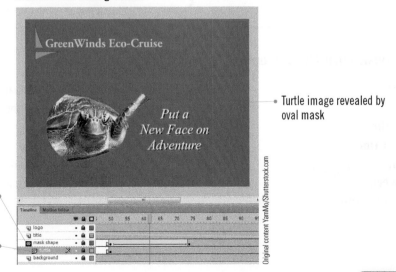

• Turtle image revealed by oval mask

Mask shape layer contains • mask shape that reveals content below

Masked layer contains the • content being masked

Original content YanMo/Shutterstock.com

Creating Animation

Practice

Concepts Review

Label the elements of the Flash screen shown in Figure D-37.

FIGURE D-37

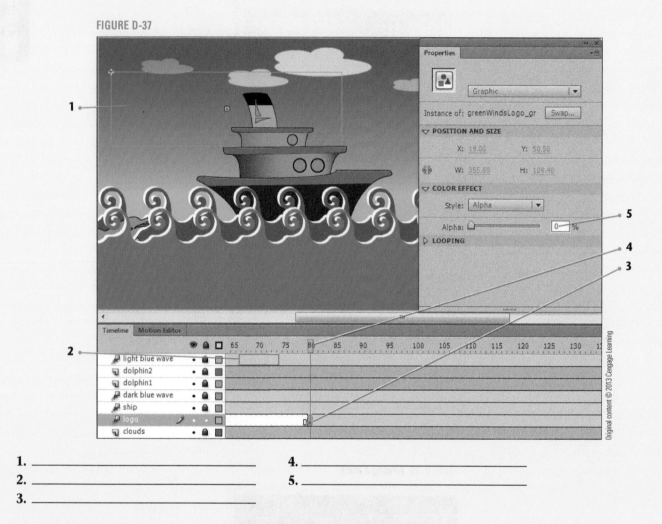

1. _____   4. _____
2. _____   5. _____
3. _____

Match each term with the statement that best describes it.

6. **Shape hint**
7. **Mask**
8. **Nested symbol**
9. **Frame-by-frame animation**
10. **Motion tween**
11. **Property keyframe**

a. Manually creating every frame in an animation
b. A marker used to better control how to morph one shape into another
c. A symbol placed in another symbol
d. Shows a change in color, position, or size
e. Uses the shape of one object in a layer to reveal content in another shape
f. Shows movement or transformation in an animation

Select the best answer from the list of choices.

12. Which animation method does not use symbols?

a. Motion tween

b. Shape tween

c. Frame-by-frame

d. Classic tween

13. What is the main difference between a keyframe and a blank keyframe?

a. Whether the frame contains artwork

b. The color of the tween span

c. Whether the frame contains animation

d. Whether the object is a symbol or a shape

14. Which of the following is *not* associated with changes in a motion tween?

a. Transparency

b. Tint

c. Shape hints

d. Location

15. Which easing value shows an object starting slow and ending fast?

a. 0

b. –100

c. No value

d. 100

16. Which of the following is probably true if an object fades out in a movie?

a. The alpha setting is 0 in the last blank keyframe.

b. The alpha setting is 100 in the last blank keyframe.

c. The alpha setting is 0 in the last keyframe.

d. The alpha setting is 100 in the last keyframe.

Skills Review

1. Understand animation.

a. Describe the role keyframes play in an animation.

b. Explain the difference between frame-by-frame animation and tweened animation.

c. Describe the difference between a motion tween and a shape tween.

2. Use frames.

a. Start Flash, open the file FL D-5.fla from the location where you store your Data Files, then save it as **LightFootRecycling_animation_FL-D.fla**.

b. Unlock the newspaper layer, then using a keyboard command, extend the frame span of the newspaper layer to frame 120.

c. Reduce the frame span of the newspaper layer back to frame 100, then lock the layer.

3. Create a motion tween and a motion path.

a. Unlock the title layer, click frame 1 in the title layer, drag an instance of the title_gr symbol to the Stage, then set the X value to **–230** and the Y value to **38**. (*Hint*: The symbol will extend into in the work area.)

b. Click the title layer's frame span, verify that the title object is selected, create a motion tween, click frame 1, select the instance, then set the alpha setting to **0**.

c. Insert a keyframe in frame 24 of the title layer, select the instance, set the alpha to **100**, then set the X value to **153**.

d. Scrub the playhead over the frames.

e. Test the movie, lock the title layer, then save the document.

4. Copy a motion path.

a. Unlock the plastic bottle 1 layer and the plastic bottle 2 layer.

b. Select the frame span in the plastic bottle 2 layer, then copy the motion.

c. Select the frame span in the plastic bottle 1 layer, then paste the motion.

d. Click frame 100 in the plastic bottle 1 layer, click the plastic bottle object, set the Rotate value to **25°** on the Transform panel, set the X value to **353**, then set the Y value to **240**.

FIGURE D-38

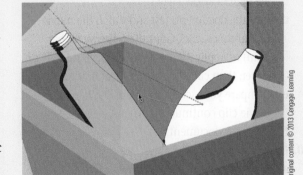

e. Using Figure D-38 as a guide, use the Selection tool to adjust the motion path so it dips down slightly.

f. Test the movie, lock the plastic bottle 2 layer, then save the document.

Skills Review (continued)

5. Use easing.

    a. Click the tween span in the plastic bottle 1 layer, set the Ease in value to **–50**, then test the movie.

    b. Set the Ease in value to **–70**, then test the movie.

    c. Set the Ease out value to **10**, then test the movie.

    d. Lock the plastic bottle 1 layer, then save the document.

6. Create and animate nested symbols.

    a. Create a new layer named **arrow movie clip** above the background layer.

    b. Create a new movie clip symbol named **symbolArrows_mc**. (*Hint*: Use a command on the Insert menu.)

    c. In the symbolArrows_mc editing window, drag an instance of the symbolArrows_gr symbol to the Stage, then set the X value to **0** and the Y value to **0**.

    d. Insert a frame in frame 9, click the frame span, then create a motion tween.

    e. Click frame 9, select the object on the Stage, then rotate the arrows **100°**. (*Hint*: You can use the Transform panel.)

    f. Scrub the playhead across the Timeline, then return to Scene 1.

    g. Click frame 1 in the arrow movie clip layer, then drag an instance of the symbolArrows_mc symbol to the Stage.

    h. Set the X value to **80**, set the Y value to **30**, then change the alpha value to **30%**.

    i. Test the movie, lock the arrow movie clip layer, then save the document.

7. Create frame-by-frame animation.

    a. Unlock the aluminum can layer, then insert a keyframe in frames 82, 88, 94, and 100.

    b. Show the Info panel, select the can instance, then set the values shown in Table D-3 for the aluminum can instance.

    c. Set the rotate value to **25°** in frame 100.

    d. Scrub the playhead across the Timeline. (*Hint*: The motion appears jerky because the animation uses just a few frames. Smooth frame-by-frame animation requires many frames.)

    e. Test the movie, lock the aluminum can layer, then save the document.

TABLE D-3: Frame values

frame	X value	Y value
82	151	232
88	181	238
94	274	248
100	320	270

8. Create a shape tween.

    a. Unlock the big red arrow layer, click frame 29, then click frame 100 to view the starting and ending shapes.

    b. Click the frame span after frame 30 in the big red arrow layer, then create a shape tween.

    c. Test the movie, then save the document.

9. Use shape hints.

    a. Click frame 30 in the big red arrow layer, then add four shape hints to each corner, starting at the upper-left corner of the rectangle and moving clockwise.

    b. Click frame 100 in the same layer, then arrange the shape hints to correspond to their location on the rectangle in frame 30.

    c. Scrub the playhead in the Timeline, then lock the big red arrow layer.

    d. Save the document, test and watch the movie several times, click Control on the Menu bar (Win) or application menu bar (Mac) in the Flash Player, then click Loop to deselect it, if necessary.

    e. Compare your screen to Figure D-39. (*Hint*: The movie clip continues to play.)

    f. Close the document.

10. Create a mask.

    a. Open the file FL D-6.fla from the location where you store your Data Files, then save it as **LightFootRecycling_mask_FL-D.fla.**

FIGURE D-39

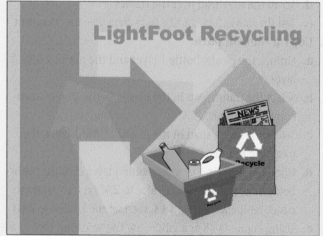

Skills Review (continued)

b. Click frame 48 on the mask layer, insert a keyframe, select the Free Transform tool, then expand the rectangle to the size of the Stage.

c. Click anywhere in the frame span, click Insert on the Menu bar, then click Shape Tween.

d. Click Modify on the Menu bar, point to Timeline, then click Layer Properties.

e. Verify that the Show check box is selected, select the Lock check box, click the Mask option button, then click OK.

f. Click the bottles layer, repeat Step d, verify that the Show check box is selected, select the Lock check box, click the Masked option button, then click OK.

g. Scrub the playhead over the animation, test the movie, then compare your screen to Figure D-40.

h. Save and close the document, then exit Flash.

© 2013 Cengage Learning

Independent Challenge 1

You work at CoasterWoop, an online source of news by, for, and about roller coaster enthusiasts. Your boss would like you to create an animation of a roller coaster. You create a movie clip and a frame-by-frame animation for the movie.

a. Start Flash, open the file FL D-7.fla from the location where you store your Data Files, save it as **CoasterWoop_animation_FL-D.fla**, then show guides, if necessary.

b. In each layer, click frame 35, then insert a frame to extend the movie.

c. Click the pinwheel instance on the Stage, convert it to a movie clip symbol named **pinWheel_mc**, then double-click it.

d. Rename Layer 1 **pinwheel**, create a new layer named **center**, insert a frame in frame 15 of both layers.

e. Click the frame span in the pinwheel layer, then create a motion tween.

f. In the Rotation section of the Properties panel, set the Rotation count to **5**, set Additional Rotation to **30°**, set the Direction to **CW**, then scrub the playhead in the Timeline.

g. Click frame 1 on the center layer, drag an instance of the circle_gr symbol to the middle of the pinwheel, then return to Scene 1.

h. Create a copy of the pinWheel_mc instance on the Stage, drag it on top of the blue pedestal on the right, then hide guides.

FIGURE D-41

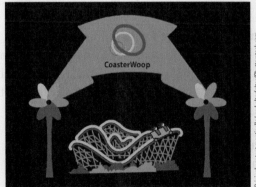

Original content monticello and afterlater/Shutterstock.com

i. Select the car instance on the Stage, click frame 1 on the car layer, zoom in as needed, then create a motion tween that moves the car along the rail. Move the car along the bottom yellow path to the top of the rail on the right. Rotate the car in a frame when appropriate.

j. Click the frame span, then set the ease out to **100**.

k. Test the movie, compare your screen to Figure D-41, save and close the document, then exit Flash.

Independent Challenge 2

As the new program director at Lingoroots, an educational website specializing in linguistics, you're constantly looking for exciting ways to engage new visitors. For the next website feature, you'll compare the evolution of written Chinese across its 4000-year history. The earliest written Chinese characters were pictures and evolved to a more stylized and artistic writing form. You want to show how Chinese calligraphy has changed over time. You complete a movie showing just a few accomplishments of Chinese culture as it relates to Chinese calligraphy.

a. Start Flash, open the file FL D-8.fla from the location where you store your Data Files, then save it as **lingoroots_animation_FL-D.fla**.

b. Unlock the calligraphy title text layer, click the title instance in the work area (above the Stage), open the Motion Presets panel, open the Default Presets folder, scroll down if necessary, click fly-in-top, then click Apply on the panel. (*Hint*: Open the Motion Presets panel from the Window menu. The Apply button may not change color.)

c. Click frame 24 in the calligraphy title text layer, click the title instance on the Stage, then set the Y value to **53**.

d. Click frame 106 in the calligraphy title text layer, insert a frame, lock the layer, then test the movie.

e. Unlock the 868 Block Txt layer, click its frame span between frames 55 and 68, then create a motion tween.

f. Click frame 55, click the 1st printed book instance on the Stage, then set the alpha to **0**.

g. Click frame 67, use the Transform panel to set the scale height and width to **130**, click the instance on the Stage, set the alpha to **100**, set the X value to **193**, set the Y value to **288**, then lock the layer. (*Hint*: Make sure the Constrain icon is locked on the Transform panel.)

h. Unlock the 868 layer, create a motion tween in frames 50 to 59, click frame 59, select the instance, set the scale height and width to **218**, set the X value to **236**, set the Y value to **299**, lock the layer, then test the movie.

i. Unlock the moon characters layer, zoom in the Stage, create a shape tween in frames 82 to 95, scrub the playhead over the frames, then lock the layer.

j. Unlock the mountain characters layer, create a shape tween in frames 76 to 89, scrub the playhead over the frames, then test the movie.

FIGURE D-42

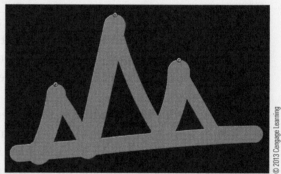

© 2013 Cengage Learning

k. Click frame 76 in the mountain characters layer, use Figure D-42 as a guide, add three shape hints, then position them as shown in the figure.

l. Click frame 90, move the shape hints to their corresponding positions in the current character, then scrub the playhead over the frames. (*Hint*: The shape hints will turn green as they snap into position.)

FIGURE D-43

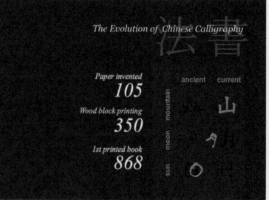

© 2013 Cengage Learning

m. Test the movie, compare your screen to Figure D-43, then lock all layers.

Advanced Challenge Exercise

- Create a new layer named **frame-by-frame animation** above the background layer, then create the frame-by-frame animation of your choice in the movie. Adjust the animation and length as needed.

n. Save and close the document.

o. Exit Flash.

Independent Challenge 3

You work for ibRobotz, an online entertainment site. Users can download ibRobotz characters or create their own to insert in stories. You've been assigned to develop a character for younger users, which you have built using Flash drawing tools. Now you apply animations to the characters.

a. Start Flash, open the file FL D-9.fla from the location where you store your Data Files, then save it as **ibrobotz_animation_FL-D.fla**.

b. Click the frame span for the itzyBOTZ layer, open the Motion Presets panel, scroll down, click wave, click Apply in the panel, then scrub the playhead over the frames.

c. Place the pointer over frame 70 in the itzyBOTZ layer, drag the ending frame to frame 60, then test the movie.

d. Click the ibROBOTZ leg layer, create a shape tween in frames 1 to 29, then test the movie.

e. Click the itzaBug layer, create an instance of the itaBug_gr symbol on the Stage, then create the motion tween or frame-by-frame animation of your choice. Adjust the motion tween as needed.

f. Select the picture_gr instance on the Stage, convert it to a movie clip symbol (give it a unique name), then open the edit symbol Document window.

FIGURE D-44

g. Create a new layer named **shape**, then insert a frame in frame 20 of both layers.

h. Click frame 1 in the shape layer, create one or more shapes of your choice in the artwork, insert a keyframe in the last frame, modify the shapes, then create a shape tween. Add another keyframe in the shape tween span, modify the shapes, then test the movie. (*Hint*: If you use two or more shapes, you must transform them as a group.)

i. Test the movie, compare your screen to Figure D-44 (your shapes will differ), then lock all layers.

Advanced Challenge Exercise

■ Add at least two additional shape tween, motion tween, or frame-by-frame animations to the movie. Copy or create shapes or symbols on new layers as needed. Adjust the animations as needed.

j. Save ibrobotz_animation_FL-D.fla, then save the document as ibrobotz_mask_FL-D.fla.

k. Create a mask for itzyBOTZ or any of the animated instances on the Stage. (*Hint:* You can convert the mask shape to a symbol and create a motion tween.)

l. Include additional layers as multiple masked layers if desired.

m. Delete layers not needed.

n. Test the movie, lock layers, save and close the document, then exit Flash.

Real Life Independent Challenge

This Independent Challenge will continue to build on the personal project that you created in Unit C. Here, you animate shapes and symbols.

a. Start Flash, open your myproject file, then save it as **myproject_animation_FL-D.fla**.

b. Create at least two shape tweens out of shapes or text. (*Hint*: If you use text, you must break it apart twice.)

c. Create at least one motion tween and one frame-by-frame animation. Adjust the animations as needed.

d. Add a mask.

e. Check your document for proper alignment and design consistency.

f. Save and close the document, then exit Flash.

Visual Workshop

Visiting websites is a great way to get inspired for your own projects. Figure D-45 shows a scene from an early animation, *Gertie on tour*. View the animation at the Library of Congress, http://memory.loc.gov/ammem/oahtml/animatTitles01.html. Click the [Gertie on tour - excerpts] link, click the viewing format best suited to your Internet connection speed, then answer the following questions. For each question, include why or how you reached a conclusion. You can open a word processor or use the Text tool in Flash to complete this exercise. When you are finished, write down the URL of the web page you selected in Step d, add your name to the document, save it, print it, then close the word processor or exit Flash. Please check with your instructor for assignment submission instructions.

a. Identify a few frames that appear to be keyframes.

b. Which parts of the animation would you tweak using Flash techniques?

c. Considering that the movie is 1 minute 22 seconds long at 24 fps, there are 1,968 hand-drawn frames in this movie. Would you have pursued a career as a tweener? What is your overall impression of the animation? How does it hold up over nearly 100 years?

d. Go to one of the following websites then answer the following questions about one of the sites you viewed. Be sure to look for sections or links dedicated to Flash sites.
   • www.thefwa.com—Click Search at the right, then search for Flash
   • www.coolwebawards.com—Click Flash Designs in the Winners section

e. Who is the target audience? How does the design (look and feel) of the website and animation fit the target audience?

f. Looking at the animation on the home page:
   • What is animated on this page? Can you guess the kind of animation used?
   • How many animations occur simultaneously?

g. Close your browser.

FIGURE D-45

Optimizing and Publishing a Project

Files You Will Need:

To view a list of files needed for this unit, see the Data Files Grid in the back of the book.

Remember that no matter how informative or entertaining your movie or application, viewers won't stick around to watch it if they have to wait too long for it to load. Fortunately, Flash provides several ways of optimizing elements to reduce loading time while preserving quality. After you finish designing your Flash projects, you can publish them in several formats. The format you choose should suit your goals and be targeted to the viewing audience. For most Flash projects, such as a banner ad, you will want to publish the movie to the web. For other projects, such as applications to run on computers, netbooks, laptops, tablets, smartphones, and TVs, you publish them using Adobe AIR. In addition to publishing the entire movie in a different format, such as a stand-alone projector file, you can export a single frame from a movie and save it in an image file format. 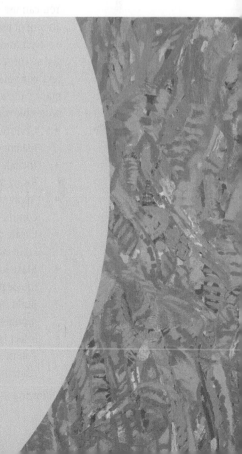 Your boss, Vanessa, asks you to review concepts for making the GreenWinds project accessible, as well as optimize images in the movie, publish it in different formats, and export an image file from a single frame.

OBJECTIVES

Make Flash content accessible

Optimize a movie

Understand publish settings

Publish a movie for the web

Create and export a publish profile

Create a projector file

Export image files

Understand AIR publishing

Making Flash Content Accessible

Flash movies and other applications containing rich media content are compelling because of their dynamic visual and auditory appeal. However, those same components can limit the user experience of those with physical challenges such as visual, hearing, or mobility limitations, or those with cognitive disabilities. Flash projects should be compatible with standard **assistive technologies**, which are used by individuals with disabilities that allows them to interact with the document or perform tasks they might not otherwise be able to do. Creating Flash projects that are accessible reaches more users in your target audience and complies with federal standards. ▓▓▓▓ You want to make sure the ad for GreenWinds can reach as many potential customers as possible. You decide to familiarize yourself with the basics of creating accessible content.

DETAILS

Building in accessibility in a Flash document involves the following:

QUICK TIP

Assistive technologies provide captioning of video and audio content.

- **Incorporate principles of accessible design**
  - Flexibility—Build a user interface that users can customize based on their needs and preferences.
  - Choice of input technique—Make common tasks accessible via keyboard, simple mouse access, or touch-screen controls.
  - Choice of output methods—Allow users to choose alternate outputs of sound, visuals, text, and graphics.
  - Consistency—Ensure the interaction between the Flash content and other applications is consistent and predicable.
  - Compatibility with assistive technology accessibility aids—Build content using standard and common user interface elements that are compatible with accessibility aids, such as screen readers, voice synthesizers, captioning, mouse-free navigation, keyboard commands, magnifier, large text, and so on. Figure E-1 shows the U.S. Department of Education web page on standards and design requirements for assistive technology.

- **Use Flash features to build in accessibility**
  You can use the Accessibility panel, shown in Figure E-2, to prepare individual elements such as dynamic and input text, buttons, and movie clips, or apply accessibility features to an entire Flash application so that a screen reader responds when users navigate the interface. For example, when you label Flash elements by giving them an instance name on the Properties panel, screen readers provide blind users with a descriptive text equivalent for all nontext elements, such as audio, video, graphics, animation, buttons, and image maps. Adobe.com provides Flash designers and builders extensive support and guidelines for creating accessible content. Figure E-3 shows an overview of best practices from Adobe.com.

QUICK TIP

Text equivalents replace the visual image, just as alt text provides a text equivalent describing the functionality in web pages when the user points to or places the mouse over an image or tool.

  - Control the reading order of labeled contents, reduce the file size, apply ActionScript to direct the reading order, or copy a version of the content and place it offstage in an easy-to-read column.
  - Include scalable graphics and magnification so users can zoom in on rich media content without losing quality. Add synchronized narrative audio for large blocks of text.
  - Apply video control skins that support closed-captioning and are easy to see and use. Allow users to control motion.
  - Create customized color swatches with high-contrast color palettes. Users should not have to rely on color alone to interact with content.
  - Make looping elements such as movie clips or movies inaccessible. Screen readers will respond to the movie playing and will start reading at the top of the page.
  - Build in voice and keyboard controls so that users can navigate rich media content using touch- or mouse-free navigation.

QUICK TIP

Some features, such as advanced antialiasing, should not be used for fonts larger than 48 points.

  - Select text based on size requirements. Antialiased text has smoother edges, which is preferred when you need to show text at small sizes. In contrast, antialiased text that is animated is more difficult to read; the Flash Player can turn off antialiasing when text is animated.

Optimizing and Publishing a Project

FIGURE E-1: Assistive Technology web page

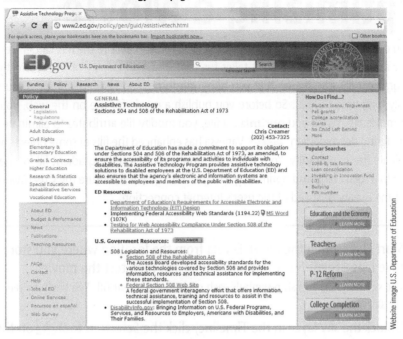

FIGURE E-2: Accessibility panel

Delivers accessibility information to a screen reader

For movie clips; ensures that nested symbol information is delivered to screen reader

Tells Flash to automatically label buttons with nearby text

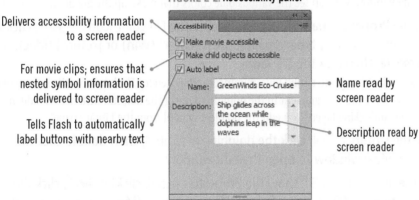

Name read by screen reader

Description read by screen reader

FIGURE E-3: Accessibility best practices web page

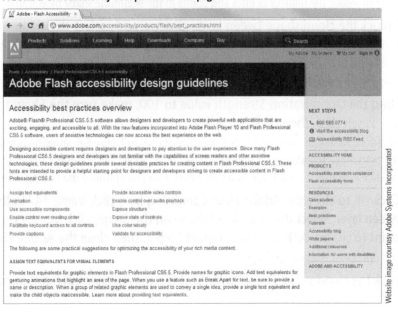

Optimizing and Publishing a Project

Optimizing a Movie

As you create and modify shapes for your movies, you add data to the file. Larger files need more processing power and slow down the time it takes for your movie to display objects correctly in a browser. Shapes with gradient fills and shapes that you have transformed and edited with many curves can take an exceptionally long time to load. So before you publish a movie for use on the web, you should optimize your Flash movie file. When you **optimize** a file, you modify file attributes to eliminate bottlenecks in a given frame during downloading. ▚▚▚▚▚ Vanessa has enhanced the fills of some objects which has increased the overall file size significantly. You reduce file size by replacing the gradient fill for the sky and dolphin symbols with a solid color, and optimizing a shape. Your goal is to ensure the GreenWinds ad plays well regardless of the quality or speed of the user's Internet connection.

STEPS

1. **Start Flash, open the file FL E-1.fla from the location where you store your Data Files, save it as GreenWinds_optimized_FL-E.fla, then test the movie**

   The sky, dolphin, and ship symbols each contain a gradient fill. You begin by removing the gradient from the sky symbol.

TROUBLE
You might need to scroll down to see the sky layer in the Timeline.

2. **Unlock the sky layer in the Timeline, click the Selection tool 🡅 on the Tools panel, then double-click the sky instance on the Stage to open the edit window**

   In the edit window, you can see the various blue colors that make up the gradient, as shown in Figure E-4.

3. **Show the Properties panel if necessary, click the Fill color icon 🖌 ▬▬, click the hexadecimal text box, type #0033FF, press [Enter] (Win) or [return] (Mac), return to the main movie, then lock the sky layer**

   The shape color changes to a solid blue, eliminating the need for Flash to store the intermediary blue colors. Next you remove the gray gradient in the dolphins. One of the dolphin instances is hidden on the Stage, so to save time unlocking layers, you edit the dolphin symbol from the Library panel.

4. **Show the Library panel, click the dolphin_gr symbol, then double-click the thumbnail in the preview window to open the edit window**

5. **Click the gray dolphin fill, show the Properties panel, click 🖌 ▬▬, click the hexadecimal text box, type #999999, press [Enter] (Win) or [return] (Mac), then return to the main movie**

   The dolphins are now a solid gray color. Next, you want to optimize the cloud shape used in the shape tween. You can reduce the number of lines and points in the beginning shape by eliminating some of the curves.

6. **Unlock the cloud shape tween layer, click frame 1, select the cloud shape on the Stage if necessary, click Modify on the Menu bar, point to Shape, then click Optimize**

   The Optimize Curves dialog box opens, as shown in Figure E-5. You can reduce the number of curves in the shape and view optimization results.

QUICK TIP
Select the Preview check box to view the changes to the shape.

7. **Drag the Optimization Strength value to 100, make sure the Show totals message check box is selected, then click OK**

   An Adobe Flash CS6 (Win) dialog box opens, as shown in Figure E-6, showing how many curves remain and the percentage reduction it achieved. Ideally, the changes do not affect the shape's appearance. It's good practice to optimize each shape in a shape tween, so you optimize the ending shape in the last frame.

8. **Click OK to close the Adobe Flash CS6 dialog box, click frame 147 in the cloud shape tween layer, select the final cloud shape on the Stage, click Modify on the Application bar, point to Shape, click Optimize, repeat Step 7, then close the Adobe Flash CS6 dialog box**

   You optimized the ending shape.

9. **Lock the cloud shape tween layer, test the movie, then save the document**

FIGURE E-4: Viewing a gradient fill in a shape

Gradient consists of many
shades of blue

FIGURE E-5: Optimize Curves dialog box

When selected, Flash will display •
optimization results

Click to deselect and view •
original shape

• Set optimization
strength here

FIGURE E-6: Viewing shape optimization results

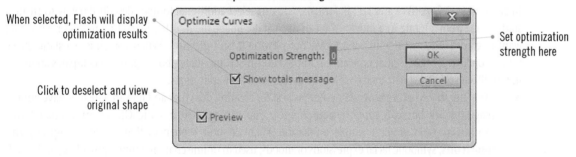

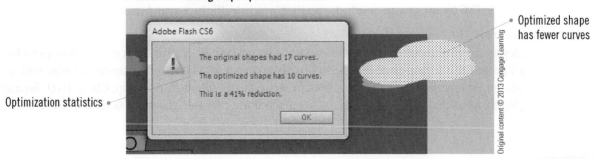

• Optimized shape
has fewer curves

Optimization statistics •

Optimizing and Publishing a Project

Understanding Publish Settings

After you optimize a movie or application file, you are ready to publish it so users can view it as a banner ad or on a mobile device. When you **publish** your movie, you instruct Flash to create the files necessary to display it on the web or deploy it to other platforms. You use the Publish Settings dialog box to choose the desired file format. ████████ Before adjusting settings for the GreenWinds Eco-Cruise project, you review the different types of publish settings and their associated file formats so you can explain them to Vanessa.

DETAILS

When you publish files using the Publish Settings dialog box, you can:

- **Choose output formats**

  You select a publishing file format on the left side of the Publish Settings dialog box, as shown in Figure E-7. On the right, you specify the file name and location Flash will use to publish each file, and adjust options specific to that format. To change the name of the file, click the text box to the right of the file format you selected, and edit the text. To change the destination for the published files, click the Select Publish Destination button ▣ to the right of the selected file format, then navigate to the location you want.

  When you first open the Publish Settings dialog box, the Flash (.swf) and HTML Wrapper formats are selected by default. You learned earlier that SWF files are the output file format for Flash movies. You can export a Flash file as an SWF with or without exporting an HTML file. You can select publishing options to suit your needs. For example, if you created different animation or content on separate layers, you can hide layers and only publish content on visible layers. This allows you to test several different versions of work easily from a single document. To publish an app to a mobile device, TV, or a computer, select a version of AIR, such as AIR 3.2 for Android, or AIR for iOS. Figure E-8 shows the available player target devices for Flash output.

- **Choose still image file formats**

  In addition to default SWF and HTML formats, you can select additional formats described below to create a static image from a frame in a movie. You can use a static image file in other marketing pieces or when you want to go over the main points of a movie but viewing it isn't practical. When you choose a static image format, options for that format type appear in the Publish Settings dialog box. Figure E-9 compares an image in GIF, JPEG, and PNG file formats, which are compressed bitmap formats.

  - **GIF (Graphics Interchange Format)** is best for creating drawings and line art. GIF files have limited image quality but can support transparency. You can publish a static GIF or an animated GIF. **Animated GIFs** support simple animation, such as short sequences that repeat in clip art, and **emoticons**, symbolic facial expressions or moods, used in online chat programs, apps, blogs, and email.
  - **JPEG (Joint Photographic Experts Group)** is a versatile and popular file format for photographs and gradients. JPEGs are used extensively for optimizing images for the web because they maintain their image quality even when they are highly compressed.
  - **PNG (Portable Network Graphics)** file format supports higher-resolution images and transparency. PNG is the native file format in Adobe Fireworks, and for assets used in Android apps. When you publish in PNG format, you can select whether the file includes the background color.

- **Choose stand-alone file formats**

  If you want to distribute your movie to users who may not have Flash Player, you can create a projector file. A **projector** is a stand-alone application that plays a movie without using a computer's browser software or (for Flash projectors) Flash Player. You can play projector files from a desktop, CD, or DVD. Because projector files contain all the data needed to run the movie, they are significantly larger than SWF files.

Optimizing and Publishing a Project

FIGURE E-7: **Publish Settings dialog box**

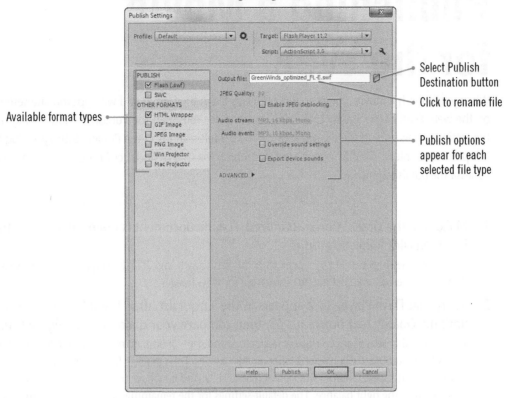

Available format types •

• Select Publish
  Destination button

• Click to rename file

• Publish options
  appear for each
  selected file type

FIGURE E-8: **List of publish targets**

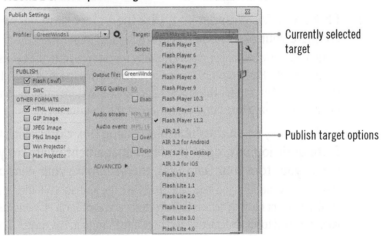

• Currently selected
  target

• Publish target options

FIGURE E-9: **Comparing image file formats**

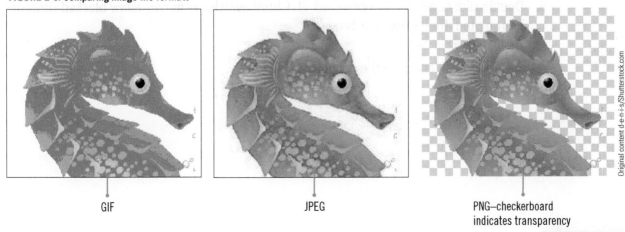

GIF

JPEG

PNG–checkerboard
indicates transparency

Original content d-e-n-i-s/Shutterstock.com

Publishing a Movie for the Web

When you publish a movie, you prepare your Flash file in the format and with appropriate settings for use on the web. Flash makes it easy to publish your movie. You open the Publish Settings dialog box, adjust the settings, then publish the movie. Most of the default settings in the Publish Settings dialog box make this process seamless. ░░░░ You are ready to publish the GreenWinds EcoCruise ad for the web and show Vanessa the published movie.

STEPS

QUICK TIP
You can also press [Ctrl][Shift][F12] (Win) or [option] [Shift][F12] (Mac) to open the Publish Settings dialog box.

1. **Make sure the GreenWinds_optimized_FL-E.fla document is open, click File on the Menu bar, then click Publish Settings**

   The Publish Settings dialog box opens with the Flash (.swf) and HTML Wrapper format types selected by default. You decide to adjust the quality setting for JPEG images.

2. **Verify that Flash Player 11.2 appears in the Target list, drag the JPEG Quality value left until the Quality text box reads 65, then compare your dialog box to Figure E-10**

   The JPEG quality setting affects the image quality—and size—of bitmap images in your document. In general, values between 80 and 100 create higher-quality images. For a smaller file size with often-adequate image quality, try setting the quality value between 50 and 79. You may have to experiment with different settings until you find the right balance. The default settings for the remaining options on the Flash tab are appropriate for the GreenWinds movie.

QUICK TIP
You can also select the Loop check box to have the movie play continuously.

3. **Click the HTML Wrapper text, click the Detect Flash Version check box to select it, then compare your dialog box to Figure E-11**

   Options for HTML Wrapper specify how the movie appears in the browser. Selecting the Detect Flash Version check box tells Flash to prompt users to update their version of Flash Player if necessary to view content in the SWF file. You can set the movie's dimensions so it matches the Stage size, is a fixed pixel width in the monitor, or is sized based on a percentage of the monitor's size.

QUICK TIP
To view your movie in a browser from Flash quickly and as your user will view it, click File on the Menu bar, point to Publish Preview, then click HTML. Flash uses the last settings selected in the Publish Settings dialog box, so HTML must be selected.

4. **Click Publish, when the Publishing dialog box closes, click OK to close the Publish Settings dialog box, open the file management utility for your computer, navigate to where you store your Data Files, then compare your window to Figure E-12**

   Flash creates the files you selected: an HTML file and an SWF file. It also generates the swfobject.js file, a small JavaScript file that detects if the correct version of Flash Player is installed. **JavaScript** is a programming language used to add interactive and dynamic features in web pages. The HTML file inserts the Flash content in the browser. You want to show Vanessa how the movie looks on the web, so you open the HTML file.

5. **Double-click GreenWinds_optimized_FL-E.html, watch the movie, allow blocked content if prompted, then close your browser**

   The movie plays in the browser.

6. **Return to Flash and save the document**

FIGURE E-10: Viewing Flash (.swf) publish settings

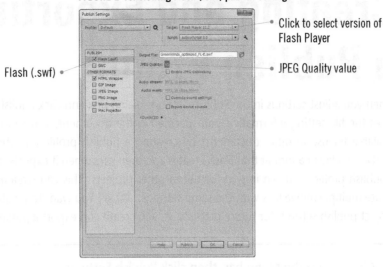

Flash (.swf) •

• Click to select version of Flash Player

• JPEG Quality value

FIGURE E-11: Viewing HTML Wrapper publish settings

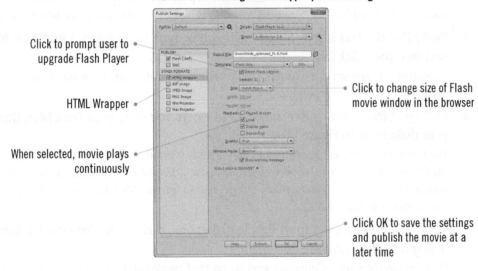

Click to prompt user to upgrade Flash Player •

HTML Wrapper •

When selected, movie plays continuously •

• Click to change size of Flash movie window in the browser

• Click OK to save the settings and publish the movie at a later time

FIGURE E-12: Viewing published files (Win)

Macintosh window will differ •

Your path might differ •

Your browser icon might differ •

Detects current version of Flash Player •

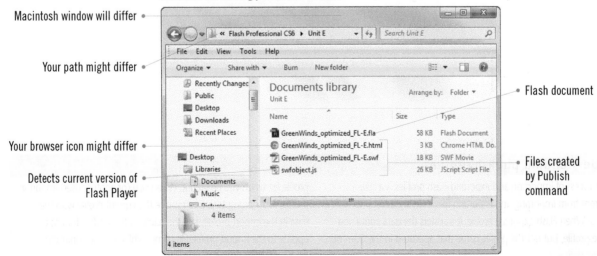

• Flash document

• Files created by Publish command

Creating and Exporting a Publish Profile

When you adjust settings in the Publish Settings dialog box and click Publish or OK, Flash automatically saves the file setting information you specified in the document. You can make these publish settings available for use in other documents by creating a publish profile and then exporting it. A **publish profile** is a file in a format that Flash creates and then uses when it exports data. Once you have created a publish profile, you can import for use in other projects. This can streamline the process you use to create multiple movie files with the same settings. ●●●●● You want to be able to reuse the GreenWinds project publish settings for future projects, so you create and export a publish profile.

STEPS

1. **Click File on the Menu bar, then click Publish Settings**
   The default profile appears at the top of the Profile list in the dialog box.

2. **Click the Profile options button ◙ at the top of the dialog box, then click Create profile**
   The Create New Profile dialog box opens, as shown in Figure E-13. You give the current profile a unique name.

3. **Verify that the text is selected in the text box, type GreenWinds1 in the Profile name text box, then click OK**
   "GreenWinds1" appears as the current profile name in the dialog box. To be able to use the profile in other documents, you need to export it.

QUICK TIP
You can rename the profile in the dialog box if you wish.

4. **Click ◙, click Export profile, navigate to where you store your Data Files, then compare your dialog box to Figure E-14**
   The Export Profile dialog box opens, and the currently selected profile name, GreenWinds1.xml, appears in the File name text box (Win) or Save As text box (Mac). The profile has an .xml extension, indicating that it is an **XML (eXtensible Markup Language)** file, an Internet file format similar to HTML that describes and stores information and data.

5. **Click Save to close the Export Profile dialog box, click OK to close the Publish Settings dialog box, then save the document**
   Flash exports the profile. Colleagues working on the GreenWinds project can now import it after Vanessa provides them with the file location.

6. **Navigate to where you store your Data Files, verify that the XML file is present, then close the file management window**

Understanding publish profiles

The process of importing and exporting Flash profiles is a little different from importing and exporting files in many other programs. When Flash exports a profile, it transfers the data contained in the profile, but not the profile name that appeared in the Current profile list when you created it. When you (or another user) import a profile, Flash prompts you to replace the current profile with the data in the import profile, but the name of the profile does not update to the import profile file name, which can be confusing.

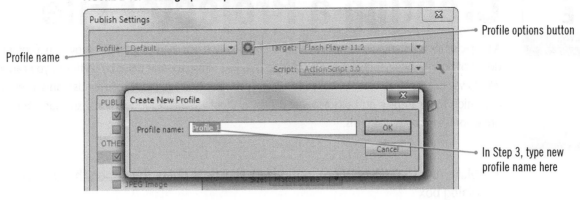

FIGURE E-13: **Creating a publish profile**

Profile name

Profile options button

In Step 3, type new profile name here

FIGURE E-14: **Exporting a profile**

Macintosh Finder will differ

Name of currently selected profile

Creating XML files and XMP metadata

XML files store and transport data in a format accessible by other programs. The XML format allows others to build, modify, and collaborate on projects using shared files by adding **tags** that describe the data; it is an uncompressed version of an FLA file. You can edit individual elements of a project in Flash, then save the file as an XFL file. **XFL** is also a default file format for FLA files. XFL files are uncompressed, incorporate XML, and enable designers and developers to collaborate on Flash projects. Flash automatically creates a series of XML files for project elements. Advanced users can modify an element directly in the XML file—without having Flash installed.

You can embed additional data into a published SWF file, such as digital photograph, video, or audio settings, copyright status, editing history, and other descriptive content. For example, as others work in the file, their changes can be reflected in the XMP data.

Adobe uses the **eXtensible Metadata Platform (XMP)** format, which is metadata able to be indexed by search engines (thus improving the file's placement in search results) and is also viewable in Adobe Bridge. On mobile devices, SWF metadata controls the background color, frame rate, size, and other attributes.

To add XMP data, open the Publish Settings dialog box, click the Flash (*.swf) check box, expand the Advanced section, click the Include XMP metadata check box, then click the Modify XMP metadata for this document button 🔍. A dialog box opens, where you can add content in several categories. Add a title, description, and keywords to improve the content for search engine optimization. You should also set the copyright status and enter the name of the copyright holder in the Copyright Notice section. While adding a copyright notice is not required for a work to be protected, it's always a good idea to add it.

Creating a Projector File

A projector file is a stand-alone, self-running application that lets users play a Flash movie on a computer that does not have browser software or Flash Player installed. Projector files differ by platform; you cannot run a Windows projector on a Mac, or vice versa. ▓▓▓▓ Vanessa tells you that GreenWinds wants a version of the animation that can play on both Macs and PCs, without the need for additional software. You publish a projector file for both platforms.

STEPS

1. **Make sure that GreenWinds_optimized_FL-E.fla is open, then open the** Publish Settings **dialog box**

2. **Click the** Flash (.swf) **and** HTML Wrapper **check boxes to deselect them, click the** Win Projector **check box, then click the** Mac Projector **check box**

   Because the projector file generates the necessary code and files to play the SWF file in the Flash Player, you only need to select the Projector check boxes. You can publish both projector files from either a PC or a Mac, but you can only open the one associated with your computer's platform. See Figure E-16.

3. **Click** Publish, **then when the Publishing dialog box closes, click** OK **to close the Publish Settings dialog box**

   > **TROUBLE**
   > Mac users may not see the .app extension; also, Mac projector files export to a folder on a PC.

4. **Navigate to where you store your Data Files, double-click** GreenWinds_optimized_FL-E.exe **(Win) or** GreenWinds_optimized_FL-E.app **(Mac) to play the file, then close the Flash Player window**

   The movie plays in Flash Player. Notice in your file management utility that the projector file is much larger than the SWF file, as shown in Figure E-17.

5. **Save the document**

Exporting a QuickTime movie

You can export Flash projects to other popular movie formats and easily expand the ways users can access your movie. **QuickTime** is a popular export format because QuickTime movies (.mov) play animation well, and play on both Macintosh and PC computers. QuickTime software comes standard with the Apple operating system, but Windows users who want to play movies in this format may need to download the free QuickTime plug-in from www.apple.com.

To export a Flash movie to the QuickTime format, you must have the latest version of the QuickTime Player installed on your computer. Click File on the Menu bar, point to Export, then click

Export Movie. Select QuickTime as the save as file type, navigate to where you want to save the file, then click Save. In the QuickTime Export Settings dialog box, you can choose whether to include the Stage color or have a transparent background, determine when the movie stops exporting, and where to store temporary data needed to play the movie. Click Export, then wait a few moments for Flash to complete the export. Flash generates a text report listing how QuickTime captured each frame in the animation and alerts you where to view it. QuickTime movies generated from Flash are much larger than the SWF movie, as shown in Figure E-15.

FIGURE E-15: Playing a QuickTime movie

QuickTime Player
window (Win)

Size comparison of
QuickTime and SWF files

FIGURE E-16: **Selecting projector formats**

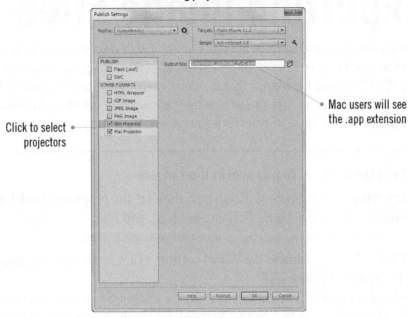

Click to select projectors

Mac users will see the .app extension

FIGURE E-17: **Playing a projector file**

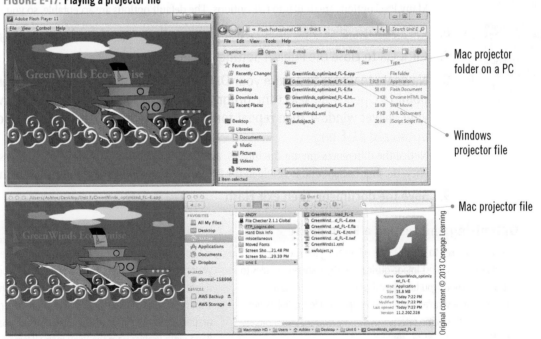

Mac projector folder on a PC

Windows projector file

Mac projector file

Original content © 2013 Cengage Learning

Optimizing and Publishing a Project

Flash 117

Exporting Image Files

If you want to create a static image from your movie, you can export a scene from a single frame or simply export an object to insert in a web page. You can select three image file formats for export: GIF, JPEG, and PNG. Vanessa has learned that the client would like some static images from the GreenWinds animation, but you're not sure exactly how the client wants to use them. To provide the most flexibility, you export a frame in three file types. First you move to the frame you wish to export.

STEPS

1. **Drag the playhead to frame 99 in the Timeline**

2. **Open the Publish Settings dialog box, deselect the projector check boxes, then select only the GIF Image (.gif), JPEG Image (.jpg), and PNG Image (.png) check boxes**
   Options for each graphic type appear when the image type is selected.

> **QUICK TIP**
> Generally, an animated GIF file works best with simple graphics and motion.

3. **Click GIF Image, expand the Colors section, examine the options, then compare your dialog box to Figure E-18**
   GIF options focus on color, but they also offer the possibility of exporting an animated GIF file, by clicking the Playback list arrow, then clicking Animated. You can also select whether you want areas of the image to be transparent. The default options are acceptable, so next you view the options for JPEG files.

> **QUICK TIP**
> You can export an image with limited adjustable settings by clicking File on the Menu bar, pointing to Export, clicking Export Image, and then selecting a format.

4. **Click JPEG Image, examine the options, then compare your dialog box to Figure E-19**
   In addition to size and quality options, you can select Progressive, which will load the JPEG image incrementally in a browser. Users will see the image gradually improve as it loads, instead of seeing nothing until the entire image appears. The default options are acceptable, so you view the options for PNG files.

5. **Click PNG Image, then examine the options**
   Many PNG options are similar to GIF options. The default options are acceptable, so you're ready to publish.

> **TROUBLE**
> Flash publishes PNG files with a transparent background even if you select a background color in the Flash document.

6. **Click Publish, click JPEG Image, click Publish, then repeat for the GIF Image**

7. **Click OK to close the Publish Settings dialog box**

8. **Navigate to where you store your Data Files, right-click GreenWinds_optimized_FL-E.gif, point to Open with, select the program you want to preview the images with, close your viewer window, then repeat for GreenWinds_optimized_FL-E.jpg and GreenWinds_optimized_FL-E.png**
   Notice the differences among the images, as shown in Figure E-20. Although PNG files support transparency, the blue background is visible in the PNG file because it is a shape in the Flash document.

9. **Save the document, then exit Flash**

Optimizing and testing a Flash movie

In general, the key to optimization is balancing file size and download time against image quality, but there are no set rules to follow. The actions you take vary depending on your movie contents. Some simple optimization steps include the following:

- Reduce the frame rate.
- Use symbols.
- Optimize and resize bitmap images before importing them.
- Replace gradient fills with solid colors.
- Use alpha transparency sparingly.
- Use tween animation instead of frame-by-frame animation.
- Compress sound files.
- Use solid lines created with the Pencil tool.

For more advanced options that perform a technical test of your movie, you can simulate the download experience users might have using the Download Settings and Simulate Download commands on the View menu in the Flash Player. To view a graphical representation of each frame's download time, open the Bandwidth Profiler from the View menu. Here you can view how much content loads in each frame. To further analyze movie data, open the Publish Settings dialog box, click Flash (.swf), expand the Advanced section, click the Generate size report check box, click Publish, then open the .txt report file. The report lists the size of each frame, shape, text, sound, video, and ActionScript script by frame.

FIGURE E-18: GIF Image options

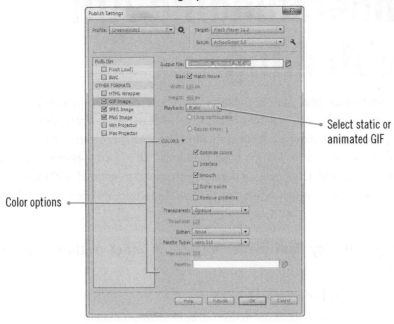

Color options ●——

—— Select static or
animated GIF

FIGURE E-19: JPEG Image options

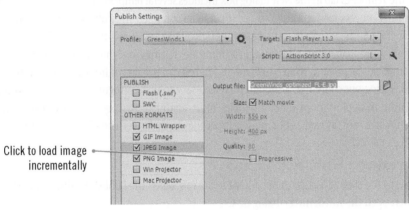

Click to load image ●——
incrementally

FIGURE E-20: Viewing GIF, JPEG, and PNG image files

GIF   JPEG   PNG

Optimizing and Publishing a Project

Understanding AIR Publishing

So far, you've seen how you can publish Flash files to be viewed in a browser as an SWF file. For smart phones and other devices, you must publish Flash files so they can play without a browser. For these applications, you use the **Adobe Integrated Runtime (AIR)** program, designed to deploy the rich media content you've created in Flash on other platforms. AIR is a cross-platform application for viewing Flash content on a PC or Mac computer or deploying an app to an Android or iOS mobile device. ▓▓▓ Vanessa asks you for an overview of how she can incorporate apps for mobile devices in her marketing plan.

DETAILS

When you deploy flash movies for use on other platforms, you should understand how to:

QUICK TIP
To create an AIR application for a TV, desktop, or laptop, select the AIR option in the Target list or the File, New menu.

- **Create apps for mobile devices**

  Creating applications for mobile devices can be more time-consuming than creating a simple SWF. For example, the coding and content rendering requirements for the best-selling Android or iPad games are quite complex. However, you can create Flash documents whose publish settings are set for AIR, AIR for Android or AIR for iOS applications, which simplifies the process. You can create either document using the File, New menu. Additionally, the Templates tab in the New dialog box includes several templates for AIR for Android documents.

  The publishing process for apps is also more involved. First, open the Publish Settings dialog box, select the appropriate target, then click the Player Settings button 🔧, as shown in Figure E-21.

  For Android apps, you must add or adjust multiple settings on the General, Deployment, Icons, Permissions, and Languages tabs, shown in Figure E-22. You can test an Android app on a mobile device that you've connected to your computer, although it is necessary to first configure the device for testing.

  Users wanting to deploy to an iPhone or iPad must complete settings on the General, Deployment, Icons, and Languages tabs, as well as obtain developer files from Apple. The AIR for iOS Settings dialog box is shown in Figure E-23.

- **Convert an existing Flash file to an app**

  You can convert a file created as a Flash document to an app. Open the Publish Settings dialog box, select an AIR target, then open the AIR Settings dialog box.

  In Adobe AIR, you can use FLV video files as source files, which allows the video to be embedded, streamed, or downloaded progressively. You learn more about working with video in Unit F.

- **AIR support**

  Adobe AIR supports the following mobile systems:
  - Android™ 2.2, 2.3, 3.0, 3.1, 3.2, and 4.0
  - iOS 4.2 and higher

Understanding rich media publishing

Certain methodology and processes are crucial when deciding how or whether you should use rich media for your projects, whether they are web-, desktop-, or mobile-based. Consider the need and user benefit of including interactive and 3D elements, audio, video, complex information, and transitions, as well as cross-platform issues. You should rely on the contract, design specifications, and overall expectations you have with your client. Your analysis, interpretation, and recommendations should be clear and documented.

Be sure to build in testing for the various playback environments users will experience, such as target playback devices, mobile and desktop operating systems, screen size and resolution, web browsers, and connectivity speed.

FIGURE E-21: Opening Player Settings in the Publish Settings dialog box

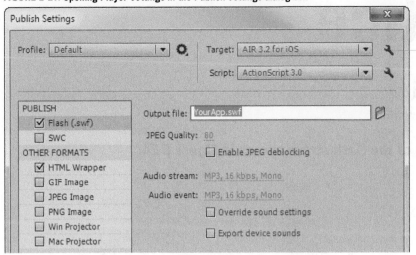

Player Settings button

FIGURE E-22: Viewing AIR for Android Settings dialog box

Settings tabs

FIGURE E-23: Viewing AIR for iOS Settings dialog box

Settings tabs

Optimizing and Publishing a Project

Practice

Concepts Review

Label the elements of the Flash screen shown in Figure E-24.

FIGURE E-24

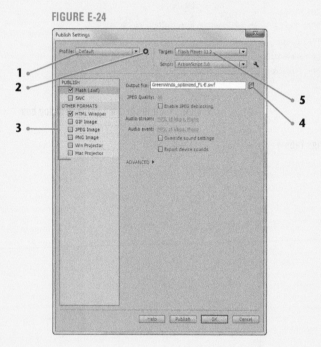

1. _____   4. _____
2. _____   5. _____
3. _____

Match each term with the statement that best describes it.

6. **Projector file**   **a.** Two or more colors that blend together in a pattern
7. **Publish profile**   **b.** Stand-alone application that can play a Flash movie
8. **Gradient**   **c.** To reduce file size while maintaining an acceptable level of quality
9. **AIR**   **d.** Publish settings saved in an XML file
10. **Optimize**   **e.** Image file format that can support transparency and high quality
11. **PNG**   **f.** Runtime selection for publishing Flash movies that do not play in a browser

Select the best answer from the list of choices.

12. **Which of the following is not a file extension for a static image file type?**
    a. .xml   **c.** .png
    b. .gif   **d.** .jpg
13. **Which are the default file types for publishing a movie to the web?**
    a. XML and MOV   **c.** SWF and HTML
    b. HTML and XML   **d.** SWF and MOV

14. Which of the following is necessary to run a projector file?

 a. Web browser

 b. Flash Player

 c. Tablet or smartphone

 d. CD or DVD

15. Which of the following is not an action you can take to make a movie accessible?

 a. Control the reading order of labeled content.

 b. Create color swatches in high-contrast colors.

 c. Add unsynchronized narrative for long text blocks.

 d. Allow users to control motion for video.

16. Which of the following is *not* an available format you can publish using Flash?

 a. AIR

 b. EXE or APP

 c. JPG

 d. MP3

Skills Review

1. Make Flash content accessible.

 a. Explain how assistive technologies can help you reach more users.

 b. List three items for which a screen reader can provide a text equivalent.

 c. List three outputs that users should be able to choose alternate methods.

2. Optimize a movie.

 a. Start Flash, open the file FL E-2.fla from the location where you store your Data Files, save it as **LightFootRecycling_optimized_FL-E.fla**, then test the movie.

 b. Change the frame rate in the Timeline to 12 fps.

 c. Unlock the background layer, select the diamond shape (called square_gr) behind the bag, change the alpha to **100%**, then lock the layer.

 d. Unlock the arrow movie clip layer, select the arrows instance on the Stage, then change the alpha to 100%.

 e. Open the symbolArrows_mc edit window, then double-click the symbol on the Stage to open the symbolArrows_gr edit window.

 f. Select the three arrows if necessary, click the Fill Color icon on the Properties panel, click the hexadecimal text box, then change the color to **#FFD300** in the color pop-up window.

 g. Return to the main movie, lock the layer, then move the arrow movie clip layer to the bottom of the Timeline.

 h. Test the movie, then save the document.

3. Understand publish settings.

 a. Describe the process of publishing in Flash.

 b. List the three image file formats you can use to publish an image, and describe what they publish.

 c. Explain why you would want to use a projector file to show a Flash movie.

4. Publish a movie for the web.

 a. Use a command on the File menu to open the Publish Settings dialog box.

 b. Set the JPEG quality to **60**.

 c. Show options for HTML Wrapper, select the Detect Flash Version check box, publish the movie, then close the Publish Settings dialog box.

 d. Navigate to where you store your Data Files, then view the LightFootRecycling_optimized__FL-E.html file in a browser.

 e. Close your browser, then save the document.

5. Create and export a publish profile.

 a. Open the Publish Settings dialog box.

 b. Use a command on the Profile options menu to create a new profile named **Lightfoot1**.

 c. Use a command on the Profile options menu to export the profile to where you store your Data Files.

 d. Close the Publish Settings dialog box, then save the document.

 e. Verify that the .xml file was created and stored in your Data Files location.

Skills Review (continued)

6. Create a projector file.

   a. Open the Publish Settings dialog box.

   b. Select only the projector check boxes, publish the movie, then close the Publish Settings dialog box.

   c. Navigate to where you store your Data Files, then play the projector file applicable to your operating system.

   d. Close Flash Player, then save the document.

7. Export image files.

   a. Drag the playhead to frame 100.

   b. Open the Publish Settings dialog box.

   c. Select only the GIF Image, JPEG Image, and PNG Image check boxes.

   d. Change the JPEG quality to **100**, and accept default settings for the Gif and PNG images.

   e. Publish the images, then close the Publish Settings dialog box.

   f. Navigate to where you store your Data Files, preview the image files, compare your screens to Figure E-25 (note that the background color of your PNG file may differ), then close the viewer windows.

   g. Save and close the document, then exit Flash.

FIGURE E-25

  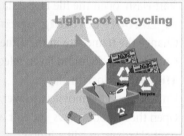

© 2013 Cengage Learning

Independent Challenge 1

You work at CoasterWoop, an online source of news by, for, and about roller coaster enthusiasts. You've animated and enhanced the appearance of several objects in the movie. Now your boss asks that you optimize the movie as much as possible and export static image files from a frame in the movie.

   a. Start Flash, open the file FL E-3.fla from the location where you store your Data Files, then save it as **CoasterWoop_optimized_FL-E.fla**.

   b. Test the movie, change the frame rate to **12 fps**, then test the movie.

   c. Unlock the entrance layer, then open the sign_gr symbol in an edit window.

   d. Select the light blue sign shape, change the color from a gradient to **#00CBFF**, return to the main movie, then lock the entrance layer.

   e. Unlock the background layer, then select the rounded shape on the lower half of the Stage.

   f. Change the color of the shape fill to **#000066**, lock the background layer, then test the movie.

   g. Open the Publish Settings dialog box, select the Flash (.swf) and HTML Wrapper check boxes if necessary, select HTML Wrapper, detect the Flash version, click the Size list arrow, click Percent, type **40** in the Width and Height text boxes, then publish the movie.

   h. Navigate to where you store your Data Files, then view the CoasterWoop_optimized_FL-E.html file in a browser.

   i. Use the Publish Settings dialog box to publish a JPEG image of frame 20 using the default settings, view the JPEG file, compare your screen to Figure E-26, then close the view window.

   j. Save and close the document, then exit Flash.

FIGURE E-26

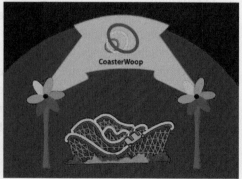

© 2013 Cengage Learning

Independent Challenge 2

As the new Program Director at Lingoroots, an educational website specializing in linguistics, you're constantly looking for exciting ways to engage new visitors. For the next feature, you'll compare the evolution of written Chinese across its 4,000-year history. The earliest written Chinese characters were pictures and evolved to a more stylized and artistic writing form. You want to show how Chinese calligraphy has changed over time. You completed a movie showing just a few accomplishments of Chinese culture and Chinese calligraphy, but now you want to optimize it so the greatest number of users can view it regardless of their computer or platform.

a. Start Flash, open the file FL E-4.fla from the location where you store your Data Files, then save it as **lingoroots_optimized_FL-E.fla**.

b. Unlock the calligraphy title text layer, click frame 1, click the instance in the work area above the Stage to select it, set the alpha to **100%**, then lock the layer.

c. Unlock the background layer, double-click the large Chinese characters to open the Group edit window, then select the characters. (*Hint*: Use the Selection tool to draw a selection box around the characters.)

d. Open the Fill color pop-up window, set the alpha to **100** and the color to **#660000**, then return to the main movie.

FIGURE E-27

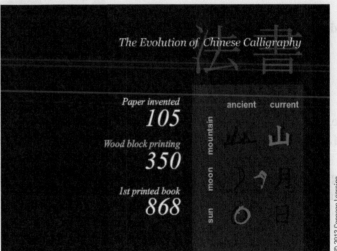

© 2013 Cengage Learning

e. Select the rectangle on the Stage, open the Fill color pop-up window, set the alpha to 100 and the color to **#330000**, then lock the background layer.

f. Unlock the text layer, shift-click to select the sun, moon, mountain, ancient, and current text boxes on the rectangle on the Stage, open the Text (fill) color pop-up window, set the alpha to 100, set the color to **#CCCCCC**, lock the text layer, then test the movie.

g. Open the Publish Settings dialog box, select the Flash (.swf) and HTML Wrapper check boxes if necessary, publish the movie, then close the Publish Settings dialog box.

h. Navigate to where you store your Data Files, view the lingoroots_optimized_FL-E.html file in a browser, then close the browser.

i. Use the Publish Settings dialog box to publish a GIF image of frame 89, view the GIF file, compare your screen to Figure E-27, then close the view window.

j. Use the Publish Settings dialog box to publish a projector for the computer platform you use, navigate to the location where you store your Data Files, play the projector file, then close the Flash Player if necessary.

k. Save the document.

Advanced Challenge Exercise

■ Publish a JPEG image of the frame of your choice, then preview the image file. Experiment with different quality settings until you find the lowest setting that generates an acceptable image. (*Hint*: Unless you save the JPEG with a unique name, Flash replaces the JPEG file each time you publish it.)

■ Create a publish profile named **lingoroots_JPEG**, then export the profile to the location where you store your Data Files.

l. Close the document, then exit Flash.

Independent Challenge 3

You work for ibRobotz, an online entertainment site. Users can download ibRobotz characters or create their own to insert in stories. You've been assigned to optimize the movie and publish image files users can download to their computers.

a. Start Flash, open the file FL E-5.fla from the location where you store your Data Files, then save it as **ibrobotz_optimized_FL-E.fla**.

FIGURE E-28

b. Test the movie, change the frame rate to **12 fps** test the movie again, then change the frame rate back to **24 fps**.

c. Unlock the furnishings layer, double-click a stem instance to open an edit window of stem_gr, then select any stem of the yellow flower. (*Hint*: Zoom in as needed.)

d. Using the Optimize command on the Modify, Shape menu, set the Optimization strength to **100** in the Optimize Curves dialog box, then click OK.

e. Note the number of fewer curves and the percentage of curve reduction, then return to the main movie.

f. Double-click the flower pot instance to open a symbol edit window, double-click the bottom of the pot to open the Drawing Object edit window, then click the bottom pot object to select it.

g. Set the color in the Fill color pop-up window to **#FF6532**, then return to the flowerPot_gr edit window.

h. Double-click the pot rim object to open a Drawing Object edit window, click the pot rim object to select it, set the color in the Fill color pop-up window to **#FEB998**, return to the main movie, then lock the furnishings layer. (*Hint: You won't see the color change until you return to the main movie.*)

i. Test the movie, publish the movie to the web using default settings, view the HTML file in a browser, then close the browser.

j. Publish a static GIF image of frame 27 using default settings, view the image, compare your image to the sample shown Figure E-28, then close the view window.

k. Keep the same frame selected, open the Publish Settings dialog box, select JPEG Image as the format, change the JPEG file name to **ibrobotz_optimized_JPEG60_FL-E.jpg**, set the JPEG quality to **60**, then publish the image. (*Hint*: Click the file name in the Output file text box, then type changes.)

l. Change the quality to 100, change the JPEG file name to **ibrobotz_optimized_JPEG100_FL-E.jpg**, then publish the image and close the Publish Settings dialog box.

m. Compare the three images, then save the document.

Advanced Challenge Exercise

- Export two publish profiles named **ibrobotz_JPEG60_ACE_FL-E.xml** and **ibrobotz_JPEG100_ACE_FL-E.xml**, respectively, to your Data Files location for the JPEG images you created in Step k and Step l above. (*Hint*: Reset the quality settings as needed.)

n. Close the document, then exit Flash.

Real Life Independent Challenge

This Independent Challenge will continue to build on the personal project that you have been developing since Unit B. Here, you optimize the movie, and publish and export files.

a. Start Flash, open your myproject file, then save it as **myproject_optimized_FL-E.fla**.

b. Use the skills you learned in this unit to optimize the frame rate, tweens, curves, and colors in your movie. Test the movie.

c. Publish the movie to the web, choose a setting to detect the Flash version, then adjust the settings as needed.

d. Publish at least one frame in the file format of your choice, adjusting settings as needed.

e. Create a projector or QuickTime movie.

f. Deselect all objects, open the Accessibility panel from the Window, Other Panels menu, then add a name and description for the movie on the panel.

g. Save and close the document, then exit Flash.

Visual Workshop

Visiting websites is a great way to get inspired for your own projects. Figure E-29 shows the home page for NASA's Global Climate Change website. View the page at http://climate.nasa.gov/. Click several items on the page, then answer the following questions. For each question, include why or how you reached a conclusion. You can open a word processor or use the Text tool in Flash to complete this exercise. When you are finished, add your name to the document, save it, print it, then close the word processor or exit Flash. Please check with your instructor for assignment submission instructions.

a. What is the website's purpose and goal?

b. Who is the target audience? How does the design (look and feel) of the website fit the target audience?

c. Did the site indicate which version of Flash Player users needed?

d. Which components of the animations would you optimize?

e. How many viewing formats were available? Could you download a movie? If so, how large was it?

f. Looking at the animation in the introduction and on the home page:

- What is animated on this page? Can you guess the kind of animation used?

- How many animations occur simultaneously?

- What is your overall opinion of the design, organization, and function of this page? How would you improve it?

g. Close your browser.

FIGURE E-29

Website image NASA/JPL-Caltech

Integrating Content with Other CS6 Programs

🛑 ***This unit assumes you have Fireworks CS6, Photoshop CS6, Dreamweaver CS6, and Illustrator CS6 installed on your computer, and understand how to start the programs.***

When you create a Flash project, you often work with a team using media in different programs. In this unit, you'll see how Flash content interacts with other programs in the Adobe Creative Suite 6, specifically Adobe Flash, Adobe Fireworks, Adobe Photoshop, Adobe Dreamweaver, and Adobe Illustrator to create graphics, animation, apps, and web pages. You will also explore the issue of copyright law and publicly available material. The marketing team at GreenWinds Eco-Cruise wants to explore how they can use other Adobe products with their Flash movie. You first need to review the concept of integration. Then you can import and edit media from Fireworks and Photoshop, insert and edit a movie from Dreamweaver, import artwork from Illustrator, and review concepts related to copyright law.

OBJECTIVES

Understand Flash integration

Import a Fireworks PNG file into Flash

Use roundtrip editing

Import a Photoshop PSD file into Flash

Edit a Photoshop image from Flash

Insert a Flash movie into Dreamweaver

Edit a Flash movie from Dreamweaver

Import an Illustrator AI file into Flash

Understand copyright

Understanding CS6 Integration

As you have seen from your own projects and from exploring the web throughout this book, Flash projects rarely stand alone; they usually rely on the other Adobe Creative Suite 6 programs to supply them with graphic objects and give them context. Flash animations consist of graphics in various formats and are usually part of a larger project, such as a mobile app or web page. ▓▓▓▓▓ Vanessa asks you for an overview of how to integrate Flash movies with other Adobe Creative Suite 6 programs.

DETAILS

When you use Flash projects with other Adobe programs, you should understand how to:

- **Integrate files**

  To create and use content effectively, you should know how Adobe Creative Suite 6 (CS6) program files can work together to create powerful visual experiences for your users. **Integration** is the process of combining elements from other programs into Flash and incorporating Flash animations into elements such as movies or apps, that can be used for other purposes. Figure H-1 shows a NASA website about the Hubble Telescope that incorporates objects created in Fireworks, Flash, Dreamweaver, and other programs in CS6, including Adobe Premiere Pro, Illustrator, and Bridge.

- **Use Adobe programs together**

  You can create graphics and illustrations for your Flash movies in conjunction with the following programs, as shown in Figure H-2:

  - **Adobe Fireworks** lets you create and edit bitmap and vector images, as well as create web page prototypes, which are models of what a web page should look like. When you import a Fireworks image into Flash, it becomes a noneditable bitmap image. However, you can use roundtrip editing (described below) to modify layers in Fireworks.
  - **Adobe Photoshop** lets you create bitmap images in which you can manipulate practically every aspect of their appearance. After you customize an image, you can import the layered Photoshop PSD file into Flash, where you can specify how you want it to appear.
  - **Adobe Illustrator** lets you design and edit vector graphics, which are best for detailed graphic designs, illustrations, logos—any graphic that needs to be resized and still maintain its clarity.
  - **Adobe Dreamweaver** lets you create web pages in several different file formats, such as XHTML, HTML, HTML5, JavaScript, CSS, or XML. You can place a Flash animation on a Dreamweaver web page or save it as its own HTML document, as you did in Unit E.

  To create original art and manipulate photos in these Adobe programs, you would need to know how to use each one. But even if you only understand Flash basics, you can still import and edit objects that were created using those programs.

- **Use roundtrip editing**

  You may find that after you create an object such as a graphic or an animation and place it in another program, you then want to change it. Instead of deleting the imported object, changing it in its original application, and reimporting it, you can use **roundtrip editing**, meaning that you can edit the imported item within Flash using the tools of the program that created it. Because editing is a frequent and usual part of creating animations and web pages, roundtrip editing can save you considerable time during the course of a project.

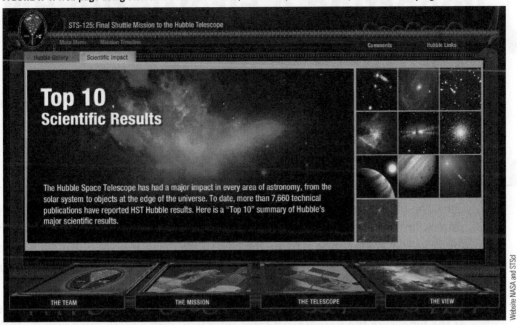

Website NASA and STScI

FIGURE H-2: How you can integrate CS6 programs

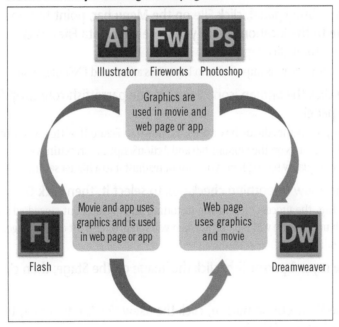

Understanding usability testing

To build a successful Flash project, you'll need to understand what it's like to interact with your project as a new user. A best practice is to analyze feedback from how real users in your target audience interact with your website or interactive Flash project. Often, usability testing involves a user performing several tasks while sitting down with a trained observer who may take notes, but not explain how to do something. A typical test plan involves developing a plan, identifying the user audience, obtaining test participants, testing, analyzing results, and finally, implementing the results into your project. Test results can show you what is or is not working, how easy it is for users to perform tasks, how they use interactive elements, even how they feel while interacting with your project. Users' feedback, which can be recorded as a video or completed through a questionnaire, provides invaluable information you can use to improve the user interface, and thus interest and approval from your target audience.

Importing a Fireworks PNG File into Flash

Designers often use Fireworks PNG files in Flash documents. You can import the image as a single **flattened bitmap**, which compresses all layers into a single layer. ▓▓▓▓ You want to import an image in the PNG format into a new movie in Flash. You're not sure if you'll be able to edit it in Flash or Fireworks, so you first import the image in Flash.

STEPS

1. **Open the file management utility for your computer, navigate to the location where you store your Data Files, click the file** parrotfish.fw.png, **copy and paste a copy of the file in the Data Files folder, then rename the copied file** parrotfish-roundtrip.fw_FL-H.png

   You work with a copy of the Data File so you can preserve the original if you need it later or want to redo the steps.

2. **Start Flash, click** File **on the Menu bar, click** New, **make sure ActionScript 3.0 is selected as the type, click the** Background color color box, **click a** black color swatch, **click** OK, **then save the document as** parrotfish_FW-layers_FL-H.fla **in the location where you store your Data Files**

   > **QUICK TIP**
   > You can also press [Ctrl][R] (Win) or [⌘][R] (Mac) to open the Import dialog box.

3. **Click the** Library panel, **click** File **on the Menu bar, point to** Import, **click** Import to Stage, **navigate to the location where you store your Data Files, click** parrotfish-roundtrip.fw_FL-H.png, **then click** Open

   The parrot fish image is imported into Layer 1 as a flattened PNG file, as shown in Figure H-3.

4. **Double-click the** bitmap icon ▓ **next to the parrotfish-roundtrip.fw_FL-H.png file in the Library panel**

   The Bitmap Properties dialog box opens, as shown in Figure H-4. Here you can apply different compression and quality settings on the Options tab and ActionScript export settings on the ActionScript tab. Note that if you set a low quality setting here, you cannot readjust it to a higher setting in the Publish Settings dialog box.

5. **Click the** Allow smoothing check box **to select it, then click** OK

   Smoothing, the process of reducing distortion and evening out jagged edges in a bitmap image, ensures that the bitmap image will look good when you rotate or resize it on the Stage. The Bitmap Properties dialog box closes.

6. **Rename Layer 1** parrot fish, **click the** image on the Stage, **then click the** Transform panel icon ▣

7. **Click the** Skew option button, **click the** Skew Vertical text box, **type 1, then press** [Enter] (Win) **or** [return] (Mac)

8. **Click the** work area, **then compare your screen to Figure H-5**

9. **Save and close the document**

Working with Adobe Fireworks

Fireworks is a graphics program intended specifically for images and media for the web and other devices. The program includes powerful vector and bitmap tools that allow you to work with multiple objects on a single layer, and is an integral component of Adobe Creative Suite 6. Fireworks is perfectly suited to prototyping a website, layout, or app, and optimizing graphics and designs created in other applications. For example, a page in Fireworks stores all the layers in a document. You can create multiple **pages** in a document that have variations on common elements, such as a different color, or you can create new pages that store only certain layers.

FIGURE H-3: Imported Fireworks PNG file

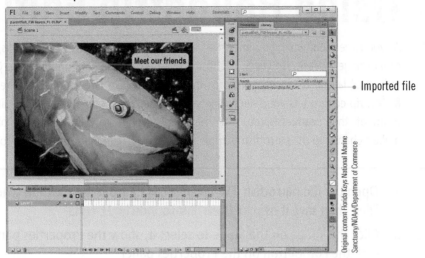

Imported file

Original content Florida Keys National Marine Sanctuary/NOAA/Department of Commerce

FIGURE H-4: Bitmap properties dialog box

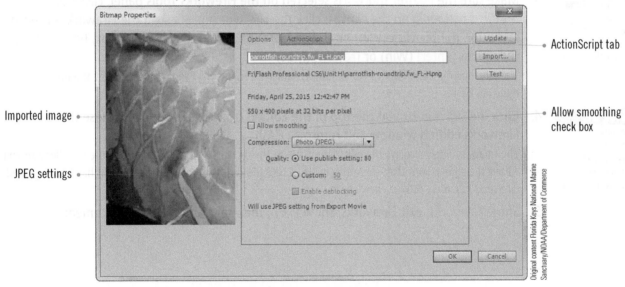

ActionScript tab

Imported image

JPEG settings

Allow smoothing check box

Original content Florida Keys National Marine Sanctuary/NOAA/Department of Commerce

FIGURE H-5: Viewing image edited in Flash

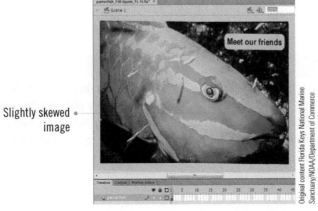

Slightly skewed image

Original content Florida Keys National Marine Sanctuary/NOAA/Department of Commerce

Using Roundtrip Editing

As you have seen, when you import a flattened bitmap image from Fireworks, you can modify it like any other image in Flash. However, because you import it as a flattened bitmap, you cannot edit content on individual layers; to do so, you must instead open it in Fireworks using the roundtrip editing feature. Roundtrip editing lets you select a file you've inserted in one application, edit that file in its native environment, then seamlessly return to the open program to view the edited object. ▰▰▰ You need to make a change to the parrotfish graphic, and decide to use roundtrip editing to make the edit in Fireworks.

If Fireworks is not selected as the default PNG image editor, follow the instructions in the Selecting an image editor sidebar below.

1. Open the file parrotfish_FW-layers_FL-H.fla from the location where you store your Data Files, then save it as parrotfish_FW-roundtrip_FL-H.fla

2. Click the image on the Stage to select it, show the Properties panel if necessary, then click the Edit button on the Properties panel

The image opens in a Fireworks editing window, as shown in Figure H-6. The Fireworks interface has features similar to Flash. You change the color of the rectangle using tools on the Fireworks Property inspector at the bottom of the screen.

The Pointer tool ▸ in Fireworks operates similar to the Selection tool ▸ in Flash.

3. Make sure the Pointer tool ▸ is selected on the Fireworks Tools panel, click the gray rounded rectangle on the canvas, click the Fill color box ▨ on the Fireworks Property inspector, double-click (Win) or click (Mac) the value in the HEX text box, type #FFD24D, then press [Enter] (Win) or [return] (Mac)

The rectangle fill color changes to yellow, as shown in Figure H-7. You're done editing the image, so you return to Flash.

The Property inspector in Fireworks is similar to the Properties panel in Flash.

4. Click the Done button at the top of the Editing from Flash window to close the Fireworks editing window and return to Flash

The image in Flash displays the edits you made to the rectangle fill, as shown in Figure H-8. Because you edited the source parrotfish-roundtrip.fw_FL-H.png file directly in Fireworks, it, too, has been updated. Fireworks remains open, so you close it.

5. Show Fireworks, exit Fireworks, show Flash, then save and close the document

---

Selecting an image editor

You can use either Fireworks or Photoshop as the default image editor for image files. By default, Photoshop edits PNG files. To select a different image editor, select the image on the Stage, right-click (Win) or [control]-click (Mac) the image, then click Edit with. In the Select External Editor dialog box, navigate to the location where you store your Adobe CS6 program files, click the program's .exe file, then click Open.

To always edit in Fireworks, right-click (Win) or [control]-click (Mac) the image, then click Edit with Fireworks (Win) or Edit with Fireworks CS6 (Mac). Note that when editing in Fireworks, you might be prompted to open a JPEG as a PNG.

FIGURE H-6: Viewing the roundtrip editing window in Fireworks

Pointer tool

Roundtrip editing window features

Property inspector

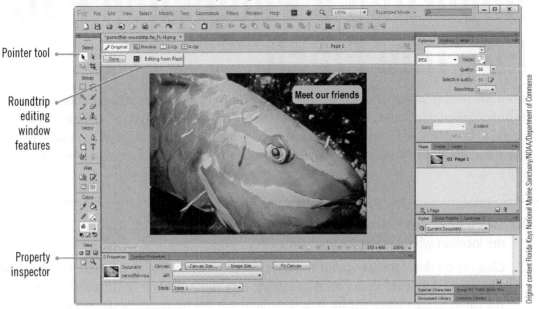

FIGURE H-7: Modifying the fill color of an object in Fireworks

Done button

New fill color

Fill color box

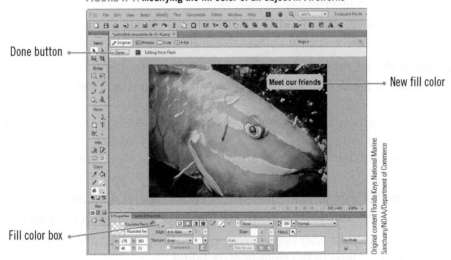

FIGURE H-8: Viewing the Fireworks-edited image in Flash

Updated image

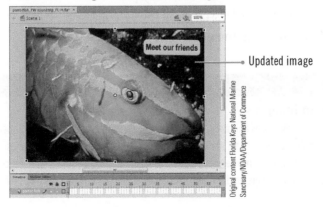

Importing a Photoshop PSD File into Flash

When you need to include photographs in your projects, you can easily incorporate Photoshop images. When you import a Photoshop PSD file into Flash, you can choose which layers to include and whether the layers will be editable in Flash. You can also set import preferences for Photoshop files in the Preferences dialog box. ▨▨▨ The marketing department has created a new logo for a river cruise. You import the file into Flash.

STEPS

1. **Start a new** ActionScript 3.0 **file, then save the new file as** china_rivers_PS_FL-H.fla **in the location where you store your Data Files**

2. **Click** File **on the Menu bar, point to** Import, **click** Import to Stage, **navigate to the location where you store your Data Files if necessary, click** china_rivers.psd, **then click** Open

The Import to Stage dialog box for Photoshop opens and lists the objects in the PSD file, as shown in Figure H-9. The name of the file you're importing appears in the title bar. Here you can select which layers to import and specific options for each layer type. You can choose whether the Photoshop layers are imported as layers or keyframes in Flash, and whether the Stage should resize to the size of the Photoshop image. You view the options for different layers.

3. **Click each** layer **and view the options for each one**

Each graphic layer is set to be imported as a flattened bitmap image, which is what Vanessa wants.

4. **Select the** Set stage size to resize to same size as Photoshop canvas **check box at the bottom of the dialog box, click** OK **to import the image, show the** Library, **then click the work area**

The china_rivers.psd file is imported into several layers in the Timeline, and a folder named china_rivers.psd Assets appears in the Library panel, as shown in Figure H-10. Because you chose not to retain editability by importing each layer of the image as a flattened bitmap, you can delete two layers from the imported image and the original Layer 1 layer as they no longer affect the appearance of the object.

5. **Click the** MASK **layer in the Timeline, press and hold [Ctrl] (Win) or ⌘ (Mac), click the** Shape 5 **layer, click** Layer 1, **then click the** Delete button 🗑 **at the bottom of the Timeline**

6. **Click the** Expand folder icon ▶ **next to the china_rivers.psd Assets folder in the Library, then click** ▶ **next to the Dragon mask folder**

All objects in the Library panel are visible.

7. **Press and hold [Ctrl] (Win) or ⌘ (Mac), click the** MASK **and** Shape 5 **objects, then click** 🗑 **at the bottom of the Library panel**

The document no longer contains extraneous objects that may increase file size, as shown in Figure H-11.

8. **Save and close the document**

Design Matters

Animating bitmap images

Animating a bitmap image is as easy as animating a vector image, but beginning Flash animators should always remember the effect an animated bitmap image has on the movie or app's performance. Even after you optimize a bitmap image, and the file's overall file size seems acceptable, performance can suffer because of the data load in individual frames. As you learned in Unit E, it's good practice to experiment with the compression settings for JPEG images to understand the trade-off between quality and performance.

FIGURE H-9: Import to Stage dialog box (Photoshop)

Click name to view
layer import options

Click to exclude layer
from importing

Click to reset
Stage size to
image size

Click to
select how
layers import

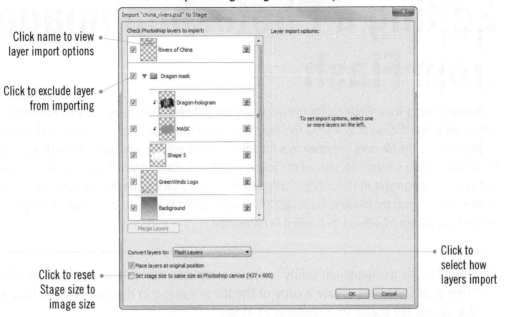

FIGURE H-10: Viewing an image and layers imported from Photoshop

Imported image

Imported
folder in
Library Panel

Imported layers
in Timeline

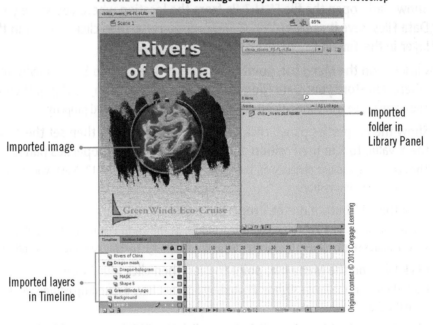

FIGURE H-11: Viewing imported image edited in Flash

Objects
deleted from
folder in the
Library

Layers deleted
from the
Timeline

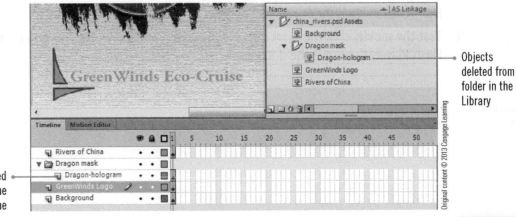

Editing a Photoshop Image from Flash

Roundtrip editing from Flash to Photoshop is slightly different than from Flash to Fireworks. You can import an image file, such as a JPEG file, that was created in Photoshop into Flash and then edit it in Photoshop, but the file does not open in a roundtrip-specific editing window in Photoshop; it opens in a Photoshop editing window. So, instead of clicking the Done button, as you do in Fireworks, you must save and close the document in Photoshop. Flash updates the changes automatically in the image when you continue working on the movie in Flash. ▓▓▓▓ Vanessa would like you to insert a new background image for the GreenWinds movie and then edit it in Photoshop.

STEPS

1. **Open the file management utility for your computer, navigate to the location where you store your Data Files, create a copy of the file ocean.jpg in the same folder, then rename the copied file ocean_PS-roundtrip_FL-H.jpg**
   You work with a copy of the Data File so you can preserve the original.

2. **Show Flash, open the file FL H-1.fla from the location where you store your Data Files, save it as GreenWinds_imports_FL-H.fla, then click frame 1 in the ocean layer in the Timeline**

3. **Click File on the Menu bar, point to Import, click Import to Stage, navigate to the location where you store your Data Files, click ocean_PS-roundtrip_FL-H.jpg, then click Open**
   The ocean image is imported directly to the Stage, but it is not aligned properly.

4. **Show the Properties panel, click the image on the Stage, then set the X value to 0 and the Y value to 0 in the Position and Size section of the Properties panel**
   The ocean image aligns perfectly on the Stage, as shown in Figure H-12. Next, you use roundtrip editing to open the file in Photoshop.

5. **Click the Edit button on the Properties panel**
   The image opens in a Photoshop editing window, as shown in Figure H-13. The Photoshop interface has some features similar to Flash. You decide to blur the image to remove some of its graininess.

6. **Click Filter on the Menu bar, point to Blur, then click Blur More**
   Photoshop blurs the image slightly. Photoshop does not have a roundtrip editing window, so you save and close the file.

7. **Click File on the Menu bar, click Close, click Yes (Win) or Save (Mac) to save your changes, then exit Photoshop**
   Photoshop closes, and the changes to the image appear in Flash.

8. **Test the movie, click the Start button, compare your screen to Figure H-14, close the Flash Player, then save the document**

FIGURE H-12: **Viewing imported and aligned image**

Imported ocean photo

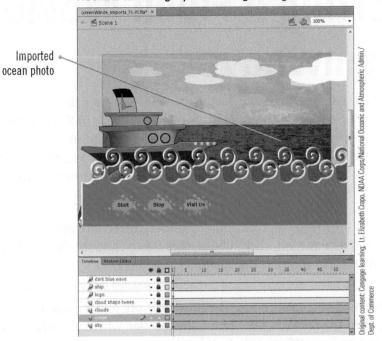

Original content: Cengage learning. Lt. Elizabeth Crapo, NOAA Corps/National Oceanic and Atmospheric Admin./
Dept. of Commerce

FIGURE H-13: **Viewing image in Photoshop**

Menu bar (Win)

Filter menu

Original content Lt. Elizabeth Crapo, NOAA Corps/National Oceanic and
Atmospheric Administration/Department of Commerce

FIGURE H-14: **Viewing Photoshop-edited image in Flash**

Edited image with blur filter

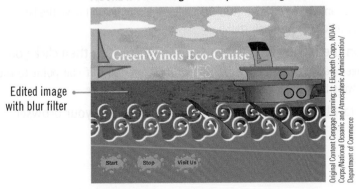

GreenWinds Eco-Cruise

Start   Stop   Visit Us

Original Content Cengage Learning. Lt. Elizabeth Crapo, NOAA
Corps/National Oceanic and Atmospheric Administration/
Department of Commerce

Integrating Content with Other CS6 Programs

Inserting a Flash Movie into Dreamweaver

As you use Dreamweaver to design web pages, you will often want to include Flash movies. You can insert a Flash movie in a Dreamweaver document as part of an existing HTML document or as its own web page in an HTML document. You need to publish the Flash movie to an SWF file before you insert it in Dreamweaver. Vanessa wants to show management how versatile Flash movies can be in Dreamweaver. She asks you to insert the GreenWinds movie in a Dreamweaver web page.

STEPS

1. **Click File on the Menu bar, click Publish Settings, make sure only the Flash (.swf) check box is selected on the left, click Publish, click OK to close the Publish Settings dialog box, then save and close the document**

   Now that you've published the SWF file, it is ready to be inserted into a Dreamweaver document.

2. **Start Dreamweaver, create a new Dreamweaver site folder named GreenWinds if desired, open the file FL H-2.html from the location where you store your Data Files, then save it as GreenWinds_DW_FL-H.html**

   An HTML document opens with a blue background, as shown in Figure H-15. To insert the movie, you can set the insertion point at the desired location in the document. In this document, the insertion point is already set to the top center, which is perfect for this project.

3. **Click Insert on the Menu bar, point to Media, click SWF, navigate to the location where you store your Data Files, click GreenWinds_imports_FL-H.swf, then click OK (Win) or Open (Mac)**

4. **Type GreenWinds Movie in the Title text box of the Object Tag Accessibility Attributes dialog box, then click OK to close the dialog box**

   Screen readers will be able to read this object title. Also, the title text will appear in your browser when a user moves the mouse pointer over any part of the movie. A placeholder for the SWF file appears in the document, and options and information specific to the placeholder appear on the Property inspector, as shown in Figure H-16. You can play the Flash movie in Dreamweaver using controls on the Property inspector.

   TROUBLE
   Mac users will not see a Play button on the Property inspector.

5. **Click the Play button on the Properties panel, click the Start button in the movie, watch the movie for a few seconds, then click the Stop button on the Property inspector**

   Clicking the Play button on the Property inspector opens the Flash Player in Dreamweaver. It doesn't play the movie if buttons have ActionScript to control that action; clicking the Stop button on the Properties panel closes the Flash Player. The movie plays with fully functional buttons in the HTML document.

6. **Click File on the Menu bar, click Save, then click OK in the Copy Dependent Files dialog box**

   Flash saves the two dependent files, expressInstall.swf and swfobject_modified.js, to a Scripts folder in the site folder location where you store your Data Files. If a user doesn't have the latest version of Flash Player installed, they'll be prompted to install it.

   TROUBLE
   If the SWF doesn't play properly, open the Publish Settings dialog box, click the Publish Target list arrow, then click Flash Player 10.3.

7. **Click File on the Menu bar, point to Preview in Browser, then click your default browser**

   The web page opens in your browser, as shown in Figure H-17. If you point to the movie, a ScreenTip appears, showing the title you assigned to the movie in Step 4 above.

8. **Click the Start button, click the Stop button, then close your browser**

FIGURE H-15: Viewing an HTML document in Dreamweaver

Flash movie will be inserted here

Blank HTML document

Your path will differ

Your folders might differ

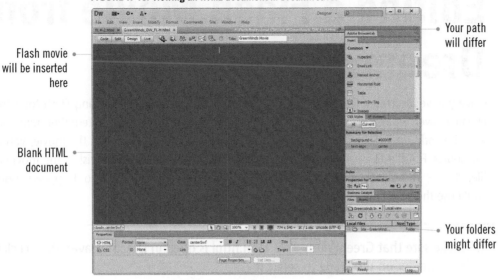

FIGURE H-16: Viewing a selected Flash placeholder

Insert menu

Selected Flash movie placeholder

SWF file name

Click to edit movie in Flash

Click to play movie in Dreamweaver

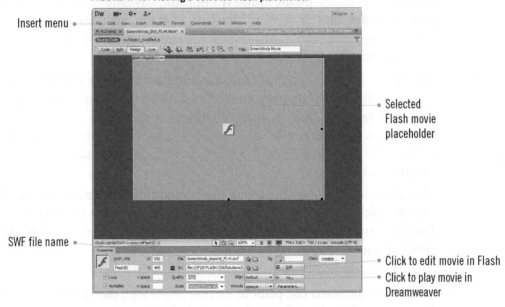

FIGURE H-17: Previewing a Flash movie in a web page

Movie title

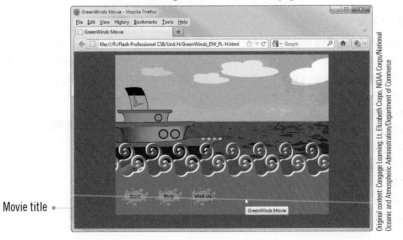

Original content: Cengage Learning; Lt. Elizabeth Crapo, NOAA Corps/National Oceanic and Atmospheric Administration/Department of Commerce

Integrating Content with Other CS6 Programs

Editing a Flash Movie from Dreamweaver

Once you've inserted a Flash movie into Dreamweaver, you can edit it using Flash tools from within Dreamweaver. Flash and Dreamweaver have the same roundtrip editing integration functions as Flash and Fireworks. In Dreamweaver, you insert a published SWF file; so to edit the movie, you first locate the source FLA file to open it in Flash. Dreamweaver automatically republishes the movie as an SWF file. You decide to convert the bitmap image to a vector image so it appears more stylized. You'll use the trace bitmap feature to accomplish this.

STEPS

1. **Make sure that GreenWinds_DW_FL-H.html is open in Dreamweaver, then click the placeholder on the Stage to select it**

   Options for the placeholder appear on the Property inspector. You want to edit the movie in Flash, so you use the roundtrip editing feature.

2. **Click the Edit button on the Property inspector, navigate to the location where you store your Data Files, click GreenWinds_imports_FL-H.fla, then click Open**

   The movie opens in a roundtrip editing window in Flash, as shown in Figure H-19. You decide to edit the ocean image to make it less realistic.

TROUBLE

Depending on the size of the image, rendering a bitmap image to a vector image requires significant processing power from your computer.

3. **Click the ocean image on the Stage, move to frame 1 in the Timeline if necessary, click Modify on the Menu bar, point to Bitmap, click Trace Bitmap, type 50 in the Color Threshold text box, click OK, then click the work area**

   Flash converts the ocean bitmap image to a vector image, which matches the overall design, as shown in Figure H-20. You're satisfied with its appearance and are ready to return to Dreamweaver to preview the web page in a browser.

4. **Click the Done button at the top of the Editing from Dreamweaver roundtrip editing window, click the movie placeholder in Dreamweaver, click the Play button on the Property inspector, click the Start button, click the Stop button on the movie, then compare your screen to Figure H-21**

   Flash automatically republished the SWF movie.

5. **Click File on the Menu bar, point to Preview in Browser, click your default browser, click the Start button, then close all open browser windows**

6. **Close GreenWinds_DW_FL-H.html and FL H-2.html in Dreamweaver, then exit Dreamweaver**

Swapping a bitmap image

If you have two or more images or symbols in a document, you can swap one image or symbol (technically, its instance) for another right on the Stage. **Swapping** substitutes a new image or instance in the same location along with its attributes, such as size, color, or button states. If you have applied an animation to one instance and then swap it with another, the swapped-out instance has the animation applied to it, instead. To swap an object, select it on the Stage, then click the Swap button on the Properties panel. The Swap Symbol or Swap Bitmap dialog box opens, shown in Figure H-18, depending on the object selected. You can swap an object with any other similar object in the Library:

a symbol with a symbol (either graphic, button, or movie), or a bitmap image with another bitmap image. You can also duplicate a symbol in the Swap Symbol dialog box, which is a great time-saver if you need to modify the same symbol many times in a movie.

FIGURE H-18: **Swap Bitmap dialog box**

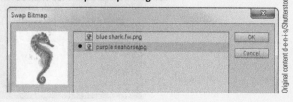

FIGURE H-19: Viewing the Flash roundtrip editing window

Roundtrip
editing window
features

FIGURE H-20: Viewing results of Trace Bitmap command

Modify menu

Ocean bitmap
converted to
vector shapes

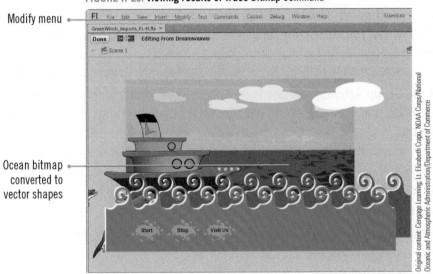

FIGURE H-21: Previewing edited Flash movie in Dreamweaver

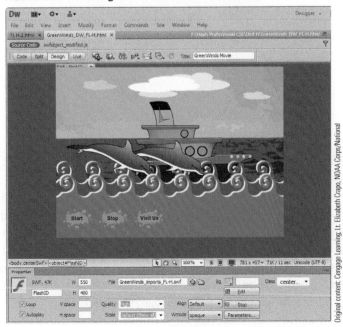

Importing an Illustrator AI File into Flash

If you plan to import many Illustrator files into Flash, you can customize import settings in the AI File Importer category of the Preferences dialog box. For example, you can select default options for text, import paths, images, groups, and layers. When you import a file, you can further specify which layers you want to remain editable and other options. ▰▰▰▰ You begin work on an activities project for kids by importing an Illustrator file into Flash. You decide to use the default AI import preferences but customize how this individual file is imported into your Flash document.

STEPS

1. **Open the file** FL H-3.fla **from the location where you store your Data Files, then save it as** sea_ponies_FL-H.fla

2. **Click** File **on the Menu bar, point to** Import, **click** Import to Stage, **navigate to the location where you store your Data Files, click** sea ponies.ai, **then click** Open

   The Import to Stage dialog box for Illustrator opens. Here you can select which layers you want to remain editable, how to import to Flash layers, and whether to import the entire image as a single bitmap image.

QUICK TIP

You can also copy artwork in Illustrator and paste it into Flash.

3. **Click the** Group Activities for Sea Pony Sailors layer, **then compare your dialog box to Figure H-22; make any necessary changes so that your settings match those in the dialog box**

   Import options for the selected layer appear on the right. For text layers, the Editable text option is selected by default.

4. **Click** OK, **compare your screen to Figure H-23, then click the** work area

   The artwork is selected, and you can see individual elements are selectable. You want to edit the text block.

5. **Click the** Text tool T **on the Tools panel, select the** text block, **type** Sea Pony Adventures, **then click the** work area

   The text block is changed. See Figure H-24.

6. **Save and close the document, then exit Flash**

Importing and exporting Illustrator AI files

Adobe Illustrator is a highly sophisticated and feature-rich vector drawing program, so conflicts can sometimes occur when importing an AI file into other programs. If settings in an AI file have compatibility issues with Flash, an Incompatibility Report button appears in the Import to Stage dialog box. Click the button to view the report and recommended fix. For example, a common incompatibility might be the color mode. Because Illustrator is used for print projects, the color mode is set to CMYK (cyan, magenta, yellow,

black) by default instead of RGB (red, green blue), the color mode used for computers, mobile phones, and similar screens. Simply set the color mode to RGB in Illustrator, then reimport the file into Flash.

Once you've adjusted artwork in Flash, you can export all the elements on the Stage or just a selected element as an .fxg file that you can open and edit in Illustrator. Select the artwork on the Stage, click File on the Menu bar, point to Export, select an option, then click Save.

FIGURE H-22: Import to Stage dialog box (Illustrator)

Text import options

Selected layer remains editable

In Step 3, make sure this option is selected

Click to select how layers import

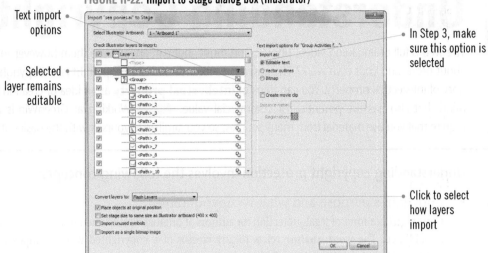

FIGURE H-23: Viewing imported Illustrator AI artwork

Imported art is editable

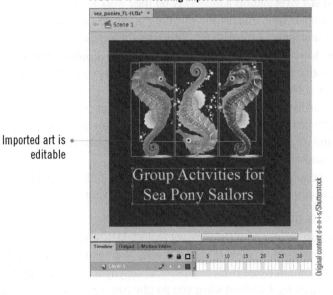

FIGURE H-24: Edited text

Integrating Content with Other CS6 Programs

Understanding Copyright

The web is full of engaging video, photos, and music, but can anyone use them however they wish? What about protecting your own work? The answers lie in understanding copyright law. Copyright law is a category of intellectual property. You can think of **intellectual property** as an idea or creation from a human mind that also has the potential for commercial value. ▓▓▓▓ Working at GreenWinds Eco-Cruise will require that you use material from many sources, so you familiarize yourself with the basics of copyright law.

DETAILS

Understanding copyright protection involves the following concepts:

QUICK TIP

The familiar copyright notice, "©2013 Cengage Learning" or "Copyright 2013 Cengage Learning," is not required to show that your work is protected, but it's always a good idea to include it.

- **Copyright's purpose and what is copyrightable**

  Copyright is a form of legal protection for authors of original works, whether those works are published or unpublished. The word **author** refers to any creator of a copyrighted work—composer, photographer, writer, or Flash animator. Copyright law gives authors exclusive rights to control how their work can be used, and it protects literary works, music, books, movies, art, dance, and computer code, among others.

  Purpose. The purpose of copyright law is to balance the interests of authors with the interests of the public. Copyright law gives authors a monopoly on their work for a set amount of time, but the law also dissolves that monopoly by eventually allowing the work to be accessed by the public, which presumably would build upon and improve the work for the progress of society.

  Copyright law defines copyrighted works as "original works of authorship fixed in any tangible medium of expression." In other words, the result is something created by you that someone else can experience. The major components of copyright consist of:
  - Originality: An independent creation with a small amount of creativity; doesn't have to be unique.
  - Fixation: Established in a tangible medium; this is the defining aspect of a work being copyrightable. The work exists, and it can be experienced, from a full-length movie to a digital work stored for a nanosecond in computer RAM.
  - Expression: A person's unique output or take on an idea. An idea is not protected (deciding to take a photo on the beach), but the expression of that idea is (clicking a camera at a particular moment).

QUICK TIP

In the United States, nearly every work created prior to 1923 is in the public domain.

- **Copyright protection**

  Start and duration. A work acquires copyright protection *as soon as* you create it. Generally, for an individual, copyright lasts the life of the author plus 70 years. You don't have to register your work with the U.S. Copyright Office, shown in Figure H-25, to prove your copyright or use the copyright symbol (©), but you establish your strongest legal position when you do (the cost is $35 for an online submission or $65 for a paper submission at the time of this book's printing).

  Your rights. Copyright law protects your work by giving you the right to reproduce a work, create a new work based on the original (known as a **derivative work**), distribute copies, and perform or display a work publicly and digitally. Cropping or applying a filter to a photo would be considered making a derivative work.

QUICK TIP

Common citation styles include APA, MLA, and Chicago. For an example, visit www.apastyle.org, then click a link, such as Learning APA Style.

- **Public domain, flexible licensing, and permissions**

  You should assume that every text and media file (audio, video, image) on the Internet has copyright protection or protection under another category of intellectual property law. Works no longer protected by some form of intellectual property law are in the **public domain**; therefore, no one owns them or controls their use. You can use and modify public domain content however you wish. Even if a work is protected, you can obtain written permission from the owner, thus ensuring your ability to use the work. If you want to keep some rights to your work (such as being credited), but share the work so others may build upon it, learn about Creative Commons (CC) copyright licenses, shown in Figure H-26. Want maximum flexibility in using a CC-licensed work? Then only choose works that require attribution, and always be sure to credit the creator, such as Courtesy Jane Doe or Credit: John Doe. You should always cite websites and media you download from the Internet, although attribution is never a substitute for permission.

FIGURE H-25: The U.S. Copyright Office home page (www.copyright.gov)

FIGURE H-26: The Creative Commons home page

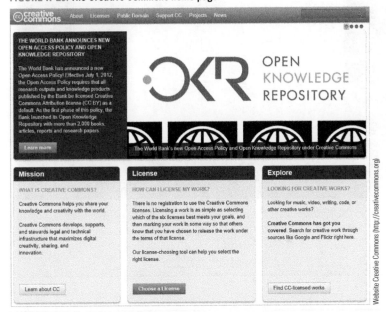

Understanding copyright infringement and fair use

Copyright infringement is the unauthorized use of one or more of the rights of a copyright holder. The penalty per infringement of a registered copyright can be tens of thousands of dollars. Even accidental infringement can lead to penalties. The assumptions and burdens of proof governing copyright infringement are based on civil law, which has broader rules of evidence. Civil law does not require proof of infringement beyond a reasonable doubt. The court's assumption may be that you are guilty, and the burden of proof is on you to prove that you're not.

The **Fair Use Doctrine** is a built-in limitation to copyright protection that allows users to copy all or part of a copyrighted work in support of their First Amendment and other rights. You do not need to ask permission from the copyright holder for a fair use of the work. For example, you could excerpt short passages of a protected film or song, or parody a television show, even though your use may have commercial value. Determining whether fair use applies to a work depends on the purpose of its use, the nature of the copyrighted work, the amount you want to copy, and the effect on the salability or value of the work. Courts also consider whether the use is **transformative**—does the new work add new meaning, insights, or information to the original? Fair use is used as the defense in many copyright-infringement cases, but it is always decided on a case-by-case basis—there is no set legal formula.

Practice

Concepts Review

Label the elements of the screen shown in Figure H-27.

FIGURE H-27

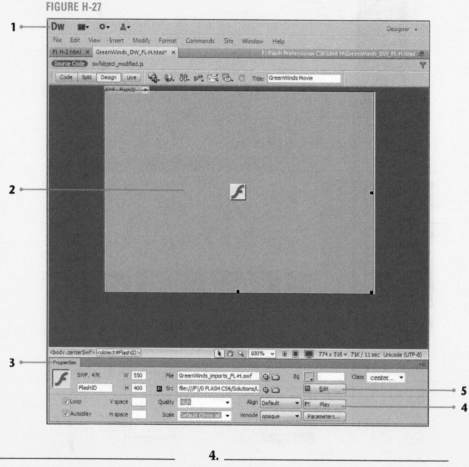

1. _____
2. _____
3. _____
4. _____
5. _____

Match each term with the statement that best describes it.

6. **Single flattened bitmap**
7. **How an SWF file appears in a Dreamweaver document**
8. **Copyright infringement**
9. **Roundtrip editing**
10. **Intellectual property**

a. Allows you to edit a file in its native program and return immediately to another program
b. An idea or creation from a human mind
c. A placeholder
d. Is imported into the selected layer in Flash
e. The unauthorized use of a work in violation of someone's copyright

Select the best answer from the list of choices.

11. **In Flash, on which panel do you find the Edit button?**
    a. Library
    b. Roundtrip edit
    c. Info
    d. Properties

12. **What are the built-in exceptions to copyright law known as?**
    a. Copyright infringement
    b. Fair use
    c. Open access
    d. Public domain

13. **What is the native file format for a Fireworks document?**
    a. PSD
    b. PNG
    c. PHP
    d. FLA

14. **Before inserting Flash media in Dreamweaver, what action should you perform in Flash?**
    a. Publish the document as an HTML file.
    b. Publish the document as a JPEG file.
    c. Publish the document as an SWF file.
    d. Do not publish the document.

15. **What is a flexible range of copyright protection known as?**
    a. Public Commons
    b. Creative Commons
    c. Creative Copyright
    d. Copyright Free

16. **What is the native file format for an Illustrator document?**
    a. AS
    b. AI
    c. AIR
    d. API

17. **When you import files into a Flash document, which of the following programs allow you select content in layers to remain editable?**
    a. Illustrator and Photoshop
    b. Fireworks and Photoshop
    c. Illustrator and Fireworks
    d. Illustrator, Fireworks, and Photoshop

18. **Which information is visible to indicate that you are using the roundtrip editing feature?**
    a. The Done button and the type of edit you're performing.
    b. The Done button and the name of the program you're editing in.
    c. The Done button and the name of the program you're editing from.
    d. The Done button and the Save or Save As buttons.

19. **Which Adobe program does not use the roundtrip editing window?**
    a. Photoshop
    b. Illustrator
    c. Dreamweaver
    d. Fireworks

Skills Review

1. **Understand Flash integration.**
   a. Describe how integration can work in Adobe Creative Suite 6.
   b. List two programs commonly used to create source bitmap or vector artwork for your projects.
   c. Describe how roundtrip editing works.

2. **Import a Fireworks PNG file into Flash.**
   a. Open the file management utility on your computer, navigate to the location where you store your Data Files, copy the file recycling.fw.png, then rename it **recycling-roundtrip.fw_FL-H.png**.
   b. Start Flash, then open a new file, then save it as **recycling_art_FW_layers_FL-H.fla** in the location where you store your Data Files.
   c. Use a command on the File menu to import to the Stage the file recycling-roundtrip.fw_FL-H.png, then compare your screen to Figure H-28.
   d. Save and close the document.

3. **Use roundtrip editing.**
   a. In Flash, create a new file and save it as **recycling_art_FW_roundtrip_FL-H.fla**.
   b. Use a command on the File menu to import to the Stage the file **recycling-roundtrip.fw_FL-H.png**.
   c. Select the image on the Stage, then use a button on the Properties panel to edit the image in Fireworks. (*Hint*: Depending on the file associations set up for your computer, you might need to right-click the image on the Stage, click Edit with, then select Fireworks.exe.)
   d. In Fireworks, click the text object on the canvas (Stage) to select the text, click the Fill color box on the Properties panel to open the color pop-up window, double-click (Win) or click (Mac) the hexadecimal value, type **#660000**, then press [Enter] (Win) or [return] (Mac) to close the color pop-up window.
   e. Click the Done button in the Editing from Flash roundtrip window to return to Flash.
   f. Deselect the image, compare your screen to Figure H-29, then save and close the document.
   g. Show Fireworks, then exit Fireworks.

FIGURE H-28

Bin there, do it

Original content Matt Gitson

FIGURE H-29

Bin there, do it

Original content Matt Gitson

Skills Review (continued)

4. **Import a Photoshop PSD file into Flash.**

   a. In Flash, create a new file, then save it as **recycling_puzzle_PS_FL-H.fla** in the location where you store your Data Files.

   b. Use a command on the File menu to import to the Stage the file **recycling_puzzle.psd** from the location where you store your Data Files, then in the Import to Stage dialog box, make sure each individual layer will be imported as a flattened bitmap image if that option is available. Select Flash Layers as the convert layers type if necessary, then set the stage size to be the same as the Photoshop canvas.

   c. Click the work area, then delete the Layer 1, Mask, and Shape 3 layers in the Timeline, show and expand folders in the Library, then delete the MASK and Shape 3 objects from the puzzle piece folder in the Library.

   d. Compare your Stage, Timeline, and Library to Figure H-30, then save and close the document.

5. **Edit a Photoshop image from Flash.**

   a. Use the file management utility on your computer to navigate to the location where you store your Data Files, create a copy of the file lightfoot_texture.jpg, then rename the file **lightfoot_texture-roundtrip_FL-H.jpg**.

   b. In Flash, open the file FL H-4.fla from the location where you store your Data Files, then save it as **LightFootRecycling_imports_FL-H.fla** in the location where you store your Data Files.

   c. In the Timeline, make sure that frame 1 is selected on the lightfoot texture layer, use a command on the File menu to import lightfoot_texture-roundtrip_FL-H.jpg to the Stage, then set its X value to **0** and Y value to **0** in the Position and Size section of the Properties panel, if necessary.

   d. Use a button on the Properties panel to open the image in Photoshop for editing. (*Hint*: If Photoshop is not set up as the default image editor for JPEG files in Flash, you must set it as the default image editor. Right-click the image on the Stage, click Edit with in the context menu, navigate to where you store your Adobe program files, click the Photoshop folder, double-click Photoshop.exe, then click Open.)

FIGURE H-30

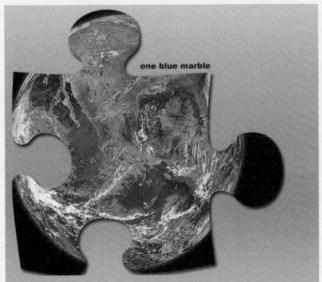

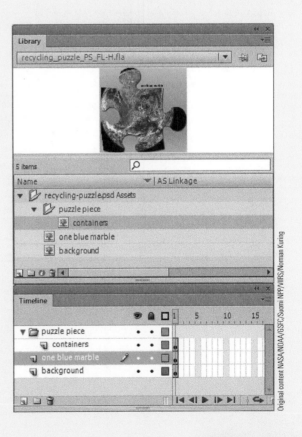

Skills Review (continued)

e. In Photoshop, click Filter on the Menu bar, point to Stylize, click Wind, click Blast in the Method section, then click From the Left in the Direction section.

f. Compare your dialog box to Figure H-31, then click OK to close the Wind dialog box.

g. Click File on the Menu bar, click Close, save your changes, exit Photoshop, then show Flash, if necessary.

h. Test the movie, click the Start and Stop buttons, close the Flash Player, then save the document.

6. Insert a Flash movie into Dreamweaver.

a. Publish the LightFootRecycling_imports_FL-H.fla file as Flash (.swf) only, then save and close the document.

b. Start Dreamweaver, open the file FL H-5.html from the location where you store your Data Files, then save it as **LightFootRecycling_DW_FL-H.html**. (*Hint*: Create a new site folder named Recycle.)

c. Click Insert on the Menu bar, point to Media, click SWF, navigate to the location where you store your Data Files if necessary, click LightFootRecycling_imports_FL-H.swf, then import the movie.

d. Type **LightFoot Animation** as the title text, then click OK.

e. Use a button on the Property inspector to play and stop the movie (Win).

f. Save the document, then use commands on the File menu to preview the web page in your browser.

g. Use the buttons to start and stop the movie, then close your browser.

FIGURE H-31

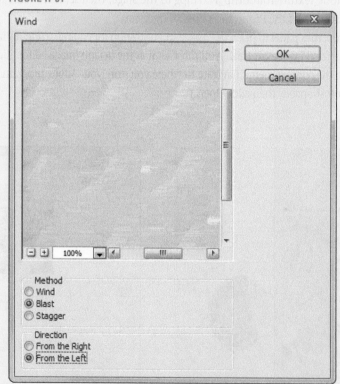

Skills Review (continued)

7. Edit a Flash movie from Dreamweaver.

  a. In Dreamweaver, click the placeholder on the Stage, use a button on the Property inspector to edit the movie in Flash, navigate to the location where you store your Data Files, then select and open the file LightFootRecycling_imports_FL-H.fla.

  b. In the Timeline, click frame 160 on the Actions layer (the top layer), press and hold [Shift], click frame 160 in the lightfoot texture layer (the bottom layer), then use a command on the Insert menu to insert a keyframe in those layers. (*Hint*: Extending the Timeline will make the movie play longer before it moves back to frame 1.)

  c. Click the Done button in the Editing from Dreamweaver roundtrip editing window to return to Dreamweaver. (*Hint:* Move to Dreamweaver, if necessary.)

  d. Save the file, use a command on the File menu to preview the web page in your browser, click buttons, compare your screen to Figure H-32, then close your browser.

  e. Close FL H-5.html and LightFootRecycling_DW_FL-H.html, then exit Dreamweaver.

FIGURE H-32

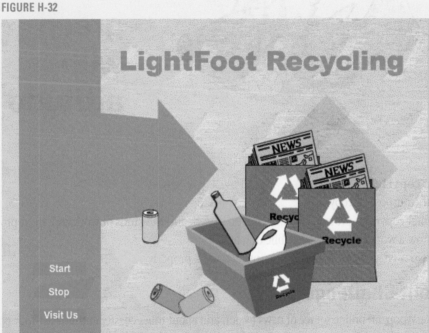

8. Import an Illustrator file into Flash.

  a. Open the file FL H-6.fla from the location where you store your Data Files, then save it as **LightFoot Recycling_attitude_FL-H.fla**.

  b. Import the file shark.ai with all layers editable (default settings).

  c. Click the Text tool on the Tools panel, select the text block, then change the font to Arial.

  d. Compare your screen to Figure H-33, then save and close the document.

  e. Exit Flash.

FIGURE H-33

Go green with attitude

Original content MisterElements/
Shutterstock.com

9. Understand copyright.

  a. Describe the purpose of copyright.

  b. Discuss when copyright protection is attached to a work and the kinds of work copyright protects.

  c. Describe how a work can enter the public domain.

  d. Describe two ways you can ensure you are using a work properly.

Independent Challenge 1

You work at CoasterWoop, an online source of news by, for, and about roller coaster enthusiasts. Your boss wants you to create a new Flash document with a unique image, and then add a background image to the CoasterWoop movie.

  a. Open your file management utility, navigate to the location where you store your Data Files, copy the file ejector-air.fw.png, rename it **ejector-air-roundtrip.fw_FL-H.png**, copy the file amusementPark.jpg, then rename it **amusementPark_PS_FL-H.jpg**.

  b. Start Flash, create a new file and save it as **coaster_fantasy_FW_FL-H.fla** in the location where you store your Data Files, import to the Stage the file ejector-air-roundtrip.fw_FL-H.png, then make sure the X and Y values are 0.

Independent Challenge 1 (continued)

c. Edit the image in Fireworks, select the Text tool on the Tools panel, select the text object on the canvas, select the text, then change the text to the color and font of your choice, as shown in the example in Figure H-34.
d. Return to Flash, then compare your screen to Figure H-35. (*Hint*: Click the Layers panel tab in the Pages panel group to view objects on layers.)
e. Save and close the document, then exit Fireworks.
f. In Flash, open the file FL-H-7.fla from the location where you store your Data Files, then save it as **CoasterWoop_imports_FL-H.fla**.
g. Import to the Stage the file amusementPark_PS_FL-H.jpg. (*Hint*: Depending on the file associations set up for your computer, the image may simply import to the Stage.)
h. Edit the image in Photoshop, click Image on the Menu bar, point to Adjustments, click Posterize, type **3** in the Level text box, view the result, then type **6** in the Levels text box.
i. Click OK, save and close the file, exit Photoshop, then show Flash. (*Hint*: Depending on the file associations set up for your computer, you might need to right-click the image on the Stage, click Edit with, navigate to the location where you store your Adobe program files, click the Photoshop folder, then double-click Photoshop.exe.)

FIGURE H-34

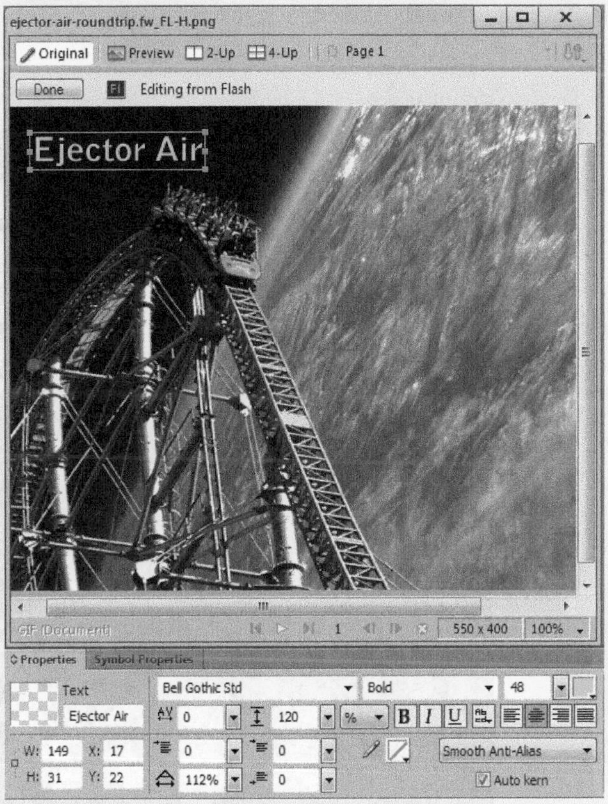

Original content Ben Garney, NASA/JPS/UCSD/JSC

FIGURE H-35

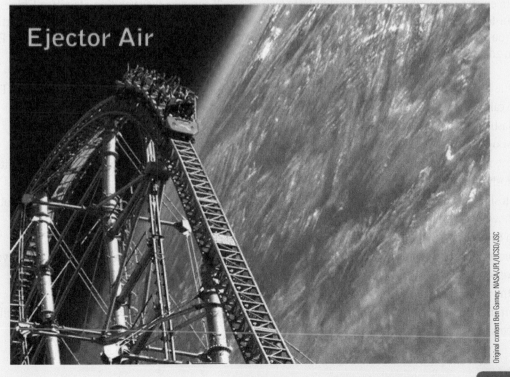

Original content Ben Garney; NASA/JPL/UCSD/JSC

Independent Challenge 1 (continued)

j. Test the movie, compare your screen to Figure H-36, then close the Flash Player.

k. Save and close the document, then exit Flash.

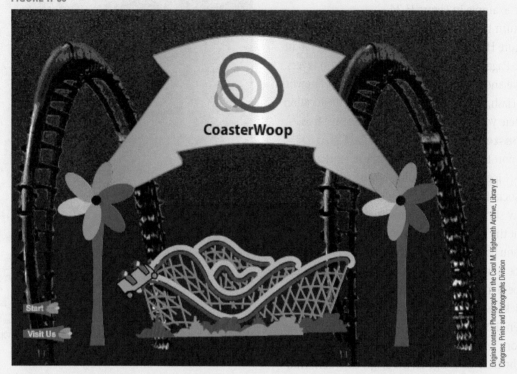

Independent Challenge 2

As the new Program Director at Lingoroots, an educational website specializing in linguistics, you're constantly looking for exciting ways to engage new visitors. For the next website feature, you'll compare the evolution of written Chinese across its 4,000-year history. The earliest written Chinese characters were pictures and evolved to a more stylized and artistic writing form. You want to show how Chinese calligraphy has changed over time and you decide to create a new Flash document. You add a background image to the existing Flash movie, then insert the movie in a web page.

a. Open the file management utility on your computer, navigate to the location where you store your Data Files, copy the file calligraphy.jpg, then rename it **calligraphy_PS_FL-H.jpg**.

b. Start Flash, open the file FL H-8.fla from the location where you store your Data Files, save it as **lingoroots_import_FL H.fla**, then click the calligraphy layer to select it.

c. Import to the Stage the file calligraphy_PS_FL-H.jpg, set the X and Y values to 0, then open the image for editing in Photoshop.

d. In Photoshop, click Filter on the Menu bar, point to Blur, click Blur More, save and close the file, exit Photoshop, then show Flash.

e. Publish the document as a Flash (.swf) file only, then save and close the document.

f. Start Dreamweaver, open the file FL H-9.html, from the location where you store your Data Files, then save it as **lingoroots_DW_FL-H.html**. (*Hint*: Create a new site folder named Lingo.)

g. Insert the file lingoroots_imports_FL-H.swf, then type the title text of your choice.

h. Use buttons on the Property inspector to play and stop the movie (Win), edit the movie, then select the file lingoroots_imports_FL-H.fla to open in Flash.

Independent Challenge 2 (continued)

i. In Flash, extend the length of the movie by inserting a keyframe in frame 180 on all the layers in the Timeline, then return to Dreamweaver.

j. Save the document, use a command on the File menu to preview the web page in your browser, click buttons, compare your screen to Figure H-37, then close your browser.

k. In Dreamweaver, close FL H-9.html and lingoroots_DW_FL-H.html, then exit Dreamweaver.

Advanced Challenge Exercise

- Open the file management utility on your computer, navigate to the location where you store your Data Files, copy the file calligraphy_brushes.fw.png, then rename it **calligraphy_brushes.fw_FL-H.png**.
- In Flash, open a new file and save it as **calligraphy_brushes_ACE_FL-H.fla** in the location where you store your Data Files, import to the Stage the file calligraphy_brushes.fw_FL-H.png, then open it for editing in Fireworks.
- In Fireworks, click Commands on the Menu bar, point to Creative, click Add Picture Frame, click the Select a pattern list arrow, click Course-Orange, double-click the Frame Size text box, type **12**, then click OK.
- Return to Flash, adjust the Stage color and size as desired, then save and close the file.

l. Exit Flash.

FIGURE H-37

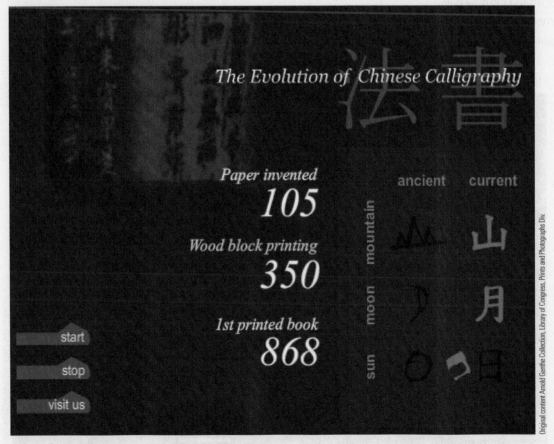

Independent Challenge 3

You work for ibRobotz, an online entertainment site. Users can download ibRobotz characters or create their own to insert in stories. Your boss wants you to add an image to the movie, then insert the movie in a web page.

a. Open the file management utility on your computer, navigate to the location where you store your Data Files, copy the file ancestorbot.fw.png, then rename it **ancestorbot.fw_FL-H.png**.

b. Start Flash, open the file FL H-10.fla from the location where you store your Data Files, then save it as **ibrobotz_imports_FL-H.fla**. (*Hint*: Create a new site folder named robotz if desired.)

c. Import to the Stage the file ancestorbot.fw_FL-H.png, set the X value to **192**, set the Y value to **20**, then open it for editing in Fireworks.

d. In Fireworks, click the robot image on the canvas, click Filters on the Menu bar, point to Sharpen, click Sharpen, then return to Flash.

e. Publish the document as a Flash (.swf) file only, then save and close the document.

f. Start Dreamweaver, open the file FL H-11.html, from the location where you store your Data Files, then save it as **ibrobotz_DW_FL-H.html**.

g. Import the file ibrobotz_imports_FL-H.swf, then type the title text of your choice.

h. Use buttons on the Property inspector to play and stop the movie (Win), then edit the file by selecting the file ibrobotz_imports_FL-H.fla to open in Flash.

i. In Flash, select the ancestor robot portrait on the Stage, use the Free Transform tool to edit it as you wish, then return to Dreamweaver.

j. Save the document, preview the web page in your browser, mouse over the buttons, compare your screen to Figure H-38, then close your browser.

FIGURE H-38

Integrating Content with Other CS6 Programs

Independent Challenge 3 (continued)

Advanced Challenge Exercise

- In Flash, open ibrobotz_imports_FL-H.fla, then save it as **ibrobotz_imports_ACE_FL-H.fla**
- Import the file decoration.ai as a single flattened bitmap, then resize and move it as desired. (*Hint*: Depending on where you want the decoration to appear, you may need to move the decoration image to a new layer and move it in the Timeline.)
- Rename the layer, test the movie, then save the document.

k. Close all files, then exit Flash.

Real Life Independent Challenge

This Independent Challenge will continue to build on the personal project that you have been developing since Unit B. Here, you import images and edit them in their native programs, and insert the movie into a Dreamweaver document.

a. Start Flash, open your myproject file, then save it as **myproject_imports_FL-H.fla**.

b. Obtain images for your movie. You can obtain images from your computer, the Internet, a digital camera, or scanned media. When downloading from the Internet, you should always assume the work is protected by copyright. Be sure to check the website's terms of use to determine how you can use the work.

c. Use the skills you learned in this unit to import and edit images, and insert an SWF into a Dreamweaver document. (*Hint*: Create a new site folder named myproject if desired. If you are not familiar with Dreamweaver, open one of the .html Data Files you used in this unit, then save it as **myprojectDW_FL-H.html**. To change the background color, click the Page Properties button on the Property inspector, click the Background color swatch, then select a new color.)

d. Test the movie and the buttons.

e. Save and close the document, then exit Flash, Dreamweaver, and other open programs as necessary.

Visual Workshop

You want to learn more about how to share your content with others while keeping some, but not all of the rights granted under copyright law, and how to find work you can use. Figure H-39 shows the Case Studies page page from the nonprofit organization Creative Commons. Go to http://wiki.creativecommons.org/Case_Studies, then read a few case studies. Answer the following questions. For each question, include why or how you reached a conclusion. You can open a word processor or use the Text tool in Flash to complete this exercise. When you are finished, add your name to the document, save it, print it, then close the word processor or exit Flash. You decide to learn more about Creative Commons and gather ideas on how to manage copyright policies for works you create.

a. Creative Commons allows you to search for public domain and open access work, and attach copyright to your own work based on which rights you want to keep and which you want to waive so that others may use your work. Which license, if any, would you be interested in using for your work?

b. Have you tried to find work you can use for your projects? If so, were you sure you could use the work legally?

c. Have you given much thought to how you want to avoid copyright infringement? Does it vary depending on where you sit in the copyright scenario—as a user of protected work or as a creator of protected work?

d. How do you think using media from various sources could complicate your use of them and how you license your own work?

e. Identify the advantages and disadvantages to having a body of work available to the public for free and legal sharing, use, repurposing, and remixing. What is your personal opinion?

f. Close your browser.

FIGURE H-39

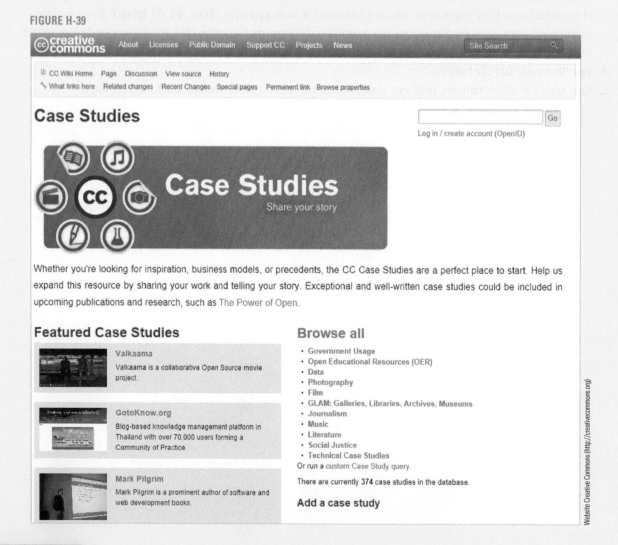

Data Files List

To complete the lessons and practice exercises in this book, students need to use Data Files that are supplied by Cengage Learning. Below is a list of the Data Files that are supplied and the unit and practice exercise to which the files correspond. For information on how to obtain Data Files, please refer to the inside front cover of this book. The following list includes only Data Files that are supplied; it does not include the website files students create from scratch or the files students create by revising supplied files

Unit	Location file is used in unit	Folder location for files	Files supplied
BRIDGE UNIT	Lessons (The Striped Umbrella site)	Bridge folder	blooms_banner.jpg
			blue_footed_booby.jpg
			boardwalk.png
			boats.jpg
			butterfly.jpg
			butterfly1.jpg
			butterfly2.jpg
			cafe_photo.jpg
			cc_banner.jpg
			cc_banner_with_text.jpg
			children_cooking.jpg
			chives.jpg
			chocolate_cake.jpg
			club_house.jpg
			coleus.jpg
			cookies_oven.jpg
			crabdance.swf
			family_sunset.jpg
			fiber_optic_grass.jpg
			fish.jpg
			fisherman.jpg
			garden_quote.swf
			gardening_gloves.gif

Unit	Location file is used in unit	Folder location for files	Files supplied
			girl_floating.jpg
			hanging_baskets.mp4
			iguana_and_lizard.jpg
			interviews.mp3
			lady_in_red.jpg
			llama.jpg
			machu_picchu_from_high.jpg
			machu_picchu_ruins.jpg
			marshmallows.jpg
			one_dolphin.jpg
			peruvian_appetizers.jpg
			peruvian_glass.jpg
			pie.jpg
			plants.jpg
			pool.jpg
			river_guide.jpg
			river_scenes.swf
			rose_bloom.jpg
			rose_bud.jpg
			rt_banner.jpg
			rt_logo_gif
			ruby_grass.jpg
			sea_lions_in_surf.jpg
			sea_spa_logo.png
			sealions_video.mp4
			seeds_audio.mp3
			su_banner.gif
			trees.jpg
			tripsmart_banner.jpg
			tripsmart_gradient.jpg
			tulips.jpg
			two_dolphins.jpg
			two_roses.jpg
			umbrella_anchor_video.mp4
			walking_stick.jpg
			water.jpg
			water_lily.jpg
			young_paddler.jpg

Unit	Location file is used in unit	Folder location for files	Files supplied
DREAMWEAVER UNIT A	Lessons (The Striped Umbrella site)	Unit A folder	dwa_1.html
		Unit A assets folder	pool.jpg
			su_banner.gif
	Skills Review (Blooms & Bulbs site)	Unit A folder	dwa_2.html
		Unit A assets folder	blooms_banner.jpg
			tulips.jpg
	Independent Challenge 1 (TripSmart site)	Unit A folder	dwa_3.html
		Unit A assets folder	tripsmart_banner.jpg
DREAMWEAVER UNIT B	Lessons (The Striped Umbrella site)	Unit B folder	dwb_1.html
		Unit B assets folder	su_banner.gif
	Skills Review (Blooms & Bulbs site)	Unit B folder	dwb_2.html
		Unit B assets folder	blooms_banner.jpg
	Independent Challenge 1 (Rapids Transit site)	Unit B folder	dwb_3.html
		Unit B assets folder	rt_banner.jpg
	Independent Challenge 2 (TripSmart site)	Unit B folder	dwb_4.html
		Unit B assets folder	tripsmart_banner.jpg
	Visual Workshop (Carolyne's Creations site)	Unit B folder	dwb_5.html
		Unit B assets folder	cc_banner.jpg
DREAMWEAVER UNIT C			No Data Files supplied
DREAMWEAVER UNIT D	Lessons (The Striped Umbrella site)	Unit D folder	spa.doc
		Unit D assets folder	sea_spa_logo.png
	Skills Review (Blooms & Bulbs site)	Unit D folder	gardening_tips.doc
		Unit D assets folder	butterfly.jpg
	Independent Challenge 1 (Rapids Transit site)	Unit D folder	dwd_1.html
		Unit D assets folder	rt_banner.jpg
	Independent Challenge 2 (TripSmart site)	Unit D folder	dwd_2.html
		Unit D assets folder	tripsmart_banner.jpg
	Visual Workshop (Carolyne's Creations site)	Unit D folder	dwd_3.html
		Unit D assets folder	cc_banner.jpg
			pie.jpg

Unit	Location file is used in unit	Folder location for files	Files supplied
DREAMWEAVER UNIT E	Lessons (The Striped Umbrella site)	Unit E folder	dwe_1.html
		Unit E assets folder	boardwalk.png
			club_house.jpg
			su_banner.gif
			water.jpg
	Skills Review (Blooms & Bulbs site)	Unit E folder	dwe_2.html
		Unit E assets folder	blooms_banner.jpg
			lady_in_red.jpg
			rose_bloom.jpg
			rose_bud.jpg
			two_roses.jpg
	Independent Challenge 1 (Rapids Transit site)	Unit E folder	dwe_3.html
		Unit E assets folder	river_guide.jpg
			rt_banner.jpg
	Independent Challenge 2 (TripSmart site)	Unit E folder	dwe_4.html
		Unit E assets folder	blue_footed_booby.jpg
			iguana_and_lizard.jpg
			tripsmart_banner.jpg
	Visual Workshop (Carolyne's Creations site)	Unit E folder	dwe_5.html
		Unit E assets folder	cc_banner.jpg
			peruvian_glass.jpg
DREAMWEAVER UNIT F	Lessons (The Striped Umbrella site)	Unit F folder	dwf_1.html
		Unit F assets folder	family_sunset.jpg
			su_banner.gif
			su_banner.gif
			two_dolphins.jpg
	Skills Review (Blooms & Bulbs site)	Unit F folder	dwf_2.html
		Unit F assets folder	blooms_banner.jpg
			plants.jpg
			ruby_grass.jpg
			trees.jpg
	Independent Challenge 1 (Rapids Transit site)	Unit F folder	dwf_3.html

Unit	Location file is used in unit	Folder location for files	Files supplied
		Unit F assets folder	rt_banner.jpg
			young_paddler.jpg
	Independent Challenge 2 (TripSmart site)	Unit F folder	dwf_4.html
		Unit F assets folder	tripsmart_banner.jpg
	Visual Workshop (Carolyne's Creations site)	Unit F folder	dwf_5.html
			dwf_6.html
			dwf_7.html
		Unit F assets folder	cc_banner_with_text.jpg
			children_cooking.jpg
			cookies_oven.jpg
			fish.jpg
			peruvian_appetizers.jpg
DREAMWEAVER UNIT G	Lessons (The Striped Umbrella site)	Unit G folder	café.doc
		Unit G assets folder	cafe_photo.jpg
			chocolate_cake.jpg
	Skills Review (Blooms & Bulbs site)	Unit G assets folder	chives.jpg
			composting.doc
			gardening_gloves.gif
	Independent Challenge 1 (Rapids Transit site)	Unit G folder	rentals.doc
		Unit G assets folder	girl_floating.jpg
			rt_logo.gif
	Independent Challenge 2 (TripSmart site)	Unit G folder	walking sticks.doc
		Unit G assets folder	tripsmart_gradient.jpg
			walking_stick.jpg
	Visual Workshop (Carolyne's Creations site)	Unit G assets folder	marshmallows.jpg
DREAMWEAVER UNIT H	Lessons (The Striped Umbrella site)	Unit H folder	crabdance.swf
			dwh_1.html
			dwh_2.html
			dwh_3.html
			interviews.mp3
			umbrella_anchor_video.mp4

Unit	Location file is used in unit	Folder location for files	Files supplied
		Unit H assets folder	boats.jpg
			fisherman.jpg
			one_dolphin.jpg
			two_dolphins.jpg
	Skills Review (Blooms & Bulbs site)	Unit H folder	dwh_4.html
			dwh_5.html
			dwh_6.html
			garden_quote.swf
			hanging_baskets.mp4
			seeds_audio.mp3
		Unit H assets folder	butterfly1.jpg
			butterfly2.jpg
			coleus.jpg
			fiber_optic_grass.jpg
			water_lily.jpg
	Independent Challenge 1 (Rapids Transit site)	Unit H folder	river_scenes.swf
	Independent Challenge 2 (TripSmart site)	Unit H folder	dwh_7.html
			dwh_8.html
			sealions_video.mp4
		Unit H assets folder	llama.jpg
			machu_picchu_from_high.jpg
			machu_picchu_ruins.jpg
			sea_lions_in_surf.jpg
	Visual Workshop (Carolyne's Creations site)		
DREAMWEAVER UNIT I			**No Data Files supplied**
DREAMWEAVER UNIT J			**No Data Files supplied**

Data File Supplied	Student Creates File	Used In	
PHOTOSHOP UNIT A			
Lessons			
PS A-1.psd	birdie_PS-A.psd	Lessons 3- 4	
	birdie_PS-A.tif		
	birdie_PS-A.jpg		
PS A-2.psd	birdie resize_PS-A.psd	Lesson 5	
PS A-3.psd	birdie magazine_PS-A.psd	Lesson 6	
	birdie web graphic_PS-A.psd		
	new document_PS-A.psd	Lesson 7	
PS A-4.psd	parrots_PS-A.psd	Lesson 8	
PS A-5.psd			
PS A-6.psd	estonia house_PS-A.psd	Lesson 9	
PS A-7.psd	hotel postcard_PS-A.psd	Lesson 10	
Skills Review			
PS A-8.psd	tallinn_PS-A.psd		
PS A-9.psd	eagle resize_PS-A.psd		
	skills new_PS-A.psd	Skills Review	
PS A-10.psd	title_PS-A.psd		
PS A-11.psd	email postcard_PS-A.psd		
PS A-12.psd	san francisco_PS-A.psd		
IC1			
PS A-13.psd	web graphic 1_PS-A.jpg		
PS A-14.psd	web graphic 2_PS-A.jpg	Independent Challenge 1	
PS A-15.psd	web graphic 3_PS-A.jpg		
IC2			
PS A-16.psd	triptych_PS-A.psd		
	triptych_PS-A.jpg	Independent Challenge 2	
PS A-17.psd			
PS A-18.psd			
IC3			
PS A-19.psd	bookmark_PS-A.psd	Independent Challenge 3	
Real Life IC			
PS A-20.psd	mother's love_PS-A.psd	Real Life IC	
	mother's love_PS-A.jpg		
Visual Workshop			
PS A-21.psd	visual solution_PS-A.psd	Visual Workshop	
PHOTOSHOP UNIT B			
Lessons			
PS B-1.psd	selections puzzle_PS_B.psd	Lessons 1-3	
PS B-2.psd	air balloon_PS-B.psd	Lesson 3	
PS B-3.psd	save selections_PS-B.psd	Lessons 4-5	
PS B-4.psd	apple edges_PS-B.psd	Lesson 6	
PS B-5.psd	vignette_PS-B.psd	Lesson 7	
PS B-6.psd	eagle silhouette_PS-B.psd	Lesson 8	
Skills Review			
PS B-7.psd	shapes_PS-B.psd		
PS B-8.psd	clown posterize_PS-B.psd		
PS B-9.psd	skills edges_PS-B.psd	Skills Review	
PS B-10.psd	apple silhouette_PS-B.psd		
IC1			
PS B-11.psd	magic wand mask_PS-B.psd	Independent Challenge 1	

Data File Supplied	Student Creates File	Used In
IC2 PS B-12.psd	orange balloons_PS-B.psd	Independent Challenge 2
IC3 PS B-13.psd PS B-14.psd	iq test_PS-B.psd	Independent Challenge 3
Real Life IC PS B-15.psd	posterized woman_PS-B.psd	Real Life IC
Visual Workshop PS B-16.psd	visual solutions_PS-B.psd	Visual Workshop
PHOTOSHOP UNIT C		
Lessons PS C-1.psd PS C-2.psd Colosseum.psd	roman holiday 1_PS-C.psd roman holiday 2_PS-C.psd	Lessons 1-2 Lessons 3-8
Skills Review PS C-3.psd PS C-4.psd PS C-5.psd Globe.psd	shining future 1_PS-C.psd shining future 2_PS-C.psd bright shining future_PS-C.psd	Skills Review
IC1 PS C-6.psd	roman numerals_PS-C.psd	Independent Challenge 1
IC2 PS C-7.psd Dolphin Sky.psd	dolphin moon_PS-C.psd	Independent Challenge 2
IC3 PS C-8.psd	double dolphins_PS-C.psd	Independent Challenge 3
Real Life IC PS C-9.psd Annie.tif Jenny.tif	sisters postcard_PS-C.psd	Real Life IC
Visual Workshop PS C-10.psd	three glowing globes_PS-C.psd	Visual Workshop
PHOTOSHOP UNIT D		
Lessons PS D-1.psd PS D-2.psd PS D-3.psd PS D-4.psd PS D-5.psd	grayscale_PS-D.psd adjust brightness contrast_PS-D.psd adjust white and black points_PS-D.psd rgb_PS-D.psd color balance_PS-D.psd	Lessons 1-2 Lesson 3 Lessons 4-5 Lesson 6 Lessons 7-8
Skills Review PS D-6.psd PS D-7.psd PS D-8.psd PS D-9.psd	grayscale skills_PS-D.psd brightness contrast skills_PS-D.psd levels skills_PS-D.psd color balance skills_PS-D.psd	Skills Review
IC1 PS D-10.psd	hay bale_PS-D.psd	Independent Challenge 1
IC2 PS D-11.psd	sailboat_PS-D.psd	Independent Challenge 2

Data File Supplied	Student Creates File	Used In
IC3		
PS D-12.psd	color flowers_PS-D.psd	Independent Challenge 3
Real Life IC		
PS D-13.psd	canyon_PS-D.psd	Real Life IC
Visual Workshop		
PS D-14.psd	visual solution_PS-D.psd	Visual Workshop
PHOTOSHOP UNIT E		
Lessons		
PS E-1.psd	set type_PS-E.psd	Lessons 1-2
PS E-2.psd	bevel type_PS-E.psd	Lessons 3-5
PS E-3.psd	making the gradient_PS-E.psd	Lessons 6-7
PS E-4.psd	clip layers_PS-E.psd	Lessons 8-9
PS E-5.psd	fade type_PS-E.psd	Lesson 10
Skills Review		
PS E-6.psd	set skills type_PS-E.psd	
PS E-7.psd	bevel skills type_PS-E.psd	Skills Review
PS E-8.psd	gradient skills_PS-E.psd	
PS E-9.psd	skills clip layers_PS-E.psd	
PS E-10.psd	fade skills type_PS-E.psd	
IC1		
PS E-11.psd	black on blue_PS-E.psd	Independent Challenge 1
IC2		
PS E-12.psd	sunset gradient_PS-E.psd	Independent Challenge 2
IC3		
PS E-13.psd	sunset stroke emboss_PS-E.psd	Independent Challenge 3
Real Life IC		
PS E-14.psd	sunset clipped_PS-E.psd	Real Life IC
Visual Workshop		
PS E-15.psd	radial gradient_PS-E.psd	Visual Workshop
PHOTOSHOP UNIT F		
Lessons		
PS F-1.psd	connect the dots_PS-F.psd	Lessons 1-2
PS F-2.psd	flip flops_PS-F.psd	Lesson 3
PS F-3.psd	hsb_PS-F.psd	Lessons 4-5
PS F-4.psd	replace color_PS-F.psd	Lesson 6
PS F-5.psd	color fan_PS-F.psd	Lesson 7
PS F-6.psd	colorize_PS-F.psd	Lesson 8
Skills Review		
PS F-7.psd	dots_PS-F.psd	Skills Review
PS F-8.psd	heels_PS-F.psd	
PS F-9.psd	replace color skills_PS-F.psd	
PS F-10.psd	b&w skills_PS-F.psd	
IC1		
PS F-11.psd	stop sign_PS-F.psd	Independent Challenge 1
IC2		
PS F-12.psd	green dress_PS-F.psd	Independent Challenge 2
IC3		
PS F-13.psd	newsletter_PS-F.psd	Independent Challenge 3

Data File Supplied	Student Creates File	Used In
Real Life IC		
PS F-14.psd	pylon_PS-F.psd	Real Life IC
Visual Workshop		
PS F-15.psd	snow cones_PS-F.psd	Visual Workshop
PHOTOSHOP UNIT G		
Lessons		
PS G-1.psd	colorize with color mode_PS-G.psd	Lesson 1
PS G-2.psd	final roman holiday_PS-G.psd	Lessons 2-4
PS G-3.psd	silver streak_PS-G.psd	Lessons 5-6
PS G-4.psd	non-destructive filters_PS-G.psd	Lesson 7
PS G-5.psd	distort_PS-G.psd	Lesson 8
charlie billboard_PS-G.psd		
Skills Review		
PS G-6.psd	colorize skills_PS-G.psd	Skills Review
PS G-7.psd	shining future skills_PS-G.psd	
IC1		
PS G-8.psd	color mode correction_PS-G.psd	Independent Challenge 1
IC2		
PS G-9.psd	key art_PS-G.psd	Independent Challenge 2
IC3		
PS G-10.psd	12 count_PS-G.psd	Independent Challenge 3
charlie key art_PS-G.psd		
backer_PS-G.psd		
Real Life IC		
PS G-11.psd	diver_PS-G.psd	Real Life IC
Visual Workshop		
PS G-12.psd	two motion blurs_PS-G.psd	Visual Workshop
PHOTOSHOP UNIT H		
Lessons		
Automation folder	TIFF folder	Lessons 1-3
bricks_PS-H.psd	bricks_PS-H.tif	
flowers_PS-H.psd	flowers_PS-H.tif	
marble_PS-H.psd	marble_PS-H.tif	
rice paper_PS-H.psd	rice paper_PS-H.tif	
water_PS-H.psd	water_PS-H.tif	
wood_PS-H.psd	wood_PS-H.tif	
woodchip paper_PS-H.psd	woodchip paper_PS-H.tif	
	JPEG folder	
	bricks_PS-H.jpg	
	flowers_PS-H.jpg	
	marble_PS-H.jpg	
	rice paper_PS-H.jpg	
	water_PS-H.jpg	
	wood_PS-H.jpg	
PS H-1.psd	woodchip paper_PS-H.jpg	
PS H-2.psd	it's history_PS-H.psd	Lessons 4-5
PS H-3.psd	five geese_PS-H.psd	Lesson 6
PS H-4.psd	sailboat scratches_PS-H.psd	Lesson 7
	clone options_PS-H.psd	Lesson 8

Data File Supplied	Student Creates File	Used In
Skills Review		Skills Review
Skills Automation Folder	TIFF folder	
family_PS-H.psd	family_PS-H.tif	
girl_PS-H.psd	girl_PS-H.tif	
grit_PS-H.psd	grit_PS-H.tif	
lake_PS-H.psd	lake_PS-H.tif	
petals_PS-H.psd	petals_PS-H.tif	
raindrops_PS-H.psd	raindrops_PS-H.tif	
vegas_PS-H.psd	vegas_PS-H.tif	
	JPEG folder	
	family_PS-H.jpg	
	girl_PS-H.jpg	
	grit_PS-H.jpg	
	lake_PS-H.jpg	
	petals_PS-H.jpg	
	raindrops_PS-H.jpg	
	vegas_PS-H.jpg	
PS H-5.psd	history skills_PS-H.psd	
PS H-6.psd	skills clone_PS-H.psd	
PS H-7.psd	blue birds_PS-H.psd	
IC1 and IC2		
PS H-8.psd	noise action_PS-H.psd	Independent Challenge 1
Noise Files folder		Independent Challenge 2
family_PS-H.psd		
girl_PS-H.psd		
grit_PS-H.psd		
lake_PS-H.psd		
petals_PS-H.psd		
raindrops_PS-H.psd		
vegas_PS-H.psd		
IC3		
PS H-9.psd	flowering_PS-H.psd	Independent Challenge 3
Real Life IC		
PS H-10.psd	sailboat cleanup_PS-H.psd	Real Life IC
Visual Workshop		
PS H-11.psd	dog balloon_PS-H.psd	Visual Workshop

Data File Supplied	Student Creates File	Used In
FLASH UNIT A		
FL A-1.fla	balloon-bounce_FL-A.fla balloon-bounce_FL-A.swf	Lessons
FL A-2.fla	abduction_FL-A.fla abduction_FL-A.swf	Skills Review
FL A-3.fla	wagmore_FL-A.fla wagmore_FL-A.swf	Independent Challenge 1
FL A-4.fla	heart2heart_FL-A.fla heart2heart_FL-A.swf heart2heart_ACE_FL-A.fla heart2heart_ACE_FL-A.swf	Independent Challenge 2
No Data File supplied	n/a	Independent Challenge 3
No Data File supplied	n/a	Real Life Independent Challenge
No Data File supplied	n/a	Visual Workshop
FLASH UNIT B		
No Data File supplied	GreenWinds-logo_FL-B.fla	Lessons
No Data File supplied	LightFootRecycling_FL-B.fla	Skills Review
No Data File supplied	CoasterWoop_FL-B.fla	Independent Challenge 1
FL B-1.fla	lingoroots_FL-B.fla lingoroots_ACE_FL-B.fla	Independent Challenge 2
No Data File supplied	ibrobotz_FL-B.fla ibrobotz_ACE_FL-B.fla	Independent Challenge 3
No Data File supplied	myproject_FL-B.fla	Real Life Independent Challenge
No Data File supplied	n/a	Visual Workshop

Data File Supplied	Student Creates File	Used In
FLASH UNIT C		
FL C-1.fla	GreenWinds_symbols_FL-C.fla GreenWinds_symbols_FL-C.swf	Lessons
FL C-2.fla	LightFootRecycling_symbols_FL.C.fla	Skills Review
FL C-3.fla	CoasterWoop_symbols_FL.C.fla	Independent Challenge 1
FL C-4.fla	lingoroots_symbols_FL-C.fla lingoroots_symbols_ACE_FL-C.fla	Independent Challenge 2
FL C-5.fla	ibrobotz_symbols_FL-C.fla ibrobotz_symbols_FL-C.swf ibrobotz_symbols_ACE_FL-C.fla	Independent Challenge 3
No Data File supplied	myproject_symbols_FL-C.fla	Real Life Independent Challenge
No Data File supplied	n/a	Visual Workshop
FLASH UNIT D		
FL D-1.fla FL D-2.fla	GreenWinds_frames_FL-D.fla GreenWinds_animation_FL-D.fla GreenWinds_animation_FL-D.swf	Lessons
FL D-3.fla	GreenWinds_shapehints_FL-D.fla GreenWinds_shapehints_FL-D.swf	
FL D-4.fla	GreenWinds_mask_FL-D.fla GreenWinds_mask_FL-D.swf	
FL D-5.fla	LightFootRecycling_animation_FL-D.fla LightFootRecycling_animation_FL-D.swf	Skills Review
FL D-6.fla	LightFootRecycling_mask_FL-D.fla LightFootRecycling_mask_FL-D.swf	
FL D-7.fla	CoasterWoop_animation_FL-D.fla CoasterWoop_animation_FL-D.swf	Independent Challenge 1
FL D-8.fla	lingoroots_animation_FL-D.fla lingoroots_animation_FL-D.swf lingoroots_animation_ACE_FL-D.fla lingoroots_animation_ACE_FL-D.swf	Independent Challenge 2
FL D-9.fla	ibrobotz_animation_FL-D.fla ibrobotz_animation_FL-D.swf ibrobotz_animation_ACE_FL-D.fla ibrobotz_animation_ACE_FL-D.swf ibrobotz_mask_FL-D.fla ibrobotz_mask_FL-D.swf	Independent Challenge 3
No Data File supplied	myproject_animation_FL-D.fla	Real Life Independent Challenge
No Data File supplied	n/a	Visual Workshop

Data File Supplied	Student Creates File	Used In
FLASH UNIT E		
FL E-1.fla	GreenWinds_optimized_FL-E.fla	Lessons
	GreenWinds_optimized_FL-E.swf	
	GreenWinds_optimized_FL-E.html	
	GreenWinds1.xml	
	GreenWinds_optimized_FL-E.exe	
	GreenWinds_optimized_FL-E.app	
	GreenWinds_optimized_FL-E.gif	
	GreenWinds_optimized_FL-E.jpg	
	GreenWinds_optimized_FL-E.png	
	swfobject.js	
FL E-2.fla	LightFootRecycling_optimized_FL-E.fla	Skills Review
	LightFootRecycling_optimized_FL-E.swf	
	LightFootRecycling_optimized_FL-E.html	
	Lightfoot1.xml	
	LightFootRecycling_optimized_FL-E.app	
	LightFootRecycling_optimized_FL-E.exe	
	LightFootRecycling_optimized_FL-E.jpg	
	LightFootRecycling_optimized_FL-E.gif	
	LightFootRecycling_optimized.png	
FL E-3.fla	CoasterWoop_optimized_FL-E.fla	Independent Challenge 1
	CoasterWoop_optimized_FL-E.swf	
	CoasterWoop_optimized_FL-E.html	
	CoasterWoop_optimized_FL-E.jpg	
FL E-4.fla	lingoroots_optimized_FL-E.fla	Independent Challenge 2
	lingoroots_optimized_FL-E.swf	
	lingoroots_optimized_FL-E.html	
	lingoroots_optimized_FL-E.exe	
	lingoroots_optimized_FL-E.app	
	lingoroots_optimized_FL-E.gif	
	lingoroots_optimized_ACE_FL-E.fla	
	lingoroots_optimized_ACE_FL-E.jpg	
	lingoroots_JPEG.xml	
FL E-5.fla	ibrobotz_optimized_FL-E.fla	Independent Challenge 3
	ibrobotz_optimized_FL-E.swf	
	ibrobotz_optimized_FL-E.html	
	ibrobotz_optimized_FL-E.gif	
	ibrobotz_optimized_JPEG60_FL-E.jpg	
	ibrobotz_optimized_JPEG100_FL-E.jpg	
	ibrobotz_JPEG100_ACE_FL-E.xml	
	ibrobotz_JPEG60_ACE_FL-E.xml	
	ibrobotz_optimized_ACE_FL-E.fla	
No Data File supplied	myproject_optimized_FL-E.fla	Real Life Independent Challenge
	myproject_optimized_FL-E.swf	
	Additional filenames will vary	
No Data File supplied	n/a	Visual Workshop
FLASH UNIT F		
FL F-1.fla	GreenWinds_buttons_FL-F.fla	Lessons
FL F-2.fla	GreenWinds_buttons_FL-F.swf	
	GreenWinds_video_FL-F.fla	
octopus.mov	GreenWinds_video_FL-F.swf	
	octopus.flv	

Data File Supplied	Student Creates File	Used In
FL F-3.fla FL F-4.fla recycle.mov	LightFootRecycling_buttons_FL-F.fla LightFootRecycling_buttons_FL-F.swf LightFootRecycling_video_FL-F.fla LightFootRecycling_video_FL-F.swf recycle.flv	Skills Review
FL F-5.fla	CoasterWoop_buttons_FL-F.fla CoasterWoop_buttons_FL-F.swf	Independent Challenge 1
FL F-6.fla	lingoroots_buttons_FL-F.fla lingoroots_buttons_FL-F.swf lingoroots_buttons_ACE_FL-F.fla lingoroots_buttons_ACE_FL-F.swf	Independent Challenge 2
FL F-7.fla FL F-8.fla robot.mov	ibrobotz_buttons_FL-F.fla ibrobotz_buttons_FL-F.swf ibrobotz_video_FL-F.fla ibrobotz_video_FL-F.swf ibrobotz_buttons_ACE_FL-F.fla ibrobotz_buttons_ACE_FL-F.swf MinimaFlatCustomColorPlayBackSeekCounterVolMute.swf robot.flv	Independent Challenge 3
No Data File supplied	myproject_buttons_FL-F.fla myproject_buttons_FL-F.swf	Real Life Independent Challenge
No Data File supplied	n/a	Visual Workshop
FLASH UNIT G		
FL G-1.fla FL G-2.fla	GreenWinds_codesnippet_FL-G.fla GreenWinds_codesnippet_FL-G.swf GreenWinds_actions_FL-G.fla GreenWinds_actions_FL-G.swf	Lessons
FL G-3.fla FL G-4.fla	LightFootRecycling_codesnippet_FL-G.fla LightFootRecycling_codesnippet_FL-G.swf LightFootRecycling_actions_FL-G.fla LightFootRecycling_actions_FL-G.swf	Skills Review
FL G-5.fla	CoasterWoop_actions_FL-G.fla CoasterWoop_actions_FL-G.swf	Independent Challenge 1
FL G-6.fla FL G-7.fla	lingoroots_actions_FL-G.fla lingoroots_actions_FL-G.swf lingoroots_actions_ACE_FL-G.fla lingoroots_actions_ACE_FL-G.fla lingoroots_mobile_FL-G.fla lingoroots_mobile_FL-G.swf lingoroots_mobile_FL-G-app.xml	Independent Challenge 2
FL G-8.fla	ibrobotz_actions_FL-G.fla ibrobotz_actions_FL-G.swf ibrobotz_actions_ACE_FL-G.fla ibrobotz_actions_ACE_FL-G.swf	Independent Challenge 3
No Data File supplied	myproject_actions_FL-G.fla myproject_actions_FL-G.swf	Real Life Independent Challenge
No Data File supplied	n/a	Visual Workshop

Data File Supplied	Student Creates File	Used In
INTEGRATION UNIT		
parrotfish.fw.png	*Used in* parrotfish-roundtrip.fw_FL-H.png	Lessons
No Data File supplied	parrotfish_FW-layers_FL-H.fla	
parrotfish-roundtrip.fw.png	*Used in* parrotfish_FW-roundtrip_FL-H.fla	
No Data File supplied	china_rivers_PS_FL-H.fla	
china_rivers.psd	*Used in* china_rivers_PS_FL-H.fla	
ocean.jpg	ocean_PS-roundtrip_FL-H.jpg	
FL H-1.fla	GreenWinds_imports_FL-H.fla	
	GreenWinds_imports_FL-H.swf	
FL H-2.html	GreenWinds_DW_FL-H.html	
FL H-3.fla	sea_ponies_FL-H.fla	
sea ponies.ai	*Used in* sea_ponies_FL-H.fla	
recycling.fw.png	recycling_art_FW_layers_FL_H.fla	Skills Review
No Data File supplied	*Used in* recycling-roundtrip.fw_FL-H.png	
recycling-roundtrip.fw_FL-H.png	*Used in* recycling_art_FW_layers.fla	
	Used in recycling_art_FW_roundtrip.FL-H.fla	
No Data File supplied	recycling_puzzle_PS_FL-H.fla	
recycling-puzzle.psd	*Used in* recycling_puzzle_PS_FL-H.fla	
FL H-4.fla	LightFootRecycling_imports_FL-H.fla	
	LightFootRecycling_imports_FL-H.swf	
lightfoot_texture.jpg	lightfoot_texture-roundtrip_FL-H.jpg	
FL H-5.html	LightFootRecycling_DW_FL-H.html	
FL H-6.fla	LightFootRecycling_attitude_FL-H.fla	
shark.ai	*Used in* LightFootRecycling_attitude_FL-H.fla	
ejector-air.fw.png	ejector-air-roundtrip.fw_FL-H.png	Independent Challenge 1
No Data File supplied	coaster_fantasy_FW_FL-H.fla	
FL H-7.fla	CoasterWoop_imports_FL-H.fla	
	CoasterWoop_imports_FL-H.swf	
amusementPark.jpg	amusementPark_PS_FL-H.jpg	
calligraphy.jpg	calligraphy_PS_FL-H.jpg	Independent Challenge 2
FL H-8.fla	lingoroots_imports_FL-H.fla	
	lingoroots_imports_FL-H.swf	
FL H-9.html	lingoroots_DW_FL-H.html	
calligraphy_brushes.fw.png	calligraphy_brushes.fw_FL-H.png	
	calligraphy_brushes_ACE_FL-H.fla	
ancestorbot.fw.png	ancestorbot.fw_FL-H.png	Independent Challenge 3
FL H-10.fla	ibrobotz_imports_FL-H.fla	
	ibrobotz_imports_FL-H.swf	
FL H-11.html	ibrobotz_DW_FL-H.html	
decoration.ai	ibrobotz_imports_ACE_FL-H.fla	
	ibrobotz_imports_ACE_FL-H.swf	
No Data File supplied	myproject_imports_FL-H.fla	Real Life Independent Challenge
	myproject_imports_FL-H.swf	
	myproject_DW_FL-H.html	
No Data File supplied	n/a	Visual Workshop

Glossary

3D Effects A process in Flash that animates 2D objects through 3D space with 3D Transformation tools.

Absolute path A path containing an external link that references a web page outside the current website, and includes the prefix http:// and the URL of the web page; *see also* URL.

Accordion A CSS style that creates a method of organizing data on a page with buttons that, when clicked, open up like an accordion with information that drops down below the button.

Action A response to an event trigger that causes a change, such as text changing color or a form being processed.

Action property Specifies the application or script that will process form data.

Actions Created, stored, and automatically saved in the Actions panel, actions execute specific procedures automatically.

ActionScript The programming language in Flash that lets you control interactivity and actions in a movie or website.

Active panel A panel displayed as the front panel in an expanded panel group with the panel options displayed.

Adaptive website A website that can adjust the page content to fit the user's needs and device type.

Add-on *See* plug-in.

Additive primary colors The primary colors red, green, and blue that combine to form white when emitted from a light source.

Adjustment layers Adjustments that exist as layers on the Layers panel.

Adjustments Operations that affect the appearance of an image, such as manipulating brightness and contrast.

Adobe Air An Adobe product used for developing content that can be delivered with a browser or as a desktop application.

Adobe BrowserLab An Adobe online service for cross-browser and cross-platform compatibility testing.

Adobe Community Help A collection of materials that includes tutorials, published articles, and blogs, in addition to the regular Help content. All content is monitored and approved by the Adobe Community Expert program.

Adobe Dreamweaver An Adobe CS6 program you use to create web pages in HTML format.

Adobe Fireworks An Adobe CS6 program you use to create and edit bitmap and vector images as well as create web page prototypes.

Adobe Flash Player A free program included with most browsers that allows you to view content created with Adobe Flash.

Adobe Illustrator An Adobe CS6 program you use to design and edit vector graphics.

Adobe Photoshop An Adobe CS6 program used to create bitmap images in which you can manipulate almost every aspect of their appearance.

Advanced style A style used to format combinations of page elements; *also called* compound style.

Alias An icon that represents a program, folder, or file stored on your computer.

Aliased edge A hard selection edge in which the "stair-stepped" pixels are obvious and the edge is noticeably blunt.

Align an image Position an image on a web page in relation to other elements on the page.

Align panel The panel used to size, align, or distribute multiple objects to the Stage or to each other.

Alpha channels Saved selections stored in the Channels panel.

Alphanumeric field A type of form field that will accept both numbers and letters or a combination of the two.

Alpha The transparency of an object.

Alternate text Descriptive text that can be set to display in place of an image or while the image is downloading.

Anchor points Squares on a vector object used to manipulate its path.

Animated GIF A generally short looped animation that plays on nearly any platform.

Animation The illusion of movement created by rapidly displaying a sequence of images.

Anti-aliased edge A crisp but smooth selection edge.

AP div A div that is assigned a fixed position on a page (absolute position); *also called* AP element.

AP Elements panel The panel used to control the properties of all AP elements on a web page.

Application bar (Win) A toolbar located above the Document window that includes menu names, a Workspace switcher, and other application commands. In Bridge, the toolbar that contains the navigation buttons, the Workspace buttons, and the Search text box.

Assets panel A panel that contains nine categories of assets, such as images, used in a website; clicking a category button will display a list of those assets.

Assistive technologies The types of technologies that allow persons with disabilities to interact with and perform tasks in a Flash document.

Authoring tool A program that creators use to develop and package content for users.

Author The creator or owner of a copyrighted work.

AVI (Audio Visual Interleave) A digital video format.

Back-end processing The end of the form processing cycle when the data is processed.

Background image An image used in place of a background color to provide depth and visual interest.

Banner An image that generally appears across the top of a web page and can incorporate information such as a company's logo and contact information.

Baseline The bottom of a line of text, not including descending portions of characters such as in y or g.

Behavior An action script that allows you to add dynamic content to your web pages by allowing an object to respond to user input or as a result of a defined condition.

Bitmap graphic Displays a picture image as a matrix of dots, or pixels, on a grid. Also called raster image.

Black point The darkest pixel in an image.

Blank keyframe A timeline element that does not contain artwork.

Blending modes Mathematical algorithms that define how pixels affect pixels beneath them to create a specific effect.

Blog A website containing regularly posted commentaries and opinions on various topics written and maintained by the website owner.

Body The part of a web page that contains all of the page content users see in their browser window, such as text, graphics, and links.

Border An outline that surrounds an image, cell, table, or div.

Bread crumb trail A list of links that provides a path from the initial page you opened in a website to the page that you are currently viewing.

Brightness Defined by a pixel's grayscale value: the higher the number, the brighter the pixel.

Broken link A link that cannot find the intended destination file.

Browser Compatibility Check (BCC) A feature on the Adobe website that is used to check for problematic CSS features that may render differently in multiple browsers.

Browser Navigation toolbar A toolbar that contains navigation buttons you use when following links on your web pages in Live view.

Buffer A temporary storage area that acts as a holding area for Flash content as it is being played.

Bullet A small image used to call attention to items in an unordered list.

Bulleted list An unordered list that uses bullets. *See also* bullet.

Button On a form, a small rectangular object with a text label that usually has an action attached to it.

Button symbol A symbol that responds to users clicking or rolling over it, which activates a different part of the movie, such as playing a movie clip.

Canvas The bed of pixels that make up an image.

Cascading Style Sheets (CSS) Sets of formatting rules used to format web pages to provide a consistent presentation for content across a website.

Cell A small box within a table that is used to hold text or images; cells are arranged horizontally in rows and vertically in columns.

Cell padding In a table, the distance between the cell content and the cell walls.

Cell spacing In a table, the distance between cells.

Cell wall In a table, the edge surrounding a cell.

Check box A classification of a form object that appears as a box that, when clicked by the user, has a check mark placed in it to indicate that it is selected.

Check Out A feature that enables only one person at a time on a team to work on a file.

Child keyword In Bridge, a keyword that is a sub-category of a parent keyword; *also known as* a sub keyword.

Child menu A submenu.

Class style A style that can be used to format any page element.

Client-side scripting A script that is processed on the user's computer.

Clip art collection A group of image files collected on CDs, DVDs, or downloaded from the Internet and sold with an index or directory of the files.

Clipping Term that refers to using artwork on one layer to mask the artwork on a layer or layers above it.

Cloak The process of marking a file or files for exclusion.

Cloning Copying pixels from one area to another.

CMYK Cyan, magenta, yellow, and black; a color model in Photoshop; the subtractive primary colors; the four process colors central to conventional offset printing.

Code and Design views A combination of Code view and Design view; each layout displays in a separate window within the Document window.

Code hint A tooltip or pop-up menu that lists possible ActionScript elements.

Code Navigator A small window that opens with code for a selected page element.

Code Snippets Predefined ActionScript code that you can add to objects on the Stage.

Code view The view that fills the Document window with the HTML code for the page and is primarily used when reading or directly editing the code.

Coder layout A layout in the Dreamweaver workspace in which the panels are docked on the left side of the screen and Code view is the default view.

Coding toolbar A toolbar used when you are working with code.

Collections panel In Bridge, a panel used to group assets located in different locations into a single collection.

Color model Defines the colors we see and work with in digital images. RGB (red, green, blue), CMYK (cyan, magenta, yellow, black), and HSB (hue, saturation, brightness) are all color models and each uses a different method for describing color.

Color panel Contains features for adjusting an object's stroke and fill colors.

Color profile A group of preset settings for controlling how color will appear on your monitor and in a printed document.

Color stops Specified colors that make up a gradient.

Comments Lines of text in the Actions panel that ActionScript programmers use to document their code; Flash ignores comments when running the code.

Compact mode A Bridge mode with a smaller, simplified workspace.

Compound style *See* advanced style.

Content panel In Bridge, the center pane where thumbnails of the files from the selected drive and folder in the Folders panel appear.

Contiguous Term referring to pixels that border other pixels.

Continuous tone A smooth transition from shadows to midtones to highlights.

Contrast Represented by the relationship between highlights and shadows.

Copyright A form of legal protection for authors of original works to control their use.

Copyright infringement The unauthorized use of one or more rights of a copyright holder.

Creep Also known as *scope creep;* the uncontrolled growth of a project scope stemming from constantly expanding the requirements.

Crop To remove a part of an image, both visually (on the page) and physically (the file size).

CSS Advisor A part of the Adobe website that offers solutions for problems with CSS.

CSS Layout Box Model A view option in Dreamweaver that displays CSS divs with the margins and padding applied.

Debug To correct errors in code.

Declaration Part of a Cascading Style Sheet rule; consists of a property and a value.

Default alignment For images, the automatic alignment with the text baseline.

Default text color The color the browser uses to display text when another color is not specified.

Definition lists A list composed of terms that are displayed with a hanging indent and is often used with terms and definitions.

Delimiter A comma, tab, colon, semicolon, or similar character that separates tabular data in a text file.

Deliverables Products that will be provided to a client upon project completion, such as the creation of new pages or graphic elements.

Deprecated A feature that is being phased out and will soon be invalid or obsolete, such as directory or menu lists.

Derivative work An adaptation of another work, such as a movie version of a book; a new, original product that includes content from a previously existing work.

Descendant selector A selector that includes two or more selectors that form a relationship and are separated by white space.

Description A short summary of website content; resides in the head section.

Design note A note directed to other content creators who are working on a website with a team.

Design view The view that shows a page in the entire Document window; primarily used when designing and creating a web page.

Designer layout A layout in the Dreamweaver workspace, in which panels are docked on the right side of the screen and Design view is the default view.

Diagonal symmetry Web page elements are balanced along the invisible diagonal line across the page.

Digital image Image that you get from a digital camera, from scanning a photograph or a slide, or that you create from scratch in Adobe Photoshop.

Distance A feature that shows you the distance between two guides.

Div A page element created with a div tag that is used to position and style content.

Div tag An HTML tag that is used to format and position divs.

Document-relative path A path referenced in relation to the web page that is currently displayed.

Document toolbar A toolbar that contains buttons for changing the current web page view, previewing and debugging web pages, and managing files.

Document window The large area under the document toolbar that encompasses most of the Dreamweaver workspace; open web pages appear in this area.

Domain name An IP address expressed in letters instead of numbers, usually reflecting the name of the business, individual, or other organization represented by the website.

Down A button state after the user clicks and holds down the button with the mouse pointer.

Download To transfer files from a remote computer to your computer.

Download time The amount of time it takes to download a file.

Drop shadow Commonly used effect and/or layer style where artwork appears to cast a shadow.

Drop zone The position on the screen where a panel that is being moved will be docked when you release the mouse button.

Dual Screen layout A layout that utilizes two monitors: one for the document window and Property inspector and one for the panels.

Dynamic content Content that changes either in response to certain conditions or through interaction with the user.

Dynamic image An image that is replaced with another image.

Dynamic text The Classic Text type used for displays that constantly update.

Easing A control on the Properties panel that speeds up or slows down the start or end of an animation.

Edit To insert, delete, or change page content, such as inserting a new image, adding a link, or correcting spelling errors.

Editable A TLF text type that allows users to select and edit text.

Editable region In a template, an area the template author creates that allows content contributors to insert text or images.

Elements of Design The basic ingredients used to produce artistic imagery.

Embedded style A style whose code is stored in the head content of a web page, rather than in a separate external file. *See also* internal style.

Emoticons A short sequence of keyboard characters that convey an inflection or expression.

Essentials workspace The default workspace in Bridge that includes all of the menus, panels, buttons, and panes that are used to organize media files.

Event A reaction to an action that causes a behavior to start.

Event handler ActionScript 3.0 code that tells Flash what event to listen for and then what to do once it hears the event.

Expanded Tables mode Displays a table with expanded table borders and temporary space between the cells to simplify working with individual cells.

Export data To save data that was created in Dreamweaver in a different file format so that other programs can read it.

Export panel In Bridge, a panel used to optimize images by saving them as JPEGs for use on the web.

Extensible Metadata Platform (XMP) standard The standard Adobe uses to save metadata.

External link A link that connects to a web page in another website.

External style sheet A single file, separate from the web page, that contains formatting code and can be attached to a web page to quickly apply formatting to page content.

Facebook A social networking site that enables a user to set up a profile page in order to post and exchange information with others.

Fair use An exemption to copyright that allows limited reproduction of copyright-protected work for certain permissible purposes such as research and reporting.

Favorite An asset you expect to use repeatedly while you work on a site, categorized separately in the Assets panel; also, the Dreamweaver Help feature that allows you to add topics to the Favorites window that you might want to view later without having to search again.

Favorites panel In Bridge, a panel used to quickly access folders that are designated as folders used frequently.

Feathered edge A soft selection edge created by blending selected pixels and the background image.

Field A form area into which users can insert a specific piece of data, such as their last names or addresses.

File field In a form, a field that lets users browse to and upload a file.

Files panel A file management tool similar to Windows Explorer or Finder, where Dreamweaver stores and manages your website files and folders.

Filter panel In Bridge, a panel used to filter files to view in the Content panel.

Fixed layout A CSS layout that uses columns expressed in pixels that will not change sizes when viewed in different window sizes.

Fixed-width text A text type whose width is limited by the size of the text block.

Fixed position A CSS property that places an element relative to the browser window.

FLA The native Flash file type; file extension for a Flash file is .fla.

Flash movie Low-bandwidth animation and interactive element created with the Adobe Flash program.

Flash Player Plug-in A program used to play an SWF in a web page.

Flash player *See* Adobe Flash Player.

Flash video A video that has been converted from a digital file format to a .flv file using Adobe Flash.

Flattened bitmap A bitmap image whose layers are compressed into a single layer.

Flipping Transformation that creates a mirror image of the artwork, vertically or horizontally.

Fluid Grid Layout A layout used for designing adaptive websites based on a single fluid grid.

FLV Adobe Flash video format.

Focus group A marketing tool that gathers feedback from a specific group of people about a product, such as the impact of a television ad or the effectiveness of a website design.

Folders panel In Bridge, a panel used to navigate through your folders to select a folder and view the folder contents.

Font The entire array of letters, numbers, and symbols created in the same shape, known as a typeface. Also called a font family.

Font-combination A set of font choices that specifies which fonts a browser should use to display text, such as Arial, Helvetica, sans serif. *Also known as* a font stack. Font-combinations that a user creates are called custom font stacks.

Font family *See* Font.

Font stack *See* font-combination.

Form A collection of input fields that allows one to obtain information from website users.

Form action attribute Part of a form tag that specifies how the form will be processed.

Form object An individual component of a form that accepts an individual piece of information.

Fps Frames per second; measurement of video-playing speed.

Frame-by-frame animation Animates an object gradually over several consecutive frames.

Frame A fixed region in a browser that can display a web page and act independently from other pages displayed in other frames within the browser.

Frame labels Frames associated with a text name that ActionScript references when running the code.

Frame rate A measurement of video-playing speed, expressed in frames per second (fps).

Frame span A group of frames in the Timeline.

Front-end processing The beginning of the processing cycle when the data is collected.

FTP (File Transfer Protocol) The technology used to upload and download files to and from a remote site.

Gestures Interactions with a touch screen, usually with a combination of fingers and a thumb.

Get method Specifies that the data collected in a form be sent to the server encoded into the URL of the web page in the form action property.

GIF Graphics Interchange Format; a still image file format best for creating drawings and line art; can support transparency.

Global style A style used to apply common properties for certain page elements, such as text, links, or backgrounds.

Gloss contours A set of 12 preset adjustments that affect the brightness and contrast of a layer style to create dramatic lighting effects.

Google Video Chat A video and audio sharing application.

Go to URL Directs the browser to use a link to open a different window.

GPS (Global Positioning System) A device used to track your position through a global satellite navigation system.

Gradient Blend between two or more colors.

Graphic A picture or design element that adds visual interest to a page.

Graphic design principles The use of emphasis, movement, balance, unity, symmetry, color, white space, alignment, line, contrast, rule of thirds, proximity, and repetition to create an attractive and effective page design.

Graphic file A graphic in digital format.

Graphic symbol A static object usually used to create an animation spanning across frames in the Timeline.

Grayscale image A digital image in which each pixel can be one—and only one—of 256 shades of gray.

Grid An alignment guide consisting of lines forming a grid of small squares on the Stage.

Group A command that manipulates multiple shapes or objects as one.

Group selector A group of rules with common formatting properties grouped together to help reduce the size of style sheets.

Guide A horizontal or vertical line that you drag onto a page from a ruler, used to position objects; guides are not visible in the browser.

Guide layer A layer that contains a shape used to trace or align objects, or to create a motion path for an animated object.

Head content Items such as the page title, keywords, and description that are contained in the head section; *see also* description, head section, keyword, meta tag, and page title.

Heading One of six different text styles that can be applied to text: Heading 1 (the largest size) through Heading 6 (the smallest size).

Head section The part of a web page that is not visible in the browser window; *see also* head content.

Height property (H) The height of an AP element expressed either in pixels or as a percentage of the page.

Hexadecimal An alphanumeric system for defining color on the web that designates each color using a set of six numbers and/or letters.

Hexadecimal value A numerical value that represents the amount of red, green, and blue in a color.

Hidden field On a form, an invisible field that stores user information.

High-res A shortened form of "high-resolution"; usually refers to images with a minimum of 300 pixels per inch.

Highlights The lightest areas of an image, represented by pixels whose value falls in the upper third of the grayscale range.

Histogram A graph that represents the distribution of pixels in the image across the grayscale; appears on the Properties panel when a Levels or Curves adjustment layer is created.

History panel A Dreamweaver panel that lists the steps that have been performed while editing and formatting a document.

Hit area The active clickable area of the button that corresponds to the button object in either the Over or Down states.

Home page The first web page that appears when you access a website.

Horizontal space Blank space above and below an image that separates the image from the text or other elements on the page.

Horizontal symmetry Web page elements are balanced across the page.

Hotspot A clickable area on an image that, when clicked, links to a different location on the page or to another web page.

Hovering A mouse action in which the user moves over or points to a button; also called rolling over.

HSB Hue, saturation, and brightness; a color model in Photoshop.

HTML (Hypertext Markup Language) The acronym for Hypertext Markup Language; the language web developers use to create web pages.

HTML5 The current version of HTML that added new ways to incorporate interactivity with tags that support semantic markup. Examples of added tags are <header>, <footer>, <article>, <section>, <video>, <hgroup>, <figure>, <embed>, <wbr>, and <canvas>.

HTML reports Five reports that check files in a website: Combinable Nested Font Tags, Missing Alt Text, Redundant Nested Tags, Removable Empty Tags, and Untitled Documents.

HTML style A style used to redefine an HTML tag.

Http (Hypertext transfer protocol) The hypertext protocol that precedes absolute paths to external links.

Hue The name of a color: red, orange, and blue are all hues.

Hyperlink *See* link.

Hypertext Markup Language *See* HTML.

Iconic view Collapsed panels that display only an identifying icon.

Image A graphic such as a photograph or a piece of artwork; images in a website are known as assets or dependent files.

Image map An image that has clickable areas defined on it that, when clicked, serve as a link that takes the user to another location.

Image size Refers to the physical dimensions (width/height) of the Photoshop file.

Import data To bring data created in another software program into Dreamweaver.

InContext Editing An online service that enables users to make changes to designated editable regions on a page while viewing it in a browser.

Index A directory, or list of files.

Info panel Shows information based on where the pointer is on the Stage, such as the color beneath the pointer, and the size, location, and color of a selected object.

Inline style A style that uses code stored in the body content of a web page. *See also* embedded style and internal style.

Input text The Classic Text type used for obtaining and processing user information.

Insert bar *See* Insert panel.

Insert panel A panel with buttons for creating or inserting objects.

Instance A reusable copy of a symbol on the Stage.

Integration The process of combining suite components into Flash and incorporating Flash animations into web pages.

Intellectual property An idea or creation from a human mind that also has the potential for commercial value; the areas of law that govern creative expressions of ideas.

Interactive content Content that accepts and responds to human actions using multimedia elements.

Internal link A link to a web page within the same website.

Internal style sheet A style sheet whose code is saved within the code of a web page, rather than in an external file. *See also* embedded style and inline style.

Interpolation Process used when an image is enlarged in which new pixels are created based on color information from existing pixels.

Intranet An internal website without public access; companies often have intranets that only their employees can access.

Inverse Kinematics (IK) Animation created with the Bone tool that creates an articulated structure that mimics natural movement.

IP (Internet Protocol) address An assigned series of four numbers separated by periods, that indicates the address of a specific computer or other piece of hardware on the Internet or an internal computer network.

ISP (Internet Service Provider) A company that supplies Internet access.

Item Each link in a Spry menu bar.

JavaScript A programming language used to add interactive and dynamic features to web pages.

JPEG (Joint Photographic Exports Group) A file format used for images that appear on web pages; many photographs are saved in JPEG format.

Keyframe A frame in the Timeline signifying change in the movie.

Keyword In Bridge, a word that is added to a file to identify, group, and sort files.

Keywords panel In Bridge, a panel that lists the keywords assigned to a file.

Layer mask Used to define which areas of artwork on a single layer are visible, not visible, or partly visible.

Layers Individual rows in the Timeline that contain content in a Flash project.

Left property (L) The distance between the left edge of an AP element and the left edge of the page or parent container, such as another div.

Library panel Contains the media used in a project, including video, sound, photos, and other graphics.

Licensing agreement Permission given by a copyright holder that conveys the right to use the copyright holder's work under certain conditions.

Linear gradient Blend that progresses straight from one color to another in a linear fashion.

Line break Code that places text on a separate line without creating a new paragraph. You create a line break by pressing [Shift][Enter] (Win) or [shift][return] (Mac).

Line number Provide a point of reference when locating specific sections of code.

Link An image or text element on a web page that users click to display another location on the page, another web page on the same website, or a web page on a different website; *also called* hyperlink.

Liquid layout A CSS layout that uses columns expressed as percents based on the browser window width, so they will change width according to the dimensions of the browser window.

List A form object that provides the user with a list or menu of choices to select. Lists display the choices in a scrolling menu.

Live view The view that displays an open document with its interactive elements active and functioning, as if you were viewing the document in a browser.

Local/Network The setting used in Dreamweaver to publish a website on either the local drive (that is, your own hard drive) or a local network drive.

Local site root folder A folder on your hard drive or other storage device that will hold all the files and folders for a website.

Locked region An area on a page that only the template author has access to change.

Loop A setting that instructs a movie to play repeatedly.

Low-bandwidth animation Animation that doesn't require a fast connection to work properly.

M

ailto: link A link to an email address on a web page for users to contact the website's point of contact.

Marquee zoom Dragging the Zoom tool on the image to magnify a specific area.

Mask An object used to expose the content of the layer beneath it. composed of the *Mask layer* and the *Masked layer*.

Mask layer The layer containing the shape or object through which content on the underlying layer is visible.

Media object A combination of visual and audio effects and text used to create an interactive experience with a website.

Media queries Style sheets that specify set parameters for displaying pages such as tablets or smartphones.

Menu A form object displayed in a shortcut menu that provides the user with a list of options to select.

Menu bar A bar at the top of the workspace with the program commands.

Merge cells To combine multiple adjacent cells into one cell.

Merge Drawing mode A tool setting that combines objects' paths.

Metadata File information you add to a file with tags (words) that are used to identify and describe the file.

Metadata panel In Bridge, a panel that lists the metadata for a selected file.

Meta tag HTML code that includes information about the page such as keywords and descriptions.

Method property Specifies the protocol used to send form data to a web server.

Micro blog A blog that only allows users to post short posts, such as Twitter.

Microsoft Visual SourceSafe A remote access option used on the Windows platform using Microsoft Visual SourceSafe Client.

Midtones Pixels whose color falls into the middle range of the grayscale.

Mini Bridge A panel that opens directly within the Photoshop and InDesign programs; a simplified version of Bridge.

Montage Multiple art components overlapping to create a single composition.

Morph How a shape tween animation changes from its starting shape into a different ending shape.

Motion Editor A Flash panel that provides detailed control over properties in every keyframe in a motion tween.

Motion tween Animates movement on the Stage as an instance moves from one position to another or changes properties such as color, size, or rotation.

MOV Apple QuickTime video format.

Movie clip symbol A mini-movie or animation within a Flash movie that has its own Timeline and plays independently of the main movie's Timeline.

MP4 The digital video compression standard.

MPEG (Motion Picture Experts) A video file format.

Multi-line text field In forms, a data entry area that is useful for entering text that may take several sentences to complete; *also called* text area field.

Multimedia Content such as text, graphics, video, animation, and sound that is integrated into technological expression.

Multiple Document Interface (MDI) All the document windows and panels are positioned within one large application window.

Multiscreen preview Dreamweaver feature that allows you to see what a page would look like if it were viewed on a mobile hand-held device, such as a smartphone or tablet. *Also known as* a 3-up preview.

N

amed anchor A specific location on a web page that is represented by an icon and an assigned descriptive name.

Navigational components Icons, menus, and similar items that help users navigate a web page or another application.

Nested AP div An AP div whose HTML code resides inside another AP div.

Nested symbol A symbol placed inside another symbol.

Nested table A table that is placed inside the cell of another table.

Nested template A template that is based on another template.

Noise A blanket of high-contrast pixels that produce a grainy effect over an image.

Nonbreaking space A space that appears in a fixed location to keep a line break from separating text into two lines or, in the case of table cells, to keep an empty cell from collapsing.

Object-oriented language A programming language that uses a modular approach to programming, including reusing elements.

Object Drawing mode A tool setting that treats the shapes as separate objects.

Ogg (Ogg Theora) Open-source video format developed by Xiph.org.

OnClick An event when a mouse is clicked on a page element that triggers an action.

Onion skinning Displays frames before or after the current frame so you can see the content.

OnLoad An event when a page is loaded in a browser window that triggers an action.

OnMouseOver An event that occurs when a mouse is placed over a page element that triggers an action.

Opacity Refers to how opaque pixels on a layer are. A layer with 0% opacity is completely transparent and not visible.

Optimize To modify file attributes to eliminate bottlenecks in a given frame during downloading.

Optional region In a template, an area that content contributors can choose to show or hide.

Ordered list A list of items that are placed in a specific order and is preceded by numbers or letters.

Orphaned file A file that is not linked to any page in the website.

Over A button state after the user rolls the mouse pointer over the button.

Pages A feature in Fireworks that stores some or all the layers in a document.

Page title The title of a page that appears in the title bar in a browser when a web page is viewed in a browser.

Panel group A set of related panels that are grouped together and displayed through the Window menu; *also called* a tab group.

Panel group title bar Dark colored bar at the top of each panel group.

Panels Individual windows that control crucial aspects of a project and display context-sensitive information and options.

Parent keyword In Bridge, the top level for a keyword with child keywords under it.

Password field In a form, a field that displays asterisks or bullets when a user types in a password.

Path The name and physical location of a web page file that opens when a link is clicked.

Path bar In Bridge, the bar where the path of the selected folder in the Folders panel appears.

Persistence of vision The capacity of the eye to retain an image for a short period, creating an illusion of continuous motion in film and video.

Pick whip A feature of the Show code panel of the Code Snippets panel that visually targets and inserts code in an instance.

Pixel The smallest square of color used to display an image on a computer screen.

Playhead A Timeline element consisting of a red translucent square that moves through the frames as a movie plays in Flash.

Plug-in A small computer program that works with a host application such as a web browser to enable it to perform certain functions; *also called* add-on.

PNG (Portable Network Graphics) A file format used for web page images; capable of showing millions of colors, but is small in file size.

Podcast (Programming on Demand) Digital media files that are downloaded from web pages.

Point of contact A place on a web page that provides users a means of contacting a company if they have questions or problems.

Pose To adjust the configuration of the joints in an inverse kinematics animation; the pose layer in the Timeline is also known as the *Armature layer*.

Posterize A special effect that is created by reducing the number of colors available for the image.

Post method Specifies that the data be sent to the processing script as a binary or encrypted file.

Preview panel A panel where a preview of a selected file appears.

Principles of Design The concepts used to determine how the Elements of Design are used in a work.

Programming on Demand *See* podcast.

Progressive download video A type of video which can be played while it is downloading to the user's computer. If the playback rate exceeds the download rate, a delay is experienced.

Project The source FLA file containing content.

Project management The process that monitors and tracks costs, schedules, and resources to successfully complete a project within a timeframe and budget.

Projector A stand-alone application that plays a movie without using a computer's browser software or (for Flash projectors) Flash Player.

Properties panel *See* Property inspector.

Property inspector A panel that displays the properties of a selected object.

Property keyframes The motion tween keyframes in the Timeline that contain the specific property values that change in that frame: position, scale, skew, rotation, color, or filter.

PSD Photoshop document; the native Photoshop Element file format.

Pseudo class style A style that determines the appearance of a page element when certain conditions are met.

Psychoacoustics The study of how the brain interprets audio.

Public domain Works no longer protected by any form of intellectual property law; you can use public domain works as you wish.

Publish Instructs Flash to create the files necessary to display it on the web or to use in other situations.

Publish profile A file in XML format that Flash creates in the Publish Settings dialog box and uses when it exports data.

Publish a website To make a website available for viewing on the Internet or on an intranet.

QuickTime A popular export format that plays animation on both Macintosh and PC computers.

Radial gradient Blend that radiates outward from one color to another, like a series of concentric circles.

Radial symmetry Balance that runs from the center of the page outward, like the petals of a flower.

Rasterize Term that means "convert to pixels." Type elements, for example, can be rasterized from vector type to pixels.

Raster image Another name for a bitmap image.

Radio button An option button on a form that appears as a small empty circle that users click to select a choice.

Radio group Two or more radio buttons grouped together on a form.

RDS (Remote Development Services) A remote access option used with a remote folder running ColdFusion.

Read Only A TLF text type that prevents users from selecting or editing text.

Reference panel A panel used to find answers to coding questions on topics such as HTML, JavaScript, and accessibility.

Registration point Appears as a small plus sign and is the default point that positions an object on the Stage.

Related Files toolbar A toolbar located below an open document's filename tab that displays the names of any related files.

Relative path A path used with an internal link to reference a web page or a file within a website.

Relative positioning The placement of div tags in relation to other web page elements.

Remote site The folder location on a web server that is connected to the Internet with software for hosting websites, not directly connected to the computer housing the local site.

Resampling Changing the total pixel count of an image when resizing an image.

Reset a form To erase the entries that have been previously entered in a form and set the values back to the default settings.

Resolution The number of pixels per inch (ppi) in a bitmap graphic. Describes the degree of clarity, detail, and sharpness of a displayed or printed image.

Revert A Photoshop command that restores the file to its status when you last saved.

RGB Red, green, and blue; the most-used color model in Photoshop; the additive primary colors of light; red, green, and blue light can combine to produce all the other colors in the spectrum; colors you see on your monitor are created by mixing varying strengths and combinations of red, green, and blue.

Rich Internet Applications (RIA) Web applications that function like desktop applications; similar to rich media applications that do not run in a web browser.

Rolling over A mouse action in which the user moves over or points to a button; also called hovering.

Rollover image An image that changes in appearance as the pointer rests on it in a browser window.

Root-relative path A path referenced from a website's root folder.

Root folder *See* local site root folder.

Rotating A transformation that moves an object clockwise or counterclockwise around a given point.

Roundtrip editing Adobe CS6 Creative Suite feature that lets you select a file you've inserted in one application, edit that file in its native program environment, and then seamlessly return to the open application to view the edited object.

Roundtrip HTML The Dreamweaver feature that allows HTML files created in other programs, such as Microsoft Expression Web, to be opened in Dreamweaver without adding additional coding, such as meta tags or spaces.

RSS (Really Simple Syndication) Regularly scheduled information downloads used by websites to distribute news stories, information, or announcements.

Rule A set of formatting attributes that defines styles in a Cascading Style Sheet.

Rule of thirds A design principle that entails dividing a page into nine equal squares and then placing the page elements of most interest on the intersections of the grid lines.

Rulers Alignment tools that appear along the top and left sides of the Stage using pixels as their unit of measurement.

Sample To select a color by picking up a color in an image.

Sans-serif font A block style character used frequently for headings and sub-headings.

Saturation The intensity of a color: how close it is to a pure hue; interchangeable with the term vibrance.

Scaling A term for resizing artwork.

Scope creep When impromptu changes or additions are made to a project without accounting for corresponding increases in the schedule or budget.

Screen reader A device used by the visually impaired to convert written text on a computer monitor to spoken words.

Scripting language A programming language used to interpret and execute user actions and tasks; Flash CS6 uses ActionScript 3.0 as its scripting language.

Scrubbing Manually dragging the playhead in the Timeline to play a group of frames on the Stage.

Seamless image A tiled image that is blurred at the edges so that it appears to be all one image, or made from a pattern that, when tiled, appears to be one image, such as a vertical stripe.

Secure FTP (SFTP) An FTP option which lets you encrypt file transfers to protect your files, user names, and passwords.

Selectable A TLF text type that allows users to select but not edit text.

Selection edge The outermost pixels in a selection.

Selector The names or tags in Cascading Style Sheets to which style declarations are assigned.

Semantic markup Coding to emphasize meaning.

Semantic web Refers to the way page content can be coded to emphasize the meaning to other programs accessing the information, such as screen readers and search engines.

Serif font A font with small extra strokes at the top and bottom of the characters; used frequently for paragraph text in printed materials.

Server A computer that is connected to other computers to provide file storage and processing services.

Server Behaviors panel The panel that is used to add, edit, and create server behaviors such as a login page.

Server-side scripting A script that processes a form on the form's host web server.

Shadows The darkest areas of an image, represented by pixels in the lowest third of the grayscale range.

Shape hints In shape tween animation, a feature that marks specific points on the beginning and ending shapes that Flash uses to transition one area into another.

Shape tweens Animation that changes one shape to another, in a process known as morphing.

Sharpness An effect created when edge pixels are high in contrast.

Shortcut An icon that represents a software program, folder, or file stored on your computer system.

Single-line text field In a form, a data entry area that is useful for small pieces of data such as a name or telephone number.

Site map A listing of all of the pages in a website.

Site usability test A process that involves obtaining website feedback from users who are not connected to the project.

Skin The bar at the bottom of a Flash video with the control buttons.

Skype A video and audio communication service.

Smart filters Non-destructive filter layers that can be shown, hidden, edited, or deleted without permanently affecting artwork.

Smart Object A Photoshop file with layers that contain image source information to allow an image to be modified while retaining the original data.

Smoothing The process of reducing distortion and evening out jagged in a bitmap image, ensures that the bitmap image will look good when you rotate or resize it on the Stage.

Snap ring An alignment aid that appears as you reshape an object on the Stage; becomes larger as it approaches a snapping point.

Social networking Any web-based service that facilitates social interaction among users.

Sort To rearrange elements on the Library panel in ascending or descending order.

Split a cell To divide a cell into multiple rows or columns.

Spry Open source code developed by Adobe to help designers quickly incorporate dynamic content on their web pages; *also called* Spry framework for AJAX.

Spry effect Screen effects such as fading or enlarging page elements.

Spry framework for AJAX *See* Spry.

Spry menu bar A preset widget that creates a dynamic, user-friendly menu bar.

Stage An interface element that contains the movie's elements—text, images, graphics, drawings, and video.

Standard mode A Dreamweaver mode that displays a table with no extra space added between the table cells.

Standard toolbar A toolbar that contains buttons for some frequently used commands on the File and Edit menus.

State On a menu bar, the condition of a menu item relative to the mouse pointer, such as Up, Down, Over, and Over While Down.

Statement A complete sentence in ActionScript.

Static position A CSS property that places an element in order with the document flow.

Static text The Classic Text default text type best used for basic content.

Status bar A bar under the Dreamweaver window; the left side displays the tag selector, which shows the HTML tags being used at the insertion point location; the right side displays the window size and estimated download time for the page displayed.

Storyboard A visual script containing captions to describe the action in keyframes in a movie; used to plan animations.

Streaming An online method of playing media before it has downloaded completely.

String Text, including letters, numbers, and punctuation, that is enclosed in quotation marks in ActionScript.

Stroke A border around a path or object.

Style Rendering toolbar A toolbar that contains buttons that can be used to display a page using different media types.

Sub keyword *See* child keyword.

Submit To send the information on a form to a host web server for processing.

Swapping Replacing an instance with an instance of another bitmap from the Library panel in the same document.

Swap Image behavior JavaScript code that directs the browser to display a different image when a mouse is rolled over an image on the page.

Swap Image Restore behavior JavaScript code that restores a swapped image back to the original image.

Swatches panel Contains colors from the active color palette, or set, of available colors.

SWF (Shockwave Format) A published output file from Flash program; used to play movies in a browser; file extension is .swf.

Symbol A copy of an object, such as a graphic or button, that can be used more than once in a movie.

Synchronize To transfer the latest version of website files to a server.

Syntax The order, structure, and use of words in a sentence of code.

Tab A CSS style that creates a method of organizing data on a page similar in appearance to a file folder tab; used for navigation above page content.

Tab group *See* panel group.

Table A grid of rows and columns that can be used to hold tabular data on a web page.

Table header Text placed at the top or side of a table on a web page and read by screen readers.

Tabular data Data arranged in columns and rows that are separated by a delimiter.

Tag An individual piece of HTML code that instructs the browser how each page element should be displayed.

Tag selector A location on the status bar that displays HTML tags being used at the insertion point location.

Target The location on a web page that the browser will display in full view when the user clicks an internal link.

Target audience The characteristics that make up the population that will be using a website, taking into consideration such factors as age, occupation, sex, education, residence, race, and computer literacy.

Template A predefined page layout.

Terms of use Rules that govern how a user may use a website's content.

Text area *See* multi-line text field.

Text block An object containing text that you can move and modify.

Text field On a form, a box in which a user can enter text. *See also* single-line text field and multi-line text field.

Text Layout Framework (TLF) The default text option that provides flexible formatting features and can accommodate advanced typographic requirements.

Thumbnail slider A sliding control that is used to change the size of the thumbnails being viewed in the Content panel.

Tiled image A small graphic that repeats across and down a web page, appearing as individual squares or rectangles.

Timeline A JavaScript feature that will cause an AP element to appear to move along a path, or change size, visibility, or position.

TLF *See* Text Layout Framework.

Tolerance A tool setting and dialog box setting that determines which pixels will be affected based upon their similarity in color.

Tools panel A Flash interface element containing tools to draw, select, modify, and view graphics and text.

Top property (T) The distance between the top edge of an AP element and the top edge of the page or AP element that contains it.

Touch gesture The actions users perform with their fingers to navigate and interact with an application on a smart phone, tablet, or other mobile device.

Trace statement An ActionScript function that makes a message appear on the Output panel when users perform an action.

Trademark Protects an image, word, slogan, symbol, or design used to identify goods or services.

Transform Operations that change the location of pixels; include scaling, rotating, skewing, and distorting pixels.

Transformation point A small circle that appears on an object when it is selected, which Flash uses to orient the object every time you transform or animate it.

Transform panel Performs the functions of the Free Transform Tool, and more precise modifications.

Transparent background A background composed of transparent pixels, rather than pixels of a color, resulting in images that blend easily on a web page background.

Tweened animation An animation with defined starting and ending keyframes where Flash automatically creates the animation between the two keyframes.

Tween span The frame span in a tweened animation.

Twitter A website where users post short messages, called "tweets."

Typeface A font family created in the same shape or style.

Unordered list *See* bulleted list.

Up The default button state, not affected by any mouse movement.

Upload To send a form or files to a host web server.

URL (Uniform Resource Locator) The address for a web page as an assigned series of numbers, separated by periods.

User interaction The way users interact with the design, function, and appearance of Flash content.

Validate markup To compare code against the current standards and identify code that is not compliant.

Variable-width text A text type in which the text block continues to expand as long as you type.

Vector graphic A scalable graphic built using mathematical formulas rather than pixels; it can be resized without losing image quality.

Vertical space Blank space on the sides of an image that separates the image from the text or other elements on the page.

Vertical symmetry Web page elements are balanced down the page.

Vibrance Intensity of a color; interchangeable with the term saturation.

Vidcast *See* vodcast.

Vignette A visual effect in which the edge of an image gradually fades away; usually created with a feathered selection.

Visited link A link that the user has previously clicked, or visited; the default color for a visited link is purple.

Vlog A video blog.

Vodcast A video podcast; *also called* vidcast.

Waveform A graphical representation of sound in the Library and the Timeline.

Web 2.0 The evolution of web applications that facilitate and promote information sharing among internet users.

Web browser Software used to display web pages.

Webcam A camera used for video communication on the web.

WebDAV (Web-based Distributed Authoring and Versioning) A remote access option used with servers such as the Microsoft Internet Information Server (IIS) and Apache web server.

Web design program A program used to create interactive web sites.

WebM Google-developed open-source video format.

Web Open Font Format (WOFF) Describes fonts available through font libraries for embedding in web pages through the CSS3 @font-face property.

Web page A page in HTML format with text combined with images and media objects in various formats.

Web-safe color palette A set of 216 colors that display consistently in all browsers, and on Macintosh, Windows, and Unix computers.

Web server A computer that is connected to the Internet with a static IP address and software that enables it to make files accessible to anyone on the internet or an intranet; *see also* IP address.

Website A collection of related web pages.

White space An area on a web page that is not filled with text or graphics; not necessarily white.

Widget A piece of code that allows users to interact with the program interface.

Width property (W) The width of an AP element either in pixels or as a percentage of the page.

Wiki A site where a user can use simple editing tools to contribute and edit page content in the site.

Wikipedia An online encyclopedia where users can use simple editing tools to contribute and edit page content.

Wireframe A prototype of each page's content and relationship to other pages in a website.

Word wrap A command that keeps all code within the width of the Document window.

Work area A gray interface element that surrounds the Stage where you can place or store object that do not appear in the movie.

Workflow reports Reports that enable you to check the progress of a project, such as a report that will list all files that have been modified recently.

Workspace The program interface area where you work with documents.

Workspace switcher A drop-down menu on the Application bar (Win) or Menu bar (Mac) that allows you to quickly change between different preset workspace screen arrangements.

World Wide Web Consortium (W3C) An international community that develops open standards for web development.

WYSIWYG (What You See Is What You Get) A program such as Dreamweaver that displays web pages as they will appear in a browser.

XHTML (eXtensible HyperText Markup Language) The current standard language used to create web pages.

XFL An uncompressed file format that enables designers and developers to collaborate on Flash projects.

XML eXtensible Markup Language file; an Internet file format similar to HTML that describes information and data.

XMP eXtensible Metadata Platform file; metadata embedded in a Flash file that is able to be indexed by search engines.

YouTube A website where you can view or upload videos.

Z-index property The property used to specify the vertical stacking order of multiple AP divs on a page.

Index